En. Astrem. 1925/32

Beveridge and the Progressive Era

BOOKS BY CLAUDE G. BOWERS

Albert J. Beveridge

BEVERIDGE
AND
THE PROGRESSIVE ERA

BY

CLAUDE G. BOWERS

WITH ILLUSTRATIONS

HOUGHTON MIFFLIN COMPANY

The Riverside Press Cambridge

1932

The Riverside Press
CAMBRIDGE · MASSACHUSETTS
PRINTED IN THE U.S.A.

PREFACE

DURING my boyhood in Indianapolis, Albert J. Beveridge, even before his election to the Senate, was one of the gods of my idolatry. Though not in sympathy with much of his political philosophy, there was no resisting the lure of his brilliant eloquence nor the charm of his personality. I knew him, then, in the home as well as on the platform. After his entrance upon the national stage, many years were to intervene before I was to make contact with him again. It was during the last ten years of his life, while he was engaged in the writing of the two great biographies that are among the classics of American literature, that I knew him most intimately.

The story of his career must be a history of American politics from 1898 until 1924, and the historian of the future will find these years among the most dramatic and significant in the life of the Republic. For these years witnessed the rise of imperialism; the organization of the powerful industrial and financial combinations; the development of the trusts: the beginning of the disintegration of political parties; the spirit of insurgency; the World War, and the hectic battles over the problems that followed in its wake.

Seldom has a biographer been more abundantly blessed with original manuscript material; never has one had such material placed at his disposal with fewer reservations. From the time of his election to the Senate until his death, Beveridge kept most of the letters he received, and retained copies of most that he wrote. These letters, many thousands of them, exchanged with the foremost figures in the political and intellectual world, throw a vivid, and frequently a new, light on events and movements of the utmost historical importance. Because he was utterly frank with his friends, to whom he wrote at length of his problems, his doubts, his motives, it has been possible to make this volume something in the nature of a biography of a mind.

In the making of history during these years, Beveridge played a conspicuous part. Thus he was the outstanding prophet and orator of the imperialism that came with the acquisition of the Philippines. This came as the realization of his dream of expanding markets in the Orient. It was foreshadowed, even to details, in his speech in Boston a week before Dewey sailed into Manila Bay. He alone, among Republican orators, took imperialism as his theme in the campaign of 1898; and it was his

Preface

first speech in the Senate on our Philippine policy that made him a national figure.

He was the first conspicuous leader of his party to meet the assaults upon the trusts with a militant defense; and among the first to realize the necessity for governmental regulation.

His history is the story of Rooseveltian days, for through all these years, in the Senate and upon the platform, he was one of the most brilliant eulogists and defenders of the virile President. His relations with Roosevelt, as we shall find, were intimate and affectionate, although occasionally they were unable to agree.

Thus, too, his story is the record of two dramatic movements that changed the course of history, concerning which historians and biographers thus far have been chary or unappreciative — the insurgency movement during the Taft régime and the Progressive Party movement that followed. Through the voluminous correspondence covering these movements I have been able to throw a new light, I hope, on the actors and their motives. Beveridge was the floor leader of the small but brilliant and able group of insurgent senators who fought the Payne-Aldrich tariff act with magnificent courage and effect through the spring and summer of 1909. In the Progressive Party movement he, after Roosevelt, was the most important party leader to bear the brunt of the battle. Both movements resulted in a rich correspondence with the participants, to which I have had free access.

Since this is the story of an era, it has been necessary, in the telling, to make more than a casual reference to many of Beveridge's contemporaries. Thus Roosevelt and Taft, Coolidge and Harding, Aldrich and Quay, Platt of Connecticut and Hanna, Lodge and Knox, La Follette and Dolliver step in and out of the story as they did in life.

In dealing with phases of Beveridge's career with which, politically, I am unsympathetic, I have sought to let the record tell the tale, without prejudice, and, as much as possible, from his point of view. My purpose has been to paint a living portrait of a great orator, statesman, and biographer against the background of his stirring times.

I am under obligations to many men and women who have been of service in the collection of material — too many to enumerate here. To these I have made my personal acknowledgments.

CLAUDE G. BOWERS

CONTENTS

BOOK I: AN AMERICAN ROMANCE

Contents

road tax cases — The insurance company case — How Beveridge entered
the case — His brief — Leo Rothschild — Standing in the profession —
Enter Philander C. Knox

Contents

BOOK II: IMPERIALISM

Contents

Contents xi

Contents

Contents

Contents

Manufacturers' Association favors commission — It solicits Beveridge's help — A letter from its spokesman — 'Full of graft' — The Beveridge bill — Not hopeful for the session — Roosevelt reported for it — Support from business bodies — Encouraged by Senate reaction — National Manufacturers' Association lobby appears — Justice Harlan warns Republicans — Stand-pat leaders' stubborn stand — Beveridge carefully prepares speech — Urges manufacturers to ask Roosevelt's support — Payne gives a hearing — Amused toleration — Cannon's rebuke — Payne's talk — Attempt to destroy effect of Beveridge's Senate speech — Payne's insinuation — Beveridge's sharp letter — Payne's apology — The Beveridge speech — Payne's meaningless substitute — Roosevelt's attitude — Confers with Beveridge and Aldrich — Aldrich's impossible substitute — National Manufacturers' Association satisfied — Why Beveridge accepted — Why Ames was against it — Manufacturers intrigue against Beveridge — The four-battleship program of Roosevelt — His fight — Leaders turning upon him — His waning power — Beveridge leads in his battleship fight — His motive questioned — Has a brush with Hale — Lodge with Roosevelt's enemies — A dramatic debate — Beveridge scores the oligarchy — A fighting speech — Is attacked by Aldrich and Hale, while Lodge prompts them — Hand-to-hand fight — Personalities — A moral victory — Press praise for Beveridge — The oligarchy's death-blow

Contents

Contents xvii

Contents

Contents

Contents

Contents　　　xxi

Contents

Contents

BOOK VI: THE IVORY TOWER

Contents

ILLUSTRATIONS

Portraits of George W. Perkins and Matthew Stanley Quay are by
courtesy of the Keystone View Company

ILLUSTRATIONS

Beveridge and the Progressive Era

.·.

BOOK I
AN AMERICAN ROMANCE

Beveridge and the Progressive Era

.·.

CHAPTER I

BOYHOOD

I

ON THE morning of October 6, 1862, the people of the North, poring over their newspapers at the breakfast-table, read of 'the terrible battle of Corinth,' where the enemy had been repulsed 'with great slaughter.' [1] Less than a month before, the northern section of the country had been in the slough of despondency, with many of the stoutest hearts ready to abandon the struggle for the preservation of the Union. James Russell Lowell had thought that only a miracle could prevent the triumph of the armies under Lee, whose genius thus far had not been approached by any of the commanders of the Federal forces. With his victory at Corinth, Grant emerged as the possible military master, and the Radicals launched their first campaign against him. At Faneuil Hall in Boston, Charles Sumner spoke for two hours on the Emancipation Proclamation to 'an assemblage of fanatics met to worship Charles Sumner and his dangerous and detestable sentiments.' [2] This, too, was on the 6th of October. That also was the day that Lincoln, weary of procrastination, sat down and wrote his order to McClellan to cross the Potomac into Virginia and give battle to Lee.

And on that day of rejoicing over the victory at Corinth, a company of raw recruits, responding to the call of the President, tramped noisily over a dirt road in Highland County, Ohio, and before an isolated farmhouse on a hill. Women looked out of the house and waved their hands. There were no men about to cheer the raw recruits on their way, for the head of the household and his sons had marched away to the battle-fields weeks before. It was in that comfortable-looking house on that memorable day that Albert Jeremiah Beveridge was born. He came into the world at a dramatic moment, with men clashing in deadly combat in Kentucky, in Virginia, Mississippi, Tennessee, and Maryland. The roar of artillery, the clash of steel, the fluttering of tattered flags — the day was to be symbolic of his career.

[1] *New York Herald*, Oct. 6, 1862.   [2] *Boston Post*, Oct. 7, 1862.

II

Thomas Henry Beveridge, the father, a Virginian of Scotch descent, had gone to battle some time before as the captain of a company he had helped to organize. He came of a family of small planters and slave-owners. His grandfather, John, the founder of the family in America, was a hearty, blithesome spirit, who had died jauntily at an advanced age from an accident in the hunting-field. His father had owned slaves and lands, but, financially unfortunate, he had lost both; and, dying soon afterwards, left a widow and eleven children in straitened circumstances. Unwilling to face the humiliation of comparative poverty in the community where she had been more happily situated, the widow had moved to Ohio with most of her children. Thomas Henry, at the age of nine, was left in Virginia to the none too tender mercies of his uncle Noble Beveridge. This guardian of the boy was one of the large landowners of Loudoun County, and lived in a pretentious brick house at Middleburg, which he had built and patterned after the home of James Monroe near by. This house is still standing and doing service as an inn. The uncle was unmarried, morose, exacting, and one day the boy followed a man driving a drove of cattle to Ohio, and joined his mother.

At the age of twenty, he was married to Elizabeth Lamb at Zanesville, and there were six children by this marriage. Later he moved to Highland County, where he acquired a farm on the West Fork of Ohio Brush Creek, three miles from the village of Sugar Tree Ridge, and immediately became one of the solid men of the community. He was in comfortable circumstances and of high standing, when, after the death of his first wife, he married Frances Eleanor Parkinson in 1861.

Her family had been among the earliest pioneers of the county. Her grandfather, Oliver Ross, a Scotch Presbyterian, born in County Tyrone, in Ireland, and educated in Londonderry, had migrated to America in 1783, and had followed the blazed trail through the wilderness and founded the New Market settlement in Ohio. Before leaving Ireland, he had married Frances Eleanor St. Clair, a woman of gentle blood. He was a real personality, imbued with the spirit and imagination of the pioneer, shrewd, and abundantly blessed with the blarney of his native isle. He soon ingratiated himself into the favor of the Governor, and was commissioned the first law officer within the present limits of Highland County. In 1803, his daughter, Rebecca, who, with the spirit of a Spartan woman, had accompanied her father into the wilderness as his tent-keeper, married George Washington

Parkinson, who had migrated from Pennsylvania the year before and established a small hat factory. During the war on the Canadian border in 1812, Parkinson joined the army, and he fell into the hands of the British when Hull surrendered without the firing of a shot.

Of his nine children, we are interested in but one — Frances Eleanor, named for her grandmother, and born in 1824. At the time of her birth, Highland County was ninety per cent dense forest, with dangerous wild beasts prowling through the woods and with wild turkey abundant. She was held, as a child, on the knees of the pioneers who had faced and fought the red men and driven them toward the sunset. Her girlhood knew the simple, severe pioneer conditions that often give strength to mind and character and fortitude to the soul. Along with this, she had inherited from the Rosses and the St. Clairs an attractive warmth and an impulsive sympathy for suffering. In her seventeenth year, she was married to Philip Doyle, the young carpenter who had built most of the houses of the community. There were to be thirteen years of married life and seven years of widowhood before her marriage to Thomas Henry Beveridge in 1861. Scarcely had she assumed charge of the farmhouse swarming with children, when the war-clouds lowered. At the time of the marriage, she was thirty-seven and her husband was forty-three; and one year later the only child of the union, the future Senator, was born — with the father far away upon the battle-field.

III

The earliest home of Beveridge was an old-fashioned farmhouse in the open country, some distance from the nearest village. To the house the father had added a large columned portico extending almost the width of the building in reminiscence of the Virginia homes of his childhood. It had the usual huge fireplace for logs, with a great stone chimney on the outside. The customary dinner bell to summon the workers from the fields hung in the yard. The barn overshadowed the house in dimensions, and there was a milk-house 'with a spring of water gurgling through the floor,' which was of 'flat slabs of rock, kept scrupulously clean.' [1] Many years later, the boy who was born in the house was to retain pleasant memories of it. 'I can see it now,' he wrote, 'the hill on which the house stood, the country road winding before it and down into the valley of the creek that flowed beneath it; the circling hills, covered with trees; the hill-surrounded level sweep of hundreds of acres of farmland that stretched be-

[1] Beveridge's MS. Autobiography.

hind. The house was quite large for those days, and the outlook was noble: the green of the forest rolling away before it — those forests which, in autumn, looked like a million banners of countless hosts marching to war.'[1]

It was in this house, among these hills and valleys, that Beveridge spent the first and happiest years of his childhood, romping with his older half-brothers and sisters. If the shadows of the war did not oppress him, they rested none the less upon the home. The responsibility of superintending the sowing and the reaping rested upon the women of the household and two veteran field laborers who had been in the employ of the family for many years.

But, aside from the management of the farm, there were other duties for the mother. The war feeling was intense. Daily in almost every household the Cincinnati papers were anxiously scanned for the names of the wounded and the dead upon the battle-fields. The gossip heard by the children was mostly of war — the struggle in Kentucky for the mastery, the rumors of the approaching attack on Cincinnati, the daring raids of Morgan. With the men fighting, there was war work for the women left at home. Every week Frances Beveridge would saddle three horses, and, with her child in her arms, mount one and ride from house to house until two other women were found who could spare the time, and away they would go from farm to farm collecting food, clothing, and other comforts for the soldiers. Of these patriotic expeditions the child was to remember nothing. Indeed, his earliest recollection was of the close of the conflict when the warriors returned. 'My earliest recollection,' he wrote, 'dim and yet strangely distinct, is of the blue-clad soldiers marching home after the war was over, to the strange wild music of the fife and drum. It echoes in my ears, and I think I can see more distinctly now than I could then the stained and torn old flags they carried.'[2]

Home from the war, the father resumed his work upon the farm, and for a time prospered as before. But times were hard, and farmers were hurt more than any other element in the economic readjustments that followed. Many of the soldiers found themselves in desperate need of help, and the head of the Beveridge clan could not be unmindful of the plight of his comrades. To assist some of these, he signed promissory notes; and to others he loaned money for doubtful business ventures. It fell to him to bear the loss of the loans, to pay the notes. A man of stern integrity, it did not occur to him to seek an avenue of

[1] Beveridge's MS. Autobiography.
[2] *Ibid.*

ALBERT J. BEVERIDGE AS A BOY

escape. He paid the penalty of his folly, if such it was, and within two years after the war, when his youngest son was in his fifth year, he was compelled to give up the homestead. Thereafter there was to be a constant battle against misfortune. It was just before the ruin that the youngest Beveridge had the first triumph of his life — he rode his pony at the county fair and won a prize.

The father, now in his fiftieth year, with a large family and his prospects swept away with his means, remained a very short time in Ohio, seeking, without success, to rehabilitate himself. Humiliated by the failure of fortune, he began to look elsewhere for the opportunity to recover his former state. The rich black soil of Illinois seemed to offer the greatest promise. Thither he went with his family in 1868. The happiest days of the childhood of the youngest son were over, and for a long while he was to look back upon the lost Ohio home with the yearning of a Sentimental Tommy for the remembered glories of Thrums.

IV

The father, courageous and audacious in the face of adversity, leased an immense farm, a full section, in Moultrie County, Illinois, in the hope of speedily recouping his fortune through production upon a large scale. A part of the farm was virgin soil, never before having been turned by a plow. The soil itself was rich and black. But only an optimist could have hoped for profitable results under the agricultural conditions then existing in the Middle West. The farmers were suffering from the inequalities of the tariff and taxation, and the harder they worked, the less they had. The exorbitant railroad rates absorbed the profits of a season's toil, and there were discriminations in the rates. The railroads were working in harness with the grain monopolies of the Chicago markets, and when the roads sought to crush the independent grain-elevator companies by refusing to carry their grain, the farmers of Illinois rose in righteous wrath and forced the passage of the Warehouse Act of 1867. At the same time an effort was made to end the trading in futures, but without success. Meanwhile, the prices of farm products were falling and the indignation of the farmers was rising, when Thomas Beveridge took possession of his farm. Within a few years the Illinois farmers would compel the enactment of a comprehensive railroad law fixing maximum rates; the Grange Movement would be in full swing, putting the fear of the Lord into the hearts of the politicians and the railroad-dominated courts, and paving the way for the creation of the Federal Interstate Commerce Commission; but by that time the immigrant from Ohio would no longer be concerned.

An intense individualist, relying on his own resources and energy, he employed a number of farm laborers and invested generously in the new farm machinery. His son was to boast, in later years, of having driven one of the first self-binder harvesters turned out of a factory,[1] for he was scarcely out of his mother's arms before he was in the fields. He was only eleven when he ran his first furrow, and he was doing a full man's work at twelve.[2] And these were not happy days. Because of the malaria from the undrained fields and swamps, some of the family were sick most of the time, and years later Beveridge was to 'remember the horror of strong men sitting for hours before the stove shaking like leaves in a storm.'[3]

If he himself was affected, there is no record. He threw himself into the work with a zest that was to make him unpopular with the hired men, who did not relish the pace he set.[4] Day after day, before the rising of the sun he had left his bed to feed and curry the horses, to have his breakfast and to reach the fields by dawn. When other boys of his age were fishing or swimming in spring and summer, nutting in the fall, or skating in the winter, he was busily employed. Sometimes, when it rained, he would seek a quiet corner in the house and turn the pages of a book; but usually there was harness to be mended, fences to be repaired, seed corn to be shelled, or broken implements to be fixed.[5] And yet the exuberance of a natural optimism sustained him, and he found his dull routine not without its recompense. 'To follow the plow, barefoot, in the early spring morning,' he wrote; 'to see the brown earth flow and turn before the gleaming share; to breathe the clean and delicate odors of the field, made daintily pungent by the smell of freshly upturned earth; to hear the mingled million sounds of insects busy in the stubble and grass, or whirring through the air,' was joy to him.[6]

But he felt a sense of isolation. There was nothing exhilarating in the life of the nearest village, which could be reached only after a hard ride over long heavy roads, into which, in spring and winter, the wheels sank deep. But he was happy enough in the pride of helping his father, and the nominal pay he received was being carefully put aside with the view to college later on.

But, alas, it was all love's labor lost. The first year a drought came, the harvest failed, the season's end found the father deeper in debt than ever. The disaster was irreparable; the farm was abandoned, and the family moved into the little county seat

---

[1] *Readers' Magazine*, May, 1907.   [2] MS. Autobiography.   [3] *Ibid.*
[4] L. H. Rose, MS. sketch.   [5] MS. Autobiography.   [6] *Ibid.*

of Sullivan. During the remainder of his childhood, his father was to support the family on contracts of various kinds. He had a turn for invention, and he made a hay press on which he took out a patent in 1874.[1] But, stern realist that he was, he instantly abandoned it on seeing a press he thought better. Although untrained, he possessed some engineering ability, and this brought him the contract for building a section of one of the numerous railroads then spreading, fanlike, in all directions. The son contributed his full share toward the building of the section, though only in his fourteenth year.

A year later, when his father took the contract to furnish a railroad with a great amount of lumber, the fifteen-year-old boy was put in charge of the logging-camp — the loneliest, hardest labor his childhood was to know. For the first time he had to leave his home, for the camp was in the woods at Buffalo Hart, in the northeastern part of Sangamon County. Here he was entrusted with the management of a rough group of illiterate men, physically powerful, and impatient of discipline or restraint. By doing his full share of the manual labor, he soon commanded the respect of the men, although they frequently got out of hand and drove him to despair. He became an expert in the loading of logs, and occasionally he drove the loads to town. The unimproved roads literally were streams of black sticky mud into which the wagons sank to the hubs. More than once the horses fell from exhaustion in the traces, and some died. It was there, in the logging-camp, that he became addicted to profanity, finding it his most effective weapon in subduing the elemental men he managed to his will. On one occasion, when the men were drinking, quarreling, and fighting, he quelled the riot that might easily have ended in a killing by tongue-lashing them until they paused in amazement at his temerity, and the fight ended in a good-natured laugh.

But not always was he able to curb these tumultuous spirits. Overhearing them planning a drunken debauch in town, he pleaded and threatened without effect. He followed them to the little town of Illiopolis, seeking to dissuade them, but they were out of control, and when they turned their backs upon him, he ran to an empty tool shack near by, and, throwing himself face downward in the shavings on the floor in black despair, sobbed without restraint. In the last year of his life, when driving by the shack, which was still standing, he recalled the incident as the one that plumbed the depths of the darkest misery of a none too happy childhood.

And yet, even among these uncouth and quarrelsome men in

[1] This is still in possession of the family.

the depths of the woods, his youthful faith and spirit buoyed him up. He always loved the forest with its silence and freedom and its streams, and found peace and repose in its bosom. There were moments of surcease from labor, and he had provided for himself the only fun that could be had by taking some books along. 'It was at this period,' he wrote, 'that I found Emerson, in the deep woods, among the roughest of men.... His essay on "Self-Reliance" was just what my soul needed, and I went over it again and again until I could repeat it from memory. His poems, too, gave me strength — almost physical strength. Especially "Wood-Notes," "The Problem," "Character," and "Guy." Emerson introduced me to Plutarch, and here, indeed, was the victualing of my ambition. I found Plutarch absorbing as my dime novels, and indeed a good deal like them; and when I found that Plutarch was an immortal classic, it dawned upon me that blood and color and human incident are quite as important in history as dates.' [1]

So real did Cæsar become to the boy that he could tell the illiterate loggers, gathered about the camp-fire in the night, of his campaigns, and they listened eagerly, and grew excited in debating the strategy of his battles. Unconsciously the orator was in training, mastering the art of simple human narrative that anyone could understand. Incidentally, his faith in the sound common sense of the plain people was impressed upon him as well. Thenceforth, through life, he had confidence in 'the sound judgment and sheer mental ability of the people — for these crude men were, indeed, the people.' [2]

Thereafter the loggers called him their 'historian,' and from time to time asked him for news of the Romans. A hard, rough life with privations it was, but it strengthened his self-confidence, and his health improved in the outdoor life of vigorous exercise.

V

Meanwhile, he had regularly attended the public schools. His first school had been in a country schoolhouse a mile and a half from the farm, to which he trudged through mud, slush, snow, and rain. Nothing fascinated him so much at first as geography, with the maps drawn upon the blackboards, the reproduction of the earth's surface, the oceans, continents, islands. 'Even then,' he wrote, 'I could feel the stirrings of the wanderlust in my blood, and to this day I have never got over it.' [3] Some of the maps he then drew, beautifully drawn and colored with extreme neatness, are still preserved.

[1] MS. Autobiography.   [2] *Ibid.*   [3] *Ibid.*

The Progressive Era 9

The records of his early school days are scant, but report cards for parts of two of his high-school years show him to have been above the average, except — of all things! — in composition, in which he was marked but 75. In civil government he invariably received 100. He was not, however, the type to confine his studies to the prescribed course in the schools. It was during his high-school days that he read Gibbon's 'Decline and Fall of the Roman Empire,' and the novels of Scott, Dickens, George Eliot, and William Black. But his most passionate interest, even then, was in government and politics. He read the speeches published in the press, attended political rallies with his mother, and haunted the courthouse to listen to the arguments of the lawyers. Even before his high-school days, he frequented the law office of Isaac J. Mauser, who, attracted to him by his brightness and earnestness, advised him in his studies. Even then he was obsessed with the importance of thoroughness. One of his boyish ambitions was to become the master of a large vocabulary and he carried a little notebook about with him in which he wrote new words each day, and went over them until he had mastered their meaning and proper use. While still living in the country, he had attended the meetings of the debating society in the country schoolhouse, where the doctor, merchant, shoemaker, farmer held forth, with more heat than light, upon the burning topics of the times. The ambition to speak and sway men by the spoken word took possession of him in childhood.

But he was not confined in his studies to the example of the local Ciceros. It was the period of tempestuous political debates. The prejudices and hates of the Civil War still were inflamed. The political campaigns were intense and venomous. Popular orators traversed the country, more bent on arousing the passions of the people than on informing them. In the Middle West the rallies were held in groves or in the fairgrounds, and the faithful flocked to the meetings from miles around. When the speaker was a party leader, entire families abandoned work and went in wagons or on horseback, taking their dinners with them.

To these meetings young Beveridge's instinct led him. He was an ardent Republican, with all the deep-seated prejudices of the decade, but he could not resist a Democratic meeting because of his interest in oratory. Having heard the orators, he tried to reframe their speeches when he was alone in the woods or on the highway. It annoyed him to find that he could not recall much the orators had said that seemed worth repeating. There had been too much fustian and too few facts. When he tried to reproduce the speech, he was amazed at the poverty of the real material, and somehow he could not throw himself into a passion over the little he found. He wondered at the wild enthusiasm in which he had shared, to which he, with his childish voice, had contributed.

The campaign of 1876 had been more than ordinarily bitter. The Democrats, having tasted blood in the congressional elections of 1874, were hard on the trail of victory. Never had their campaign ammunition been so abundant — the numerous malodorous scandals of the Grant régime — the Whiskey Ring scandal, Babcock, Belknap, the New York Custom-House, Crédit Mobilier, the corruption with which the Nation reeked. To the Democrats' fierce denunciation of the Administration there was no answer to be made. But the Republicans replied with quite as much heat and passion, evoking all the memories of the war of eleven years before, and denouncing Democrats as traitors and murderers of Union soldiers in prison camps. 'Every man who poisoned the wells of loyal communities was a Democrat!' screamed the most cultured of these orators.[1] And Beveridge, the boy, caught momentarily in the hysteria, found himself strangely cold and wondering after the meetings were over and the music of the band had died away and the débris of the barbecues and the dinners on the grass had been cleared.

That year he listened to a typical 'bloody-shirt' speech by John A. Logan, and determined, first, to reconstruct the speech in his mind and then attempt to deliver it. 'Next day,' he wrote later, 'following the plow, with my bare feet in the mellow, fragrant furrow, I went over that speech. I wondered if ever I could say such wonderful things.' There was no one within hearing distance of the field — only the horses in the fence-corner. Mounting a stump, the embryo orator launched forth — but it was no use. He could not go on. 'There was nothing definite, nothing concrete, that I could think of to say — nothing to prove, and nothing to prove it with. I almost cried with humiliation,' he wrote in later years. 'Plain as it was that oratory was the road to distinction, it was even plainer to me that I could never be an orator. Such was the beginning of my learning how to speak.'[2]

A few days later, he stood in a country store listening to amateur debaters discussing the issues of the campaign. It was all so confusing, he thought to make it clear to himself by restating the arguments in his own way. As he trudged along the road, oblivious to his surroundings, spouting boyish eloquence, he was startled by a voice. An old free-thinker of the neighborhood had come up behind him in a buggy and overheard. 'Good for you, Allie!' he exclaimed. 'You have made

[1] Robert G. Ingersoll.   [2] MS. Autobiography.

the best speech I have heard this campaign. Keep that up and you'll be a great speaker some day.' The boy hung his head in shame.

But the interruption was to bear fruit. The free-thinker spoke to the county chairman, and the boy was permitted to speak at a country schoolhouse. Looking back, in later years, upon that first campaign speech, he knew he had torn a passion to tatters and given an immature imitation of the orators he had not quite liked.[1]

Then came the most ambitious oratorical flight of the Sullivan days when the Murphy Temperance Movement swept the country, bearing multitudes of temperance societies in its wake. In almost every little community of the Middle West one of these sprang up, and Beveridge was invited to address that in his home town. Laboriously he wrought an oration of an hour's length, committed it, practiced it in the woods, and delivered it triumphantly to his neighbors. It was long to be remembered in the community.

VI

But along with the exultation of such boyish triumphs was the numbing realization of the almost insurmountable obstacle to a higher education. The money he had accumulated with the view to college had been given to his father to assist him in tiding over the hard times. Convinced that his plan was impossible, the youth turned his thoughts to West Point. It was not without effect that he had been born when the cannonading was echoing in the Kentucky hills. Never had military renown seemed fairer. The officers of the army had come back home to be received with adulation and to be advanced rapidly in the public service. And warfare appealed to young Beveridge powerfully, then, and ever afterward. Clearly, West Point offered the one opportunity for higher education, and, possibly, ultimate fame.

Being designated for the examination, along with other candidates in the congressional district, he went to Mattoon, in a neighboring county, confident of passing the ordeal there. He had ranked beyond the average in mathematics, in government, and geography in school. But, alas, in the midst of the examination, an amusing comment from a wag caused the country boy to laugh aloud. For that harmless laugh he was marked down, and, in the end, he lost to the winner by one fifth of one per cent. But for that joke and laugh, he would have gone to West Point

[1] MS. Autobiography.

and his life would have moved in lines remote from those he was to follow.

Utterly crushed with humiliation and despair, he could not reconcile himself to abandoning his ambition for an education. Taking his courage in both hands, he wrote a letter to be sent to the heads of a number of colleges. It was crude and unpromising enough to have wrecked all his prospects. 'I want to go to college,' he wrote. 'I have been through our high school, but I have no Latin and Greek. I have no money, either. I mean by that, I have no money at all; but I feel that I must go to college. Can you tell me how I can get through college in this condition and how much it will cost?'

Having mailed the letters, he waited anxiously for replies. With one exception, there were not even acknowledgments of those pathetic little notes. But the president of DePauw (then Asbury) University at Greencastle, Indiana, wrote kindly, though offering no encouragement. Evidently he knew no way to enter college with 'no money at all.' He merely gave the minimum cost of a year in his institution.

Reduced to despair again, hopelessly discouraged for the first time, the youth's mental anguish was too apparent in his face to escape observation, and one day, on the street, he was accosted by a lumberman (E. P. Anderson) for whom he had worked, and asked the cause of his trouble. Young Beveridge explained.

'Don't let that bother you,' said the lumberman heartily. 'I'll back you. When must you start?'

That was Saturday.

'College opens next Wednesday,' the boy replied.

'All right, come around to the office Monday morning, and I will stake you for the money.'

And thus it was that a joyous but anxious youth, with fifty dollars in his pocket and his personal belongings in a trunk, boarded the train in the early autumn of 1881 for Greencastle. With no Latin, little money, a meager wardrobe, and with none too much encouragement at home, the future would have seemed far from promising to the average boy. But he had passed by grim determination and force of character through the preparatory school of privation; had held his own with the rough characters of a logging-camp; and he carried with him an ardent ambition to get ahead. His work would not be easy; but it never had been. In addition to his regular work, he would have to take the Latin course in the preparatory school at DePauw, and somehow find the means constantly to replenish his purse as he went along.

And he boarded the train without the shadow of a doubt of winning.

CHAPTER II
DePAUW DAYS

I

A LEAN-FACED, strong-jawed youth, with a veritable mop of hair, and blue-gray eyes, alighted from the train at Greencastle, and, after arranging to leave his trunk temporarily at the station, which was at the edge of the town, set forth with hurried strides in search of room and board. Even then his instinct for going directly to those highest in authority led him to President Martin of the university. He found a kindly, shrewd Scotchman, whose real scholarship was mellowed by humanity and an intuitive understanding of the needs of youth; and the raw youth went directly to the point. He wanted a boarding-house, and the cheapest possible. The president gave him a note to the mistress of a students' boarding-house where he could get room and board for two dollars a week. That arranged, he hurried back to the station, lifted the heavy trunk on his shoulders, and, resting occasionally, carried it through the streets to his room.[1]

The university, then known as Asbury, but soon to be called DePauw, had been established forty years before as a Methodist institution, and it was the Alma Mater of two of the greatest figures Indiana had ever given to the Senate, Daniel Wolsey Voorhees and Joseph Ewing McDonald. At the time young Beveridge made his initial bow to the college with his trunk on his back, it had but few buildings — the Main College, with its famous Meharry Hall, with which his triumphs were to be associated; the West College, then the preparatory school; and the Music Conservatory. Other buildings, including a girls' dormitory, were to be constructed during his time there. Throughout the whole of his course the boys were to live in boarding-houses or in clubs of their own. Greencastle, seat of a rich agricultural county, had a population of less than four thousand, and the university gave the tone to the community. Then, as now, it was an attractive place, its comfortable homes with front porches set back in lawns, its streets lined with great trees, beautiful and fragrant in the spring and autumn. The town and gown mingled on the best of terms.

That first year was to be one of loneliness and bitter struggle. Having neither Greek nor Latin, Beveridge could not enter even

[1] MS. Autobiography.

the freshman class, and with his meager means it was impossible
to engage a Latin tutor. Nothing daunted, he enrolled in the
Latin class of the preparatory school, determined if possible to
do two years' work in one. This, together with other college
studies, would have been a strenuous undertaking, but he also
had to find means for the replenishment of his slender purse.
That year he was scarcely to sleep at all, and indeed through his
four years' course he was to sleep none too much. Very early
in his first term he determined to 'scorn delights and live laborious days.' To make every waking moment count, he put his
time on a budget system. He balanced his minutes as scrupulously as a banker his books. Beginning before the other students were up, he entered upon his schedule. Every minute was
assigned, and if at times he borrowed from one item in the time
account, he made it up as meticulously as a good business man
dealing with money. He spared but little time for play, and did
not ordinarily attend the parties until his last year, when he fell in
love. One of his classmates, Frank C. Payne, who has a vivid
memory of his college days, is sure that 'until his senior year
he probably never held a girl's hand,' though he occasionally
took one of the girl students to a lecture, as was the custom. He
had no moments of leisure. The time not given to the studies for
the classroom was spent in the college library; and he took a
special course in the reading of history under the guidance of Dr.
John Clark Ridpath, vice-president of the university and Professor of Belles-Lettres and History, who had written an entertaining history of the world which had an enormous sale. This was
entirely independent of the regular college course.

A miser of his time, Beveridge crossed the campus and went to
his boarding-house with rapid strides and was impatient with
classmates who hailed him for a chat. The marvel is that he was
not decidedly unpopular, for he not only took little time for play,
but he carried himself with an air of super-self-confidence, and
he 'had a snappy, assertive manner which did not take kindly
to contradiction.'[1] His strong chin and square shoulders were a
challenge. Ever fond of congenial society and the best of company, he was always to be irritable over interruptions in his
work.

And yet, despite it all, he immediately won the respect and
admiration of the more serious and ambitious of his fellow students, and was taken into the Psi Phi chapter of the Delta Kappa
Epsilon fraternity, a group which 'had become a by-word for
its hard-headedness and hard-fistedness — the ambitious chaps,
the prize-takers. Their name was arrogance with just a touch

[1] Frank C. Payne to the author.

of the bully in them.'[1] It was then that he conceived the idea of organizing a fraternity boarding-house and becoming the steward.[2] This fed him and reduced expenses a very little. We have an indication of his standing with his fraternity brothers in the letter of a committee which sent a note of thanks to his mother for three huge cakes she had baked for the boys. 'More than once,' runs the letter, 'we have rejoiced at our good fortune in securing Bro. Beveridge as a member of our fraternity. His ability, energy, and ambition have given him a high rank in his class, while his gentlemanly deportment and dignified, courteous behavior have made him a favorite among his fraternity brothers and the college in general.'[3] This was within four months of his entrance at the university.

But worries and humiliations pursued him. Always interested in military matters, he was eager to join the company of cadets, to whom the Government had assigned an officer to drill them. Here, too, was an opportunity for good-fellowship, but the cadets wore tight-fitting gray suits, and the outfit cost close to twenty-five dollars. It was at this time that he sent his father an itemized account of all his expenditures down to an item of fifteen cents for postage stamps, ending with the pathetic line: 'At this time on hand, $2.15.' In sheer desperation he turned to his father for a loan to buy the suit.

'The above is a correct account to the cent of my expenditures. I have tried to improve it. Not a penny has gone foolishly. What about my cadet suit? Suit, cape and all, will cost from $21.50 to $25.50. If I get one I stand a good show of promotion this year. They wear well, some of the boys having worn them three and four years. They are the regular school suit. Please decide this at once. If I do not get it, I must get a hat, for my old one is about worn out.'

Evidently there was no favorable response to the plea, and a little later, when a student offered to advance him enough money for the outfit, he wrote his father for his consent to accept. 'You know,' he wrote, 'there is just a little pride in everybody, and I would like to come home in this suit. I trust that it is excusable. The suit is modest, neat, very durable, and not at all showy.'[4]

Meanwhile, despite his humiliations over money, he was able to write home with evident satisfaction of his progress in the university. 'You will receive a paper in a day or so,' he wrote, 'the "Asbury Monthly." The article on "The Rise and Fall of

[1] MS. Autobiography.   [2] *Ibid.*
[3] J. W. Finch, Douglas Morris, and R. R. Overstreet, Feb. 1, 1882.
[4] Sept. 15, 1881.

Human Intelligence," by Luther Liquid, is by me. Big honor for a freshman.' He had passed in all his examinations, and been chosen by the Platonian Literary Society to read Washington's 'Farewell Address' before the student body. Within three months of his matriculation, he was able to write home that he had satisfied his professors, finished six months' work in Latin, received the highest grades in all his studies, and become leader of one faction of his class in politics. 'I feel guilty every morning on arising that I am not doing all I can,' he concluded, with a conciliatory gesture to a stern, exacting father who brooked no nonsense.

II

The Platonian Literary Society, to which reference has been made, was known affectionately as 'Old Plato,' and contributed to the development of the eager youth as a ready debater. It also seethed with politics. It was not until the second term of the first year that he became an active member and was assigned for a debate on the tariff question, on the side of Protection. Because he was untried, he was given the middle place, leaving the opening and the closing to more experienced men. Years later, he was to recall the incidents of that evening. 'I was so nervous when I rose to reply,' he said, 'that I was sure I would fail. But by the time I had uttered my first sentence, all nervousness went away. Also I lost sight of my prepared argument. I pounced upon my opponent's slip in logic, and on that destroyed his whole effort. I also had prepared some two minutes of "glittering eloquence" to close the debate with. But I sacrificed it to deliver blow after blow of practical argument.... And so I ended. Applause broke out from both sides. I had succeeded. I had found myself.' [1] Thereafter he was regularly to participate in the debates and to be the leader of his faction in the politics of the society. The leader of the opposing faction was a tall, slim, long-haired youth from Winchester, James E. Watson, who was also to reach the Senate of the United States and to cross his path many times.

Rapidly as he developed as a debater, Beveridge ranked higher in college as an orator, and it was the dire need of money that drove him into his first contest for the E. H. Staley Prize. He knew, from observation in the debating society, that at least three of his competitors were better speakers. There was just one chance — it was stipulated that, all else being equal, the oration having the largest percentage of Anglo-Saxon words

[1] MS. Autobiography.

was to be awarded the prize. After writing his speech, he shut himself up in his room with Crabbe's 'Synonyms' and Roget's 'Thesaurus' and 'dug out every Latin derivative by the roots.'[1] That accomplished, he critically studied his delivery and found it faulty. Thereafter, until the contest, every morning before dawn found him hurrying away to a beech wood, where he practiced to the trees.[2] Taking as his subject 'The Ideal Philosophy,' he donned the armor and fought zealously for Christ against Confucius, Buddha, and Plato, and won the award.[3] His financial pain momentarily was eased again.

As the last term drew to a close, he astounded the Latin teacher, Dr. Henry B. Longden, to whom he was devoted, with the demand that he be examined on two years' work. Unable to dissuade him, the Professor gave him the examination, and he passed. 'I am glad to hear of his great success,' wrote his half-sister Eva to his parents. 'That speaks well for him. He signed his letter "your loving Yaller Hammer brother." You know we girls used to call him that when provoked by him.'[4]

That summer found him working in the harvest fields of Illinois, and he returned in the autumn with seventy-five dollars.

III

The beginning of the second year was to be memorable in marking the beginning of a beautiful and intimate friendship that was to persist through life. Among the freshmen was a fat, rosy-cheeked youngster responding to the name of David Graham Phillips, destined to literary renown in later years. The first meeting remained a vivid memory to the future novelist into middle age. The freshman was talking with a friend in the corridor of one of the buildings when Beveridge entered in his usual hurried manner. 'He was a strong, straight figure,' wrote Phillips later, 'short rather than tall, dressed in a baggy old suit that yet somehow deceived you into thinking it was all right; a pallid, keen, alert face with a powerful jaw and gray-blue eyes that suggested a runner in sight of the goal; longish fair hair, a perfect mop of it. I remember his voice, too — someone stopped him in his quick, almost sharp walk, and introduced us. The voice was curiously clear and penetrating — almost painfully penetrating then.... "You may not like him at first," said the boy who had introduced us when he had gone on, "but you will as soon as you know him better." It so happened that I did like him, however, for there was a fascination to me in strength —

[1] MS. Autobiography. [2] *Ibid.*
[3] Contemporary Greencastle paper. [4] February 5, 1882.

and this new acquaintance of mine, with his unkempt hair and his burning eyes and his voice like a trumpet, was obviously strong mentally and physically.' [1]

The friendship of these youths was instantaneous and it was to intensify with the years. Soon they were rooming together, in the home of Professor John B. DeMotte on College Avenue, South [2] — the son of a banker and the boy of the logging-camp. There were no secrets between them. Phillips knew of Beveridge's poverty, and marveled greatly at his ability to do his work, win contests, and 'make a living — a good living — in addition.' He would have thought it incredible had he not seen it with his own eyes. He noticed that there were months, hard winter months, when the schedule of his friend allowed him but four hours' sleep a night. 'Many mornings,' he wrote, 'I have seen him long before sunrise start across the snow into the woods to practice his voice, which meant several hours of exhaustive exercise; and he would get back in time to study Shakespeare or the great orations for an hour before breakfast.'' [3]

Often he would leave the sitting-room where the boys were idly chatting, and be back before his absence had been generally noticed, but in that hour he had prepared for a recitation or two. Phillips observed that, eager as any for a lark, the moment it was over Beveridge was back at his work while the others wasted hours discussing the good time they had had. [4]

Having found himself, he was much happier in his second year. But having tasted the fruits of victory, he was eager for more contests, and he still needed money. There were several contests to be won. The boys of his fraternity entered into a conspiracy to win them all. It was Beveridge's idea to purchase from Washington C. DePauw a large mirror for the fraternity house before which members could practice for their speeches. [5] He thought it important that they should study their facial expression as well as gesticulation. It was in the days when oratory carried the highest honors at DePauw and when he who won a contest was as much a hero as he who was received into the Porcellian Club at Harvard, or one who made the crew or team at Yale. In later life, Beveridge was to insist that he had no natural aptitude for oratory, but manifestly he had. His temperament was always oratorical, however much discouraged he may have been at first with its mechanics. He was disgusted with himself in the fraternity-house days because the studied gesture was be-

---

[1] *Success Magazine*, August, 1905.   [2] Now the home of Professor Edwin Post.
[3] *Success Magazine*, August, 1905.   [4] *Ibid.*
[5] It is still hanging over the fireplace in the smoking-room of the present Deke House.

yond him, and he was unable to run the gamut of tones. He hated it. Why should not an audience be viewed as a composite man — a single being? Why not talk to a crowd precisely as one would talk to an individual, 'excepting only that the statements should be simpler and clearer, the strokes of the argument bigger and plainer, the tone of the voice and method of speaking just enough greater to make each unit of this big personality, the audience, feel that you are talking quite naturally?'[1] Indeed, this was the method of direct address he adopted almost from the beginning; and this it was which set him apart from most of the aspiring college orators. One of his classmates, after almost fifty years, remembered that 'as a speaker he differed from most youths in that he was never so flowery and always had the modern direct manner.'[2]

Then, too, he thought the usual college method of writing speeches wrong — the selecting of a subject, the reading of whatever anyone else had said upon it, and making the speech a mosaic of other people's opinions. He would adopt a new scheme. He would read on the subject solely to get the facts, then think over the facts, and write out of his own feelings and convictions. Then he would test the soundness of his opinions by reading those of more mature minds.[3]

Thus that second winter found young Beveridge in the small hours of the morning bending over his desk writing speeches, reading the master orators; the dawn found him far away in the beech woods trying his voice against the winds; and at odd moments he took his place before the mirror to study his expression and gestures. The result was a year of triumphs.

That was the year he won the Landes Prize in Meharry Hall in a fundamentalist attack on rationalism, speaking on 'The Irrepressible Conflict,' and, incongruously enough, permitting Ingersoll to affect his style. This contest, too, was symbolic of the future, for one of his competitors was James E. Watson, who lashed the rationalists in an oration on 'The Great Conflict.'[4] That same year he won the W.C.T.U. Prize with a prohibition oration that enormously delighted the 'Organist,' the paper of the temperance society. And then the W. D. Parr Historical Essay Contest was won with a paper on 'The Influence of the Cotton Plant upon American Civilization,' tracing the Civil War to cotton.

Thereafter he won contest after contest, and in his junior year he won the Coffin-Finney Prize Oratorical Contest with 'The Impending Conflict,' in which he expressed scant sympathy

[1] MS. Autobiography. [2] Frank C. Payne to the author.
[3] MS. Autobiography. [4] Contemporary Greencastle paper.

with the complaints of labor, and impressed the local papers with his 'fiery and magnetic delivery' and his 'penetrating voice.' The young orator painted a black picture of poverty and inequality; but socialism? No, 'let socialism attempt the pillage of private property and our landowners' cannon will answer.' After all, genius on the one hand and drink on the other explained the inequality, though privilege should be driven out.

It was this year, too, that he won his largest prize, the De-Pauw Oratorical, open to one freshman, two sophomores, three juniors, and four seniors. When it was learned he was planning to enter, the other contestants waited upon the head of the Department of Oratory, Joseph Carhart, to announce that they would not enter if Beveridge, an almost certain winner, did. 'Very well,' said the Professor, 'we will set up a standard and Beveridge will contest against that standard, and, if he surpasses it, he wins, that's all.' The others carried out their threat, and the one-man contest became the gossip of the town and campus. On the appointed day the hall was packed; and when the speaker closed, he was given an ovation, and a hundred dollars in gold was dropped into his hand.[1]

IV

But still money was the problem; and in the summer of his junior year he contracted as a book-agent, but, finding the sales bad in the small county seats, he wanted to throw up the contract. His father protested that 'a contract is sacred'; and so he struck out into the country with his books. He took along an umbrella, three shirts, two suits of light underclothing. Each night he would carefully collect information on the houses where he would call the following day. He learned the names, politics, religion, favorite child, who was the dominant figure in the family. 'Von Moltke could not have planned the invasion of France with more careful detail than I arranged my daily assault on the homes of the countryside,' he wrote later.[2] To the pious he talked religion; with the politically minded he discussed politics; and drink, horses, cattle-raising to those interested. That fall he returned to college with two hundred and twenty-five dollars, and during his junior year dressed better than he ever had before. So impressed was the book company with his prowess as a super-salesman that the next summer he was given the entire State of Iowa. Selecting a group of college boys eager for a lark as agents under his command, he

[1] Richard Lloyd Jones, *Collier's*, Oct. 15, 1910.   [2] MS. Autobiography.

chartered a car, 'dined at Chicago, lunched at Davenport, and dumped off at West Liberty and Des Moines.' [1] As commander-in-chief, Beveridge established his headquarters at Des Moines, whence he directed the operations in the field, and his Des Moines experiences were to trail pleasant memories through the years. His campaign was a monetary success. Years later, soon after his election to the Senate, he found himself seated at dinner beside Senator Allison. Turning a reproving eye upon him, the venerable Iowa statesman, asked:

'Are you the man who is responsible for "Error's Chains" in Iowa?'

'I am,' Beveridge answered.

'Well, Iowa is snowed under with it.'

Senator Dolliver insisted in later years that there was not a center table in the parlor of a country house in Iowa that did not have 'Error's Chains' beside the Bible.

But that summer in Iowa was to introduce him to two orators who entered into his own life. It was the year that the youthful Dolliver, destined to be his comrade in arms in the most bitter senatorial battle of his career, sprang into fame in a speech of spectacular brilliance as keynote speaker in the Iowa State Convention. Far back in the hall, young Beveridge listened in amazement and admiration.

But even more eventful to him was his opportunity to hear Ingersoll, in those days the *beau idéal* of every budding college orator. That summer Ingersoll lectured in Des Moines, and the eager young orator got a seat in the front where he could study the master at close range. He was near enough to observe that Ingersoll wore silk stockings, and that made an impression; also that he was 'perfectly groomed and dressed' and wore patent-leather pumps. The fact that he 'wore evening clothes which fit him to perfection,' and that 'his whole physical impression on the audience was one of extreme neatness,' entered at once into the young man's conception of the proper accessories of oratory at its best. He observed that the lecture was not all committed to memory, and that the orator 'laid his roll of manuscript on a little table in the rear of the stage.' Then, too, he noted carefully the great artist's approach to his audience. Delighted with the beauty of the speaker's English, impressed with the dramatic manner of the delivery, he was puzzled at the occasional witticisms or stories, 'not necessary to the argument.' So long as he lived, he was to insist that there is no humor in the world's great orations and he was never to resort to it. [2]

Thus he carried away from Des Moines the memory of two

[1] *Asbury Monthly*, October, 1884.   [2] MS. Autobiography.

notable experiences — the triumph of young Dolliver and the eloquence of Ingersoll.

V

It was the year that Beveridge was to make his initial bow upon the stump. A sagacious party leader in Greencastle, with an eye to new and promising recruits, persuaded the Republican State Committee to use him in the Blaine campaign. Delighted with the opportunity, Beveridge abandoned all thoughts of returning to the university until the close of the campaign. Years later, he was to recall the assiduity of his preparations. 'For weeks,' he said, 'I labored over the writing.... I put in, here and there, imitations of Ingersoll. I had a passage on "the wings of the morning" that made the American eagle look like a young robin just thrown from the nest.'[1] Naturally he did not fail to wave the 'bloody shirt' a bit, and much waving was necessary to divert attention from some unsavory incidents in the career of Blaine. Indeed, before the convention Beveridge had favored Arthur!

It was in a blacksmith shop in Parke County that he made his first appearance, and the next night in the same county he spoke in a barn. If the speech, two hours in length, had the crudities of his inexperience and the intolerance of the times, it pleased his fellow partisans, and the Democrats conceded him the gift of expression. The 'Rockville Tribune'[2] thought that 'brilliant' was the right word, since the argument was scant and the 'facts' were 'horrible.' Even so, 'his youth, vivacity, and general style made his address wonderfully attractive.' But why, at the end of each rhetorical passage, did he fall back, strike an attitude, and make a 'dramatic pause' such as was taught in the schools? A little campaigning in the country would rid him of that vice.

His boyishness and obscurity brought some embarrassing moments, as at Bloomington, where a company of local dignitaries, expecting Governor Beveridge of Illinois, appeared at the station to receive the honored guest becomingly. As the passengers alighted from the train, the committee peered anxiously into each face, but Beveridge was ignored. Assuming that the speaker was being sought, he introduced himself. 'What, you!' they exclaimed in a chorus. The carriage was dismissed and the committee walked their speaker to the hotel in sullen silence. The chairman of the meeting refused to serve, and another, in pity, volunteered. Within a few moments the delighted crowd of partisans were cheering wildly, and the in-

[1] MS. Autobiography.   [2] Sept. 25, 1884.

cident was to enter into the folklore of the community. When, a little later, he spoke with Fred Douglass, the Negro, at Bethany Park, the party press began to notice him and comment on a style resembling that of 'Harrison, the boy preacher'; upon his 'magnetism,' his 'short, incisive sentences,' his 'command of language.' He spoke with the former Secretary of the Navy, Richard W. Thompson of the 'silver tongue,' at Milroy. A relative, meeting him in Indianapolis and learning from others of his triumphs, wrote the good news to his mother. 'Allie is indeed a bright boy,' the letter ran, 'and a bright future is before him if he does not fall in love with some confounded girl. I gave him a lecture on that subject tonight.... I think there is a girl in Greencastle that has the young man by the ear.' [1] When Blaine swept through the State in a private train, young Beveridge's cup of joy was running over when he was assigned to accompany the party as far as Worthington, where Blaine was to remain and address the multitude. After Ingersoll, no one appealed quite so much to his imagination as the 'plumed knight,' and he 'listened to Blaine even more carefully than he had to Ingersoll.' The magnetic politician impressed him even more than his first idol because of the absence from his speech of 'thrilling flights of eloquence.' He observed that Blaine 'had no time or ammunition to waste,' 'made every shot count,' and spoke so simply that 'the dullest could understand.' But one impression was disappointing — it seemed to the boy that the great man was 'unfair.' [2]

So ended the interlude in his college work. He had heard Dolliver, Ingersoll, and Blaine, and he carried new impressions back to the university, from which he would profit in the contests ahead.

VI

Never parsimonious, Beveridge's earnings from the Iowa venture had dwindled sadly, and he again found himself embarrassed as to means. One day he walked briskly into the office of Professor Joseph Carhart, the teacher of oratory. The warm friendship of the two had come from a struggle and a surrender. The professor had found him difficult at first, because 'his mind was combative rather than receptive.' [3] At first believing Carhart's methods wrong, he had opposed them in the presence of the class and had been roughly handled. Seething with indignation, he had carried his grievance to Dr. John Clark

[1] C. W. Doyle to Mrs. Beveridge, Oct. 18, 1884.
[2] MS. Autobiography.   [3] Collier's, Oct. 15, 1910.

Ridpath, who finally persuaded him to call upon Carhart at his home. After a long talk, he admitted his error and wanted to apologize before the class, but was told to do his work and all would be forgiven.

'Professor,' he said, as he rushed into his office, 'I need about a hundred dollars to finish here at DePauw.'

Sitting down at a table, he took a pencil and began to write down the various prizes that were open — the Historical, Latin, Home Oratorical, State Oratorical, Interstate Oratorical.

'Now, you see, if I get all these, I shall have a balance,' he said.

Carhart looked at him incredulously, but encouraged him to try. Before the year was over, he had won all but the Latin Prize.[1]

And this, too, despite diversions he had not permitted before. It was at this time that he had his first taste of liquor, when, celebrating a football victory of the university in another town, some of the boys swaggered through the streets singing:

> 'I take my whiskey straight,
> And I drink my lager b-e-e-r;
> For I'm a roaring, rollicking son of a gun,
> And the son of a gambolier.'

It was to be his last diversion of the sort for a long while, for there was a more attractive diversion that year at DePauw. One of the outstanding men in the community was Colonel George J. Langsdale, editor of the local paper, and a politician whose influence extended far beyond the section in which he lived. Later, he was to be the head of the commission in charge of the building of the Soldiers' and Sailors' Monument in Indianapolis. But Beveridge was not so much interested in him as in his daughter, who lived in the large old-fashioned brick corner house and was a student in the university. Kate Langsdale, pretty, vivacious, with dash and poise, was the belle of the community and the school, and after Beveridge met her, during the remainder of his college days 'a girl in Greencastle' verily 'led him by the ear.'

VII

The supreme honor in DePauw was to represent the university in the State Oratorical Contest in Indianapolis. Beveridge aspired to the distinction as a matter of ambition, but he needed the money, too. Ten entered the contest, but these had dwindled to two when it occurred, and Beveridge won easily with an

[1] *Collier's*, Oct. 15, 1910.

oration on 'The Conflict of Capital and Labor.' At Indianapolis his triumph was repeated after the oration had been carefully revised, and the press there was more than kind in its comments. One of the papers, finding his carriage graceful, his accentuation good, and his voice excellent, thought his delivery 'somewhat too forceful.' [1] Another, finding him 'impressive,' thought that 'his words and gestures seem to be the outburst of an inward fire.' [2]

But now the Interstate Contest was ahead, and for weeks there was little sleep for the young orator. Out from these contests were to come some of the famous orators of the generation. In the University of Wisconsin, young Bob La Follette had won the Interstate with an oration on 'Iago,' and in Illinois a young man named Bryan was to win a second place. It meant something to win in an Interstate, and long before dawn Beveridge could be seen hastening to the beech woods. His roommate, David Graham Phillips, marveled at his fortitude as he peered through the window upon his retreating figure.

The oration had been prepared with meticulous care for the third time, scanned critically for the elimination of every useless word and of every unnecessary 'flight of eloquence.' The sentences were made short and dynamic. The purport of it all was that we were drifting into a class conflict that justice could prevent. Not in equality of condition, which he rejected as impossible, but equality of rights — there he sought the remedy. Education, conscience in the business field, and Christian faith — these he thought could reconcile capital and labor to each other. It was an earnest paper of the sort that appealed to the conservative instincts of the times.

It was characteristic of young Beveridge that he set forth for Columbus, where the contest was held, with the utmost confidence. The speaker from Illinois who preceded him had spoken beautifully and charmed the audience, which was clearly impatient when Beveridge rose. 'Consciously or unconsciously,' said Carhart, telling the DePauw students of the contest, 'the speaker was unfavorably affected by the sentiment which dominated the audience. He who had been a stranger to defeat, who heretofore had never blanched in the presence of an audience, appeared uneasy. The directness of his manner was in striking contrast to the insinuating style of the speaker who had preceded him, and appeared harsh to the audience. The head wind against which he began the voyage is rising and threatens to become a gale. He seems to waver and struggle like a ship stemming wind and tide. But it was only for a moment. The

[1] *Indianapolis News.*　　[2] *Indianapolis Herald.*

sensuous pleasure which he had disturbed has given place to a higher mental state. The audience is beginning to think.' [1]

And the result was victory. The 'Ohio State Journal' thought his speech 'made undoubtedly the finest impression of the evening,' but found him 'so free from embarrassment and restraint that the criticism might possibly be made that he lacked dignity.'

When the news of the victory reached Greencastle, the students went on a rampage, marching in groups to the homes of the professors and cheering until after midnight. Preparations immediately were made for a warm welcome home. When he alighted from the train, artillery roared a salute, the reception committee, headed by the president of the university, showered him with congratulations, and he was marched to a carriage between lines of the Cadet Corps presenting arms. Another salute was fired as the procession reached the grounds of the university, and the victor was conducted to the platform in Meharry Hall to the enthusiastic acclaim of the student body. Carhart described the contest, Dr. Martin spoke for the faculty, Mayor McClary for the town, and then the spokesman of the students stepped forward and James E. Watson, future Senator, paid his tribute. The victor responded modestly in sentimental mood, and the glories of the day were over. It had been a great day. 'I can see the procession winding through the streets of the town, with everybody watching it and cheering,' wrote David Graham Phillips many years afterward. [2]

That night Beveridge, Phillips, and other students sat in the room the two occupied while the hero gave his version of the victory; and when all were gone, Beveridge sat down at a table to work while Phillips went to bed. At the Commencement, Beveridge spoke on Robert Burns; and, perhaps a little too exuberant in confidence, he turned to face the world.

VIII

But Nature had exacted her penalty for the flagrant disregard of her laws, and he emerged from the university badly broken in health. The physician he consulted in some consternation found him suffering from nervous exhaustion, and urged him to go to Arizona or Colorado and remain until restored. But this required money, and he had none. While he was puzzling over his predicament, a young man in Sullivan suggested that they follow the sunset trail to western Kansas, then sparsely settled and given over largely to cattle-raising and cowboys. It meant outdoor air

[1] Contemporary Greencastle paper.　　　[2] *Success Magazine*, August, 1905.

GROUP AT DEPAUW UNIVERSITY

Beveridge is second from the right in the middle row. David Graham Phillips is in the center of the back row.

and exercise, and young Beveridge seized the opportunity. He needed time to readjust himself, for, penniless, and broken in health, the 'old terror of the world' which had oppressed his childhood came back to him, and he literally was soul-sick. The inevitable reaction from his triumphs had set in.[1]

Many years later, while passing through this country on a campaign tour, he wrote his young son of the then far-off adventure: 'When I graduated from college, I came out here for my health, which was sadly broken by overwork. At Wichita we bought two broncos and a light wagon and started westward. When we got to Dodge City, we sold our outfit and came by railway to Garden City. It was a hard trip — cowboys shooting, and all that. From Garden City we went on by stage to Dighton, Kansas. There was no railroad. Dighton had half a dozen sod houses — houses made by piling strips of sod on one another. I stayed there for three months. I became a partner of a cowboy named McClelland, and made several hundred dollars "locating settlers" on Government land. They came in by the hundreds, whole families dwelling in covered wagons searching for free lands and new homes.... At that time the country was a "range"; it was very dry and impossible to make crops grow. There were droves of wild antelope and many wild horses. There were literally millions of prairie dogs — little animals that look not unlike squirrels — and tremendous rattlesnakes. Now the country is all fenced into farms and the people are well-to-do.'

Thus he was personally to witness and be a part of the romantic drama of the western drift of population, to see and welcome the long processions of covered wagons bearing the hopes and fortunes of robust Americans, to mingle with the cowboys and the lusty, gusty pioneers, descendants of the followers of Daniel Boone. Always he was to remember these experiences and to love the West. But he was narrowly to escape the bullet of a bad-man.

The western Kansas of that period was primitive and rough. No railroad penetrated to the tiny settlement with its sod houses, and it was only when the stage-coach operating between Fort Dodge and Fort Wallace clattered into Dighton, the halfway point, that the settlers heard by word of mouth from the outside world. The land as yet was for the most part uncultivated, and the vast lonely prairies stretching to the horizon on all sides were abandoned to the cattle industry. The very small towns scattered here and there were dominated by the saloons and bullied by the gamblers, and the rough population administered justice without much recourse to the courts. The village of

[1] MS. Autobiography.

Dighton grew apace, and with the cowboys in picturesque costumes, the swaggering gamblers, the impoverished settlers, the pale and broken student from DePauw mingled on terms of familiarity. Immediately he found something to do.

He formed a partnership, as we have seen, with a cowboy for 'locating settlers.' The cowboy knew every inch of the ground, every section line and surveying stone; and the student's persuasive talking powers were expected to draw business. Almost immediately the firm was the most flourishing in the settlement. Determined to miss no opportunity, Beveridge took out a claim for himself five miles from town and on the line of a prospective railroad. Soon he was interested in a real estate venture, for many of the settlers, penniless and impatient, were willing to part with their claims for a song. The town itself was building up, and tradition has it that Beveridge first platted it off in town lots that were for sale. Certainly he considered himself a real estate broker for a time.[1]

Meanwhile the outdoor life, abundant exercise, plain wholesome food, and freedom from anxiety were restoring his nervous energy, and he found amusement enough in the *opéra bouffe* life of the community — the cowboys in from the range firing their revolvers, drinking, pouring their hard-earned wages into the eager palms of the worst of gamblers. Fist-fights flourished, hatreds the most elemental and fierce were engendered, and no one interfered. There was little ordinary crime, like stealing, for, in the absence of courts, the penalty was speedy under the administration of the mob.

Living on terms of equality with these rough men, Beveridge made friends. His education set him apart in the eyes of these illiterates. They rather plumed themselves on having him among them. His life in the logging-camp had brought him an understanding of both the hearts and psychology of such people. Many of them he liked. When one of these, a cowboy, became ill, he took him into his own room and nursed him through his sickness. It was not long until the grateful cowboy was able to repay him in full measure.

The stealing of a horse had left Dighton seething with excitement. A well-digger, drunk to inarticulation, had been found staggering about with a halter in his hand which was identified as having been on the lost animal. The circumstantial evidence was damning. The well-digger was too drunk to explain, or even to understand. His silence seemed more damning still. A lynching party was instantly organized, the well-digger was roughly seized, and was being dragged along to his death. The

[1] MS. Autobiography.

boy coldly, and he marched the stage-driver at the point of the gun out on the country road and warned him that he would be shot like a mad dog if he returned. The discomfited bully made no reply, but strode hurriedly down the road, never to be seen again at Dighton.[1]

Thus narrowly did Beveridge escape an untimely end.

The incident illustrates three qualities of the man — his keen sense of justice, his hatred of mob rule, his courage in the face of danger. These qualities, together with his breezy comradeship, had made him an outstanding man in the settlement. For a time he thought of remaining, of practicing law, of dealing in real estate, and of ultimately entering politics. But the temptation was fugitive. His ambition was pitched upon a higher plane. It was only when he had definitely determined to leave that he wrote to his father. It was to report the complete restoration of his health and his plan to return to Indianapolis and enter a law office. 'If I stay here,' he wrote, 'I can make money, but I can never be much of anything. If I return to Indianapolis, I can't make any money for some years, but I can become a first-class lawyer. This town will be as large or much larger than Sullivan in five years, and I can be the chief man of the place. I can make $10,000 or $15,000 in the next ten years, but I can never be a master in anything. If I go to Indianapolis, it will be a long hard pull, but some day I'll be a first-class lawyer and speaker. What do you say?'[2]

We have no record of the father's response, but the son took his courage in both hands and turned eastward. He had four hundred dollars in his purse when he reached the Hoosier capital, but much of this went almost immediately to relieve the necessities of his father. He found himself facing some lean years.

[1] Interview with Colonel Tom Gallegher, *New York Sunday Telegram*, Feb. 25, 1900; Beveridge to McClure Newspaper Syndicate, March 26, 1908.

[2] Beveridge to his father, September, 1886.

blood of the mob was boiling and it was in no mood to brook interference when young Beveridge happened upon the scene. The injustice of the thing appalled him, and at the deadly peril of his life, for all were armed and some were drunk, he managed to stop the procession and make it listen. With all his persuasive powers he pleaded for the well-digger's life. The sheer audacity of the pale-faced youngster made them listen. The mob had no right to take human life, he said. There were courts somewhere to pass upon the guilt of the accused. He had been denied a hearing or an opportunity to explain, since he was too drunk to talk. Had he not always borne the reputation of a hard-working, honest man? He had a bitter enemy, and was it not possible that the enemy had placed the halter in his hand?

On, on he talked, until the mob relented, and the intended victim was given his freedom. Beveridge had won his first case.

But in winning for the well-digger, he had made a mortal enemy of one of the worst characters in the community — the stage-driver known to be a deadly enemy of the man found with the halter in his hand. Every member of the mob had understood the allusion of the orator. That day at the dinner-table the stage-driver sought to force a quarrel with Beveridge, and he was met halfway. Infuriated at the bullying manner of the bad-man, the youth expressed his opinion of his tormentor with picturesque freedom and force. Springing to his feet and striking the table with his fist, the stage-driver left the room swearing he would have the life of his white-faced accuser. It was no idle threat. As Beveridge was returning to the shack he called his office, his foe stepped from behind a small building and confronted him with pointed pistol, his face drawn with passion. The unarmed youth, assuming himself doomed, launched upon a savage denunciation of the cowardice of the tense man with the pointed gun. All the while his amazement grew that his enemy did not shoot. Instead, he stood cowed-fashion, shifting from foot to foot, the pistol no longer pointed straight at the heart. At length Beveridge turned to walk away, and there behind him stood his friend the cowboy and a gambler, each with a pistol covering the cowering bully. Having witnessed the scene at the table, the cowboy had followed the boy who had nursed him, with the view to protecting him against assault.

'Are you through skinnin' him, Mr. Beveridge?' he asked in even tones.

'Steve!' exclaimed Beveridge, recovering from his astonishment. 'Yes, Steve, I guess I have given him the best I have in the shop.'

'Well, then, I'll take charge of him for a while,' said the cow-

CHAPTER III
AT THE BAR

I

BEVERIDGE reached Indiana in the midst of the congressional campaign of 1886, and a zest for the fight, whetted by his triumphs of two years before, led him into the field. Soon he was busily engaged upon the stump and the press was giving him notice seldom accorded to one so young. The Republican press was extravagant in its praise of the 'young man eloquent,' and the Democratic papers were contemptuous in their sneers. This hostile attitude of the opposition was invited; for, taking his cue from his elders in his party, he was scarcely ingratiating to the foe, and far from fair. Cleveland was President, and the young orator was not alone in finding him wicked and unpatriotic in his policies. The exuberant young man was waving the rather frayed 'bloody shirt' with the best of them, and after a fashion that was to embarrass and disgust him many years afterward. 'The present Administration,' he exclaimed to rapturous applause in Kokomo, 'is built upon blood and fraud. It is the creature of the shot-gun policy of the South. It owes its existence to the night rider and assassin. It is a structure cemented with the blood of a thousand black freedmen.' If this seems ridiculous today, it was the fashion then, and the 'wise and the good' and the 'pure of heart' shouted their approval heartily.

Scarcely less strange, and yet remarkable in view of the orator's attitude ten years later, was his speech at Wabash. 'The Administration,' he declared, 'is an Administration of gold bugs. Silver is the money of the people. There is just so much gold, silver, and paper money in the country to buy everything purchasable. Wall Street has the gold, the people the silver and paper. If the silver should be piled up in the vaults of the Treasury, if its coinage should be contracted, if the paper currency should be limited, the value of gold would be doubled or trebled or quadrupled. The people would lose, Wall Street would gain. The people would become poor, Wall Street wax fat in wealth and riches. That thing a Democratic Administration of a New York President, with a New York Secretary of the Treasury, a New York Secretary of the Navy, and New York officials throughout the Treasury Department, is trying to bring about.' [1]

[1] Early scrapbook clippings.

Strange! — and yet many Republican national leaders were sharing such views ten years before the great struggle came when the money question became an issue, and the young man's argument was in no sense displeasing to the party managers in Indiana.

Thus, by plunging again into the State campaign, the young orator maintained and advanced the prestige he had won as a speaker. Even so early he was promoted from the barns and blacksmith shops to more æsthetic platforms.

II

In seeking a mentor for his legal studies, Beveridge followed the custom of his life in aiming high. The Indianapolis of the latter part of the eighties was less than a hundred thousand in population, and a little drab, but it had a distinguished bar. The foremost Republican in the town was Benjamin Harrison, soon to be elected to the Presidency, and the confident youth fared forth to ask permission to sit at his feet as a disciple in the law. Had not Harrison been on the Blaine train in 1884, and had not Beveridge met him? Of course he would be remembered, cordially received, and sympathetically advised. But it appears that he who later was to reveal a veritable genius for affronting party leaders and senators with his cold and aloof dignity was not in the melting mood when the young man called. Years later, Beveridge was to retain a resentful recollection of that visit. 'I had met him three or four times in the Blaine campaign,' he wrote, 'and supposed, of course, that he would remember me. So I asked him if I could read law in his office. He dismissed me with a coldness and curtness that both angered and hurt me.' [1]

But he was not discouraged. Rather did the rebuff put him on his mettle. There was another leader of the bar, who professionally and intellectually was fully the equal of Harrison, and in the human qualities his superior. Joseph E. McDonald had been one of the ablest members of the United States Senate, and was still conspicuous enough in Democratic politics to be mentioned frequently for the Presidency. Associated with him in the practice of law was John M. Butler, a man of enormous legal erudition and a Republican advocate who set an example in dignity and restraint that few followed. The firm had the largest practice in the State, and to these two men Beveridge turned after his curt dismissal by Harrison. The reception he received from Senator McDonald was always to linger in his memory.

[1] MS. Autobiography.

'He received me with great kindness,' he wrote, 'listened to me patiently and sympathetically.' [1] Within a week he had been given a chair in the office, but without salary and with no definite promises. It was enough.

It would not have been enough with one of less courage and iron will. Most of the money he had brought from Kansas was gone. He had no source of income. He himself has given us an idea of what these early months with the firm meant. 'When I went into that office, I did not read law, I devoured it. In those days, and for years after, I was a veritable ball of fire, with night and day very much the same with me. For three or four months I managed to live on a single meal a day.' But instead of resenting his fate, he sought in every unobtrusive way to make himself useful, and in six months he was given twenty dollars a month; at the end of the year he was advanced over several senior clerks to the chief clerkship of the office. Two months later, when the junior partner was forced temporarily to retire because of a breakdown, Beveridge was summoned by McDonald and informed that he would be given the major part of the work the ailing partner had done. Just for a moment the young man doubted his capacity. His advance had been too rapid, he thought, and he frankly expressed his misgivings. The kindly old statesman laughed indulgently.

'Well, it's our funeral; if we can stand it, you ought to.'

And so it was settled. Thereafter, as long as he remained with the firm, he not only met every expectation, but profited enormously from his contact with two really superior minds. But it was a struggle. 'I hardly went to bed at all,' he said. 'I ate my noonday lunch in about a minute and a half.' [2] Living, literally, on his nerve, he then for a time fell into the habit of drinking for stimulation, but never to excess.

But he was happy in his expectations. It was at about this time that he found a room on the charming little shaded street sacred to Hoosiers because of its association with James Whitcomb Riley, who had written a poem to it. It was before the poet had taken up his residence on Lockerbie Street with the Holsteins, and Beveridge never was to become really intimate with Riley. But in those days of lonely struggle he was befriended by Colonel Charles L. Holstein, an able lawyer of courtliness and charm, and his beautiful wife. His gratitude for their sympathy and kindness and for the hospitality of their home was never to cool.

[1] MS. Autobiography. [2] *Ibid.*

III

But throughout these years, it was his association and conversation with McDonald and Butler that furnished him his exhilaration. The former was a lover of literature, and in moments of relaxation he would chat with charm and enthusiasm of the books he loved. He belonged to the generation that found no sense of humiliation in confessing to partiality for Thackeray and Scott. When young Beveridge tried to engage him in talk on works of political economy, he found him not so helpful. This impressed the student as strange, and he finally concluded that McDonald 'was a natural political economist.' Between the old man and the young — both had been students at De-Pauw — there developed a feeling that 'transcended friendship.' In many ways the kindly old Senator was the younger man's Great Stone Face. He admired 'the lion's heart in him,' and liked to think that 'through his veins there flowed the blood of Scottish heroes.' But, admiring and loving him as a man, he found in him the ideal qualities of the high-minded lawyer. The youth, studying his manner and methods in court, found him 'infinitely at ease,' with 'the repose of strength,' and as 'deliberate as Nature.' He admired and sought to imitate the older man's 'supreme gift of statement which carried its conclusion with it without argument.' He noted, too, that he 'loathed a trick, despised the shadow of sharp practice, and in the heat of conflict never ceased to be a gentleman.' [1]

That the student repaid the master for the latter's attentions we may be sure. McDonald was a master in his analysis of men and he found enough of the unusual in his chief clerk to make him an interesting study. One day, after reading for the first time some of the nationalistic decisions of John Marshall, and finding them perfect expressions of the philosophy he had imbibed from childhood, Beveridge hurried to the old Senator with his discovery.

'Senator,' he said, 'the man who wrote this great state paper called Marshall's Opinion in McCulloch *vs.* Maryland was a soldier.'

The patient old man sat back in his chair and smiled.

'What makes you think that?' he asked.

'Internal evidence,' said the cock-sure student. 'Just look at this paragraph, it has in it the blast of bugle, the thump of drum, the tramp of charging squadrons. Nobody but a soldier could have written that; nobody but one who had seen armed service could have conceived it.'

[1] From Beveridge's tribute, *Indianapolis Journal*, June 25, 1891.

the jury brought in a verdict for a thousand dollars, which Judge Baker of the Federal Court, who presided, thought generous enough. The verdict, however, was set aside on the petition of the railroad. In the second trial the jurist noticed, as Beveridge spoke, that the jury sat 'with elbows on their knees, drinking in the eloquence, pathos, and wit of the orator with the eagerness with which the young robin watches the return of the mother bird with its morning meal.' Swept off their feet, the jury brought in a verdict for twenty-five hundred dollars. When the leading railroad lawyer of the State made a motion for a new trial on the ground that the damages awarded were too great, the Judge, admitting that the verdict probably was 'two or three times as much as it ought to be,' denied the motion with the observation that he was afraid to set the verdict aside, 'lest if Mr. Beveridge had a chance to try the case a third time, he would persuade the jury to give his client a verdict of five thousand dollars.' [1]

A few notable cases in which Beveridge participated will suffice to indicate his professional status. One of the most important, finally passed upon by the Supreme Court of the United States, grew out of an act of the Legislature of 1891 providing that, while the property of individuals or ordinary corporations could be assessed by county officials, the assessment of railroad property should be committed to the State Board of Tax Commissioners, composed of the Governor, Secretary of State, Auditor, and two appointees of the Executive. The assessment of the roads resulting involved $22,666,470; and the roads commenced a suit in the Superior Court of Marion County to restrain the collection of the taxes on the double ground that the act itself was unconstitutional and that, if constitutional, it had been so administered as to create an illegal assessment of the company's property. The railroads were represented by eminent counsel, and the State engaged attorneys to assist the Attorney-General. It was in the days when the venerable Alvin P. Hovey was Governor, and Beveridge probably owed his retention, two years after he had entered upon his independent practice, to the admiration and affection of the older for the younger man. The State was sustained in the Superior Court and also by the State Supreme Court, and an appeal was taken to the Supreme Court at Washington. The part assigned to Beveridge, along with John W. Kern, was the preparation of the brief, and his work was warmly commended by representatives of the Democratic Administration which was in power in Indianapolis when the case was advanced to the

[1] Judge John H. Baker, *Dinner in Honor of Senator Beveridge, 1899*, 17.

highest tribunal. 'To my mind it is a clear, strong, terse statement of the entire matter, and unanswerable,' wrote the State
Auditor, to whom a copy had been sent.[1]

The decision of the Court criticized the manner of fixing the
valuation, but sustained the method, and this was hailed as a
notable victory for the State; and while young Beveridge's part
was confined to the preparation of the brief, a work in which he
always excelled, the victory added to his prestige.[2]

VI

More interesting, among the notable cases in which he had a
part, was that of John H. Holliday *vs.* the State Board of Tax
Commissioners of Indiana in 1897. The commissioners, seeking
to tap new and additional sources of revenue, conceived the idea
of taxing insurance-policy-holders upon the so-called paid-up
and surrender value of their policies. This was something entirely new in the world, since nothing of the sort had ever before
been attempted anywhere. It was of vital concern, not only to
the policy-holders, but to every life insurance company in the
country. John H. Holliday, formerly editor and founder of the
'Indianapolis News,' filed a bill of complaint in the Marion
County Circuit Court, and the issue was made. The original
attorneys for the policy-holders were distinguished lawyers of
long experience,[3] and there was some mystery as to how young
Beveridge entered the case. The explanation is found in the
Beveridge Manuscripts.

For some years he had been an intimate friend of George W.
Perkins, of the New York Life Insurance Company. The latter
had written Beveridge, as a friend, of the case, in which all the
insurance companies were interested, and asked his reactions.
While nothing more than an informal opinion was expected,
Beveridge, deeply interested in the taxation policy involved,
made an exhaustive research of the authorities and prepared an
elaborate brief as answer. On reading it, Perkins, very much
impressed, sent it to another insurance company with the comment that, while it appealed to him as very able, he could not
trust his own judgment because of personal friendship for the
lawyer, and asking an impartial judgment upon it. He was soon
called to the telephone by the company to which it had been sent
and told that the man who wrote the brief should by all means
be added to the legal battery. Thus Beveridge entered the case.

In the original trial in the Marion County Circuit Court, the

---

[1] Captain D. F. Allen.   [2] U.S. Reports, 154, 439–47.
[3] A. G. Smith, Charles A. Korbly, and John N. Finch, a specialist on insurance law.

evidence was soon in and the arguments continued for two days. On the first day Beveridge spoke an hour and a half. Four days later, the court held for the complainants and enjoined the taxation of life insurance policies. The State appealed to the United States Supreme Court, and the Beveridge brief went in. He did not participate in the oral arguments in the higher court, but his brief was followed largely in the opinion of the majority of the Court, sustaining the opinions of the lower tribunals.

The Beveridge brief attracted much attention in life insurance circles and among lawyers at the time. It bristled with citations, and marshaled the arguments with the dash and precision of battalions on the march. Touching, as the case did, unbroken fields, the brief was a statesmanlike discussion of the relations of insurance to society; it lifted the argument to the high plane of national policy and was written with the boldness of a pioneer who knew his directions. It was in cases of this character, touching on public policy and constitutional interpretation, that Beveridge was to find his keenest interest in the law.

VII

The most interesting criminal cause in which Beveridge appeared was one that stirred the entire Commonwealth to its foundations. The head of one of the oldest and presumably soundest banks in Indianapolis, and his son, were indicted for a criminal misuse of funds after the crash of their institution. The failure of the bank was almost incredible; it had seemed as solid as the Soldiers' Monument. But even more startling than the closing of the bank was the discovery that it literally had been systematically looted by one of the most trusted and admired men in the community. The district attorney likened this man's fall to the sudden crash in a serene atmosphere of a giant oak that had dominated a forest for generations. The banker not only was prominent financially and socially, but had long been one of the pillars of the leading Methodist Church, which Beveridge attended.

The trial of the father, in which Beveridge had no part, had been a community spectacle. The most brilliant lawyers in the city had been engaged on one side or the other, and the arguments, powerful beyond the average, had been heard by a packed courtroom, and published in full in the newspapers. The head of the bank had been convicted and sent to prison, and he was serving his sentence when his son was brought to trial, with Beveridge one of the principal attorneys for the defense.

The social and business prominence of the defendant crowded

the courtroom with men and women of the *élite*, and this was especially true when Beveridge, who had become a favorite subject of gossip in the town, made his argument. With the ending of the evidence, he had resorted to the unique method of writing his speech in full, and within twenty-four hours he delivered it without one deviation from the manuscript, without reference even to notes, and it was in the newspapers and on the streets almost as soon as he had finished. He did not seek in his argument to minimize the seriousness of the offense, but dwelt especially on the fact that the illegal proceedings through which the bank had been looted had been going on long before the son of the banker had entered the business. This he pleaded in extenuation. It was more a plea for mercy than a defense.

It was in closing that he caused a stir in the courtroom when he personally appealed to Frank B. Burke, the brilliant district attorney, whose extraordinarily effective speech in the prosecution of the father justified the fear of a similar performance in closing the arguments against the son, Beveridge making the most of the general sympathy for the wife and mother, facing the tragedy of being left alone in her country home.

'Tomorrow,' said Beveridge, in closing, 'is God's holy day. Shall the church bells, sounding to the city the Master's message of "peace on earth, good will to men," ring for this defendant the chimes of peace or toll for him the death of hope? Who demands the last? Not justice, for justice pleads for the defendant. Not mercy, for mercy pleads for this defendant. Who demands the last?'

And then, turning dramatically to Burke — 'Not you, great-minded, golden-hearted man whom I love as a brother, not you!'

It just so happened that when on Sunday morning the jury, ready to report, filed into the courtroom, the church bells were ringing; and the verdict was acquittal. The case had attracted State-wide attention, and Beveridge was deluged with congratulations; but newspapers denounced the verdict and ascribed it to the 'sentimental twaddle' of the attorneys for the defense. One paper wondered why Burke lost interest when he had as good a case as that against the father. 'Was he, like the extremely sympathetic jury, entirely overcome by the heart-rending picture painted by Mr. Beveridge of his young client, the curled darling, in prison garb, or was it something else?' asked the 'Lafayette Courier.' But the Beveridge speech had been effective, and it was to enter into the conversation of the people of the town for a long time.

VIII

This was the most notable criminal case in which Beveridge appeared before a jury. His real interest in the law was in civil cases having a constitutional slant, and on these he worked with special enthusiasm. In his arguments before courts he confined himself rigidly to the law and the facts, but he spoke with the fluency of one who had exhausted the authorities. Within a few years he was conceded a place among the ablest members of an exceptionally strong bar. If his practice was not as lucrative as some, it was sufficient to maintain him in the way he wished to live. It is the fate of lawyers to win at best but an ephemeral renown, for there is nothing so uninteresting or so quickly forgotten as the average case that has been adjudicated. In the ten years of his practice he had his full share of cases that interested the public at the time; but few of these are now remembered, and most of the lawyers with whom he crossed swords have long since passed to their reward.

He was never to take a partner. At the time he finally abandoned the practice of the law to enter public life, he shared offices with Larz Whitcomb, a young man destined to a high professional standing and to be elected Speaker of the Indiana House of Representatives the year Beveridge was elected to the Senate. With him, too, was a young Jewish youth whose devotion through life was of the rarest sort. Quite early, when Beveridge himself had but a meager practice, Leo Rothschild, to whom he was an idol because of his political speeches, walked in upon him with a letter of introduction. Short, rotund, rosy-cheeked, with smiling, friendly eyes peering through glasses, he was not then needed, but he could not be resisted when he asked permission to remain as a clerk. He was told to 'hang up his hat,' and thus began a relationship of which we shall have much evidence as we proceed.

The rules Beveridge had laid down for the conduct of his office in the beginning were adhered to scrupulously. It was never to become a lounging place for the gossips, but to be maintained as a workshop. The older lawyers of established reputation were cultivated until they took him under their wing. If Harrison was never to become an intimate or wholly reconciled to the younger man's belligerent manner, he was speedily to recognize his ability and proclaim it. Judge John H. Baker of the Federal Court, who had been amused at the law student's challenge to Harrison, soon became an ardent admirer and an adviser. No lawyer who found himself pitted against him in a case but realized the necessity of a thorough preparation to meet his own; for he was always prepared, was seldom taken off his guard, and usually was found on the offensive, pressing his opponent with a fighter's gayety. Within ten years a leader of the bar found that 'he has reached the very highest mark that a lawyer can gain in his profession.' [1]

And it was in those young buoyant days at the bar that out of his association in a case with a young Pittsburgh lawyer sprang a mutual admiration that deepened into a friendship that was to extend into the political careers of both and continue unbroken until the death of Philander C. Knox; and Beveridge was to be chosen to pay the tribute at the memorial meeting for the great Senator and Secretary of State.

[1] John B. Cockran, *Dinner in Honor of Senator Beveridge, 1899*, 38.

CHAPTER IV
SPRINGTIME IN INDIANAPOLIS

I

BUT ten years intervened between Beveridge's admission to the bar and his election to the Senate at the age of thirty-six. These years were passed in Indianapolis, with occasional excursions to the larger cities to make the speeches that spread his fame. Nowhere could a more ideal spot have been found for this period of rapid growth. There was an exuberance and charm to the Indianapolis of the nineties that had not appeared before, and was soon to disappear, with greater wealth and a more crowded industrial life. Early in the decade the mud roads became a memory, along with the horse-drawn cars and the disreputable transfer station in the heart of the town. But throughout the nineties the town retained something of simplicity and bucolic charm. Most of the inhabitants were Hoosiers, racy of the soil — descendants of those who had moved in with the founding of the capital, and people of comfortable means who had come from the smaller towns. The factories, home-owned, were institutions, and so placed as not to mar the residential section with unsightly buildings and unsavory smoke. Designated as the State capital before a house was built, the city had been carefully designed somewhat after the L'Enfant plan for Washington, with its four avenues spreading fanwise from the center, where the Governor's mansion had its seat. In the days of Beveridge the mansion had disappeared, and in its place, during much of the decade, the great Soldiers' Monument that dominates the city's skyline now was slowly creeping upward from behind a high wooden fence that encircled the grounds.

It was a city of homes, for it was not until the close of the decade that Lew Wallace built the first apartment house from the proceeds of the sale of 'The Prince of India.' The aristocracy, by no means ostentatious, dwelt for the most part on Meridian, Pennsylvania, and Delaware Streets, from within four blocks of the principal business thoroughfare to Sixteenth Street on the north. Here were the old-fashioned, commodious brick houses, set back in woodsy lawns shaded by great elm trees. Stone images of lions and dogs sentineled not a few, for it was the 'mauve decade.' Most of the prosperous professional and business men walked to their daily work, but their comfortable carriages and well-groomed horses were known to the multitude. Every morning Negro servants drove the cows of leading citizens to the grazing beyond Pogue's Run. Every evening in the long summers the people sat back on the lawns of the more pretentious homes, and on the front porches, and there was much visiting back and forth. It was in the golden days when shirt-sleeves were not taboo and too much formality was confused with pretense.

It was a friendly city. An interesting item in the evening paper would send a neighbor strolling across the lawn to discuss it with the family next door; the best of men would pause to refresh themselves at the old town pump by the blackish Federal building and to exchange pleasantries; and all through the Sunday afternoons young men in silk hats and with canes would stroll in small groups from house to house calling on the young ladies, who invariably were at home.

The Indianapolis of the nineties suggested the expansiveness and romanticism of Elizabethan days. Indeed, it was a little proud. The Middle West was just awakening to its power, and Chicago's phenomenal growth was as cake and wine to the spirits of the young. Soon the monument in Indianapolis would reach higher than any other dedicated to the soldier dead, and in the course of a promenade one might meet not a few local and national celebrities. A short, dignified man with wrinkled face and graying beard, with silk hat and cane, and leading a small child by the hand, is passed. He bears himself with a dignity proclaiming his abhorrence of familiarities, but his eyes twinkle as he lifts his hat. This is Harrison, no longer President, now living in the brick house without a fence because the souvenir-seekers in 1888 had cut it to pieces.... Another impressive gentleman, similarly attired — a serious-faced man with a penetrating eye — is recognized as Isaac Pusey Gray, former Governor, superb campaigner, dreaming of the Presidency. Soon he will go to Mexico as United States Minister and die there, and there will be an imposing funeral with military music.... Another, dressed as for a promenade, though on his way to business — a bearded man with an ingratiating smile — this is Albert G. Porter, once Governor, and later Minister to Italy.... Now comes a little dapper man, evidently a dandy in his tastes, holding his head a wee bit to one side, peering quizzically and satirically upon you through his glasses as he saunters along lazily — James Whitcomb Riley.... Another small man, stepping briskly and holding himself erect as on parade, and with the sharp, stern countenance of a commander, and you bow to Lew Wallace, whose pen is mightier than his sword.

Proceeding up Pennsylvania Street, your companion, likely as not, will call attention to a brick house, vine-covered, at the corner, and gossip a bit about the indolent young man who might make something of himself if he would — a young Princetonian who romped all night at parties and shamelessly slept all day. The secret of his sloth is still in hiding, but soon the story of all-night vigils with pen and pad of young Booth Tarkington will be told with the triumphs of 'The Gentleman from Indiana' and 'Monsieur Beaucaire.' Young authors are not numerous, though the pale, slim gentleman of the press bearing down upon us has recently stamped the name of Meredith Nicholson on a slender volume of poems, and soon 'The House of a Thousand Candles' will illuminate his fame. Young orators are more conspicuous at the time, and we observe one approaching now. Slender, moving briskly with the stiff military carriage of a West-Pointer, gloved, silk-hatted, his pale, thin features a bit sternly set, we know him at a glance. It is young Beveridge, the 'brilliant orator,' who, along with the corpulent, cherubic-faced John Lewis Griffiths, divides the honors of the town on the platform. They are said to dislike each other, but one will go to the Senate and become the premier orator of his party, and the other, as Consul-General in London, will thrill and delight Englishmen with an eloquence of a high order.

II

In this Indianapolis of the nineties, Beveridge was the favorite subject of the gossips. His brilliancy was conceded, his eloquence acknowledged, and the town liked both. There was something almost too clever in the oratory of this young man. The gossips talked about his speeches; his mannerisms; his supreme self-confidence, which some likened to that of Sentimental Tommy; his expanding fame. They even commented on the dashing manner with which he ushered people to their pews on Sunday mornings at the Meridian Street Methodist Church. Thither the young lawyer had been attracted by the polished eloquence and scholarship of Horace A. Cleveland, the minister, who would have shone as a Professor of Belles-Lettres at a great university. There is a tradition, which probably grew out of some facetious statement of his own, that when invited to membership Beveridge had accepted on condition that he would not be disciplined because of profanity. Aside from the intellectual stimulus of the pastor's sermons, he profited through the friendships and associations formed at the church. Years later, Meredith Nicholson was to remember him in the rôle of usher. 'He was a gallant

usher in those days,' he wrote,[1] 'meeting everybody with a wel-
coming smile.' Another tells us that 'he ushered pewholders
to their seats with the grace of a Chesterfield, and passed the
plate as though he were granting a favor.'[2] After services, he
would hasten to the rear of the church to exchange greetings with
friends.[3] We shall find a little later that one of the pews will be
used in electioneering for him for the Senate. Certainly the
friendships there formed were of the utmost value. Indianapolis
was essentially a religious community, the churches were a vital
part of the social system, and this particular church in those
days was almost a religious adjunct of the Republican Party.

III

But Beveridge's interest in the church was matched by his
enthusiasm for the stage. In the nineties the greatest actors and
actresses, closing their New York engagements in the early
spring, went forth on tour, and always appeared in Indianapolis.
The coming of these artists was eagerly awaited; the press teemed
with stories of the players and the plays. When the play was
published, anyone making a Sunday call previous to the Monday
appearance of Irving or Mansfield would be apt to find a copy
of the play on the table of his host or hostess. The drama was
taken seriously by the Indianapolitans, and the artists were as
old friends to be discussed eagerly before they came and after
they had gone. When Mansfield made his first appearance in
'Cyrano,' a line extended for three blocks through the night of
sleet and rain before the opening of the box office. It was not
a solitary incident. The wealthy sent their servants and the
poor accepted the ordeal themselves. It was in the days when
Morris Ross was writing elaborate criticisms for the 'Indianapolis News,' and everyone was following him devoutly. When
a new critic on the 'Journal' noted that his more humble offerings attracted no attention, he hit upon a ruse to force it. Learning that Julia Marlowe was the favorite actress of the town, he
awaited her coming. To Ross, the autocrat of dramatic criticism,
she was worth two columns. The new critic wrote a short,
restrained criticism, and outraged the community with a stinger
at the close — the opinion that Marlowe 'gives much promise.'
The town instantly was arrayed in hostile camps, with the Marlowe faction and the scoffers at each other's throats, and young
Meredith Nicholson, then an underling of the 'News,' viewing
the feud of the critics with much joy.[4] Beveridge, caught by the

[1] To the author.   [2] James W. Noel to the author.   [3] *Ibid.*
[4] The *Journal* critic was Frank C. Payne.

glamour of the footlights, was a regular attendant at the plays, and at one time appeared anonymously in the rôle of critic for the 'Journal.' Just before a famous player's week's engagement in Shakespearian plays began, the young lawyer met the 'Journal' critic, a classmate at DePauw, and asked permission to criticize the performances. Both amazed and amused, the friend readily agreed, and thus that year, unknown to the players or the public, the criticisms of the 'Journal' were sometimes from the pen of Beveridge. But it was a secret that was guarded zealously.

IV

In this decade Indianapolis took fervently to song, and Beveridge was caught and carried in the musical current of the times. In rollicking mood he joined a small group of young men in an attempt to give the town a summer opera in Ayres's cow pasture north of Fall Creek, and some of the company sang well enough and later rose to fame in the East.[1] It was soon afterward that Beveridge was made a director of the May Musical Festival, an annual event for a decade that brought the world's greatest artists to the town. Interested from the beginning, he was drawn to some extent within the magic circle of social and business leaders sponsoring the festivals, by his friend John C. Shaffer. Through him he saw something more of the artists than could be seen from the audience. On some occasions, when a tribute was to be paid to Nordica or to Melba, it was his eloquence, patterned still somewhat after that of Ingersoll, that was requisitioned. None of the artists — and Melba and Calvé were among them — made quite the appeal of the beautiful and gracious Nordica, who always received marked social attentions. Indeed, it was on the occasion of one of these festivals that her marriage to Zoltan Doehme, another singer, occurred in Indianapolis. She was easily accessible to her Hoosier friends, and to one of these I am indebted for a story that made an indelible impression on Beveridge, who looked upon oratory as an art kindred to that of the singer. This friend [2] lunched with her the day after she had sung Senta's prayer from the 'Flying Dutchman.' At her suggestion he had gone to the top gallery in Tomlinson's Hall to hear her sing it, and it had proved 'one of the most haunting songs.' One note had made a deep impression on the friend in the gallery — 'a note so zephyrlike that it fell upon one's ear-drum like the illusion, say, of a snowflake softly settling on the back of one's hand,' and he thought 'the beauty as well as artistry of that one note tran-

[1] Gavin L. Payne to the author.   [2] Gavin L. Payne.

scended the mechanics of voice culture.' Speaking of the impression to Nordica, he had asked whether it was her 'incomparable throat' that made possible 'that gossamer note.'

'No, no, no!' she replied, laughing; 'that one note was weeks of work, work, work — over, over, over — study, study, study! You remember how the old Greek sculptors, after chiseling their marble, polished it until the human eye could not detect a roughness on the surface; then, not content with that, they would rip the nail from their thumb, and test the smoothness of the marble with the quick of the flesh underneath their nail? That is the way I obtained that note.'

Chatting with Beveridge, who had been impressed by that gossamer note, the friend told him Nordica's story of its mastery. 'The comparison of the Greek sculptors and Madame Nordica's struggle affected him — he paused a minute or two.

'That is it!' he exclaimed vehemently. 'That is IT!'

The artist in the orator responded to that in the singer and in the ancient Greek masters; it was a lesson he was to take to himself.

In 1892, Shaffer was president of the festival, and Walter Damrosch, then in the dawning of his brilliant career, who had contributed notably to the artistic triumph of the week, was given a dinner, where Beveridge toasted him as 'the coming captain of all the hosts of song.' [1] Thus the young orator, doing his part to crown the festivals with success, was finally made president for 1898.

Eager to make that of '98 outglitter any other, he and the directors made their plans early in the autumn before. Frank von der Stucken, with his Cincinnati orchestra, was engaged, and during the frequent meetings in the winter a warm friendship developed between Beveridge and the artist. The veteran musician, who recalled to some an old steel engraving of Beethoven, and carried with him 'the aura of artistic grace,' delighted the younger man, and the relation grew intimate enough to permit some challenging of the conductor's theories.

One clash came from Beveridge's plan for a Verdi night. The great composer had recently died, and, with an intensified interest in his compositions and a desire to pay tribute to his memory, there was certain to be a good reaction at the box office. Von der Stucken had planned a more classical program, viewed from the angle of German classicism, and was obdurate. The debate increased in animation, but all the while the conductor was driving Beveridge, who knew little of music, to the wall. At length, after a pause of sheer disgust, he burst forth:

[1] *Indianapolis Journal*, May 27, 1892.

'Look here, Von der Stucken, do you mean to tell me that Verdi's Requiem Mass is not in the high realms of music?'

'Well,' came the soft reply, 'no one suggested anything but Verdi opera.'

And so there was no Verdi night, but Beveridge had his way about the Requiem Mass — it was the principal number of one program.

It was a busy winter for the young president of the festival, attending rehearsals, speaking to musical societies that were coöperating, arousing the enthusiasm of the community;[1] but in April the Spanish War burst upon the country to divert attention, and it was evident there would be a financial failure. Distressed over the danger, Beveridge personally appealed to all the leaders of society to assure the usual attendance. Why not convert at least one meeting into a patriotic demonstration? The idea was debated by the directors and all agreed to a dramatic song to harmonize with the mounting nationalism of the people.

'I know the song!' Beveridge exclaimed, with bubbling enthusiasm — 'the grand song. We will have the "Battle Hymn of the Republic" — nothing less than that!'

'And we'll have one of the great sopranos sing it,' another added.

'Soprano, nothing!' snapped Beveridge. 'We'll have the biggest man voice we can get to hurl out that song. That is the song such as a grand old patriarch might sing' — and he began to hum it.

And thus it came about that David Bispham raised a great audience to a pitch of enthusiasm seldom seen before, and thousands joined fervently in the chorus and greeted the singer at the close with frenzied cheers and shouts.

Three nights of song, and one of Ysaye as the star, but the deficit was larger than usual, and it was to be the last of the festivals; though Beveridge was not to mourn over the defeat of his hopes — he was entering that year upon his march to national renown.

V

During these ten years Beveridge found another source of mental exhilaration in the Indianapolis Literary Club, formed in the early seventies under the more snobbish name of the Gentlemen's Literary Club. Among the charter members were Walter Q. Gresham, Secretary of State under Cleveland; Jonathan

[1] *Indianapolis Journal*, Jan. 18, 1898.

W. Gordon, the brilliant lawyer and forensic orator, famed for his defense of the Knights of the Golden Circle; William P. Fishback, whose literary taste was as notable as his legal acquirements; Livingston Howland, whose sons were long to be intellectual leaders of the community,[1] and Governor Porter. Among its most notable members were one President of the United States, Harrison; three Vice-Presidents, Thomas A. Hendricks, Thomas R. Marshall, and Charles W. Fairbanks; two United States Ministers, Albert G. Porter accredited to Rome, and Addison C. Harris to Vienna. Included were really great jurists, as Byron K. Elliott; eloquent ministers, as Dr. Cleveland, Myron D. Reed, and Bishop William A. Quayle; novelists, as Booth Tarkington and Meredith Nicholson; accomplished journalists, as Louis Howland and John H. Holliday; and James Whitcomb Riley.

Through all the years it had been a mark of distinction to be invited in. Matthew Arnold had been discovered by the members of the club long before he had been acclaimed by the critics generally, and there was an old-fashioned interest among them in Ruskin and Carlyle. 'When the talk turned on theology,' one old member recalls, 'someone was bound to bring in Newman and the Tractarian Movement, or to cite Dr. Briggs and the Andover case.' The essayist of sensibility was inevitably unhappy, for the discussions of the papers were without restraint, and always there were satirists among them to probe the tender parts of an argument.

During the years of his active affiliation, Beveridge read a number of papers that attracted attention, but most of these are lost. One, on American trade, is biographically important in tracing the beginnings of the author's imperialistic ideals. But the most sensational of his essays, which rattled the dry bones of the community with its audacity, was a lawyer's argument to prove that Sir Walter Raleigh wrote Shakespeare plays.

'A genius wrote the plays,' he began, 'but genius does not supply facts, learning, experience. These plays were the great repository of his time. They abound in accurate legal learning; in all the medical learning of the day; in all the historical learning then current. They are full of rabbinical lore. They bristle with the kind of martial facts which are to be learned only on the field of battle. They are saturated with personal experiences upon the high seas; salt gales blow through every page. Only a sailor could have written the storm scene in "The Tempest"; only a soldier could have written the "Histories"; only a Jewish

[1] Louis Howland, editor of the *Indianapolis News*, and Hewitt Hanson Howland, editor of the *Century*.

scholar could have written "The Merchant of Venice" and parts of the other plays; only a linguist could have written most of the plays, since most of them were taken from works in foreign languages, then untranslated. But Shakespeare knew no French, no Italian, no German, no Danish, no Hebrew, probably even no Latin. He knew no law except that of the money-lender which he applied to his own business. He knew no medicine, no science. He was untraveled; he was never out of England; he never got as far as Scotland or Wales. He was never a soldier. He took no sea voyage. He was never at court.'

Thus disposing of Shakespeare, he brushed Bacon aside as a contender for the honor. 'A cold diplomat' and 'corrupt intriguer,' he 'had no warm generous blood.' 'Intrigue with a woman would have been impossible with this slow-pulsed, calculating politician. Yet the plays flame with animal passion. Some parts of them run even to licentiousness. Some sonnets are almost indecent. Everywhere the spasm of propagation is in full ecstasy.' And Bacon knew only two kinds of men, 'the most artificial varieties of all, the courtier and the lawyer,' while the plays hold the mirror up to every variety — the courtier, lawyer, soldier, sailor, peasant, ruffian, priest, queen, maid, courtesan, laborer, merchant, miser, profligate. With a few of these William Shakespeare was acquainted; with two of them, Francis Bacon; but neither knew half of them, nor did both together know all of them.'

But Raleigh was a brilliant Oxonian, excelling in languages, oratory, poetry, philosophy; a natural gallant, hot-blooded, and capable of seducing the Queen's maid at forty; a versatile scholar who read foreign literature in the original; a student of law at the Middle Temple; adviser of Elizabeth; the most gallant and daring soldier of his time, familiar with the French scenes in plays described; an accomplished sailor who had seen the Bermudas of the 'Tempest' scene; a consummate courtier; and so interested in medicine that in the Tower he had been busy with his crucibles and retorts. More: the author of the plays had studied madness, and Raleigh had feigned it in the Tower. The critics had puzzled over reference in the plays to 'men whose heads do grow beneath their shoulders,' and Raleigh had brought the legend back from South America and used it in his book on Guiana. Commentators had stumbled in explaining where Shakespeare got the story of Ariel imprisoned in the heart of a tree by Sycorax, and this, taken from the mythology of the South American Indians, had been brought back by Raleigh, who had known them.

Why, then, the concealment of the authorship? Because

a courtier suspected of writing the plays, with Elizabeth furious over many lines, would have been ruined. To have proclaimed the truth on the scaffold would have robbed his wife and children of their heritage. So ran the argument.

If such rollicking audacity was intended to arouse the members of the club to indignant protest, it failed of its purpose, for they heard it in a stunned silence. After thirty-five years Meredith Nicholson remembers that it was 'so plausible that it knocked the members cold, and the conversation did not come up as usual.' [1] Some assumed that it was written as a hoax, and the blue-stocking of the town,[2] hearing it read later before a woman's club, could only murmur that 'he is merely exercising his intellectual ingenuity.' Certain it is that in later life he fain would have had it forgotten and he was a little sheepish about it. But he appears to have taken it seriously at the time, since it was submitted to several magazines, only to be rejected. 'We find,' wrote the editor of the 'Century,' 'the argument ingenious and forcible, but not at all convincing to our mind.'

And so the paper was filed away and forgotten, for the author was hastening to the triumphs of his political career.[3]

VI

It was midway in the decade when Beveridge made his first journey to Europe, and wrote his 'Notes of a Hasty Journey' for the 'Indianapolis News.' While the articles in parts are deliciously naïve, they reveal, thus early, the methods of investigation he was ever after to employ on more important journeys of the sort. Thus, curious to know the European estimate of Americans, he talked with all classes — shoemakers, shopkeepers, lawyers, cab-drivers. His interest in the armies discloses his imperialistic slant and his zest for martial glory.[4] Thus the Beveridge of these ten years was intensively engaged in all interesting phases of community life, playing his part, and always with an enthusiasm to attract attention. His minor triumphs, together with his colorful personality, made him the subject of conversation. He had his enemies who were uncompromising, playing upon what they called his 'egotism'; but he had his fighting friends, making the most of his undoubted brilliance.

Among the latter, aside from those previously mentioned,

[1] Letter to the author.　　　　[2] Catherine Meredith.

[3] Years later, Henry Pemberton wrote his *Shakespeare and Sir Walter Raleigh* on the same theme.

[4] *Indianapolis News*, September–December, 1894.

were the Horace Bennetts, at whose home he stayed frequently on his returns from Washington in later years, and Mrs. Ovid B. Jameson, sister of Booth Tarkington, then young, vivacious, brilliant in conversation, whose friendship, ever loyal, was greatly cherished. Insisting always on his summer vacation, even when he could ill afford it, Beveridge frequently accompanied a group of his friends to Cape Cod or the White Mountains — the Shaffers, Colemans, Kenyons, Thompsons. These were happy days. The law student, living on one meal a day, within ten years had become an outstanding figure in the professional, social, and artistic life of a conservative people. But he was becoming a challenging political figure too.

VII

All the while he was making the most of every opportunity to enhance his reputation as an orator with the view to ultimate political preferment. The campaign of 1888 was one of more than ordinary animation, even for Indiana; for Harrison was the presidential nominee, and the parading of pilgrims, the music of bands, the shouting of partisans, extended through the summer and autumn. Into this campaign Beveridge plunged with eager zest; and if the extracts from his speeches at twenty-six bear but a remote resemblance to those of a little later, he was following the fashion of his time. It was enough that the Republican papers exhausted superlatives in describing his progress through the State. To him the contest was one between Beef (Cleveland) and Brains (Harrison). If he discussed the tariff in a manner satisfactory to his fellow partisans, the Democratic press thought he discussed it 'as intelligently as a Market Street Chinaman would discuss immigration.'[1]

Four years later, he was regarded as one of the most eloquent and effective Republican orators in the State, regardless of age, and in a conservative community dominated by hard-headed politicians and accustomed to hearing Blaine, Ingersoll, Depew, Cockran, Voorhees, and Breckinridge he was assigned as the sole speaker at a mass meeting in Indianapolis. All over the State he had gone, heralded everywhere by the party press as 'Beveridge the Brilliant.' The 'Journal' correspondent at Madison excitedly wrote that 'even a fire alarm which was sounded in the city failed to break the magic spell.' 'Incisive argument,' 'biting epigram,' 'scintillating wit,' 'thrilling pathos,' 'beautiful imagery' — such the descriptions of the speech which some Madisonians thought superior to those of Ingersoll. That year

[1] Early scrapbook.

he defended the tariff and ridiculed the idea that the tariff is a tax. The Cleveland vetoes of private pension bills furnished the theme for the 'thrilling pathos,' and tributes to the old soldiers who were wronged, for the 'beautiful imagery.' A Richmond paper [1] reported that he had carried the audience 'by storm from the beginning,' and that 'while his eloquence is too florid to measure up to the highest standards of taste, it loses nothing in its effect on that account.'

But it was the Grand Opera House speech in Indianapolis that marked a distinct ascent on the ladder he was climbing. The 'Journal' account was a rhapsody. The house was packed, and 'hundreds of ladies shared the pleasure which followed the climaxes of oratory,' and 'hundreds of young men drank deep of the fires of patriotism.' And the orator, 'young in years, youthful in appearance, fluent of tongue, as rich in rhetoric as he was strong in logic, piquant in wit as he was subtle in pathos or fierce in invective, achieved a brilliant success.' In truth, the vices of the speech were the vices of the time, and the audience was enormously impressed. For days it was the talk of the town and the subject of acrimonious quarrels among the children in the public schools. What though the 'Indianapolis News' did pick him up on facts confused, one of the soundest critics in the town wrote him he had 'at one bound outclassed our political orators, young and old,' and that 'at least no man stands between you and Ingersoll today in the ranks of American orators.' [2] Thus at thirty, Beveridge was acknowledged the premier orator of his party in the State, with many thinking him unsurpassed in the Nation. The next four years were to find him more assiduous on his oratory than ever before, and scanning the national horizon anxiously for an opportunity beyond the boundaries of the State.

VIII

The six years between 1892 and his election to the Senate marked a change in his style of oratory. The 'bloody-shirt' rhetoric could no longer rouse the rabble. Thereafter he was to discontinue long and bathetic references to the 'old soldiers' and the war. He would soon become incapable of the 'beef and brains' alliteration, applied to Cleveland and Harrison. He was to reach a national recognition by an unusual route. Having found that short speeches, compact, epigrammatic, dynamic, and seriously treating contemporary conditions, made an impression, he speedily developed into an after-dinner and special-

[1] *Daily Item*, Nov. 1, 1892.   [2] Augustus Lynch Mason, Nov. 5, 1892.

Violently disagreeing with his views, though Beveridge himself
had urged them in the campaign of 1886, he was too much the
artist to underestimate Bryan's oratory. 'I was charmed,' he
wrote later. 'What he said was all so simple and natural.'[1] Soon
afterward he had the opportunity to study the artistry of Bourke
Cockran, and he thought him 'marvelous.' But, talking with men
in the audience, he found that the brilliant Celt's reputation for
insincerity neutralized the effect of his eloquence, and he made
a mental note of that.[2]

IX

Never, perhaps, has Indiana been so rocked with political passion as in the campaign of 1896. Bryan entered the State to be
received with a frenzy of enthusiasm, and a young god he seemed
to all who saw and heard him. Never had such enormous throngs
crowded to hear a presidential nominee; children literally were
crushed in the crash, and women fainted. That year, anxious
to plume his wings in a National Convention, Beveridge was
eager to go as a delegate; but he was warned against his ambition
by Louis T. Michener, a practical politician who had managed
Harrison's campaigns and been tarred by the brush of the
Dudley 'blocks of five.' He was practicing law in Washington
and was one of the advisers of the young orator at this stage of
his career. 'There is likely to be a very nasty mess,' he wrote
Beveridge, 'and I don't want you connected with it, especially
as the supporter of a man whose nomination will be succeeded by
scandal after scandal.... My dear boy, I want you to realize
that our party never yet has sold a nomination,[3] either wholly or
partially.'[4]

Whatever the reason, Beveridge did not go as a delegate,
but no one enlisted more zealously for the campaign that followed. It was toward the close of the campaign, when he was
worn and weary from constant speaking in the State, that he
received, on short notice, the invitation to close the Republican
campaign at Chicago in the Auditorium. The managers of the
meeting thought they had a definite engagement with Harrison
to make the final speech, but he declined to serve. When a committee went to Indianapolis to importune the stubborn statesman, the members were advised by Harrison to get Beveridge.
It meant a supreme opportunity, but he would have preferred

[1] MS. Autobiography.   [2] Ibid.
[3] A reference to the charge that Hanna had bought delegates for McKinley in the
South.
[4] Michener to Beveridge.

more notice. The meeting was almost upon him and he had speaking engagements in the meanwhile. In the interval he traveled about the State, speaking in small towns and hiding in cheerless hotel rooms to work upon the Chicago speech. It was to be published in the press; it had to be written under every disadvantage and memorized as well. Ordinarily the committing would have been a simple task for him.

His theme was a congenial one. Four years before, John P. Altgeld had become Governor of Illinois. He was a man of intense convictions, with profound sympathies for the lowly and a rare capacity to arouse the emotions of great audiences. Soon after entering upon his duties, he shocked the conservative by pardoning some anarchistic agitators in prison for complicity in the Chicago Haymarket Riot of 1886. A study of the record had convinced him that the trial had been a farce, the jury packed, the judge prejudiced. Even more shocking to the conventional was the powerful State paper in which he justified the pardon. This State paper has constantly grown in impressiveness with the passing of the years, but at the time the author was the object of unmeasured criticism. When, during the Pullman strike of 1894, President Cleveland, without a request from either Governor or Legislature as provided in the Constitution, sent Federal troops into Illinois and crushed the strike, Altgeld made a vigorous protest, based on constitutional grounds and the rights of the States. The floodgates of abuse were opened upon him. His critics treated his constitutional objections as flippancy, and to the country at large grossly exaggerated the degree of disorder. During the campaign of 1896 he had made a notable speech at Cooper Union, New York, in defense of his action — and Beveridge was to answer him.

The theme — Nationalism against Altgeld's State Rights — fitted in perfectly with Beveridge's most intense conviction that State Rights had been shot to pieces in the war of the States.

Thus he set to work with a zest upon his manuscript, sometimes by the light of kerosene lamps in country taverns. But for the first time he found it almost impossible to commit. He was suffering from utter physical weariness and brain-fag. On the morning of the day he was to speak, he awoke to the realization that he had not mastered his manuscript. Reaching Chicago, he excused himself from the committee that met him, retired to his room, and 'literally went to bed with the speech.' [1] But it was no use. Night came. Nearer panic than he had ever been before, he dressed and went to the Auditorium; and as he appeared in the wings and the great organ pealed forth, some-

[1] This was told the author by Beveridge in 1919.

thing seemed to hit him in the pit of the stomach, and he had to sit down. When summoned to the platform, he went 'precisely in the spirit of one going to his execution.' But the audience, noting his youthful appearance, was clearly sympathetic, and that helped. And when he stepped to the front, he felt at ease and the words came trippingly to the tongue as they never had before. Keyed up to high nervous tension, he had never appeared in such fine fettle, and soon the great crowd was swaying before his philippic against Altgeld. One of the papers said that 'the young barrister sounded the tocsin of liberty and honor and prosperity until the audience was wild with enthusiasm,' and that he spoke with an eloquence unsurpassed by the most celebrated orators in the Nation.[1]

'Events, not politicians, have shaped and shifted the issue of the campaign,' he began. 'Six months ago the issue was national prosperity. One month ago the issue was national honor. To-day the issue is national life. Are the American people a nation, or are they an aggregation of localities?... Shall the National Government enforce its laws... or shall it first get permission of local satraps called governors? Which is supreme, the general government of the whole people or the caprice of the executive of a State? Which is sacred, the decision of the court or the decree of a caucus? Is the Stars and Stripes the flag of a vital nation of invincible people or is it as meaningless as idiocy and powerless as burnt powder?'

Thus he swept into the full flood of his extreme Federalism. Was not the Government established to assure tranquillity? Who was to be the judge as to when tranquillity was destroyed and the intervention of Federal power necessary? 'Governor Altgeld,' he continued, 'tells the American people that the local authorities are on the ground and can best decide. Yes, they are on the ground, and therefore most influenced by local conditions — by the hope of winning votes by pandering to temporary passions.' Is it not true that the local authorities are 'responsible to no one save the people where frenzy lays prostrate the laws?' And true that 'mobs can never overthrow the law in any locality until their number is so great... as to constitute, if not a majority, at least a formidable array of voting power?' And true that when this formidable array appears, the local officials 'temporize with lawlessness,' and thus encourage it? 'The danger that threatens our future is local demagogy, and not Federal despots.'

Thus, in the heat of advocacy, he swept State Rights aside and gave the Federal power the right to enter any State at any time with its armed forces under the guise of maintaining law

[1] *Chicago Inter-Ocean*, Oct. 30, 1896.

and order. 'Governor Altgeld is not the issue; his official acts or omissions are not the issue. The principle implied is the issue' — the principle that the Federal Government may send troops into any State whenever it sees fit.

Asserting this extreme nationalism, he swept beyond most champions of centralization, while the great crowd shouted, cheered, laughed, and swayed. The Chicago papers published the speech in full, featuring it in the day's news of a great city, praising the speaker and the speech.[1] Parts were copied in the party press throughout the country. In Indianapolis, men stopped one another on the streets to talk about it and to agree that the young orator had moved toward the head of the procession of expounders. From Michener came congratulations: 'You have made a fine impression upon Senator Quay and other men of power in the eastern part of the country,' he wrote.[2]

Looking back upon this speech and its effect in later life, Beveridge was convinced that it paved his way to the Senate two years later. It stamped him as a militant champion of centralization — as a Hamiltonian without compromise — as a protector of property rights against the mob. Soon he would expand upon that theme and associate himself more than ever with that theory.

x

The opportunity came when his friendship with Philander C. Knox brought him an invitation to speak before the Allegheny Bar Association at Pittsburgh. Taking as his subject 'The Vitality of the Constitution,' he boldly read into the Hamiltonian doctrine of implied powers the right of the central government to do whatever it sees fit. From Marshall's decision in the case of McCullogh *vs.* Maryland, he reviewed the steady processes through which the doctrine of strict construction had been overthrown, down to the action of Cleveland in the Chicago strike; and approved. 'For in any event,' he said, 'the people will grow; in any event, problems undreamed of by the writers of the Constitution will be evolved from changed conditions and unprecedented social and industrial situations. And if the Constitution is not self-adapting to the march of history and the progress of the people, revolution will rend the Constitution to pieces.' True, Cleveland's action in Chicago went beyond any previous formal interpretation of the fundamental law — but it marched in the long line with Hamilton and Marshall.[3]

---

[1] *Chicago Chronicle*, Oct. 30, 1896.
[2] Michener to Beveridge, Nov. 10, 1896.   [3] Pamphlet speech, Jan. 4, 1898.

Within a month, the 'young man in a hurry' had penetrated
to the heart of the East and won the acclaim of New York City.
The occasion was the annual Lincoln Day Banquet of the
Republican Club; his subject, 'Abraham Lincoln'; and here he
struck another note, not new with him, destined to be heard
recurrently the rest of his days — the discipline and regulation
of great business and financial power. Chauncey M. Depew
was in the chair; and beside him, as a fellow speaker, was a young
man then Assistant Secretary of the Navy — Theodore Roosevelt. Beveridge had scarcely uttered three sentences before he
had caught the crowd. His sentences were short, sharp, like
cracks of a whip, and soon they were punctuated by cheers and
shouts. It was a daring speech for such a company, and its very
audacity won its way. Denouncing the fomenters of social dis-
content, he turned suddenly on the vices of the rich:

'There are abuses of capital,' he said, 'which furnish the pil-
lagers a war-cry — improper uses of riches which the Catilines
use as examples to discredit all wealth; vulgar ostentation of
money which unsheathes envy and whets hatred; a meddling
with the making and the execution of the laws; a controlling of
the natural laws of trade by unlawful devices. But these financial
developments are not structural defects. They are merely
a natural tendency developed beyond their rightful sphere, and
requiring rebuke, regulation, and restraint.'

At this point he was interrupted with applause and 'three
cheers for Beveridge!'

'They demand,' he said, 'that the party of Abraham Lincoln
shall with one hand take by the throat that idiot Greed, who
gives the demagogue his incendiary text, and with the other
hand take by the throat the demagogue himself, and knock
their heads together until robbery is knocked out of the one
and anarchy out of the other, and common sense and patriotism
knocked into the heads of both.'

This brought the great demonstration of the evening; and
when he had finished, Roosevelt, who followed, referred to him
as one 'than whom I have never heard anyone expound the
principles for which Abraham Lincoln lived and died more ably.' [1]

That evening was to be memorable in Beveridge's life. It
brought him for the first time into contact with Roosevelt, won
him the lasting friendship of Depew, and carried his reputation
as an orator to the East. 'Holland,' the correspondent, wrote
glowingly of the speech as 'thoughtful' and 'profound,' and its
effect upon the audience as comparable only 'with some of
the higher intellectual utterances which have become traditional

[1] Republican Club Report, Feb. 12, 1898.

here.'[1] A quarter of a century later, Beveridge was to write 'Holland' that his friendly article had given him his first recognition in the East, 'and helped to start moving the forces that finally landed me in the Senate.'[2]

Thus, by the winter of 1897–98, though but thirty-five, and but ten years removed from the sod huts of western Kansas, he had been recognized as the most brilliant and dynamic Republican orator in the State; had commanded the warm appreciation of Chicago, and gained his spurs in a brilliant oratorical tournament in New York.

XI

During the preceding four years, by associating his name with certain theories of government and society, he had become to many something more than a mere orator. An intense nationalist and centralizationalist of the Hamiltonian school he had always been, imbibing this feeling with his mother's milk. But he had phrased a philosophy of conservatism that was rather too rare. Hostility to demagogy meant to many, if not most, subserviency to wealth, an utter indifference to the rights of men or the obligations of power. Beveridge had no more patience with that point of view than with that of the demagogue, and knew that the protection of property and the stability of society rests upon the decent restraint of power. Because he favored a powerful government, he resented the pretensions of great fortunes to immunity from its regulations. This was to remain his idea through life and to involve him in political difficulties in the future. He thought it the conservatism of common sense for great corporations to be honest, humane, and just. These views attracted national attention beyond the party wall. 'The point that impresses and rejoices me in your utterances,' wrote John Temple Graves, the orator and journalist of Georgia, 'is the fact that joined to your loyal and strenuous advocacy of your party ... is an unvarying expression of consideration for the suffering masses of the common people, and a fearless reminder to your party, and the vast property interests that compose it, of the duty of consideration and helpfulness to this element of our population.' And he concluded with an appeal: 'My dear Mr. Beveridge, if there is any hope for the country, it is in conservatism like this. If there is a mission on earth for a voice noble and eloquent as yours, it is to stand in the ranks of your great party and preach this wholesome conservatism to the massed

[1] *Philadelphia Press*, Feb. 12, 1898.
[2] Beveridge to E. J. Edwards (Holland), June 17, 1923.

and mighty capital which is fronting the ever-increasing army of the discontented and desperate poor. May God give you strength to fulfill the mission for which your splendid talents seem to be set.' [1]

Thus, at thirty-five his views on political and social policies had turned inquisitive eyes upon him; and he was ready to strike out upon a career.

Five days after the New York speech, the Maine went to the bottom in the harbor of Havana.

[1] John Temple Graves to Beveridge, July 7, 1897.

CHAPTER V

PROPHET OF IMPERIALISM

I

From the moment the Maine went down in the waters of Havana Harbor, war was inevitable. Generations of Americans, coveting the Pearl of the Antilles, had been clamoring for the expulsion of the Spaniards; and the ruthless methods of General Weyler, called 'The Butcher,' sent from Madrid to give short shrift to the insurrection on the island, had aroused the bitter resentment of the American people. It mattered little whether the Maine explosion was from within or without the vessel, the excuse sufficed. Politicians in Congress echoed the demands of the people. Thurston of Nebraska moved the sentimental with a lachrymose oration in the Senate, and Proctor of Vermont, in a cold matter-of-fact recital of what he had seen in Cuba, was thoroughly convincing. War was declared. The Nation entered the struggle with the zeal of the old crusaders and in the rôle of liberators of oppressed peoples. McKinley reluctantly yielded to public clamor, and the war was on.

The excitement after the declaration was out of all proportion to the magnitude of the struggle ahead. We had not engaged in a foreign war since the far-off days when Western boys swept on Mexico and added a new empire to the Republic. But this was not a war against a minor nation. We were faring forth to face one of the great monarchies of the Old World, which, in its golden days, had been the dominating power of the earth. There was something of dignity, aloofness, and romance about Spain. It seemed like the twentieth century meeting the sixteenth in combat. And the cause of Cuba — beautiful, bleeding Cuba! The call for volunteers was not unheeded. Crowds gathered about the recruiting office in Indianapolis. Strangely enough, as we look back upon it in perspective, there was an undercurrent of uneasiness. After all — the fortunes of war. Who knew? — perhaps we might lose. And then there was the possibility that Spain might find an ally. Had not the French papers referred to our crusade with cynical contempt? There was intense excitement and some sober thinking among the thoughtful, but in the streets where newsboys hawked the newspapers with flaming headlines the people were marching, shouting, following the band.

To Beveridge the turn of events was thrilling. That the flag would sweep on to ultimate victory, he had no doubt. It might be a prolonged struggle, he thought, but not likely. And unlike many other Americans of the moment he was getting his greatest thrill over that which would follow the triumph. Had he not read a paper before the Literary Club eight years ago on American Diplomacy, criticizing our failure to go forth aggressively for the markets of the Orient — to assume our place as a world power by virtue of our strength? And here was the opportunity. There is something almost uncanny in the manner in which he envisioned the whole scene for the next few years.

For a moment he was inclined to lock his law office and go forth to battle. Always the thought of the thunder of artillery and the clash of steel had enthralled him — a heritage of his childhood. Narrowly he had missed West Point, because of his boyish giggle at the examination. Napoleon was his idol — Napoleon and all the tribe of conquerors. And then, too, so many others among the young men of his circle in Indianapolis had been commissioned as officers; for the moment the idea appealed to him.

At that time his close friend Charles G. Dawes was in Washington as Comptroller of the Treasury, and Beveridge wrote him on the possibility of getting a commission that would speed him to the fighting. Evidently there was some red tape, some uncertainty as to the meaning of a commission, for Dawes's reply was unsatisfactory.

'I have your esteemed letter of the 22d,' Beveridge wrote him, 'and thank you for it. My only objection to your suggestion as to the manner of getting my military commission would be that I do not care to go in at all unless I can go in for actual service in the field, for actual out-and-out warfare. I will not consent for a moment to be a carpetbag soldier.... I leave tonight for Boston, where I speak before the Middlesex Club at the Grant anniversary banquet at the Brunswick Hotel on next Wednesday night, April 27. I wish you would run up there. It would do you good to take a day off.'

It was on this occasion before the Middlesex Club that Beveridge fired the first shot for that policy of imperialism that was to follow hotly in the wake of war. A little later, he would write Theodore Roosevelt, who was raising his regiment of Rough Riders, in the interest of a youth who wished to join. 'He wants to go with Roosevelt,' he wrote, and then added, a bit wistfully, 'and I don't blame him.' [1]

[1] Beveridge to Roosevelt, May 3, 1898.

II

At the time of the Banquet of the Middlesex Club, not a shot had been fired. The minds of the masses were on Cuba, few dreaming of a spot so remote as the Philippines, of which few had ever heard. Military men were thinking of coming events in the Pacific, but even the press had little to say. And all that was being said in the streets was that we were going to free Cuba and send the Spaniards speeding back to their own country. There was no reason for the guests of the Middlesex Club to expect anything from the comparatively unknown young Mid-Western orator beyond a tribute to Grant, on whom he was to speak.

And he threw a bombshell among the tables.

A few sentences on the Republicanism of Grant, a few more on the gold standard, and then he began to skirt the edge of the war about to begin in earnest.

'He [Grant] never forgot that we are a conquering race, and that we must obey our blood and occupy new markets, and, if necessary, new lands,' he said.

There was a stir at the tables. What strange talk was this? 'Must occupy new markets and new lands.' But he had just begun.

He had the prophet's seer-like sight which beheld, as a part of the Almighty's infinite plan, the disappearance of debased civilizations and decaying races before the higher civilization of the nobler and more virile types of men.

This, indeed, was imperialism; and how reconcile it with the traditions of the Republic? The prophet of imperialism answered:

He understood that the axioms applicable to thirteen impoverished colonies have been rendered obsolete by history. An echo of the past is not to stay the progress of a mighty people and their free institutions. He had the instinct of empire.[1] He dreamed the same dream that God put in the brain of Jefferson and Hamilton, of John Bright and Emerson, and all the imperial intellects of his race — the drama of American extension till all the seas shall bloom with that flower of liberty, the flag of the great Republic.

Still there was silence. Perhaps the young man, inebriate on rhetoric, was speaking at random, without a realization of what he was proposing. But no — the next paragraph proved that he was not thinking in terms of mere sentiment.

[1] A reference to Cuba and Santo Domingo.

The Progressive Era 69

American factories are making more than the American people can use; American soil is producing more than they can consume. Fate has written our policy for us; the trade of the world must and shall be ours. And we will get it as our mother [England] has told us how. We will establish trading-posts throughout the world as distributing-points for American products. We will cover the ocean with our merchant marine. We will build a navy to the measure of our greatness. Great colonies governing themselves, flying our flag and trading with us, will grow about our posts of trade. Our institutions will follow our flag on the wings of our commerce. And American law, American order, American civilization, and the American flag will plant themselves on shores hitherto bloody and benighted, but by those agencies of God henceforth to be made beautiful and bright.

The astonished banqueters, no longer doubtful of his meaning, responded with 'tremendous cheers.' American imperialism, frankly, defiantly avowed, was that night receiving its first tribute of applause. And a prophet was speaking.

If this means the Stars and Stripes over an Isthmian canal... over Hawaii... over Cuba and the southern seas... then let us meet that meaning with a mighty joy and make that meaning good, no matter what barbarism and all our foes may do or say.

The crowd again responded with rapturous cheers. Many hard-headed business men had been a bit cynical over the sentiment of the war — but this was business. But the audacity and novelty of it, in Irish Boston, this:

If it means Anglo-Saxon solidarity; if it means an English-American understanding upon the basis of a division of the world's markets so that the results may be just, upon the basis of justice to Ireland so that the understanding may be enduring; if it means such an English-speaking people's league of God for the permanent peace of this war-worn world, the stars in their courses will fight for us and countless centuries will applaud.

The crowd was now cheering wildly, and General Champlin, springing to his feet, called for 'Three cheers for Beveridge!' and they were given lustily. A moment later, when the fervent orator sternly warned, 'And let those beware who prove apostate to our destiny,' three cheers were given again.

The guests now knew they were listening to the first voice that had yet been raised to define the real significance of the war, but they did not know how accurately he was defining the policy that was to be. Neither did they realize how uncannily he was foreshadowing military events, before a shot was fired, when he continued:

What should be the policy of the war?... It is our military duty to strike her [Spain] at her weakest point before we strike her at her strongest points. Cuba must fall into our hands, but that will be only when Spain is conquered.... In the Pacific is the true field of our earliest operations. There Spain has an island empire, the Philippine Archipelago. It is poorly defended. Spain's best ships are on the Atlantic side. In the Pacific the United States has a powerful squadron. The Philippines are logically our first target.

At that moment, unknown to a single man in the room and to few in the Nation, Admiral Dewey was moving on the waters upon the Philippines, and three days after the delivery of the speech, he moved to glory in the triumph of Manila Bay.

The audience in Boston applauded his victory before it was won; applauded the policy we were to pursue before it had officially been defined, and applauded through the prophecy of Beveridge. Imperialism, defiant, unafraid, had found a voice.

III

And Beveridge had confidence in his policy and prophecy. When his speech was published and distributed among his friends, some were sympathetic and others hostile. His replies to the letters throw a vivid light on the fervor of his belief. To his friend George W. Perkins he unbosomed himself:

With this mail I hand you my recent speech in Boston, which I have marked. I delivered that speech in the very home of Mugwumpery; in a town where it was supposed that the blood of its citizens was so cold that it no longer had American enterprise; but when I came to that point where I advocated the extension of our territory, there was a greater demonstration even than there was at the Delmonico dinner.... Out here in the West the young men are for it almost to a man — I mean the full-blooded young men....

I have no words sufficiently withering to designate those sugar-beet apostates to our destiny, like Thurston of Iowa [Nebraska]. It is unthinkable that any man should be so little of a statesman and so much of a politician as to throw himself against the current of events in order to take political advantage of what they think is a prejudice of the people in favor of the old Washington dictum about isolation. There is no such thing as isolation in the world today. They say that Cuba is not contiguous;... that the Philippines are not contiguous. They are contiguous. Our navy will make them contiguous.

The commercial extension of the Republic has been my dream since boyhood. Eight years ago I read a paper in the Gentlemen's Club in this city on our diplomatic relations in which I outlined the imperial policy we are now beginning and which your letter so eloquently advocates. At that time not one single member of the club except myself was in favor of it.[1]

[1] Beveridge to Perkins, May 3, 1898.

It was in a letter to Charles G. Dawes that he revealed the passing of an ambition for a military commission, and confessed his intense desire to enter public life and help work out what he conceived to be certain—an imperial national policy. He had expected such a policy inevitable in time, but had not expected it to come so soon. 'But,' he wrote, 'now all at once the fierce light of war reveals to the American people that this policy, which I thought would be delayed for years, is upon us, and so it is, for the first time in my life, I wish I were in public station where I could partly shape the events that are now upon us. I would rather take part in organizing our colonial system than to do anything else on this earth. I would rather map out and advocate the imperial policy of the Republic than to have been the leading statesman of the late war. It means more for humanity, more for our country, and a larger place in history.' [1]

But not all his friends were able to go with him in his enthusiasm over the new departure. When Henry D. Estabrook, a brilliant Chicago lawyer and orator, who had been captivated by his Chicago speeches, wrote at length to combat his views, Beveridge was unmoved. 'Territorial extension,' he replied, 'is not desirable for itself alone. It is and will be merely an incident of commercial extension. And commercial extension is the absolutely necessary result of the overwhelming productive energy and capacity of the American people. So there you are, and what are you going to do about it?' [2]

When his friend and admirer John Temple Graves wrote more in sorrow than in anger to protest against his radical imperialistic views, Beveridge replied that 'if Fate could lay before me the choice of a place in history as a free gift from the gods, I would rather be the forming and the shaping mind which is to mark out our foreign policy from now on than to have been the greatest statesman of the period of the Civil War, for, after all, the latter will be more or less local, the former will be universal.' [3]

None of his friends were more heartily in accord with him than Perkins. When Thomas B. Reed, Speaker of the House, was assuming a belligerent stand against imperialism, Perkins urged Beveridge to write to him. To Reed the young Indianian was probably unknown. Beveridge had the better judgment and declined. 'I feel that any effort of mine,' he wrote, 'upon the Gibraltar-like mind and will of the Speaker would be absolutely ineffectual.' [4]

[1] Beveridge to Dawes, May 10, 1898.
[2] Beveridge to Estabrook, May 20, 1898.
[3] Beveridge to Graves, July 15, 1898.
[4] Beveridge to Perkins, May 31, 1898.

But his imperialism was literally flaming now. When Perkins sent him an article he had written on Gladstone, Beveridge wrote him of his ideal of statesmanship. As to Gladstone, 'he did not do things — he talked.' Beveridge preferred 'great constructive minds' — Bismarck, Disraeli, Hamilton, Cavour — 'and that quality of mind and purpose.' To his mind 'the heroic statesmanship of Disraeli in securing for England the control of the Suez Canal was more admirable than all the talk in which Gladstone ever indulged.' [1]

And by that he meant, do things materially, imperially. Never was he so much a Hamiltonian as at the beginning of his career.

IV

As we shall learn later, he was planning even then, with superb audacity, to march defiantly over the plans of the politicians and bosses to the senatorial election. A few days before the Middlesex Club speech, he had presided over the Marion County Convention at Indianapolis, and aroused the delegates to a high pitch of enthusiasm in a speech which was more brilliant in epigrams than sound in logic. It was an uncompromising partisan speech deliberately designed to please the partisans. A fling at the Democratic Convention which had been disorderly — the Republicans would 'nominate its candidates by roll-call and not by riot'; a word upon the trusts — if Democrats mentioned trusts, 'pick up the names of Whitney, Brice, and Gorman and fling them in their teeth'; and just a hint at imperialism. The declaration of war had just been made, and that could wait. But he was straining at the leash. 'Mighty events,' he said, 'sleep in the Republic's shotted guns — Cuban liberty is there; Cuban independence is there; and finally, not today or tomorrow, but worked out in the processes of time, Jefferson's dream of an Anglo-Saxon civilization for Cuba under the Stars and Stripes, is there for realization and fulfillment.' [2]

Even then he was planning to challenge Destiny in a race for the United States Senate; and with that in view he was eager for the chairmanship of the State Convention and the opportunity to sound the tocsin of the imperialism that obsessed him. But that was not to be. He wrote to Perkins about it, and to Perry Heath, an influential politician then in Washington, but Senator Fairbanks insisted on his right. This aroused the ire of some of the youthful followers of Beveridge, and he wrote one of his managers that it had done him 'more good than presiding

[1] Beveridge to Perkins, June 6, 1898.
[2] *Indianapolis Journal*, April 17, 1898.

over a dozen conventions.' But he was sick at heart, nevertheless. 'I sincerely regret that I did not have charge of the Convention today,' he wrote, 'because I will never live long enough to make the speech I would have made this morning. The occasion was here, the subject was at hand, the delegates and the people were prepared. It was an infinite opportunity. Had I conducted the Convention today, I would, in a single day, have done seventy-five per cent of the work which will be on our shoulders this fall and winter.' [1]

V

If he could not deliver the keynote in the Convention, he would make it for the campaign, and he was chosen to open the fight at Tomlinson's Hall. Here was the golden opportunity, and he was prepared. The stage-setting was worthy of a master. Two hundred members of the Marion Club, with torches and red lights, and preceded by a band, marched to the Beveridge home, where the orator was conducted to a carriage immediately behind the band, and with much shouting, waving of torches, burning of red fire, the procession moved to the hall. Long before it had been packed to its capacity, to the highest gallery, and hundreds were standing in the aisles. When Beveridge was introduced, the crowd roared for two minutes. And then, 'with his first gesture a complete silence fell over the hall, and with soft, but clear enunciation, he began his address.' [2] It was to be one of the greatest of his speeches in its effect upon his fortunes. The scene was inspiring — thousands expectant, animated, literally packed before him. And he had imperialism for his theme — a theme that others were not touching.

'The burning question of this campaign,' he said, 'is whether the American people will accept the gifts of events, whether they will rise as lifts their soaring destiny; whether they will proceed upon the lines of national development surveyed by the statesmen of our past; or whether, for the first time, the American people, doubting their mission, will question Fate, prove apostate to the spirit of their race, and halt the ceaseless march of free institutions.'

This was in keeping with the Boston speech, but he was now forging ahead and forcing the fighting.

'The opposition tells us we ought not to rule a people without their consent. I answer, the rule of liberty, that all just governments derive their authority from the consent of the governed,

[1] Beveridge to John C. Wingate, Aug. 4, 1898.
[2] *Indianapolis Journal*, Sept. 17, 1898.

applies only to those who are capable of self-government' — and the thousands cheered.

And how did the opposition know that consent would be refused? 'Would not the people of the Philippines prefer the just, humane, civilizing government of this Republic to the savage, bloody rule of pillage and extortion from which we have rescued them?'

The excited crowd cheered for them.

'Do not the blazing fires of joy and the ringing of bells of gladness in Porto Rico prove the welcome of our flag?'

Again a demonstration.

And, all else aside, did we not owe something to the world? 'Shall we turn these people back to the reeking hands from which we have taken them? Shall we abandon them to their fate, with the wolves of conquest all about them — with Germany, Russia, France, even Japan, hungering for them? Shall we save them from these nations to give them the self-rule of tragedy? It would be like giving a razor to a babe and telling it to shave itself.'

The tense crowd relaxed in laughter, and the orator continued:

'The proposition of the opposition makes the Declaration of Independence preposterous, like the reading of Job's lamentations would be at a wedding, or an Altgeld speech on the Fourth of July.'

And how govern our new possessions? 'Out of local conditions and the necessities of the case, methods of government will grow. If England can govern foreign lands, so can America. If it can supervise protectorates, so can America. Will you affirm by your vote that you are an infidel to American vigor and power and practical sense? Or that we are of the ruling race of the world; that ours is the blood of government; ours the hearts of dominion; ours the brain and genius of administration?'

By this time the audience, packed in tight, was cheering sentences, not waiting for climaxes, or rather finding a climax in every sentence. The young orator, glowing with the fervor of his imperialistic vision, warmed by the eager response of the crowd, now launched into his famous 'March of the Flag.' It voiced the spirit of the day and throws light on the trend of thought which determined the Nation on its departure from its earlier ideals, and is therefore of historic value.

The march of the flag. [Cheers.] In 1789, the flag of the Republic waved over four million souls in thirteen States and their savage territory which stretched to the Mississippi, to Canada, and to the Floridas. The timid souls of that day said that no new territory was needed, and, for an hour, they were right. But Jefferson, through whose intellect the centuries marched; Jefferson, whose blood was Saxon, but whose schooling was French,[1] and therefore whose deeds negatived his words; Jefferson, who dreamed of Cuba as a State of the Union; Jefferson, the first imperialist of the Republic — Jefferson acquired that imperial territory which swept from the Mississippi to the mountains, from Texas to the British Possessions, and the march of the flag began. [Applause.] The infidels to the gospel of liberty raved, but the flag swept on. [Applause.]

The title to that noble land out of which Oregon, Washington, Idaho, and Montana have been carved was uncertain; Jefferson, strict constructionist of constitutional power though he was, obeyed the Anglo-Saxon impulse within him, whose watchword then, and whose watchword throughout the world today, is 'Forward' [Applause.], another empire was added to the Republic, and the march of the flag went on. [Applause.]

Those who denied the power of free institutions to expand urged every argument and more that we hear today; but the people's judgment approved the command of their blood, and the march of the flag went on. [Applause.]

The screen of land from New Orleans to Florida shut us from the Gulf, and over this and the Everglades Peninsula waved the saffron flag of Spain; Andrew Jackson seized both, the American people stood at his back, and, under Monroe, Florida came under the dominion of the Republic, and the march of the flag went on. [Applause.] The Cassandras prophesied every prophecy we hear today, but the march of the flag went on. Then Texas responded to the bugle call of liberty, and the march of the flag went on. [Cheers.] And at last we waged war with Mexico, and the flag swept over the Southwest, over peerless California, past the Golden Gate to Oregon, and from ocean to ocean its folds of glory blazed. [Great cheering.]

And now, obeying the same voice that Jefferson heard and obeyed, that Jackson heard and obeyed, that Monroe heard and obeyed, that Seward heard and obeyed, that Ulysses S. Grant heard and obeyed, that Benjamin Harrison heard and obeyed, William McKinley plants the flag over all the islands of the seas, outposts of commerce, citadels of national security, and the march of the flag goes on. [Long-continued cheering.] Bryan, Bailey, Bland, and Blackburn command it to stand still, but the march of the flag goes on. [Renewed cheering.] And the question you will answer at the polls is whether you will stand with this quartet of disbelief in the American people, or whether you are marching onward with the flag. [Tremendous cheering.]

But did the opposition say that, unlike the other lands, these lands of Spain are not contiguous?

The orator paused and smiled indulgently, while the audience laughed.

The ocean does not separate us from the lands of our duty and desire — the ocean joins us, a river never to be dredged, a canal never to be repaired. [Applause.] Steam joins us, electricity joins us — the very

[1] This was a favorite fallacy of Beveridge frequently found.

elements are in league with our destiny. [Continued applause and cheers.] Cuba not contiguous? Porto Rico not contiguous? The Philippines not contiguous? Our navy will make them contiguous! [he thundered, as the thousands shouted their delight].

Dewey and Sampson and Schley have made them contiguous, and American speed, American guns, American heart and brain and nerve will keep them contiguous forever.

But, aside from the call of the blood, there was another reason for imperialism:

We are raising more than we can consume. We are making more than we can use. Today our industrial society is congested; there are more workers than there is work; there is more capital than there is investment. We do not need more money — we need more circulation, more employment.... Think of the thousands of Americans who will pour into Hawaii and Porto Rico when the republican laws cover these islands with justice and safety! Think of the tens of thousands of Americans who will invade mine and field and forest in the Philippines when a liberal government, protected and controlled by this Republic, if not the government of the Republic itself, shall establish order and equity there!

Swiftly, seductively, he described the resources and products of the islands — the wealth waiting to be converted through our markets; and then closed with the usual religious note of all imperialists: 'It is God's great purpose made manifest in the instincts of our race, whose present phase is our personal profit, but whose far-off end is the redemption of the world and the christianization of mankind.' [1]

He sat down in the midst of a remarkable ovation. Never had Indianapolis been more stirred by campaign oratory; never more startled by the novelty of new ideas. Its pride of race, its imagination, had been touched to the utmost. And never was Beveridge to be in finer fettle. Even the enemies of imperialism thrilled to the fervor of the delivery, the militant march of the rhetoric, and went away sadly lamenting that in the excitement they, too, had cheered.

The next day all of Indiana was reading the speech in the Indianapolis papers, and the Republican State Committee, though controlled by men unfriendly to the young man's aspirations, ordered three hundred thousand copies for distribution. Thousands were sent into other States, for no other Republican orator that year approached the fervor and effectiveness of Beveridge's speech; none other made the pulse beat faster. But in Indiana the speech was a sensation, and clamorous calls for his services on the stump poured in from every nook and corner. The very

[1] *Indianapolis Journal*, Sept. 17, 1898.

next day he spoke at Fort Wayne, the second largest city in the State, and thenceforth until the election he literally marched with the flag, speaking once and twice a day to delighted partisans from the river to the lake. Toward the close of October, the hardships of the campaign told upon him, and, ill, he dragged himself to his appointment,[1] only to be forced to bed. But three days later he was out — voicing the gospel of imperialism until the day of the balloting.

VI

The 'March of the Flag' speech also extended and increased his reputation nationally, and he became the subject of feature articles, like an actor or a candidate. To some of his admirers his imperialistic pæans were distressing, to none more than to Melville E. Ingalls, the railroad president, who wrote that he could not agree with Beveridge's dream 'of an Asiatic republic.' Nothing daunted by the implied rebuke, Beveridge replied that his dream was 'of an American supremacy in Asiatic commerce.' 'Surely,' he wrote, 'you will agree with this?' Many times he had referred to Ingalls in conversation with his friends as 'the best type of those masters of affairs which America has developed,' and he was not ready to admit that Ingalls's 'breed has run out.' No, 'there will be other hearts as strong and other kings as far-seeing who will repeat in our world commerce the industrial triumphs you have achieved here at home.' Were we not in need of foreign markets for our surplus? Did not 'Oceania and Asia afford the best market for our products?' Opposition to imperialism was unworthy of Ingalls. 'Never forget that we are Anglo-Saxon at heart,' he concluded. 'We are the only people on earth whose farmers buy the adjoining farm before they need it. We are of the blood which furnishes the world with its Daniel Boones, its Francis Drakes, its Cecil Rhodes — and its M. E. Ingalls.'[2]

It is in this letter to Ingalls that Beveridge revealed without embroidery or sentiment the dominant passion of his younger days — a passion for the American domination of the markets of the Orient. He did not mention God to Ingalls.

The young eagle had now tried his wings against a current and was persuaded that he could fly alone against any wind. As he traversed the State to be received with enthusiasm everywhere, he was busy with his plans in the event of a Republican Legislature. Among the big-wigs of the party in the State he did not enter into the calculations on the senatorship at all.

[1] At Connersville, Oct. 25, 1898.　　[2] Beveridge to Ingalls, Sept. 21, 1898.

But in the middle of the campaign he was almost confident. 'If things go on as they are,' he wrote Shaffer, 'even Mr. Fairbanks will not be able to head things off.' [1]

The election resulted in a Republican victory and a Republican Legislature that would elect a successor to Senator David Turpie, a Democrat. That day Beveridge sent a cable to his friend George W. Perkins, then in Paris: 'The Legislature is Republican. The fight will now be on. I shall need your assistance. Write or wire me when you will be home.' [2]

Three days later, the press announced that he had entered the contest for the Senate.

[1] Beveridge to Shaffer, Oct. 17, 1898.   [2] Beveridge MSS.

CHAPTER VI
THE TRIUMPH OF YOUTH

I

WHEN Beveridge sent the cable to George Perkins, he was not
acting on a sudden impulse, for his determination to challenge
the graybeards in the senatorial contest had been formed early
in the spring. 'For the first time in my life, I wish I were in public life,' he had written Perkins in early May, but he had entertained a secret ambition much earlier. Early in 1898, at a casual
meeting in the law office of James W. Noel, a personal friend,
Beveridge had bluntly announced to a group of friends of the
younger set that he was eager to go to the Senate. Among those
present were Noel, Frank Littleton, Larz Whitcomb, who shared
Beveridge's office, and A. M. Glossbrenner — all young and
comparatively inexperienced in politics. The year before,
Littleton had been a member of the Legislature, and he was
seeking renomination and reëlection with a view to the speakership of the House. It was tacitly agreed at this meeting that
Noel, Littleton, Larz Whitcomb, and Glossbrenner should be
candidates for the House with the double purpose of contributing to the election of Littleton to the speakership and of
Beveridge to the Senate.[1] A few days later, walking from the
Columbia Club with Fred A. Joss, a keen and clever young
lawyer, Beveridge confessed his ambition, and urged the latter
to contest for the joint senatorship from Marion and Morgan
Counties. A young man like Beveridge, Joss had long been one
of his admirers, but he was more stunned than impressed by the
solicitation. He did not doubt Beveridge's capacity, but he returned to his office convinced of the absurdity of attempting to
break through the line of the old party bosses who had other
plans. But soon he was importuned by Noel and Whitcomb, and
in something of the spirit of a Dumas musketeer, he fell in line.[2]
On the day Beveridge was lamenting the loss of the opportunity
of presiding over the State Convention, Joss unexpectedly entered the race for the joint senatorship, and defeated the candidate having the support of the machine. This left the graybeards gasping with wonderment, but they had no idea of the
significance of the event. The secret of the Beveridge candidacy
was zealously to be guarded throughout the campaign.

[1] Noel to the author; J. A. Coffin, *Indiana Magazine of History*, September, 1928.
[2] Joss to the author.

Very early, however, the Beveridge forces were greatly strengthened by the accession of one of the most clever and experienced of the practical politicians, when John Wingate entered Beveridge's office to tell him the hour had struck for him to strike for the Senate. 'Looking backward a long time ago,' wrote Wesley M. Girard, of Monticello, years later,[1] 'I see our mutual friend John Wingate and myself calling at your office on North Pennsylvania Street and informing you that it was time for you to come out for United States Senator.' From that time on, Wingate dedicated his skill and experience to the Beveridge cause. As the campaign progressed, with Beveridge passing through a series of oratorical triumphs from the river to the lake, the clever Wingate, with extraordinary cunning, was quietly organizing throughout the State and planning the strategy of the coming fight. It was during the campaign that encouragement reached Beveridge from a source so unexpected as momentarily to awaken the fear that the secret of his candidacy was suspected. The State editor of the 'Indianapolis Journal' at the time was Frank C. Payne, who had been a classmate at DePauw, albeit not of his circle there, and a roommate of James E. Watson. Because of the college associations, Beveridge had not thought of him as at all friendly. But the editor had been impressed with the glowing accounts of the Beveridge meetings that had poured in upon his desk from the correspondents, had given them good headlines, and been convinced of the appreciation of the party workers throughout the State. One day, at the 'Journal' office, he told Beveridge of his impressions and urged that no time be lost in announcing his senatorial candidacy. 'But I would not dare!' Beveridge exclaimed, suspecting a trap.[2] Persuaded of Beveridge's genuine reluctance and amazement, Payne pressed the project upon Mrs. Beveridge, whom he had introduced to her husband at DePauw.

Indeed, it required no little temerity even to contemplate such a course. In Indianapolis it was inevitable that a character as dynamic as the young orator would have enemies and scoffers, but Payne had found nothing but admiration reflected in the reports that came over his desk from every quarter outside the capital. Even so, while popular with the rank and file because of his campaigning, he was not a favorite of the dominant organization, which had directed party politics with an iron hand. He had not yet reached his thirty-sixth birthday and had never held public office. For years no one of either party had aspired to the Senate until well seasoned in public station. Morton, Hendricks, Voorhees, McDonald, and Turpie, had long been

[1] August 14, 1923. [2] Payne to the author.

before the public as experienced practical politicians before they
dared aspire; and while Fairbanks, elected two years before,
had held no office, he had been the boss of the party and its
financier during the lean years before. All Beveridge had to recommend him was his reputation as an original thinker with a
definite national program and his eloquence. The younger element liked him for his imperialistic views, the business men were
impressed by his grasp of business problems and his ultra-conservatism as disclosed in his speeches, and the rank and file
generally were enthusiastically friendly because of the fire and
brilliancy of his oratory. In his campaign excursions over the
State for ten years, he had frequently been entertained in the
homes of the local leaders, who had been fascinated by his
dynamic personality. But in standardized politics he did not
fit into the picture at all.

But, as the campaign progressed, Beveridge was busy extending and solidifying his strength, and Wingate was cautiously
feeling his way to the support of the local leaders of importance.
In September, Beveridge was urging him to make contacts with
Riley McKeen, politically powerful in Terre Haute and in
western Indiana, but warning against any disclosure of purpose
until satisfied of a friendly feeling;[1] and Wingate was informing
Beveridge that Charles B. Landis, a member of Congress, thought
he (Beveridge) would be a candidate and, if elected, would be
popular in Washington.[2]

II

Long before the campaign closed, the lines were being drawn
for a bitter struggle between the old organization and the insurgents over the control of the party machinery. There was no
secrecy as to the candidacy of J. Frank Hanly (afterward Governor), who promised from the first to be a formidable figure. He
was a speaker of force and eloquence, magnetic, young in years,
with a brief experience in the lower house of Congress, and his
friends were capitalizing the sordid poverty of his childhood and
touting him as 'the poor man's candidate.' He was a cunning
politician, a master of intrigue, but he was something more —
he was thought to be the most likely person to break the hold of
the old organization on the party, and the younger element
rallied to his support. It soon developed that he was to be the
beneficiary of all the accumulated grievances that spring up in
time against the party bosses.

[1] Beveridge to Wingate, Sept. 17, 1898.
[2] Wingate to Beveridge, Sept. 22, 1898.

The older organization unhappily was handicapped by having two favorites in the race, Judge Robert S. Taylor and Major George W. Steele. The former was an able lawyer, with a fine analytical mind, and was of senatorial stature. He was a favorite of Harrison, whom he greatly resembled in the dignity of his manner, which repelled all familiarities. But he was impatient of the details of organization and of the necessity of cultivating the 'mob.'

Major Steele had long been a strong figure in Indiana politics. He had marched with Sherman to the sea, had been the first Governor of Oklahoma Territory, had served with some distinction several terms in the House, and had been Governor of the Soldiers' Home at Marion. He was credited with being a consummate master in the intrigues of practical politics, and he was the favorite of the 'old soldier' element, which was still a political factor of real consequence.

The sole candidate from the southern section of the State was Francis B. Posey, who was expected to draw heavily from that quarter. But his strength was not wholly geographical. A man of commanding stature and impressive presence, he was also a campaign speaker of no mean order, and for many years he had been heard every two years upon the stump. He had served several terms in the House of Representatives. He possessed many admirable and lovable qualities.

In the early stages, other names were mentioned prominently. General Lew Wallace had expressed a willingness to serve if drafted, and Governor Mount was being discussed. But more impressive and disturbing was the movement in favor of Harrison, who was said to be willing to accept the honor if conferred upon him without any effort on his part. The time was to come when the Democrats, not without guile, were to suggest the withdrawal of all the other candidates and the selection of the former President by a bi-partisan vote, but nothing was to come of it. By that time the lines would be too strongly drawn.

Such was the company into which a young man of thirty-six, with no experience in public station, was to inject himself with the support of a small group of young men with no more experience than himself.

III

But he did not hesitate. Three days after the polls had closed on victory, he had announced his candidacy.[1] The organization work throughout the State was entrusted to Wingate and Sid

[1] *Indianapolis Journal*, Nov. 26, 1898.

Conger, another veteran politician of influence and tact, and the fight was on.

Nothing could have been more disconcerting to the two 'organization crowds' — the old and the new. Nor could anything have been more distasteful to Senator Fairbanks. He had never been numbered among the admirers of the young orator, but his candidacy gave him a legitimate reason for uneasiness. For many years Indianapolis candidates in State Conventions had run counter to a pronounced prejudice against the capital. The Senator lived in Indianapolis, and, in the event of Beveridge's success, his own continuance in the Senate might be endangered should the old prejudice against one city's domination flame again. It was commonly understood that the Indiana congressional delegation was unfriendly to the Indianapolis candidate, and Beveridge soon had the Washington reaction in a letter from his friend Michener, who had been the manager of Harrison's campaigns. It was a clever letter, but not without its transparency.

I am satisfied [he wrote], that you made a mistake in yielding to the importunities of your friends. I do not know if you can be elected or not, and I am not speaking from the standpoint of success or defeat in the election, but I do speak from the standpoint of a friend who does not want to see you, in the days of your youth, securing an election to the Senate, there to become familiar with office-holding and blinded by the shimmer and sheen of official life in Washington, to the detriment of the very great talents you possess.

It has always been my wish to see you in the Senate after you had passed the fifty milestones and had secured a competence in the way of money. I cannot bear the thought of your spending six years, or even twelve years, of your life, as Senator and then having to begin the practice of your profession at the bottom of the rung. I will further consider whether or not I will help you do yourself this injury.

I am just a little vexed with you, too, because you have been listening to the mob too much. Your wife must have been away from home when you concluded to be a candidate.[1] Notwithstanding my vexation with you, I love you just the same, but I must confess that I would like to pull your ear a little. You must not underestimate the fact that you reside within a mile of Senator Fairbanks. Ofttimes the question of locality is more potent than one of ability.[2]

Beveridge sought to reassure and console his friend with the promise that he would not succumb to Washington life, but Michener was inconsolable.

'I sincerely wish you to be thrashed,' he wrote, 'but I want to see you make a good fight just the same.'[3]

[1] I am reliably informed that Mrs. Beveridge urged him to be a candidate.
[2] Michener to Beveridge, Nov. 18, 1898.   [3] *Ibid.*, Nov. 25, 1898.

But not all Beveridge's friends outside the State were so much distressed, and Philander C. Knox had been trying to help as early as September. 'I have planted the seed,' he wrote, 'and feel satisfied that it will bear some fruit.' [1] He had sent a copy of the 'March of the Flag' speech to the brother of Mark Hanna and enclosed to Beveridge the latter's comment that 'this man will bear watching.'

Throughout November, Beveridge and his friends were constantly on the march. That he was delighted with the caliber of the men he had drawn to him is evident in letters this month to his friends beyond the State line:

To Charles G. Dawes, Nov. 18, 1898
We had a meeting of my friends the other night, and the whole matter was thoroughly organized. Absolutely the best politicians in Indiana — at the very least as good as any in Indiana — were at that meeting. They are as devoted friends of mine as you are.

To George W. Perkins, Nov. 25, 1898
My campaign is now organized by my friends and they are constantly traveling over the State on this mission.

To Charles G. Dawes, Nov. 29, 1898
Last night my friends from all over the State held the most remarkable political caucus ever held in Indianapolis. The State politicians who 'cut ice' were there in force.... The situation was gone over, district by district, and man by man from nine o'clock to one o'clock. As Bob Brown, the newly elected Clerk of the Supreme Court, and one of the strongest practical politicians in Indiana, said, 'I don't know much about Senator-making, but I do know that I can take this crowd and nominate any man in Indiana for anything.'

To David Graham Phillips, Dec. 10, 1898
We tried to have a caucus last Thursday night, but the number of politicians, cool-headed and cold-blooded, who have taken off their coats in my behalf and burned their bridges behind them, who came to the caucus from all over the State, was so large that it could not be held in any room in the hotel, and it had to be held in the Century Club rooms.

All through November and December members of the Legislature going to Indianapolis to gather the gossip and gauge the situation were received with almost suspicious cordiality on every side. Outstanding business men, manufacturers, and bankers were interesting themselves in Beveridge's candidacy, with George W. Perkins and John C. Shaffer assisting the business

[1] Knox to Beveridge, Sept. 30, 1898.

movement from behind the scenes. As the legislators reached the capital, they were taken in tow and ushered about to mercantile and banking houses and introduced to men of substance, known by reputation, who spoke in praise of Beveridge.[1] He had no warmer supporter than Charles E. Coffin, a leader in the business men's movement who found a way to utilize his pew at the Meridian Street Methodist Church for canvassing. Out-of-town legislators, in conversation with him, casually but cordially were invited to share his pew to hear Dr. Cleveland preach and were pleased with the novelty of the hospitality. 'Do you know what that means?' one was asked. 'It means you will have to vote for Beveridge.' Invariably the visiting legislators were ushered, sooner or later, into the apartment of Judge Baker of the Federal Court at the Denison Hotel. He was an impressive and dignified gentleman of real distinction, and he flattered them with the warmth of his greeting, and found a way to hint that Beveridge would make an ideal Senator.

But, alas, there were other reception committees in waiting for the flustered legislators, and many of these were accompanied up Delaware Street under the leafless trees to the home of Harrison, where, in language tactful and yet firm, they were told that they should support Judge Taylor, or, at the very least, Major Steele.

This measures the strength of the opposition Beveridge had to overcome. Harrison literally was a State institution, admired for his intellect, respected for the soundness of his judgment, and it was natural that the legislators should be impressed. And Senator Fairbanks, until then easily the second Republican in the State, was heartily, and more openly than he realized, seconding the pleas of Harrison. But the clever young men with Beveridge were only put the more upon their mettle. The Indianapolis situation did not look promising. Joss was the only representative of the capital district in the Senate who was supporting Beveridge, the other three supporting Taylor, Steele, or Hanly. And a group of Indianapolis lawyers, stung by jealousy, perhaps, or inspired by the old organization clique, were canvassing against Beveridge with a zeal that could not be ignored.

The reason urged most frequently against Beveridge was his youth and his reputation among the superficial as a mere glib talker without a background of solid professional attainment. This annoyed and irritated him and gave him a little amusement. When he heard that Clem Studebaker, the South Bend wagon manufacturer, had expressed doubts as to the wisdom of elect-

[1] James W. Noel to the author.

ing so young a man to the Senate, he dashed off an answer to the objection and commissioned Shaffer to convey it to the old man. 'Let him know that Thomas Jefferson was only thirty-three years of age when he wrote the Declaration of Independence,' he wrote; 'that Hamilton was only thirty-two when he was Secretary of the Treasury; that Andrew Jackson was in the Senate at thirty; Albert Gallatin... at thirty-two; Henry Clay... at thirty; Thomas H. Benton at thirty-eight; Martin Van Buren at thirty-eight; John C. Calhoun was Secretary of War at thirty-five; Daniel Webster was only thirty-six when he made the Dartmouth College argument; and Phil Sheridan was only thirty-four when the War of the Rebellion was over; that Pitt was Prime Minister of England at twenty-one, and Gladstone was making a stir in the world before he was thirty.'[1] It was an appalling procession of hated Democrats to parade before the affrighted vision of Studebaker, and perhaps Shaffer did not comply; but the list was to play its part in combating the dreadful offense of youth.

To offset the charge of superficiality in his profession, he had recourse to Judge Baker, the best of friends. Many years later, at the time of Judge Baker's death, Beveridge was to recall with keen appreciation the whole-hearted support he had received from Baker and his son. 'The Bakers, father and son, owed me nothing,' he wrote; 'on the contrary, their friendship had helped me greatly at the bar, and I was indebted to them. Yet, when my race for the Senate seemed hopeless, Judge John H. Baker and his son... voluntarily came to my aid with their great influence. He wrote letters for me all over the State — two hundred of them. He adjourned court and personally saw members of the Legislature in my behalf. His son threw several northern members to me without reward or hope of it.'[2] It was this letter, with the signature of the most accomplished jurist in Indiana, that made the deepest impression:

For the last six years, Mr. Beveridge has tried in the United States Circuit Court quite a number of important cases, both at law and in equity, involving difficult questions of law and fact. In the trial of these cases, he has shown himself a complete master both of the law and the facts. He exhibited learning, skill, and ability of no ordinary quality in their trial. I regard him among the foremost lawyers who practice in the court over which I preside. He is keen, logical, learned, and he shows in discussions of questions of law great ability, industry, and research. From a wide acquaintance with the leading lawyers of the State, I have no hesitancy in saying that there is no more able, learned, or conscientious lawyer of his age in this State.... Particularly in ques-

---

[1] Beveridge to Shaffer, Dec. 17, 1898.   [2] Beveridge to Mrs. Beveridge.

tions involving constitutional law has Mr. Beveridge shown a knowledge and understanding of the nature, history, and purposes of our government as comprehensive as it is profound. In addition to all this, he is a painstaking, persistent, and careful student, not only of legal questions and subjects, but of the grave and serious questions involving our national life. His legal learning and his familiarity with the interests and wants of the Nation eminently fit him for the position of United States Senator.

With this encomium from such a source, he might well have rested his defense against the charge of youth and superficiality. But nothing contributed quite so much to give an air of solidity and respectability to his candidacy as the mobilization of hardheaded business men in his support. The campaign of 1896 had resulted in the deification of the business man in politics; it had given industrial and financial leaders a sense of elation and a taste for political management, and Mark Hanna had now become the symbol of the connection between business and politics. The Republicans, keenly appreciative of their salvation two years before by the business element, had never been so prone to hearken to its advice, and, if possible, to yield to its desires. For four years Beveridge's speeches had been in harmony with business aspirations, and a group of the most substantial manufacturers, merchants, and financiers in Indianapolis met and organized a 'Business Men's Association.' With D. M. Parry, a leading manufacturer, as president, and C. E. Coffin, a financier and business man, as treasurer, more than a hundred of the cream of the business element declared for Beveridge, invited the coöperation of business men throughout the State, and raised among themselves, without the contribution of a penny from Beveridge or his political friends, $2125 to be expended on headquarters and stamps.[1]

At the second meeting, the entire State was represented, and petitions from industries — twelve leading industries of Anderson — were soon pouring in upon legislators in the interest of the Indianapolis candidate.[2] As soon as the legislators began to swarm in the lobbies of the Denison Hotel, the business men opened headquarters, and seventy-five began active canvassing. Beveridge was delighted and wrote jubilantly to Perkins: 'The labor organizations have done this same thing.... One of the candidates said last night that if I lived twenty-five miles from Indianapolis, which already has one Senator, all the rest of them might as well pack up their grips and go home.... Their only hope of defeating me is that I live in Indianapolis, which already

[1] Noel to the author.
[2] *Indianapolis Journal*, Jan. 10, 1899.

has one Senator. This is my great obstacle. But it is believed by every one of my friends that we can overcome it.' [1]

IV

This geographical objection was by odds the most serious in his way, and was used persistently by his opponents. The time came when some of his friends began to urge the withdrawal of Frank Littleton, one of his supporters, from the contest for the speakership. Two Senators and the Speaker, and all from Indianapolis! It was a flagrant challenge to the prejudice against the capital. The forces bent on Beveridge's defeat were turning with sinister intent to his friend Littleton. But Beveridge indignantly rejected the suggestion of his friend's sacrifice.

'Gentlemen, not another word,' he said. 'Frank Littleton is one of the best friends I have in the world. He is a candidate for Speaker, as I am for Senator. I would rather go down in defeat than imperil by any selfish act of mine the chance of my friend for the office that he seeks.' [2]

That such would have been his position under any circumstances is certain, for the disadvantages of the two candidacies had been measured in the beginning, and Littleton's election was thought an advantage to the Beveridge candidacy. The speakership with its power and influence could scarcely be overlooked by members of the Legislature. [3]

It was after Littleton's election was assured, apparently without checking the Beveridge sentiment, that the old machine, supporting Taylor and Steele, tossed a bomb into the lobby of the Denison. The news flashed from Washington that McKinley had announced the appointment of Addison C. Harris, of Indianapolis, as United States Minister to Austria-Hungary. It could only have been on the recommendation of Senator Fairbanks. Two Senators, the Speaker, and a United States Minister from Indianapolis! Preposterous, and just too bad, chattered the enemies of Beveridge. But the reaction on the lobby was not as hoped. It was too transparent. Many denounced it as unsportsmanlike — like a blow below the belt. [4] The sole victim of the scheme was Harris, the innocent party. For the first time the man in the street began to suspect that Beveridge had a chance.

[1] Beveridge to Perkins, Jan. 3, 1899.
[2] Coffin, *Indiana Magazine of History*, September, 1928.
[3] Noel to the author.
[4] I, a boy, curiously mingling with the crowd, witnessed the reaction.

V

Meanwhile, the Beveridge organization was moving smoothly. Wingate and Conger had been reënforced by John Bonnell, who began as a supporter of General Lew Wallace. All out-State men, each was a master of the finesse of politics. Long before the caucus, these, together with Beveridge's young men, had outlined the strategy of the fight. The bitterest feeling had been engendered between the new Hanly organization seeking the patronage and the old machine anxious to retain it; and the latter was divided between Steele and Taylor. Neither Hanly nor the old organization could afford to permit the other to prevail. If Beveridge could start in the balloting with as many as a dozen men pledged to stand to the end, the time would come when these would hold the balance of power. The plan was to secure as many first pledges as possible and then concentrate desperately on second-choice pledges. Long before the caucus met, three fourths of the legislators had pledged themselves to Beveridge as their second choice. To hold this advantage, his friends were meticulously careful to offend no one. They adopted 'Keep sweet' as their motto. They had reason to believe that rather than permit the election of Hanly, the other candidates would withdraw and throw their support to the Indianapolis candidate.[1]

And now the legislators are on the ground, swarming day and night in the lobbies of the Denison. The candidates have opened their headquarters. The pulling and hauling of excited politicians has begun. The effect on some of the candidates is depressing. Posey looks upon the undignified scramble with disgust and retires to his room. Taylor, super-dignified and with aristocratic taste, has no stomach for the carnival-like scene, and distresses and disgusts his friends by standing aloof. Occasionally he wanders into the lobby, but only to find a seat in a remote corner where he can smoke in solitude and meditate on the vanities of life. Steele mingles freely, but Hanly is seldom seen, staying in his room busily weaving the web of his intrigues. Beveridge comes and goes like a flash. 'He comes in ... as though there was a train in the rear which he is compelled to catch in just four seconds.'[2] He hurries to a little alcove, where he is surrounded by a group of men — and then as suddenly disappears. Uncommitted legislators drift into town with prepared statements announcing themselves for him. These are not unexpected, but have been held back for the culminative effect on the eve of the caucus. Now and then an accession to the Hanly

[1] Noel, Joss, and Glossbrenner to the author.
[2] *Indianapolis Journal*, Jan. 2, 1899.

ranks is announced, and the Beveridge group rejoices greatly. The sooner the danger of his election is realized, the more speedily will the second-choice votes appear.

But there are spies in the Beveridge camp — the spies of Hanly. The night before the caucus, fifteen members meet and pledge themselves to vote steadfastly for Beveridge until the end, but on the first ballot two of these will go to Hanly and never leave him. The Taylor and Steele managers declare that, if Hanly gets as many as thirty-seven votes, a break will have to come to prevent his election. The managers of Beveridge make no bargains and 'keep sweet.'

VI

The corridors of the State House are a seething mass as the legislators shut themselves in for the balloting. The balloting begins without preliminaries beyond the organization of the caucus. Each member goes forward and deposits his vote when his name is called. The first ballot discloses the hopes of Hanly — to vote full strength and take the election by storm. He receives thirty-two votes; Taylor, nineteen; Posey, fourteen; Beveridge, thirteen; and Steele, eleven. The announcement of the result to the waiting multitude is greeted with a Hanly demonstration, intended to influence the voters. The Beveridge forces are stunned — two spies in the camp the night before!

The second ballot: and Hanly loses one, Taylor three, Posey two; Beveridge gains six, and Steele holds his own.

The third ballot: Hanly polls thirty-three, Posey falls to ten, Taylor and Steele stand still, and Beveridge advances to twenty.

And so through the fourth, fifth, sixth, seventh, and eighth ballots the shifting goes, with Beveridge slowly creeping up, and Hanly leading with an impressive margin.

And now the ninth ballot — and Hanly polls the thirty-seven ballots fixed as the danger-point, the utmost limit to be allowed him. The caucus is a madhouse now, the Taylor men pulling, hauling, pleading with the Beveridge men to desert their advancing leader for the favorite of Harrison. The Beveridge group, still 'sweet,' refuse to budge. Another ballot points the way to the sole road to victory over Hanly, who loses but one while Taylor falls to nine, Steele to eight, and Beveridge advances to twenty-eight — within eight votes of Hanly's strength. It is Hanly or Beveridge. Steele's and Taylor's forces quick-step into the Beveridge camp and Beveridge wins with a margin of fifteen votes.

The doors are thrown open, the result announced to the flushed-faced throng without, and the State House rings with cheers and shouts, while George J. Langsdale, veteran politician of the old school and the father of Mrs. Beveridge, finding the announcement incredible, walks back and forth wringing his hands and exclaiming over and over, 'Impossible! Impossible! Impossible!'[1] He sees that the graybeards are passing on.

VII

Meanwhile, in his office on Pennsylvania Street, Beveridge sits at the telephone in touch with his managers at the front, eager but unperturbed. With him are Charles F. Remy (later judge of the Appellate Court) and two friends from outside the city. He answers the call of the telephone himself, takes the results of the ballots, tabulates them, informs his companions coolly. At length the news of victory flashes over the wires, and, turning quite unmoved to his companions, he says, 'Gentlemen, I am nominated.' The excited little group cheer lustily, and, thinking of the celebration even then in progress at the Denison, hurriedly don their overcoats. Beveridge remains at the receiver answering the congratulations of the youthful group who had won the battle. The friends stand impatiently beside him with his coat and hat. He rises now, puts on his coat and hat, and the party reaches the door.

'Too much haste here,' he says. 'Wait a minute.'

Taking down the receiver again, he calls his home. His voice is clear and firm, without a suggestion of emotion. 'Kitty, I am nominated,' he says. A few words more, and he turns to his friends. 'I am ready now.' The conversation with the home sobers the companions with the thought of what the victory means to the young man and his wife, and they descend the stairs quietly.[2]

But there is no quiet in the streets. A crowd is hurrying from the State House on the run, cheering, laughing, gesticulating, and the victor is swept along to the Denison and literally carried into the lobby to the most noisy of celebrations. He briefly thanks his friends, and proceeds to the State House and to the office of Governor Mount, who had been friendly to his aspiration from the start, where he finds an impromptu reception awaiting him. The Governor issues a statement in commendation of the caucus action. 'It has nominated a clean man of marked ability, who combines wisdom with the fire and vigor of youth.... In a knowledge of constitutional law and statecraft he will measure swords with the ablest in the Senate. In master-

[1] Noel to the author.   [2] Remy to the author.

ful eloquence he will be surpassed by none.'[1] At length he was permitted to go home.

VIII

The bitterness of the battle over, everyone, regardless of party, rejoiced over the triumph of virile youth, and for days the office on Pennsylvania Street was choked with letters and telegrams — one from Thomas B. Reed, whom Beveridge had declined to solicit on the issue of imperialism.[2] One week later, in a joint session of the Legislature he was elected over Senator David Turpie, the Democrat, and astonished some by the independent tone of his speech. It was then that he announced that he would 'know no master but the people.'

For some days he passed happily through a round of receptions given by friends and organizations. The Columbia Club had him and Addison C. Harris, whose diplomatic appointment was intended to defeat him, as its guests of honor at the Denison,[3] and at the Marion Club Ball, when the grand march closed, his portrait, the frame studded with electric lights, was illuminated. Charles E. Coffin gave him a dinner, where he listened to tributes from representative citizens. But he was tired, though not too weary to fill his speaking engagement at the Lincoln Banquet in Philadelphia. It was inevitable that he should urge again his imperialistic views. Not another public man in America had proclaimed them earlier or with more abandon, or made them so much his own. The story of the remarkable prophecy at the Middlesex Club in Boston before a shot was fired was now going the rounds of the press. On this issue he would stake his immediate future. This was to be his topic in Philadelphia.

But Fate did its utmost to thwart him, for, *en route*, he was caught in a snowstorm that blockaded the railroads and he did not reach the scene of the dinner until it was over. So keen, however, was the desire to hear him that the directors of the Union League Club asked him to deliver his speech at a dinner given especially to hear it. The entire country was now interested in the romantic story of his rise and triumph; and as he stood at the entrance of the banquet hall the solid men of Philadelphia filed by to grasp his hand.[4] And again he beat the tom-toms of imperialism, and, whatever we may think today, it was as music to that generation.

Civil government is to be perfected in Porto Rico [he said].... Even if Cubans are capable of self-government, every interest points to

[1] *Indianapolis Journal*, Jan. 11, 1899.   [2] *Ibid.*, Jan. 12, 1899.
[3] *Ibid.*, Jan. 31, 1899.   [4] *Philadelphia Press*, Feb. 15, 1899.

union... in the end Cuba will be part of the great Republic.... The Philippines are ours forever. Let faint hearts anoint their fears with the thought that some day American administration and American duty there will end. But they will never end.... The Republic never retreats. Its flag is the only flag that has never known defeat. Where the flag leads, we follow, for we know that the hand that bears it onward is the unseen hand of God.

So spoke the supreme orator of American imperialism to a generation that found nothing of exaggeration in the thought. It was in the day when high-school girls were poring over the 'Barrack-Room Ballads' of Kipling with flaming cheeks in every nook and corner of the country, and Tommy Atkins seemed the very evangel of the Lord. When he concluded, he was given three lusty cheers, the diners rushed forward to take him by the hand, and the correspondent of the London 'Times' hurried to the telegraph office to cable to the Thunderer of British Imperialism the utterances of a young Senator who had not yet seen his seat. There were scoffers, of course. Bryan was shocked, and even Harrison was prone to scoff. Speaking at a Presbyterian dinner on 'Predestination and the Philippines,' he found that 'our Methodist brethren are coming to this doctrine, judging from the expressions of our Senator who is saying much about the predestination of the Philippines.' [1]

But Beveridge was in dead earnest; for a few weeks only he would brood upon the future, and then, breaking all precedents for American statesmen, make his plans for going forth to meet it.

[1] *Indianapolis Journal*, Feb. 18, 1899.

BOOK II
IMPERIALISM

CHAPTER I

IN THE PHILIPPINES

I

FROM the moment of his election, Beveridge had no doubt as to where Destiny directed him to go. An earnest desire to play a part in the moulding of the imperialistic policy of the Republic had turned his thoughts on public life, and now the path was plain before him. One morning in New York, where he had spent the night with Perkins, the two friends were walking across Twenty-Third Street on their way downtown when Beveridge announced his plans. 'I am going to the Philippines,' he said suddenly. 'I have thought it all over. Every Senator who can ought to view those islands. I know that very few of us can do so, but I can, and I shall. I want to understand the situation when I take my seat in the Senate.' [1]

It was a common-sense idea, but startling in its novelty, since American statesmen had not been accustomed to investigation of the sort in foreign lands.

On his return to Indianapolis, Beveridge confidentially announced his purpose to his friend Joss, who was not surprised. He had observed for some time that Beveridge had interpreted his rôle as that of a statesman rather than a politician. But the senatorial contest had cost something, and the young Senator had never been burdened with the bump of acquisition through hoarding. Joss suggested that the journey would be expensive and inquired how he could finance it. Beveridge replied that he would manage. 'Don't save money,' he said vehemently. 'Spend it on yourself to improve yourself.' [2]

His friend thought him still a bit intoxicated by the rare opportunity that had come to him so early.

The next few weeks found him busily engaged in putting his house in order for the journey, which he was keeping largely to himself. For a time he thought to continue in the practice of the law, and he interested himself in the forming of a partnership. He had the men in mind with whom he wished to be associated,[3] but when the negotiations fell through, he was easily reconciled to the failure. After all, he thought, the study of public problems would consume his time and the public would

[1] Interview with Perkins, *Saturday Evening Post*, Sept. 8, 1900.
[2] Joss to the author.
[3] Jameson and Joss, with Shirley, of Kokomo, for trial work.

be his client.[1] But some of his friends were not so easily reconciled to the abandonment of his profession. 'In the matter of that law firm business,' wrote George Perkins, 'I hope you haven't before leaving Indianapolis tied yourself up in any permanent arrangement, because, my dear fellow, law practice will come your way in the next three or four years faster than applications are now pouring in to this home office,[2] and that exhausts comparison. In five years your name alone will be worth almost any number of thousands of dollars a year to any law firm, whether you do any work in the firm or not.'[3]

But Beveridge was not the type to sell his name without his services, and when he closed his office and turned his docket over to his friends, he passed permanently from the ranks of the practitioners. That phase of his life was over.

Even so, if not in a professional capacity, he was to be of service to Perkins and his company on his Eastern trip. The latter, who was a master in the foreign field, was interested in insurance possibilities in China, and Beveridge was to investigate and report on whether there was enough interest in insurance among the Chinese to justify an aggressive campaign there. And so, too, in the Philippines.[4] There was a rapid exchange of letters between the two friends at that time. A letter Beveridge had written Perkins had been sent by the latter to his friend, Vice-President Hobart, to be passed on to McKinley. 'I think in this way we stuck a good peg for the future,' Perkins wrote, in a farewell letter which reveals the intimacy of their relations.

Now, old fellow, save for a telegram that I will send you to wish God-speed, let this tell you what you already know, viz., that I hope you and your wife will have a most enjoyable, comfortable, safe, and in every way satisfactory voyage. Don't take any chances at all with your health or your life. Go in for all the good solid rest you can get. I wonder if you realize that the rest you ought to get out of this trip, in the long ocean voyage, coming and going, will perhaps be the last long rest of this kind that you will be able to get for a great many years. It ought to be worth millions to you in fame, fortune, and longevity. Go in and get all the solid good out of it you can. Don't be in a hurry to get back. Take your time, remembering that when you do get back, you get back to a new life — a new condition of things in all respects....

I figure that there are just three things you want to do in the present status of your career. One is to husband your strength, both mental and physical. Second: keep in the background as far as the public gaze is concerned. Third, increase your store of knowledge and information as regards the world generally. With these three things accomplished,

---

[1] Joss to the author.
[2] Perkins had become a vice-president of the New York Life Insurance Company.
[3] Perkins to Beveridge, March 10, 1899.   [4] *Ibid.*, March 17, 1899.

when the hour comes to strike, you will be physically and mentally equipped to deliver a blow that will knock out all comers.

By the way, if Mrs. Beveridge, in her sight-seeing, should run across anything that she thinks would delight the soul of another woman (I don't necessarily mean a bargain) — something that would come in handy as an ornament or a useful article or a fabric, in that ranch of ours out at Riverdale, tell her to swoop down upon it, gather it in, and I will make good the price when you get home.[1]

Futile advice! The dynamic traveler was about to subject himself to every hardship, spare himself nothing day or night, to be under fire in more than one engagement; and, coming home, to find himself in the white glare of a publicity seldom, if ever, thrown before upon a new Senator.

The day after the receipt of the letter, Beveridge and his wife left for Vancouver, British Columbia, whence they set sail on the Empress of India, the finest passenger vessel in the service to China. It was not until the morning of his departure that the Indianapolis papers announced that he was on his way. Even then they knew little of his plans. He was going to China for a rest, believing a sea voyage would be beneficial, and he might even go to the Philippines. So, leaving many of his friends wondering, he set forth with letters of introduction to the military authorities in Manila.

II

It was a critical period in the development of the new control in the islands. With the situation in part, Beveridge was familiar when he sailed. When the ratification of the peace treaty was assured, the Filipino army, which had been coöperating with ours, attacked the American army in Manila. Two weeks before, the insurgents had set up a Philippine Republic, based on a Constitution adopted by a Congress at Malolos, with Aguinaldo as President and Commander-in-Chief of its armed forces. The aspirations of the people for independence dated far back into the days of Spanish rule, and the more ardent of the patriots were maddened by the thought of a mere exchange of masters. The Philippine President was deservedly popular with his people because of 'his patriotic services, his attested honesty, and his remarkable gift of surrounding himself with able coadjutors and administrators.'[2] Intent on doing all within his power to conciliate and win the insurgents, President McKinley had appointed a commission of 'civil advisers' to proceed to the

[1] Perkins to Beveridge, March 17, 1899.
[2] J. G. Schurman, *Philippine Affairs: A Retrospect and Outlook*, 6.

islands, and Jacob Gould Schurman had been persuaded to go as chairman. He had protested that he was opposed to the Administration's Philippine policy, and 'never wanted the Philippines,' and the President had replied:

'Oh, don't let that trouble you; I didn't want the Philippines either; and in the protocol of the treaty I left myself free not to take them, but in the end there was no alternative.[1]

Reaching Manila April 2, 1899, and establishing headquarters in the Audiencia, a large building within the walled city near the headquarters of General Otis, the Commission found that the authority of the United States was limited to Manila and that there was much sympathy for the insurgents among the people even there.[2] Assuming that the insurrection was due to a misunderstanding among the many, imposed upon by the ambitious few, the Commission issued a proclamation announcing that the authority of the United States would be rigidly enforced, but that all civil rights would be protected, the greatest liberty consistent with the maintenance of order would be granted, and that the exploitation of the natives would not be tolerated. Thousands of copies in Spanish and the dialect languages were published and posted, but the insurgents had destroyed them when unguarded and had threatened the natives found reading them. However, it had some effect.[3]

Toward the end of April, as Beveridge was approaching the islands, Colonel Arguelles had been sent as an emissary of the insurgents to ask a suspension of hostilities to permit a calm discussion of the terms of the proclamation. The suspension was denied, but the American terms were carefully explained; and, notified of the incident, Secretary of State Hay had cabled an authorization to the Commission to announce the form of government favored in Washington. This had but slight effect. The fighting continued, and the last of March the American forces captured Malolos, the Philippine Government fled to the northern provinces, and the fight went on.

It was in the midst of the fighting and the typhoons that Beveridge reached Manila from China. Two months before, the city was an uncomfortable place for the relaxation of a tired man. Incendiary fires were a daily occurrence, business was at a standstill, and, with the sound of firing audible in every house, the community was passing through a reign of terror. There was something of sinister aspect even in the deserted streets, for such of the native population as had not fled had shut themselves up in their houses.[4]

[1] J. G. Schurman, *Philippine Affairs: A Retrospect and Outlook*, 2.
[2] *Ibid.*, 6.   [3] *Report of the Philippine Commission*, Jan. 31, 1900, I, 9.
[4] *Ibid.*, I, 176.

The American soldiers had redeemed Manila when Beveridge reached the scene.

III

He entered Manila the first of May, to find the city seemingly safe and rigidly sentineled. He was eager to get to his work at once. That first night, when dining at the officers' mess where he had his headquarters, he expressed a wish to make his formal call on General Otis early the next morning. Why not at once? he was asked. It was not a swivel-chair contest in which the army was engaged, and the Commanding General usually worked until almost midnight every night at his quarters. Eagerly Beveridge acted upon the suggestion. It was then within two hours of midnight, and the streets were utterly deserted, since a military order confined everyone to his home after eight o'clock. As he walked through the streets with his guide, the low, sharp challenge of sentries frequently brought them to a stop in the two-mile interval between the mess and the office of the military governor.

For two hours, or until after midnight, Beveridge bombarded Otis with rapid-fire questions; and when he left, he was familiar with the military situation and had secured a pass to take him through the lines and the right to go armed.

Thus he began the rest cure Perkins had prescribed. He was there primarily to investigate the requirements of government, to mobilize his arguments for imperialism, but the mere presence of the soldiers awakened the military instinct within him. Instantly his plans were made. He would interview all sorts and conditions of men on the governmental needs of the islands, would study the commercial possibilities, the business opportunities, but he would see the fighting, too, mingle with the soldiers, eat with them, ride with them to the far outposts. The romance within him urged him to this course, and there was fighting but a little way distant in Luzon.

Soon he was with General Lawton, an Indianian, like himself, and found him fascinating — the dashing dare-devil, and yet the cool and collected soldier who all too soon was to be one of the casualties of imperialism. Thus the young Senator soon found himself witnessing the assault at Taytay. He was riding beside Lawton when in this stronghold of the insurgents three thousand Filipinos, the cream of their army, were awaiting the assault from behind the entrenchments. Desultory firing was going on all the while. A short time before, two men standing on the very spot where Lawton and Beveridge sat upon their horses had been killed. The civilian was astonished to find that he felt no fear. The drama of the scene entranced him. It seemed more like a play than stark reality. He was standing beside the General when the Twelfth Regulars were ordered to the charge, and he saw them dash with shouts across the third of a mile of open space of level ground and take the enemy by storm. The whole scene delighted him; it was exotic, with the little rice ridges that alone relieved the table-like ground. Most of all was he delighted with the soldiers, who 'charged with a smile.' [1]

It was here that he owed to the wrath and soldierly profanity of Lawton his friendship with John McCutcheon, the cartoonist. Beveridge was mounted and with the General's party, when the enemy, finding it offered an attractive target, opened fire. Lawton ordered the others to cover. Beveridge was in the act of dismounting when he observed that Lawton remained unmoved upon his horse and the civilian seated himself firmly in his saddle. A moment later, the General, turning, furiously ordered his guest off his horse and out of range. He took refuge behind some kind of protection where others were crouching. 'Hello, there,' said one of the company, beginning a conversation. It was McCutcheon; and there, under fire in the Philippines, was formed a friendship that was to persist through the future years.

Again he was with Lawton at Pasig, where he was impressed with the soldier's recklessness of danger. 'Lawton, sometime you will be killed if you keep this up,' he said. The General replied that he had figured out mathematically a table of averages on which an army officer might calculate his chances of death. 'But,' he concluded, 'this is my profession, Senator.' [2] To a civilian with a partiality for fighting men, Lawton was the ideal — 'like Napoleon's marshals... so little self-conscious in the hour of battle that he was literally unconscious of danger.' [3]

Soon he was finding General MacArthur equally admirable, and with him witnessing the fierce fighting at the battle of San Fernando. He spent a memorable evening with him at his headquarters there.

We were sixteen miles away from our source of supplies [he wrote]. The line of communications was almost unguarded, so limited were the number of troops. Around us on either flank was an army of Filipinos, well equipped with Mauser rifles, outnumbering our forces five to one.

The moon had gone down behind the horizon; the bamboo and banana thickets blended the sky and earth with a smudge of deeper darkness. Out over the fields that stretched southward came the hoarse howl of a pack of starving dogs, left homeless and without food

[1] *Saturday Evening Post*, March 17, 1900.
[2] *Indianapolis Journal*, Dec. 26, 1899.   [3] *Ibid.*, Dec. 20, 1899.

by the war, driven by hunger and desolation to a state of wildness like that of wolves. Once the weird sound was punctuated by a shot. A scout had just arrived with the statement that Luna might attack that night or in the morning. The Commanding General himself went to the headquarters of his officers and gave directions against any possible surprise. Our walk took us through the plaza, and in front of the great church which the Filipinos had fired some days before, and which was still burning. The roof had fallen in, the flames had eaten out the doors, the ruins stood erect like a specter of departed power which had dwelt within their walls.[1]

In his eagerness to miss nothing, Beveridge was to place himself in deadly danger many times. Riding one day at one of the outposts on a road leading across an open plain to the Filipino lines, he dismounted. The trees and undergrowth ended abruptly where he stood, giving an uninterrupted view across the plain. Down the white road he could see, with the aid of a glass, the insurgents moving about. The idea that modern guns could do damage at that distance did not occur to him. He moved farther into the open, thinking with the use of the glass to get a still better view. Suddenly an amused Kansas soldier stood beside him.

'If you stand there long, Senator, you'll get hell shot out of you.'

'Why, can they shoot this far?' gasped the astonished civilian.

'Yes, and farther too. The air was full of holes here not an hour ago.'[2]

But it was not so much his indifference to danger that impressed these seasoned soldiers as his physical endurance, riding by the hour under blazing skies or through torrential rains. He was to prove his mettle in this respect on his journey to the southern islands, for he penetrated to where none other but the soldiers went. They liked him for his comradery, and he repaid them with open admiration.

Determined to penetrate the thickets of the southern islands where many of the soldiers were, the military authorities sent him on board the Charleston under the command of Captain Whitney; a pleasant journey with the sailors greeting him with a complimentary song to the air of the Elephant Song in 'Wang.' It was after breakfast on the Charleston that Captain Whitney introduced him to Dr. Harry L. Gilchrist, surgeon of one of the regiments, who was to take him ashore and act as his guide through Iloilo. That morning the rain fell in torrents; and, knowing the hardships of travel from his own experience in reaching the ship, Gilchrist sought vainly to persuade him to

[1] *Saturday Evening Post*, March 31, 1899.   [2] *Ibid.*, March 17, 1899.

wait awhile for his explorations. The young doctor never was to forget that wild trip across Iloilo Bay. The two sat in the cabin while Beveridge fired questions with the rapidity of a Gatling gun. He wanted to know about military conditions in that quarter, about the country, most of all just then about the private soldiers' morale under the punishment of such weather. There, in the stuffy little room, he made his plans for the day. When they reached shore, the rain had abated, and the two men started for headquarters, but suddenly the storm returned in all its fury. Two drenched men, dripping pools of water, finally reached the office of the provost marshal, and the surgeon never was to lose the vision of the expression of Major Park's face when he learned the identity of his rain-soaked visitor. There a two-wheeled conveyance was furnished, and the two slushed through the rain to headquarters, a mile distant. As they were ascending the old-fashioned mahogany stairs of the house occupied by the officers, Gilchrist was doubtful of his hearing when Beveridge turned on him with the proposal that they make a tour of the outposts that afternoon. The surgeon had hoped to remain snugly indoors, but he dared not weaken before a civilian, and so arrangements were made for the long damp journey.

When they started for the headquarters of the First Tennessee Regiment, Beveridge appeared with an outfit complete — service hat, blue flannel shirt, soldiers' trousers, colored leggings, and poncho over his shoulders. When at length they appeared on the stairs of the old convent converted to military purposes, and Colonel Childers was brushing by them without a glance until he was halted and introduced, the surgeon was amused again at the expression of incredulity on the Colonel's face. These soldiers had seen few Senators like this bedraggled man in soldiers' garb. The party went to the office of Major Cheatham, son of the famous Confederate general, but Beveridge was eager to be upon his way. Cheatham and Lieutenant-Colonel Baille volunteered to join the party, and arrangements were made to meet after luncheon at an old bridge. That was the hour of the hardest downpour. But by this time everyone had entered into the venture in the spirit of a lark. Across a level strip of country, submerged eight to ten inches in water, they rode to the first outpost, where, under a thatched roof, they found four husky Tennessee soldiers high and dry. They sprang to salute at the sight of the officers, and the Major told them that a Senator had journeyed thousands of miles to see them, and introduced him. This was unexpected, but off came the Senator's hat while the rain beat upon his head.

AT THE HEADQUARTERS OF THE FIRST TENNESSEE VOLUNTEER
INFANTRY, ILOILO, PHILIPPINE ISLANDS

Senator Beveridge (second from left) with officers of the regiment

'Gentlemen,' he said, 'I am glad to see you. I came out in this storm this afternoon to see what soldiering is like during the disagreeable season. I am proud of you. I want you to know that we, back in the States, have been thinking of you, have appreciated your great work, and when your work is completed, we know you will come back with flying colors. I wish you good luck.'

The soldiers gave three cheers, and the little party pushed on in the rain, leaving the American lines and taking a beach road; and for an hour they rode through a forest of bamboo, coconut, and tall palms and ferns, and finally reached a peaceful little town behind the lines. At Yaro the river had overflowed its banks and the town was submerged in the rushing flood. The officers tried to persuade Beveridge to abandon his purpose, but to no avail; so the party rode through the town on their ponies, nothing of the animals visible but their necks. Thence on to Lopaz, completely submerged, where the soldiers of the First Tennessee Regiment were amusing themselves sailing around on rafts or in native boats.

At headquarters a goodly crowd of soldiers had assembled, and here Beveridge made another talk, mostly humorous, partly patriotic, and the men in uniforms, delighted, cheered lustily. 'I bet,' wrote Gilchrist later, 'the insurgents over at Santa Barbara six miles away went for the mountains, thinking from the continuous cheering that the Americans were surely after them.' From Lopaz the party turned back and reached headquarters in safety, Beveridge hilariously gay, and apparently untired by the hard trip.[1]

It was on this southern journey which took him into Sulu and Cebu that Beveridge, unarmed, braved one of the most ferocious and malicious of the insurgent generals in his camp. When the Governor of Cebu took command of the island a little before, the American troops were confined to the town; and just beyond the boundaries were the insurgents. There had been no fighting, but there was something sinister in the inactivity. The Governor finally determined to call upon Maxelion, the rebel chief, explain the American purpose, and conciliate him if possible. The visit had been made. When, a few days later, Beveridge reached Cebu and heard of the incident, he was captivated by the idea of visiting a rebel camp. The Governor agreed to accompany him, but other officers dourly declined. Taking along as interpreter a man condemned to death by the insurgents, Beveridge rode boldly, jauntily, into the presence of the dreaded Maxelion,

[1] Letter of Dr. Gilchrist to his parents; quoted in the *Indianapolis Star*, Sept. 12, 1899, from *Cleveland Leader*.

unarmed. The Governor introduced him, and Maxelion, who had everything of the courtly courtesy and verbal warmth of the Spaniard, received him and conversed with him a few minutes. During the interview, the insurgent chief was surrounded by his staff, while from seventy-five to a hundred insurgent soldiers stood without. Finally the visitors, bowing politely, took their departure unmolested.[1]

Thus Beveridge saw the war and saw the army in action, making friends of the officers, mingling with the men, eating with the privates in the shade of a bamboo tree on the banks of the Bagbag River,[2] visiting the hospital at Manila, and talking with the wounded — insurgents and Americans — of their treatment there. Always he was in the saddle by sunrise, and at night he was busy with his interviewing of natives and foreigners on the governmental requirements of the new imperialism. He was to carry with him always a vivid memory of the private soldiers. 'I cannot get away from the impression of youth,' he wrote later, 'a youth that seems that it would be youth forever — that fairly gleams with virile life from the faces of these boys of ours.'

IV

Meanwhile, even in the midst of his soldiering, he was zealously marshaling the arguments to be used in support of his idea of American imperialism. He had neither time nor inclination for mere functions, and when Señor Abren in Manila gave a dinner and reception for the American Commissioners and General MacArthur, Mrs. Beveridge went without him, for it was about the time he was engaged in his adventures among the southern islands.[3] He returned from the south in time to witness the opening of the Supreme Court, to talk at length with the judges, and to conclude that but one was capable.[4]

On reaching Manila he had purloined for his notes a little book, three by six inches in size, evidently purchased there by Mrs. Beveridge, since it bears her initials. It lies before me now, battered and pocket-worn, but the hurriedly written notations in ink are as clear as on the day they were written. It would be absurd to say that he was an impartial investigator. He had gone with a fixed idea and as a lawyer goes in search of evidence to support his case. Occasionally he was to interview natives, but not often. He was more interested in the views of foreign

---

[1] *Saturday Evening Post*, March 31, 1899.   [2] *Ibid.*, March 17, 1899.
[3] *Indianapolis Journal*, May 28, 1899.
[4] MS. Philippine Notebook.

business men living in the islands, and of the intelligentsia and
the wealthy among the natives.

It was characteristic of him, first of all, to seek Robert Wood,
then manager of the largest business concern in the islands, and
they became warm friends. Beveridge found him 'self-contained,
keen and able.' From conversations with him, Beveridge jotted
down in his little book that the country was 'enormously rich'
and that commerce would be 'immense' with 'only ordinarily
good government'; and that 'the people are quite incapable of
self-government' with the exception of a few. Indeed, Wood
thought that 'for years to come a very strong government will be
necessary.' Having in mind the possibility of American migra-
tion to the islands, Beveridge was interested in the effect on
foreigners of the climate. Wood, who had lived there eighteen
years, assured him that his health had 'never been better.' [1]

The next day Beveridge interviewed R. N. Brown, agent of
the bank, as they cantered over the roads on horseback. The
bank agent also thought business would be enormously improved
under 'good government,' and was positive that it would 'be
folly to give the natives any part of consequence in the government,' since not more than half a dozen had the necessary capacity. 'Anything but a strong government at first will result in
disaster,' he insisted. And 'Don't put courts into their hands at
all except the village courts,' he added. In municipal government in the small towns they might be given some power. [2]

The next day found the investigator with Father Sino of Saint
Ignatius — a Spaniard, a Jesuit teacher, speaking English
fluently — 'very intelligent and accomplished.' And from him
he heard that the United States should 'introduce a strong decisive government,' and that self-government was an impossibility.
He was not hopeful of the early suppression of the insurrection.
'Our natives,' he said, 'are like buffalo bulls — they get mad
and then want to fight, no matter whether right or wrong. You
cannot possibly deal with them by gentle means. They mis-
understand such treatment. While in arms they must be fought,
fought, fought ceaselessly and remorselessly.' [3] From another
Jesuit teacher, Father Algie, Director of the Observatory, the
same ideas were gleaned. He thought it 'would take a long time
to prepare the people for self-government,' and he was afraid
the insurrection would 'last for years.' It was from him that
Beveridge first heard that much of the trouble would have been
averted had the United States announced 'a definite policy'
without delay. [4]

When occasionally Beveridge met a man with some sympathy

[1] MS. Philippine Notebook.   [2] *Ibid.*   [3] *Ibid.*   [4] *Ibid.*

for the insurgent point of view, he prodded him with leading
questions. The most cunning of these he found in Francesco
Hizon, a Chinese, but 'said to be a pure Filipino,' a planter and
a business man. The claim that he spent part of his time within
the American lines and part within those of the insurgents impressed the interviewer with his craftiness. 'He is more characteristic of the Filipino people than anyone I have met,' runs the
Notebook. It was clearly annoying to find him always evading
a direct answer, and even his views were contradictory. True,
he said, the common people were not interested. It was hard to
tell how long the fight would last. Bad things had been heard
about the Americans, and the people wanted to rule themselves.
Beveridge plainly looked upon this man as an 'unwilling witness,' to be cross-examined closely. 'If you give these islands
a government where justice would be administered truly and
without price, property protected, and free speech secured, you
ask me if the common people would be satisfied,' said Hizon,
repeating the question. 'I do not know,' he answered. After
all, he thought, the ignorant masses would follow their intelligent
leaders. Complete self-government, with the protection of the
American fleet, was what was wanted.[1]

But the next day a native was found in Dr. G. Gonzales,
a physician, living in 'a delightfully constructed house,' to offset
Hizon. He found the leaders wanting independence, and the
masses 'probably socialistic' if they knew at all what they
sought. True, if given 'pure government, free speech, they would
not understand or appreciate at first, but later they would.'
And then the commercial note introduced by Beveridge. 'Oh,
yes, the islands are marvelously rich,' Gonzales said, 'and under
good government will pay their way many times over.'[2]

At Iloilo the investigator found his own views reflected in
those of two Englishmen, Fyfe, the British vice-consul, and
Hubert Fox, an English merchant. Both were impressed with
the enormous commercial possibilities of the islands under good
government, with the richness of the resources of the islands
scarcely touched, and with the utter incapacity of the people to
rule themselves. Both criticized the Americans for their tardi-
ness with a definite plan. The natives should not be indulged in
'any nonsense about self-government.'[3] It was in this province
that Beveridge saw the richest man in the islands, Don Cornello
Milliza, seventy-four years old, and the owner of many planta-
tions, ships, and houses. He spoke the language of his class. He
was sure the common people wanted to 'get back to work.' They
had no opinions, and not twenty-five per cent were competent to

[1] MS. Philippine Notebook. [2] *Ibid.* [3] *Ibid.*

vote for legislators. If Americans would give a good government, with free speech and justice in the courts, the people would be satisfied.[1]

Such was the tenor of the questions and replies that found their way into the little red notebook, to be read later to the Senate with the names omitted. He had convinced himself on evidence that the people were unfit for self-government; that the country was enormously rich with resources scarcely touched because of the lack of capital; that commerce would thrive under a stable government; that the climate was fit for American occupation. He also had sustained his theory that a definite plan should be made at once, and that, pending the restoration of order, the war against the insurgents should be waged relentlessly and with all the power of the Republic. He left the islands completely satisfied with the result of his investigations, more intimately familiar with the conditions and necessities than any other Senator possibly could be.

V

Obsessed with his subject, he did not discontinue his research when he reached China and Japan. He wanted to talk with British officers in China on the British method of dealing with subject races, and at Hongkong he saw Colonel Ellsdale, Imperial British Engineer, who told him the United States had made a serious mistake in not calling the insurgents in and telling them precisely the nature of the system to be imposed.[2] He went to Lake Chuzengi to get the views of Colonel The O'Gorman, second in command of the British forces in South China, with extensive experience in dealing with Oriental peoples. 'I think,' said the Colonel, 'you must do nothing but fight them. When we are in a row with Orientals, that is the way we do. They do not understand anything else.' [3]

But it was in Tokio that he had his most fascinating experience when he sat down for a long and frank discussion of America's new problem of colonialism with Marquis Ito, whom he considered one of the three or four great world figures. He was the Prime Minister at the time and not in position to speak for publication on the problems of other nations. Though almost sixty, Beveridge found him 'hard as a nail, full of vitality and good for ten or twenty years yet.' After the interview he set it down that Ito was 'one of the few great men I have met.' Previous to the meeting, Ito had sent him his book on 'The

[1] MS. Philippine Notebook.
[2] *Ibid.*   [3] *Ibid.*

Constitution of Japan.' This interview, published now for the first time, is worth recording from the Notebook:

Our interview lasted two hours and a half. After personally thanking him for his book, I said I personally wanted his frank and confidential views on the Philippine situation. I told him I would be frank with him as to my views, although not one man in the Far East knew what my views were except him. I told him I wanted him to be frank with me, and that he might know I concealed nothing from him. Then I asked him what he thought we ought to do.

First he asked me about the people. I told him all, good and bad. Then he said he had been told that our Constitution and institutions would not permit the kind of government which he thought ought to be adopted. I told him that this was not true, briefly, because of the principle of implied powers.

Then he said: 'That clears up the air. In that case it is clear what you should do. You have been frank with me. I will be as frank with you. First you must keep the islands.'

I asked him why?

'Because,' he said, 'your national honor is involved; because it is to your interest, not at once, but greatly, almost incontestably so in the future; and because if you do not, another Power will immediately take them, involving the world in war in all probability, for which you will be responsible. From what you say, I think self-government is out of the question, and even their participation in your government should be regulated and limited with great caution.

'As to the form of government, you should have a Governor-General of great ability, firmness, and purity. Under him, sub-officials of the districts, all appointed by the superiors and not chosen by the people. You should employ the ablest natives in the islands in the Government service in some way, so as to enlist them on your side. The courts are the most important consideration of all. You will make a mistake if you put natives in charge of the courts. Don't do it. That may come later, but not now. They must be given minor military positions, but not important ones. Don't do too much for them at the beginning — do it gradually, as the years go by.

'Now in Formosa we have adopted practically this system and it is working well. There was difficulty at first, and that is necessary, but things are beginning to move well.

'As to your present situation, I think your course is clear, most clear. Don't treat with them until you definitely defeat them. First you must do that. You cannot treat and fight. Of course make the English language the language of courts and schools and everything else. Do away with the court interpreters as soon as may be. After a while, when the people have sent their children to America to be educated, all things will be much better.

'Let me impress upon you the necessity of conferring your benefits upon them quite gradually. If you give them too much, they cannot appreciate or understand or rightly use them, and they will thus be

Tokio, Japan

July 26th '99, Marquis Ito:
68 years old but hard
as a nail, full of
vitality & good for
10 or even 20
years yet. He is one
of the keenest men
in the far east &
one of the few great
men I ever met.

After my former
interview which
resulted in the friendly
relations culminating
in this one, he sent
me his book "The
Constitution of Japan
with commentaries"
I wrote thanking him
for it & saying that
I would give to his

thrown away. But if you give them the blessings of free institutions gradually, you furnish a source of constant gratitude. In the other way you exhaust yourselves at the beginning. In short, I think you should be guided by the experience of all mankind, throughout all history.' [1]

Here Beveridge had precisely his own views reflected and from a source that left him in no doubt as to the soundness of his own theories.

Meanwhile, as he lingered in the Orient, Colonel J. F. Bell and George F. Becker, United States Geologist in charge, were busily getting together papers and suggestions Beveridge had asked for, and these reached him in Japan in two letters.[2] The letter from Bell referred to 'propaganda' in behalf of the natives, manufactured, as he said, in Hongkong, issued by the Filipino Junta there, and put out in form by 'one Howard W. Bray,' described as 'a refugee Englishman from here, who has a slight faculty for arraying sophisticated arguments.' This 'propaganda' was described by Bell as 'a tissue of falsehoods and transparent platitudes which appear rather formidable until punctured with the truth.'

A letter from General Lawton also overtook him in Japan soliciting his influence in securing for the officer the grade of Brigadier-General created by the retirement of General Shafter. Beveridge had told Lawton in their rides in the islands of the desire of Indianians to bestow some honor upon him. 'If my friends in Indiana sincerely desire to honor me,' he wrote, 'I will feel grateful to them if they will let it come to me in the line of my profession. I will be glad to have the State of Indiana, represented by yourself, appeal to the President to favorably consider my claims in connection with the coming vacancy.' [3]

Within four months Lawton was to fall upon the field of battle.

VI

During the latter part of July, the American press carried a story that Beveridge had been quarantined on a plague ship off Nagasaki, Japan. The newspaper story was all the more sensational because based on a letter presumably smuggled ashore by the Senator. His friends were alarmed, since, were the story true, Consul C. G. Harris at Nagasaki might be in ignorance of his countryman's plight. At the instance of friends, John Hay, Secretary of State, cabled the consul: 'Reported

[1] MS. Philippine Notebook. The interview was on July 26, 1899.
[2] Bell to Beveridge, Aug. 19, 1899; Becker to Beveridge, Aug. 1, 1899.
[3] Lawton to Beveridge, Aug. 21, 1899.

Senator Beveridge on board plague ship off Nagasaki. Cable his condition. His friends anxious.' [1] The next day brought a reassuring reply: 'Beveridge all right.' [2] He had really been in quarantine, but in no danger, and there was nothing spectacular about the incident except in the press, but this served to keep him and his mission in the public mind. Later there was a mystery as to his whereabouts, and a false report that he was returning by way of San Francisco, where emissaries of some magazines and publishing houses were waiting to secure his signature to a contract for the story of his experiences. [3] In truth, he returned by the Empress of China and reached Victoria, British Columbia, on August 10. Refusing to give interviews, he disappeared again, for he went into hiding at Banff Springs in the Rocky Mountains to rest. Mrs. Beveridge was not well. It was the beginning of her fatal illness. [4]

When the time of his homecoming was learned, the Marion Club in Indianapolis arranged for a hearty welcome. It sent a reception committee to Chicago to meet him and Mrs. Beveridge and accompany them home. When the traveler emerged from his car at Indianapolis, he found the entire club, in uniforms of white duck trousers, dark coats, and straw hats, awaiting him; and, headed by a band, the procession moved to the clubhouse on Meridian Street, where electric lights in front blazed forth a 'Welcome Home.'

'How about the Philippines, Senator?' shouted one of the crowd. 'Let's not talk about the Philippines,' he replied; 'let's talk about home.' Again, steadfastly, though courteously, he refused to be interviewed on his journey. He was saving his observations for the speech he planned to make as his initial bow to the Senate. 'I am hearing on all sides,' wrote Perkins, 'the most favorable comments from the dispatches to the newspapers, to the effect that you are back from the Philippines, but are not going to talk. You are extremely wise in this, and while Munsey will be actually disappointed that you cannot write him an article, I think you want to hold close and fast to your original proposition that you went out for blood for use in the hard work you are going to have in Washington. The people will respect you for such a course.' [5]

A few days later he appeared in Washington, summoned thither by President McKinley, who wished to hear his report on the conditions in the islands. He was the guest while there of Charles G. Dawes, but much of his time was spent at the

[1] *Indianapolis Journal*, July 29, 1899.   [2] *Ibid.*, July 29, 1899.
[3] *Ibid.*, July 31, 1899.   [4] *Ibid.*, Aug. 10 and 12, 1899.
[5] Perkins to Beveridge, Aug. 14, 1899.

White House. He had a conference with McKinley the first day and the conversation was continued during a long drive around the city. It was observed that the conference 'was one of the longest ever had by anyone since President McKinley entered the White House.'[1] The next day the conference was resumed before the Cabinet meeting, and again after it had adjourned, with Secretary Elihu Root sitting in.[2] The third day found Beveridge in another conference at the White House.[3] No other civilian in America had such a wealth of information of the sort required, but the frequent conferences intensified popular interest in the new Senator.

That he was happy, we may assume. As he paced back and forth in the lobby of the Riggs House, he attracted the favorable notice of Senator John W. Daniel of Virginia, as he sat in conversation with Senator Thomas Martin. Turning to Martin, the 'lion of Lynchburg' said: 'There's a fine-looking young man, Tom. He's handsome enough to be a Virginian. He's probably going to call on some lovely young lady tonight, and he looks as happy as if he were going to the White House.' At that moment Beveridge turned sharply, and, recognizing Daniel, whose oratory he admired, he advanced on the two Senators, holding out his hand.

'Is this Senator Daniel?' he asked.

'Your most obedient servant,' replied the courtly Virginian. 'I am very glad to see you, sir. I was just speaking about you, my young friend, and I told Senator Martin' — patting the young man familiarly on the shoulder — 'that I knew you were a Virginian the moment I saw you. Do you know Senator Martin? No? Then permit me — Senator Martin, I want to present to you my young friend from ——'

He paused, slightly embarrassed. The young man began to flush.

'No, don't tell me!' cried Daniel, 'I'll place you in just one moment. Ah, yes, I remember now. You are the nephew of my dear old honored friend, Colonel ——'

'Pardon me, Senator Daniel, you are mistaken. I am sorry to say I have never had the pleasure of seeing you before tonight. I have always wished to know you. I am Senator Beveridge from Indiana.'[4]

Concluding his conferences with McKinley, Beveridge went to New York to visit Roosevelt at Oyster Bay. He, too, wanted reports from the Philippines. He was delighted with the new

[1] *Indianapolis Journal*, Sept. 8, 1899.
[2] *Ibid.*, Sept. 9, 1899.　　[3] *Ibid.*, Sept. 10, 1899.
[4] *Indianapolis Journal*, quoting *Cincinnati Enquirer*, Oct. 8, 1899.

statesman and his opinions. 'Senator Beveridge was out here yesterday,' Roosevelt wrote Henry Cabot Lodge the next day. 'He has just come back from the Philippines. His views on public matters are almost exactly yours and mine. I want you to meet him.' [1] It had been said in the press that his views were not in accord with some of McKinley's. [2]

At length he had reached the theater toward which he had been striving, heralded as few new Senators have ever been by the press.

[1] *Roosevelt-Lodge Correspondence*, I, 421.
[2] *Indianapolis Journal*, Sept. 11, 1899.

CHAPTER II
PEAK AND ABYSS

I

WHEN Beveridge turned to Washington, he left in Indianapolis to guard his interests a friend as devoted as Herndon was to Lincoln. This was the Jewish youth, Leo Rothschild, whose infectious smile had so captivated Beveridge that he had taken him into his office when he did not need him. The youth was older now, but his big round face still fairly radiated kindliness and good will toward men and on his lips still hovered the smile of suavity. Among all the friends and well-wishers of the young Senator there was to be none more abundantly blessed with penetration, prescience, and an intuitive judgment of men. From time to time we shall have occasion to marvel at his wisdom.

It was with some naïveté that the young statesman had planned his position in the Senate. He had an extravagant notion of what he should have in the way of committee assignments. His continuing triumphs from his DePauw days, his easy victory over competitors, his spectacular advance, were to exact their penalty. He appeared upon the theater of his activities in Washington in the late summer of 1899 without the shadow of a doubt. Not only did he want to be on the new Committee on Philippine Affairs, for which he was better fitted then any other member of the Senate, but he expected to have the Committee on Foreign Relations as well, and possibly a place on the Judiciary Committee. He made no secret of his expectations. If he seemed a bit immodest in senatorial circles where seniority is a religion, he was not without company. Theodore Roosevelt, who might have known better because of his experience at the capital before the Spanish War, had been so favorably impressed during that Sunday afternoon conversation at Oyster Bay that he had written his friend Henry Cabot Lodge, urging that Beveridge would be 'a good man on the Committee on Foreign Relations,' since 'he seems to be sound on those matters.'[1] All through the late summer, Perkins had been pulling the strings with the same thing in view. 'No opportunity has been lost to keep the matter of the committees before all the powers that be,' he had written Beveridge. 'Everything seems to be moving all right in connection with them....

[1] *Roosevelt-Lodge Correspondence*, I, 426.

I think you ought to write Allison and Hobart now, saying that you are back; that you have worked very hard; that you have information which you believe will be of service to you on both the Foreign Relations and Judiciary Committees.'[1] Strange that Perkins, now vice-president of the New York Life Insurance Company and in touch with W. C. Beer, its legislative agent, who knew his Washington forward and backward, knew no better. If the Young-Senator-in-a-Hurry had some absurd ideas, he shared them with Roosevelt and Perkins. It remained for Lodge to explain the rule of seniority to the lay mind in a letter to Roosevelt. He wrote that Beveridge was 'a very bright fellow, well informed and sound in his views,' but that he had arrived in Washington 'with a very imperfect idea of the rights of seniority and with a large idea of what he ought to have.' Not only did he expect the chairmanship of the Philippines Committee, 'which is going to be one of the biggest committees in the Senate' which they had 'forced' upon Lodge, but he wanted to be on the Foreign Relations Committee as well. So the big-wigs 'put Beveridge on the Committee on the Philippines — which I think he was fortunate to get,' and Lodge was 'very glad to have him there.'

And so the laymen learned that the mere possession of more extensive and profound knowledge of a subject than any other Senator possessed merely made the possessor 'lucky' to be placed where he could use it.[2] Even so, as custom ran, Beveridge was fortunate to be given a place on the committee at all. It would deal in that session and for some time with matters uppermost in the public mind. The political lines were being closely drawn for the contest. The Democratic Senators were preparing to go forth to battle in the armor of the Declaration of Independence to put Imperialism to the sword. A few Republicans, like Hoar of Massachusetts, were up in arms against the new departure. The fighting was still in progress in the Philippines, and whatever was to be the ultimate determination, it was imperative that a definite policy be speedily announced. As we have seen, almost everyone with whom Beveridge had talked in the islands had urged the necessity of a clear-cut and positive declaration of intent. The Republican members of the committee were agreed upon it, and there were numerous conferences regarding its phrasing. When Lodge, Platt of Connecticut, the ablest member of the Senate, Cushman K. Davis, chairman of the Foreign Relations Committee, and the venerable Allison assembled to frame the declaration, young Beveridge sat among

[1] Perkins to Beveridge, Aug. 14, 1899.
[2] *Roosevelt-Lodge Correspondence*, I, 427.

them on invitation. I have before me in his own handwriting the Beveridge draft, which differs but slightly from that finally adopted. Thus, before the new Senator had warmed his seat, he sat with the party leaders in the determination of a vital policy. They 'Resolved, that the Philippine Islands are territory belonging to the United States; that it is the intention of the United States to retain them as such, and to establish and maintain such governmental control throughout the archipelago as the situation may demand.'

II

It was natural and proper that Beveridge should speak upon this resolution. Tradition had foolishly ordained that a new member should sit mute and humble for a year after entering the Senate, leaving his constituents voiceless for that period. Under ordinary circumstances it would have been exceedingly dangerous to have challenged that unwritten rule. But Beveridge had caught the imagination of the country by his unprecedented enterprise in making a tour of personal investigation through the islands. The press had teemed with commendatory editorials. The country, knowing little about the new 'possessions,' was curious to hear a report from the field. The sphinxlike silence the traveler had maintained since his return and the three-day conferences with McKinley had accentuated the curiosity. He had placed himself in a position clearly above the rule of silence, and it was generally understood that he would make his report to the American people from the floor of the Senate.

Keenly realizing the importance, to himself, of the speech, he wrote it with meticulous care and finished it one night in the home of Perkins at Riverdale. Returning to the house late at night, and noticing lights burning in the guest-room, the host broke in upon his friend in the throes of composition. 'Get out of here!' he shouted. 'Come back in an hour.' When Perkins re-entered the room an hour later, the speech was finished, and far into the night the two friends sat, while Beveridge read it from beginning to end.[1]

Following his policy at this period of submitting important speeches to the criticisms of competent friends, the manuscript was left with Perkins for a careful reading and for submission to others. Soon Beveridge had a report on the reaction of the readers. 'Your speech has been pawed over almost constantly since you left here,' Perkins wrote. '... There is no doubt in the world, old

[1] Perkins's story, *Saturday Evening Post*, Sept. 8, 1900.

man, that the people are eager and anxious to hear practical truths about the Philippines, and the closer you can confine your remarks to this phase, the more dead certain you are to make a profound impression on the country.' [1]

Enclosed was a criticism by Ira S. Dodd, of Dodd, Mead and Company, publishers. He thought the speech 'brilliant,' and would be 'disappointed if it does not attract more than ordinary attention when it is given to the country.' It had 'force, not only as the utterance of an able lawyer, but as that of a man who has seen for himself and has shown himself as an exceedingly good observer.' The tone was 'impressive,' not only because of its 'profound conviction,' but because of its 'high ideals.' Indeed, the reader found 'something noble about it,' and the references to the destiny of the Anglo-Saxon race were 'eloquent and inspiring.' So ran the tribute; but Dodd was not so sure of its effect at that time. The path of conquering peoples had always been 'an awful one' and 'been marked by dark stains in the past.'

And there was a note from President McCall, of the New York Life Insurance Company: 'I have read the Senator's speech. It is great. I should like to hear him deliver it.'

Satisfied with his manuscript, Beveridge shut himself in to commit it and to await the day of its delivery.

III

The announcement that he would address the Senate on the Philippines was enough to shake blasé Washington out of its inertia and lead to a clamorous demand for gallery tickets. An hour and a half before the Senate was called to order, the galleries were packed, and at noon a long line of men and women strung out from the doors through the corridors. Hundreds were to keep their weary vigil throughout the delivery of the speech in the hope that some would leave the galleries, but none did. The diplomatic gallery, usually deserted, was filled, the representatives of England and Japan predominating. The press gallery was packed from exordium to peroration. No such scene had been witnessed on the occasion of a maiden speech since another Indiana orator, and a fellow alumnus of DePauw, Daniel Wolsey Voorhees, had made his initial bow to the Senate, but he had long been a favorite in the capital in the House and in the courts.

It was observed [2] that when Beveridge first appeared at the

[1] Perkins to Beveridge, Dec. 30, 1899.
[2] J. S. S. in *New York Mail and Express*, Jan. 10, 1900.

Capitol, he was nervous, and much paler than usual. Like a war-horse awaiting the bugle call, he was restless and kept flitting to and from the cloakroom. A hundred glasses were trained upon him constantly from the galleries.[1] Upon his desk there was not the usual depressing array of reference books, and it was free of anything suggesting statistics.

When he rose to speak, all his nervousness miraculously disappeared and he seemed the most composed man in the room. His slight form and thin, pale face made him appear even younger than he was, but his voice, 'clear and musical as a bell,' and the perfection of his modulation and the rapidity of his utterance instantly denoted the practiced orator. Gesticulating sparingly, scarcely raising his voice above the conversational pitch, he still managed to convey the impression of intense earnestness. For two hours he held the crowded Chamber and was the complete master of his audience.

In the beginning he startled many by the uncompromising imperialism of his tone:

Mr. President, the times call for candor. The Philippines are ours forever: 'territory belonging to the United States,' as the Constitution calls them. And just beyond the Philippines are China's illimitable markets. We will not retreat from either. We will not repudiate our duty in the archipelago. We will not abandon our opportunity in the Orient. We will not renounce our part in the mission of our race, trustees under God, of the civilization of the world. And we will move forward to our work, not howling out regrets like slaves whipped to their burdens, but with gratitude for a task worthy of our strength and thanksgiving to Almighty God that He has marked us as his chosen people, henceforth to lead in the regeneration of the world.

Having thus struck the usual religious note of all imperialistic enterprises, he turned abruptly to more practical appeals — the commercial advantages in the retention of the islands. The markets of the future are in the Orient. 'China is our natural customer,' and the islands 'give us a base at the door of all the East.' 'The power that rules the Pacific is the power that rules the world,' and with the Philippines 'that power is and will forever be the American Republic.' The trade of China is 'the mightiest commercial fact in our future,' and 'that statesman commits a crime against American trade — against the American grower of cotton and wheat and tobacco, the American manufacturer of machinery and clothing — who fails to put America where she can command that trade.'

But the trade of the rest of the Orient aside, the Philippines alone are valuable enough to hold. 'I have cruised more than

[1] *Indianapolis News*, Jan. 9, 1900.

two thousand miles through the archipelago, every moment a surprise at its loveliness and wealth. I have ridden hundreds of miles on the islands, every foot of the way a revelation of vegetable and mineral riches.' He dwelt enthusiastically on the 'fertility of the plains and valleys of Luzon,' on 'rice and coffee, sugar and coconuts, hemp and tobacco,' and told of seeing 'hundreds of bushels of Indian corn lying in a road fringed with banana trees.' Why, 'the wood of the Philippines can supply the furniture of the world for a century to come.' He had been reliably informed that forty miles of Cebu's mountain chain were 'practically mountains of coal.' And then, with Hoar the anti-imperialist utterly amazed, he went on: 'I have a nugget of pure gold picked up in its present form on the banks of a Philippine creek. I have gold-dust washed out by crude processes of careless natives from the sands of a Philippine stream.' And more: 'In one of the islands great deposits of copper exist untouched.' And then:

'If we are willing to go to war rather than let England have a few dozen feet of frozen Alaska, which afford no market and commands none, what should we do rather than let England, Germany, Russia, or Japan have the Philippines?'

And could Americans live there? It has 'the best tropical climate in the world.'

And the Filipinos? 'It is barely possible that a thousand men in all the archipelago are capable of self-government in the Anglo-Saxon sense. My own belief is that there are not a hundred men among them who comprehend what Anglo-Saxon self-government even means, and there are over five million people to be governed.' Among all the natives, he had found but three commanding intellects — Arellano, Mabini, and Aguinaldo. The first, 'a profound lawyer and a brave and incorruptible man'; Mabini, 'the most constructive mind the race has yet produced'; and Aguinaldo, 'a clever, popular leader, able, brave, resourceful, cunning, ambitious, unscrupulous, and masterful' — a natural dictator. And where did he get these impressions? From 'conversations had informally at dinner tables, on journeys, and always under conditions favorable to entire frankness.'

At this point he produced the little red book, reading the notations but not the names which are given in the previous chapter. This he followed with the views of Ito, described as 'a Japanese statesman.'

And how establish peace and hold the islands? 'A lasting peace can be secured by overwhelming forces in ceaseless action until universal and absolutely final defeat is inflicted on the enemy.... Even then we shall not dare rest; to treat at all is to admit that we are wrong.'

And our treatment of the natives cruel? 'I have been in the hospitals and seen the wounded Filipinos as carefully, tenderly cared for as our own.' No, 'our mistake has not been cruelty; it has been kindness. We smiled at intolerable insult and insolence until the lips of every native in Manila were curling in ridicule for the cowardly Americans.' Yes, 'soldiers, and plenty of them, the only way.'

And a governmental system? He set forth his own ideas:

An American Governor-General in Manila with power to meet daily emergencies; probably an advisory council with no power except that of discussing measures with the Governor-General; American lieutenant-governors in each province, with a similar council; frequent and unannounced visits of provincial governors to the districts of their province; a Philippine civil service with promotion for efficiency; the abolishment of duties on exports from the islands with such discrimination in favor of American imports as to prevent cheaper goods of other nations from destroying our trade; complete tax reforms, beginning with the land tax based on valuation; the granting of franchises and concessions to develop resources.

Turning now to the attacks on imperialism: 'The administration of good government is not a denial of liberty.' 'The Declaration of Independence has no application to the present situation. It was written by self-governing men for self-governing men.' The Declaration of Independence applies to all men? How dare we, then, deny its application to the American Indians?

No constitutional power? 'Is there a geographical interpretation to the Constitution? Do degrees of longitude fix constitutional limitations? Does a thousand miles of ocean diminish constitutional power more than a thousand miles of land?'

And then, concluding, he sounded, lyrically, the imperialistic note again:

God has not been preparing the English-speaking and Teutonic peoples for a thousand years for nothing but vain and idle self-contemplation and self-admiration. No! He has made us the master organizers of the world to establish system where chaos reigns.... He has made us adepts in government that we may administer government among savages and senile peoples.

Pray God the time may never come when Mammon and the love of ease shall so debase our blood that we will fear to shed it for the flag and its imperial destiny.... And that time will never come. We will renew our youth at the fountain of new and glorious deeds. We will exalt our reverence for the flag by carrying it to a nobler future, as well as in remembering its ineffable past.... And so, Senators, with reverent hearts, where dwells the fear of God, the American people move forward to the future of their hope and the doing of His work.

Adopt the resolutions offered that peace may quickly come and that we may begin our saving, regenerating, and uplifting work. Adopt it, and this bloodshed will cease when these deluded children of our islands learn that this is the final word of the representatives of the American people in Congress assembled. Reject it, and the world, history, and the American people will know where to forever fix the awful responsibility for the consequences that will surely follow our failure to do our manifest duty. How dare we delay when our soldiers' blood is flowing?

IV

As he resumed his seat, the galleries roared their applause, and Senator Frye in the chair, refraining from the usual pounding of the gavel, awaited its termination, and then made the customary announcement that applause was not permitted. The galleries laughed. The venerable Allison, who sat beside the speaker studying him carefully, was the first to grasp his hand. The bellicose Tillman of the Opposition strode across the Chamber with his congratulations, and in a moment he was surrounded by Senators and Congressmen. But one Senator stood aloof, with flushed cheeks. To Hoar of Massachusetts the sentiments of the speech were treason to the Republic of the Fathers. The business imperialism of America had swept by him and he had not seen it pass. There were many like him. Now in his seventy-second year, he had entered Congress when Beveridge was a child of six. He had not intended to speak, but he could not mutely acquiesce in the general approval accorded the young orator. As soon as he could get the eye of the presiding officer, he rose, face flushed, voice trembling with sincere emotion.

I have listened, he said, delighted, as I suppose all the members of the Senate did, to the eloquence of my honorable friend from Indiana. I am glad to welcome to the public service his enthusiasm, his patriotism, his silver speech, and the earnestness and courage with which he has devoted himself to the discharge of his duty to the Republic, as he conceives it.

Yet, Mr. President, as I heard his eloquent description of wealth and glory and commerce and trade, I listened in vain for those words which the American people have been wont to take upon their lips in every solemn crisis of their history. I heard much calculated to excite the imagination of youth seeking wealth, or the youth charmed by the dream of empire. But the words Right, Duty, Freedom, were absent, my friend must permit me to say, from that eloquent speech. I could think of this brave young Republic of ours listening to what he had to say, of but one occurrence:

'The devil taketh him up into an exceeding high mountain, and showeth him all the kingdoms of the world, and the glory of them: and saith unto him, All these things will I give thee, if thou wilt fall down and worship me. Then saith Jesus unto him, Get thee behind me, Satan.'[1]

And so the curtain fell upon the Senate drama of that day, and Beveridge's spectacular triumph was the talk of the town and country. One must search far in parliamentary and congressional history for a similar reception of a maiden speech. It was a first-page story in papers from coast to coast, and Washington correspondents were to write about it for several days to come. The Associated Press said that 'the occasion was inspiring, and Mr. Beveridge arose to it brilliantly. His oration — for properly it was an oration — was deeply interesting. It was replete with striking sentences and well-arranged information. Spoken with all the earnestness, vigor, and eloquence of a fine orator, enthusiastic, who rose at times to his subject with a power of passionate dramatic utterance, the speech created a profound impression.' Walter Wellman, the correspondent of the 'Chicago Times-Herald,' wrote that 'his was a speech such as we hear in the Senate Chamber once or twice only in a decade,' and continued: 'He seized the psychological moment in the tide of our national affairs and made himself famous at a leap. It takes genius to do this, and Albert J. Beveridge is a genius.... He had to stand or fall today — fall as a presumptuous, self-advertising upstart, or stand as a man of originality, of intellectual force, of ability to guide, instruct, and be one of the leaders of his people in an epoch of new activity and construction which they are just entering. He stands. And hereafter his personal foibles will be scored not against him. He has the license of a genius.'[2] Editorially the 'Chicago Daily News' struck a typical note: 'Like all really great orations, his speech is unanswerable. As to the magic of his eloquence, that was born of his subject and of transcendent events, and it is praise enough to say that Senator Beveridge rose to the height of his great theme.'[3] From the State of Hoar, however, came a jarring note from the 'Springfield Republican,'[4] expressing the opinion 'that Mr. Beveridge talks like a young Attila come out of the West, and if his Americanism is now the true brand, then indeed is the Republic no more.'

For days telegrams poured in upon Beveridge from the four corners. George B. Cortelyou, Secretary to the President,

[1] *Congressional Record*, Jan. 9, 1900.
[2] *Chicago Times-Herald*, Jan. 10, 1900.
[3] *Indianapolis Journal*, Jan. 12, 1900.   [4] Jan. 10, 1900.

wrote that 'the promptness with which the attempt will be made to refute your arguments and question your statements will show how vigorously you presented the matter.'[1] Theodore Roosevelt telegraphed from Albany: 'Just a line to say how delighted I was with your speech. After Hoar's reply, I felt like sending him Whittier's Ichabod.'[2] Philander C. Knox found the speech had come up to his expectations, which were great.[3] Commandant Clifford H. West, United States Navy Yard, New York, wrote that the speech had 'created a great sensation throughout the land,' and that 'naval officers are greatly pleased with it.'[4] From Henry D. Estabrook, who had deprecated the imperialistic tone of the 'March of the Flag' speech came a recantation: 'I am not yet released from the spell of your resounding sentences and masterful fervor. You speak with the authority of a genius. Forward, then, and may God bless you.'[5]

From his Indianapolis friends came similar expressions of jubilation. 'On Tuesday evening there was nothing else talked about,' wrote Larz A. Whitcomb. 'I was at the Columbia Club, the Marion Club, and at a ball given by Mr. Malott.[6] At all three places it was the absorbing topic of conversation.'[7] Rothschild, microscopically scanning the newspapers of the country, hurried to him the comments, good and bad.

Thus literally, like Byron, Beveridge awoke on the next morning to find himself a national figure within little more than a month after taking his seat. Among the younger men, and especially the military group, he became an idol. Young Archie Butt, later military aide to Presidents Roosevelt and Taft, and long a social favorite in the capital, had hastened from the Senate Chamber to leave his card and a note at Beveridge's apartment. 'Never has the Senate given such attention in a similar case before. Wish you could hear half what is being said.'[8] A month later, *en route* to the Philippines, Butt wrote from Portland, Oregon, that 'here, as everywhere else, there is the same interest in you,' and that 'the editor of "The Oregonian" called upon me and he agreed with me that a new light has arisen in the East.'[9] And a few days later, as Butt was waiting for his transport: 'As I write, you are looking down upon me from out your photograph with the same kind, calm influence I felt the day I met you. It gave me great pleasure to find that through the South, and even in the arid deserts of the West, there was the greatest interest felt in you.'[10] Only here and there a break in the harmony of praise. Peter F. Dunne, whose 'Mr. Dooley' articles were then

[1] Beveridge MSS.   [2] *Ibid.*   [3] *Ibid.*   [4] *Ibid.*   [5] *Ibid.*
[6] Volney Malott, banker.   [7] Beveridge MSS.   [8] *Ibid.*
[9] *Ibid.*   [10] *Ibid.*

delighting the country, made the speech the subject of one of his satires.

With his triumph complete, the young Senator found himself literally on a dizzy height. He had dared precedent, crashed through custom, bowled over age-old prejudice, and in one stride placed himself among the most famous of the Senators. Delighted with his success, he clearly had no appreciation of his perilous altitude. Would he rest for a while on his laurels or would he tempt Fate by attempting too soon to repeat the performance? Some of his friends were worried. A tactful note of warning had reached him from Larz Whitcomb: 'There has been expression here from some source that your great success will probably militate to your ultimate downfall. They proceed upon the theory that whom the gods would destroy they first make mad. They have said that so much compliment and praise will completely turn your head and that you will lose yourself; that you will be speaking on every occasion that you can catch the President's attention. Of course, we who know you better know that no such thing will happen. From conversations we have had, I know that you appreciate the value of silence.' [1]

In a month he had attained the heights; in two months he would be plunged momentarily into the depths — because he did not 'appreciate the value of silence.'

V

In the legislation of the session relating to the government of the new dependencies, the Democrats proposed to make the imperialistic features as shocking as possible, while the Administration was eager to soften them. Imperialism logically was to be the charge and the issue of the minority in the elections that year. No one until then had questioned that the Constitution ordained that customs duties should be uniform in all the ports of the Nation. On this ground, insisting that the 'Constitution follows the flag,' the Democrats demanded free trade between our possessions and ourselves. The sponsors of protective tariffs rose in wrath at the mere suggestion, but consoled themselves with the conviction that the Supreme Court would find a way around.

This made the Message of McKinley at the opening of the session fall among the protectionists like an exploding bomb. Its feeling reference to the plight of Porto Rico in losing its principal markets in Spain and Cuba, 'without a compensating

[1] Beveridge MSS.

benefit in this market,' seemed unnecessary to the faithful, but the recommendation hurt most of all. 'Our plain duty,' wrote McKinley, 'is to abolish all customs tariffs between the United States and Porto Rico and give her products free access to our markets.'

There was a special reason why the United States at the moment should have been particularly tender toward the island that had accepted American domination without a struggle. Through a hurricane she had been desolated, and her people were in dire need. This, however, furnished the House with an excuse to fix tariff duties with the understanding that the revenue received should be expended on the care of the afflicted subjects. To this was added a vague promise of reciprocity later on. It was after this that McKinley asked for the two million dollars already collected from the tariff to be used for the benefit of the Porto Ricans — and the Senate fight was on.

The President, the Democrats, many Republicans, and practically all the independent and Democratic papers persisted in the demand for free trade, but the protectionists, making a fetish of protection, met the issue stubbornly. The free-traders, however, were split, largely on party lines, with the Democrats declaring that the Constitution follows the flag in all respects and the Republican imperialists necessarily ridiculing the idea. It was a controversy later to be resolved in favor of imperialism by the Supreme Court in an opinion holding that, without an act of Congress, there was not a single guarantee in the Constitution that applied to our possessions. This was to make an issue in the campaign.

Had Beveridge been well advised, he would have stood aloof from the contest, but had he not written Dawes that his sole reason for aspiring to the Senate was to help frame the policies called for by the new departure? Here was a problem of some magnitude, and he had pronounced views. He did not believe that the Constitution followed the flag, and did believe that we could do whatever we wished in regard to customs duties. But he thought conditions dictated a free-trade policy and that the economic rehabilitation of Porto Rico would be to our advantage. The people there had accepted our rule without a challenge, and he felt this fact deserving of a gesture of good will.

There were other Republicans who shared his views, but with less danger to themselves. They were veterans; he was a raw recruit. In the numerous conferences of Republican Senators seeking an agreement, he participated, without making any secret of his position. He knew he was reflecting the sentiment of his own people, for the Indiana press and his correspondence left him in no doubt. 'Two weeks ago,' wrote Morris Ross of the 'Indianapolis News,' 'the Republican Party looked to me like an army with banners. Today I doubt very much whether the Republicans will carry Indiana next fall for McKinley if the Porto Rican tariff is passed.... I have not seen a Republican, high or low, that is not hot in indignant opposition to the Porto Rican tariff bill.... I give it as my firm opinion that the passage of the Porto Rican tariff bill means the loss of Indiana for Mc-Kinley.'[1] But more persuasive on Beveridge was the stout conviction of Henry W. Bennett that justice and the sentiment in Indiana sustained him in his position. Then and throughout his life he found this friend loyal in his allegiance and sound and conservative in his advice. 'My Lord Burleigh,' he was wont to call him; and he too had written that 'the Republican Party in Indiana was never more unanimous on any question.'[2]

It was at this juncture that Shaffer sent Beveridge the suggestion that he propose as a solution of the problem of party harmony the imposition of a three to five per cent duty on some one article of small importance as an assertion of the constitutional right to levy duties.[3]

Beveridge had been thinking somewhat along this line, and it was such encouragement as this which impelled him to assume a leadership that was not to be relished by his seniors. Nine days later, he spent a day in submitting a plan he had worked out to the members of the Republican harmony committee. This plan provided for free trade, but stated that 'this act shall not be construed as extending the Constitution of the United States, or any part thereof, over Porto Rico.' This compromised no imperialistic plan for the ruling of the new possessions, while it conformed to the public sentiment for free trade with the island. Nearly all the committee were favorably disposed.[4] When these consultations closed at night, it seemed more than possible that they might be adopted. When, on the following morning, the plan was submitted to McKinley and given the stamp of his approval, Beveridge was confident.[5]

Then it was that he made a tragic blunder because of his inexperience and his ignorance of the traditional attitude toward new members. Instead of turning his plan over to the committee of the elders to be submitted as their own, he introduced it, in substance, in the Senate on his own responsibility. That

---

[1] Ross to Beveridge, Feb. 28, 1900.
[2] Bennett to Beveridge, March 4, 1900.
[3] Shaffer to Beveridge, March 10, 1900.
[4] Walter Wellman, *Chicago Times-Herald*, March 20, 1900.　　[5] *Ibid.*

aroused the wrath of the guardians of the temple. And when the rumor spread that he would speak upon it, they began to rustle about for the hickory branch of chastisement. A week before, the 'Baltimore Sun' reported that the graybeards were seeking the opportunity 'to clip his wings.' [1] When Rothschild, in the watch-tower in Indianapolis, heard that his idol was to tempt Fate with another speech, he made a mild protest. 'It strikes me as a very dangerous thing to do,' he wrote. 'I was in hopes that you would make no speech whatever.... Besides, unless you have some understanding with the Congressmen of the State, it will make a feeling not congenial at all.' [2] But by this time Beveridge had succumbed to the lust for battle and there was no power to persuade him to his tent. Two days before he spoke, he was described by the 'Washington Post' as 'the busiest man in twenty States,' with floods of telegrams, conferences, and consultations.[3] He had no thought that some of his own people had hickory branches up their sleeves. He was like a well-meaning lamb frisking to the slaughter.

VI

He was to have spoken on March 30, but through the courtesy of Senator Proctor he was given the floor the day before to permit him to hasten to the bedside of his dying wife. She had been desperately ill in a sanatorium at Dansville, New York. She had been gradually sinking, but until now she had forbidden anyone to notify her husband. Even now, she insisted that he remain at his post until the fight was over. He arranged to rush from the Senate Chamber to the station the moment he concluded his speech, and there was not one member of the Senate who did not know the strain under which he was laboring. But that did not move them in the least. Their plans were made. The incident smacks of a schoolboys' conspiracy with all the schoolboys' heartlessness.

The galleries were packed when he rose, the Chamber full. It was the first time that session that the galleries had been packed since he had spoken on the Philippines. But the moment he began to speak, the Senators, with few exceptions, rose and filed out into the cloakrooms, leaving the doors slightly ajar to hear and see. A few remained. Senator Foraker, in charge of the bill, was rummaging among papers or chatting with friends who stopped at his desk. Lodge remained, but was ostentatiously

[1] Quoted in *Indianapolis Journal*, March 14, 1900.
[2] Rothschild to Beveridge, March 19, 1900.
[3] Quoted in *Indianapolis Journal*, March 27, 1900.

disinterested. Fairbanks kept his seat, described in the papers as 'ill at ease,' and talked with the venerable John Sherman, now retired, until the latter, pointing to the speaker, indicated a desire to listen. Chandler remained throughout, attentive, and toward the close Gallinger entered and gave close attention. Up in the gallery, the aged former Senator Dawes of Massachusetts did not take his eyes off the speaker. But when he concluded, there were but six Republican Senators on the floor. It was a signal triumph for the graybeards. Belasco could not have staged it better. As Beveridge hurriedly took up his papers to dash to the train, he himself felt that he was ruined. Never before had he failed to hold an audience; never had he encountered such brutality — not certainly among the gamblers and the cowboys.

But the reactions of the press were not quite up to the expectations of the conspirators. The correspondent of the 'Chicago Journal' thought the conduct of mature Senators 'too mean even for Senators.' 'There was not a man of them who did not know that the speaker was racing with time to go to the bedside of his dying wife. There was not one of them who could not see, and who did not see, the traces of grief and suffering in the hollow eyes, the pale face, the dry, cracked lips. They knew that he was making his fight for conscience, while a good many of them knew that their political course was due primarily to a lack of conscience.' [1] Such was the reaction of the press gallery; and when the correspondents went into their lobby 'there were blasts of profanity and epithets which could never under any circumstances be put in print.' [2] But the 'Cincinnati Commercial-Tribune' reported that the incident was 'the talk of the town tonight,' and that many thought Beveridge was politically dead. No one was surer of it than Beveridge himself as he rode toward Dansville.

VII

After his arrival at the sanatorium, Mrs. Beveridge revived, and improved so much that she insisted, after a while, that he return to his duties. But it was a miserable spring. The insult of the Senate had cut him to the heart, and he was distressed over his wife's condition. Everything increased his irritability, and even his most loyal friends were not spared. The State organization in Indiana had fallen into the hands of his enemies, and Rothschild's assurance that if he would be 'mum and saw wood,' he would be the 'lion in Indiana' in the fall gave him no

[1] Quoted in *Indianapolis Journal*, April 4, 1900.   [2] *Ibid.*

comfort.[1] When he fell into a rage because of a peculiarly offensive attack by William E. Curtis, of the 'Chicago Record,' Rothschild was concerned over his health. 'You worry too much on things when there is no necessity,' he wrote, 'and with all the strain you have been through in Washington as well as in the sickness, it is clear to me that you want to take the best possible care of yourself.'[2] In his irritation he was falling into indiscretions in conversations of a political nature, and his enemies at home were using them to the utmost. 'This struck me as one of your impulses ... better unsaid than said,' wrote Rothschild sternly of one of his indiscreet remarks. Nothing depressed him more than the attitude of his friends toward his Porto Rican speech, for they bluntly opposed his plan for its circulation. Perkins was almost brutal:

'I want to be brutally frank with you and say that in my judgment you won't have very many calls for that speech — at least I hope you won't ....I have followed pretty nearly everything that all the daily papers... have said... and I do not gather... that the speech has struck anything like the chord that your Philippine speech did.'[3] Even Rothschild advised that the speech be 'dropped.' 'I still cling to the idea that your Porto Rican speech was great, barring the finish,[4] and there was nothing but what was best for the Republican Party, yet the Administration policy is such that it would be the height of folly for you to send it out.'[5] And later he wrote again: 'The average Republican and the politicians... are always with the Administration policy. That policy was a tariff. Your speech was against the tariff, notwithstanding you voted for it. If you frank it out, doesn't it appear to you that you are going to lay the foundations for your enemies to build upon?'[6]

Meanwhile, Mrs. Beveridge was steadily growing worse, and the end came in the midst of the Republican National Convention Beveridge was unable to attend. To get his mind off his troubles, he turned savagely to work.

[1] Rothschild to Beveridge, March 18, 1900.   [2] *Ibid.*
[3] Perkins to Beveridge, April 6, 1900.   [4] Beveridge voted for the bill.
[5] Rothschild to Beveridge, May 5, 1900.   [6] *Ibid.*, undated.

CHAPTER III
FIGHTING FOR IMPERIALISM

I

THE spring and summer of 1900 found Beveridge feverishly at work. He had agreed with George H. Lorimer, editor of the 'Saturday Evening Post,' to write six articles, in the imperialistic vein, on his experiences in the Philippines. This was the beginning of an intimacy with Lorimer that was to continue through his life, for never was he to find anyone else who ministered so completely to his need for relaxation. The business relations were to be mutually helpful, too, for within two months Lorimer was to write him that 'nothing has appeared in any magazine this year which has received the liberal and favorable newspaper notice that has been accorded the American soldier articles, and I hear from them on all sides.'[1] These articles were to be followed immediately with others, an astonishing number that first year, and were to continue periodically for a quarter of a century. That summer and autumn the 'Post' was to publish articles on Ito, Diaz, and Rhodes; an article on Russia as a youth among the nations; and a series of articles on 'The Young Man and the World,' that later were to appear in book form. Into the preparation of these papers Beveridge threw himself with the passionate intensity that marked all his activities.

This literary work, however, was only a fragment of what he did that summer, and he was to admit later that only by working literally day and night could he throw off the depression of his spirit. With the presidential campaign approaching and demands rolling in upon the Republican National Committee from every quarter for his services on the stump, he soon learned that the hazing by the Senate had in no sense diminished his popularity with the people.

In his acceptance speech, Bryan, in a powerful presentation of the case against imperialism, had made it the paramount issue of the campaign. Bourke Cockran had again espoused the Democratic cause upon this issue and was to sweep across the continent with a series of speeches of extraordinarily moving eloquence in denunciation of the departure from the traditional policies of the Nation. There were dissensions among the Republicans; and the defalcations and corruption of American post-office officials in Cuba had been discovered in the spring.

[1] Lorimer to Beveridge, April 3, 1900.

The Democrats instantly cited these as the first fruits of imperialism, and a resolution by Senator Bacon of Georgia had instructed the Senate Committee on Cuban Affairs to institute a searching investigation. To Senator Orville H. Platt of Connecticut fell the burden of the task. A real statesman, with a keen sense of responsibility, the miserable mess nauseated and appalled him. 'The Cuban scandal is really bad and mortifying,' he wrote his wife. 'The Democrats and Populists are making all they can of it, and the worst is that they have too much ground to go on.' [1] Ten days later, he wrote that the disclosures seemed 'worse and worse,' and he doubted if he could ever get to the bottom of them.[2] Not only had the situation to be met in the Senate — it would have to be met upon the stump, and the celebrity of Beveridge's Philippine speech pointed to him as the most effective orator to meet the onslaughts of Bryan and Cockran. With his characteristic wisdom, Platt made a clean breast of the scandal, conceded that it was humiliating and disgraceful to the Nation, and promised to purge the public service in Cuba. But the less said about it upon the stump, the better. Here was a call to just such militant imperialism as Beveridge's — with drums rolling, flags flying.

During the summer days and nights while writing article after article, Beveridge, preparing his campaign speeches, was in correspondence with friends in the Philippines who were fanning his enthusiasm for the cause. Archie Butt, now on the islands and under fire, was writing him that the fighting would be indefinitely prolonged, but that both officers and men were 'enthusiastic for holding the islands.' And he added: 'I think of you always, and your life and work and success is a great incentive to put forth one's best efforts. I have never been so happy as I am now, and feel all the possibilities of living, even on the roughest food and poorest water. Don't let them take an inch from the flag this fall.' [3] And two months later, he wrote again: 'I think of you always and no matter where I go.... I think of your life work and how it has been crowned by the laurel.... Everything you have written has been reprinted here in the papers, and your encomium of Generals Lawton and MacArthur has doubly endeared you to their friends. My highest ambition has been, and ever since I knew you, to accomplish something in the world that will make me worthy of your friendship.' [4]

Such was Beveridge's appeal to the militant youth of those days.

But it was from Dr. Harry L. Gilchrist, with whom he had

[1] L. A. Coolidge, *An Old-Fashioned Senator: Orville H. Platt*, 326.
[2] *Ibid.*   [3] Butt to Beveridge, June 15, 1900.   [4] Aug. 29, 1900.

made the inspection tour in the rainstorm, that he received just the message he wanted for the campaign. 'A few days after it became known here that Bryan had received the nomination,' he wrote, 'Aguinaldo published an open letter in the "Manila Freedom" in which he advised all lovers of freedom to take heart and renew the struggle, saying, by doing so, it would greatly aid the Deliverer of the Philippines in becoming the next President of the United States and then all the troops would be withdrawn and the Filipinos would be free.'[1] And a month later: 'At present we are in the midst of a sudden renewal of energy of the insurgents.... The insurgents know all about Bryan's acceptance speech... and I dare say they can repeat it word for word.'[2]

To Beveridge, who was to defend imperialism, this was ammunition; but there was another development that Bryan would pounce upon as an issue — the trusts; and few Republicans that year would have the temerity to speak out boldly in defense of the trusts. During the previous four years the big industrialists and financiers, certain of the non-interference of the McKinley Administration, had been moving with unprecedented audacity toward monopolies. The press through 1899 had fairly teemed with daily stories of these new combinations. The trusts were being discussed at breakfast-tables all over the land, and the ancient hatred of monopoly was flaming anew, with the rich and powerful the targets for denunciations. The more timid of the Republican politicians were not eager for the defense, and this gave Beveridge, whose temerity was inherent, his cue. He would defend, not only imperialism, but the trusts.

It was in this campaign that the press correspondents were impressed with his marvelous memory. During a crowded September he had worked on the preparation of a number of speeches on different subjects, some on imperialism, some on the trusts, some on markets, and no two alike. Speaking with his rapidity of utterance, any one of them would require two hours in delivery. They were scheduled to follow in rapid succession; and, as it developed, to large and tumultuous meetings, and correspondents, following the manuscripts, found him speaking without notes and without the deviation of one word from the text.

But more startling to the politicians — he was to strike a note of super-imperialism and to declare it a blunder ever to have parted with Cuba.

The Auditorium in Chicago was crowded to hear him open the Illinois campaign with a ringing defense of imperialism, and 'the applause was almost continuous from the time he came on

[1] Gilchrist to Beveridge, Aug. 18, 1900.
[2] Sept. 23, 1900.

the stage until he closed'; and Congress Street was packed from Michigan Avenue to Wabash with people unable to get in.[1]

With his opening sentences he caught the fancy of the great crowd, as was his method:

'Westward the Star of Empire takes its way.' Not the star of kingly power, for kingdoms are everywhere dissolving in the increasing rights of men; not the star of autocratic oppression, for civilization is brightening and the liberties of the people are broadening under every flag. But the star of empire as Washington used the word when he called this republic an 'empire'; as Jefferson understood it, when he declared our form of government ideal for extending 'our empire'; as Marshall understood it, when he closed a noble period of an immortal constitutional opinion by naming the domain of the American people 'our empire.' This is the 'empire' of which the prophet's voice declared 'Westward the Star of Empire takes its way' — the star of the empire of liberty and law, of commerce and communication, of social order and the Gospel of our Lord — the star of empire of the civilization of the world.

The Cuban scandals he lightly brushed aside. Were there no embezzlements among officials in America? But the high light of this Chicago speech was on Cuba. 'I am speaking for myself alone, but speaking thus, I say that for the good of Cuba... a separate government over Cuba uncontrolled by the American Government should never have been promised. Cuba is a mere extension of our Atlantic coast line.'

And the Philippines? War would cease with McKinley's reëlection. 'If from the first there had been united support of the American Government in holding aloft the American flag in the Philippines, no bloodshed would have been necessary, no lives of American soldiers required to keep it floating there.'

It was at Columbus, Nebraska, that he made his defense of trusts, anticipating the precise position Roosevelt would assume a little later. Bad trusts? Yes, and good ones, too. A good trust 'produces better goods at cheaper prices and delivers them to the consumers more conveniently than a dozen different concerns could do.' A bad trust raises prices dishonestly. Then what? The good trust should be kept; the bad one destroyed; and Bryan would destroy both. Regulation by the Government — there was the solution. State Rights? 'We have outgrown State Rights.' Were not railroads trusts, and were not their great systems better than having them cut up into small groups?

At St. Louis he spoke again in defense of imperialism under the pretext of discussing markets. We raise a surplus, he said; we must have markets; colonies make markets and open the way

[1] *Chicago Tribune, Chicago Inter-Ocean,* Sept. 26, 1900.

to others. The rights of man? 'There can be no rights of man outside of organized society.'

At Kansas City he duplicated the triumph of Chicago. His subject was 'Patriotism,' and all opposing his party's policies were put beyond the pale. When the parade with marching clubs and 'rough riders,' with bands and red fire, reached the enormous tent where the meeting was held, ten thousand were already seated. He moved the throng to such a pitch of enthusiasm that when he closed 'there was a rush for the platform, and he was nearly pulled over the railing by the wild desire of the enthusiasts to grasp his hand'; and 'time after time he started to the carriage, but was dragged back.'[1]

It was at Kansas City that he met Roosevelt, the Vice-Presidential nominee, with whom he was to work in such close harmony for seven years. The two men rode horseback together through the parks, and afterwards dined together.[2]

It was toward the close of the campaign that the 'New York Journal' posted a bulletin on the street: 'Senator Albert J. Beveridge in the presence of four witnesses said today, "I am full of fear that Bryan will sweep the country next Tuesday. I have had this feeling for several days, and other Republican leaders with whom I have talked tell me the same."' Flashed to the country, it was printed in Democratic papers everywhere, and Perkins telegraphed Beveridge to send an immediate denial to each Republican paper in New York.[3] That night at Jeffersonville, he denounced the story as 'a lie.' If he had been betrayed in private conversation there was nothing else to do, but there were many Republican leaders who shared the fear. Bryan had made a cyclonic sweep around the country, received everywhere with frantic enthusiasm. If Mark Hanna, in charge of the Republican campaign, had no misgivings, he concealed his confidence in his efforts to rally the corporations to the financial support of the party. Thus did he keep the pursestrings loose throughout the contest,[4] and the Standard Oil Company contributed a quarter of a million as in 1896.[5]

But there was no serious danger at any time. The mass of the people were indifferent to the Declaration of Independence and the feelings of the Filipinos, and only interested in wages and the price of wheat and hogs. Because of the 'campaign of education' four years before, the fear of disaster from a Bryan victory had sunk deep. If Bryan voiced their views, they gave him their cheers and marched to the polls for McKinley.

[1] *Kansas City Journal*, Sept. 29, 1900.
[2] *Indianapolis Journal*, Oct. 1, 1900.   [3] Beveridge MSS.
[4] H. D. Croly, *Marcus Alonzo Hanna*, 322.   [5] *Ibid.*, 325.

Beveridge emerged from the campaign again triumphant, so much so that Perkins thought it a friendly duty to caution him to humility;[1] and when Beveridge sharply resented the implication of the warning, his friend replied: 'I just felt that you needed a word of caution... lest you might be tempted to show, the least bit, the effects of the success you are meeting with.'[2] The close relations of the two friends were not in the least disturbed, and when, at the beginning of the congressional session, Beveridge invited Perkins to be his guest in Washington, the latter replied that he had thought of it, without an invitation, until he learned that Beveridge 'had personally superintended the decoration of the rooms.'[3] And when Beveridge telegraphed that 'for the next few months I shall dazzle the people with the most brilliant flash of silence since the age of the dumb,' Perkins was able, without offense, to reply that 'with every desire to flatter, I can truthfully say that is not bad.'

II

And Beveridge kept his word. He had learned his lesson in the hazing experience and knew now that it was considered intolerably bad taste to act upon the theory that the constituents of a new Senator had a voice in the debates. Very well, then, 'a brilliant flash of silence!' There was committee work to do, and to be taken seriously.

Immediately on convening, the Senate was put in possession of the Hay-Pauncefote Treaty, intended to pave the way to the building of the Panama Canal. The Bulwer-Clayton Treaty of many years before was a barrier to be removed, and John Hay, Secretary of State, had entered into negotiations for the abrogation of the old treaty and the substitution of a new. During the progress of negotiations he does not appear to have consulted much with his colleagues in the Cabinet, for his was the aristocratic concept of government. When the Senate examined the proffered treaty, it was found to be very much what Lord Pauncefote would want, but hardly what the American people could take. The evident acquiescence of McKinley made the situation all the more delicate. Under the treaty we could build the canal with our own money, neutralize it completely, but we could not fortify it. Nor was it at all clear that we could acquire territory in Central America to build it. In the beginning, Senator Lodge, in charge of the treaty, seemed fairly satisfied, and many senators were indifferent.

[1] Perkins to Beveridge, Oct. 1, 1900.   [2] Perkins to Beveridge, Oct. 8, 1900.
[3] Perkins to Beveridge, Dec. 5, 1900.

To Beveridge, intense nationalist and imperialist, this treaty was utterly impossible. Testing his judgment by correspondence with Albert Shaw, of the 'Review of Reviews,' he found he was not alone in the feeling that the treaty not only betrayed American interests, but, if ratified, would endanger all our future.[1] Many senators shared these feelings, and Hay began the writing of the abusive and childish letters denunciatory of senators in general as boresome obstacles to autocratic efficiency in international affairs.[2]

When Lodge explained the treaty in executive session, he was met with a bombardment of embarrassing questions. Some speeches were made, but Beveridge confined himself to Socratic questions having the effect of a speech in opposition. He wanted to know if the abrogation of the old treaty would leave Great Britain free to acquire territory in the area affected.[3] And whether the effect would be to prevent the United States from acquiring territory in Central America; and if the ratification by the Senate and the acceptance by twenty nations would prevent any modification without the consent of all the signatory powers. He wanted to know whether the new treaty would permit hostile nations to station ships in the vicinity of the canal in the event of its construction. In explaining his inquiries, he referred to the second article of the Bulwer-Clayton Treaty, which not only appeared to guarantee the neutrality of the canal, but to forbid its fortification and deny to the United States the right to acquire territory in Central America. Lodge replied that in his opinion the new treaty would prevent the United States from extending its domain into Central America. This was enough for Beveridge.[4]

Questions of this sort were fatal, and while Hay was fuming and fussing, sentiment was crystallizing against ratification, and the treaty failed. Hay proffered his resignation to McKinley, who refused it, and instructed that negotiations be renewed.

To Beveridge the part he played in the questioning was always to be a matter of keen satisfaction. Shaw congratulated him upon his course, on 'the admirable tact and discretion' he had shown. 'You have accomplished more,' he wrote, 'by asking these questions for information... than if you had made an elaborate set speech which would have seemed to put you, in the first place, in antagonism to the Administration, and, in the second place, would have seemed to some of the older senators

---

[1] Shaw to Beveridge, Dec. 12, 1900.
[2] W. R. Thayer, *Life and Letters of John Hay.*
[3] *Indianapolis Journal*, Dec. 6, 1900.
[4] *Ibid.*, Dec. 12, 1900.

as if you were too eager and strenuous.'[1] Throughout this controversy he was inspired by the vision of an expanding nation, and was moved by a determination to prevent any obstacles being placed in the pathway of the onward march of what he conceived to be the Nation's destiny. He was to appear in the same rôle that session in the formulation of our policy toward Cuba. This was to be worked out by Senator Platt of Connecticut, for whom he had a profound admiration and affection.

III

No public man, then or afterward, impressed Beveridge so much as Orville H. Platt or had a more salutary effect upon his thinking. The Connecticut statesman was more than seventy years old and had been a member of the Senate for twenty years. His personal appearance at the time may be best described by Beveridge himself. 'Senator Platt looked the part,' he said in an informal discussion of the Senate years later. 'He was more than six feet tall, slender, bony, very much the type of John Marshall or Abraham Lincoln. He reminded one of what the greatest of the Hebrew prophets must have looked like; his head was very noble, his features grave, composed, determined, and full of character; his eyes uncommonly large, deep brown in color, and fathomless; his forehead was high, broad, intellectual, and commanding. One could not look at him without repeating Milton's immortal lines, "On his brow deliberation sat, and public care." '[2]

In those days, as Beveridge himself observed, the Senate was dominated by a 'marvelous combination,' composed of Aldrich as manager, Allison as 'conciliator and adjuster,' Spooner as floor leader and debater, and Platt as 'designer and builder.'[3] When care or foresight was required in the framing of a new law or in the modification of an old one, to no one did the leaders turn so frequently for the task as to this old statesman. Beveridge thought him 'one of the greatest constitutional lawyers America has produced.'[4] His concept of government and of the national destiny precisely reflected the views of Beveridge himself. If Platt was an ultra-conservative, so was Beveridge in those early days. If Beveridge did not entirely agree with Platt in looking upon Bryan, Altgeld, and Tillman as the 'Robespierre, Danton, and Marat' of American politics, he agreed that they were bad enough. Both the veteran and the stripling had an exalted opinion of Business; both were imperialists; neither was greatly in-

[1] Shaw to Beveridge, Dec. 15, 1900.   [2] From manuscript of speech.
[3] *Ibid.*   [4] *Ibid.*

ORVILLE H. PLATT
1902

terested in money and both were forced to write for magazines for their vacation funds; and neither had time for the mere frivolities of society. Neither was a practical politician, familiar with the finesse of tricky manipulation. This was unnecessary in the case of Platt, but not so good for a Senator from Indiana, where skill in party management through intrigue meant much in power or disappointment.

The venerable Senator and his wife lived simply at the old Arlington Hotel, associated with Sumner. There he worked, studied, amused himself by reading in the original Greek to Mrs. Platt,[1] and there Beveridge found a second home. His relations with Platt until the latter's death were reminiscent of those with Judge John H. Baker in his younger days, and there was something of similarity in the intellectual processes of the two older men. From the moment Platt took him under his wing, Beveridge constantly was running in upon the old couple, seeking advice, information, or merely relaxation. There must have been much in the eagerness and impatience of the younger man that Platt would have moderated, but instantly he saw the possibilities of Beveridge's mind and he became a kind of mentor. Mrs. Platt, who liked him, assumed over him some of the maternal privileges, scolding him roundly when she thought he deserved it, and that was not infrequently. And Beveridge repaid them both with a warm affection. If he ever literally loved a member of the Senate, it was Platt. Had the latter lived into Beveridge's progressive and insurgent days, there might have been a cooling in their relations, but Beveridge always thought that had Platt lived, his powers of conciliation and compromise would have found a way around the bitter controversy of 1909.

IV

As we have seen, Beveridge thought the Teller Resolution pledging the United States to withdraw from Cuba on the establishment of a government, a great mistake. A high-flying imperialist at the time, he would have kept the island with the view to its ultimate admission as a State of the Union. Even after we had given the pledge, he felt certain that Destiny would ultimately throw Cuba into our laps. It was with keen impatience, therefore, that he observed the proceedings of the Cuban Constitutional Convention, called at the instance of McKinley. For three months the delegates, mostly radical or reactionary, talked and talked, without the utterance of a word of appreciation for the part the United States had played in the

[1] From manuscript of speech.

winning of their independence. On the cynical, but not unsound, theory that it is difficult to forgive anyone who has bestowed a favor, it was feared that the Cuban Republic might turn upon us and enter into agreements with European nations detrimental to our own interests. Beveridge insisted that something should be done to prevent such a possibility, and that, with a view to the future, it would be wise to attach a string to our withdrawal. This was likewise the view of Platt.

Out of this state of feeling came the famous Sunday afternoon meeting at the home of Senator Chandler, where the Platt Amendment was evolved which was to be adopted by a strict party vote. It prohibited Cuba from entering into any agreement with any other nation that would impair her independence; from granting colonization privileges or a military base to any other country; and from contracting a debt not provided for by a sinking fund. And there was something else that particularly delighted Beveridge — the provision that we might intervene for the preservation of Cuban independence and for the maintenance of a government capable of maintaining law and order. Being a youngster in the Senate, he did not sit in the conference that adopted the plan and cannot be credited with it. But long before those who sat in the conference had interested themselves in these provisions, the correspondence of Beveridge shows him to have been urging them vehemently. Thus he was enormously pleased with the Amendment, which he thought 'comparable with the British-North American Act' and in the 'same rank with the Ordinance of 1787.'

It was at this time that Shaffer suggested to the editor of the 'North American Review' that he get an article from Beveridge on the Platt Amendment. He knew it embodied ideas Beveridge had been urging for a year, but he was motivated partly by a wish to lift his friend from the slough of depression into which he had sunk in mid-winter. 'You cannot afford to get the blues,' he had written Beveridge the latter part of February. 'The fact that the Administration has adopted your views on the Cuban question ought to make you well.'[1] And a little later: 'It must be very gratifying to you to see the change in the sentiment of the President and the members of the Senate in regard to the Cuban question. In a very little while they will be over on your platform with both feet.... I am pained to hear that you are ill and worn out.'[2] A mercurial type, Beveridge's spirits rose and fell. He turned with pleasure to the article for the 'North American Review,' since it gave him an opportunity to call the roll of American statesmen who thought Cuba a natural part of the

[1] Shaffer to Beveridge, undated.   [2] Shaffer to Beveridge, Feb. 26, 1901.

United States. By laying some stress on the right of intervention, he could show that the possibility of an ultimate annexation was not destroyed, while accepting as a gracious experiment the granting of independence. Shaffer had written that he should make it 'a keynote that will be heard all over the land,' and that his Southern friends had 'expressed keen interest in it.'

David Graham Phillips, to whom the manuscript was submitted, being an idealist on international affairs, scarcely realized what his friend was about. He was not pleased. The article impressed him as 'sober and monotonous' in form, and the argument 'not consecutive.' In parts he found it 'specious.' It should be rewritten with more 'dash and spirit.' Since the purpose was to show that McKinley found in the Platt Amendment 'a reasonable, honorable carrying out of the Teller Resolution,' would it not be well to call it 'Keeping Faith with Cuba'? [1]

That which Phillips did not see was that the primary purpose was deftly to show that there was still a possibility to acquire Cuba for the United States.

It was during this short session that Beveridge won the friendship and admiration of Mark Hanna by refusing a request. During the campaign of 1896 the latter had clearly entered into an agreement for a ship subsidy, and he was pressing his Ship Subsidy Bill. The popular reaction was bitterly against it. If Beveridge had ever thought upon the project, it does not appear in his correspondence. The Democrats were arrayed in militant ranks against it, charging it as part of a bargain for campaign funds in 1896. Hanna was zealously canvassing the Senate for support and was eager to lift the Senate's embargo on a Beveridge speech. Approaching him one day, and placing his hand on his shoulder with the breezy familiarity of the Mid-West, Hanna asked him to make a speech for his bill. Beveridge replied that, not having studied the bill, he was in no position to make a promise, but that he would consider it if Hanna would send all available literature on the subject to his rooms. Twenty or thirty books were sent to Beveridge's hotel and he made a study of the bill and the books and decided he could not make the speech.

He lost nothing in Hanna's esteem by his action, and from that hour he was cordial and even affectionate, and for the brusque business man in politics who did things, Beveridge formed a sincere admiration. It was Hanna's custom to give an

[1] Phillips to Beveridge, March 15, 1901.

eleven o'clock breakfast every Sunday morning in his rooms at the Arlington, to which public men were invited. Soon it was thought a distinction to be asked. It was shortly after this incident that H. H. Kohlsaat, the Chicago editor, attending one of these breakfasts and noting a vacant chair, remarked to Hanna that one of his guests had not responded. 'Oh, yes, all did,' said Hanna. 'But I notice that one chair is vacant,' persisted the journalist. 'Oh, yes,' Hanna replied. 'We keep that for Senator Beveridge, and he comes whenever he can.'[1]

Thus, before the adjournment of the short session, Beveridge had recovered the ground lost in the Porto Rican fight and immeasurably strengthened his position with the strong men in the Senate. But he had kept his promise of 'a brilliant flash of silence.'

VI

But only in the Senate.

The new home of the Columbia Club in Indianapolis was formally opened with a New Year's Eve dinner, with all leading Republicans about the board and with a brilliant array at the speakers' table. There were former President Harrison, Beveridge, Fairbanks, and John Lewis Griffiths to speak, and James Whitcomb Riley to read a poem. The interest centered in the speeches of Harrison and Beveridge because of their clashing views on imperialism. Only a few weeks before, Harrison had delivered a forceful lecture at Ann Arbor University combating the imperialistic philosophy of the times, and insisting, with the Democrats, that the Constitution follows the flag. He had but recently published a magazine article to the same purports. Utterly without reason, we think, it was bruited abroad that, so deep were his feelings he might break with his party on the issue. In the Ann Arbor address he had taken sharp issue with Beveridge's theory of the status of the inhabitants of our insular possessions.

On the program, Harrison closed the speaking, immediately preceded by Beveridge, and while their subjects promised nothing spectacular, there was a feeling that they might clash on imperialism. And so it happened. It was nearly one o'clock when Beveridge was reached in the speaking. The audience was tired and worn, but perked up at the prospect of a debate. Beveridge was to talk on 'The Twentieth Century,' and Harrison's toast was, 'Hail, Columbia.' Some who were present

[1] As related by Kohlsaat to John C. Shaffer, Shaffer to James W. Noel, Jan. 24, 1898.

insist that both speakers disregarded their prepared speeches and launched vigorously into the debate. The speeches actually delivered may have been lost. Even so, the press reports indicate a clash.[1]

Beveridge literally lunged into the fight.

Before the clock of the century strikes the half-hour the American Republic will be the sought-for arbitrator of the disputes of the nations, the justice of whose decrees every people will admit, and whose power to enforce them none will dare resist. And, to me, the Republic as an active dispenser of international justice is a picture more desirable than a republic as an idle, egotistical example posing before mankind as a statue of do-nothing righteousness. A new day had dawned. Civilization will never loose its hold on Shanghai; civilization will never depart from Hongkong; the gates of Pekin will never again be closed against the methods of modern men. The regeneration of the world, physical as well as moral, has begun, and revolutions never move backward.

And constitutional limitations — on which Harrison had dwelt?

Give posterity a clean future. Stretch no treaty prohibitions across our tide of time. Clear the way for the coming race. Give the children of today and the children yet unborn the liberty to solve the questions of their own day in their own way. How awful is the egotism that would fasten about the brow of future generations the steel band of our little thought! We cannot foresee all the problems that will arise after we are gone, any more than the fathers foresaw the problems that arose after they were gone — problems that our elders have had to solve according to the wisdom of contemporaneous circumstances, and in the solving of which they discovered new powers in the Constitution undreamed of by the men who wrote that immortal document.

An ovation greeted his close; an ovation greeted the rising of Harrison, who had but three months to live. He accepted the challenge of Beveridge:

At first we talked of English rights, but it was not long until we began to talk of human rights. The British Parliament was, under the British law, supreme — could repeal the Magna Charta. We turned to the colonial charters, surely they were irrevocable grants, but the crown courts held otherwise. What kings and parliaments had given, they could take away. And so our fathers were driven to claim a divine endowment, and to allow it to all men, since God had made all of one blood. To write the argument otherwise was to divest it of its major premise. The grand conclusion — no king or parliament can rightfully take God's gift of liberty from any man — was thus riveted to the eternal throne itself. We made our convenience an exception in the case of the black man; but God erased it with a sponge dipped in the white man's blood.

[1] James W. Noel to the author.

And then, striking clearly at Beveridge, he concluded:

I have no argument to make against territorial expansion, but I do not, as some do, look to expansion as the safest and most attractive avenue of national development. By the advantages of abundant and cheap coal and iron, of an enormous supply of food products, and of invention and economy in production, we are now leading by a nose the original and greatest of the colonizing nations.... Great Britain cannot hold the trade of her colonies against American offerings of a better or cheaper product. The Central and South American States, assured of our purpose not only to respect, but to defend, their autonomy, and finding that peace and social order which a closer and larger commercial intercourse with the world will bring over to our commerce a field, the full development of which will realize the El Dorado. Hail to Columbia, the home of the free, from which only freedom can go out.[1]

The audience was thrilled by the polite encounter, and filed out into the night discussing it, and the next day the unheralded debate was the chief topic of conversation. Beveridge was satisfied, and wrote Perkins he had never delivered any speech in his life as well.[2]

Through this first phase of his public life he was obsessed entirely with his ideas of expanding trade through colonialism. In April he spoke at a banquet in Des Moines before the Grant Club on his favorite topic, declaring that the Philippines, acquired 'by conquest and purchase,' were ours forever. Civilization had imposed a duty upon us. 'We cannot hand it over to Germany, who is anxious to undertake it; we cannot deliver it to England, who is willing to undertake it; we cannot surrender it to Japan, who is eager to undertake it.' Thus we were bound by necessity to press forward. And Cuba? The Platt Amendment had temporarily settled that, and more — it had paved the way for the ultimate domination of other nations to that extent. 'No man can now deny,' he said, 'that the Republic may be suzerain whenever the interests of the American people or the peace of the world may make that form of control convenient.'[3]

It was here at Des Moines that coming events cast their shadows before. He was entertained by Governor Shaw and Senator Dolliver, and in his speech he proposed a policy of reciprocity, lest other nations pass tariff laws against us. He was not quite satisfied with the tariff policy even then.

But his interest in colonial government held him; and for weeks he had been meditating another Oriental journey to study trade methods and conditions in the Far East. His Philippines experiment had persuaded him that only through

[1] *Indianapolis Journal*, Jan. 1, 1901. [2] Beveridge to Perkins, Jan. 2, 1901.
[3] Pamphlet speech, April 27, 1901.

study on the ground could statesmanship fit itself to deal with foreign problems. Perkins, whose opinion had been asked, thought, on the whole, that he should go. It would be an expensive trip, but if Beveridge would let him 'be of some assistance in this direction,' he would be 'mighty glad to do it.' And he had added in merry mood, 'I don't see, when you come to think of it, why I should not chip in, so that when I am Secretary of State I will not be constantly feeling that my chief has never been abroad, and therefore I must know a great deal more about international subjects that come up than Bertie the lamb.' [1]

But Beveridge had other plans for financing the journey. He had written Albert Shaw that he expected to pay his way by writing magazine articles on his observations, and had talked about it with Lorimer, of the 'Saturday Evening Post.' His only source of revenue, he wrote, was in his writing, for he had determined while in the Senate he would never 'buy or sell any stocks or anything of the kind.' If English statesmen, like Lord Curzon, could write, he could find no compromising of dignity in it. It was in this letter that he explained the motive of the trip:

'I take this trip because the Oriental question is the world question from now on for the next quarter of a century.... The trade of the Orient is ours because of nearness to our Pacific coast, and it will ultimately be divided between Russia and us. European statesmen become acquainted with the situation in the lands where their government operates by personal inspection. American public men have not done so prior to my trip to the Philippines. This trip will make me easily the authority on the Orient in American public life.' [2] He proposed to visit St. Petersburg and Moscow; travel through Siberia and Manchuria, observing the Russian penetration there; and pass on to Japan, China, and the Philippines.

He was to do much more than he had planned.

[1] Perkins to Beveridge, April 20, 1901.   [2] Beveridge to Shaw, May 2, 1901.

CHAPTER IV
AN IMPERIALIST IN RUSSIA

I

BEVERIDGE was moved to make the Russian journey by his desire to understand the political and economic situation in Manchuria and the Far East, and there was another reason which
crops out continually in his narrative of his travels. He had long
been impressed with the colonizing, organizing genius of the
British, and here was a fresh race, just awakening, and faring
forth on a venture not dissimilar to ours in the Philippines. Perhaps from them we might learn.

Then, as always, he made laborious preparations for the
journey, reading dozens of books on the various phases of the
countries he would visit, consulting with the nationals of these
nations in America, and getting letters of introduction to important personages he hoped to see. Sailing from New York on
May 16, 1901, he lingered long enough in England to talk with
James Bryce, Joseph Chamberlain, and Ambassador Whitelaw
Reid, and then proceeded to Germany, where he had interviews
with Count von Bülow, the Chancellor, with Baron von Rhein-
baben, and others. While he was in Germany he was a guest on
the estate of Prince Hatzfeldt in Silesia, where he studied rural
conditions. This visit resulted in a warm friendship for the
Prince and Princess that was to continue through the years and
be renewed on his last journey to Germany.

When he reached St. Petersburg, he found Ambassador
Charlemagne Tower, with Consul-General W. R. Holloway, a
friend from home, awaiting him with the offer to facilitate his
researches through official channels. Immediately he was deep
in discussions with A. A. Ristein, the banker, on the commercial
and industrial conditions of the empire, and with M. De Witte,
Minister of Finance; Count Lamsdorf, Minister of Foreign Affairs; Prince Khilkof, Minister of Railways; and M. Pobiedonostsev, Procurator-General of the Holy Synod. He found
Lamsdorf charming with his Old-World courtesy, but it is significant of his inherent admiration for sheer relentless power that
he reserved his keenest enthusiasm for the Minister of Finance
and the Procurator-General.

At that moment Witte was at the zenith of his power and
unpopularity in reactionary circles, and much too busy to minister gladly to the idle curiosity of tourists. Even so, he dis-

cussed with Beveridge for two hours the industrial problems of the empire. The latter was profoundly impressed with the dynamic personality of the Russian statesman. 'The first thing that impresses you about Witte,' he wrote, 'is perfect simplicity.... He speaks in a low voice looking directly at you. What a steady eye! The freedom of his conversation... astonishes you. His eyes are large and brown, with an expression of patience and weariness which reminds you of what you read about the eyes of Lincoln.'

Much as he admired Witte, the great intellectual autocrat of the Russian Church, evil genius of the last of the Romanoffs, impressed him even more. The traveler has left a vivid portrait of Constantine P. Pobiedonostsev. He was found 'in a very unpretentious building which stands flush with the sidewalk,' and Beveridge entered a hall guarded by two soldiers, and mounted 'three low broad steps into another hallway or room, with lower ceiling than the first, where again two soldiers are motionless sentinels.' Thence he passed through a broad door into a large low room 'full of shadows.' He was conscious of books — hundreds of them; and then of an 'ample broad heavy desk made out of some dark wood'; and then of 'an old man whose shoulders droop with age' seated at the desk. The old man turned quickly, rose and advanced with a welcome 'in a low, pleasant voice, full of all courtesy and kindness.' The face of the grim reactionary, who blocked every liberal movement, seemed to Beveridge 'mild, even benevolent,' and the gray eyes as 'almost affectionate.' The features were 'aglow with intelligence.' The general impression made on the American was that of 'acute and profound mentality.'

The venerable reactionary made no effort to conciliate American sensibilities, but held forth contemptuously on representative government in general and against the freedom of the press. But the intense nationalism of the false adviser of the fated Nicholas was after the Senator's own heart. 'You refer to Russia as a state,' the old man said. 'No, no, Russia is no state; Russia is a world.'

A thorough Hamiltonian, wedded to the idea of a strong centralized government, and impressed with manifestations of material power, Beveridge was to find little to condemn and much to approve in the Russian system. The deep undercurrent of passionate protest from the submerged masses he appears to have missed entirely. 'I have never been impressed with the idea... that the Russian Government was destined to crumble and finally disappear, perhaps, as some writers have suggested, in a second "terror" surpassing the awful days of the French

Revolution,' he wrote at the time.[1] 'Such talk appears to me to be wild, absurd, ill-informed.' His attitude toward the Russia that even then was bounding toward revolution was precisely that of Gouverneur Morris toward the France of the Bourbons. Everywhere he saw evidence of power and authority, the raw material of immense wealth.

This point of view was scarcely one with which sympathetically to approach a pilgrimage to the home of Tolstoy, the Voice of Protest. The road leading to the philosopher's estate gave him a charming picture of rural Russia, with its gently rolling slopes and woods, and the ride was even more picturesque when his troika turned into the dirt road on the Count's estate, and continued between modest hills 'green with grass or proud with noble forests.' When he drove between two massive stone pillars at the entrance to the grounds, he noticed that one of the pillars was out of plumb; that a little pond, offering rich opportunities for loveliness, was utterly neglected; that 'the roadway had not seen gravel for a long time, and is full of furrows and ruts.' When he visited the peasant village across a ravine, some brick houses suggested 'some spurt of activity many years ago'; but everything spoke of neglect. 'Poverty, want of care, rebellion at system are visible on every side,' he thought. And as he looked upon the squalor of the estate of the friend of man, he was reminded of another peasant village on the estate of a nobleman he had visited, which was 'clean, well built, well kept, industrious, with yards and vines and fruit, and in the midst of it a schoolhouse.'

Some beggars were seated under a tree near the door of Tolstoy's house when he returned, and he observed them enter the house and emerge apparently well pleased. At length the Count appeared in the garb of a peasant, but with manners having 'a touch of the grandeur of old-time fashion.' The two men, one a philosophic anarchist having no faith in government, and the other having too much, walked together along the stately avenue of trees and talked. The old man discussed religion, America, our Philippine experiment which he abhorred, and described Witte as 'a foolish surface juggler,' and Pobiedonostsev as 'the intellectual incarnation of tyranny.' Later, when Beveridge was discussing his visit, with a lady of fashion in St. Petersburg, she said, 'Oh, yes, we all know here that Tolstoy is down on the Saviour'; and a merchant thought him 'impossible,' and said that the Russians of consequence 'pay no attention to him.'

We have the feeling that the American was glad of his assurance. He had come to learn from the Wittes, not the Tolstoys.

[1] *Saturday Evening Post*, June 9, 1900.

II

And yet there were premonitions of the Beveridge that was to emerge after a few years. He was not unmindful of the material and social status of the laborers and peasants, and with his usual thoroughness, he sought the peasant in the fields, the worker at the forge, the villager in his cabin; and before he left the capital of Nicholas, he had written David Graham Phillips that he had been 'the guest of first-class and middle-class Russian people in their homes' and had seen their life and had their views, had lunched with an officer of the Imperial Guard and had his slant, and had conversed with the extreme champions of autocracy and with men of moderate liberalism.[1] At no time, however, does he appear to have been interested in making contacts with the revolutionary element. At that time a man named Lenin was living in exile in Switzerland and meditating things not dreamed of in the philosophy of the ruling powers in Russia. But as Beveridge roamed about the cities, villages, and countryside and observed the communistic establishments everywhere, he was persuaded that 'the Russian state may be said to be at the bottom communistic.'[2] The Labor Palace in the capital, 'where tea and other refreshments were served at actual cost and free performances were given by fairly good theatrical companies,'[3] pleased him; and when in Moscow he mingled with the workers in a free amusement park and listened to the singing, he was convinced that much was being done for the working class.[4]

But his visit in Moscow to the 'human market,' where peasants seeking work offered their services, disturbed him. An open square in a congested quarter lined with vodka shops was crowded with workers of the lower class, since it was Sunday. 'Several were lying on the ground, with bundles under their heads, in the open glare of the hot sun, apparently in a state of bestial intoxication'; but he learned they were 'rugged young peasants taking a nap.'[5] Even so, he had been told that here he would see the Russian peasant and laborer at their worst. Learning that their language was shocking, if properly translated, and that guides ignored it, he was accompanied by a Russian friend, who spared him nothing.[6]

Thinking of Russia as a competitor for the markets of the Orient, he visited the iron and steel mills of Moscow and St. Petersburg and found the furnaces not of the latest types, and

[1] Beveridge to Phillips, June 7, 1901.
[2] *The Russian Advance*, 332.   [3] *Ibid.*, 247.   [4] *Ibid.*
[5] *Ibid.*   [6] *Ibid.*, 275.

the Russian workmen 'slow compared to our American workingmen, and stupid, though industrious and strong.'[1] But it
was the country, with its brooding mediævalism, that fascinated him most. Within sight of Moscow the spectacle of a
peasant, plowing with the kind of wooden implement used by his
ancestors in the days of the Tartar subjugation, startled him.
It seemed to him like the fifteenth century 'at work in the early
dawn of the twentieth.'[2] Riding over the vast estate of a count
he visited, he was astonished at the number of crude factories in
remote fields, worked by the peasants in winter; and the deference of the peasants did not seem to partake of the servile spirit.[3]

Thus, peering into the huts of peasants, rummaging in book-
stores to learn the reading taste of the people, studying the
newspapers and magazines with the aid of a translator to note
and get the trend of opinion, visiting the law courts to observe
the course of justice, he missed no detail of Russian life that was
open to him.

But nothing made a deeper impression upon him than the
deep religious nature of the people. One day he stationed himself
beside an icon on a street in St. Petersburg to note the effect on
the people passing. A poor and humble mujik passed. 'Off goes
his cap; his body reverentially bows; his lips move; meanwhile
he makes the Russian sign of the cross with his hand. A merchant passes. Off goes the merchant's cap, and he does exactly
as did the mujik.' A woman 'of good condition' passes, and is
even more reverential than the others. Then the clatter of
horses' hoofs, and 'a carriage comes along bearing an officer...
a man of high rank too... going to an audience of some kind
or other, for he wears certain orders, which his unbuttoned great
overcoat, flying back, reveals on his breast'; and 'with hardly
slackening speed, the officer and his coachman alike perform
precisely the poor mujik's obeisance, mutter apparently the same
reverent words, make precisely the same holy sign.'[4] It was in
the Cathedral of the Kremlin that he was most deeply moved as
he stood with noble and peasant, banker and worker, 'in the
very room where for centuries the monarchs had been crowned.'
This scene in the Kremlin interpreted Holy Russia to him as he
thought nothing else could.

Driving through the country, he passed a religious procession,
with men and women running through the fields to join it, with
a yellow-haired youth, trousers in his boots, bearing a banner
with a picture of a saint, his eyes lifted to it, his lips murmuring
an appeal.[5]

[1] *The Russian Advance*, 279.   [2] *Ibid.*, 333.   [3] *Ibid.*, 334.
[4] *Ibid.*, 339–40.   [5] *Ibid.*, 344.

This fervent faith he was to find, too, in Manchuria and Siberia.

III

When he turned toward Siberia, it was with none of the pre-conceived ideas of horrors to be seen, and he was to find it drab enough for the purposes of the ordinary tourist. It was the raw-ness of it and its vast possibilities that awed him. The Siberia of the political prisoners interested him less than that of the immigrants — the great throngs of men and women from Euro-pean Russia, moving in communities to a land of possibilities, their transportation furnished by the Government. Picturesque they seemed to him as they floated lazily down the Shilka and Amur Rivers on rafts, or alighted from trains in an agricultural section almost virgin and as vast and rich as the valley of the Mississippi. This he could understand; it was the Kansas of the wagon caravans.[1]

To study the state of Siberian development he undertook a long and tiresome journey that led him to Irkutsk, Blagovest-chensk, Misovaia, Sretensk, Nikolsk, Vladivostok. At Irkutsk, a thousand miles from Moscow or Pekin, in the very heart of Siberia, he was astonished to find a museum for the study of the sciences, churches of various sects, theaters not much unlike our own. He went into the stores, made an inventory of their stock, and found almost anything to be had in an American depart-ment store. He noticed many Germans there, and that piqued him. Here was something to remember — Germany's peaceable penetration of Russia for purposes of trade. At Blagovestchensk, nearly two thousand miles from Irkutsk, and almost as far from Vladivostok, he priced threshing machines, plows, and other agricultural implements of American make, and this pleased him. He was studying Russia as a potential American market, and here was evidence of the possibilities.

Thence on he pressed to Misovaia, to find Siberia at its worst, 'the abode of assassination and skulking robbery,' where his intended promenade through a purple twilight was interrupted by the warning of his guide. On now to Sretensk, three days by rail, a typical Cossack settlement with no evidence of progress, the houses 'wooden and filthy.' In the doorways chickens, pigs, children; in the mud on the river-bank an old woman in a coma of vodka intoxication. On, now, to Nikolsk, in the center of the grain district, where he was almost happy. It was there he at-tended a familiar circus, a fondness for which he was never to

[1] *The Russian Advance*, 217–19.

outgrow. But there was something else at Nikolsk that appealed to the American apostle of colonization and conquest. The town was not remote from Manchuria, where this was in progress, and it was full of barracks and thronged with soldiers drilling to the music of military bands. He watched the cavalry and artillery maneuvering as in actual battle, and found the spectacle worth traveling to see. Thence on to Vladivostok, a place of 'surpassing loveliness' with its well-paved streets, well-built docks, and one of the largest and finest drydocks in the world. Here he studied trade trends in the stores, and attended a light opera such as one might see in Berlin or Moscow. The audience pleased him — the white coats of the Cossack officials everywhere, the uniformed Cossack Governor in the box heartily applauding.[1]

The Cossacks appealed to his imagination and his love for fighting men. One night in Trans-Baikal Siberia, while chatting with a Russian officer of high birth, the strange weird notes of a Russian peasant song came through the darkness. 'The Cossacks singing to their mother Volga,' he was told. Would he like to visit their company and listen to their war songs which the officer would translate? He found the singers seated in a circle in the darkness, poor men of the humblest station. He observed that the officer with him, 'heir of one of the noblest names in Russia, approached them with the deference and courteous bearing of equality that he would have used in a St. Petersburg ballroom.' And thus Beveridge heard them sing their war songs about the Volga being their mother, and the steppes their father, and their muskets their brothers, and their knapsacks their wives; and as the camp-fire lighted their faces, he found the officer, son of a hundred nobles, watching them with a sort of paternal pride.[2]

He saw Russia and Siberia as few tourists ever had.

IV

He was now ready to proceed into Manchuria, the real object of his journey. America, even American statesmanship, was just beginning to discover this rich domain coveted by conquerors. In a vague way Americans understood that for all practical purposes the Russians were in control of this vast rich territory, but few, even among the best-informed, had any notion as to what was being done. It was known that for some reason every cabinet in Europe was anxiously observing the Manchurian experiment; that Japan, which, after her victory over China, had been expelled through some maneuver of the Western

---

[1] *The Russian Advance*, 250.   [2] *Ibid.*, 135–36.

Powers, was looking on with jealous, covetous eyes; that the mastery of this great domain might easily unlock the treasure-house of Chinese trade. Infinitely more was involved than building the Russian railroad to Port Arthur from Siberia; nothing less, perhaps, than the commercial domination of the Far East. It was the specter of 'a gray-clad, militant figure standing on the frozen shores' of the Pacific that had drawn Beveridge to Manchuria. Years before, as we have seen, he had looked to the Orient for America's future markets. He wanted to see for himself what other nations were doing there; what opportunities of ours were being wasted; what Russia was planning in that quarter; and how that autocratic nation was dealing with 'inferior peoples.' This last would be of value to us in the Philippines.

From the time of the Boxer Movement, Manchuria had been closed to the world. At this time one might enter a vestibuled train at Port Arthur and pass through to Siberia, but it does not appear that many attempted to do more.[1] Only a little while before Beveridge set forth, an English officer, attempting a tour of inspection, had been arrested and sent back. 'The lone gray figure on the frozen shores of the ocean' was guarding his secret well. But Beveridge had no difficulty. He had made a plain, blunt statement of his plans to the proper minister in St. Petersburg and had been 'accorded unqualified and absolute liberty to see what was to be seen, and to hear what was being said in Manchuria itself.'[2] As far as he could learn there was no seal of any sort upon his lips, no prohibition on his pen, for he was planning to write his story for a magazine. No one suggested a guard of Cossacks; no authority advised any particular route of travel; every imaginable barrier was let down.

Traveling by train to the Manchurian frontier from Nikolsk, he found himself with a motley company — soldiers, Chinese, Koreans, some women, three well-dressed men not Russians. Finally the train stopped where there was no station, a lonely spot surrounded by hills looming like mountains in the moonlight, and all, not authorized to enter, were ordered off, and the protests of the men and the pleas and tears of the women were unavailing.[3] They should have left the train at the frontier town of Grodekoff, where, under the electric light, they had seen some Chinamen fighting.[4] Beveridge was unmolested.

That which he saw aroused his enthusiasm and blurred his judgment. His mind then was obsessed with the thought of empire-building, of redeeming waste places, of subduing inferior

[1] *The Russian Advance*, 7.   [2] *Ibid.*
[3] *Ibid.*, 18–19.   [4] *Ibid.*, 17.

peoples to the will of the master nations, of maintaining order, setting up the machinery of civilization. That which Clive had done in India, Russia was attempting in Manchuria and America in the Philippines. Our problem was still unsolved; he would observe how Russia was solving hers.

All the while he was looking for American opportunities. He was to conclude that American capital was failing in its duty in the Orient; that American syndicates should be building railroads; that much would be gained by keeping our Pacific squadron in Chinese waters for the psychological effect upon the Oriental mind.[1]

In comparing the Russian and Chinese towns, he found the same justification for Russia's activities in Manchuria that he urged as ours in the Philippines. The Chinese towns were 'organized filthiness,' covered with a slime 'compounded from all the elements that might offend both sight and smell' in rainy weather. The houses were of mud, the shops of wood and earth. But the Russian towns that had sprung up were built of brick, the houses pleasing, the streets both broad and clean.[2] Russia was redeeming Manchuria for Manchurians. In Chinese towns nothing American could be found to eat; in the Russian towns he found bread made from American flour, American sugar-cured hams, American canned fruits, from the Pacific Coast. Therefore the civilizing processes of Russia were good for American trade.

Nowhere, he liked to think, was the martial note predominant. Everywhere he heard 'the thud of the axe in the forest, the thump of drill in the quarry, the grating swish of the mixing mortar, the click of mason's trowel on bricks of rapidly rising walls, the drone of the saw, and the drum of hammer from one end of Manchuria to the other.'[3] But he was more impressed with the martial note than he thought. That which he had preached for the Philippines, he found Russia had practiced in Manchuria. Explaining the so-called massacre of Kirin, he described the incident with evident approval:

Five Russian divisions entered from different points, and, sweeping all before them, converged upon Kirin. It was fire and sword and death. It was war. There was no attempt to pacify or cajole while villages were burning. While the condition of war lasted, Russia waged war; she waged a war of blood. And when she had finished, she had finished; indeed, just as everywhere Russia's task has been finished when once she had concluded a border conflict.[4]

The very language of the Philippine Notebook of two years before; and of the Philippine speeches!

[1] *The Russian Advance*, 192.   [2] *Ibid.*, 20.   [3] *Ibid.*, 23.   [4] *Ibid.*, 30.

And again:

For it is worth the attention of all men that when Russia has once inflicted her punishment, there has seldom been any recurrence of insurrection. Where Russian law and order and system have been established, they have remained, upheld, not by the bayonets of the soldiers who established them, but by the hands of the very people among whom and against whose resistance they were planted.[1]

Just as he admired Disraeli, who acquired the Suez Canal, more than Gladstone; just as he preferred Witte and Pobiedonostsev, who conquered, to Tolstoy, who did not, he was fascinated by the conquerors, military and economic, in Manchuria. The venerable Tugovitch, the engineer-in-chief of the Manchurian railroad, delighted him with his efficiency. General Grodekoff, the Governor of Eastern Siberia and Manchuria, commanded his unstinted admiration. 'Force, energy, keenness, masterfulness' — these were qualities that never failed to receive Beveridge's salute.[2] But he reserved his warmest appreciation for Admiral Alexeieff; and time, not remote, was to play him a scurvy trick because of it. This domineering personage, then in charge of Southern Manchuria and the Asiatic Russian squadron, was to be charged by history with the major blunders leading to the humiliation of Russia in the Japanese war. But Beveridge, noting his alert manner, impetuous step, found his talk the 'vocalization of force,' and predicted that 'all statesmen... who may... be called upon to meet in negotiations or otherwise Admiral Alexeieff would do well to understand that they are dealing with a master-mind.'[3] When, in a crisis, the Admiral failed to measure up to this portrait, Beveridge's ill-wishers were to make the most of it.

He saw, during his Manchurian trip, an irrepressible conflict between Russia and Japan. The latter had never forgiven Russian diplomacy for bringing international pressure to bear to drive her out of China; and the permission to Russia, which speedily followed, to build a railroad to Port Arthur had only rubbed salt in the sore. But it is not true, as his enemies later were to insist, that he predicted an easy victory for Russia in the war. 'War between Russia and Japan is certain,' he wrote. 'It would be raging now if Japan had the money.'[4] He conceded that Russia might be dislodged from Manchuria by the 'sword-like bayonets of the soldiers of Japan, the warships of Japan, the siege guns of Japan.'[5] He thought the issue of such a struggle doubtful, hinging on so many elements, but predicted that it

---

[1] *The Russian Advance*, 31. [2] *Ibid.*, 58–59.
[3] *Ibid.*, 60–61. [4] *Ibid.*, 122. [5] *Ibid.*

would be a great drama, and that 'when the curtain falls upon its last desperate act, the destiny of the East, and in a certain sense the future of the world, will be forecast by the flag which flies in triumph over the carnage of that final conflict.' [1] And for such a contest he did not find that Russia was prepared. [2] The Russian soldiers he found 'tough and enduring,' but the Japanese army he thought 'as well disciplined as I have ever seen.' [3] He was prophet enough to conclude that the war would be lost or won by the navies, and he found that of Japan 'one of the best fighting naval organizations in the world.' He thought the Russian navy 'not to be sneezed at.' When the Russian fleet went down before the scathing fire of Togo, the enemies of Beveridge were to laugh heartily over a prediction he had never made. 'No opinion is here ventured,' he had written, 'as to the respective fighting powers of the Japanese and the Russian ships in a combat to the death.' [4]

V

It was the middle of August when he emerged from Manchuria and arrived in Pekin, with E. Burton Holmes, who traveled with him through the Chinese provinces. He interviewed business and political leaders in China and Japan. On September 10, his boat was hailed off Nagasaki with the tragic news that President McKinley had been assassinated. This was to have a greater effect upon his career than he suspected. He had just left the Philippines at the time. While there he had gone over much the same ground he had traversed on his first trip to the islands. It was a trying experience, associated as the first trip was with his dead wife. From Manila he wrote to Graham Phillips:

It takes all my nerve. How I need you to talk to. If duty, without a speck of ambition ever made a man do work at a place where every association makes him miserable, it is making me do this.

Of course I cannot say anything in a letter about conditions — take too long. There are, as you know, serious disturbances in three or four places. I went to San Fernando today — went through the American-taught schools, talked to children, teachers (American and Filipino both), with Filipinos I talked with two years ago, etc. It will take about a week to see all I saw then, find how they talk now, note changes, etc. That is, it will take that long the way I work, that is day and night. I must not remain long or I shall go mad.... Our withdrawal of troops was a mistake — our prestige suffered badly. [5]

[1] *The Russian Advance*, 128.   [2] *Ibid.*, 131.
[3] *Ibid.*, 144.   [4] *Ibid.*, 147.   [5] Beveridge to Phillips, Aug. 27, 1901.

Beveridge reached home October 8, after five months of hardships and dangers, returning on the same ship with Marquis Ito. He found a letter awaiting him at home from Dr. Albert Shaw, who had lunched with Roosevelt, now President, and reported that the latter was anxious to have the benefit of his observations. After finishing at the White House, he was to hurry to New York where Shaw and Perkins would be waiting 'with bulging eyes and open mouths and splitting ears for your wondrous tales of travel and adventure.'[1]

Two days later, Beveridge was in Washington dining with Roosevelt and discussing the Philippine situation with him.[2] The next day he lunched again at the White House, and returned in the evening.[3]

Meanwhile, he had planned his articles on his travels during the homeward voyage, and within a month, Albert Shaw, reading the articles on Manchuria, was writing him that they were 'magnificent.' 'They tell more about Manchuria than all the other articles and books put together that I have ever looked through.... They are like a flashlight through a dark night.'[4] That month these articles began running in the 'Saturday Evening Post' and continued until late in the spring of 1902, and through them millions of Americans discovered Manchuria for the first time.

Such was Beveridge's 'vacation' during the summer of 1901. He now turned eagerly to Washington where death had wrought a revolution.

[1] Shaw to Beveridge.   [2] *Indianapolis Journal*, Oct. 10, 1901.
[3] *Ibid.*, Oct. 11, 1901.   [4] Shaw to Beveridge, Nov. 4, 1901.

CHAPTER V

PERSONALITY AND FRIENDSHIPS

I

HERE we may profitably pause, on the threshold of the Rooseveltian days, for a more intimate view of Beveridge — then, as always, a colorful personality — and for an introduction to notable friendships that he cherished.

Though but of medium height, Beveridge's military carriage gave distinction to his appearance. He was muscularly built, with broad and powerful shoulders, but throughout his life he retained the slender figure of his youth. He walked rapidly with the sure stride of the enthusiastic pedestrian. His head was beautifully formed; his face lean and strong; his eyes, blue-gray in color, were keen, penetrating, and expressive; and his well-shaped mouth had the mobility of the natural orator. In conversation, as on the platform, he spoke rapidly, earnestly, with a pronunciation so unusual in its purity that it was not easy for a stranger to associate him with any section of the country. This was due in large measure to the meticulous training to which he subjected himself in youth in pronunciation and enunciation.

Soon after entering the Senate, he took up his residence in the Portland, on Fourteenth Street, near Thomas Circle. There, on the sixth floor, he had two rooms — a sitting-room and a bedroom. The furniture, mostly of ebony, he had picked up in Japan. Some of his friends thought the effect gloomy. A dark wood cabinet, filled with souvenirs of his visits in the Orient, did not have a brightening effect. Here for years he lived, worked, planned his battles. He was served by a colored man, known in the parlance of Washington as a 'sundown valet' — an employee of the Government who took service for the extra pay after the Government offices were closed for the day. He looked after Beveridge's rooms and clothes, but he became a heavy trial to the secretarial staff because of his habit of getting into trouble from which they were called upon to extricate him without recourse to the Senator.[1]

At no time during his senatorial career did Beveridge mingle much with the congressional social set, but such time as he could spare from his work he gave to residential society. He was an intimate in the family of Senator Elkins, whose daughter, Kath-

[1] Thomas R. Shipp to the author.

erine, was one of the belles of the capital. Frequently he was a guest at the home of Mrs. Wadsworth on Dupont Circle, who claimed and held her Thursday evenings even against the White House. And he thoroughly enjoyed his associations with the Larz Andersons and the Pinchots.

But much of his time outside the Senate and his office was spent in the Portland apartment which frequently had more the appearance of a workshop than a home. There frequently, if not usually, he prepared his speeches by dictation. His method of work was to continue into the days of his literary achievements. His secretary, summoned to his rooms, would find him with his stenographer, dictating. He would think and talk standing, pacing up and down the room. Before him on the floor in a semicircle, would be spread a great number of books and papers. 'Don't touch these,' he would say sternly; 'I know just where everything is.' And as he dictated, he would stoop and take up a book at one end of the semicircle and then dart to the other end for another. Often in the preparation of a speech he would work on until three o'clock in the morning, and at times all night. After the dictated speech had been transcribed, he would work it over and over again — frequently as many as ten times.[1] These were the speeches, delivered with infinite ease and consummate art, that many thought were spun out of his head without thought or research.

This extraordinary power of concentration and endurance was a constant source of amazement to his secretaries. Tom Shipp, the most efficient secretary he ever had, was never able to learn just when he memorized these speeches, and concluded that in the act of dictating and correcting, he became almost word perfect. He illustrated Beveridge's method to me with an interesting story. One day Justice Harlan, of the Supreme Court, called at his office with an invitation to deliver the Commencement Address before the Law School of George Washington University. Beveridge instantly accepted; but scarcely had Harlan left the room when Beveridge, overburdened by work in the Senate, turned furiously and unfairly upon his office force to demand why they had permitted him to do anything of the sort when he had no time. But at once he dictated the speech on 'The Extra-Territorial Powers of the Constitution,' and ordered it filed away. This was three weeks before the date for the delivery. A week before, Shipp reminded him of it, and was impatiently brushed aside, with dour remarks on the stupidity of his acceptance. Three days before, the alert secretary placed the manuscript on the table before him. Indignantly he was

[2] Thomas R. Shipp to the author.

ordered to put it away. The same thing happened on the morning of the day. At three o'clock in the afternoon, Beveridge rushed into the room like a cyclone. 'Now all of you people clear out!' he said sharply. 'Where is that speech?... Take the receiver off the hook.' The office force instantly disappeared. An hour and a half later they returned, and learned that Beveridge had been gone half an hour. But there was a note for Shipp. He was to call for Beveridge at the Portland with a carriage just in time to reach the hall. When Shipp reached the Portland, he found Beveridge dressed, but with his dress-coat off, seated in his shirt-sleeves before an open window, with the manuscript in one hand and the other clinched and pounding the air as the orator sought to drive the speech into his mind.

'My God!' he exclaimed, 'is it time?'

'We have just time to get there,' he was told.

Putting his coat on, he turned to Shipp: 'This is the first time, Tom, since my DePauw days that I haven't had my speech. Oh, well, if I forget parts, it will be the gain of the audience, and maybe I can make up on delivery.' Folding the manuscript, he gave it to Shipp: 'Put this in your pocket and keep out of my sight,' he said.

That night Shipp curiously followed the manuscript as Beveridge spoke, and he was amazed to find that only a word here and there was changed. The speech was a brilliant success, and the audience rose and cheered for a minute and a half.

Shipp once asked him for an explanation of his phenomenal memory. 'I have what is called the photographic memory,' he replied. 'As I speak, I see the manuscript clearly before me, each page, each paragraph and its beginning, and in my mind I literally turn the pages.'

Shipp was to witness, too, his power to shift, while speaking, from one speech to another, without betraying the transition to the audience. In one campaign he had prepared a speech on Roosevelt of which he was very proud. On the night of its delivery, Shipp sat on the stage to enjoy the triumph. Something was wrong, with the speech or the audience. When the orator rolled forth passages and awaited a demonstration, there was silence. After each failure he would turn toward Shipp with a puzzled expression. Very soon Shipp observed him shifting from this speech to another, imperceptibly to the crowd, and soon demonstration followed demonstration. After it was over, Beveridge turned to his secretary as they went away: 'Tom, that Roosevelt speech is not worth a damn.'

More or less temperamental, often irritable under pressure and impatient, his occasional outbursts were a sore trial to the staff. Once, when he had flamed up against Shipp for disregarding an order because of unforeseen events, the secretary returned to the office righteously indignant and hurt; but within a few minutes Beveridge rushed into the room, placed his hand on Shipp's shoulder, and motioning the entire force about him with the explanation, 'I want you all to hear this,' made a sweeping apology and thanked his assistant for using his own judgment. If, under irritation, he was unjust, he never failed to make amends handsomely immediately afterward. These impatient outbursts were to do him much harm among people he met infrequently and but casually. They were not about when the reaction came and they treasured a resentment.

No one understood this weakness better than Beveridge himself. One day he entered the office, sat down at the table, and printed out in large letters the word 'C–O–N–S–I–D–E–R–A–T–I–O–N.' Turning to Shipp, he said: 'Tom, this is an order. Every morning when I come down, I want you to place this on my desk so it will be the first thing I see when I come in.' Thus did he try to discipline himself to patience and justice.

Contrary to the popular idea, he invited the criticism of his tried friends. Always sensitive to the press, he once asked Shipp what the newspaper men were saying about him. 'Why, they say you flit about the Senate Chamber constantly as though you were the general manager of the Senate,' was the reply. Shipp was referring to his manner on the floor. Nervous, impatient, he found it difficult to sit quietly in his seat. He was up and down constantly, running about the Chamber to talk with this man and that, rushing into the cloakroom and out. Beveridge heard the criticism thoughtfully. The next day, Shipp was instructed to take two women to the gallery and remain until summoned by a motion to the floor. Soon Beveridge entered the Chamber quietly, nodding pleasantly to Senators, took his seat, folded his arms, and sat motionless. Shipp, noting his subdued manner, wondered if he were ill. At length he was summoned to the floor and led into the lobby. 'Was that better?' Beveridge asked. Then Shipp understood. 'It was perfect,' he said. 'Then I will do it!' said Beveridge. But never was he to be able to keep that promise to himself.

His weaknesses were in little things; in things worth while he was always big.

To all in intimate contact with him, he made no secret of his ambition for the Presidency. From the moment of his election to the Senate, it remained his goal. His close friends knew it, as we shall find. It was understood by his secretaries. In the early days he was wont to take Shipp with him on long walks in the evening, and the secretary noticed that no matter where they began they invariably ended at the White House. There they would walk around and around the grounds, and more than once Beveridge, indicating the mansion, would exclaim, 'Tom, as surely as there is a God in heaven, I will be there some day.'

It was on these night walks, too, when he was in a confiding mood, that he talked freely about his faults — as though he were passing judgment upon a third party. Always he was trying to govern his impatience. Looking up at the stars, he more than once quoted the lines of Emerson:

> 'Teach me your mood, O patient stars,
> That climb each night the ancient sky,
> And leave on space no trace, no scars,
> No sign of age, no fear to die.'

Thus, the subordinates who worked with him and suffered frequently from his outbursts of impatience came to understand him and to be devoted to him. From his intimates he held no secrets and to them he was ardently devoted. With them he was himself, with nothing concealed of his faults or virtues. No man ever had better friends, and his friendships were a precious part of his life. And on neither side did they cool. Because they meant so much to him politically and personally, it is important that a record of the more notable friendships be set forth.

II

The oldest and best-loved friend of all was David Graham Phillips. We have observed the beginnings of this tender relationship during the DePauw days when they roomed together, and the future novelist, from the window on a winter's dawn, watched the future statesman setting forth to the woods to practice oratory. It was in those days that Beveridge turned his friend's mind to writing, with the observation that if he could master the art of writing as he talked he would succeed brilliantly. When Beveridge graduated, Phillips left DePauw and finished at Princeton, and from the beginning his career was brilliant. Commencing as a reporter on the 'New York Sun,' in the days of Dana, he passed to the 'New York World' in the days of Pulitzer, who sought to train him in the great editor's theory of journalism. He wrote editorials, and for a time represented the 'World' in London. Meanwhile, he turned his attention to fiction, producing novels notable for realism and sincerity, culminating with the 'Grain of Dust' and 'Susan Lenox.' He wrote plays, some of them successful; and, passionately hating injustice and profoundly moved by the unhappy lot of the many, he became a magazine crusader against evils in our social and political life. But his genius found expression in his novels. And his was the genius of infinite pains, not unlike that of Beveridge. He had remarkable powers of concentration, and, again like Beveridge, he was a tireless worker. One of his novels was written by hand three times before he was satisfied. In his studio apartment in the National Arts Club in Gramercy Square, he worked standing at a writing-desk often through the night. Behind the plot in his stories was a profound conviction of some sort, an outraged sense of justice, a great pity. Frank Harris, in the London 'Academy,' thought him the greatest of American novelists. 'Since Balzac,' he wrote, 'no one has studied society with such a union of creative power of temperament and the critical power of the intellect.' By the time Beveridge reached the Senate, his friend's reputation had been made and his character formed. As we shall see in the letters, as we proceed, Phillips early became a militant reformer, with some radical ideas on social rights and wrongs, and these he constantly was to impress upon his friend.

Until Phillips's tragic death, the college days intimacy, confidence, mutual admiration and affection continued. Each rejoiced in the triumphs of the other; each sought to advance the other's interest. And both felt free to criticize adversely without apology. Phillips, perhaps, was the more ruthless critic. He minced no words on his friend's manuscripts. If he thought them heavy or crude, he blurted it out spasmodically; or if he thought them tending to a compromise with principle, he protested vehemently. But he was just as generous in his praise, and even through his criticism ran an undertone of tenderness. Beveridge seldom found anything but praise for Phillips's work. Occasionally, on the appearance of a new Phillips novel, Beveridge would dart into every bookstore he passed to inquire regarding the sales, and if he got a favorable report, he wrote jubilantly to his friend about it. 'How proud we ought to be of David Graham Phillips,' he wrote after the appearance of 'The Deluge.' 'How splendid to see his talent flower into genius as it is doing every year.' When 'The Master Rogue' appeared, Beveridge wrote his friend that it was infinitely stronger than 'The Golden Fleece,' though he mildly criticized: 'I can only regret that you saw fit to state the bitter side of the man of affairs. Yet I can see an excuse for that too. The book has in it such sincerity, such conviction, and, in short, it smells so thoroughly of the truth.' [1]

[1] Beveridge to Phillips, Nov. 27, 1903.

When Beveridge wrote an article not uncomplimentary to the Senate, Phillips was not pleased. 'I have read your scream on the Senate, and I'll try to answer it in two or three months,' he wrote. 'You and Tillman and La Follette might at least refrain from defending the indefensible. But after all, that is your business, not mine.'[1]

Whenever he was in New York, Beveridge was with Phillips, dining, going to the theater, or, better still, having an hilarious time in the studio apartment in Gramercy Square, with a few mutual friends. When he spoke in New York, Beveridge would hurry from the meeting to sit up until the small hours with Phillips before the fire, getting his talk out; and many times on these occasions he ended by lying down on a large couch in the living-room and sleeping the night there.

Whenever either found time from exacting labors to relax, their minds traveled to each other. Time and again Beveridge in a flood of feeling would urge his friend to join him wherever he might be. 'Come up here, Graham, I am always hungry to see you' — and he was. Nothing in the correspondence of the two throws a tenderer light on the novelist and his loneliness than the letter he wrote on the birth of Beveridge's first child. 'You get everything, don't you?... I envy you, Bev, I do — that baby.'[2] Thus the friendship was like a poem until the end when Beveridge took charge of Phillips's funeral. It had its effect on Beveridge's life. It is possible, from the correspondence, to believe that the banker's son contributed something to the progressivism of the boy of the logging-camp.

III

The friendship with John C. Shaffer, the publisher, developed, as we have seen, within a few years after Beveridge left DePauw, when he entered into the inner circle of Beveridge's friends. When Beveridge needed friends, Shaffer was as dependable as the North Star. A man of influence and substance, he was in position to advance the younger man's interest professionally and otherwise. When he moved to Chicago, the friendship persisted, and Shaffer was in the background, but active, during the spirited first contest for the Senate. He was won by Beveridge's mentality, his sincerity, industry, genius for public life, and the spirit and substance of his speeches. No blood brother could have been more obsessed by, or concerned with, Beveridge's career. The moment he entered the Senate, Shaffer began to dream of his friend in the Presidency, and it remained in

[1] Phillips to Beveridge, July 31, 1906.   [2] Phillips to Beveridge.

the foreground of his thought for thirty years. Two years after Beveridge entered the Senate, Shaffer acquired the 'Chicago Post.' 'If you want to have the honor of writing the first editorial on our "plain duty" to the Cubans for the "Post,"' he wrote, 'the opportunity is herewith offered.'[1] Later, the older man reached out into the publishing field and acquired the 'Rocky Mountain News' of Denver, the 'Indianapolis Star,' the 'Terre Haute Star,' and the 'Muncie Star.' With all the fervor of friendship all these papers were put behind the career of Beveridge.

But this did not measure the intimacy of their relations. For more than a third of a century, Beveridge appealed to the judgment of the publisher on every important act of his career. The correspondence was voluminous. It lacked the playfulness of the correspondence with some of the others of the inner circle, for Shaffer was an earnest, serious-minded man, intensely interested in the political advancement of his friend. They wrote at length on public and party questions. Only when one or the other was ill or ailing did the note of tenderness creep in, and then it never was absent. When they differed on public policy, as they sometimes did, they had it out at length; for neither liked to be at cross-purposes with the other. More than once Shaffer, wishing a portrait of his friend, asked him to sit for an artist. In more than one crisis in Beveridge's career, it was Shaffer who went to the front for him. As we proceed with the unfolding of the drama of these pages, we shall find ourselves indebted to the free exchange of opinion between these two men. Only once in this voluminous correspondence does Shaffer write in a critical spirit, and even then with affection. It was when the crisis of 1912 was approaching, and Shaffer was seeking to reconcile some of his friend's foes, that he complained of Beveridge's distaste for conciliatory methods.

For the last thirty years [he wrote], we have had an intimate relationship. During these three decades I have not only admired you, but have had a deep affection for you. Both have grown with the years. During that time I have met a great many prominent men — some prominent in business, others in politics, still others in educational work. None, however, except Mr. Roosevelt, have impressed me so strongly with their mental power, creative genius, and scholarly attainments as you. The gold coin of your realm must have some alloy in it or it would be so fine and soft that it would soon wear away. So in each life there is more or less alloy, and you are not exempt from it, nor I, nor anyone else. You are a scholar and a statesman, but, as I have studied your characteristics and achievements, it has seemed to me

[1] Shaffer to Beveridge, March 22, 1901.

that the alloy in your make-up is your lack of receptivity to suggestions or criticisms offered by others to your plans or purposes. Another place where it is in evidence is your disposition to drive your lieutenants and followers rather than attempt to persuade them to your point of view when they differ with you.[1]

Among the friends of the inner circle such frankness was not resented. The time was to come when the two friends would disagree on phases of the World War and the League of Nations and the World Court, but the friendship was to remain undiminished.

IV

Some years before either had risen above obscurity, the intimacy of Beveridge and George W. Perkins began. At the time the former was approaching the Senate, the latter was revealing his extraordinary qualities to the New York Life Insurance Company, of which he was a vice-president, by negotiating settlements with the Governments of Switzerland, Austria, and Germany. These matters had long been pending and their settlement required the genius of a diplomat. It was soon after this, when Beveridge had been in the Senate less than two years, that Perkins, as the head of the Palisade Commission, called on J. Pierpont Morgan for a contribution. As he was signing a check, the premier financier of America said casually:

'I'll give you a hundred thousand dollars a year, Perkins, if you'll move over here and take that seat.'

'Are you joking?' asked Perkins.

'Certainly not. I feel the need of an energetic young man in this office and have had my eye on you for some time.'

Nothing had impressed Morgan more than Perkins's successful negotiations in Europe, and with the Morgans he was to have much to do with international affairs. The qualities that appealed to Morgan were inherent, and it was these that appealed to Beveridge, when, as a young man, he met Perkins, no better known than himself. A keen mind, a Beveridgean energy, a Napoleonic imagination, vision, enthusiasm, he had, in business, the qualities that Beveridge dedicated to politics. The two men met when both were twenty-six, and they were mutually attracted. Each saw the other rise rapidly in his chosen field, each applauding every upward step. The time was to come when Perkins would be pictured in political circles as a ruthless champion of monopoly, but his vision reached farther into the misty field of industrial social reforms than that of any other business

[1] Shaffer to Beveridge, Jan. 3, 1912.

GEORGE W. PERKINS

man of his time. He conceived the business world as built on Men, Money, and Machinery; and felt that while inventive and financial genius had satisfactorily met the problems of the last two, too little had been done for the first. He was the first to propose profit-sharing, insurance, sick benefits, old-age pensions. As a director of the United States Steel Corporation and the International Harvester Trust, he proposed service bonuses and the granting of permission to employees to buy stock at less than market value. He pioneered the thought that such powerful corporations were public institutions and urged the publication of their reports.

These ideas had vaguely been those of Beveridge from his DePauw days, and this drew the two eager young men together. Their intimacy long antedated Beveridge's aspirations for the Senate. The moment Beveridge determined to be a candidate, he cabled Perkins in Paris. It was with Perkins he consulted on his Philippine trip; Perkins who sent him the farewell letter, and advised him to reticence on his return. It was Beveridge who scoured the shops in China and Japan for odds and ends for the Perkins house at Riverdale. It was in this house that Beveridge completed his first Senate speech on the Philippines, and Perkins who first heard it as Beveridge read it in the small hours of a winter morning. So the relation continued until the demise of the Progressive Party in 1916.

So sacred did Beveridge consider this friendship that he would never accept financial help from Perkins, even in his campaigns. We shall find proof of this as we proceed.

The correspondence of these two was as voluminous as that with Shaffer, and while much of it was serious, dealing with large matters, it was enlivened with a humorous vein, satire, bantering. Some of these letters — the letters of men worked to the limit of endurance — were as frivolous in their deliberate foolishness as those of schoolboys. The full extent of the intimacy of the two will appear as we go along.

V

None of the inner circle of Beveridge's friends influenced him more in his literary work and in oratory than Dr. Albert Shaw, editor of the 'Review of Reviews.' The friendship had an unusual beginning, being deliberately sought by Beveridge. He had been impressed with the editor through his work, and, soon after entering the Senate, Beveridge walked into Shaw's office, introduced himself, and expressed his admiration and the hope that they might be friends. From that hour the friendship began and continued until the death of the statesman. They corresponded copiously on public questions and policies. Most of Beveridge's most important speeches were submitted to Shaw's criticism, and many of his problems for Shaw's advice. Frequently he was a guest at Shaw's home, and when he was planning his battle against the packers for a meat inspection bill, he drove with Shaw through the countryside discussing the possible effect on his political fortunes. It was Shaw's conservatism in expression that impelled Beveridge, within a few years of his entrance to the Senate, to moderate the rhetorical features of his orations.

The Shaw friendship, more than that of any other of the inner circle, was valuable when Beveridge left the arena for the ivory tower and entered seriously into the writing of the 'Life of John Marshall.'

VI

The friendship with Frank A. Munsey, the publisher, began with the early Senate days. Years before, this unusual man had appeared in New York from Maine, where he had begun life as a telegrapher, with forty dollars and a shibboleth — 'Forty Dollars, Forty Years, Forty Millions.' With pitifully meager resources he launched his magazine, the 'Golden Argosy,' for children. By working eighteen hours a day, writing his own serials at night, and living leanly, while pouring all his profits into advertising and promotion, he established himself. The 'Golden Argosy' was soon 'The Argosy' for adults, and 'Munsey's Magazine' was launched and enthusiastically received, and within twelve years his magazines were earning him seventy thousand dollars a year.

That was five years before Beveridge entered the Senate.

In less than two years after, Munsey purchased the 'Washington Times.' Thenceforth he was committed to journalism, and at times he owned papers in Baltimore, Philadelphia, and Boston. He entered the New York field with the 'New York Press,' and four years later he was the proud owner of the 'New York Sun' and the 'Evening Sun.' Four years more and he had acquired the 'New York Herald.' There was a Napoleonic audacity in the manner in which this rangy Yankee disregarded sentiment and tradition in his mergers, which swept historic newspapers out of existence. Before he was through, he had reduced the number of morning papers in New York from seven to four, and the evening papers from seven to five. This was his business genius at work, seeking 'fewer and better and sounder papers.'

Meanwhile, he was deeply involved in the business field with United States Steel and other corporations, and was numbered among the very rich men of the community.

Beveridge was attracted by the Napoleonic qualities of the man, the ideals of service that inspired him, his courage and independence. Munsey, who made intimates cautiously, was fascinated by Beveridge's romantic rise and his intense nationalism. Both were serious-minded. Soon they were very close. While the man in the street thought of the journalist as a money-maker, interested solely in the counting-room of his paper, Beveridge thought of him as the directing mind of a great newspaper. They met frequently, spent hours together, and talked on public questions and politics, not on money. They had common habits of industry. When Munsey was asked his favorite recreation, he replied, 'Hard work.' Beveridge could understand the type. And Munsey warmed to the statesman who thought so passionately in terms of nationalism. Like Shaffer, he concluded early that Beveridge had the qualities for the Presidency.

When Munsey lived at Sherry's, and later, when he had apartments at the Ritz Carlton, Beveridge seldom failed to spend hours with him when in town. At the Ritz on winter evenings they would sit before the open fire and talk on public matters until three in the morning. If, because of a crowded program, Beveridge failed to call, he would receive a letter of rebuke. But as they grew older and late hours had their aftermath, they came to dread these meetings by the fire. They would agree to break up early, but they never could. There was a real affection between them. Only once did they approach a break, and that was because of Munsey's leadership of the movement for the amalgamation of the Republicans and Progressives in 1913. But as late as 1923, Munsey was writing Beveridge from Paris that he had a vision of a President which, while vague, bore a strange resemblance to his friend.

VII

With none of the inner circle did Beveridge enjoy himself more keenly than with George Horace Lorimer, for many years editor of the 'Saturday Evening Post.' This friendship had its origin in a professional relationship. When Beveridge returned from the Philippines, Lorimer, but a short time in the editor's chair, went to Washington to persuade him to write a series of articles for the 'Post.' From that time on, intermittently until Beveridge's death, he continued as a contributor. Lorimer found him a sore trial at times because of the frequency of his revisions, even after his articles had been set in type. Their correspondence was not so rich as that of Beveridge with others, for the editor was too busy for lengthy letters. Though brief, his were seldom without wit or satire. But whenever Beveridge was in Philadelphia or within easy reach, he would spend the night at his friend's place twelve miles from town; and when utterly weary, he would make a special trip to laugh it off with Lorimer. We are indebted to the initiative of Lorimer for the fragmentary autobiography of Beveridge's early years, which was abandoned. The latter was impressed by the dynamic qualities of the editor, his rare capacity for sensing the public wants, his unusual combination of business acumen and taste.

Another of Beveridge's editorial friendships was with Joseph Sears, which began when the latter, then with the Harpers, was seeing Beveridge's first book on Russia through the press. This relationship was mostly social, and the Sears home at Oyster Bay was also a favorite playground.

VIII

In the early days in the Senate, Beveridge and Charles G. Dawes were warm friends. Their friendship had its beginning in Chicago at a much earlier date. Both were keenly ambitious, reeking with plans, and eager to talk about them. It was Beveridge who introduced Dawes to Perkins, and the trio frequently met at Perkins's house in Riverdale. The latter was as ambitious as the others, and just as keen about his plans. 'Any two of the three,' writes Dawes, 'constituted a tribunal before which the other one exploited his plans and hopes as long as they were willing to listen. I remember Mrs. George W. Perkins approaching us one evening when the three of us were gathered in strenuous conversation on the porch at the Riverdale home, and saying, "Which one of you is talking about himself now?"'[1]

In his enthusiasm about his friends, it was inconceivable to Beveridge that any one of them should not be drawn to another. It was his custom, when planning a visit to New York, to telegraph them all to meet him, and it was unknown to him that some of them never would have met but for their common attachment to him. These meetings were talk-fests, bubbling with enthusiasm, and, with Beveridge and Perkins present, these usually held the floor. When it was Beveridge and Roosevelt, then came the tug of war. Both were teeming with ideas and wanted to express them, but Roosevelt, being the President, had the advantage. When Roosevelt got the floor, Beveridge

[1] Dawes to the author, Nov. 27, 1930.

had to grind his teeth in impatience. But when Beveridge was in a flood of talk, Roosevelt would sternly exclaim: 'Wait a minute, Beveridge! Sit down! Let me talk!' [1]

In the company of his friends, Beveridge had no reticences. Everything he thought and felt came out. Nowhere was he more warmly welcomed than at Riverdale, which for many years was as a second home. There he sometimes went, not only for the joys of companionship, but for seclusion when he had a speech to write. We have seen how he ordered the master of the house out of the room when he broke in on his guest in the throes of composition. One night Beveridge and Sears spent the night at Riverdale. They stayed up far into the night in the billiard-room, and there was a fusillade of talk, with Beveridge walking about the room, pausing now and then to emphasize a point by pounding the table with his fist. Partly serious, partly in merry mood, he parceled out the appointments he would give his friends when he was President. Perkins looked on awhile with a satirical smile, but soon he was caught in the sweep of the enthusiasm and was pounding the table too. Even Sears found the enthusiasm contagious. The incident gives us a picture of Beveridge's social sessions with his intimate friends. [2]

Working always under pressure, with speaking engagements just ahead, Beveridge continued his work at odd moments at the homes of his friends. One day, when a guest of Sears at Oyster Bay, the host returned to the house to find his guest out. Learning that he had gone for a walk in the direction of the chestnut woods, Sears started in pursuit. As he approached the woods, he heard an earnest voice and concluded someone was having a row. At length he came in sight of Beveridge, walking up and down, apparently making a speech, using his arm for emphasis. 'For Heaven's sake, Beveridge,' he exclaimed, 'stop that! Someone will have you pinched.' 'Hush,' said Beveridge, 'don't interrupt me now.' Then Sears noticed a young woman sitting on a stump taking notes and knew his guest was dictating a speech. He had sent to the Village for a stenographer and was taking advantage of an idle moment. When he had finished the passage that had been interrupted, he laughingly explained that he could think better in the open and that dictating outdoors was good for the voice. [3]

Among his friends with whom he stayed it was understood just what he wished for breakfast. There had to be poached eggs — and poached with cream. The Lorimers never failed him. But one night he stayed with Sears, and the host, going downstairs in the early morning, heard Beveridge's voice in the

[1] Sears to the author.   [2] *Ibid.*   [3] *Ibid.*

kitchen. There he found Beveridge in very earnest conversation with the cook, who clearly was intimidated by the earnest manner of the speaker. 'What — you don't know how to poach eggs?' he was saying. 'You use cream! Got any cream? That is what makes a poached egg.' Sears motioned him out of the kitchen. 'Better be careful with that cook,' he warned, 'she might leave.' 'She ought to leave!' snorted Beveridge. 'Doesn't know how to cook eggs! What a cook!' A little later, he returned to the kitchen and poached the eggs as he would have them.

Thus his intimate friends knew a very human, Johnsonian Beveridge, and loved him.

As we proceed, we shall find this Beveridge quite as human, impetuous, enthusiastic in public life as he was in the inner circle of his friends. And we shall find these friends zealous in their devotion to him.

CHAPTER VI

DRAMA AND MELODRAMA

I

BEVERIDGE returned to a Washington that was throbbing with expectation and change. The death of McKinley ushered in a new era and completely changed the complexion of politics. However cordial the relations of McKinley and the young Senator, the former belonged to the old régime, the latter to one just coming on. The dead President had risen to power through the conventional processes of congressional influence and association, and it is probable he looked with some amazement upon a young man who, in one long stride, passed from private life to the Senate. Calm, patient, compromising, preferring concessions to a fight, he was the very antithesis of Beveridge, with the uncompromising impatience of youth. And then, too, in the unfortunate conflict that was rapidly developing between the two Indiana Senators, there were reasons that would have arrayed him on the side of Fairbanks, who had been one of the sponsors of his nomination and chairman of the convention that named him.

The magnetic, dynamic, unconventional, swashbuckling Roosevelt, with none too much reverence for traditions in politics, had ridden into the White House on his Rough Rider charger. He had been nominated for the Vice-Presidency for two well-understood reasons — one to give a speedy burial to his vaulting ambitions, and the other to prevent him from blocking the exploiting scheme of great corporations from the gubernatorial office. His enemies, and Fate, had played into his hands. And as he took up the reins of government there was no little apprehension among the groups that long had dominated the affairs of the Nation. Brilliant, volatile, pugnacious, he was viewed with sincere alarm.

To Beveridge, the change was pleasing. He had much in common with the new chief in temperament. Both were brilliant and eager for real public service; both were fighters; neither was awed by precedent. When for the first time they met at Oyster Bay, one Sunday afternoon, they found much in each other to admire, and Roosevelt had urged on Lodge the new Senator's immediate appointment to the Committee on Foreign Relations. Later, in the campaign of 1900, they had found much more in common on the horseback ride through the environs of Kansas

City. They were prepared to get along when, on his return from Russia and the Philippines, Beveridge, on invitation, called at the White House. Outwardly there was to be a momentary lull, but the masterful man in power was chafing at the bit during the period decency demanded for mourning. All over the country, there was an air of expectancy.

When, on the visit at the White House, the President suggested that they ride together occasionally, since both were equestrians, Beveridge put upon Perkins the responsibility of selecting 'an excellent and fine-looking horse.'[1] At the same time he was writing Shaffer to find him a German valet to care for his rooms at the Portland and look after his clothes,[2] and a week later one was found.

The gloom that had rested upon him like a pall was lifting. The puerile hazing of the Senate was now forgotten, or, in the light of after events, now seemed inconsequential. He was still the object of criticism, but the Washington correspondents who indulged in it were tempering it with praise. Sam Blythe, of the 'New York World,' was merciless in his sarcasm and satire, but he found his victim 'a good sport,' and, after quarreling violently with him, became his friend.[3] But when the graybeards of the Senate conceded the fundamental soundness and strength of the young Solon, and made him a member of the important Steering Committee to determine the course of legislation, his senatorial future seemed secure. Within two years he was sitting with such veterans as Allison, Hale, Aldrich, Spooner, Cullom, Hanna, and Lodge in the forming of the legislative program, and this definitely fixed his status as a party leader.

Throughout the winter and spring he was writing his Russian articles, which were being carefully read by his colleagues, and his rare friendship with Platt of Connecticut was ripening. It was the Manchurian articles that won him, and he was warmly recommending them to friends. The venerable Frye of Maine told Senator Hale that they were 'second only to Parkman.' When an English paper in Shanghai, owned and edited by British subjects, attacked the Russian articles, Beveridge was more pleased than otherwise. The English 'bitterly resent anything said that may be favorable to Russia,' he wrote Perkins.[4] Lorimer, who had found him a valuable contributor, requested an article on Perkins, whose spectacular ascent in the financial field was creating a vast curiosity as to his personality, but Albert Shaw advised against it, 'on the ground that your friendship with Perkins is of such a character that you shouldn't even in the

[1] Beveridge to Perkins, Nov. 11, 1901.　　[2] Beveridge to Shaffer, Nov. 7, 1901.
[3] Blythe to the author.　　[4] Beveridge to Perkins, Jan. 19, 1902.

smallest degree... exploit your intimacy.' This but confirmed Beveridge in his own impression and he declined.[1]

It was at this time, too, that his personal friendship with William Allen White began, growing out of the reading of his 'marvelous article' on Platt of New York, and of his book, 'Stratagems and Spoils.' 'I was so captivated,' he wrote Lorimer, 'that I immediately sat down and wrote him a letter of appreciation.' Why should not White displace Senator Harris, the Populist, the next year? Why should not Lorimer take it up personally with White, and push it? 'If I ever get to know him in a personal way, I shall jab him fuller of this with the hypodermic syringe of suggestion than the cocaine fiend fills himself with dope.' Out of this correspondence of White and Beveridge grew a friendship that never failed.

II

That winter, a dramatic and bitter controversy over the appointment of a Federal Judge in Indiana accentuated the differences between the two Senators from that State. The contest involved the political prestige of both, but it meant much more to the younger man. As we have seen, Judge John H. Baker, of the Federal Court in Indianapolis, had been more father than friend to him in the days of his early struggles in Indianapolis. He had been taken into the Baker home and treated like a son. In his race for the Senate, the jurist's son, Francis E. Baker, had shared his father's warm partiality and participated actively and effectively. It was the father's dearest wish to see the son upon the bench, and when a vacancy occurred, Beveridge rushed to the opportunity. Every effort was made to persuade Senator Fairbanks to join in the recommendation, but without success. Meanwhile, the exploitation of the controversy by the press involved the prestige of both men. The ugly specter of party faction loomed threateningly, and the fight intensified. When Shaffer, seeking harmony, urged Beveridge to get along with his colleague, a hot reply was sent. 'I have done everything under Heaven,' Beveridge replied, 'much more than I have ever heard of any other man doing.... There is only one way that I can meet your views in regard to agreeing with Fairbanks and that is to resign.... I will say that I do not think it is the fault of Fairbanks either, but that it is the fault of interested parties and of newspaper men.'[2]

The fight waxed warm when charges that Baker was opposed to the foreign policies of the country were made to Roosevelt,

[1] Shaw to Beveridge, April 21, 1902.   [2] Beveridge to Shaffer, Nov. 7, 1901.

and men who knew better were hurried to the President and Attorney-General Knox, and easily convinced them.[2] Thoroughly aroused, Beveridge bombarded the White House with letters from such men of outstanding importance as Judge Elbridge Gerry. It was soon evident that Fairbanks was fighting a losing battle, for both Roosevelt and Knox were friends of his colleague and in sympathy with his motive, and Rothschild was sure Fairbanks would have surrendered long before but for 'the feeling of loss of prestige in Indiana.'[2] But the struggle continued for months afterwards, and it was not until the middle of January that the nomination was confirmed by the Senate.

The after-effects might have been less disastrous to the relations of the two Senators but for the mysterious manner in which a personal letter of Beveridge's, rejoicing over his triumph, fell into the hands of his colleague. It was a chatty letter to the wife of an intimate friend (Horace Bennett) addressed on a Senate envelope without the frank or a stamp; and the Senate post-office, guessing at the identity of the sender, sent it to the Fairbanks office. There it was read and a copy made, and later carried by Senator Fairbanks to Roosevelt with the evident expectation that it would be damaging to the writer. The effect was otherwise, and Beveridge was notified of the incident by the White House.

There never had been friendly relations between the two Senators, and after this the antipathy grew stronger. The momentary superficial effect of the episode was to increase the prestige of the younger man. He, and not Fairbanks, was now the White House favorite. The tables had been turned by the shot at Buffalo.

III

Throughout the session, Beveridge maintained his 'flash of silence' in the Senate, but he made two notable speeches outside which marked a definite departure from his previous style. His Washington Birthday Address before the Union League Club in Chicago, prepared with scrupulous care, was a comprehensive survey of the Nation's pending problems at home and abroad and a plea for discipline and foresight. The manuscript was submitted to Albert Shaw with a request for brutally frank criticism. The result was a moderating of the tone. Why suggest our 'monopoly' of Oriental trade? asked the critic. 'Isn't monopoly too big a word?' And why use the word 'never' in reference to

---

[1] Rothschild to Beveridge, Nov. 22, 1901.   [2] *Ibid.*

our withdrawal from the Philippines? 'Never is a very long time, you know. George III said "never," but here we are. Isn't it possible that we may take the greatest pleasure a hundred years hence in setting up a Philippine Republic?'[1] Beveridge acted on most of the suggestions, but clung to 'never.' 'I believe it to be true that a people of our blood never leave a land they have once occupied.'[2]

The speech was a success, and James J. Hill, the railroad magnate, to whom the eager Perkins sent a copy, wrote the latter that 'it contains perfectly sound and practical advice, and is expressed in language that has a strong flavor of Carlyle.' He had not read anything that was better or more to the point.[3]

But it was on his State Convention speech that Beveridge was staking most. In the Middle West, where the sentiment ran strongly against trusts and monopolies, he determined to defend industrial combinations. To Perkins he appealed for data on the prices of steel girders and beams used in building years before, and then. 'Any other facts showing increased services, better materials, cheaper prices, larger employment of labor, and generally the benefits, to the producer and the Nation, of the corporations, instead of the various mills which operated separately, will be of value,' he added. Shaw, who read the manuscript, was pleased by the absence of flamboyancy and colorful rhetoric, for no one of the critics whose judgment influenced Beveridge had done more to discourage decoration, 'eloquence,' and 'flights.' 'Your last two pages,' wrote Shaw, 'must be tolerated because they are intended for momentary effect upon your audience. They will sound much better than they will ever look in print.'[4] 'You are right,' Beveridge replied. 'This is a State Convention and I have already so thoroughly pared down the speech that very little opportunity is left for "enthusiasm."'[5] But to Rothschild, the more sober, compact, simple style was not so pleasing. 'I believe,' he had written, 'your speech should be on the enthusiastic order — not epigrammatic — but one of those short, terse, clear sentence speeches of yours.'[6] It was in reply to this that Beveridge formally took leave of his old oratorical manner and method.

Concerning the speech, I do not agree with you. I think that the speech should not be in any sense a rabble-rouser. I think it should be a speech of reason and instruction. Further, I think it should be exhaustive — one that will be read, and read over again. I have about completed the draft of it, and I suspect you will find it quite common-

---

[1] Shaw to Beveridge, Feb. 11, 1902.   [2] Beveridge to Shaw, Feb. 12, 1902.
[3] Perkins to Beveridge, Feb. 26, 1902.   [4] Shaw to Beveridge, April 9, 1902.
[5] Beveridge to Shaw, April 12, 1902.   [6] Rothschild to Beveridge, March 25, 1902.

place. It appears to me, however, that the period of my life of the spell-binding speech, the 'great cheers' speech, and the 'touch to tears' speech is over.[1]

The 'Baron' was far too faithful to find fault; and in commending him for his acquiescence, Beveridge wrote:

As to catching the crowd: You will observe that my tendency for the last two years has been steadily toward simplicity of style and the elimination of mere phrase. I must keep on at that. The day of the other things has gone by for me.[2]

But he was to be less embarrassed over the problem of style than by the danger that before delivery his defense of trusts would be reduced to absurdity by the greed of these combinations. He had predicated his defense on the theory that industrial combinations, by reducing the cost of production, would decrease the price of the products; and that no swinish greed would take the benefits and penalize the public by increasing costs. The enemies of the trusts were saying that, whenever these new combinations broke competition down, they would exact the utmost penny from the consumers; and Beveridge was replying that business men were too intelligent, public-spirited, and just. But scarcely had the speech been put in type when the beef trust greedily increased the price of meat. How could the speech be delivered to people thus gouged? Indignantly he wrote to Perkins:

The idiotic operations of the beef trust in unjustly and arbitrarily raising prices is causing, and very justly, indignation throughout the country. It gives demagogues an unjust opportunity to answer my arguments. Cannot you bring these foolish persons to terms? I am aware that you have your hands full, but it seems to me that the general policy which I understand trusts are pursuing — the best possible service, the cheapest possible rates to the people — you can do nothing better than to see these people and give them a little sense.[3]

However embarrassed, he persisted in his purpose, and delivered the speech to an approving convention. Hundreds of thousands of copies were distributed, and the State Committees in Idaho and Oregon made it a campaign document. The demand for the speech almost equaled that for the speech on the Philippines.[4] Trusts and combinations, he insisted, were but meeting the needs of the time; making for greater efficiency, greater employment, better wages. Evils? Yes — his mind on the beef trust — but these would be cured by national supervision.

[1] Beveridge to Rothschild, March 26, 1902.
[2] Beveridge to Rothschild, April 7, 1902.
[3] Beveridge to Perkins, April 8, 1902.   [4] Beveridge to Perkins, May 1, 1902.

The Sherman Anti-Trust Law was dead — archaic. The Nation's problem was our growing surplus, and this called for markets; and our expansion in the Far East holds the key to these. Corruption in the mail frauds of Cuba? Well, Neely was in prison. And the brutality of American soldiers in the Philippines? This was slander. Had he not listened to the evidence and seen the charge crumble before the questions of inquisitors?

IV

For Beveridge sat as a member of the investigating committee in the rôle of attorney for the defense for many days, crossing swords with the fiery and brilliant Carmack of Tennessee, the able Culberson of Texas, and Patterson of Colorado.

Serious charges concerning the conduct of the troops had been reaching the press, with former soldiers standing sponsor. Tales were told of the wanton burning of Filipino villages, the murder of prisoners, the raping of native women, the torture of the 'water cure.' Songs and ditties, brought back from the islands, gave color to the rumors, and the very children in American schools were singing one of these with special gusto:

> 'Damn, damn, damn the Filipino.
> Underneath the starry flag,
> Civilize them with a Krag.'

When it was reported that the 'water cure,' consisting of prying the victim's mouth open and pouring water down his throat until he was in agony or on the point of suffocation, had become a favorite torture of the troops, and especially of their Macabebe scouts; when it was charged that a soldier, under the immediate command of General Frederick Funston, had helped administer the torture to one hundred and sixty natives, with fatal results to twenty-six, an investigation was ordered by the Senate. Funston had written Elihu Root, Secretary of War, that the charge was a lie, though 'occasionally the Macabebe scouts, when not under the direct control of an officer, would resort to this means of obtaining information.' [1]

The hearings before the committee began in January and continued until in June. An imposing company of witnesses passed in procession — Taft the Governor-General, Admiral Dewey, Generals MacArthur, Otis, and Hughes. Henry Cabot Lodge, presiding as chairman of the Philippines Committee, took but a scant part in the questioning, and the burden of the defense fell upon Beveridge, who alone was familiar with the scenes of the

[1] Senate Doc. 205, Part I, 57th Cong. 1st session.

outrages charged. There were enough of these to whet the appetite of the Democratic members for more, and Carmack, Patterson, and Culberson were vigorous and resourceful prosecutors. The army was on trial. Beveridge was its attorney. The tongues of the three Democrats were sharp, and there were frequent acidic exchanges. When Beveridge persisted in interrupting the questioning of the Democrats, Patterson declared that were he an attorney in court he would be fined for contempt and sent to jail.[1] But the court in this instance was Henry Cabot Lodge, there were no rules of evidence, and the duel of wits was frankly partisan.

Taft was a good-natured witness seeking no party advantage, and Beveridge frequently forced him to statements that could be used in the defense before the people. At times the Governor-General admitted ignorance, with the comment that Beveridge had been on the ground and knew some particular point better than he.[2] At times they disagreed. When Taft spoke favorably of a popular assembly, Beveridge asked if 'the experience in Hawaii inspired him with very brilliant prospects.' At times the huge man in the witness chair was forced to sit back as a spectator of the sword-play of the Senators. Apropos of the theory that the insurgents could be put down by drastic measures and then conciliated by kindness, Patterson said:

I have heard it illustrated in this way, Governor: Take a wild horse; use the spur, use the quirt, and use the snaffle to conquer him, and then keep him in subjection by kindness. You pat him on the neck, you stroke his coat, and you call him kind names, and do things of that sort.

Senator Allison — You have heard this particular situation illustrated that way?

Patterson — I have heard the affair in the Philippines illustrated that way.

Beveridge — Did you go on and say that they gave that horse oats and all that?

Patterson — Oh, yes.

Beveridge — And that he had an excellent stable and good treatment?

Carmack — Treated him like a horse in every respect.

Beveridge — That is your theory?

Patterson — That if the Filipinos were horses, they would be in no danger, by reason of the treatment they are receiving, of their ever again bucking against the American Government.

Taft — I hope I am not to be asked to furnish the committee with metaphors for either side.[3]

It was when the soldiers with their charges began to file be-

[1] Senate Doc. 331, Part I, 57th Cong., 1st session.
[2] *Ibid.*, Part I, 78.   [3] *Ibid.*, Part I, 297.

fore the committee that public interest perked up. It was soon clear that the charge of using the water cure would have to be conceded; that the defense that this was the work of native scouts when alone would have to be abandoned. The testimony was conclusive. Beveridge, therefore, interested himself in making the best of a bad situation. Did anyone die under the treatment? he asked. None did. Were they able to walk away afterward? They were. Were the prisoners treated well and well fed? They were. When sick or wounded, were they treated precisely as American soldiers? They were. Thus each damaging witness was subjected to this unvarying bombardment of questions.[1]

The charges of rape and the burning of entire villages he found more difficult to manage, and sometimes he was driven to take a harsh military position. Had not soldiers been fired upon from some of those houses containing women and children? And under the rules of war, was not the firing of the town permissible?[2] There were numerous embarrassing moments for the defenders of imperialism; and when one witness jauntily testified to an imaginary order to take no prisoners in battle, to the raping of a beautiful native by four American officers, to the use of dum-dum bullets by the American army, to the deliberate desecration of a church, Beveridge fell upon him with cold, relentless fury in a fiery cross-examination. Under his red-hot probing, the witness weakened, and one by one his charges were utterly discredited. If the most damaging witness of the many weeks of hearings was utterly destroyed, it was due solely to the searching cross-examination of Beveridge.

One thing had been established — that American soldiers in isolated cases did torture with the water cure; and one other, that soldiers were sometimes as careless with their fire in the Filipino villages as Sherman was on his march to the sea. But the honor of the army, as an army, had been vindicated.

In the bitter debate that followed in the Senate, Beveridge continued to lead for his party, denouncing the anti-imperialists for featuring isolated cases of brutality as the rule. When the charge was made that his Philippine speech had fanned the flames of insurrection, he called upon the army, in letters to Generals MacArthur, Hughes, and Otis, to confute it; and they responded that the Beveridge speech had not been circulated among the insurgents, who had, however, built high hopes on a Bryan victory in 1900.

[1] Senate Doc. 331, Hughes, Part I, 650; Hallock, Part II, 1984; Evans, Part II, 2063; Richard Hughes, Part II, 2241.
[2] *Ibid.*, Part II, 2904–05.

The officers of the army were over their heads in party politics. Then, and for years afterward, Beveridge was to be popular in army circles. The charges and hearings had shaken the equanimity of the Republican Party, and if it emerged but slightly ruffled, no little of the credit was ascribed to the one man on the committee who had been upon the ground, seen the fighting, mingled with the soldiers, and talked with the natives. But his fighting for the session was not over.

V

This session was memorable in the senatorial career of Beveridge in marking the beginning of one of the most stubborn and historic contests over the conversion of Territories into States in the history of the Union. He had not coveted the chairmanship of the Committee on Territories. It had made possible the removal of his offices from the drab Maltby Building to the Capitol, and for the moment that seemed the sole advantage. But he now found himself confronting a serious problem, involving what he thought to be the first principles of sound State-building. A bill had been rushed through the House[1] providing for the immediate admission of Oklahoma, Arizona, and New Mexico. The moment it reached the Senate, that master of finesse in management, Senator Quay, took charge and began pressing for speedy action. When it was referred to Beveridge's committee, he determined that it should stay there until he was familiar with all its ramifications and with the actual conditions in the Territories. The eagerness with which powerful corporations and conspicuous public men were demanding action piqued his curiosity and aroused his suspicions. From Albert Shaw he received a warning and the suggestion that investigation precede a favorable report upon the bill, and reminding him that Benjamin Harrison, when chairman of the committee, had made a profound study of the problems of State-making.[2]

Beveridge made it clear that he would not act precipitately in the dark, and instantly he was deluged with letters importuning him for an immediate favorable report. The tone of most of these letters was frankly partisan. The son of Oliver P. Morton, Indiana's Civil War Governor, then in Arizona, urged that the admission of that Territory would mean two more Republican Senators.[3] Another wrote that the admission of Arizona would be 'a good paying political move.' He offered an explanation for the failure of the Territory to go Republican. It was due to

[1] The Moon Bill, H.R. 12, 268.   [2] Shaw to Beveridge, Jan. 8, 1902.
[3] C. P. Morton to Beveridge, June 3, 1902.

'the apathy... of the officials of... the Santa Fé and the Southern Pacific, and the managers of the great mining corporations.' These were indifferent because of the 'very ordinary timber sent to the Legislature which was easily controlled.' There was no motive for their participation in politics, since it had 'always been easy for these corporations to get through any legislation they desired in their interest.' But with admission to statehood, involving the election of United States Senators, these corporations, ninety per cent of whose officials were Republicans, would 'arouse themselves and take an active personal interest, and put up money for needed campaign expenses' and 'control elections.'[1] Ardent partisan though he was, these letters shocked Beveridge, who replied curtly: 'I assume, of course, the matter will be decided purely on its merits.'[2]

About the same time he was reading a letter from Governor N. C. Murphy of Arizona, who wrote 'confidentially' that Arizona, admitted, would send two Republican Senators to Washington, since the 'large and influential corporations' that had taken no interest in elections would become active and these corporations were controlled by Republicans.[3] Again astounded at such an approach, Beveridge replied that he was 'quite sure... it is the desire of every member of the committee — certainly of every Republican member — to pass upon the matter purely on its merits.'

By this time Beveridge had heard enough to be suspicious of the bill; and the hectic activity of Quay, who had a personal motive, interested him most of all. He thereupon moved a postponement of action until the next session, and the motion carried in the committee by a vote of 6 to 4.

Then the storm broke. The delegate from Arizona wrote that the action taken had 'filled his cup of disappointment to overflowing.' If the bill had only been sent to the calendar 'it would have been worth thousands of votes to the Republican organizations in the territories.' It was 'passing strange' to him that the members of the Senate committee did not 'look at this matter from the standpoint of Republicans, living there. Governor Murphy, then in Washington, wrote in bitter protest.

To the cunning and resourceful Quay the day was not yet lost. He redoubled his activities, slipping about quietly, whispering in the ears of senators, planning to muster a majority to take the bill out of the possession of the committee. To Beveridge, it seemed not impossible that he might succeed. One day

[1] S. M. McCowan to Beveridge, May 26, 1902.
[2] Beveridge to McCowan, May 29, 1902.
[3] Murphy to Beveridge, May 13, 1902.

he had a conference with Quay and the Territorial representatives in the House. 'To go on with your contention,' he said, 'would be neither good management nor good politics. You are likely to alienate senators who would be with you next winter.'

The wily Quay seemingly agreed, but it was with the view to a surprise attack.[1] Four days later, Quay made his motion; Beveridge explained his reasons for delay; and Quay lost. It was not without a struggle, however. Both Quay and Beveridge had been feverishly canvassing for votes. A cable was sent to Senator Chauncey M. Depew in London asking him to release his pair with Platt of New York, who was pledged to Quay. Depew refused.[2]

It was the first hand-to-hand encounter Beveridge had had with one of the most consummate of the veteran leaders, and he had won. But it was only the beginning of the struggle, as we shall see.

VI

An actual physical encounter was all that was required to make this a real fighting session, and this, too, he was to have. He was to suffer a physical assault on the floor of the Senate. The incident grew out of a controversy between Senator Joseph W. Bailey of Texas and W. L. Penfield, Solicitor of the State Department, over the official actions of the latter in an action on contract brought by one Bielenberg against S. W. Scott, in Mexico. The case was lost by Scott in the State Court of Nuevo Leon; again in the Supreme Court of that State; again in the Federal District Court; and at the time of the incident it was pending in the Supreme Court of Mexico. Senator Bailey, interested in Scott, had insisted that the State Department intervene in his behalf. It was a dangerous intervention under the circumstances, but 'out of extraordinary deference to Senator Bailey,' instructions were sent to Ambassador Powell Clayton asking him to invoke the good offices of the Mexican Government in securing 'a most careful consideration of the case.'[3] This did not satisfy Bailey, who became embittered against Clayton, and finally against Judge Penfield upon whom and whose Department the Senator made a savage attack. The man thus denounced, an Indianian and a friend of Beveridge, at his request, prepared a memorandum on the case for Beveridge's guidance.

Senator Bailey was a remarkable man in many ways and the most impressive orator on the Democratic side. His mentality

[1] *Indianapolis Journal*, June 20, 1902.   [2] *Ibid.*, June 26, 1902.
[3] Judge Penfield's statement for the Beveridge MSS.

was far beyond the average. Physically, he was imposing. Tall, powerfully built, broad of shoulder, thick of chest, he would have stood out in any crowd because of his physical proportions. Few men had a more profound understanding of the Constitution, and no man drew greater crowds to the gallery on the announcement that he would speak. His voice was melodious as a fine organ. In temperament he was difficult, dictatorial by nature, and quick to take offense. In early life he had been embroiled in some unfortunate fighting in Mississippi and had gone to Texas, where no one dared cross him lightly. His sense of dignity was a bit pretentious.

In the course of Beveridge's speech in defense of Penfield, he referred to the Bailey speech as 'an unwarranted attack.' No one was shocked at the expression. Discussing the facts, it was merely the expression of the opinion that the facts did not warrant such an assault. But Bailey rose:

Mr. President, the Senator from Indiana, I think, upon reflection, will hardly be willing to stand here and charge me with making an unwarranted attack. I ask the Senator here and now to withdraw that insinuation.

If the Senator thinks it is an insinuation, I will withdraw the insinuation [Beveridge replied]. I make no insinuation. But my words mean what they mean. If the Senator will withdraw his words about a high official of the State Department, I will be very glad, indeed, to withdraw mine, but not until then, because I think the Senator will admit, when the ardor of debate and of advocacy is not upon him, that those words, used in reference to the Solicitor, were most unwarranted.

If the Senator from Indiana will permit me [Bailey went on], I want to say that it was far from my purpose to provoke in this Chamber an insult from any Senator. If the Senator chooses to resent what I feel it my duty to say... then that is his concern. But I want to say to him now that the statement on this floor that a Senator has made an attack upon a man whom he describes as being as honorable as the Senator himself, or anyone else, is offensive, and I think it deserves a reply that the rules of the Senate will not permit me to make here. But I want to say, and say it without any kind of passion, that neither the Senator from Indiana nor any other Senator can insult me and then require me to withdraw what I have said in the performance of my duty before he withdraws his insulting words.

Beveridge replied that the words 'unwarranted attack' were not an insult, and Bailey knew it. Meanwhile, others entered the discussion, and Bailey's attitude toward Beveridge was one of studied insult. When at one time he said a distinction had been drawn 'obvious to every Senator except the Senator from Indiana,' and Beveridge replied sharply, Bailey answered that Beveridge's opinion was not of the slightest weight with him.

'I can fathom the intelligence of every other man in the Senate Chamber, except that of the Senator from Indiana,' he continued. 'I am very glad to find the Senator beyond his depth,' Beveridge retorted, and the galleries laughed.

It was evident to all but Beveridge that Bailey was in a white heat, and when the Senate went into executive session, Bailey sat quietly in his seat. It was clear to those who knew his temperament that he was waiting for Beveridge to leave the Chamber after adjournment. The latter sat in his seat laughing and chatting with friends. At length the Texan went over to Beveridge's seat and sat down beside him and began talking in low tones.

'Beveridge, I want you to retract what you said about me today. I wanted you once to retract in open session, but I will be satisfied if you retract to me now,' he began.

'Retract what?' asked Beveridge.

'You said that I had made an unwarranted attack against Penfield, and you coupled it with a quotation from my speech, saying that any man who made an unwarranted accusation was worse than a corrupt official. Your inference was that I was worse than a corrupt official.... I want you to withdraw that insinuation and do it right now.'

'I didn't insult you,' Beveridge replied with warmth. 'I said your attack was unwarranted, and I mean it, but that was no insult.'

'Then you will withdraw the statement?' Bailey pressed, still in low tones, but with blazing eyes.

'No,' was the reply.

'Then, damn you, I will make you!'

He sprang to his feet, towering like a giant over Beveridge, a much smaller man, and it seemed to the spectators that he seized him by the throat. Beveridge said afterward that, while such was the intent, Bailey had been caught before he reached him. Beveridge sat quietly in his seat, not lifting an arm. At this juncture Senator Spooner and the doorkeeper sprang upon the Texan, Senator McComas caught him by the coat, and two or three other Senators assisted in dragging him away. Senator Bacon of Georgia led the infuriated assailant toward the cloakroom, talking with him earnestly, and Spooner tried to persuade him to apologize. Beveridge lingered in the Chamber awhile longer, calmly smoking a cigar.[1]

The incident created much discussion throughout the country, and Beveridge was warmly commended on his restraint and conduct. The correspondent of the 'New York Times' wrote

[1] *New York Times*, July 1, 1902.

that the 'prevailing view of the affair was that Senator Bailey's vanity was hurt through Mr. Beveridge's sharp thrusts and ridicule, and that he lost control of his temper and made a silly brutal exhibition of himself'; and editorially, the 'Times' said, since no one in his right senses would consider the words used by Beveridge insulting, it was 'a compliment to Mr. Bailey that more is expected of him in the way of good manners.' [1] When Shaw telegraphed his congratulations of Beveridge's 'splendid self-control' the latter replied that he had been surprised at the publicity and had thought so little of the incident that he had gone that night to the theater with Platt of Connecticut. [2] It was there he learned from reporters that he was in for more notoriety than he wished, when he was called out and told what the papers were saying. [3] Letters and telegrams of congratulation poured in upon him. John Temple Graves wrote that the whole of Georgia 'condemns the haste and temper displayed' by Bailey, while having 'the highest admiration for the intellectual qualities' of the Texan and his genius as a leader and statesman. [4]

It was left to Elbert Hubbard in the August 'Philistine' to cap the comments with a sarcastic article. 'I would rather be Beveridge who ruled his own spirit,' he concluded, 'than Bailey who fell a-cursing like a very drab — a scullion — meeting logic with blows.'

Thus Beveridge emerged from the encounter with all the laurels. He had outwitted, outmanaged Quay in a battle of wits, and prevailed over Bailey in the matter of dignity.

VII

It had been a hard session, and the moment of release found him speeding to Lake Tahoe in the Sierras for a typical Beveridgean vacation. His camp was remote from railroad, telegraph, and interviewer, but he took with him, besides a guide, his stenographer; and as he tramped the mountains felling trees, he found the time to dictate his speeches for the fall campaign. [5]

Meanwhile, the dynamic Roosevelt was disturbing the serenity of the camp of conservatism. David Graham Phillips, observing his actions from the not wholly disinterested atmosphere of New York, wrote Beveridge that 'Roosevelt is riding tremendously hard in the first quarter,' and that he would 'be blown by the time he reaches the home stretch.' The novelist

[1] *New York Times*, July 2, 1902.   [2] Beveridge to Shaw, July 4, 1902.
[3] Beveridge to John Temple Graves, July 7, 1902.
[4] Graves to Beveridge, July 3, 1902.   [5] *Indianapolis Journal*, Sept. 9, 1902.

was anxious that Beveridge 'be careful about tariffs, Philippines, and trusts,' since 'the best attitude on all debatable questions is that of a willingness to learn, not only of the people, but of the trusts.' Beveridge, he wrote, should stick to his principles. 'You are young. You can live down anything but a conviction in the public mind that your principles are not well embedded. That cost Webster the Presidency. See how much the people forgive McKinley because he was steadfast to his principle of protection, that is, to the plausible, pocket-tickling idea of "home markets and high wages." But don't forget that he lived to see the time was at hand for a "reinterpretation" of his gospel.' [1]

Toward the end of August, and in early September, Roosevelt sallied forth on a tour of New England towns, and launched his campaign for the governmental regulation of trusts. The decision in the Northern Securities Case was not to be handed down for almost two years, and no one knew what power the Government possessed. Roosevelt was demanding legislation to fix the power. 'We must get power first,' he said in Boston, 'then use that power fearlessly but with moderation, with sanity, and with self-restraint.' He was not asking for power that he might turn it against property. 'I am acting in the most conservative sense in property's interest,' he declared. 'I am advocating action to prevent anything revolutionary.'

And then came the anthracite coal strike, and the Rooseveltian gesture which did not suit the 'trustees under God.' [2] The conservatives were decidedly worried. From Perkins, Beveridge received a letter of prayerful admonition. He found 'a good many things in the political situation' he did not like. 'Meanwhile,' he wrote, 'for Heaven's sake, keep out of the public eye all you can.' It would be better to speak only 'when you are absolutely obliged to.' It was clear to Perkins that 'a great many capital mistakes have been made, and it looks as though the party was not done with them.' [3]

Whatever the views of Perkins at the time, Beveridge was in hearty accord with the idea of regulating the great corporations. Being in the Far West, he opened the campaign for his party at Ogden in Utah, spoke in San Francisco and Denver, and later in New England and West Virginia. He appeared with Hanna and Foraker in Cincinnati, and launched the Republican campaign in Michigan at Detroit, where he was introduced by Senator William Alden Smith as the successor of Roosevelt in six years.

[1] Phillips to Beveridge.
[2] Baer's expression on the function of the operators.
[3] Perkins to Beveridge, Sept. 29, 1902.

These speeches were devoted largely to the further exposition of his Philippine views, to the Oriental market, and to the trusts that he defended, albeit he urged governmental regulation. Everywhere he was received with enthusiastic acclaim, and in Indiana his campaign was the usual series of ovations.

It was at this time that Roosevelt went to Indiana, where he was joined by Beveridge at Logansport. The President was suffering from an injury to his leg that required surgical attention. Beveridge telegraphed Dr. John H. Oliver, the leading surgeon in Indianapolis, to be prepared, and he was waiting at the station there when the presidential train arrived. Roosevelt was hurried to St. Vincent Hospital where a minor operation was performed, with Beveridge in the room.[1]

Even then the popularity of Roosevelt was increasing by leaps and bounds because of his demands for legislation for regulation, and the Republicans swept the country in the congressional elections.

The moment the polls closed, Beveridge found work to do. He would take a sub-committee of the Committee on Territories to Arizona and New Mexico and investigate the statehood situation on the ground. In a few days he was off.

[1] *Indianapolis Journal*, Sept. 24, 1902.

BOOK III
ROOSEVELTIAN DAYS

CHAPTER I

A DUEL WITH QUAY

I

ALL through the campaign Beveridge was absorbed with the statehood fight, planning the battles with Quay that were inevitable. In the midst of his campaigning he was writing Albert Shaw for the names of professors at Columbia, Yale, Harvard, and Princeton who could testify before the committee concerning the aridity of the soil in the Territories and the impossibility of its sustaining a much greater population until irrigation could do its work. With the view to interesting the public in the fight, he planned to place Owen Wister, the novelist, and Remington, the artist, on the stand.[1] Anticipating a 'desperate fight,' he arranged immediately after the election to take a sub-committee to the Territories to study conditions on the ground, and he again wrote Shaw of his desire to get the testimony of Charles F. Adams, author of 'The Country We Forgot,' and Maxfield Parrish, the illustrator for the 'Century.' 'My thought is,' he explained, 'that if we can add to the prestige of the committee's visit the testimony of men whose names in literature are household words, it will greatly influence the country.'[2] He was now convinced that Democrats in the Senate would favor admission, because 'after the first senators these Territories constantly will send Democratic senators to Congress.' And Quay?

'It already appears in the record that Mr. Quay's interest... is due to Pennsylvania capital building a railroad under the direction of Mr. Andrews, who, up to four years ago, was a Pennsylvanian and a lieutenant of Mr. Quay, and was known as "Bull" Andrews; and that Senator Penrose's brother-in-law is a miner in Arizona; and if the Territories are admitted, the bonds of the road can be sold for several points higher. So far as my attitude is concerned, I shall take positively no partisan ground, dealing impartially and dispassionately with the merits of the case.'

Just as the sub-committee was about to start, Beveridge wrote Shaw that it was to be no junket trip, but serious hard work from early morning until late at night. Could Shaw lead off in the 'Review of Reviews' with a review of the facts and get them before the editor of the 'Independent'? If, in addition, the editors of the 'Christian Advocate' and the 'Outlook' could

[1] Beveridge to Shaw, Oct. 19, 1902.　　　[2] Beveridge to Shaw, Nov. 3, 1902.

be interested, 'the conservative thought of the country will be with us.'[1]

The day this letter was written the sub-committee (composed of Senators Beveridge, Dillingham, Burnham, and Heitfeld), accompanied by stenographers and interpreters, left Chicago in a private car; and when, at the first town after crossing the New Mexican border, the senators found waiting a reception committee, headed by a brass band, it was disclosed that enough receptions, fêtes, and entertainments had been planned in the Territory to consume all the time. Politely but firmly these social attentions were declined. In each community postmasters, editors, ministers, business men, and lawyers were invited to testify on commercial, agricultural, mercantile, mining, and industrial conditions. No possible detail was overlooked. On one occasion a night trip of seven hundred miles was made to save time. Thus Arizona, New Mexico, Oklahoma, and Indian Territory were thoroughly combed for essential facts. The irrepressible Rothschild, who was along with his infectious smile, was the life of the party, and became a prime favorite with the senators.[2]

On returning to Indianapolis, Beveridge found a discouraging letter from Shaw. Owen Wister knew practically nothing, but was informed it was best to travel by day because of train robberies. Remington had not been in the section for years. Parrish, interviewed by Winston Churchill, the novelist, was found to have but a superficial knowledge. The same difficulties were encountered in the case of the professors.

Reporting to Shaw on his general conclusions, Beveridge wrote that 'Arizona is a mining camp, and the bill admitting her is gerrymandered so shamefully that if the Republicans were to carry the State by ten thousand, she would still send two Democratic senators to Washington'; that New Mexico was 'in a much worse state educationally and her senators will be dictated by certain interests'; and that 'the whole thing comes down merely to this: Mr. Quay is anxious to help his old friend "Bull" Andrews to a seat in the United States Senate and also to help him sell his bonds for his new railroad down there, not yet built.'[3]

But as he turned toward Washington, Beveridge entertained no illusions as to the bitterness of the impending struggle.

[1] Beveridge to Shaw, Nov. 10, 1902.
[2] *Indianapolis Journal*, Nov. 27, 1902.
[3] Beveridge to Shaw, Nov. 29, 1902.

II

Matthew Stanley Quay was one of the most consummate and unscrupulous politicians in American history. At the time of his bitter battle with Beveridge, he was in his seventieth year and had been a member of the Senate when his young antagonist was a student of the law. Maturing politically under the régime of the Camerons, he had mastered, under the supervision of experts, the art of manipulation, proper and improper alike. A machine politician in the most unsavory sense, he was a genius in organization. He had successfully managed the Republican presidential campaign in 1888, and rumor had it that Harrison's defeat for re-election had been due in a measure to the slighting of Quay in the matter of patronage. The head of a powerful personal organization in the Republican State of Pennsylvania, he exerted an influence on public affairs that was not reflected in his senatorial status. He was not a member of the recognized Senate oligarchy. He was a free lance, quite capable of coping with any situation on his own resources.

Physically he was not impressive. He was little more than five feet, six inches in height. His large, finely moulded head gave him the appearance of distinction, and Beveridge thought it one of the 'finest' he had ever seen.[1] He had a broad, prominent brow, and his eyes were large and set far apart. One of his eyes was of the sort usually described as 'cock-eyed.' In dress he was utterly indifferent.

His sartorial indifference went well with his character as a student. Few outside his intimate circle thought of him as anything other than a rather unscrupulous type of practical politician. But no other member of the Senate had a finer library or enjoyed one more. In some far-off time he had become enamoured of the Greece of Pericles, who was his special hero. He read omnivorously and only the best literature. He loved historical discussions and had been known to keep important political leaders waiting while he finished a discussion of Pericles' career with someone well informed. It was Beveridge's conviction that he would have been 'a notable author had he turned his brilliant mind to literature instead of politics,' and that he was a man 'of astonishing intellectuality.' Years after the contest on which we are now entering, Beveridge was to say that 'he was the only man I ever knew who, in lightning rapidity of thought, accuracy of decision, fruitfulness of imagination, and other like qualities, deserved to be called by that misused word, "genius."'[2]

[1] Speech at La Porte. [2] *Ibid.*

As a political director he thought Quay 'the greatest practical politician in American history, excepting only Thomas Jefferson, and in the technique of party management he was almost superior to that wonderful general.' [1] When, on one notable occasion, there was an insurrection against his leadership in Pennsylvania, and he alighted from a train to learn for the first time from reporters that the leading business men had held a meeting to assail him, he said, in an inspirational flash, 'I appeal to the man in the blouse,' and thus had a winning slogan. When, in the same fight, he had the audacity to go into the 'Scotch counties,' where the revolt was fiercest, he faced a tumultuous audience until it quieted, and then began softly: 'We are of the same blood, ye and me,' making an effective appeal to racial kinship. And on the same evening he flashed a message over the wires — 'Across the hills and valleys of Pennsylvania, I send the burning cross of regularity.' Thus he was a master of mass psychology and a phrase-maker of real genius who knew how to reach the emotions of men.

Gentle in manner, unpretentious, soft-spoken, he awakened no prejudices. He spoke only when necessary; but when he did, he spoke a language chaste and often picturesque. Yet he was moved by intense likes and hatreds, and he made no secret of his feelings. He despised hypocrisy, but unhappily his cynic nature persuaded him that men who spoke for righteousness spoke the language of pretense.

For this weird combination of high and low, of good and bad, Beveridge had a profound admiration. He always uncovered before brilliancy or strength — even when it was misused. Such was the man he returned to Washington to face and fight.

III

Beveridge was motivated primarily by the conviction that the creation of a State concerns the Nation and not alone the Territory involved. He knew that more than one Territory with the population of a congressional district in Ohio had been hurried into the Union to gain electoral votes in some particular election or to acquire senatorial strength for some hard-pressed party measure. It had been scandalous enough in the mad-dog days of Reconstruction. Through the creation of States out of Territories with a scant population, he could see how the minority of the people of the country might dominate the legislation of the Senate. His objection to the admission of Arizona and New Mexico was based on what he thought the insufficiency of their population.

[1] Speech at LaPorte.

MATTHEW STANLEY QUAY

As the fight developed and he got beneath the surface of events, he saw sinister motives. It was clear enough that Quay was moved to herculean efforts to serve his friend 'Bull' Andrews. Though he assumed that the senatorial aspirations of the latter were involved, he was certain that his business plans were decisive in the struggle. Writing an explanation of his position to a friend, Beveridge placed special emphasis on the railroad Andrews was promoting from Santa Fé into the timber region. 'Part of this railroad is built,' he wrote, 'part graded, and the greater part surveyed, as I understand it. In a Territory, neither the Territorial Government, a county, or any municipality can go in debt over four per cent of the assessed valuation of its property. Therefore, they cannot vote subsidies to aid railroad promoters. When a Territory becomes a State, this limitation is removed. Therefore, most of the Western States, as witness Kansas, Nebraska, and others, were induced to vote enormous subsidies to build railroads and the people were saddled with wicked debts for one and even two generations.'[1] This was an ugly personal phase that could not easily be brought into the foreground of debate, but it was in Beveridge's mind all the while.

He was embarrassed by the platform pledges of both parties to admit the Territories. In the Convention of 1896, the Republican platform had favored their admission 'with due regard for the interests of the Territory and the people of the remainder of the Nation.' But in the Convention of 1900, Senator Penrose, the colleague of Quay, and Senator Foraker, a friend of his, were on the platform committee and had a straight pledge of admission substituted for the qualified promise of four years before. Constantly throughout the debate that was to follow, Quay and Foraker were to dwell with much emotion on the sanctity of a platform plank.

When the Senate convened, Beveridge submitted his report, recommending the indefinite postponement of the admission of Arizona and New Mexico and the merging of Oklahoma and Indian Territory and their admission as a State. He was not deserted by the party leaders because of the platform pledge. On the first day of the session he submitted his plan to a conference of leaders, including Aldrich, Allison, Hale, Platt of Connecticut, Cullom, Lodge, and Hanna, and received their sanction. The managerial genius of Quay shines forth in the fact that this imposing combination did not settle the question.[2]

A few days later, Quay submitted his report in favor of the

[1] Beveridge to F. P. Dunne, Jan. 11, 1903.
[2] *Indianapolis Journal*, Dec. 2, 1902.

House bill; Beveridge offered his report as an amendment, and the gage of battle was thrown. Instantly Quay began to force the fighting. The day after the Beveridge report with the testimony was ordered printed, and before a word was in type, Quay demanded an immediate vote. Beveridge protested that there could be no intelligent action until senators were in possession of the report and evidence, and he prevailed.[1]

Meanwhile, Quay, suave, subtle, tireless, was canvassing the Senate. When Beveridge inquired if he planned extended remarks, he replied that he was 'not one of the wranglers of the Senate except on very special occasions,' and added, a bit viciously, that nothing was apt to change his views 'as enunciated by the Republican National Convention, in consonance with the views of the Senator from Indiana at that time.'[2] He was ready for a vote without discussion.[3] Nothing could have seemed more ominous, since Quay was too good a general to invite an engagement before he was ready with the votes.

The debate began, but after a day it was postponed until after the Christmas recess. Writing Shaw of the progress of the fight, Beveridge said:

'We have anticipated every move the enemy have made and checkmated them.... There is some proposition on our side from Hanna, among others, to let the bill come to a vote, and if we are beaten have the President veto it. I put my foot down on this thing yesterday...; that I myself would prevent it if I had to read the Century Dictionary, the Hebrew Scriptures, and everything else in the course of the three weeks' speeches. The point is that it is neither fair nor right to put the burden on his shoulders unless we are driven to it as a last-ditch measure.'[4]

Knowing that Quay had the votes he needed, Beveridge was playing for time to permit the crystallization of public opinion. The independent magazines were lining up, and the metropolitan press — the 'New York Times,' 'Philadelphia Press,' 'Chicago Tribune,' 'Chicago Inter-Ocean,' and 'Washington Star,' were supporting his position. The 'Washington Post' was fighting with Quay and Foraker.

Then a bomb fell into the Beveridge camp.

Early in the session, without a consultation with the committee, Roosevelt had fallen into the opposition's trap and expressed satisfaction with a compromise admitting Arizona and

[1] *Congressional Record*, Dec. 11, 1902.

[2] Beveridge did not attend the Convention in 1900 because of Mrs. Beveridge's illness. Her death occurred during the Convention.

[3] *Congressional Record*, Dec. 15, 1902.

[4] Beveridge to Shaw, Dec. 19, 1902.

New Mexico as one State. But under protests, he receded from that position.[1]

With the resumption of the debate, the fiery and brilliant Foraker entered the fray in defense of the platform pledge he had helped to frame, and there were frequent coldly courteous exchanges with Beveridge.[2] As he sat down, Quay rose jauntily to demand a vote. 'We have the votes to pass it,' he announced. Beveridge replied with a denunciation of the resort 'to convention and combination methods.' And the platform? 'Was there an issue on statehood?' he asked. 'Was there a speech made upon the subject? In the address of the temporary or permanent chairman, was the question mentioned? Was it talked about even in the lobbies of the hotels where the delegates gathered?' Aldrich, with characteristic cynicism, added that he knew too much about the making of platforms to feel especially bound.[3]

The struggle had just begun. Throughout the three months of the short session, both principals in the fight were in a constant state of tension, with no opportunity for relaxation. Neither dared leave the floor for a moment without leaving a trusted lieutenant on guard, and even then there was danger of sharp practice. One day when Beveridge was at lunch, Quay began pressing vigorously for a vote; and, notified immediately, Beveridge dashed through the swinging doors of the Senate Chamber waving his napkin, and launched into a long extemporaneous speech, clutching the napkin in his hand.[4] Another time, when he had three men pledged to speak against time, he learned that two had failed him. Chauncey M. Depew was just finishing a two hours' speech when Beveridge learned of his predicament. He hurriedly scratched a note, and a moment later Depew paused in his speech to read it. 'Go on, for God's sake, or we are lost! I have no other speaker.' Smiling blandly, the orator took up 'another branch' of the subject and went on.

Knowing of the deep-seated antipathy between Quay and Hanna, Beveridge bitterly assailed the suave Pennsylvanian, cunningly drawing him into a reiteration of previously made reflections on the National Committee. Hanna, enraged, rushed into the debate and spoke for hours in opposition to his enemy.

But the next day the tireless little genius seemed on the verge of victory. The excitement of the Chamber had extended to the town, and crowds were now filling the galleries daily. It was so

[1] Beveridge to Shaw, Jan. 10, 1903.
[2] *Congressional Record*, Jan. 15–16, 1903.   [3] *Ibid.*, Jan. 20, 1903.
[4] *St. Louis Globe-Democrat*, quoted in *Indianapolis Star*, July 2, 1906.

when the Beveridge party sought to stave off a vote by moving an executive session. Here, apparently, was a test — and Beveridge lost by ten. With all the excitement and blood lust of the hunter that has his quarry cornered, Quay turned tauntingly upon Beveridge, daring him to a vote, but the latter only smiled.[1] The debate was now all drama. Intimidating letters poured in on the Indianian,[2] and one day he found himself in receipt of a block of mining stock which he speeded back to the owner. Its retention, in time, would have made him independently rich.[3]

With little more than a month of the session remaining, Quay sought to hold the Senate in continuous session, but it was impossible to maintain a quorum. Almost gayly, the two antagonists moved about the floor and cloakrooms, always canvassing. Time and again their rapiers flashed, but always with a smile. 'Cannot the Senator fix a day when we may vote?' Quay asked purringly. 'I regret that I am not able to accede to the Senator's request,' was the courteous response. 'The Senator certainly sees that such consent is impossible? But four prepared arguments have been made on our side... but two upon the Senator's.'[4] That very day Nicholas Murray Butler was sending Beveridge word, through Shaw, to let the issue reach a vote if assurance of a ringing veto could be had from Roosevelt,[5] but this plan was put aside. The interminable talk went on, Beveridge constantly interrupting, interjecting, even when his own men were speaking, to consume time. For it was a battle against time. When Quay moved that a date be fixed for a vote, Aldrich, Lodge, and Spooner assailed him for proposing cloture.[6]

The contest took on the character of a drama — at times melodrama. The time came when Beveridge had exhausted his parliamentary resources to prevent a vote — and Quay had the votes. As chairman of the committee there would be no vote in the absence of Beveridge. It was imperative to gain time. There was one recourse left — he could disappear! On the third floor of Gifford Pinchot's home at 1615 Rhode Island Avenue there was a small monastic den familiar to Beveridge. One night he went into hiding in the little room, and there he remained a week. Day by day the fiery Foraker would descend in stormy mood on Beveridge's office to demand of Shipp the lost Senator's address. 'You know!' Foraker would say explosively. 'I am sorry, Senator,' replied Shipp suavely; 'I haven't the remotest idea.'

[1] *Indianapolis Journal*, Jan. 22, 1903.   [2] *Ibid.*
[3] *Indianapolis Star*, July 2, 1906.   [4] *Congressional Record*, Feb. 3, 1903.
[5] Shaw to Beveridge, Feb. 3, 1903.
[6] *Congressional Record*, Feb. 14 and 18, 1903.

And at night Shipp would slip to Pinchot's and report to Beveridge, restless as a caged tiger. At length the confinement was too much — he could stand it no longer. He would go to Atlantic City and hide in a big hotel. Thus, one night Shipp appeared at the Pinchot house with a cab, Beveridge dashed across the pavement, the blinds were drawn, and the cabman, following Shipp's instructions, drove to the Baltimore and Ohio freight yards as near the train as possible. With his hat pulled down over his eyes and his coat-collar turned up, the nervous Senator made his successful dash for the train.[1]

On Washington's Birthday, after five days of desperate maneuvering to consolidate as much Republican strength as possible, Beveridge and the leaders went into a conference to plan a compromise. This, beginning on Saturday, continued all day and through the night, through Sunday and until Monday morning at five o'clock, with Beveridge, Aldrich, Spooner, Allison, and Platt of Connecticut sitting in. It was resumed at eight o'clock Monday morning, and was concluded before dinner in the evening.[2] Out of this emerged a compromise which the Democrats instantly rejected. Thereafter Quay made daily demands for a vote, with Beveridge objecting, and the session ended without action. Quay had the votes, but the parliamentary tactics of Beveridge had robbed him of a triumph. It had been a bitter, brilliant exhibition on both sides, and Beveridge had won — won what he himself described as 'the hardest and most notable fight perhaps seen in the Senate for many a year.'[3]

IV

Three fighting months for Beveridge; for he was in the thick of the acrimonious debate on the court-martials and charges of cruelty in the Philippines. As in the hearings, he again bore the brunt of the defense. The charge had been made and sworn to by American soldiers that Father Augustine had been murdered by native soldiers in American uniforms, and when Senator Rawlins referred to it as a 'cold-blooded murder,' Beveridge, in apparent heat, denounced him as slandering the whole American army. It was hardly a fair denunciation, and Hoar and others protested. Brushing these aside, Beveridge continued: 'Simply because they wear our uniform is no reason why they are outragers of women and murderers of men.'

This aroused the ire of the combative Carmack. 'Of all the

[1] Shipp to the author.
[2] Beveridge to Shaw, Feb. 24, 1903; *Indianapolis News*, Feb. 23, 1903.
[3] Beveridge to Shaffer, Feb. 28, 1903.

mean and miserable lies that crawled through the last campaign, this charge that we [the Democrats] have assailed the American army is the meanest, the lowest and the dirtiest of them all. It has been the very vermin of this debate; and I am greatly surprised to find it crawling in the hair of the honorable Senator from Indiana.'

When he added the charge that, through the chicanery of Lodge, evidence of outrages in the Philippines had been suppressed, Beveridge grappled with him in vigorous denial, but the facts set forth and not specifically denied bear out the Carmack charge.[1]

And so that fight went on — with no one in America greatly interested. Already the Philippines seemed as remote as one of the possessions of ancient Rome. There was not to be a time in thirty years when a book upon the Philippines would have more than a meager sale in the United States.

The grueling struggles of the session exacted their toll of both Quay and Beveridge. The former was more frail than ever when the adjournment came, and Beveridge, nervously exhausted and afflicted with a severe cold, hurried to Atlantic City for rest and recreation.

v

Thence he returned to Indianapolis, sat for a portrait to Steele, the artist, and attended the wedding of Mark Hanna's daughter at Cleveland and a dinner for Roosevelt. He followed the course of Hanna in the Ohio Convention in reference to Roosevelt with concern and sorrow. 'Hanna made a break and a bad one,' he wrote Shaffer. 'I admire Senator Hanna and love him; but this play was bad sense, bad politics, and bad everything else.'[2] On the battle-field of Shiloh, he delivered a Periclean oration at the unveiling of the Indiana Monument.

Having no other thought than of returning to the Senate the next year, he was eager for the prestige of being temporary chairman and keynote speaker in the National Convention.[3] Throughout the early part of the summer many stories associating his name with the vice-presidential nomination were running in the press.[4] Ira Bennett, of the 'Washington Post,' had written approvingly of the rumors. 'But, my dear Bennett, I am not and will not be under any circumstances a candidate

[1] *Congressional Record*, Jan. 28, 1903.
[2] Beveridge to Shaffer, May 28, 1903.
[3] Beveridge to Shaw, July 6, 1903.
[4] *Indianapolis Journal*, June 9, 1903, and other papers.

for Vice-President,' Beveridge wrote. 'It has caused me more trouble than anything else.... I have my hands full getting rid of this confounded thing.'[1] These rumors interested Shaffer none the less, and in June, lunching with Roosevelt, he had discussed them with the President.[2] A bad summer, with the vice-presidential rumors embarrassing him in his aspirations for re-election to the Senate, and the 'Indianapolis Journal' passing to the unfriendly Fairbanks interest. But in the midst of all his numerous activities and worries, he managed to keep his articles running rather regularly in the 'Saturday Evening Post.' His Manchurian articles had made a deep impression, and Henry Cabot Lodge was writing Roosevelt that he had been 'thinking a great deal about Manchuria,' and that, in view of our growing trade there, 'we ought to take very strong grounds.'[3] Beveridge was planning the publication of his Russian articles in book form, and with these in his bag for critical revision, he turned in late June toward Rangeley, Maine, which was to become a favorite playground of his.

Out in the woods he had hoped to be uninterrupted in the writing of 'The Russian Advance,' and in his rambles through the pines. Within a few days he was writing furiously to Tom Shipp, his secretary, and to Rothschild for letting people descend upon him there and for sending him clippings on rumors, and 'a whole lot of idiotic matter about Ade, McCutcheon, and myself.' All through July he was working with absorption on the book, and Senator Platt of Connecticut was writing him 'the loveliest scolding letters you ever saw telling me I do not know how to rest.'[4] He promised himself to relax, but he was apprehensive about his first literary venture between covers. 'You are the only person on earth that could have persuaded me to publish this book,' he wrote Shaw. 'I am afraid to do it. I am afraid the critics, the newspapers, and everybody else will jump on it. I am afraid the pro-English fellows will swear it is not so, and a whole lot of other afraids.'[5] Determined to check every point, he wrote Gifford Pinchot to go to his apartment in the Portland and send him seven enumerated volumes he had on Russia, Siberia, and China.[6]

Thus, when he emerged from the woods in early September, he had rested little if at all; and returning to Indiana, he was instantly engaged on a series of non-partisan speeches, mostly out-of-doors under the trees. October found him campaigning

[1] Beveridge to Bennett, June 16, 1903.
[2] Shaffer to Beveridge, July 14, 1903.
[3] *Roosevelt-Lodge Correspondence*, II, 15.   [4] Beveridge to Shipp, Aug. 1, 1903.
[5] Beveridge to Shaw, July 20, 1903.   [6] Beveridge to Pinchot, July 22, 1903.

vigorously for a week for Hanna in Ohio. And in the midst of these trying, nerve-racking activities, he found time to write Shaw about the book. 'Of course this book is on my mind day and night,' he wrote. 'You see, I never published a book before, and I am just like a woman who has never had a baby before. In her opinion it is the only child ever born, and she wonders whether it is going to be an idiot or the most beautiful creature that ever blessed the earth.... So I am fearful, worked up, and worked down, and worked all around. Well, well, God help us all!'[1] And a month later: 'I do hope you like it. I would rather you like the book than to have the public itself like it. You were its inspiration. But for you, it never would have been written. Such as it is, however, it is written, and there you are.'[2] Meanwhile, Shaw was responding with encouragement. He had discussed the project with Roosevelt, who understood that Beveridge and Pinchot did not agree about the Russians, but for that he 'did not care a rap.' 'He agrees with me that to bring out the book would strengthen your reputation, and, to quote him directly, "Whatever strengthens one of my friends, strengthens me."'[3]

It was at the beginning of winter that he attended the installation of Dr. Edwin H. Hughes as President of DePauw University, and at the same time he was initiated into Phi Beta Kappa Society 'for scholarly attainments in college and since.'

He returned to Washington refreshed by the contact with the scenes of his youthful triumphs. It was not to be a session of great importance. A presidential campaign was approaching, and the least said or done the better. The nomination of Roosevelt was a forgone conclusion, and the secret hostility of powerful interests and political leaders made the uninitiated wonder. The chief interest now centered in the vice-presidential nomination, and both senators from Indiana were being mentioned. Early in the winter, Beveridge was quite willing to get behind the very evident ambition of Fairbanks for the nomination, as his correspondence clearly shows. No one longer doubted that ambition, and Henry Cabot Lodge, after a conversation with Fairbanks in New York wrote Roosevelt that while coy the Indianian 'did want it and is after it — and means to get it,' and that the President should 'tread warily and say nothing.'[4] The very day Lodge was writing thus, Beveridge was writing Shaw to ascertain whether 'Washington has decided on Fairbanks's nomination,' and whether Roosevelt

[1] Beveridge to Shaw, Oct. 21, 1903.   [2] Beveridge to Shaw, Nov. 23, 1903.
[3] Shaw to Beveridge, Oct. 14, 1903.
[4] *Roosevelt-Lodge Correspondence*, II, 79.

wanted Beveridge to nominate Fairbanks or make a seconding speech for himself.[1] Nothing that Shaw could learn led him to assume that Roosevelt wanted Beveridge to place Fairbanks in nomination.[2]

Meanwhile, with Roosevelt's nomination certain, Lorimer, of the 'Saturday Evening Post,' was asking Beveridge to write an article on the President, and, despite his admiration for Roosevelt, Beveridge was embarrassed. At first he agreed. Then he reconsidered, and his reasons in his letter to Lorimer are interesting in throwing a light upon the two men who were to work together in so many historic contests. 'I am a little afraid to do it,' he wrote. 'I am not sure that he would be pleased with it, and there is no use risking the matter. While I would want to make it lively and entertaining, I should at the same time want to present a calm, sensible, rational view — one that would appeal to voters. I think, on the whole, for the reasons that you, Phillips, and myself went over carefully, that I had better leave it alone.'[3] To Shaw he wrote a similar explanation with an addition: 'I am a little bit afraid the President, who wants the most extravagant things said about him, might not be pleased with my view as to what is best for the purpose of getting votes.'[4] He finally compromised by writing an article on the Roosevelt Administration.[5]

Nearer to the heart of Beveridge than the vice-presidency was his wish to be temporary chairman of the National Convention. Never had he wanted anything more. Hanna was interested, but had become involved in some arrangement with Senator Allison and was pledged to Robert G. Cousins of Iowa, who was 'not a Roosevelt man.' Personally and politically, Beveridge did not need the honor at the moment, but he was looking to the future. Cortelyou and Charles G. Dawes, he understood, were quietly working in his interest, and he had been told that Perkins 'holds the key to the situation.' He had talked with Perkins, but did not know how far he would go. It was important to keep the negotiations from the press. In the meanwhile, he wrote, he would 'go to work during the coming months' and prepare the 'speech of his life.'[6] But the Administration had other plans, and Elihu Root was to be chosen.

[1] Beveridge to Shaw, May 27, 1904.
[2] Shaw to Beveridge, June 1, 1904.
[3] Beveridge to Lorimer, June 1, 1904.
[4] Beveridge to Shaw, undated.
[5] *Saturday Evening Post*, Sept. 10, 1904.
[6] Beveridge to Shaw, Jan. 21, 1904.

VI

While all these secret political negotiations were in process, Japan struck at Russia with her fleet, and 'The Russian Advance' entered into the list of the 'best-sellers.' That which the book had predicted was inevitable had come. It had expressed no opinion on the outcome of the struggle, but Beveridge's ill-wishers were to insist that he had prophesied a Russian triumph. Two weeks before the war began, the 'Chicago Tribune' had cited the book as 'a masterpiece of observation,' and described the author as one of two senators with 'at least a spark of the divine fire.' [1]

As the situation rapidly developed, his familiarity with the scene of the conflict and the character of the two peoples brought Beveridge into frequent conferences with Roosevelt and John Hay, Secretary of State. He was besieged by press correspondents and forced to refuse interviews. While his enemies were laughing over the failure of the Russians to 'advance,' more discriminating critics were finding the book illuminating and useful, and Senator Hoar was writing that 'the effect of reading the chapter on 'Three Russians of World Fame' had raised his opinion of four men — the three Russians and Beveridge.' [2] Henry White wrote from the Embassy in London that the book was favorably discussed there.[3] And John Goodnow, of the Consulate at Shanghai, wrote that the book confirmed him in the opinion that 'few men understand the East as well as you, and no one better.' [4]

The 'child' at least was not an 'idiot.'

VII

The winter and spring were to be notable politically because of the passing of two of the greatest party managers of generations. Hanna was not to interfere with the Rooseveltians in the Convention. In February he was stricken, and, speaking at the Lincoln Dinner at the Columbia Club in Indianapolis, Beveridge, referring to his illness, described him as a 'man whom every Republican holds in dearest affection,' and asked the diners to rise and drink 'to the recovery of this great and good man.' [5] Two days later, Hanna was dead; and Beveridge, returning to Wash-

[1] The other was Spooner.
[2] *Indianapolis Star*, March 4, 1904.
[3] White to Beveridge, March 4, 1904.
[4] Goodnow to Beveridge, May 10, 1904.
[5] *Indianapolis Star*, Feb. 13, 1904.

ington, went directly from the train to the Arlington Hotel to pay his tribute.

Three months later, a great political general of an earlier day passed, in the death of Quay. His death had been hastened by the bitter battle with Beveridge on the statehood bill. It was his most spectacular defeat, and he had fought with all his genius only to find his smiling opponent his equal as a tactician and parliamentarian. Accustomed to break the deadening routine of a session by occasional trips of recreation to Florida, Quay had been forced to remain throughout the session of the combat under nervous pressure. He had told Beveridge that his fight was killing him, and talked quite casually of his approaching end. But Quay admired a fighter, and almost always, during the exchanges of debate, Beveridge had treated him with a courtesy and respect that was sincere.

In the closing days of his life, Beveridge called upon the old man, now frail and haggard. Sitting at the window looking out, Quay said, as the younger man was taking his leave: 'I shall be dead in a few months, and the papers will say, "Matt Quay, Boss, is dead." Had I lived my life differently, they would say: "Death of Matthew S. Quay, Statesman." Take warning by me, young man.' Then, taking up a copy of 'Peter Ibbetson,' he wrote upon the fly-leaf the enigmatic words, 'Dream true,' and gave it to Beveridge as a parting gift.

With the passing of these two masterful leaders of the old school, a new era dawned in American politics; new leaders, with new ideas and ideals and methods, were to assume command for a while, and Roosevelt was to symbolize the new day.

CHAPTER II

THE DAWN OF GREAT EVENTS

I

BEFORE the end of the winter, the rumors that Beveridge would be opposed for reëlection within his own party died down. The Republican Editorial Association declared unanimously for his reëlection in January.[1] Long before the State Convention, it was clear that only a Democratic victory would deprive him of his seat, and the heady tribute to him in the platform amounted to a renomination.[2] It was quite as evident that all the party enemies of Roosevelt had been crushed or intimidated into silence, and that his would be the only name presented for the presidential nomination in Chicago. The interest of Indiana in the National Convention was in the candidacy of Fairbanks for the vice-presidential nomination. The State delegation, canvassing the situation in advance, had concluded that Beveridge should be the chairman and Fairbanks should go on the Committee on Resolutions. No other thought was in the minds of many when the special train bearing the Hoosiers drew out of the Union Station in Indianapolis.[3]

But for reasons of his own Fairbanks had other plans and soon made his wishes known. The purveyor of the change in plans was James P. Goodrich, the State Chairman, who rushed into the room of Beveridge at the Auditorium with the tidings. 'Senator,' he said, 'I am sorry, but Senator Fairbanks wants to head the delegation.' He was assured that there would be no friction and that the junior Senator would yield. But the news spread through the lobbies, and many of Beveridge's friends insisted that he make a fight. He counseled peace. The delegation met in an atmosphere far from pleasant. The selection of a chairman and of the member of the Platform Committee was postponed until the last. At length Goodrich turned to Fairbanks with the blunt question, 'Do you want to head the Indiana delegation?' 'All I want is what the delegation desires me to have,' he replied. Turning to Beveridge, Goodrich asked, 'What about yourself and the chairmanship of this delegation?' 'Since the name of Senator Fairbanks is now mentioned, I gladly defer to him and shall take pleasure in placing him in nomination for that position,' Beveridge replied.

[1] *Indianapolis Journal*, Jan. 23, 1904.   [2] *Ibid.*, April 3, 1904.
[3] *Indianapolis Star*, June 19, 1904.

Thus a threatened rupture was prevented, and Beveridge went on the Resolutions Committee, acting as one of the sub-committee that actually framed the platform. There he, who so soon was to undergo a change of heart, appeared as a strong advocate of a 'stand-pat' tariff plank. It is not at all fair to assume from this that he was not even then in favor of a revision. The time was not ripe.

Roosevelt had clearly advised against it. Just before the Convention he had read a letter from Henry Cabot Lodge:

Moody [Attorney-General] is uneasy over the tariff situation. He thinks, and I find that there is a strong northwestern sentiment for tariff revision, and that, though the bulk of the party is resolute on the protective idea, there is a strong minority which is much disaffected and which is inclined to feel that we ought to have a revision. Warn me if any Boston reciprocity people are coming on here. Moody is much impressed with the reciprocity movement.[1]

Within two years, Beveridge was to be one of the 'strong minority,' and it is not without significance that the tariff plank he favored carried a modifying clause to the effect that whenever revision became necessary it should be made by the Republicans.[2]

However, Beveridge was not to be wholly buried in the committee room of the platform-makers. He was to emerge to second the nomination of Roosevelt in a speech concededly the most brilliant and effective in the Convention,[3] and, in the opinion of Sam Blythe, in no sense partial to the orator, not only the best, but the only speech.[4] It was but twenty minutes in length, dynamic, epigrammatic, militant, and as the speaker proceeded, his enthusiasm glowed and the convention reflected the fervor of the orator. His collar wilted in the heat, which was intense, the perspiration rolled down his face; yet he did not rant, and his penetrating voice reached every corner of the hall as few others did.[5] Strangely enough, Shaffer was not pleased with it, and Beveridge was hurt, but the general acclaim salved his wound.

Despite the friction in the organization of the delegation, he loyally supported Fairbanks's aspirations for the second place on the ticket. When Jonathan P. Dolliver had concluded his speech placing him in nomination, Beveridge mounted a chair and led the delegation as its cheer leader. Only once were the Indianians flustered. A young inexperienced Georgian,[6] seconding Fairbanks's nomination, began with a startling

---

[1] *Roosevelt-Lodge Correspondence*, II, 81.   [2] *Indianapolis Star*, June 23, 1904.
[3] *New York Tribune, New York Sun, New York World*, June 24, 1904.
[4] *New York World*.   [5] *Indianapolis Star*, June 24, 1904.   [6] H. Blunn.

sentence: 'The State of Georgia realizes that sound money makes sound banks, and sound banks make Senator Fairbanks.' There was some amazement, a little tittering, but something was forgiven to the young man's good intentions.[1]

The end of the convention found Beveridge hurrying to the Maine woods to recruit his strength for the strenuous campaign expected. He stopped at Oyster Bay for a conference with Roosevelt, and lingered to enjoy the fireworks for the President's children on the lawn.[2]

Thence to Rangeley, Maine, where he spent five or six weeks tramping through the pine woods, untempted by the deer in the forest and the fish in the streams. He loved the water, and for five days he paddled in a canoe through miles of the lakes and streams. Living out-of-doors, walking, rowing, lounging, permitting no political interruptions, he ended his vacation with the Allagash trip with George Bramwell Baker as his companion.

It was in Maine that he opened his campaign with two speeches for Senator Eugene Hale; and then he started home, brown and ruddy, spending an afternoon at Oyster Bay, chatting with the President on his experiences in the woods.[3]

II

After the conventions, it was apparent to the Democrats that they did not have a chance in Indiana. The 'gold telegram' of Alton B. Parker, the Democratic nominee, sent to the convention after his nomination, had created an ugly, incurable disaffection among the followers of Bryan, composing the major part of the party; and throughout the campaign local Democratic candidates were afraid to mention the name of their leader in their speeches. The large campaign fund expected did not materialize. The Indiana Democrats were hopelessly defeated in July, but the Republicans did not realize it until November. Roosevelt was to be uneasy about the State to the very end, and in mid-October was writing Lodge of 'disquieting reports from Indiana,'[4] and on the eve of the election he wrote again that 'Indiana, I fear, is doubtful.'[5]

This inexplicable sense of uncertainty affected Beveridge, who needed money for his fight, but refused to take it when offered by his friend Perkins. He had declined his proffer of financial help, and when it was renewed, he wrote:

[1] *Indianapolis Star*, June 24, 1904. [2] *Ibid.*, July 6, 1904.
[3] *Ibid.*, Sept. 3, 1904.
[4] *Roosevelt-Lodge Correspondence*, II, 103.
[5] *Ibid.*, 106.

Dear George: But I mean what I said. I have thought it all over and I cannot accept financial help even from my best and closest friend. So I return the draft you were so kind as to send me. Be sure your generosity is appreciated — it could not possibly be more appreciated. The more I see how money is spent in politics, and how thereafter they pose as honorable men, even as examples in our political life, I am disgusted. I am the more determined to win or lose on my merits. Of course it is a fight against odds, but no matter. Had the National Committee seen fit to help the purely legitimate expenses of carrying the Legislature — and only legitimate expenses would have been accepted even from the committee — they could have sent the aid to Mr. Pettit, who has the legislative campaign in charge. But since it is otherwise, let it go.[1]

This was his attitude throughout toward wealthy friends with powerful corporate connections. In one campaign he turned the checks of such over to Charles E. Coffin, with instructions to lock them in a safe and return them with thanks after the election.[2]

In the midst of his financial worries, he was delighted to learn from Shaffer that he had signed a contract for the purchase of the 'Indianapolis Star,' the 'Terre Haute Star,' and the 'Muncie Star,' but his jubilation was premature, for years were to intervene before the consummation and he was to pass through the whole of his senatorial career without powerful newspaper support.[3] But always, in the end, Beveridge's strength was on the stump before the people, and he could find nothing in his receptions to depress him. He was convinced that the speaking campaign should be short and sharp, raised immediately to a high pitch of enthusiasm and held there. When he heard that George B. Cortelyou was planning to launch the campaign early, he sent a protest.

I think this is a serious mistake. Very emphatically I am against it. As I said to you in our conversation in Washington, this is to be a peculiarly personal campaign. It is largely to be a campaign of enthusiasm. In no sense is it to be a campaign of education.... Therefore, a long speaking campaign is not only unnecessary, but most unwise. You will find that the enthusiasm of your audiences and the power of your speakers will be lagging toward the latter part of the campaign, at the very time when it ought to be increasing to its final culminative power.[4]

From over the country the Macedonian cry reached Beveridge for help at the very moment he was foolishly uneasy about his own campaign. No other Republican was in such demand.

[1] Beveridge to Perkins, Oct. 3, 1904.   [2] Mr. Coffin's statement.
[3] Shaffer to Beveridge, Oct. 11, 1904.
[4] Beveridge to Cortelyou, Aug. 9, 1904.

He was wanted in New York, New Jersey, Iowa, Ohio, whence Senator Dick appealed, and Wisconsin, where Senator Quarles was pleading for him. Even from rock-ribbed Republican Vermont came Senator Dillingham's appeal.[1]

And, with the Roosevelt landslide in the very air, Beveridge was sending forth appeals of his own. Lodge could not respond because Senator Hoar was ill.[2] Spooner, in a losing fight with young La Follette, replied that 'the situation in this State is hell,' and he could not leave.[3] But Allison, Dolliver, and Clapp of Minnesota spoke in Indiana — and Beveridge was a host within himself.

He opened his campaign for reëlection at a great meeting in Tomlinson's Hall in Indianapolis. The place was packed, the aisles were jammed, and great numbers who could not get in were addressed by speakers from the balcony. As the crowd pushed into the hall, young men at the doors distributed a pamphlet attacking Beveridge's labor record. He was assailed for his attitude on the eight-hour law, on the injunction, on the ship subsidy for which finally he had voted. But the pamphlets were soon in the street under the feet of the crowd. His arrival at the hall was announced by the roar of cannon. The meeting had been staged for enthusiasm — and enthusiasm it was to have. Taking as his keynote and subject, 'All is Well with the Republic,' he concentrated in the first paragraph the gist of the argument of his party in that landslide year.

'All is well with the Republic. Other nations are in battle or within the possibilities of war; the Republic is without an antagonist. The debts of other nations increase; the debt of the Republic diminishes, and its bonds are the best security in every money market. The Republic's foreign trade is greater than ever before in our history — greater than the foreign trade of any nation, ancient or modern, and the balance in our favor since McKinley's inauguration until now is ten times greater than the entire balance in our favor from the adoption of the Constitution in 1787 to McKinley's election in 1896. The commerce of the American people among themselves is larger than the international trade of all the other peoples of the earth combined. In farms and mines, in shops and roads and trade; in everything that makes for comfort and prosperity, all is well with the Republic.'

Then, he asked, what was the campaign all about? Was anyone dissatisfied? Anyone want an election, even? Or would there be one but for the constitutional mandate? Everyone was

[1] Beveridge MS.   [2] Lodge to Beveridge, Aug. 30, 1904.
[3] Spooner to Beveridge, Oct. 14, 1904.

prosperous, and statistics proved it. Labor was prosperous — it was consuming more sugar and coffee than ever, and had more money in savings banks. Strikes? Well, strikes come when times are good. The Democratic issues? Militarism — with Roosevelt, the Man on Horseback?[1] 'Two thirds of a soldier for every thousand citizens,' Beveridge counted. Tariff revision? With a Republican Senate, Parker, if elected, could do nothing, but confusion would result and business suffer. And, besides, 'if there is a branch needing pruning, those who planted the tree and have guarded its growth should do it.' The Democratic idea of changing a single tariff schedule here and there? No, no, 'the Republican theory is that there is no industry in this country which stands by itself — that all depend on each, and each depends on all; that the American people are one great industrial family, brothers within a single nation, sons of a single flag.' And trusts? Regulate them if need be, but destroy them never. And imperialism? The party of imperialism had no apologies to make — it was doing the will of God in redeeming backward peoples.

And what could be expected from the Democrats? They were divided against themselves. And what of Roosevelt? That which he had given — for example, the Panama Canal which will give the Nation 'a continuous coast line — one vast maritime semicircle of safety.' And more: 'The election of Theodore Roosevelt means that no power in this Republic, however strong or rich, no organization, however numerous and determined, is too great for the sovereignty of the law; no citizen, however poor or humble, no interest, however small or weak, is too insignificant for the law's protection. And just this was the largest issue of the campaign — that common equality before the law which Theodore Roosevelt's public personality represents.'

The speech was constantly interrupted with applause and laughter, and occasional shouts; Beveridge had pitched the fight upon the plane of enthusiasm, and that which he did so well in Indiana, others, with varying success, were doing elsewhere.[2]

It had its effect. A reactionary element within the Democratic Party was balking Parker's desire for a courageous tariff fight, and the 'gold telegram' hung about his neck like the Old Man of the Sea. When he made the perfectly accurate charge that the great industrialists and financiers were contributing generously to Roosevelt's campaign fund,[3] the latter vigorously denounced it as a lie, and the man in the street shouted his approval and the contributors smiled behind their hands. The

[1] Henry Watterson's description.   [2] *Indianapolis Star*, Sept. 29, 1904.
[3] Afterwards admitted by Roosevelt.

President had captured the popular imagination. Bryan swept through Indiana speaking from breakfast until midnight, but doing more harm than good by recommending Parker as the lesser of two evils. And Beveridge was touring the State from the river to the lake, arousing enthusiasm, cheered by multitudes. 'The shifting sands of politics may unseat Mr. Beveridge,' said the 'Indianapolis Star'[1] editorially, 'although it is not likely; but no matter what comes to him as a result of the election, he can hold in grateful remembrance the enthusiastic tributes that have been paid to him the past month by the people of his great State.'

The result was the landslide — Roosevelt swept Indiana by an unprecedented majority, the Legislature was overwhelmingly Republican, and Beveridge's reëlection was assured. To most letters of congratulations he replied that the country had 'gone Rooseveltian, not Republican.'

III

This did not end his anxiety over the election, for he was concerned lest an enemy be elected to succeed Fairbanks, but soon he was reassured. After he had returned to Washington, Shaffer went to Indianapolis, conferred with Rothschild on the senatorial situation, and talked with James A. Hemenway in the office of the 'Star.' 'He assured me,' wrote Shaffer to Beveridge, 'that his going to the Senate means absolute harmony in working out all plans with you, and I assured him under that condition he would have our hearty coöperation and support. He told me that he had had a talk with you, and that everything was satisfactory, and Mr. Rothschild brought me a message from you that everything was satisfactory to you.'[2] Thus it was arranged, and Hemenway entered the Senate a secret enemy of his colleague, soon to disclose his hostility in the open.

With the retirement of Fairbanks, a vacancy was created on the Committee on Foreign Relations, to which Beveridge had looked with longing from the moment he entered the Senate. Two and a half years before, it had been agreed among the older senators that he should go on at the first opportunity. But when a vacancy occurred, Fairbanks had insisted upon the place for himself. Senator McMillan of Michigan and others sought to dissuade him, and Beveridge appealed to him, but in vain, and he had had his way. Now, with another opportunity at hand, Beveridge was anxious. He took his anxiety to Shaw:

[1] Nov. 7, 1904.
[2] Shaffer to Beveridge, Dec. 5, 1904.

Last summer I wrote Hale, who is my warm personal friend, calling attention to the general understanding that this place was to be mine, and had from him an extremely satisfactory letter. I am sure that he will do all he can.... In addition to this, I have written today to Senator Platt of Connecticut, who is my father, or who is as dear and close to me as if he were my father. I have a feeling that the President may in some way or other push Knox for this place. I would write the President personally, but I feel some delicacy in doing so, because, after all, he might not be considering Knox for this place; and my relations with the President are so intimate, so perfect, and have grown so very close during the campaign — much closer than ever before — that I do not feel personally like taking the matter up with him.... Knox [1] is my warm personal friend. We were devoted friends for several years before I went to the Senate. Our friendship began here in Indianapolis, and has steadily grown until this very hour. If I were to stand aside for anybody on earth, it would be Knox. I have earned the Foreign Relations and I want it.[2]

He was to get it, but unhappily at the time he was about to concentrate on domestic problems of reform and become one of the Rooseveltian crusaders; and from the hour he went upon the committee he was, until the end, to be constantly engaged in battle after battle. Too frequently the other more pressing duties were to keep him from the committee meetings, and Senator Cullom, the chairman, was to complain of this in his memoirs. It just so happened that the international problems that deeply concerned him came before he went on the committee, or after he had left the Senate.

But his position at this time was one of commanding importance. He had taken his place among the recognized leaders of the Senate, albeit he never was to be taken into the little oligarchy that was dominated by Aldrich.

IV

The short congressional session was to accomplish little beyond the passing of the supply bills, but it was to foreshadow the bitter struggles of the next winter. The statehood bill was to be made the unfinished business and was not to be finished or taken up. Beveridge, nevertheless, was busy with correspondence upon it.

The drama of that struggle was not in the Senate Chamber only; much was being enacted behind the scenes. It was again to command the attention of the senators, but no one hoped for action in the three months. Benjamin Ide Wheeler was writing from California that Senator Perkins had aligned himself against the Beveridge plan under pressure from that State. If

[1] Philander C. Knox.   [2] Beveridge to Shaw, Nov. 10, 1904.

Beveridge would undertake to counteract it, Wheeler would have leading men, organizations, 'and everybody else wire him.'[1] To Gifford Pinchot, who was an expert on land grants, Beveridge had written for suggestions on amendments covering that phase, and Pinchot had responded in a carefully prepared letter.[2]

The preceding summer a number of members of the House had made a junket trip into the Territories, engineered by the railroads. 'It appears that three of these gentlemen have stock in Arizona mines,' Beveridge wrote Pinchot. 'Wouldn't that jar you? You will remember that when I was down there I quite accidentally — quite accidentally — met an Indianian who also accidentally owned a mine, and when I got back he accidentally sent me a block of stock in the mine. Well, I just as accidentally returned it to him — damn him.'[3]

But all his troubles did not come from those financially interested. Some of his correspondents were concerned about the sale of liquor, some about votes for women, some about mixed schools. Susan B. Anthony had written him in anger because the word 'sex' had appeared in an earlier bill, and she later wrote of her gratification that it was omitted from the new. But now, she noticed, the words 'male citizens' appeared. 'Now,' wrote the militant suffrage leader, 'I would ask that the word "male" be stricken out in each of these places and that the bill shall read, "all citizens, persons, inhabitants, etc.," and not discriminate against any sex any more than against any color.' And the fee system — why retain it? 'When I voted in 1872, from the saloon lounger who entered complaint to the United States Marshal and the District Attorney, all the men who had anything to do with the trial, each and every one of them got a fee. I do not believe I would have been prosecuted if it hadn't been for the money there was in it for individual office-holders.'

And Susan B. Anthony had more. Since Beveridge had asked frank criticism, he should have it. It was fine, she thought, that the proposed use of public money for sectarian schools was abandoned, but why provide for colored schools? Indian children — were they colored? All this was wrong — the same schools for all — that was the American idea. And suffrage — what about that?[4]

Meanwhile, the statehood fight was opened early and continued sporadically for weeks. The climax of the debate came a month later, when Senator Foraker, upon whose shoulders the

[1] Wheeler to Beveridge, Feb. 2, 1905.   [2] Pinchot to Beveridge, Jan. 16, 1905.
[3] Beveridge to Pinchot, Oct. 23, 1905.
[4] Susan B. Anthony to Beveridge, Dec. 3 and 22, 1904.

mantle of Quay had fallen, made a hot attack upon the bill. Separate statehood for Arizona and New Mexico, he said; or at least let the people of each State vote separately upon the proposed consolidation. But it was absurd to make one State out of two that had a natural barrier between them. Beveridge replied, submitting a report from the director of the Geological Survey that there was 'no natural barrier between the Territories,' that the boundary line was 'wholly arbitrary' and 'might have been drawn anywhere.'

Pitching his argument on the high plane of national statesmanship, he argued that the controversy did not concern the people of the Territories wholly or even chiefly. 'It chiefly concerns the Nation.' Because the founders knew it chiefly concerned the Nation, Congress had been given absolute constitutional power in the matter of State-making. 'It may fix boundaries where it will; it may determine numbers as it will; it may impose any condition not expressly prohibited by the Constitution itself.'

Two years before, when the union of Oklahoma and Indian Territory was first proposed, it was resisted by the politicians in both, and the country was indifferent. Now the people of the two Territories were a unit for it, and the politicians had agreed. Time would bring the same result in Arizona and New Mexico. For these mergers were in accord with logic. Oklahoma had fields and mines, and Indian Territory had vast beds of coal, great mineral deposits, and marble beds. Thus they complement each other. And so with Arizona and New Mexico; for Arizona had gold, silver, and copper, but no coal or coke, and New Mexico lacked what Arizona had, and had what Arizona lacked.

Difference in race? An argument that, for the merger. 'It is said ... that the most of the people of New Mexico are of Mexican descent,' he continued. 'Very well. If that Territory is admitted separately, we shall have imported into the Union a condition nowhere duplicated within the Republic — a State where a great majority of its citizens are not of the blood and speech that is common to the rest of us.' But unite the Territories and with 'the Mexican population in the middle, masses of Americans to the east of them, masses of Americans to the west of them — a situation ideal for Americanizing within a few brief years every drop of the blood of Spain.'

Was it said that the union would make the State too large? 'Too large! Too large! Why, you might add to this proposed new State the States of Massachusetts, Connecticut, Rhode Island, Delaware, and Maryland, and then it would not be as large as the State of Texas.'

Interrupted throughout the speech, the interruptions played into the speaker's hands. He knew the selfish personal interests behind the opposition, the case of Andrews, the railroads, the mine-owners, but these topics he did not touch in the debates. Then, suddenly, an interruption from Senator Russell B. Alger, who unfortunately had been Secretary of War during the clash with Spain.

'I made some investments there [Arizona] that I will sell in a minute if this goes through,' he said.

'Oh!' Beveridge exclaimed, pausing to let the significance of the statement sink in. 'Oh! After that, there is nothing more to be said.'

He closed with a glowing peroration, describing 'Arizona the Great,' and the galleries rang with applause.[1]

The debate droned on. The amendment stage was reached. Liquor was excluded from Indian Territory for twenty-one years. Another amendment to create separate States was voted down by a narrow margin of two. The measure permitting Oklahoma and Indian Territory to form a Constitution and State Government was passed, with one vote to spare. The House disagreed, the conferees of the two houses disagreed; and for another session the statehood bill was dead.

But with Beveridge, the fight had just begun, and he foresaw a crucial test in the coming session.

V

And other future events cast their shadows before — pointing toward bitter party struggles. Roosevelt, swept into office by an imposing majority and having a personal mandate from the people, was girding his loins for action. In his Message he had ventured to discuss the controversial subject of railroad rates. He was not prepared to clothe the Interstate Commerce Commission with the power to fix rates; but, in the interest of the shippers, the Commission might well be empowered to determine a reasonable rate, after a hearing, and subject to judicial review, when an existing rate was challenged.[2] He was not concerned so much with the effect of the rates on consumers.

The conservatives listened aghast. The progressives took courage. The House, under the leadership of William P. Hepburn, framed and passed a bill that went far beyond the presidential recommendation, and this was killed by the failure of the Senate to act. It was the beginning of the fierce struggle that was to fascinate the country the next winter.

[1] *Congressional Record*, Feb. 5, 1905. [2] Message, Dec. 6, 1904.

But even more disturbing to the reactionaries of the party was the discovery that Roosevelt did not consider the tariff sacrosanct. No one yet had been quite able to fathom the mind of the President at this juncture. The platform had made no revision pledge. The country was fairly prosperous. But the press was discussing revision sympathetically, and no man ever was more sensitive of the Fourth Estate. The correspondence of the time shows that the conservatives were apprehensive, alarmed. Soon after the election, Roosevelt, discussing plans with Senator Aldrich, suggested that some tariff revision would be necessary. The wily Senate dictator, custodian of the covenant of privilege, assumed a poker face. 'Possibly,' he said, but with studied coldness. He understood that Roosevelt was hinting at an extra session, and forthwith wrote Platt of Connecticut of his experience.[1] Shocked at the news, Platt hurried to Roosevelt, to be told that the President had understood Aldrich to indicate that something should be done about the tariff.

'I should have said, offhand, that there was absolutely no demand for tariff revision, and was greatly surprised at the President's feeling, and I am yet at a loss to know where the pressure comes from,' Aldrich replied.[2]

Had he known as he wrote that La Follette and Cummins of Iowa were in conference with the President at the White House, he might have suspected the source of the pressure.

It was Platt's understanding that Roosevelt proposed at least to broach the subject in his Message, possibly following it up with a Special Message and an extra session. But why, asked Platt — why the necessity? None, said the President, except a political necessity. He found the sentiment for revision much stronger than Platt imagined. The latter was incredulous. He had heard nothing of the sort among the men with whom he associated.[3] Returning to his home, he wrote a strong remonstrance to Roosevelt. He found 'no Republican' who favored revision, and the very suggestion would disturb business.[4]

Meanwhile, Speaker Joseph G. Cannon was struggling with his astonishment. He had received a letter from Roosevelt setting forth a tentative plan of legislation and broaching tariff revision. He noticed that this reference was in quotation marks. Why? Was it a quotation from the forthcoming Message? This was alarming enough. Reaching Washington, Cannon called at the White House and protested that to open a tariff discussion would mean a congressional session through the next summer.[5]

[1] N. W. Stephenson, *Life of Nelson W. Aldrich*, 252. [2] *Ibid.*
[3] L. A. Coolidge, *An Old-Fashioned Senator: Orville H. Platt*, 285–86.
[4] *Ibid.*, 387–91. [5] L. W. Busbey, *Uncle Joe Cannon*, 207–08.

Even so the conservatives awaited the Message with fear and trembling. It was bruited abroad that the tariff recommendation was included; it was insisted, afterward, that it was in the copy furnished the Associated Press and was canceled later. But it did not appear.

Nevertheless, the anxiety continued. Roosevelt was getting on the nerves of the reactionaries. Everything had been so peaceful before. But nothing definite was heard until within two weeks of the end of the session. It was then that Roosevelt summoned the conservative leaders to the White House. When Cannon arrived, he found in the Cabinet room Senators Aldrich, Allison, Hale, Platt of Connecticut, Cullom, and Penrose; and Representatives Payne, Dalzell, Grosvenor, Tawney, and Dolliver. Rushing breezily into the room, Roosevelt announced briefly, almost casually, that he had been urged to press for revision in his Message of the next December. What did the assembled leaders think? Strangely enough, Aldrich commended the suggestion. 'I knew,' wrote Cannon, 'or at least I thought I knew, that he was opposed to any revision at that time, but whether he did not want to lead the opposition to the President or thought it was politics to wait for a more favorable opportunity, I do not know.' Allison and Hale followed with qualified approvals. It was an amazing exhibition. When Payne, Tawney and Grosvenor fell in, Cannon was dumbfounded. But Platt of Connecticut voiced a vigorous and determined dissent, and Cannon said that Platt had voiced his views.

All the while, Roosevelt sat on a table, swinging his legs, now and then injecting a sharp question. When Cannon finished, Roosevelt got up, grinned, and said: 'It is evident the consensus of opinion is that the tariff should not be revised until after the next presidential election.'

Six had agreed to revision, two opposed, and Roosevelt found the consensus of opinion against the idea, remembering Talleyrand's definition of the use of words. What was his own idea? No one knew. No one ever was to know positively. But he had thrown the fear of the Lord into the conservatives, and afar off they could smell the smoke of the coming battles.[1]

VI

It was clear to Beveridge that the coming session would be one of titanic struggles and that he would be deeply involved. His continental campaign tours had given him a better insight into national opinion than was possible to the conservatives sum-

[1] Busbey, *Uncle Joe Cannon*, 212–13.

moned by Roosevelt. He sensed an undercurrent of resentment against existing conditions, and knew the power of Roosevelt with the masses.

When Congress adjourned, he was badly worn. Since entering the Senate he had enjoyed no real vacation. The summer of 1899 had found him enduring the hardships of the Philippine journey. That of 1900, following the extraordinary activities of his first session and the death of his wife, was spent at Rangeley, but he could not rest. That summer, too, he had prepared eight speeches, each of two hours' length, and committed them to memory. When the vacation of 1901 came, he had made the wearisome investigation in Russia and Manchuria and had returned fatigued in mind and body. He had gone to the Rocky Mountains in 1902, but had nearly died of melancholy until he sent for his stenographer and dictated speeches for the campaign. So it had been each year. And now he was tired — dead tired — and confronted with the necessity of completing the essays for the book, 'The Young Man and the World.' Some of these were then running in the 'Saturday Evening Post.'

Shaffer, a bit concerned, urged him to go to Europe and socially meet the political and literary leaders and 'get the physical rest you need and ought to have, and the mental recuperation which you would get from contact and association with the people you would meet there.'[1] But Beveridge could see no rest in such contacts. 'I had thought,' he wrote, 'that I would, this summer, go to Europe and just drift around, not knowing any person where I went, not seeking to know any person, and going by the untrodden paths, along the byways and hedgerows of the country, resting, utterly resting without definite aim or purpose for once in my life.'[2] He still thought he might, but he was 'sick and tired to the point of exhaustion of great men and statesmen,' and would 'like some repose, some simplicity, some affection.'

In April he went to Greenfield, Ohio, to the home of his cousin, Edward L. McClain, for whom he had a great affection, taking with him the unfinished manuscript of 'The Young Man and the World.' He had to write some new chapters and add several thousand words to those that had been written. There 'in the country and amid the scenes where I was born,' he hoped for relaxation, but Shaffer was now urging him to make a Canadian trip and write articles tending to bring the two countries closer together.[3] Hardly had he reached his cousin's home, where the whole house was put at his disposal, when he almost collapsed,

[1] Shaffer to Beveridge, March 11, 1905.
[2] Beveridge to Shaffer, March 15, 1905.
[3] Shaffer to Beveridge, April 12, 1905.

and on top of the nervous exhaustion he caught a cold. 'So here I am,' he wrote Shaffer, 'nine tenths sick, and yet working all I can, notwithstanding. It is an ideal place for my condition and necessities. My cousin and his wife think a good deal more of me than they ought to think, their children are delicious.' Every afternoon he was taken out for a drive. And, to 'cap the climax, this is the country where I was born. So if there is a place on earth where I can work and get well, I guess it is here.' The Canadian project? It meant too much work. Out in the woods of Wisconsin, on the border of a lake, and surrounded by primeval woods, Bob DePauw [1] had offered him his camp, and he thought he would take it. [2]

But in the mean time Beveridge had arranged to go with his cousin to Europe, sailing May 9 on the Kaiser Wilhelm der Grosse, landing at Bremen, where he took an automobile to Lucerne, thence by train to Lake Como, and then to Genoa and Naples, and home by June 6. On returning, he went to the camp, which he dubbed 'Camp DePauw,' in the pine forest of Wisconsin, where guests were not permitted to indulge in 'serious talk' and where he 'could play red Indian.' [3] It was the first rest he had had for years, and he would need it.

The Rooseveltian period was about to open in earnest, with furious fighting henceforth to the end — the lustiest, gustiest period in American politics since the fighting days of Andrew Jackson.

[1] The son of the benefactor of DePauw University.
[2] Beveridge to Shaffer, April 14, 1905. [3] Beveridge to Shaw, undated.

CHAPTER III

CLEANING THE AUGEAN STABLES

I

THE congressional session beginning in December, 1905, was to be one of gusty battle, of broken bones and bloody noses, and was to mark a new departure in Beveridge's career. He who had interpreted national prosperity in terms of great railroad systems, powerful corporations, and mass production, became aware of the average man. He was no longer quite so certain of the inherent righteousness of Big Business, and was realizing that the partiality of government, positively or negatively disclosed, had been creating something of a Frankenstein monster. And he had been hearing things — the talk of the streets, of the Pullmans, of the farms and factories. This had produced a state of mind quite different from that of former years. He had an intuition that there was something wrong, something of unrest stirring beneath the sunny surface.

It was at about this time that he wrote Lorimer that when home he intended 'to get in close touch with the current opinions of the common man, the street-car conductor, the clerk in the store, the banker, and so on.' He was beginning to wonder if the fat dividends of a few great trusts were contributing to the satisfaction of the masses. 'I tell you, there is something going to happen in this country as sure as you are a foot high,' he added.[1] And Lorimer was quite as certain that there was something wrong. When Roosevelt made his famous 'muckrake speech,' and Beveridge wrote Lorimer that 'no scoundrel can hide behind his words,'[2] Lorimer replied that there was muck enough, and that no one who was familiar with it was going to go after it with a gingerly rake. The magazines, he thought, had 'only scratched the surface.'[3]

To Shaffer, Beveridge wrote more fully:

I have been carefully studying the present unrest and interviewing numbers of people about it. I am coming to the conclusion that it is not a passing whim, but a great and natural movement such as occurs in this country, as our early history shows, once about every forty years. It is not like the Granger episode or the Debs episode. The former... affected only the farmers; the latter, only the workingmen. The present unrest, however, is quite as vigorous among the intellec-

[1] Beveridge to Lorimer, March 13, 1906.   [2] Beveridge to Lorimer, April 18, 1906.
[3] Lorimer to Beveridge, April 20, 1906.

tuals, college men, university people, etc., as it is among the common people.[1]

But Shaffer was not impressed. The people seemed 'prosperous and reasonably happy' to him. Of course there had been a hue and cry to put some prominent men in the penitentiary. The Hearst papers had started it; then Munsey had got Ida Tarbell to write her 'Standard Oil'; and then had followed Lawson on 'Frenzied Finance,' and Stebbins's articles on graft, and David Graham Phillips's 'Treason of the Senate.' But there had been more noise than effect.[2] But Beveridge was not reassured, and was beginning to entertain some 'radical' ideas of his own. In this frame of mind he wrote an article on 'The Rich Man in Politics,' and sent it to Lorimer to read, but not for publication. As he followed the proceedings in the Senate, soon afterward, he began to yield to the editor's importunity to publish. 'I am not so dead sure,' he wrote, 'that I don't feel like letting you print that article on "The Rich Man in Politics," after all. It surely needs to be done by somebody, and on the other hand, a defense of the Senate as an institution is needed to be printed by somebody, although, God knows, there could be no defense of some of the men of that body.'[3] In the end, the article was published and attracted much attention:

We must always remember that this is a government of the people; but if public office is occupied by possessors of great wealth, the mass of the people, among whom, after all, throughout all history, the ablest governing ability has always been found, will be excluded from practical participation in the management of public affairs....

Yes, and a man who is rich and personally agreeable can secure the nomination for, and election to, an office over a man who is far better equipped for public duty....

Capital is all right in its place. It has a mission, and a mighty and beneficent mission it is. I do not object to capital. I defend it — only let it attend to its own business. And public life and special legislation for its own benefit are not its business....

But the vote of the rich man in public life, cast in the interest of his own investments, is only the beginning of his practical mischief. Universally such men are great entertainers. They give sumptuous and delightful dinners. They are friendly men, too; and in addition to that tremendous ability which won their immense wealth, they frequently have a singular charm of manner. Thus they make personal friends among their associates — and blood is thicker than water in public life just as it is anywhere else.[4]

[1] Beveridge to Shaffer, March 27, 1906.
[2] Shaffer to Beveridge, March 31, 1906.
[3] Beveridge to Lorimer, March 13, 1906.
[4] *Saturday Evening Post*, June 16, 1906.

Such was the tenor of the article, and the effect was to embarrass some of the rich members of both houses up for reëlection. Beveridge, supplicated by a number to speak in their behalf, refused on some pretense in some cases, but he did go to the support of Frank Lowden of Illinois, who he thought 'deserved it.'[1]

Beveridge had always thought himself a progressive; now he was becoming one.

II

Nothing did more to hasten his new alignment than the bitter and brilliant battle over the rate regulation bill which Roosevelt had urged. A year before,[2] Roosevelt had recommended that the Interstate Commerce Commission be clothed with the power to pass upon a rate that had been fixed, after a full hearing and judicial review, and to fix a reasonable substitute. He was not then in favor of giving the Commission the authority to initiate rates in general. The House, as we have seen, running beyond him, had passed the Hepburn Bill which died in the Senate on the expiration of the Congress. At the beginning of this session he had reiterated his position and made it plain that he did not ask that the Commission be granted the power to 'initiate or originate rates generally,' but only to change a rate already fixed.[3] But the House swept beyond him, as before, and re-passed the measure sponsored by William P. Hepburn.

The reactionaries of the Senate were waiting for it with knives when it appeared. Aldrich had marshaled his forces for the fight. Meanwhile, Roosevelt was being swept along by public sentiment favoring general regulation. It was in this epochal battle of wits that Jonathan P. Dolliver first unsheathed his sword to do battle for the public and to repudiate the leadership of Aldrich. When Aldrich's proposal of a compromise was rejected by Roosevelt, the former planned to push full steam ahead regardless of Executive displeasure; but when the venerable Cullom, resting in Florida, telegraphed instructions to record his vote for the unamended Hepburn Bill, the dictator changed his tactics. Thus, defeated on the main proposition of the power to initiate the rates, Aldrich, like a nimble cat landing on its feet, saved himself from utter discomfiture. If the Commission was to have the power, the courts should have the broadest possible power of review, and on this demand Aldrich and his followers gave

[1] Beveridge to Lorimer, June 23, 1906.
[2] Dec. 4, 1904.
[3] Message, December, 1905.

battle. Some of the more radical, suspicious of the courts, would have denied the right of appeal.

Through many days the memorable debate ran on, brilliant and able beyond all precedent for a generation. A bit of Aldrich strategy set the capital to shaking with laughter. In ordinary course, Dolliver, whose apostasy had infuriated Aldrich, would have sponsored the bill, reporting it from the committee. The brilliant Iowan was keen about it. Whereupon, in spite, the Aldrich manikins on the committee turned it over to the fiery Tillman, a Democrat, to report.

There was a reason for the laughter. Tillman was a man of great capacity, sterling integrity, and debating power, but at the time he was not on speaking terms with Roosevelt. But the latter, who was not squeamish about his weapons in a fight, announced his satisfaction with the support of Tillman and promised to work with him, and the laugh turned sour. In the end, the bill, with weakening compromises, was passed.

During the debate, Beveridge, intensely occupied with other matters as we shall see, took no major part, but constantly he supported Roosevelt in the votes and in the running debate. This was to have its effect upon his status in the Senate. Aldrich fumed, then raged. Democrats? They were expected, with few exceptions, to be against him. Men like the chronic insurgents could be forgiven — nothing was expected from them. But Beveridge! Member of the Steering Committee, slowly but surely being inducted into the inner circle of the oligarchy — it was too much! If Beveridge the conservative, defender of the trusts, panegyrist of Big Business, was to desert, what would happen next? This desertion could not go unscathed. When it was finally apparent that he had gone over, bag and baggage, to the progressive group on the bill, Aldrich momentarily lost his temper, and snapped at him on the floor of the Senate: 'We'll get you for this.'[1]

Henceforth, beneath the surface, the fight was on. Dolliver had been affronted; Beveridge threatened.

III

But Beveridge, that winter, spring, and summer, was busy with other things.

The idea of an effective meat inspection law had been incubating in his mind for many months. In studying our trade relations with Europe, he had been impressed by the rule that before the meat of our packers could reach the foreign market,

[1] Stephenson, *op. cit.*, 266.

it had to pass inspection. He knew that the canned meat for the British army had to be inspected and bear the date of the canning on the label. He wondered why it was thought less important to protect the American people than the European and the British soldier. He remembered his embarrassment over the rotten canned meat served American soldiers in the war with Spain. Years later, he was to write Mark Sullivan of the origin of the inspection plan:

Before I had seen Upton Sinclair's book, late one night in my study, I got to going over the law of Moses, as I often do just to amuse myself, and I was greatly interested in the extreme care taken by the Jewish theocracy that the Jewish people should eat only pure fish and birds — those that did not carry disease. This led to an investigation, just as a matter of interest and nothing more, of the Kosher slaughter-houses which to this day keep up the old Jewish custom of testing food. Thereupon I looked at our own meat inspection laws, and was horrified to find that, while our laws demanded careful inspection of meats intended for foreign consumption (simply because other countries would not otherwise take them), there was practically none at all for meat sold to our own people.[1]

It did not occur to him that there would be much opposition to a meat inspection bill.[2]

It was while he was meditating action that the country was shaken by the appearance of Upton Sinclair's powerful novel, 'The Jungle,' describing with sickening realism the conditions in the great packing-houses of Chicago. Written with the fervor of a crusader, it shocked a whole people. It told of the preparation of meats for consumption in the midst of filth and nauseating sanitary conditions, of packing meat from tubercular cattle and diseased hogs, of corruption and inadequate inspection by governmental agents. For a moment America sickened at the very thought of meat.

As much as a year before, the London 'Lancet' had run a series of appalling articles describing the scenes and methods of the American packing-houses. These were brutally frank in their seeming fidelity to the truth. They set forth that 'several nations of the more civilized parts of the world have thought it necessary to enact special laws against Chicago,'[3] that 'the representatives of the majesty of the law [inspectors] condescended' to work on the 'foul and abominable premises'[4] and they described the scenes of the slaughter-houses — 'the splashing of

[1] Beveridge to Sullivan, March 12, 1927.
[2] Frederick Boyd Stevenson, *Brooklyn Eagle*, May 17, 1908.
[3] *Lancet*, Jan. 7, 1905.   [4] *Ibid.*, Jan. 14, 1905.

offal, and the sputum of tuberculous workers' accumulating for
'weeks and months.'[1] A dreadful picture — the windows
'heavily caked with dirt,' the closets out of order and offensive,
the condemned carcasses of diseased animals in the same room
where meat was being prepared for human consumption.[2]
These 'Lancet' articles were threatening our markets for meat
throughout Europe. They carried, not merely an indictment of
the packing-houses, but a condemnation of the United States
Inspection Service.

Meanwhile, the Department of Agriculture, writhing under
the insinuations, began an investigation from within, and Roosevelt, mindful that the investigation might be discredited, named
investigating commissioners of his own[3] not associated with
the department under attack. The department investigators'
report, suggesting the defensive, was damning enough with its
story of rats nibbling meat and of filthy conditions, but the
Neill-Reynolds report was all dynamite.

In the mean time, Beveridge was preparing for action. His
first step was to consult with Lorimer of Philadelphia, and this
was in March. The latter, who had published the defense of
Armour, the packer, against the Sinclair charges, had at one
time been advertising manager of the Armour house. He warned
Beveridge he was working on a 'hard proposition,' and would
have to fight one of the 'most powerful combinations in America.'[4] Undismayed, Beveridge went to New York to consult
with Albert Shaw, who took him out to drive and discussed with
him the possible political effects upon his fortunes.[5] At the time
he had no intimation that the Department of Agriculture was
considering the subject,[6] and it was not, in fact, until weeks
later that its committee of investigation was named.

Before seeing Lorimer or Shaw, Beveridge had called Roosevelt's attention to 'The Jungle,' not knowing that the manuscript
of the novel had been seen by him.[7] It was after his return from
Philadelphia and New York that Beveridge determined upon
his course. His own story appears in a letter to Shaw.

After I came back from your place, I called Gifford Pinchot and
James A. Garfield to my room one morning before breakfast and told
them that I had made up my mind to draft a meat inspection bill and
asked their opinion and coöperation. They heartily endorsed the idea
and got me some data. About this time I went to the President and
told him that I was preparing a meat inspection bill, and he said,

[1] *Lancet*, Jan. 14, 1905.   [2] *Ibid.*, Jan. 21, 1905.
[3] Charles P. Neill and James B. Reynolds.
[4] Stevenson in *Brooklyn Eagle*, May 17, 1908.
[5] Beveridge to Shaw, July 1, 1908.   [6] *Ibid.*   [7] *Ibid.*

'Bully, but you'd better wait until Neill and Reynolds get back from Chicago.' At that time I did not know that Neill and Reynolds had gone to Chicago.[1] When they returned, I consulted with both of them, and with Reynolds many times. Meanwhile, several drafts of the bill had been drawn by me. About this time I met Secretary Wilson [2] one evening at dinner at the Pinchots'. Of course I was full of the subject and talked about nothing else; whereupon Wilson said that they were also thinking about it and were drafting a bill upon the subject which they were going to send to the President. I didn't like the idea of some person else introducing a bill on which I had been working, and I went to the President and told him to have Wilson send the bill over to me. This was the time I saw you when you were down here to see the Halsteads. Since Wilson at first hesitated, this is what I complained of to you about, and you and I went to the President the next morning on the subject.

The bill which Mr. Wilson sent me was drawn by young McCabe, Solicitor of the Agricultural Department.... I rejected it *in toto*, excepting only the section on fees, which I retained — it being drawn by Wilson himself.... After this ... I think I drafted the bill about twenty times. Every third or fourth draft I would send to Wilson for his comment.... I finally completed the bill to my satisfaction on the Sunday before I introduced it on Monday. I went over to the President and told him that I would introduce it that day, and asked him if he would send in his Message. He said he could promise nothing. I told him that I was going ahead and introduce the bill anyhow — which I did that day. The rest you know.[3]

This bill provided for the thorough, rigid inspection we now have, for the payment of the cost of inspection by the packers, and for placing the date of canning on canned meats.

And then began the tumult and the shouting.

IV

The packers and cattlemen of the western plains made common cause against the bill, and launched the most transparent propaganda. Instantly Beveridge drove them to a momentary acquiescence by laying his cards face upward on the table. There was nothing they feared so much as the publication of the report of Neill and Reynolds; and if they made a fight, the President would send it to Congress with a Message. Four days after the introduction of the bill, Beveridge had a conference with their representatives. He promised if they would support the measure, he would let it pass in silence; but otherwise he would take the floor and discuss the need of the law with the utmost frankness.

---

[1] Roosevelt began investigation after Isaac Marcosson had shown him the manuscript of *The Jungle*.

[2] Secretary of Agriculture. [3] Beveridge to Shaw, July, 1908.

That was in the morning. At three o'clock in the afternoon they surrendered, and the bill was put in as an amendment to the agricultural appropriation bill, and passed.

But it was a packers' retreat, not a surrender.

The strategy of the packers and their allies was to wreck the bill by amendments in the House. In anticipation of this very plan, Roosevelt had warned that if the measure were materially changed, he would send in the feared report with a Message.[1] Within a few days, members of both houses were deluged with protesting telegrams from all over the country, and the similarity of their phrasing left no doubt as to their common inspiration. Clearly they had been hurried from Chicago ready for signatures. The thing was so brazen that Senator Redfield Proctor of Vermont denounced it on the floor.[2] The Capitol was congested with lobbyists.

The fight in the House committee was prolonged and bitter, and one by one the teeth of the measure were being pulled. So stubbornly did Beveridge struggle against all changes that even Roosevelt at times was prone to criticize his uncompromising attitude. The President, however, entered the fray with his usual zest, protesting against House amendments tending to encourage appeals to the courts and to reduce the Secretary of Agriculture to a mere ministerial officer without power.[3] He was not so set as Beveridge against the Wadsworth amendment putting the cost of inspection on the people rather than on the packers. In the heat of the controversy, a misunderstanding, due to a difference in interpretation, threatened for a moment to disturb the relations of Beveridge and Roosevelt. The former, interpreting one of the House amendments as meaning no inspection of the plants at night, protested to the latter, who, in turn, made his protest to Wadsworth. Beveridge was mistaken, and Roosevelt flew into a rage. To callers at the White House he seemed a seething volcano, expressing his displeasure freely.[4] Beveridge insisted on his interpretation of the effect of the amendment.

With the White House deeply engaged in day and night conferences with members, with Beveridge making a personal canvass of the House, with inspired telegrams pouring in, with the packers threatening to pass on the cost of inspection to the consumers and the cattle-raisers, the President struck. Responding to the resolution of a Democrat, he sent the report of Neill and Reynolds to Congress.

[1] Beveridge to Shaw, May 26, 1906.   [2] *Congressional Record*, June 20, 1906.
[3] Roosevelt to Wadsworth, June 15, 1906.
[4] *Indianapolis Star*, June 17, 1906.

Setting forth the methods of the packers in plain language, the report made a profound impression on the country and threw the enemies of real inspection into a perspiration. Roosevelt was denounced on the floor of the House for dealing a deadly blow to a great industry.[1] Shaffer reported to Beveridge that in Chicago there was 'intense bitterness... among the business men and bankers against the President.' The publisher had attended a meeting of the business men's and bankers' associations where he found 'the expressions almost unanimously against the President.' He was amazed. Some of the business leaders declared they would vote for Bryan in preference to Roosevelt in another election.[2] It was at this juncture that the long intimacy of Beveridge and Charles G. Dawes was broken, not to be resumed until ten years later.

When the bill emerged from the House, most of the teeth had been put back, but the people, not the packers, were to pay the inspection costs and the date of canning was not to be put upon the cans.

Back in the Senate the fight centered on these amendments. In reporting the inability of the conferees to agree, Senator Proctor denounced the organized propaganda, and Beveridge immediately took the floor.

Just before, the English Minister of War had been asked in the Commons if it were true that the British soldiers were being fed packed meat without the date of packing on the can, and the Minister indignantly had replied that they were not. Taking his cue from this episode, Beveridge asked why Americans should eat what the British soldiers would scorn. The grocers would suffer if people knew the canned meat on the shelves was old? 'Is that a defense for fraud upon the purchaser?' he asked. And the cost of inspection a hardship on the packers? Under existing conditions, would not the packers be glad to pay twice the cost to restore confidence in their products? The farmer of North Dakota, taking his wheat to market, paid the cost of inspection — was the packer alone sacrosanct? And the agitation hurting business? 'It does not hurt any business to tell the truth about it and to correct the evils which that truth reveals. Any business that can be permanently hurt by telling the truth about it, ought not only to be hurt, it ought to be destroyed.'

Senator Warren, described later as 'the greatest shepherd since Abraham,' replied for the packers and served notice that they would pass the cost of inspection on to the consumers and the cattlemen.[3] Bitter and in jeering mood, he made a personal

[1] *Congressional Record*, June 12, 1906.
[2] Shaffer to Beveridge, June 12, 1906.   [3] *Congressional Record*, June 20, 1906.

attack on Beveridge, who ignored the personalities and sought in vain to pin him down as to the date upon the cans.

It was this arrogance of the packers and their allies that aroused the wrath of the venerable Gallinger of New Hampshire, himself a physician with a professional interest in the reform. 'After the wretched and revolting exposé... I have very little sympathy for the men who have made their millions and their tens of millions, and who, if they had been men of public spirit and correct impulses, would have made their packing-houses as free from filth and disease-breeding conditions as is this Senate Chamber.' [1]

The Senate voted to insist on its bill, and asked a conference with the House. Four days later, Proctor reported the result — the House had stood unfalteringly against the date upon the cans and for the cost of inspection on the people. The comments were scathing. [2] Two days later, the debate was resumed, with Proctor witheringly denouncing the shameless methods of the monopoly and its 'cheapness.' And then Beveridge took the floor to accept the best that could be had and to pledge himself to renew the fight in the next session against the House amendments.

'There is a reason,' he said, 'why I dislike to see the Senate forced to the necessity of surrendering to the packers in this manner. The Senator from South Carolina (Tillman), in his dramatic way and with his picturesque language, has exposed the surrender which the Congress has just made to the Standard Oil monopoly. Indeed, it was a disgraceful surrender, but a surrender possibly made necessary to save the life of a great measure — the rate bill — just as in this case it seems that surrender is necessary to save the life of another great measure — the Agricultural Appropriation Bill, and a system of inspection of meat and meat food products.

'Now, right upon the heels of this surrender to the Standard Oil Company, immediately after we have struck our colors to that great and grinding monopoly, to surrender again to the next biggest monopoly in the United States is, to me, full of humiliation and shame. Yet that is what it is.' [3]

Thus was the measure passed, with a surrender on the two issues; but even so, it was one of the most important measures for the protection of the people ever enacted into law. Something had been done to introduce the humanities into statesmanship, and to Beveridge belonged the laurels. Roosevelt himself bestowed them in sending him the pen with which he had signed the bill, with a note definitively crediting him with the reform:

[1] *Congressional Record*, June 23, 1906.   [2] *Ibid.*, June 27, 1906.
[3] *Ibid.*, June 29, 1906.

My Dear Senator Beveridge:

You were the man who first called my attention to the abuses of the packing-houses. You were the legislator who drafted the bill which in its substance now appears in the amendment to the agricultural bill, and which will enable us to put a complete stop to the wrongdoing complained of. The pen is worth nothing in itself, but I am glad to send it to you as the expression of my acknowledgment of your services.

Faithfully yours

THEODORE ROOSEVELT [1]

With this triumph, Beveridge had taken a long stride forward as a progressive and compromised some of his old relationships. He had discovered that bigness and power do not necessarily make for the good of humanity.

V

Meanwhile, during this hectic session, the statehood bill again called forth his utmost exertions. During the preceding vacation he had been intensively engaged in the organization of public sentiment for his plan. Delegations from Oklahoma had made a pilgrimage to Indianapolis for a conference. In that Territory he had become a hero — a savior. All objections to joint statehood with Indian Territory had faded away. The situation still was different in Arizona and New Mexico, but the fight was being waged in these Territories too. With the foes of joint statehood marshaling their forces for a decisive battle, Roosevelt was becoming annoyed that he had burned his bridges.[2] An imposing lobby of business men and men of great wealth, representing great interests, had descended on the capital to fight the Beveridge bill. The spectacle was shocking to Beveridge, who wrote in disgust to Shaw: 'I don't want anybody ever again to tell me about the high moral tone of wealthy men when their pocketbook is touched. These fellows are indulging in the crudest kind of scoundrelism. They are inspired by nothing in the world except a desire to escape taxation. The mining corporations of Arizona have taken out of the Territory over $400,000,000 of mineral wealth; and they have paid the Territory nothing in the way of taxes.'[3]

As the fight waxed warm, with the press reporting the progress of the fight, Shaffer wired his friend to 'drop all newspaper and other matters and fight and win the statehood victory';[4] and Beveridge replied that he had dropped everything but statehood, but thought it extremely doubtful whether he would win.

---

[1] Roosevelt to Beveridge, June 30, 1906. [2] Roosevelt to Beveridge, June 16, 1906.
[3] Beveridge to Shaw, Dec. 7, 1905. [4] Shaffer to Beveridge, Feb. 6, 1906.

There was no longer any doubt about Oklahoma — Beveridge had won there; and the fight in the Senate was to revolve around the proposition to permit Arizona and New Mexico to vote, as a unit or separately, on entering the Union jointly. Senator Joseph Benson Foraker, an able, dashing, slashing, resourceful debater, was proposing that they vote separately. This strategy was born of the belief that in her impatience to get in, New Mexico would vote heavily for joint statehood.[1] Beveridge was now insisting that the Territories vote as one people.

The debate though brief was brilliant. After the opening speech of the opposition, Beveridge took the floor and launched into his remarkable speech, 'Arizona the Great.' He painted glowingly the future of a mighty State such as could be made from the two Territories; but on the whole it was a fighting speech in which he analyzed the opposition with brutal frankness. The politicians wanted separate States, since that would double the offices. The cattle interests were against his bill because the grazing lands on which they had been fattening their herds would be taken up by the school grants provided in the measure. The railroads were against it because they would be subjected to taxation from which they then were immune. The mining interests were against it for a similar reason.

'Arizona,' he said, 'possesses subject to taxation more than $400,000,000 worth of property, and yet returns less than $50,-000,000 worth on the tax list. The railroads are worth about $70,000,000 and are returned for less than $7,000,000.' Thus, steeped in his facts, he easily met all interruptions and struck with all his might at the motives he thought behind the opposition. Crowded galleries listened to the speech, and cheered its close.

Foraker replied in his best manner; and Spooner, paying tribute to Beveridge's eloquence, made a short, strong speech insisting that the party platforms had pledged the honor of the Nation. Beveridge closed in a brief and moving rejoinder, pitched on the national plane — the responsibility of the Nation in the making of a State. Foraker offered his amendment for a separate vote, the roll was called, and Beveridge lost by forty-two to twenty-nine.[2]

Some years before, Beveridge had started out against the most virulent opposition, brilliantly led and powerfully supported, to make two States of four Territories. He had won on Oklahoma and Indian Territory; he had no illusions about Arizona and New Mexico. His part in the making of Oklahoma was enthusi-

[1] J. B. Foraker, *Notes of a Busy Life.*
[2] *Congressional Record*, March 8–9, 1906.

astically acknowledged by the Governor of the Territory. 'We look forward,' he wrote, 'to the time, in the not far distance, when you will pay us the honor of a visit, when you will be able to see for yourself the debt we all feel we owe you.'[1] When Roosevelt signed the statehood bill, he reached across the table to grasp Beveridge's hand and say:

'Senator Beveridge, the congratulations are due you, and now with all my heart I congratulate you upon the great work finished and a great battle splendidly fought.'[2]

But to the recipient of the congratulations the fight was not yet over. He had done his part, was willing to do more, but the battle-field henceforth was to be in Arizona and New Mexico. Notifying Governor Hagleman of Arizona of the action taken, he called on the people of the Territories favorable to joint statehood to organize for the elections.[3] And when he was informed that the Republican and Democratic State Chairmen had agreed in conference jointly to denounce joint statehood, he wrote: 'I am in Washington and can put the bill through, but you people in Arizona must do the campaigning. If you cannot do it with all the literature you have at your disposal and with all the arguments, then, of course, it will have to go.'[4]

For the moment he was worn and weary, and a bit disgusted, but we shall find him fighting throughout the summer as best he could.

VI

He had looked forward to leaving in June for Paris to deliver the Fourth of July oration there to the American colony on its invitation. It was not the first time the invitation had been extended, but this year he had agreed, and had prepared his speech with the utmost care to make it a document of some importance. His membership on the Foreign Relations Committee and his personal intimacy with the President promised to arouse more than casual interest in the speech. He had completed the manuscript in May and was ready to 'begin the polishing process.'[5]

Then, unhappily, the 'Washington Star,' announcing the speech, made the comment that 'if it is true, as reported, that he has discussed the terms of his speech with the President and that the latter is aware of what he intends to say, there may be some

[1] Governor Frantz to Beveridge, June 23, 1906.
[2] *Indianapolis Star*, June 17, 1906.   [3] Beveridge to Hagleman.
[4] Beveridge to C. F. Ainsworth, June 22, 1906.
[5] Beveridge to Perkins, May 28, 1906.

significance in the remarks.' It was the very thing that could not be said. Elihu Root, Secretary of State, had made much of the point with Roosevelt that neither of them should see the speech in advance. On the publication of the 'Star' article, Roosevelt, unduly excited, wrote: 'Will you glance at the enclosed clipping from the "Evening Star"? It contains, of course, just what must not be said about your speech. Can't you make it understood that I have not seen your speech and am, of course, not in any way responsible for it, and that it has simply the significance that attaches to the speech of a member of the Foreign Relations Committee who has been in close agreement with the President's policy; or (if you prefer to put it that way) who together with the President and the other Republican members of the Foreign Relations Committee has had for the last four and a half years followed substantially the same policy? Of course what is necessary is that there shall not be any impression conveyed that you are the spokesman of the Administration, or that your utterances have any official weight as representing the Administration save from the standpoint of our general sympathy and friendship.'[1]

Thus, it seemed, there was to be a penalty attached to his fidelity to the President and his policies, and he was to be called upon publicly to proclaim his insignificance as far as the Administration, to which he had given the last ounce of his energy, was concerned.

The letter did not change his plans in the least. As a member of the Foreign Relations Committee he was under no obligation to remain silent or to embarrass himself by proclaiming that the President was not responsible for his public utterances.

But the speech was not to be delivered. He was to have sailed on June 23, his reservations were made, his trunk packed, but at the moment the fight on the meat inspection bill was at a critical stage and he had to cancel his engagement. It was just as well. He had performed herculean labors during the session. It had been a constant battle. He had suffered some disillusionments and had been forced to fight powerful reactionary forces and make enemies in high quarters. He needed rest. The day Congress adjourned, he hurried to Philadelphia to revive his spirits and play a bit with the congenial Lorimer, his favorite playfellow; and then he turned toward the pine woods of Maine.

[1] Roosevelt to Beveridge, May 23, 1906.

CHAPTER IV

FORWARD MARCH

I

'YOU cannot imagine or believe the comforts of camp life until you experience them,' Beveridge wrote Shaw from Rangeley, Maine. 'No bed you ever slept in equals the pine-bough beds in which we sleep. They are very smooth and springier than any mattress you ever slept on.'[1] The moment he reached the pine woods of Maine, he was floating in canoes with guides down the streams reflecting the trees that bordered them, and this close communion with Nature speedily restored his strength and spirits. The excursion was made all the more enjoyable by the company of George Bramwell Baker, a Boston banker of Indiana origin of whom Beveridge was very fond.

To Roosevelt he wrote of his experiences and plans: 'I have been in the depths of the Maine woods with two of the most intelligent guides in this country — indeed, two as intelligent men and as well read (which is very remarkable) as one ordinarily finds.... Immediately after the adjournment I plunged into the deep wilderness on a long canoe trip. It made a new man of me. I could not have believed that a human being could have been so restored in so short a time. I am finishing the work of resting here [Rangeley]. After I open the Maine campaign at Portland, August 22, I am going on another long canoe trip. Gifford Pinchot arrives home from abroad just in time to take the trip with me. I am wondering whether you would feel like urging him to do it. I just have a letter from him in which he says he wants to, but there is some meeting or other out in Idaho in which Heyburn [Senator Heyburn] is interested and Gifford wants to be on the ground to stand by the fellows who stood by him. Nevertheless, Pinchot needs an outing.'[2]

Roosevelt replied from Oyster Bay, 'Oh, how I wish I could be off on a canoe trip in the great woods myself!' However, he had had a delightful summer and a real rest and could not grumble. 'I shall see if I can get Gifford Pinchot and make him go with you,' he continued. 'I am not going to promise until I see him, because I do not know just how much weight he puts upon the other appeals made to him.'[3]

[1] Beveridge to Shaw, July 6, 1906.
[2] Beveridge to Roosevelt, Aug. 8, 1906.
[3] Roosevelt to Beveridge, Aug. 15, 1906.

Within a month after Beveridge, 'not much more than a
fishworm physically,' plunged into the forest, he was so thoroughly restored that he wrote in merry mood that he would
challenge the champion heavyweight but for the fear of hurting
him.[1] However, his mind was busy. More and more impressed
with the iniquities and inequalities of the tariff, he was positive
there should be an early revision. He talked upon the subject
with everyone he met. The expression, 'stand-pat,' had become
revolting to him, and the day before he opened the Maine
campaign he wrote to Roosevelt:

Those fellows who are trying to make tne tariff the only... issue, or
some other tommyrot the issue, and who are trying to leave out the
tremendous work of this Administration, will not have their way —
shall not have their way. You are the issue — whoever fights on that
issue will win....

There are a great number of business men at this hotel from all over
the country — many from Massachusetts, several from New York, and
several from Philadelphia. I have talked with them all, and not one
single man of them who does not say that some schedules of the tariff
ought to be changed — and all of them are protectionist Republicans.

Also every solitary man who has talked to me... declares that he is
sick and tired of that false, reactionary, and foolish motto, 'Let well
enough alone.' Mr. Cannon in his speech at Danville, has utterly
missed the meaning of the times. He entirely fails to comprehend the
great movement of the American millions which you are leading; he is
utterly ignorant of the spirit that is now spreading over this Nation.
I am sorry, a good deal sorrier than I can say. For I had come to like
him tremendously and admire his immense strength of character and
mind. It puts me in mind of the words of the Saviour as reported by
Matthew: 'When it is evening, ye say, It will be fair weather; for the
day is red. And in the morning: It will be foul weather; for the sky is
red and lowering. Oh, ye hypocrites, ye can discern the face of the
sky; but can yet not discern the signs of the times.'

The truth about it is that nearly all the older politicians are like a
bunch of belated travelers who have come to catch a train and stand
on the platform waiting for it, when as a matter of fact the train has
passed on a long while ago. Their watches are bad, that is all.[2]

But Roosevelt was still chary about grappling with the tariff,
and gave his reasons in his reply:

As to the tariff, the trouble is that of which those business men with
whom you spoke ought to be aware — that when it comes down to the
practical work of reforming the tariff, no two men want quite the same
reform. As you know, I have for a couple of years been desirous of
seeing the tariff revised; for while its protective features should be

[1] Beveridge to Judge Francis E. Baker, Aug. 1, 1906.
[2] Beveridge to Roosevelt, Aug. 22, 1906.

ALBERT J. BEVERIDGE
1906

maintained, a number of schedules should be materially lowered. But I confess I do not see how we are going to accomplish this just at this time unless there is a change in the temper of the people, as reflected by their Congressmen.[1]

Before he had read this letter, Beveridge had opened the campaign in Portland with the declaration that the tariff had to be revised along Republican lines and by the friends of protection — but revised. It was the first such declaration from a Republican leader of the conservative school and attracted attention all over the country, and called forth many editorial expressions. A little later, in the same State, Taft was to make a similar declaration, but it was Beveridge who was to hammer away on the theme from time to time in the campaign that fall.

Meanwhile, as he floated lazily down the streams under the canopy of the trees and tramped sturdily through the pine woods, a crisis came in Cuba which instantly rekindled the old imperialistic flame within him. During the four previous years the island had prospered and grown materially, but the Administration of Tomas Estrada Palma had ignored the constitutional provisions regarding the independence of the judiciary and the autonomy of municipalities. Despairing of any redress at the polls, after the election preliminaries had reeked with frauds, and finding recourse to the courts impossible because manned by enemies, the Liberals issued a revolutionary manifesto in June and the insurrection immediately assumed dangerous proportions. The Government of Palma had neither the moral support of the people nor the physical power to cope with the situation, and Palma made repeated appeals to Washington for intervention. At length mediators were dispatched to Cuba and failed to find a compromise, and in late September, Palma resigned, Congress adjourned without choosing a successor, and the island was on the verge of anarchy. To meet this emergency, Roosevelt proclaimed a provisional government the next day, and through the remainder of the year peace was maintained. The situation was delicate and was handled carefully, the United States making no display of military force.

From the beginning, Beveridge was convinced that the hour had struck to take over the island. He had resented, as a sentimental blunder, the pledge made at the close of the Spanish War, but had thought time would serve the purpose of imperialism, and the time would come when there would be no other way but annexation. And now the day had come, he was persuaded. Nor did he make a secret of his idea. In mid-September, on emerging from the woods and before entering the fall cam-

[1] Roosevelt to Beveridge, Aug. 23, 1906.

paign, he had spent a day and night with Roosevelt at Oyster Bay. The record of that visit was set down by Roosevelt in a letter to Henry Cabot Lodge. Beveridge had urged a revision of the tariff, and Roosevelt had combated the idea on the ground that it would be impossible to have a revision 'without inviting disaster in the Presidential election.' These considerations, Beveridge had pronounced 'irrelevant.' And on Cuba: 'His advice as regards Cuba was simple, namely: that I should at once take the island — advice about as rational as requests I used to get at the time of the anthracite coal strike to " take the coal barons by the throat." However, I will do him the justice to say that he is far better than Foraker who telegraphed me his judgment that I could not intervene at all.'[1]

Knowing the view of Roosevelt, when he returned to New York Beveridge announced that there would be intervention only as a last resort.[2]

But when he took the stump, and he opened the Republican campaign in eight States, beginning with a great meeting in Chicago, he urged tariff revision, and supported the presidential policy of non-intervention in Cuba — in his own way. If the fighting there continued, intervention would be necessary; if, again, we raised the flag in Cuba, it must never be lowered again. The fervent manner of this declaration invariably aroused enthusiasm, and he did his best to create sentiment favorable to the permanent acquisition of the island.[3] Nor did he miss the opportunity to report to Roosevelt on the popular reactions:

Tariff revision is always heartily and instantly cheered. Also in talking with our people before the meetings I have found but one sentiment, and that expressed without any expression of my views. It is that there must be some tariff change.

Second: Your course in Cuba arouses unlimited enthusiasm. It is the universal belief, so far as I can find it expressed, that Cuba in the end will be permanently under American authority. I have not found a single man or woman who does not believe that any reëstablishment of the Cuban Government will be followed by another insurrection. The statement that should it become necessary to raise our flag again in Cuba it will be raised to stay, brings a response very much like the wild enthusiasm that preceded the Spanish War.[4]

Roosevelt, seeking to maintain order in Cuba until an election could be held and some reforms wrought to satisfy the people, and without intervention in a permanent form 'at present,'[5] was annoyed, and left no doubt of his annoyance.

[1] *Roosevelt-Lodge Correspondence*, II, 233–34.
[2] *Indianapolis Star*, Sept. 16, 1906.   [3] *Ibid.*, Sept. 23, 1906.
[4] Beveridge to Roosevelt, Oct. 1, 1906.
[5] *Roosevelt-Lodge Correspondence*, II, 235.

Your friends 'Tom, Dick and Harry' simply do not know what they are talking about if they say 'it is nonsense to keep on setting up one Cuban Government after another.' If they believe this, it then becomes apparent that even the most ignorant have their limitations, and that it is not safe to follow the advice, even of those who know nothing about the subject — as in the case of the 'Tom, Dick and Harry' of your letter. One Cuban Government has been tumbled over. It would come perilously near bad faith if we do what would amount to seizing this excuse immediately to conquer the island. I could not do it on my own responsibility. It is not a task to be undertaken with less than twenty-five thousand troops, and perhaps more would be needed, while probably it would take at least a year. For such a move the consent of Congress would have to be obtained. However, if it should prove true that 'as fast as one Cuban Government is set up, it will be knocked over,' I think that you will find that all Americans will stand behind the policy of taking possession of the island in some form or other. But they would like to be sure that first we have in good faith striven to avoid the necessity.

P.S. Your second letter has just come. It is interesting and important. You may have noticed that I have been scrupulous not to hoist the American flag in Cuba because I do not want to hoist it again unless it becomes necessary to raise it in such a way that it has got to stay. I am mighty glad to hear from outside sources of the extraordinary enthusiasm with which you have been greeted whenever you have opened the campaign.[1]

A few days later Roosevelt wrote again.

I am much struck by what you say about the attitude of the West toward Cuba. It would not have done to have acted otherwise in this matter, for it would have looked as if this nation was not behaving in good faith; but of course if there is a fresh breakdown of the Cuban Government, I feel that all need on our part for exercising further patience will be at an end.[2]

In the midst of a whirlwind campaign, Beveridge found time for a hasty trip from New York to Washington to confer with the President,[3] and immediately afterward to write Roosevelt some suggestions as to his Message, and chide him on his jeer at 'Tom, Dick and Harry.'

I have read over again your kind letters since our talk and cannot resist saying to you in writing what I said to you in our last conversation, 'Tom, Dick and Harry' have been your sources of power. It was their faith in you which enabled you last winter to get from a reluctant Congress laws needed by the people. I am wondering if you remember our long ride from Kansas City six years ago. I cannot but reflect that it was this same 'Tom, Dick and Harry' with whom Napoleon was able to overthrow Europe.

[1] Roosevelt to Beveridge, Oct. 6, 1906.
[2] Roosevelt to Beveridge, Oct. 7, 1906.   [3] *Indianapolis Star*, Oct. 14, 1906.

I must again repeat that constant touch with the people is bringing me to believe that there are very few ignorant among them. The ordinary citizen is better posted than the average Senator or Congressman — the reason is that they read more current literature. In this connection I see only one danger — and it is a grave danger — the purchase by corporations which have 'interests to protect,' and by enormously wealthy men who have ambitions to serve, of so many newspapers. Newspapers thus owned give the people only such information as will help their owners, suppressing all information that might injure them, on the one hand; and on the other hand, giving them information that will help the owners. This, of course, poisons the source of the people's information, and, as far as their influence goes, makes them a good deal worse than ignorant because it makes them misinformed.[1]

Thus, throughout the summer and autumn of 1906, Beveridge was putting a great distance between himself and the philosophy of 'Let well enough alone.'

II

The campaign was a hard one, and, in the development of the Beveridge of reform, an important one. Opening the campaign in Chicago, he was constantly busy until the closing of the polls, addressing great meetings in many of the significant centers of the West. In Boston, a painful affliction of the throat confined him to his room in the home of George B. Baker, but, disregarding the doctor's orders, he was speaking in Carnegie Hall, New York, within two days. The last two weeks were spent in Indiana on the stump.

Here Bryan, never more popular, was arousing the fervent enthusiasm of his followers, and soon he and Beveridge were engaging in long-distance debates. The positive note of progressivism in the latter's speeches was causing comment, and it was not lost on Bryan. When Beveridge declared that vast wealth was the greatest peril of the age, that an income tax was coming, and, in the meanwhile, an inheritance tax to limit 'the unhealthy fortunes so that they will not go on increasing in the idle hands of heirs who never earned a dollar,' [2] Bryan welcomed him into the Democratic Party, and formed the habit of taking texts from the speeches of the Indiana orator. Immediately after the address just quoted, Bryan, speaking in Evansville, found his text in the same speech, reading it from the paper slowly:

Every reform measure and every proposed law for the Nation's good has been fought by mighty financial interests whose practices and im-

[1] Beveridge to Roosevelt, Oct. 16, 1906.
[2] At Dunkirk, *Indianapolis Star*, Oct. 21, 1906.

munities the proposed law threatened. There seems to be a strange insanity created in the piling up of unhealthy fortunes, with unhealthy haste, by unhealthy methods — an insanity that makes men who are worth scores of millions fight a law which will reduce even a small percentage of their enormous profit.

Laying the paper down, Bryan smiled broadly, and said: 'This might be attributed to a Democratic speaker and no one would ever notice the mistake. But what is to be said when a Republican Senator uses this language? I rejoice that such a brilliant man as Senator Beveridge has become converted to this good Democratic doctrine.'

It was a compliment not to be relished by Beveridge, beset on every side by the reactionaries of his own party as more Democratic than Republican, and he parried the blow by inviting Bryan and the Democrats to make it unanimous for Republican policies. Throughout the remainder of the campaign the two men fired Parthian shots at one another. When Beveridge described him as a 'dreamer,' Bryan responded with his classic Bible story of Joseph, driven away by his brothers as a dreamer, and later found by them in Egypt in possession of the corn they needed.

Tariff revision downward — an inheritance tax — the limitation of swollen fortunes; and then, in his closing speech at Indianapolis, Beveridge sowed more dragons' teeth, when, ignoring the protests of the politicians, he declared for nominations for office in primaries instead of in conventions. 'The people have a right to elect whom they please to any office,' he said. 'But the people cannot elect whom they please because they must vote, not for candidates the people name, but for candidates conventions name. And sometimes these candidates — those named by conventions — are selected by one or two men who manipulate conventions. Consider Quay of Pennsylvania, or Platt of New York, or bosses anywhere. Let the people really govern, not govern in pretense, but govern in reality.'[1]

The old-line politicians, already astonished by the demand for tariff revision and an inheritance tax, lifted their eyebrows a little higher, and shivered in their shoes.

III

The campaign ended in a Republican victory, for the Rough Rider was still at the height of his popularity, and Beveridge had put his finger on the only issue that really counted — the President himself.

[1] *Indianapolis Star*, Nov. 4, 1906.

But Beveridge was not wholly pleased with the November polling, for up from Arizona and New Mexico rolled the tidings of defeat. Throughout the summer and autumn, he had been in touch, through correspondence, with the fight down there. Too wise to enter the campaign in person to persuade the voters to demand joint statehood, he advised his friends by mail. It seemed a hopeless prospect. The major part of the practical politicians were against it, but there was certain fatality in the open opposition of the Federal office-holders. In August he was receiving bitter complaints of Roosevelt's neutrality. 'While we assert and believe,' wrote one irate champion, 'that he is sincere in his desire to have Arizona and New Mexico admitted as a joint State, we are met constantly by numbers... who hold office at the President's disposal saying... the President is only making this talk for political strength for himself.... Governor Kibbey and Judge Kent [1] were a short time ago in consultation with the President, and they report here that the President is satisfied with their course. If this be true, there is no use in our trying to carry the joint statehood proposition in Arizona. These statements of theirs are borne out by the fact that Kibbey is allowed to remain as Governor which is practically at the head of the Republican Party.[2] But Roosevelt, if not indifferent to the cause, was adamant against coercion. When approached, he said he had 'no desire to coerce the action of any man in Arizona.' The Federal office-holders had the same right to an opinion and a vote as any other citizens, so long as they do not use their offices 'to control or influence the popular vote.' Otherwise, they absolutely were 'untrammeled.' That said, he might add that the President hoped the joint statehood would carry, since otherwise Arizona might have to wait for years, for another chance.[3]

But as the fight waxed warmer, the man in the Maine woods began to stir uneasily under the prodding of complaining letters about the Territorial Governor. He wrote to Roosevelt that the removal of Kibbey would make for a fairer count, since, otherwise, he and his subordinates would manipulate the election boards. Charges had been filed against him. 'You will know,' he continued, 'whether they are sufficient for your action — and, indeed, of course you will know whether it is best to take any action at all. It was 'disheartening to the supporters of joint statehood to have Federal officials insisting openly that the President was in sympathy with their opposition.'[4]

[1] Opponents of joint statehood.

[2] Charles F. Ainsworth to Beveridge, Aug. 21, 1906.

[3] Roosevelt to Dr. Mark A. Rodgers, Tucson, June 27, 1906.

[4] Beveridge to Roosevelt, Sept. 20. 1906.

But Roosevelt replied that 'the one thing that would be absolutely certain, not only to hurt the cause of joint statehood... but to do serious damage to the Republican Party... would be the removal of Governor Kibbey or anyone else for exercising his right to do as he thinks... in the joint statehood matter.' He described the removal of the Governor as 'the kind of violent measure that can always be counted upon to make a bad condition worse.'[1]

Thus no aggressive help could be had from Washington, and the friends of joint statehood had to rely upon themselves. They did all they could. A speaking campaign was launched and a daily newspaper devoted solely to the issue was published.[2] An effort was made to enlist the influence of Senator Smoot with the Mormon bishops in Arizona, but he replied that conversations with Mormons in Utah persuaded him that his people favored joint statehood without suggestion.[3]

But the corporations, along with the politicians and Federal office-holders, were against it, and the result was that joint statehood carried in New Mexico and lost in Arizona. Thirty per cent of the registered Arizonians failed to vote, but, out of a total of 21,500 votes, a scant three thousand were cast for the unification of the Territories. Two thirds of the voters in New Mexico supported joint statehood.

Beveridge had fought his last fight upon that issue, and, though disappointed, he turned to other things.

IV

For months, he had been preparing to fight to end child labor in factories, mines, and shops, assembling an arsenal of statistics, combing every possible source of information on the evil. He had touched upon the subject in campaign speeches, and at Symphony Hall, Boston, within hearing of the mills, had denounced the economic exploitation of childhood. Just after the campaign he had announced his purpose at Richmond, Indiana,[4] and a month before he had urged Roosevelt to recommend an adequate child-labor law in his forthcoming Message.[5] A few days after the announcement of his purpose, he had sent a copy of his bill to the President and followed it with a letter.

The bill sent you is admittedly constitutional; nobody will question its constitutionality. No constitutional argument, plausible or other-

[1] Roosevelt to Beveridge, Sept. 22, 1906.
[2] Ainsworth to Beveridge, Sept. 25, 1906.
[3] W. H. Andrews to Beveridge, Aug. 17, 1906.
[4] *Indianapolis Star*, Nov. 19, 1906. [5] Beveridge to Roosevelt, Oct. 16, 1906.

wise, can be made against it.... The bill... is a gradual extension of national power for the purpose of curing nation-wide evils under the interstate commerce powers of Congress and not open to constitutional objection.... If it is not too late, I am hoping that you can make favorable mention of this proposed legislation in your Message. The country is quite ripe for it, as I have informed you in the various reports I have had the honor to submit during the campaign. The proposition to remedy the child-labor evil by national law met with great enthusiasm every place I spoke throughout the country and was excelled only by the retention of Cuba and equaled only by the declaration that we would renew the battle on the two points in the Meat Bill on which we lost, date on the cans and cost on packers.[1]

When Shaffer, a bit concerned with the abandon with which his friend was challenging the enmity of powerful business elements, wrote to warn him that such legislation might discourage business expansion, he replied, with heat, that he himself had worked as a child from the age of twelve, and had he not been 'blessed with an optimistic turn of mind and had not fallen under the best influences,' he could see how he might have 'developed into a bitter and anarchistic hater of society.' With these personal memories, he could see how, 'when these children grew up and understood how they had been ruined for life, there is developed the classes which we all fear and have reason to fear.'[2]

But when the letter to Roosevelt reached him, he had already incorporated a recommendation in his Message that such legislation be left to the States. In harmony with this idea, Senator Lodge, who knew of Beveridge's purpose, appeared in Washington with a child-labor bill applicable only to the District of Columbia — where there were no factories! Loeb, the President's Secretary, wrote Beveridge that Roosevelt was 'very glad to learn what you are doing about the subject of child labor,' and wished he had known of his plan before writing his Message. Time was to show, however, that Beveridge was to receive no assistance from Roosevelt, and was to be embarrassed by him in some ways.[3]

Nothing daunted by Loeb's reply, Beveridge prepared to force the fighting. He faced a crowded session. He would launch the fight to end child slavery; he would renew the fight to strengthen the meat inspection law; and he would actively participate in the fight over the seating of Senator Smoot. Each of these fights would increase his enemies among the powerful. He was thinking, too, about the revision of the tariff, and,

[1] Beveridge to Roosevelt, Nov. 24, 1906.
[2] Beveridge to Shaffer, Nov. 20, 1906.   [3] *Indianapolis Star*, Dec. 7, 1906.

in urging Roosevelt to mention it in his Message, he had written that Indiana was 'practically a unit, as far as business men are concerned, about the revision of the steel schedule.' [1] He was unhappy, too, about Cuba, and wrote the President that we had 'redeemed our pledge under the Teller Amendment when we left Cuba the first time'; that American occupation was the inevitable permanent solution; that if the island did not become American under Roosevelt, it would under someone else. And he had added, cannily: 'It would break my heart to see that historic occurrence under anybody else than yourself.' [2]

It was to be his last appeal on Cuba. Without the occupation, stability was to be restored, and never again in his time was the opportunity for the acquisition of the island to come. Henceforth he was to be engaged more and more with progressive battles for domestic reforms.

V

That session there was to be a tempest in a teapot because Roosevelt had discharged Negro soldiers for rioting in Brownsville, Texas. The fiery Foraker, valiantly bearing the 'bloody shirt' into his generation, impetuously rushed to the defense of the Negroes with slashing attacks on the conduct of the President. The drama was to culminate at the Gridiron Dinner in a sensational verbal duel between the President and the Senator. In this contest Beveridge was to play an inconspicuous part, supporting Roosevelt and voting for the Blackburn amendment to the Foraker resolution disclaiming any intention to deny the President's right to discharge the troops. He had been one of the first of the Republicans to declare for the amendment, and here he came into conflict with Lodge, who had been doing his best to have the amendment tabled.

Watching the picturesque personal contest from the sidelines, Beveridge was to enjoy the battle and to express his admiration for the volcanic Foraker who dared to measure swords with the head of the Nation in a public arena.

The political and journalistic leaders had assembled for the festivities of the Gridiron. Foraker had spoken and criticized the presidential action, and Roosevelt, replying, had made a furious onslaught. Foraker, pale and grim, sat listening. When the President concluded, Sam Blythe, presiding, rose. The atmosphere was already tense. Many thought Roosevelt had forgotten himself and the dignity of his position. 'The hour for bloody sarcasm having arrived,' said Blythe, 'I take the liberty

[1] Beveridge to Roosevelt, Oct. 16, 1906.   [2] *Ibid.*

of calling upon Senator Foraker for some remarks.' By this time the President, accompanied by his party, had left the room.

The reply of Foraker was a brilliant invective, delivered with smashing effect, and with all the forensic talent he possessed. Beveridge was fascinated by the spectacle. Here was a politician, evidently sincere, assailing the foremost political figure of the day at the height of his popularity. The moment he sat down, Beveridge scribbled a note on a card and sent it to him.

Dear Senator — I am against you, but I have never so admired you as at this instant. You are game, and you are masterful. You were altogether thoroughbred tonight.[1]

To Beveridge the incident was regrettable. He felt that Foraker should not have been literally pitched into the fray by Blythe, and wrote as much to Roosevelt. In his reply, Roosevelt revealed his state of mind when he rose to speak:

That was awfully nice, but, mind you, I agree with you. Foraker ought not to have been called upon to speak; but as he was called upon, I do not blame him much for the speech he made. I was in two minds about what to say in answer. I was inclined to make a Berserker speech myself and go over the whole business, and perhaps this would have been better; but in the few minutes I had to decide, I concluded that I would merely make a flat contradiction of what he had said, point out the fact that I, and not he, would pass judgement upon the case, and that I should absolutely disregard anything except my own convictions, and let it go at that.[2]

But Beveridge was too intensely engaged in conflicts of his own to be greatly concerned over the verbal duel.

On the first day of the session, he had introduced his bill to restore the date on the can and the cost of inspection on the packers in the meat inspection law. Referred to Senator Proctor's committee, it entered upon a long drowse. Toward the last of January, Beveridge inquired when a report might be expected. Proctor replied that he had assumed there was no hurry and that the bill would be added as an amendment to the Agricultural Bill. Beveridge took the floor.

Holding before the Senate an enormous advertisement of the packers making the most of the fact that their meat was now Government-inspected, Beveridge said: 'That is the kind of advertisement which the Senator from Vermont pointed out last year would be worth millions of dollars to the meat trust. Yet we are not only giving them that, but three million dollars a year in cash.'[3]

[1] J. B. Foraker, *Notes of a Busy Life*, II, 252.
[2] Roosevelt to Beveridge, Jan. 27, 1907.
[3] *Congressional Record*, Jan. 30, 1907.

The bill was soon reported, and a month later the debate began. The packers, busy with the cattlemen of the plains, had marshaled them against the measure on the ground that the cost of the inspection would be passed on to them. Beveridge was not tender of the 'cattle kings,' but ridiculed the claim that they would have to pay. And what if they did? Would it not be better that they pay the miserly price on a steer than that the American people be fed tuberculous and trichinous beef? But the cost would come from the packers, not the cattle kings. And why not? 'It is true that their business has been so unprofitable that four men in Chicago alone in the last twenty-five years have become worth altogether something like two hundred million dollars, and as to the men who are in that impecunious condition and have business so unprofitable, it is suggested that we ought not to lay our hands upon their pockets, or the pockets of their business, but on the pockets of the people which are capacious and unfailing. It is true the immigrant pays, but do not let us see the packers pay; it is true the oleomargarine manufacturer pays for the inspection of that product, but for Heaven's sake let us protect the poor cattlemen of the western plains!'

But the packers had their forces well in hand, and the scheme already had been devised to rule the bill out on a point of order. When, during Beveridge's speech, Senator Gallinger, the physician, entered the chamber and commented upon the rumor, he suggested that in the event the plan was carried through, Beveridge introduce the bill again at the next session, 'and see whether the American people are going to be taxed for this matter.'[1]

The fight was lost before it had begun. The Senate accepted the provision for the date upon the can, but a point of order was made against the payment of the cost of inspection by the packers, and Fairbanks, in the chair, sustained the point. Even the acceptance of the date upon the can was a mere gesture. The House conferees, under the leadership of James W. Wadsworth of New York, refused to accept it, and the Senate conferees meekly surrendered with a smile.

Beveridge promised to renew the fight, but this caused no consternation. The packers had their congressional forces well in hand.

[1] *Congressional Record*, Feb. 25, 1907.

CHAPTER V
FIGHTING FOR SOCIAL JUSTICE
I

MORE important to Beveridge at this time than all else was his projected fight to end child slavery in America. At this time millions of children, ranging in age from seven and eight to fourteen and fifteen, were being literally wrecked physically, mentally, and morally by the exploitation of their labor. Ruthlessly, heartlessly, they were given to the machine of industry to be ground out as dividends for their exploiters. All attempts to destroy this legalized and perfectly respectable ruin of American childhood through State legislation had failed. Great humanitarians, like Felix Adler, fine and self-sacrificing women like Florence Kelley and Jane Addams, had been spending themselves without stint in an effort to reach the conscience of the Nation. Magazines and newspapers had carried the most appalling stories of the personal investigations of the most reliable of men and women. John Spargo had written his moving book on 'The Bitter Cry of the Children'; Florence Kelley had published her illuminating work on 'Some Ethical Gains Through Legislation.' A National Child-Labor Committee had been formed, and was zealously working for reforms. Organizations of women everywhere were demanding the ending of the incredible crime against humanity. Men of science were warning that unless something were done, we should ultimately be a race of weaklings.

All these books, articles, reports had been studied by Beveridge, and they had aroused his wrath and impelled him to the preparation of a bill to stop the slaughter of the children. Strangely enough, he had not anticipated the hostility of organized wealth and industry. He had gone over his plans with Perkins and asked him to arrange a meeting with John Pierpont Morgan for a discussion of the problem.[1]

If he had thought it a simple matter to put through his program of social justice and humanity, he was speedily disillusioned. On his arrival in Washington, he had found that Henry Cabot Lodge, representing a constituency teeming with factories profiting on the labor of childhood, had prepared a bill to soothe the public conscience, prohibiting child labor where it did not exist — in Washington! Beveridge made no secret of

[1] Beveridge to Perkins, Dec. 11, 1906.

his indignation, and wondered if Roosevelt in any sense had been responsible.[1] This indignation cooled into a cold disgust on learning that the Lodge measure had no national scope and was patterned after his own. This embarrassment was not lightened by Roosevelt's action in taking the position that all such legislation should be left to the States. Many, discouraged, were ready to give up the battle against such odds. To rally the friends of his bill, Beveridge instantly announced that the President was not against national legislation, and gave out the equivocal letter from Loeb. Whether this was a mere bluff to save the situation or not, we shall never know. Beveridge had written Roosevelt of his plans fully three weeks before the delivery of the Message.[2] Time was to show that Roosevelt at no time had favored national legislation to end child slavery.

Meanwhile Lodge, with more than a touch of malice, was deriding the idea that there was anything novel in the proposal of a national child-labor law, and saying that it had first been suggested by Fairbanks in Kansas City four years before, and by Senator Hoar and Mr. Roosevelt. There was no escaping the animus of the statement, but reason to doubt its fidelity to the truth. It was news to Beveridge that Fairbanks had been crusading for humanity four years before, and an investigation failed to discover anything to justify the statement of the Massachusetts Senator. Beveridge thereupon issued a reply, expressing his pleasure at having Lodge's support for a national law — which was also malicious. It seemed all too evident that Lodge, having heard of Beveridge's intention, had prepared his bill to head the other off, and thus save the manufacturers in Massachusetts from annoyance. This was all the more apparent when Beveridge announced that he would add his bill as an amendment to the Lodge bill, and hysterically was importuned to do nothing to endanger the prospects of a measure that would stop child slavery in the mines, factories, and sweatshops of Washington City! But he refused to recede, and the bill was added as an amendment.

II

There was no possibility of passing such a measure in the three crowded months of the short session, but Beveridge was preparing, not for a battle, but for a war. He knew, from the experience of England, that the fight might be prolonged, but he proposed to initiate his fight with the most impressive and damning statement he could make, descriptive of the evil. He

[1] Beveridge to Lorimer, Dec. 3, 1906; to Shaffer.
[2] Beveridge to Lorimer, Dec. 3, 1906.

planned to prick the conscience of the Nation, to shock it into sensibility. He knew that comparatively few had the most remote idea of what was going on within the sweatshops, mines, and factories. He would lift the veil.

Thus for many days he worked on the preparation of his speech until two and three o'clock each morning, mobilizing his facts and authorities, marshaling them in orderly procession, and, as he wrote, 'reading an enormous pile of stenographic notes and verifying the authorities until now my eyes are practically out.' [1] To the authors of books and articles describing the barbarous working conditions of the children, he appealed for affidavits under oath on the truth of their statements, and they responded.

Thus he was thoroughly prepared when he rose to begin his remarkable four days' speech. He began under the most trying circumstances. For an hour and a half after he was to have had the floor, senators were debating the increase of their salaries with much feeling. Meanwhile, his speech had been released to the press, and his irritation was evident. The galleries were full. He sat impatiently behind a veritable barricade of books and documents piled high upon his desk and on the desks of neighboring senators — and the debate on the salary increase droned on. When, at length, he got the floor, his irritation took the form of sarcasm.

'Now that we have voted ourselves an increase in salary,' he said, 'perhaps it is proper to call the attention of the Senate to some other matters of almost as much importance to the Nation.'

But the lunch hour was past and senators had postponed lunching until after they had increased their salaries, and they trailed out of the Chamber into the restaurant. Beveridge proceeded, reading the descriptions of the inhumanity of child slavery from eye-witnesses — dreadful tales of human cruelty at the expense of mere mites of humanity for the sake of the rich man's dividends. Children of ten and twelve working with bleeding hands in the breakers of the mines, breathing the germs of death; children, under twelve, working twelve and fourteen hours a day for a pittance; a wan girl of nine working from dusk to dawn cleaning bobbins for three cents an hour.

Some senators smiled.

'Does the Senate find that amusing?' asked the speaker — 'a girl going a mile or more across a windswept valley to begin work at half-past six at night, and working until six in the morning for three cents an hour? If so, I shall present some examples from other States that perhaps will amuse the Senate still more.'

[1] Beveridge to Shaffer, Feb. 4, 1907.

And then, striking at the heart of the cynical opposition:

'It is said that certain industries are even now at work opposing this bill.... It is said that the great Southern Railroad... a large part of whose business and a good fraction of whose profits comes from these cotton mills, is against this, or any similar reform. It is said that the enormous coal industries of Pennsylvania... with their immense power and the railroads that gridiron that portion of the State and that carry the produce of these mines — the Pennsylvania, the Lehigh Valley, the Delaware and Lackawanna, and the Delaware and Hudson — will oppose it.'

And thus, striking directly at the cynics, he went on reading from the evidence a record as brutal and horrible in its inhumanity as anything the pen of Dickens ever painted — a record of dwarfed bodies, of stunted minds, of tainted morals — of vicious greed fattening on the blood and sweat of children of from eight to fourteen in mills, mines, and sweatshops.

'Of course, these are not our children. They are the children of somebody else that are working twelve hours at night. If they were our children, we would forget lunch and not sit up at nights contriving arguments to show that the Constitution won't let us rescue them.'

As he paraded these children, pale, anæmic, tottering, vacant-eyed, before the Senate, members ceased to smile. Decency had its fling. The press of the reactionary school began to make excuses, to minimize the importance of the disclosures. The 'New York Sun' rose to the occasion editorially:

'It is likely enough that many of these child laborers will grow up into capitalists and become "too rich," like their present oppressors.'

Beveridge quoted this in his speech and rang the changes on it.

'As I read the conditions of these children in the coal-breakers of Pennsylvania, in the cotton mills of the South, in the cotton mills of Maine, in the glass works of West Virginia, and in the sweatshops of New Jersey, you will see the material out of which our future "capitalists," according to this paper, are to be made.'

As he proceeded, hour after hour, with the procession of horrors, he was to remember the 'Sun's' editorial defense time and again. Thus, after describing the conditions in an eastern Pennsylvania mill, where young girls under sixteen in short dresses worked all night, wan and weary unto death, he paused with a scornful smile: 'Future mothers, you know, of the "capitalists" of the "New York Sun's" prophecy.'

As the thoroughness and authenticity of his information

dawned upon the Senate, it began seriously to listen — child labor was no longer a joke for the senatorial lunch hour. Robust humanitarians, like Tillman, broke in with indignant comment on the outrage. Senators whose States were touched became sensitive. The child slave was getting a hearing.

And now the speaker passed on to the effect on the health of the oncoming generations, summoning physicians as his witnesses; citing the physical degeneration of the English, discovered during the Boer War, as a warning; paying a glowing tribute to Lord Ashley, Earl of Shaftesbury, who had made the fight against child slavery in England.

I have heard it whispered about the corridors that we must not go too fast, that we are bound to have an 'investigation.' Oh, no, let us not go 'too fast!' The evidence is before the Senate of the slow murder of these children, not by the tens or hundreds, but by the thousands. But let us not 'hasten' to their rescue 'too fast!' Let us 'investigate,' just as the manufacturers of England asked when they were confronted by the same kind of a reform. 'Why not investigate?' said they.

Now, Mr. President, it has got to be stopped, and stopped now! We all agree upon that — anyhow, everybody says that he agrees it must be stopped; only some, say, 'Let us be careful about the Constitution.' But, never mind, child labor has got to be stopped. How? The States cannot stop it.

And why?

If one State passes good laws and enforces them, and another State does not, then the business men in the former State are at a business disadvantage with the business men in the other State. The business men in the State that has good laws suffer from the very righteousness of that State's laws, and the business man in the State that has bad laws profits by the very wickedness of that State's laws.

Three days of the scathing indictment of a savage system in the interest of greed had passed, and the infamy of child labor was now conceded; and Senators threw up the Constitution as a barricade, with Spooner and Bacon proclaiming the unconstitutionality of a national law. The remainder of the speech, with interruptions and counter-contentions, was a brilliant forensic exhibition. Beveridge insisted that, under the power to regulate interstate commerce, there was a constitutional right to forbid interstate commerce in goods made by the labor of childhood. He closed with a fervent peroration that brought applause from the galleries.[1]

A more remarkable and exhaustive exposé of a crime had never

[1] *Congressional Record*, Jan. 23, 28, 1907.

before been heard in the Senate Chamber. It was more than an argument — it was a treatise of history, constitutional law, and facts. Printed in a pamphlet of one hundred and seventy pages, it was sent broadcast throughout the country to awaken the public conscience and arouse the people to action.

Nothing more was expected from the initial engagement. Letters of approval flooded the Beveridge office. A judge of the Supreme Court of Mississippi wrote for twenty copies for distribution among the leading members of the Legislature, for the women of the State were pressing child-labor legislation upon that body. 'I think,' wrote the Southern jurist, 'one of the most grotesque spectacles ever presented to the American public is the frantic and clamorous defense, now being made on all hands by the railroad corporations, of the doctrine of states' rights.' [1]

To a Tennessee woman, wishing to know if the bill would be reintroduced, and planning to enlist the State Federation of Women's Clubs behind it, Beveridge revealed his thought: 'When I first announced my determination to introduce this bill, I said I thought it would take five years to pass it — it took Shaftesbury fifty years to do the same thing in England. But so fast was the progress that I hope to pass it next session. However, passed it shall be, whether it is next session or some future session.' [2]

Even before the session closed, he actually was preparing feverishly to press for action in the next.

III

Meanwhile, he had been engaged in another fight that brought him under criticism. Four years before, Reed Smoot, a high functionary of the Mormon Church, had been elected to the Senate from Utah. A successful banker and manufacturer, an industrious man of modest manner, there was no justification for denying him his seat. But he had his enemies, and these raised the hue and cry that he was a Mormon in sympathy with polygamy; and soon the charge was made that he practiced it himself and was a man of low character. There was just enough of the religious issue to fan the flames of that fanaticism which has never died since men burned each other at the stake in the name of God. The churches and church people were aroused, and for a time it seemed America was to have a Dreyfus case.

Listening to the evidence as a member of the Committee, Beveridge had been appalled that such passionate hate could be

[1] Judge A. H. Whitefield to Beveridge, April 29, 1907.
[2] Beveridge to Mrs. J. C. Tyler, May 16, 1907.

mustered on evidence so puny. Three years before, he had written in utter disgust to his old friend, Judge John H. Baker:

The investigation thus far is disgusting. As a lawyer, your wrath would have been aroused at almost every stage of the game. Hardly a scrap of testimony has yet been offered that you would have tolerated for a moment as a judge upon the bench, and of course the committee, in a sense, is a judicial body. Thus far not a word of evidence has been offered against Smoot. The only testimony connecting Smoot with anything was as follows:

A Mormon bishop had contracted an irregular connection with two or three wives in the last two or three years. He was sent for to come down to Provo, where Smoot lives, and where Smoot interviewed him. On his way home from this interview, the deputy sheriff arrested him, took him to Provo, the Church authorities removed him from his office and membership in the Church, and he was prosecuted and sent to the penitentiary — all at the instance of Smoot himself.... I have not formed any opinion on this case yet, and of course shall not do so until all the evidence is in and arguments of the counsel are made. Then I shall form an opinion, and, under my oath, do justice as you would have me do, and just as you would do were you in my place — and this, too, without fear of any public clamor or coercion from any public sentiment.[1]

During the taking of testimony at that time, Beveridge had asked a question which called forth an answer favorable to Smoot, and instantly church women in Washington, attending the hearings by courtesy of the committee, denounced him as a champion of polygamy; and it was taken up by a group of women in Indianapolis. Some ministers of his own church, who had been guilty of the same offense during the trial of Andrew Johnson, undertook to dictate the judgment of the senators in a judicial proceeding; and this had in some cases been so brutally offensive that the venerable Senator Hoar had replied to one minister that were he actually sitting on the bench he would send the cleric to jail. Beveridge had written indignantly to a friend in Indianapolis [2] of the attempted interference of church women and ministers.

The case had been unsettled all this while, and now it was coming up for final action. Prejudice had been furiously fanned by intolerant religionists, and politicians had demagogically joined in the sorry work for the sake of votes. At the head of the senatorial witch-burners was Julius C. Burrows of Michigan, and Beveridge thought he understood the motive. 'Burrows of Michigan is up for reëlection,' he had written in the beginning,

[1] Beveridge to Baker, March 18, 1904.
[2] Charles E. Coffin, March 24, 1904.

'and until recently had opposition; and like a certain class of public men is playing to the galleries.'[1]

He was still playing to the galleries when the final fight was being made at this session. The galleries were daily packed with enemies of Smoot, ready to hiss or cheer in the name of religion. When Burrows reached the climax of his speech with the exclamation: 'I protest against this effort to drag the Christian churches of the land down to the low level of this abomination,' the galleries had roared their delight.

It was in this atmosphere, heavily charged with prejudice and fanaticism, that Beveridge rose to champion the cause of Smoot. Casting aside discretion, he rose to heights of eloquence never surpassed by him and seldom equalled.

No wrong is blacker [he began] than the ruin of the reputation of a man or woman whose life has been stainless. No public policy can justify the damnation of a man by his countrymen upon error. And where liberty reigns, truth will vindicate the wronged man in the end. This is true, even though millions, misinformed, clamor against a man.'

And what had been the nature of the clamor?

The average man and woman had been told for three long years that Reed Smoot is a criminal, guilty of a disgusting and filthy crime — a crime abhorrent to our race and destructive of our civilization. The country has been told that this man is a polygamist. That is the charge on which he has been tried before the bar of American public opinion; that the charge on which he has been condemned by the millions; and that the charge that has injured him as deeply as Dreyfus was injured. And that charge is utterly false.... Not only is this true, but the evidence shows that, from the first, Reed Smoot has been the leader of the younger, wiser, and more modern element of his Church that oppose that insult to marriage.

Charging that these slanders had been deliberately spread by 'unscrupulous and lying propagandists,' citing the press story that Burrows had said Smoot had been 'cohabiting with five wives,' he analyzed the evidence and laid bare the dearth of any evidence to sustain a single charge.

And treason? Treason because he owed a higher allegiance to his Church than to his Nation? True, six had testified that the oath of the Church called for vengeance on the Nation. But five of the six had been impeached, and the sixth had not used the word 'Nation.' And who were these witnesses? Three were drunkards, one insane! 'The testimony of these witnesses would not be received by a court of justice.'

And then, with the Smoot baiters in the galleries struck dumb

[1] Charles E. Coffin, March 24, 1904.

by the devastating nature of the philippic, he launched into his peroration:

Religious liberty! Religious intolerance has stained crimson more of this earth than any other cause.... And this, in the final analysis, is the ultimate issue before us. For polygamy I have hatred made stronger by disgust. For enemies of our Government, I have a hatred intensified by the period and circumstances of my birth. But we have seen that this accused man is not a practicer of this revolting crime, but its enemy. We have seen that he is not a traitor, but a loyal man. And so the only question that remains is that of the tolerance of his religion. And though his religion is to me incomprehensible, grotesque, and absurd, I hate intolerance of it and all religions as much as I hate treason.

As he concluded, the hostile galleries paid him the rare compliment of applause.

The roll was called and Smoot was vindicated. But Hemenway of Indiana had voted for his expulsion.

IV

The opposing votes of the two Indiana senators meant nothing significant outside of Indiana. But it was not an isolated case of the Hoosiers working at cross-purposes. That same session Beveridge had hotly defended the forestry policy of Gifford Pinchot and paid him a rare tribute, and Hemenway had voted against the liberal appropriation asked. Fairbanks, with whose group Hemenway was acting, had ruled Beveridge's amendment, to put the cost of inspection on the packers rather than the people, out of order. That spring, too, there was an ugly conflict between the two senators on patronage.[1] More and more Beveridge was being isolated as far as the politicians were concerned. The press was harping more and more on 'factions,' and this could not possibly accrue to his advantage. Fairbanks was an active candidate for the presidential nomination the next year, and all the drums were beating. To make matters worse, the 'Chicago Post,' owned by Shaffer, was a little critical in its analysis of Fairbanks's aspirations, and conspicuously mentioned Beveridge as a possibility.

Eager to prevent serious dissensions, Beveridge wrote to Shaffer:

I have just been shown a copy of the 'Post' containing correspondence from here on the subject of the Presidency, in which my name is conspicuously mentioned.... If it is not asking too much, I would be pleased if you will keep out all such comment. I am not a candidate

[1] *Indianapolis Star*, March 9, 10, 12, 13, 1907.

and will not be a candidate; and any mention of my name in that connection is most distasteful to me.

I am for Vice-President Fairbanks, have said so publicly, and intend to do all in my power to secure his nomination, if I am permitted to do so. In this connection my attention has been called to a fact that occasionally there is some reference to Mr. Fairbanks in the 'Post' that is not advantageous to him. I am well aware that you have little to do with this and cannot overlook every word, or perhaps any of your correspondents' matter; nevertheless, if such slighting references would not appear any more, I would be very happy. The fact of our close friendship gives grounds for evil persons to suggest that I am not displeased with such references; because my home papers, which are popularly supposed to be run in the interest of Mr. Fairbanks, make such continual slighting references to myself.... Some people, therefore, think it natural that I should be glad to see my newspaper friends retaliate; but... I am distinctly displeased.[1]

Shaffer replied that special instructions would be given to delete any matter reflecting on Fairbanks's character or integrity, but, being a public man, all references to him could not be censored. He recognized Beveridge's right to appeal to him on the basis of friendship, but that did not place him under obligations to act on his request.[2]

Never had Beveridge been quite so unfavorably situated as to press support in Indianapolis as in 1907. The pages of the 'Indianapolis Star' for the year are uniformly unfriendly; and newspaper articles about him, not unfriendly, were generally relegated to obscure sections of the papers.

But throughout the year he was receiving an abundance of national publicity through his debates with Bryan in the 'Reader Magazine.' Some time before, Hewitt Hanson Howland had conceived the idea of a series of debates between the two men in the magazine. Their disposition to cross swords in the campaign of 1906 had inspired the thought. Beveridge readily agreed; and Howland hurried to 'Fairview,' the country home of Bryan in Nebraska, to persuade him to the plan. 'I shall have to speak to Mrs. Bryan,' the Commoner replied, and she consented. The announcement called forth much discussion, since Bryan's nomination for the Presidency the next year was a foregone conclusion. Many Democratic leaders and papers thought it would be a blunder for him definitely to commit himself in advance on all the issues. Some of Beveridge's friends were concerned lest Bryan trip him. 'Mr. Beveridge must be alert in this debate,' said Senator Allison, 'for he has in Mr. Bryan an able antagonist who knows how to evade as well as assert'; and the unfriendly

[1] Beveridge to Shaffer, Feb. 4, 1907.
[2] Shaffer to Beveridge, Feb. 7, 1907.

'Indianapolis Star' headlined this statement: 'Bryan Debate Too Big for Beveridge.' [1]

Under the plan adopted, each wrote in one number on a given issue, and in the next each answered the other. The discussion included the Jeffersonian and Hamiltonian concept of the Nation, trusts, imperialism, tariff, railroads, and labor. On most subjects there was nothing more than a reiteration of their well-known views. In his tariff article, Beveridge vigorously advocated the creation of a scientific tariff commission, for he was to be found battling for it within a year. The railroad question caused him the most concern. In sending Roosevelt the manuscript of his trust article, he referred to his uncertainty regarding the valuation of the railroads.

Beveridge to Roosevelt, May 7, 1907

In our last conference I took a decided position against the policy of the valuation of railroads for the many excellent, and to me, at the time, conclusive, reasons which I gave you. I then intended to put a paragraph to that effect in my Galena speech,[2] but, on thinking it over, I withheld it. I still feel that the valuation of railroads is a bad policy, and all of the reasons I gave you in support of that conclusion still hold good with me; but somehow or other I have a 'hunch' — as Stewart Edward White would say — that that subject had better not be touched upon at the present time. The public mind is moving rapidly, and minute, painstaking study of other questions like this franchise plan [3] has so caused me to change my views in one or two instances that I think it discreet and altogether wise to say nothing at present on the valuation problem.... However, if I were compelled to declare at the present moment, I should declare against the policy of the valuation of railroads, although with a feeling of misgiving. In short, it is a subject upon which I feel that I would like to wait awhile and think it over.

Roosevelt to Beveridge, May 9, 1907

I have your letter of the 7th instant. Events have moved so fast in the valuation business that I think it is impossible to avoid taking a conservative ground in its favor. The Northern Pacific has offered a physical valuation of its road before the Interstate Commerce Commission. Two other big systems are making physical valuations themselves. I think this means there must be physical valuation.

Beveridge to Roosevelt, May 15, 1907

Answering your letter of May 9th about valuation: all right. I shall follow where you lead. As you observe from my letter, my own mind was subconsciously tending in the same direction.

[1] March 22, 1907.
[2] April 27, 1907.
[3] Proposed by Bryan in the debate on trusts.

The magazine debate was followed by the great industrialists and financiers, and most were pleased with Beveridge's treatment of the trust question. This had been prepared with meticulous care, and Judge E. H. Gary, of the United States Steel Corporation, had furnished some of the data. But Beveridge had conceded that one of the vices of great corporations and trusts was in their seeking privilege through campaign contributions. A railroad president took issue with the criticism. 'Without question,' he wrote, 'more money was contributed to the Republican campaign fund in 1896 by the corporations and individuals than had ever been contributed in any four national campaigns in the history of the Nation. I think you will agree with me that not a single dollar of the vast contribution referred to was for improper purposes.'

Indeed, he said, no President had ever been elected by the corrupt use of money. To this Beveridge did not agree:

No, I am sorry that I cannot agree with you that no President has ever been elected in this manner. On the contrary, I think more than one President has been elected in this manner. Nor do I agree that the enormous campaign funds raised in the past by both parties have not been spent improperly; they have been spent improperly....

But a large part of the campaign funds in the past have been used for the direct corruption of voters at the polls. It is an actual fact that many members of the legislatures are picked out and elected by rich men or the representatives of corporations by the direct use of actual money on the spot.... I have no objections to great corporations contributing to a campaign fund, providing that they do not use such contributions as a sort of mortgage upon the Administration they elect.[1]

Thus, with rapid strides, Beveridge was moving into conflict with the major forces of his party at the time. Within a few months he had invited the hostility of the manufacturers and operators using child labor, the railroads carrying their product. He had agreed to the physical valuation of railroads and written a railroad president in denunciation of the use of corporation money in the corruption of the voters.

That spring he spoke at Galena on Grant's birthday, addressed the Academy of Political Science in Philadelphia, and delivered a notable progressive address at Yale University. But his mind and heart were occupied with other things. If he was tired, he was too happy to notice it until in May he was seized by dizziness and forced to go to bed for several hours.[2] But when Shaffer asked his company on a motor trip through France and England, he

[1] Beveridge to W. C. Brown, president, New York Central Railroad, May 20, 1907.
[2] Beveridge to Shaffer, May 28, 1907.

declined. He was suffering from brain-fag and would go to Europe, but he would not go to London, where he would have to see Ambassador Reid and other public men, since he was too weary to brace up to it.[1]

But he was not entirely frank — he had other plans for that summer.

V

Three years before, Catherine Eddy, a young woman of charm and beauty, visiting Mrs. Slater in Washington, was asked whom she would care to meet. She mentioned Beveridge, in whom she had become interested through his book and speeches. She was the daughter of Mr. and Mrs. Augustus Eddy, of Chicago, and had spent much of her time abroad.

But it was not until two years after that first meeting, when she was again visiting her friend in Washington, that the romance really began. The next winter, when her mother took an apartment in the capital, Beveridge had the opportunity to see her often, and when she returned to Chicago in the spring of 1907, they were engaged.

A little later, she sailed with her parents for Europe, and Beveridge, with his friend, John McCutcheon, followed in a few weeks. It was arranged that the wedding would be solemnized in the German capital, where the bride's brother, Spencer Eddy, was first secretary of the American Embassy.

Because of Beveridge's wish to be married on technically American soil, the Embassy was chosen for the wedding. Before his arrival in Berlin, the Foreign Office had granted the dispensation, waiving the usual restrictions. The civil contract was signed at noon on August 7 at the Town Hall, in accordance with German usage, and the religious ceremony was performed half an hour later at the Embassy by Dr. Thomas C. Hall, a friend of the bride's family, then professor at the Union Theological Seminary. It was a grief to Beveridge that his friend Phillips was ill and could not act as best man, but in the small company that had gathered for the occasion were some old friends. Shaffer was there, and Elmer Roberts, a classmate at DePauw, and Edward L. McClain, the favorite cousin, and Senator Dillingham of Vermont. The wedding breakfast followed in the apartments of Spencer Eddy, where happy speeches were made by Charlemagne Tower, the Ambassador; Dr. Hall and Senator Dillingham, and the bridegroom responded in joyous mood. The honey-

[1] Beveridge to Shaffer, May 23, 1907.

moon was spent in the Dolomites at Borca di Cadore in Northern Italy, one of the loveliest spots in Europe.

There were to be several weeks of freedom from official care and political annoyances before they reached New York on the Kaiser Wilhelm II on September 24, and hurried on to Indianapolis, to take up their residence in the leased house next to the ground where, amidst great forest trees, their own house was to be constructed; and instantly Beveridge was swept into the whirlpool again.

CHAPTER VI

FIGHTING UPSTREAM

I

NEVER was Beveridge to suffer more disappointments and disillusionments nor encounter a more venomous hostility than during the session opening in December, 1907. Even so, his buoyancy of spirit sustained him, and Archie Butt, now military aide to the President, was writing his mother that Beveridge was 'just the same enthusiastic youthful-looking fellow he was when he was in Manila,' and just as sure that the old walls of that city should be demolished.[1]

Returning from his honeymoon, he found a disturbing letter from Florence Kelley, a leader in the fight against child labor, warning him of 'a very active subterranean propaganda' against his child-labor bill, then being carried on by a woman conspicuous in philanthropic work.[2] Beveridge, however, was more concerned at the moment over the attitude of Roosevelt. 'Very confidentially,' he wrote in reply, 'I am sure that they have done everything they can with the President, but I suppose, of course, that they have not been able to move him. Whatever you, Miss Addams, Miss McDowell, and others who are working in harmony for the support of this bill, and all of whom are friends of the President, might do to counteract anything that may have been done with him along this line, will be helpful. I do not in the least think they have shaken him, but it is my tactics in a fight not to overlook any point.'[3] But Miss Kelley was pessimistic, finding that lukewarm friends 'tend to grow chilly.'

That month, Beveridge sent Roosevelt an exhaustive lawyer's brief on the constitutionality of his bill, citing judicial decisions to sustain his contention that the power to regulate interstate commerce carried the power to prohibit any article of commerce; that the power over foreign commerce is precisely the same as over the interstate; that it was just as constitutional to exclude child-made goods as goods made by convicts; and that the possible abuse of power was no argument against its existence. To these legal arguments he added a fervent appeal, urging the support of the measure by organized labor. 'We cannot end this infamous evil,' he continued, 'except by national action; it is constitutional to vote such action; the sentiment of the country is

---

[1] *Letters of Archie Butt*, 13. [2] Miss Kelley to Beveridge, Aug. 5, 1907.
[3] Beveridge to Miss Kelley, Oct. 8, 1907.

tremendously aroused upon it; it is wise statesmanship and it is good politics.' [1]

Two days later, he wrote one of the leaders in the fight 'to get to the President so that he will be sure to incorporate it in his Message,' since 'the other side has been at him ever since Congress adjourned.' [2] The earnest support of Roosevelt was absolutely necessary to success, for he had been warned that even the National Child-Labor Committee had divided, and that a resolution against the bill was possible.[3] When he had written Lindsay, urging that he and Felix Adler 'block that,' he learned how completely the ground had been cut from under him. Lindsay corroborated the bad news. He had not had the heart to warn him. 'Practically the whole bunch of people of the National Committee seem to be reactionaries.... We are right in the center of the hostile anti-Administration forces here in New York, and I get precious little sympathy in any quarter.' It was even possible that Lindsay might lose his position with the committee, but he was 'ready to walk the streets for a while if necessary.' [4]

But Beveridge soon was to learn that the 'anti-Administration forces' were in the White House, too, under the aggressive leadership of the President himself. In reply to an appeal for a recommendation of the measure in the Message, Roosevelt replied with evident hostility.

'It simply cannot be that "organized labor is overwhelmingly for this bill — militantly for it,"' he wrote. 'Gompers and twenty labor leaders came in to see me Saturday, and when I asked them about the bill, not a single one of them would admit that he favored it.' [5]

And so 'Gompers and twenty labor leaders' were worse than lukewarm! The President was hostile, and the National Child-Labor Committee was preparing to block the measure.

Thoroughly aroused now, Beveridge turned to Big Business. He had discussed the project with Isaac N. Seligman and Paul Warburg at dinner, and he wrote the former he was ready at any time to resume the conversation at a luncheon:

I am not in the least interested and shall not spend any time upon certain persons well known to both of us who at heart are more interested in unrighteous profits wrung directly or indirectly from this iniquity. I think I am perhaps as active a defender of honestly gotten wealth and of legitimate business as any man now vigorously in public

[1] Beveridge to Roosevelt, Oct. 28, 1907.
[2] Beveridge to Samuel M. Lindsay, Oct. 30, 1907.
[3] Miss Kelley to Beveridge, Oct. 30 and 31, 1907.
[4] Lindsay to Beveridge, Nov. 8, 1907.
[5] Roosevelt to Beveridge, Nov. 12, 1907.

life. I went to the Senate as a Conservative, and my public speeches show that I have stuck to that creed. But it is just such villainies as child labor defended by some apparently respectable people that in the public mind casts discredit upon all business, both good and bad.... As I told you at the dinner at Mr. Warburg's, my experience has been that when we want to stop an evil like this, everybody apparently is for scrapping the evil, but the worst enemies to the reform are those who say they want to stop it, but are always against any effective means of stopping it; and I do not recall a single instance where their ostensible opposition to any effective measure has not been on so-called 'constitutional' grounds.[1]

Two weeks after this letter was written, the National Child-Labor Committee compromised its differences by agreeing to do nothing for a year until a report had been made from the national investigation ordered. This was tantamount to a desertion; but, nothing daunted, Beveridge promptly introduced his bill and continued his agitation. When, five months later, he inquired of the chairman of the committee to which it had been referred when a report could be expected, Dolliver replied that great questions were involved and hearings could not be given until the next session.[2] This was equivalent to a burial. But there was nothing more to be done. Beveridge was convinced that the burial had been effected through the united efforts of Southern cotton mills, the silk and glass factories of New Jersey and West Virginia, the New England interests, and the railroads carrying the products of child labor.[3]

It was to be the end of any serious attempt to end child labor until Woodrow Wilson personally insisted on action, and got it, some years later. Nothing ever had absorbed Beveridge more. He had written the introduction to Mrs. Van Vorst's book, 'The Cry of the Children'; had personally sought to interest David Warfield, the actor, in a play on the subject; and had read and criticized another drama which he found powerful but of such 'desperate sadness' that it would not fit the stage.

II

Equally futile was his attempt at this session to push through his bill compelling the packers to put the date of canning on the cans. He had reintroduced the measure on the opening of Congress, and now six months had passed. Meanwhile, he had been desperately ill from ptomaine poisoning, 'caused by eating some

[1] Beveridge to Seligman, Nov. 13, 1907.
[2] *Congressional Record*, May 6, 1908.
[3] Beveridge to Henry Beach Needham, April 9, 1908.

canned-meat product on the train which undoubtedly was eight or ten years old,' and he had learned from his physician that 'nearly all cases of ptomaine poisoning came from just this cause.'[1] But when, toward the close of the session, he asked Senator Warren when the Agricultural Committee would be ready to report, he learned that the Committee had 'just taken it up,' and since 'grocers and others' wished hearings, nothing could be done that session.

'I have never yet heard one single objection to this measure of human safety to the health and life of the people,' said Beveridge.

And when, in reply to Warren's assertion that no Senate Committee had passed on the date on cans and Beveridge reminded him that a bill containing the provision had passed the Senate twice to be thrown out in the House, he was met with the cynical rejoinder: 'That is true, because it was well known when it passed here that it would be thrown out in conference.'

Thus no action was taken then; nor has any been taken in the quarter-century that has intervened.

III

Thus, with his cup of disappointment running over, he could see the end of the trail in the statehood controversy, with every indication that Arizona and New Mexico would enter as separate States. It did not contribute to his happiness to find Roosevelt in full retreat. The President had no stomach for fighting against sentiment, and he was convinced that the majority of the people in the Territories wished separate statehood. Then, too, his Rough Rider friend, George Curry, was Governor of New Mexico, and was urging immediate action for party purposes. He had met Beveridge in the Philippines when one was an army officer and the other a civilian senator galloping with the troops, and he sought his conversion. Since the beginning of the fight, he urged, the population of the Territories had increased, railroads had been built, mines opened. If admitted to statehood at once, New Mexico would send Republicans to House and Senate in 1908; if action were delayed, the settlers pouring in from the South would make it Democratic.[2] But Beveridge resented the political reference. 'The political argument you make was urged upon me six years ago,' he wrote. 'Neither then nor now does such an argument impress me as so tremendously important a matter in the making of a State which is to stand as long as the Republic endures. While some temporary political advantage

[1] Beveridge to Shaffer, Feb. 28, 1908.
[2] Curry to Beveridge, Oct. 16, 1907.

might be gained, the higher, broader, and more statesmanlike purpose should outweigh it.' [1]

But Roosevelt, a consummate politician always, had been won over to the political consideration. He had written Beveridge of his change of heart, and the latter had asked him to 'make no public utterance' to that effect 'until I have an opportunity to confer with you.' [2]

Undiscouraged still, he again began to mobilize the agencies of public opinion. To Albert Shaw he wrote of the Roosevelt letter and his reply. 'Bring your guns to bear upon this question or we will find ourselves in a dreadful tangle,' he wrote. 'I think quick work is necessary. The President's sudden determination is undoubtedly due to the presence of Governor Curry, a member of the President's regiment, and this is somewhat increased by political considerations.' [3] Similar appeals were sent to Hamilton Wright Mabie, of the 'Outlook,' and to George Harvey. 'It is said,' he wrote Harvey, 'that the President has decided to favor admission of these Territories, but I do not believe that he will do anything of the kind.' [4]

But he was only whistling to keep up courage. It was all too evident that Roosevelt had gone over to the enemy, bag and baggage.

IV

Fighting still for the causes lost, he plunged with impetuosity and enthusiasm into another fight that was not to contribute to his popularity with the ruling forces in House and Senate. A zealous protectionist always, he had long resented the inequalities and iniquities of the existing tariff act framed through the usual processes of shameless bartering and logrolling. Two years before, in Maine, he had urged the necessity of a downward revision, but he knew that another revision in the old slovenly fashion, with the interests knowing precisely what they wanted and the major part of Congress inadequately informed, would mean but a repetition of the venerable scandal. He saw the need of a fact-finding body of experts to assist Congress in intelligent action, and his mind turned to a tariff commission. Then it was, during the debate with Bryan, that he proposed the establishment of such a commission as a part of Republican policy. In Germany he had found time to study the German method. From Elmer Roberts, a classmate at DePauw, then representing the Associated Press

[1] Beveridge to Curry, Oct. 19, 1907.
[2] Beveridge to Roosevelt, Oct. 5, 1907.
[3] Beveridge to Shaw, Oct. 8, 1907.   [4] Beveridge to Harvey, Oct. 26, 1907.

in Berlin, he learned that the most competent man on the Roosevelt Tariff Commission to Germany the year before was N. I. Stone, the tariff expert of the Department of Commerce and Labor; and the 'stand-patters' had feared him because of his intimate and technical knowledge of the tariff. Having prepared his tariff commission article for the magazine in Germany, he submitted it to Stone immediately on returning to America; and, after a revision, sent it to the magazine. He had sent proof-sheets to Roosevelt, who had been so favorably impressed with the idea that he was thinking of including a recommendation in his Message.

But with the publication of the article, the sponsors of the old system were enraged. Rumors of Roosevelt's intention reaching John Dalzell, representing the House organization, he made such a vehement protest that the President was dissuaded for the time. This incident led to an exchange of letters between Beveridge and Dalzell. When the latter complained that the plan provided for the transfer of the power to levy tariff taxes from the Congress to an appointive body, Beveridge explained:

I would not put in the hands of such a commission the fixing of any schedules, nor in any sense the taking of our tariff out of the hands of Congress where the Constitution places it, and where it properly belongs. But there ought to be a commission of experts which will get the facts for Congress, acting purely as a servant of Congress for that purpose. Why not let the commission, which would be nothing more than a bureau of one of the departments, get to work upon the facts and keep at work until the time Congress reassembles after the presidential election, and then let its statement be made before the proper committees of the two Houses for their information. It will save time, labor, and make for accuracy.[1]

The reply of Dalzell, who specialized on tariffs, was significant of the reasoning of his tribe:

I shall be very glad to discuss with you the matter of such a tariff commission as you seem to favor when opportunity shall offer, although I cannot agree with you that there is any necessity for such a commission. It must be borne in mind that we have been making tariff bills for more than a hundred years, and that each bill furnishes the groundwork for its successor. All the schedules have been perfected, all subjects covered, and it is, with us, only a matter of readjustment of particular items.

To which he added, with a touch of malice:

Of course, the problem would be a different one if we were going to change from a tariff built on protection lines to a tariff for revenue only.[2]

But Dalzell was comparatively mild. Not so sweetly reason-

[1] Beveridge to Dalzell, Nov. 1, 1907.   [2] Dalzell to Beveridge, Nov. 8, 1907.

able was Senator Eugene Hale of the Senate oligarchy. To him the Beveridge suggestion had seemed treason, and on Beveridge's return to Washington he was summoned to Hale's residence where he was confined by illness. Beveridge found him in a rage as he attacked the magazine article violently and demanded to know how Beveridge had dared attempt to commit the party to such a policy. It had been understood that Beveridge was to have the next vacancy on the Finance Committee, and he was bluntly informed that persistence on the tariff commission idea would mean his exclusion from the Committee. The veteran was told that the fight would be waged, though he were denied the coveted position and thrown off every other committee in the Senate.

It was a quarrel — the Beveridge insurgency had begun.

V

The rage of the 'stand-patters,' as the Bourbons were called, was due in part to terror. A powerful movement had been launched within the organization of the National Association of Manufacturers for just such a reform as Beveridge had proposed. The resolution favoring a tariff commission had unanimously passed its convention. A poll later of the 1800 members had revealed all but 350 in favor of a revision, and these were opposed on the sole ground of expediency. The poll on the commission plan had revealed 1221 for it and but 153 against. It was a complete vindication of Beveridge's contention the year before that business men and industrialists were demanding both revision and a new method.[1]

The moment he reached home, Beveridge had been importuned to join the manufacturers in the fight for the commission plan, and H. E. Miles, of the Tariff Committee of the manufacturers' organization, had written him a denunciation of the old method:

We all know how full of graft the tariff is. When there were few trusts and almost everything was made on a competitive basis at a low cost, with a very small margin of profit, it made small difference how high the tariff was, as the manufacturer was unable to take advantage of the tariff opportunities. There were some as far back as we can find who added a large part of the tariff to their prices. Now, when everything is trust-made, or, if not trust-made, is made with better understandings, sometimes very complete ones between competitors (though only of a verbal and loose nature not within the cog-

[1] H. E. Miles, chairman, Tariff Committee, National Association of Manufacturers, to George E. Wells, Dec. 2, 1907.

nizance of the law), the tariff is added to the price, however high the tariff is, on most everything that is made in a big way....

Too much cannot be made of the fact that the manufacturers themselves, in whose interest the tariff is made, are in very large numbers bitterly opposed to it, because the practical uses now made of unjust schedules is favoring some manufacturers almost to the ruin of others. For instance, it is the cause of the excessive profits of the steel industry, and that same steel tariff is the cause of the very small profits made in almost all industries that use steel as their raw material. It is limiting export business most unfortunately with this latter class, though the steel companies themselves go abroad and sell against European competition at a splendid profit and at prices which, if granted to our home manufacturers, would enable a great increase in export business on steel.

The present situation is simply unendurable. The Standpatters propose by specious talk... to hold the present situation over the next election and then give us the old sort of revision. If by any chance they should do all this, the people would rebel against that revision and that tariff would have to be made over, in my judgment, within twelve or twenty-four months.

Substantially the manufacturers are Republicans as well as Protectionists. They have no end of information showing that the Republican Party has sold out the consuming public, that is, the whole country, every time in our generation that it has made a tariff. We do not want to publish that information.[1]

Seldom has so much prophecy been crowded into so few words.

Firmly convinced that business men were with him, and that his idea in no way ran counter to the Republican concept of protection, Beveridge prepared his bill with the coöperation of Stone, the tariff expert.[2] The bill provided for a commission of seven members, three representing the producing interests, with one lawyer familiar with customs and tariff laws, with one member experienced in the administration of such laws, one acquainted with the customs and tariff laws of other countries, and one economist and statistician who had made a special study of the prices and cost of production as affected by the tariff. The commission was to be empowered to take testimony, under oath, and to require the production of books and papers. It was 'to investigate immediately the cost of production of all articles covered by the tariff, with special reference to prices paid American labor in comparison with the prices paid foreign labor, the prices of raw materials, whether domestic or imported, entering into manufactured articles, the condition of domestic and foreign markets as affecting American products, and all other facts

[1] H. E. Miles, of the National Association of Manufacturers, to Beveridge, Oct. 2, 1907.

[2] Beveridge to Bross, July 22, 1913.

which, in the judgment of the commission, may be necessary or helpful to Congress in providing equitable rates of duties on any article.'

As Congress opened, Beveridge expected no favorable action during that session, and wrote confidentially to that effect to an Indianapolis manufacturer, warning him against the over-confidence of Miles: 'If Miles or anyone else thinks they can get the tariff commission bill through, I shall be rejoiced to have somebody else take the laboring oar, and I will help with all my might.'[1]

It was about this time that Miles was persuaded, after a talk with Roosevelt, that the President was 'heart and soul, to use his own words, for a tariff commission.' He had refrained from recommending it in his Message, since it was a function of Congress and would have been injurious. He suggested that farmers and manufacturers be urged to deluge Congress with letters.[2]

In January the measure was introduced and the president of the Manufacturers' Association sounded the tocsin to its membership; commercial and industrial bodies began pouring in commendatory resolutions; and the manufacturers' lobby took up its residence in Washington. Though not entirely satisfied with the bill, the popular reaction encouraged Beveridge in the hope that after all it might be passed at that session. He found more favorable sentiment in the Senate than he had expected.[3] He had been encouraged when at a dinner Justice Harlan said, and thrice repeated to Roosevelt and some Senators, that 'unless you gentlemen in Congress establish a tariff commission and get ready to revise the tariff, the Republican Party — my party — will be swept off the face of the earth in the coming election.'[4] The old crusading zeal possessed Beveridge again; and soon Miles was writing Franklin Pierce that 'Senator La Follette is a terror on the floor' and would 'give them naked truth in sensational fashion,' and that Beveridge would 'be more conservative, but quite as able.'

Meanwhile, in possession of ugly facts on previous scandals of tariff-making, Miles was bluntly serving notice that it was 'up to the politicians whether they want these figures given to the public or whether they will give us a commission.' To the politicians he was speaking a language they could understand. 'You are counting too much upon the fealty of Republican manufacturers

[1] Beveridge to D. M. Parry, Dec. 4, 1907.
[2] Hearings on Maintenance of a Lobby, S.R. 92; A. B. Farquhar to J. W. Van Cleave, Dec. 7, 1907, I, 1194.
[3] Beveridge to Van Cleave, Jan. 10, 1908.
[4] Beveridge to Van Cleave, Jan. 16, 1908.

and business men, who prefer the Republican Party to Bryanism and Free Silver, and other heresies, but who have less reason to fear Democratic success now than before in a dozen years.'[1] Payne, Cannon, and Dalzell were dumbfounded by the demands of their own people, but were determined to stand out against the 'heresy' of a scientific tariff.

In the preparation of his speech, Beveridge, with his genius for research, was mobilizing facts intended for the public generally as much as for the Senate. He postponed the date for its delivery until in February, and sent Miles an explanation: 'This will give opportunity for your delegation to visit the President and Congress; and if you get a rebuke from the Speaker or Mr. Aldrich, as may be the case, this speech, and what I hope will be your reception of it, will show that you are in earnest and not to be rebuffed.'[2]

VI

Thus (February 4, 1908), representatives of the manufacturers, of the Tariff Reciprocity League, of the National Grange, and the National Live Stock Association filed into the hearing granted by Cannon and Payne. These leaders received them with amused toleration, listened to their arguments, and announced their opposition. Cannon spoke glowingly of 'this glorious country,' with a market for ninety per cent of all it could produce. And what was the matter with the country? Was it not prospering under the existing law? Experts? Where a greater expert than Payne? And who could approach the experts of the Treasury? Payne was equally decisive. Why a commission, anyway? 'We know where to get the Government experts for information about the intricacies of the operation of the various schedules. We know where to get the information from manufacturers, or merchants, or mechanics the country over. Shall we get this information at first hand?'

And then, again, the quibble about the Constitution granting power over revenue measures exclusively to the Congress.

The hearing was over; nothing had been accomplished; the fight was on.

VII

Every effort was made to destroy the effect of the Beveridge speech before its delivery. The 'Indianapolis Star' conceded

[1] Miles to Hon. J. J. Jenkins, Jan. 14, 1908.
[2] Beveridge to Miles, Jan. 29, 1908.

that there would be a large gallery attendance and a 'feast of oratory,' but gleefully declared the speaker might as well 'direct his remarks against the Soldiers' and Sailors' Monument.' It described Cannon placing his hand on the shoulders of Payne, and saying, 'I don't believe there is a man in the United States who knows as much about the tariff or is as well equipped to revise it as my friend Payne.' The latter's reported comment that 'You probably know where it [Beveridge's bill] was prepared,' brought a sharp rebuke from Beveridge, to whom Payne apologized.[1]

The galleries, indeed, were packed, and largely with a sympathetic audience, when Beveridge spoke. It was a statesmanlike presentation of the argument. Did the proposed commission deprive Congress of its constitutional function of framing tariff laws? It did not; it merely created a body to assist Congress to a just and reasonable conclusion by assembling essential facts with scientific accuracy. 'If any man needs the facts more than any other,' he said, 'it is the protectionist like myself; because we cannot wisely protect any business unless we know the facts about that business.' With thousands of items, it was impossible for Congress to get all the facts bearing on each. Calling the roll of the members of the Finance Committee of the Senate, he showed from their other committee obligations the impossibility of any of them mastering all the facts without expert aid. When the Dingley Bill was framed, the members of the Ways and Means Committee included two lawyers, one wood manufacturer, and an editor — none qualified to act authoritatively without assistance. And if Congress had the facts when it framed that measure, did the Senate and House, which conflicted on many items, have the same facts? Hearings? Yes, but all were congested, and some were private.

The interruptions were few and without consequence. When Senator Stone, from the Democratic side, interrupted with congratulations to the speaker on having joined the Democrats, Beveridge replied that he would 'never join any organization which makes the American tariff the football of partisan politics.'[2] This covered the interruption of Senator Scott of West Virginia, who rose indignantly to announce himself a Republican.

The sponsors of the commission movement, immensely pleased with the speech, ordered seventeen thousand copies for immediate distribution. But the fight had just begun. Beveridge had mortally offended the dictators of his party's policy in the Senate. Soon they would strike.

[1] Beveridge to Payne, Feb. 10, 1908; Payne to Beveridge, Feb. 13, 1908.
[2] *Congressional Record*, Feb. 5, 1908.

VIII

But the pressure of outside sentiment was pushing the gray-beards of House and Senate hard. The press had been responsive, and resolutions were pouring in from trade associations. The Manufacturers' Association was making progress among business men, and Beveridge, relying largely on public sentiment, kept urging them to still greater activity. 'These are golden hours,' he wrote them. Meanwhile, working constantly among his colleagues, he was not even neglecting Aldrich. By the last of the month he was able to report that the dictator had agreed to report the bill. 'And though he may report adversely,' he added, 'that gets the bill before the Senate and I can then move to take it up.'[1] Payne in the House both amazed and grieved by the developments, was seeking a way out through a compromise that would mean nothing. He was proposing to appoint a 'commission' from among the members of the Ways and Means Committee. 'It shows how thoroughly we have them on the run,' wrote Beveridge.[2] Every effort was being made to bring Roosevelt to the firing line. 'I have had a long talk with the President,' he wrote '— he is for us, horse, foot and dragoon — but confidentially I am afraid he thinks that you gentlemen[3] will not keep up the fight until it assumes the proportions of an irresistible movement.'[4]

Two days after this letter was written, Roosevelt was reading a vigorous letter from Miles, warning that the developments threatened to injure the Republican Party and cost it the Presidency. It was too bad that some of the 'Standpatters are likely to insist upon our proving them before the whole people arrant cowards and knaves,' but if they insist, it was their feast or funeral. Would the President look over the enclosed pamphlet, which would be published in a few days, on how tariffs had been made and on the part Payne had played in making them?[5]

A few days later, the pamphlet was in the mails speeding to the four corners.[6] In this slashing article 'Old Schedules,' as Payne was often called, was literally pulverized on his own confession, in 'The Making of America,' that logrolling had brought some scandalous results. It went into damaging details on the steel schedule.

[1] Beveridge to Van Cleave, Feb. 29, 1908.   [2] *Ibid.*
[3] The National Manufacturers' Association.
[4] Beveridge to Van Cleave, Feb. 29, 1908.
[5] Miles to Roosevelt, Feb. 21, 1908.
[6] *Tariff-Making: The Old Way and the Right Way; Remarkable Statements of Hon. Sereno E. Payne, Chairman of the Ways and Means Committee.*

Thus, all through March the battle raged, with Aldrich suavely seeking a meaningless compromise. Roosevelt was still holding back from a public declaration of his position, conferring the while with both Aldrich and Beveridge. When Beveridge in a letter urged a declaration in a Message, the reply came from the President's Secretary, promising 'careful consideration.'[1] But the very next day Miles was writing an interested party in Chicago that 'today the President is just on the point of sending a message to Congress with a word in it in our behalf.' The House was reported 'in a turmoil,' with 'two thirds of the members fighting for us, with most of the remaining worried and indifferent, and a very few Standpatters at bay, fighting back.' In the Senate, Aldrich was proposing to report the Beveridge bill with the recommendation that the work be done by Treasury experts; and Miles was strangely pleased. 'This concedes our principle and is a wonderful advance toward right methods of tariff-making,' he wrote. Now if Aldrich only would agree that the President should appoint three outsiders.[2]

Three days later, Beveridge and Aldrich conferred with Roosevelt, and the former was not so enthusiastic over the Aldrich plan as Miles. 'It involves giving in all along the line.' The battle seemed lost for the session, and utterly weary, he wrote: 'In my judgment the very best that can be done is to get a joint resolution declaring for tariff revision by a special session... elected at the next Presidential election, providing that subcommittees of the Senate and House shall sit during the recess and that the President shall designate experts from the departments to do the work provided for in our bill.... We are lucky to get this much.'[3]

But through April the fight went on, with members of the Manufacturers' Association canvassing the House and finding members timid and reticent. Butler Ames of Massachusetts frankly was against a commission because 'an examination by a non-political commission would expose conditions to the Democrats'; and Weeks of Massachusetts confided that the manufacturers were most unfortunate in choosing Beveridge and La Follette as their advocates. This was to appear increasingly in the correspondence later to be brought out in the Mulhall investigation.[4] Meanwhile, an attempt was being made to commit Payne to the plan with a platform declaration in the New York

[1] Beveridge to Roosevelt, March 12, 1908.
[2] Miles to James S. Agar, March 13, 1908.
[3] Beveridge to Miles, March 16, 1908.
[4] Unsigned letter to Miles, April 8, 1908; Hearings on Maintenance of Lobby, II, 1527–29.

State Convention through the influence of Roosevelt. J. Sloat Fassett had already written the tariff plank under Payne's direction, declaring 'for revision of the tariff at the proper time'; and when informed by the anonymous correspondent that the President that very morning had said, in the presence of an agent and Beveridge, that he wanted a tariff commission plank, Fassett agreed to make the substitution on a written request from the White House. Beveridge agreed to see Roosevelt, but Fassett reached the White House first, greatly flurried, according to Loeb, the President's Secretary.[1]

Payne prevailed; there was no tariff commission plank in the New York platform.

And so the flurry continued to disturb the sweet serenity of the session, without resulting in any action; but it was only the first skirmish. The fight would be continued.

IX

It had turned glowering glances on Beveridge from the 'leaders' of the old régime. They had viewed the course of the 'upstart' during the entire session with increasing irritation. They had growled; but when immediately afterwards he led a dramatic fight against them on the four battleship program of the Administration, they began to snap. The man in the White House had long been a prickly nuisance to the 'leaders,' but they had been forced to tolerate his manners and measures by fear of popular chastisement. Now he was approaching the end of his term. Their release was not remote. Soon his successor would be nominated in Chicago, and the power of the 'Big Stick' would be an ugly memory. When the leaders lined up against Roosevelt on his desired appropriation for four battleships and proposed two instead, some of the more ardent Rooseveltians organized for combat and asked Beveridge to lead them. The Administration's wishes were in harmony with his own views; he stood for a powerful navy; and he was loyal to the man in the White House. But it required no little temerity for him to step out in front and fight. His own State had never been a 'big navy State,' and his enemies were certain to make the most of his 'indifference to the sentiment of his constituency.' But he entered the fight on principle, knowing that the Administration program would be voted down.[2] The fact that his colleague Hemenway was aligned against the Roosevelt program accentuated the issue in Indiana.

[1] Hearings on Maintenance of Lobby, III, 2780.
[2] *Indianapolis Star*, April 23, 1908.

Soon Beveridge's enemies in Indiana were making the most of a conversation with William C. Beer, described as a 'lobbyist of the Steel Trust,' in the Marble Room, the absurd insinuation being that the friend of Perkins favored the larger program because the Steel Trust would more largely profit.[1]

It was at the time when Roosevelt was preparing to send the fleet on a cruise around the world, and this was thought obnoxious because the Senate Committee on Naval Affairs had not been consulted. The Senate had been snubbed; something would have to be done about it; and the battleship program offered the opportunity. The word was passed around to defeat the President's plan, and success seemed easy. Even Lodge had intimate relations with the conspirators. He would have to work surreptitiously, but he would find a way.

When Beveridge, accepting the leadership of the four-ship party, thought of introducing a four-ship amendment, and attempted to discuss it with Hale, he was met with an icy hauteur.

'But my dear sir,' said Hale, 'you cannot do that.'

'Why not?' asked Beveridge.

'Because we do not desire it.'

'Who are "we"?' persisted Beveridge.

'The leaders,' said Hale, with a note of finality.

'Well, well,' said Beveridge. 'I did not know my actions were controlled by any self-constituted leaders. Let's find out about this.'[2]

Thus the battle began; the canvassing of the Senate commenced; and Piles of Washington introduced the amendment. The President himself, deeply interested, and following the fight closely, learned to his amazement that his friend Lodge was either lukewarm or hostile to his program. This attitude of Lodge was being used among the enemies of Roosevelt to show that he was not in earnest. Piles hurried to the White House to protest, and Roosevelt wrote sharply to Lodge. 'I wish you would tell Piles that of course you are heartily for the proposition,' he wrote. 'It is a simple outrage from the national standpoint not to provide for these four battleships.'[3] We do not have the reply of Lodge, but he persisted in attacking openly and covertly the Senators who were waging the President's battle.

The afternoon devoted to the debate was one of drama. After Piles opened the debate on his amendment, and Hale and Aldrich sought to lead him into the admission that he contemplated

[1] *Indianapolis Star*, April 25, 1908.
[2] *Saturday Evening Post*, May 23, 1908.
[3] *Roosevelt-Lodge Correspondence*, II, 293.

a war with Japan, Beveridge entered. He opened with an offensive, with a sharp challenge on Hale's comment when the amendment was first introduced, that it would be futile to discuss a matter on which the Senate's mind was made up.

I know, Mr. President, that the Senator did not mean a certain interpretation which might be put upon those remarks by persons unkinder than myself. It is inconceivable that in this body... a question involving, in the opinion of the Chief Magistrate, the defense and honor of the Nation, should be determined without any deliberation at all. It is inconceivable that the Senate of the United States, in what the future may show to be one of its historic moments, had 'made up its mind' before a fact has been adduced, before an argument has been presented, before one word of discussion has been heard. So I am sure that the Senator from Maine did not mean that the Senate had 'made up its mind' without consideration. Surely he did not mean that this 'greatest deliberative body in the world' is a mere automaton whose votes are herded and cast as the springs are pulled.

This was insurgency dangerously expressed. Hale protested that he had no thought of closing debate. He would gladly hear what Beveridge had to say, but would not bother with a reply.

It was a quaint conceit that this lofty indifference would break the spirit of this insurgent. He continued more bitingly sarcastic than before. He was sure he had properly interpreted the observation of Hale. Of course he meant that all the Senators had thoroughly studied the matter; and yet, though perhaps 'speaking against a Senate already convinced in a silent and secret way,' the minority would be permitted to voice their opinions as a matter of justice to themselves. Whence the danger to the Nation? He did not know. A crisis often comes unexpectedly. The Mafia incident in New Orleans came in a flash and might easily have led to war with Italy. Perhaps Hale was too certain and optimistic. When the speaker, in his article on Manchuria, confidently predicted war, had he not discussed his conclusion with Hale, who ridiculed the thought? 'He showed me so conclusively,' he continued, 'that it could not come, that the enlightened opinion of the world would prevent it, that I actually modified the chapter upon that subject, saying it was a "probability" instead of a "certainty."'

But, interrupted Hale, why did Beveridge now fear war? It was a blunder.

'What the Executive may have in his possession no man knows,' he replied. 'I have gone over the other messages of President Roosevelt and nowhere can I find the solemn words which he there uses, and that is the reason why I do not answer.'

There was audacity, perhaps impropriety, in this pointed

observation. Lodge now broke into the discussion with little pin-pricks at the insurgents without actually touching the issue seriously; and Beveridge closed with a fervent appeal for the President's program.[1]

The incident enraged the Senate oligarchy, which determined to make short shrift of the trouble-makers and to rebuke the man who led them. This process was to follow on the morrow. Then it was that Aldrich, who seldom spoke, took the floor to devote himself exclusively to Beveridge in a speech of studied insult. Ridiculing the importance of the issue, he hurried on in arrogant tones to a rebuke of Beveridge and Piles for presuming to speak for the President. 'In my opinion neither the Senator from Indiana nor the Senator from Washington had any authority to speak for the President of the United States.'

'Neither the Senator from Washington nor myself said to the Senate that we spoke on the authority of the President,' Beveridge replied. 'I made distinct reference only to the Message.'

But the afternoon entertainment had been carefully planned, and Hale joined Aldrich in the attack, while Lodge sat at the elbow of Hale with eager suggestions. The stage-setting so clearly disclosed a conspiracy to crush Beveridge that the men in the press gallery settled down to the enjoyment of the drama. The exchanges between Aldrich and his intended victim grew constantly more peppery, but it was noticed that while the 'dictator' was struggling with his rage, Beveridge was smiling as he fought back.

'I venture to deny for the President,' stormed Aldrich, 'and for the members of the Committee on Foreign Relations, who I hope will be heard from in this connection, that there are any facts in connection with our relations with any friendly power that if they became known would affect the question now pending before the Senate.'

He knew that Lodge, the President's intimate, would be 'heard from,' for that was prearranged; and though Lodge knew, from the letter from Roosevelt in his possession, that Beveridge was fighting the President's battle, he would manage to do his bit.

The personal animus appeared all too clearly when it developed that in the hope of making Beveridge ridiculous, Hale had spent the previous evening poring over 'The Russian Advance' to find predictions that events had overthrown. He rose happily to say that the whole tenor of the book had been that no nation in the East could stand before Russia; which was an utterly false statement, as we have seen. But the gallery laughed;

[1] *Congressional Record*, April 24, 1908.

and when Aldrich interposed with 'that is my recollection of the book,' it laughed again. If Beveridge's pride was hurt, he did not show it. He recalled again that Hale had taken issue with his prediction that Russia and Japan would be at war within a few years. He had scouted the idea as impossible, 'and yet within three months the war was raging.' The gallery now laughed at Hale.

Meanwhile, with Aldrich continuing his attempt to crush the insurgent, it was becoming increasingly difficult for the galleries to determine who was getting the most lashes. Once Beveridge flashed forth an indignant protest against the impertinence of the 'dictator' in attempting to control the opinions of Senators.

Aldrich — I do not find fault with the judgment of the Senator at all. He has a perfect right to his own judgment and to his own opinions; and I hope he controls his own vote.

Beveridge — The Senator knows I do — nobody knows it better than he.

When Aldrich closed, Lodge rose to support the President with many acknowledgments that he was forced 'to agree with the Senator from Rhode Island' and with criticisms of the man who was leading the President's fight. But when, in closing, Beveridge vigorously denounced his critics for deliberate misrepresentations, as shown by the 'Record' to be false, the galleries heartily applauded. The conspirators had presumed too far in their right to dictate. And when Senator William Alden Smith of Michigan finally rose to protest against the purpose of the conspiracy, there was a hush in the Chamber.

The American people are accustomed to listen to the Senator from Indiana and to recognize his brilliant attainments. There is not a Senator upon this side of the Chamber who does not recognize his ability when help is needed in elections and campaigns. He is able to state his views then to your satisfaction and sometimes to your advantage. It is his ability and his character and courage that have again and again come to the rescue of Senators in doubtful States when their elections were pending.

The galleries now roared their approval.

When by the hardest work in years the senatorial oligarchy was unable to prevent almost a third of the Senate from following Beveridge, it was plain that the moral victory was with the insurgent.[1] It was more than that — the insurgents had forced a compromise in the pledge of two battleships a year. The press reports were favorable to Beveridge, the 'New York Times' describing his speech as 'one of the most eloquent heard this

[1] *Congressional Record*, April 24, 1908.

session';[1] and, commenting on the desertion of two fifths of the Republicans, the 'New York World' saw in the incident the passing of the power of the old oligarchy:

> The passing of the Senate leaders of old time was illustrated strikingly in Mr. Aldrich's speech.... He has been a cloakroom leader, a committeeman leader, who has never appeared on the floor except to voice some partisan principle. In the galleries today the comment was that the scepter was passing from the old coterie that has ruled the Senate for so many years, and that its chief has been forced into the arena in open debate and free discussion. The young Republicans from the West... are said to be responsible. They have forced the Senate oligarchy into a defensive position and put an end to the method of silent rule.[2]

The Washington observer for the 'Saturday Evening Post' reached the same conclusion. 'The Senate oligarchy is in a bad way. It is tottery and wobbly at the knees. Its members do not know just what it was that hit them, but they do know that they have been hit hard.'[3]

And in their rage they blundered again, through hate. Just after the vote was taken, the clerk began reading a Message from Roosevelt urging action on his legislative program. Hardly had the reading begun when Aldrich suggested that the reading be postponed and Foraker moved an adjournment. It was, as it was intended, a studied discourtesy to Roosevelt.

Beveridge was jubilant and content. 'It was a glorious victory after all,' he wrote Perkins. 'It is the last victory of the old gang. By next year we will be strong enough to do things.'[4]

The battleship fight is historically important only in that it marks the beginning of the end of the domination of the Aldrich oligarchy, and the beginning of the insurgency that was to make history within two years.

[1] April 25, 1908.   [2] *New York World*, April 26, 1908.
[3] *Saturday Evening Post*, May 23, 1908.
[4] Beveridge to Perkins, April 28, 1908.

CHAPTER VII

'SPECIAL TRAIN FOR ATKINS'

I

THE campaign of 1908 found Beveridge as fiercely engaged as though he had been a candidate himself. The preliminary stages were to bring him disappointments. His intimate personal and political friend, Charles W. Miller, associated in the law with the younger Baker, was seeking the gubernatorial nomination, but Beveridge was in no position to buckle on the armor and go forth to battle wearing his friend's colors. All he could do in the way of advice he did. The autumn before, he had urged Miller to prepare a short speech for the Republican Love Feast and 'commit it so you can say it backwards'; and as an afterthought, he added: 'And when you deliver it, don't stand with your legs more than six feet apart, or your stomach more than four feet in front of you.' [1]

To make Beveridge's position all the more difficult, on the eve of his own candidacy for reëlection two years later, his political foes were organizing behind James E. Watson, who had never seriously pretended to be one of his supporters. As usual, the organization was largely dominated by his enemies. With his hands tied, it was not encouraging to learn from Miller that Senator Hemenway, who had promised Shaffer to coöperate with Beveridge, was scouring the State for Watson, promising positions that would be at the disposal of the Governor, demanding the support of gaugers and revenue men, and passing the word down to his postmasters to deliver the votes. [2] On top of it all, Watson, with an impressive campaign fund, was a consummate politician with a zealous following, and the result was inevitable. Miller was defeated.

But in the general results of the State Convention, Beveridge had less to worry him than Watson. The latter had to accept a county option plank in the platform on prohibition which threatened complications at the polls, and Beveridge was successful in securing platform endorsements of his position on a tariff commission and on child labor. When he appeared before the Convention, he was given a notable ovation, and spoke briefly but boldly. 'Two years ago,' he said, 'some of us began the tariff fight. We were met with arrogance and insult from those who think that the world does not move; from interests whom

[1] Beveridge to Miller, Nov. 7, 1907. [2] Miller to Beveridge, Jan. 27, 1908.

the tariff may have protected properly when it was made, but which changed conditions now enable to injure other honest interests; from a purchased press owned by corporations and men whose wealth has flowed and is flowing from obsolete schedules. But success is now in sight, and since Indiana led the first charge in this battle, so let Indiana lead the last charge that crowns with victory.' A commission of experts — that must come. And child labor — that must go. Thus he made his position defiantly plain. And then he closed with a pledge of fidelity to the presidential candidacy of Fairbanks.[1]

The unknown quantity in the State campaign was known to be Governor J. Frank Hanly, now approaching the close of his gubernatorial term in no happy frame of mind. He had forced the county option plank into the platform, but he was not yet through. In May, when in Washington, Beveridge had entertained him at dinner, with the Ambassadors of France and Spain, Justice Holmes of the Supreme Court, the Secretary of the Interior, the presidents of the universities of Minnesota, Michigan, Yale, Johns Hopkins, Robert Underwood Johnson of the 'Century,' Gifford Pinchot, Shaw, and Munsey as guests.[2]

Scarcely had the campaign opened when Hanly summoned the Legislature in extra session, and, forcing the county option law upon the statutes, took the power of decision from the people, aroused the fire of the liberals, and put Watson in an untenable position from which he was to find it impossible to extricate himself.

II

The presidential contest in the spring likewise was uncertain By a mere nod of the head, Roosevelt could have commanded another nomination. He had pledged himself in an impetuous moment against it, and lived to regret it. But he was pledged. Though he openly arrayed himself behind the candidacy of William Howard Taft, the favorite in his Cabinet, the politicians, eager to be rid of the dynamic executive with uncomfortable surprises up his sleeve, were fearful of a stampede to him in the Convention. It was even suspected that he might be preparing the way for it, and this, as much as anything else, was to deprive Beveridge of the coveted honor of presiding over the Convention and making the keynote speech. That there was another reason, which was to appear after the election when the reactionary wing of the party took possession of the Government, is now quite clear. A speech from Beveridge would have been a

[1] Republican Committee pamphlet.   [2] *Indianapolis Star*, May 16, 1908.

progressive pronouncement in line with the Roosevelt policies. And then, too, Roosevelt himself had requested that Beveridge be chosen. The combination of reasons was enough.

Early in March, Roosevelt had written Harry New, the National Chairman, suggesting that Beveridge would be a pleasing choice for the position, and asking New's opinion. The fact had been conveyed to Beveridge by Roosevelt himself; and Beveridge thereupon wrote the faithful Rothschild to see New and ascertain his views.[1] Within a few days, Rothschild replied that New had expressed his hearty assent, but, confidentially, he was afraid there might be opposition because Beveridge came from a State which had a candidate in Fairbanks.[2] The truth was that the Roosevelt letter gave his enemies an opportunity to snub him which they had no intention of passing by. The result was the selection of Senator Julius C. Burrows of Michigan, one of the most trusted lieutenants of Aldrich, who had no sympathy with the Roosevelt policies. There had been some discussion of Jonathan P. Dolliver, but this was intended as a blind. Senators Hale, Scott of West Virginia, and Burrows had managed the business from the beginning. Beveridge, who received two of the five votes, felt that 'the purpose was that the keynote speech should not be a progressive speech,' least of all, a downward revision speech.[3] And it wasn't.

Beveridge keenly felt the disappointment. He had been so certain of his selection, after Roosevelt informed him of his letter to New, that he had prepared the speech. Lorimer wanted it for the 'Saturday Evening Post.' 'Are you willing, and can you write that keynote speech which you are not going to deliver at the Convention, for the "Saturday Evening Post"?' he wrote.[4] But Beveridge was not willing.

Meanwhile, the press had been having much to say about the contest. The 'New York Herald' correspondent wrote from Washington that Senator Lodge, who was one of Taft's strongest supporters, was going to the Convention to head off a Roosevelt stampede, and, incidentally, to side-track Beveridge.[5] The Taft coterie even then was quite distinct from Roosevelt's, though the public understood otherwise at the time. The Indianian did not fit into the picture the reactionaries had in mind. They were tired of tributes to Roosevelt.

[1] Beveridge to Rothschild, March 7, 1908.
[2] Rothschild to Beveridge, March 16, 1908.
[3] Beveridge to Shaw, May 18, 1908.
[4] Lorimer to Beveridge, May 25, 1908.
[5] *New York Herald*, May 2, 1908.

III

Nevertheless, Beveridge took his humiliation lightly, and went as chairman of the Indiana delegation to Chicago to work faithfully for Fairbanks's nomination as a matter of duty and expediency. There had been much discussion of the possibility of his own nomination as a dark horse, and he had been forced to protest against the launching of such a movement at a banquet of the Marquette Club in Chicago, where he was to speak on Lincoln's Birthday. He had enjoined Shaffer to take the necessary steps.[1] On the very day he was writing Shaffer to prevent any such demonstration, Governor Chase S. Osborne of Michigan, who was to be one of the speakers at the Marquette banquet, was writing Beveridge:

I note that Mr. Bigelow, of the Marquette Club, stated in his letter to me that their club was grooming you as a 'dark horse.' I state this for the reason that I have gotten the idea from your letter that too much reference of this kind will embarrass you in Indiana. While you are setting me right, possibly it might not be a bad idea to keep your eye on your other friends. They are all so proud of you and so earnest and so interested, that they will need regulating.[2]

The other friends speedily were 'set right,' and nothing occurred at the banquet to embarrass Beveridge in Indiana or elsewhere. As chairman of the delegation, he did his bit for Fairbanks. He was not asked to place him in nomination, and Hanly made no brilliant job of it. Senator Burrows droned uninspiringly through the keynote of ultra-conservatism, and no one heard or cared what he said.

But Beveridge's embarrassments were not over. On the Friday morning before the Convention adjourned, Frank Hitchcock, the Taft manager, made the proffer of the vice-presidential nomination, and Myron T. Herrick and other Taft men urged it upon him. Several reasons impelled him resolutely to refuse to consider it. It would mean a dreadful summer and a position of utter uselessness — that of a mere spectator without power to propose a law, enter into debate, or affect events. Except in the case of Taft's death, it would mean the end of his career. Then, too, he considered the possibility that, after the movement might be started, either Taft or Roosevelt might for some reason of expediency oppose it, to his serious injury. He refused.

But even in the Convention he was not to escape pressure. The Nebraska delegation approached him on the floor, proposing to nominate him, anyway, and he had a struggle with them.

[1] Beveridge to Shaffer, Jan. 11, 1908.   [2] Osborne to Beveridge, Jan. 11, 1908.

'If I am placed in nomination,' he declared, 'I shall rise in my place and decline it.' Senator Smoot also joined those urging his acceptance.[1] But he was not to be satisfied with the nomination of Sherman. 'Aside from the fact that he cannot physically possibly last through the campaign... he is not a vote-getter even in New York, and is a vote-loser in the Middle West.'[2]

Very rapidly, in these days, Beveridge's progressivism was moving toward insurgency. He had been deeply impressed by the intensity of the La Follette group in the Convention, with the fervent devotion of La Follette's followers to his principles and fortunes. He had seen resolutions urged by these men voted down, and he had felt they were right. Immediately after the adjournment, he sat down and wrote La Follette:

Since the Convention I have been thinking so much about the remarkable speeches which were made by young Cochems and McGee, nominating you and seconding your nomination, that I cannot refrain from writing you about it. When any man can inspire the loyalty those two young fellows manifested for you and for the cause for which you stand, the man has done a very great thing. The only real pieces of oratory in that Convention came from the lips of these two men. They seemed inspired by the occasion; burning with the vital earnestness for the reforms in which they believed sufficiently to fight for them and to be defeated for them if need be, and the result was that, although they spoke late in the day when everybody was tired and before a Convention that was more or less hostile, they nevertheless aroused the only real enthusiasm elicited by any speaker.

Of course, your friends have told you of the remarkable demonstration with which your name was received when these two men had presented you to the Convention. It was notable and worth while. I explain it only on the ground that here was a cause, a definite, tangible cause, in which men believe with entire devotion, and that this struck a responsive chord in their breasts, no matter what the attitude of any person might be toward the reforms themselves for which you stand.

I was deeply humiliated when the Convention voted down the plank of your platform for publicity of campaign contributions — specifically voted it down; and also specifically voted down the election of United States Senators by the people, and for the valuation of railroad properties. Perhaps you observed that these planks received a heavy favorable vote from our delegation. I, as chairman, personally voted for each one of them, and being accompanied in this.... The men who voted in our delegation did so without any appeal being made to them by me or anybody else — they voted for them simply because they believed in them.... I regretted that other planks of the platform you presented were not separately presented to the Convention. There

---

[1] Beveridge to Shaffer, undated; to Mrs. Beveridge, June 13, 1908.
[2] Beveridge to Shaffer.

are three or four others for which I should have been more than happy to vote, notably that one concerning the tariff commission.[1]

Thus, when the Convention had done its work, Beveridge was not entirely happy. He intuitively knew that his party was not headed in the direction he was going, or Roosevelt, in so many instances, had gone. Burrows for keynoter, Sherman for Vice-President, and progressive planks, including those on campaign contributions and the tariff commission, voted down! There could be no doubt as to which element had been in control of the Convention. And Taft? He wondered.

Then, in early July came an invitation from Taft to join him in Hot Springs, Virginia, whither the nominee had gone, for a conference. Others were summoned at the same time, and Beveridge was not flattered by the invitation, but was glad of the opportunity to learn what Taft had in mind. The train from Washington had axle trouble, delaying it, and Beveridge enjoyed the wild scenery about him. In a two hours' conference with Taft on reaching the Springs, the candidate delighted him with his cordiality and views. Beveridge wrote Shaffer:

I had a very long and thorough conference with Mr. Taft. The other 'statesmen' tried to break into it by sending continual messages to Mr. Taft to come to the ball game, in which he was to participate, but he waved them all aside until we were through, and then went to the game just when it was closed. We talked over the chairmanship, conditions in Indiana, and his letter of acceptance, very thoroughly. I think his attitude on every question is going to please you tremendously. As he told the newspaper boys himself, he did most of the talking. I sat quietly by until he would get through a particular point and asked me what I thought of it, and he agreed with me on all of them. He impressed me as almost boyish in his simplicity and truthfulness and sincerity, and I must confess to my surprise that I liked him far better than I ever did before. I think he is going to be found very much more reliable than other friends of ours — that is to say, that he is so simple, so very truthful that he is thoroughly dependable.' [2]

From Hot Springs Beveridge went to his vacation.

IV

'We are pleasantly located here,' he wrote Shaffer from Smith's Point near Manchester-by-the-Sea. 'We have a lovely little cottage, and although the grounds are small, yet they are restful and attractive. We have trees and flowers, and the cottage fronts upon the ocean, which sweeps in, unbroken for three

[1] Beveridge to La Follette, June 29, 1908.
[2] Beveridge to Shaffer, July, 1908.

thousand miles. Big cliffs of granite drop down from our front
yard right into the sea. I don't intend to do a thing this fall but
get a good rest. When next you see me, I will be as "hard as
nails" and as vigorous as vitality itself.'[1]

From the cliffs by the sea he looked out over the national
scene that summer watching the moves upon the political
checkerboard. Bryan had been nominated by the Democrats
at Denver, and Beveridge never made the mistake of under-
estimating him, or his appeal to the people. The young man of
1896 had greatly grown. The silver issue was in the past. And
Bryan was still pioneering as a progressive. When, immediately
after the Denver Convention, he formally announced that he
would have all the campaign contributions to his party published
'before the election,' and invited Mr. Taft to follow him, Beveridge was interested. He was disappointed when Taft and Roosevelt substituted the meaningless formula of publishing after the
polls were closed. Meanwhile, Bryan was preparing a few set
speeches on outstanding issues, and Beveridge knew they could
not be ignored.

And then, too, he still feared the effect of the nomination of
Sherman. When a friend wrote that Sherman would be stronger
than John W. Kern, his opponent, Beveridge disagreed. 'I
don't agree with you that Kern is a weaker candidate than Sherman,' he wrote. 'I am very much afraid that he will prove to be a
better vote-getter.'[2] When Shaw, planning articles on the vice-
presidential nominees, wrote him for suggestions on someone to
write on Kern, Beveridge suggested Meredith Nicholson, the
novelist, and added: 'I know Kern intimately. He is a good
lawyer, has good general ability, is a good stumper, and a good
man. He is extremely popular in Indianapolis and throughout
the State.'[3]

It was a summer of mingled joy and sorrow. Real grief came
to him with the death of the venerable Senator Allison, to whom
he was devoted. One autumn he had interested himself in running about Washington seeking an apartment for him, quarreling
with the agent who wished to exact an unjust rent. When, not
long before, he had been ill and both Senator and Mrs. Beveridge had been most attentive, the old statesman had written
gratefully to the latter: 'I want you to know how greatly I appreciate your friendship for me, shown in many ways, and especially your devotion to me during my serious illness. It helped
me much, and I regret that I have not felt adequate to make my

[1] Beveridge to Shaffer, undated.
[2] Beveridge to Shaffer, July 18, 1908.
[3] Beveridge to Shaw, July 12, 1908.

personal acknowledgments before now, but I sincerely hope that
I can soon look in upon you and tell you what consolation you
and your good husband have been to me in my trials. I appreciate it all and shall reciprocate in some way, I hope, ere long, but
you both are so full of life and spirit and goodly feeling that I
fear I can do little, but that little will come to you as time goes
on. In the meantime, I hope soon to have the pleasure of looking
in on you, and am, affectionately yours.' [1]

Platt of Connecticut, Hanna — and now Allison was gone!
The old conciliators were passing out. Beveridge was unable to
leave Smith's Point to attend the funeral, for late in August Albert, Jr., was born, and the proud father was in an ecstasy of
delight. Soon he would be writing in rollicking mood to Lorimer
proposing, apropos of the birth of a daughter in the latter's
home, that the proud fathers 'revert to the ancient custom of
mankind and make a tie-up between these two young hopefuls
right now,' since he was the parent of 'unquestionably the finest
male child on earth,' and Lorimer of 'the finest girl baby,' and
Lorimer would reply cautiously that he would 'have to look at
your goods' before committing himself. 'If he takes after his
mother, we may be able to do business.' [2]

In the midst of his joy that summer by the sea, Beveridge had
to consider campaign plans, for Roosevelt was writing Lodge
that the big demands were for Taft, Hughes, and Beveridge. [3]

One thing he had determined — that he would advocate
progressive principles and reforms, flying the Rooseveltian flag,
and his talk with Taft at Hot Springs had convinced him that
this course would be pleasing to the nominee. He had written
an article for the 'Saturday Evening Post' on 'The Issue' that
must have curdled the faces of the reactionaries.

'For the last year,' he warned, 'there has been a determined
effort, not only to check, but also to turn back, this mighty movement for common honesty in trade and righteousness in business
upon which the American people have entered. Great forces —
the greatest financial forces in history — are determined that
it shall be turned back. Master minds — by far the most resourceful in the Republic or in the world — have been planning,
and are planning now, to turn it back. Unlimited wealth is at
their disposal, the craftiest minds in politics at work.'

But he was sure they would fail, that progress would go on.
'Our whole financial system, which is now a sort of chaos, must
be set in order, and put upon a solid, enduring basis. The time

[1] Allison to Mrs. Beveridge, March 20, 1908.
[2] Beveridge to Lorimer, April 17; Lorimer to Beveridge, April 21, 1909.
[3] *Roosevelt-Lodge Correspondence*, II, 323.

has come when we must abandon the logrolling, hop-skip-and-jump method of tariff building and make our customs laws upon exact information, according to modern methods of commerce.' [1]

These views, however, did not decrease the importunate demands for his services on the stump. The demands rolled in, overwhelmingly. The party managers had no objections to these views and wanted to use them for popular effect as the expression of a party purpose. Soon Taft would be interpreting the tariff plank of the platform as a pledge of downward revision of the tariff, and no responsible party leader would challenge his interpretation. He had declared for revision at Bath two years before, and at Columbus; [2] and soon he would be declaring that revision meant downward revision at Cincinnati, where he would say that the Dingley rates had become excessive; [3] at Milwaukee, [4] where he would promise downward revision; and at Des Moines, [5] where he was to declare bluntly that the tariff plank was a pledge of a 'substantial revision downward.'

All this persuaded Beveridge that the progressive policies were to continue in the event of Taft's election, and he prepared to enter the fray with enthusiasm. He did not think the fight would be a frolic. A few months before, he had written Shaffer of his fears of possible defeat. 'The business conditions are working against our party,' he wrote, 'and it would not be at all surprising if the Government had to borrow money this year to meet operating expenses.' [6] And even as he verged on the campaign, he sometimes wondered if there was betrayal ahead. 'The truth is,' he wrote a friend, 'that some men in our party do all they can to kill these [progressive] laws which the welfare of the people demand, and then go out on the stump and pretend to the people that they have been for them all the time. Sometimes I feel that public life is not worth the effort when a man gives his best efforts for the passage of righteous laws, and then, by the "ethics" of party regularity, is compelled to go out and work for the very men who were the enemies of these measures. Nevertheless, this is just what I am going to do in this campaign.' [7]

V

Late in the summer, Joseph M. Dixon, chairman of the Speakers' Bureau, wrote him that 'the entire Northwest and Pacific Coast States' were unanimously demanding him, and

[1] *Saturday Evening Post*, June 27, 1908.   [2] August 19, 1907.
[3] Sept. 22, 1908.   [4] Sept. 24, 1908.   [5] Sept. 25, 1908.
[6] Beveridge to Shaffer, Feb. 27, 1908.
[7] Beveridge to C. W. Miller, Aug. 15, 1908.

that Hitchcock, the chairman, had said Beveridge had agreed to go.[1] He was to make one of the most amazing, nerve-racking continental tours in American history, traveling more than sixteen thousand miles, speaking from early in the day until midnight, and closing one dramatic speech at two o'clock in the morning, addressing tumultuous crowds in great auditoriums and from the rear ends of private cars, and refusing the expense money sent by the National Committee. 'Like yourself,' he wrote Dixon, 'I am in this fight for the cause and am very glad to give not only my time and efforts, but also my own expenses. I therefore return this check to you.'[2]

It was to prepare for these anticipated hardships that he trained like an athlete that summer by the sea. 'I am sleeping ten hours a night and spending the whole day out-of-doors, riding a horse, rowing a boat, walking or swimming or climbing over the rocks, and mean to get into as perfect condition as ozone and exercise can make a man,' he had written Senator Flint.[3] Though he had determined not to enter the campaign until the last of September, the importunities of Taft persuaded him to open the Ohio campaign with Charles Evans Hughes at Youngstown the first of that month. Thousands of steel workers in white uniforms packed the streets and the park where the two orators expounded the gospel.[4] Three weeks later, he opened his continental tour at Carnegie Hall, New York City, with Hughes presiding. One week before, Bryan had spoken in the same hall, and Beveridge, described by the 'New York World' as 'the heaviest piece of oratorical artillery in the Republican camp,' had been chosen to follow on the heels of the Commoner from coast to coast. It was an audacious speech for the financial center of the country, for it was a spirited defense of the Rooseveltian policy of trust regulation; an explanation of the plan 'to remove the poison ivy without cutting down the oak.' The audience was attentive, even enthusiastic, and at the close rushed to the platform to grasp the speaker's hand.[5]

Three days later, he introduced Hughes in Indianapolis, and then answered Bryan on Labor Day in Terre Haute, Indiana, and was off to the golden West. As fast as steam could carry him, he sped to North Dakota, which was in an ugly mood on the tariff. In a large auditorium in Valley City, before a lusty audience of farmers, he assailed the policy of tariff for revenue only, denounced the iniquities of the existing tariff, and pro-

[1] Dixon to Beveridge, undated.
[2] Beveridge to Dixon, Oct. 1, 1908.
[3] Oct. 12, 1908.   [4] Beveridge to Shaw; *Indianapolis Star*, Sept. 6, 1908.
[5] *New York Tribune, Times, World*, Sept. 26, 1908.

posed reform through a tariff commission.[1] The next day he was speaking from the rear end of the train in numerous towns and hamlets of the State, and at Bismarck and Dickinson the business houses were closed for his meetings. Then on to Helena, Montana, to address a great throng in the afternoon; and thence by special train over the mountains to the mining center of Butte, where he was rushed from his car to the platform to face the most impressive audience of workingmen he had ever seen. The crowd was tumultuous, not altogether friendly, and replies to frequent questions from the spectators kept him on the platform until after eleven o'clock. Afterwards he was to be told that his manner of meeting the hecklers saved the State for Taft. Thence to a banquet of young Republicans presided over by a major he had met under fire in the Philippines, and it was four in the morning when he reached his bed.

At seven he was up packing his own bags to catch an early train to Missoula. The train was heated by a stove, the schedule was upset, and on reaching his destination he was hurried to the Opera House without breakfast or even a cup of coffee, to speak on 'The Bible as Good Reading' — thus following the policy of Bryan.[2] From the Opera House he was hurried to the train and was off for Washington, where ovations awaited him at every station, and he made a militant speech at Seattle for a mighty navy to protect the seaboard and the foreign trade. A triumphant tour through Washington, and he was off for Oregon for several meetings and a luncheon at Tacoma in honor of his forty-sixth birthday.[3]

The continuous speaking, with physical hardships and little sleeping, so affected his voice that when he reached Sacramento, California, he could scarcely speak above a whisper. He begged release from his engagement, but when the party leaders urged the critical labor situation there against a cancellation, he yielded and addressed the crowd, though every word caused pain.[4] Forced to rebellion by the orders of physicians, he insisted on the abandonment of the meeting at Reno, Nevada, and the special train chartered for the trip was cancelled. He went to Lake Tahoe, shut himself off from visitors, sunned himself and rested, and within two days he was off to a meeting at Salt Lake City. The rest had revived him, healed his voice, and, striking his stride again within the shadow of the Mormon Temple, he went on to Pueblo and spoke, and thence immediately to Denver, where he discussed the tariff and a commission in

[1] *Valley City Pilot*, Oct. 2, 1908.
[2] Beveridge to Spencer Eddy, Nov. 15, 1908.
[3] *Indianapolis Star*, Oct. 7, 1908.   [4] To Senator Flint, Oct. 10, 1908.

the enormous auditorium where Bryan had been nominated three months before.

But he was not to know what pressure was until he reached Oklahoma. Just before, he had a strenuous day of speaking from the rear end of his train in Nebraska, closing with a night meeting at Lincoln. The ovations made him happy, but he was pitifully tired. That day he wired Mrs. Beveridge: 'I spoke ten times to thousands of people and altogether spoke six solid hours. Am in splendid condition tonight, but desperately weary.' In Kansas through which he passed it was a repetition of Nebraska, and he wired his wife: 'It is hard work, but inspiring. I wish you were with me, not only for my comfort and happiness, but also that you might see the splendid sweep of these plains and the power, intelligence, and nobility that shines in the faces of these real men and women of the soil.'

Leaving Kansas, he was to speak *en route* at various towns in northern Oklahoma and reach Oklahoma City for a meeting at night. But the train was delayed in Kansas, and the Oklahoma towns could not be snubbed. Thus, all through the earlier part of the night he was speaking in these towns, and it was after midnight when he reached the capital of the State. It was twelve-thirty when he reached the platform and one o'clock when he began to address six thousand people who had waited patiently. It was two-fifteen when he closed, and, lingering on the platform shaking hands, it was three-thirty when he reached his car. At four o'clock he was asleep; and at seven-thirty he was speaking at McAlester in old Indian Territory to a great throng. All through that dreadful day he spoke almost continuously, closing at night at Bartlesville.[1]

He closed this amazing tour with a speech in Chicago, speaking along the lines of his New York speech. And he was sadly worn. Only his love for the crowds, the excitement, had kept him going against nature. Chairman Hitchcock had telegraphed him 'heartiest congratulations on the tremendous success' he was having 'throughout the West.' And he had expressed deep appreciation for all he was 'accomplishing for the cause.'[2] Compared with this sweep across the continent, the Midlothian campaign of Gladstone was child's play. He had slept throughout the journey on an average of four hours a night, except on Sundays, when he slept the clock around. But he had an intensive tour in Indiana yet before him. In the meanwhile, he could rest four days in Chicago with the baby.

[1] Spencer Eddy, Nov. 15, 1908; to Scott Bone, Nov. 10, 1908; *Indianapolis Star*, Oct. 18, 1908.

[2] Hitchcock to Beveridge, Oct. 8, 1908.

ON THE WESTERN TOUR IN 1908

VI

The separation from Mrs. Beveridge and the baby had been his greatest hardship, but she had taken the separation 'like the thoroughbred she is — without a whimper or complaint,' he wrote her brother. 'She walked right up to the situation in splendid style and I went away to my work encouraged instead of depressed.' [1] But now that he had four days with his family, she was in New York at the sick-bed of her mother. The baby delighted him, however, and he was in boyish mood. 'Don't believe newspaper reports,' he wrote his wife, 'for we are both perfectly sober. Albert II says he thinks the tariff should be revised and wishes Mother would see the President about it immediately. Albert II, very hilarious, proposed a toast in Latin, Greek, and Sanscrit to his wonderful mother.'

Thus, playing with the baby, sleeping, he made the four days count — for there was still heavy work ahead. Despite the spectacular triumphs and the enthusiasm of his continental tour, he could not divest himself of the feeling that there was something wrong. 'I have a vague feeling of unrest,' he wrote Shaffer, 'and am not at all sure that everything is all right.' [2] There was work to do in Indiana where Hanly's action in forcing county option upon the statutes in the midst of a campaign on that very issue was being resented, and powerful forces were aligning themselves against the Republican State and legislative tickets. Indiana was in danger.

At the beginning of the last week of the campaign, Beveridge began a hectic tour of the State. He traveled in a special train with a private car for his party, a day coach and a baggage car. Worn almost to exhaustion, he had stipulated that no politicians should be included in his party. He selected his companions with a view to as much pleasure and relaxation as possible between stops. The faithful Rothschild was in charge of the train, and his secretary was aboard; but when the train drew out of the Chicago station, it carried a brilliant company of notables having no relation to politics. Samuel G. Blythe, the clever political correspondent; George Ade, author of the 'Fables' and noted as a wit; John T. McCutcheon, the famous cartoonist of the 'Chicago Tribune'; and 'Kin' Hubbard, whose 'Abe Martin' sketches with their wise and homely philosophy had caught the fancy of the country, were along. Ade, who had intended to leave the train at Brooks, his country home, alighted there, but, just as the train was about to start, swung on again with

[1] Beveridge to Spencer Eddy, Nov. 15, 1908.
[2] Beveridge to Shaffer, undated.

the comment: 'I can't miss this.' It was a joyous, rollicking company of wits, a bit boisterous in its mirth, and thus with jest, story, and laughter the companions passed the time between stops. The wits were to be amazed and moved to admiration at the ease with which the orator would join in the hilarity until the train stopped at a station, and then rush to the platform, speak with effect, and, catching the questions of hecklers, deftly turn them to the advantage of his cause.[1]

The campaigning in Indiana was reminiscent of the ovations of the West. Inviting questions everywhere, Beveridge was frequently bombarded with them, and invariably turned them neatly. The tour was not without its exotic touches. Thus, at Gaston, a small town, where the train was to stop for three minutes, Beveridge had just begun to speak when the train pulled out, leaving a gaping crowd behind. 'Here, don't start this train,' Beveridge shouted, but it moved on. 'If you don't stop the train, I won't go!' he said to the representative of the road. 'Stop her!' someone called to the train man. 'Thunder! I can't stop her,' he replied. But the conductor finally was found just as the train reached the edge of the town, and Beveridge forced the crew to back up to the crowd, where he finished his speech.[2] It was a feverish journey; and it ended with an impressive meeting in Indianapolis.

No other Republican had rendered such notable service on the stump in that campaign.

And within three days Sereno Payne, chairman of the Ways and Means Committee of the House, began hearings on the revision of the tariff — in the old manner.

VII

Meanwhile, Beveridge was momentarily threatened with the loss of prestige at home. Roosevelt, attacked by the 'New York World' and the 'Indianapolis News' on charges relating to his manner of acquiring the Panama strip, had brought action for criminal libel against Joseph P. Pulitzer and the 'News,' with the determination to try the Indianapolis publisher in Washington. It was an audacious move, involving the vital rights of citizens, and public sentiment in Indiana veered for the moment from the President. The district attorney in Indianapolis, Joe Kealing, powerful in the organization of Mr. Fairbanks, who secretly owned the 'News,' resigned rather than prosecute. The news of Kealing's intention reached Beveridge from Taft in New York.

[1] Letters to author from Ade, McCutcheon, and Blythe.
[2] *Indianapolis Star*, Oct. 31, 1908.

He had conferred at length with Taft just before, in the home of the President-elect's brother in New York, and again was delighted. The greater part of the conversation was on policies, and Beveridge got the impression that Taft would continue the policies of Roosevelt without deviation. The next day Taft informed him of Kealing's resignation, and of the attempt being made to persuade Roosevelt to appoint one of Beveridge's most powerful foes to the vacated post. He had his heart set at the time on having the place for his friend Miller, if a vacancy occurred. To Shaffer he wrote the story:

The following day, even while preparing his speech for the Ohio Society dinner, he [Taft] called me up by telephone in great excitement and told me that —— had just telephoned him that Kealing had resigned and that Roosevelt was going to appoint —— on Hemenway's recommendation if Taft consented. Taft said that he had told —— that he probably had no objections, but that such matters were usually determined on the recommendation of both Senators. He said this startled him, so he thought I ought to know it. Of course, I went off the handle and told him I was committed to Miller.... Then Hitchcock and myself had a conference. Hitchcock then saw Taft. Taft stopped off at Washington to talk with Roosevelt about Panama and other things, and I think knocked this galley-west. At all events, when, at Roosevelt's request, I called at the White House this morning, prepared to fight... I found the President in the best frame of mind I have ever seen him. He said he would not appoint —— or anyone else I did not wish, and that he would appoint Miller, as he and I had talked that matter over extensively.[1]

Later, Kealing explained his action to Rothschild in a fashion that seemed proper to the 'Baron.' He had, as was known, intended to resign at all events, but the action in the case of the President against the 'News' had hastened his retirement. He could find no justification in the law for the Roosevelt plan, and refused to be a party to the attempt. His relations with the publisher of the 'News' meant too much to him to be broken, and he tendered his resignation in early March, and Miller was appointed. But Beveridge's triumph was to be charged against him in the day of reckoning, now approaching.[2]

Meanwhile, behind the scenes, the reactionary forces were at work to turn the course of the new Administration away from the progressive policies of Roosevelt; and while Roosevelt and Taft appeared on the surface to be as close as ever, a secret bitterness was incubating in the heart of one.

The Rooseveltian days were over.

[1] Beveridge to Shaffer and to Rothschild, Dec. 18, 1908.
[2] Rothschild to Beveridge, March 3, 1909.

CHAPTER VIII

TWILIGHT OF A RÉGIME

I

'THE King is dead; long live the King!'

The thought was singing rapturously in the hearts of the reactionaries during the three months intervening between the election of Taft and his inauguration. The popularity of Roosevelt, unprecedented since the days of Jackson, had forced his secret enemies publicly to applaud him and pretend to the approval of his policies. But for seven years he had kept the leaders of the old régime 'stewing in their juice. As never before since Jackson turned wearily toward the Hermitage after his eight years of domination, Roosevelt had assumed a leadership of the people, and in matters of legislation, had appealed repeatedly to them over the heads of the congressional leaders. His régime had been one of constant excitement. No man knew one day what he would bring forth on the morrow. Looking back upon those tumultuous years, one is persuaded that his main achievement had been to awaken the civic consciousness of the Nation and impress upon the people their power in government. Much had been accomplished. A rate regulation bill governing the railroads had been enacted after a compromise. The right of the Government to regulate the tremendous business organizations, which had had a mushroom growth in the complacent days of McKinley, had been established in the public mind. Numerous reforms had been wrought, such as the passing of the Pure Food Law, of the Meat Inspection Act, and the establishment of a conservation policy. In the international field, Roosevelt had scored some spectacular triumphs. The Panama Canal was on the way — by odds the most conspicuous actual achievement of the Administration.

But most of the reforms had been forced despite the underhand opposition of the 'big-wigs' of the old régime, and they had not been happy. They had cursed under their breath.

It had been a régime of greater social splendor than any in generations. He who ostensibly was fighting the battles of democracy was essentially an aristocrat in his personal tastes. The aristocracy had moved in on Washington, and names seldom before heard in connection with White House activities had figured prominently in the social news. Gossip was busy with the 'imperial' grandeur of the capital, and Roosevelt had been amused over the story that 'to emphasize his imperial way of living he was using gold knives, forks, and spoons, while his family used only silver and old broken china.'[1] But society had become a bit more exclusive, and, though its functions were more brilliant than before, there was less of vulgar ostentation. These affairs were no longer exploited in all their details by the press. They were of no concern to the masses. To escape the prying eyes of the reporters, it had become popular to move out for social functions to the Old Country Club at Tennallytown, since the Chevy Chase Club was no longer exclusive enough for the very smart. The favorite club was housed in a rather dilapidated country place, but the dining-room, done in crimson and velvet, with the galleries enlarged, was well adapted for dinners. There was a good chef, but some of the more magnificent of the hostesses often moved out with a goodly portion of their own *ménage*. On the veranda the hostess would receive the guests, and after dinner, except in winter, the guests would move to the spacious lawn. This exclusiveness suited the inner circle, and Archie Butt, the military aide to the President, thought it 'a great comfort to go to a dinner and not feel certain that the next morning everybody in Washington would know just where you dined, and, often, what you had to eat.[2]

The dinners and parties so crowded themselves one upon another that hostesses frequently left the selection of their guests to their butlers, who were to choose them from among the frequenters of the house. It was said that one prominent hostess did not know who her guests would be until she met them in her home. Alice Roosevelt Longworth, planning a dinner and bridge company, hurriedly instructed the butler to call up gentlemen who dined with her and then 'four ladies without husbands.' The only stipulation was that they should play bridge.[3]

It was in the days when Alice Roosevelt, but recently married, was the toast of the country; when Katherine Elkins's name was on everyone's tongue because of her romance with the Duke of the Abruzzi; when Mathilde Townsend was at the height of her brilliant beauty and charm. But it was the 'Princess Alice' who dominated the scene. Possessing magnetism, charm, and the cleverness of her father, glorying in indiscretions of wit, daring and dashing, she was all the more interesting to the gaping public because of her ardent devotion to her father.[4]

But the social center during the régime was at the White House. Its dinners were brilliant, the conversation exhilarating, for at the table, along with public men, were to be found the

[1] *Letters of Archie Butt*, 9.   [2] *Ibid.*, 16–17.   [3] *Ibid.*, 49–50.
[4] *Ibid.*, 321.

intellectual leaders of the country — scientists, poets, novelists, journalists. As the régime was ending, the Baroness von Hengelmüller, wife of the Austrian Ambassador, was heaving heavy sighs over the departing glories, certain that the next Administration would be dull. She idolized Roosevelt, who found her amusing, and once asked Butt not to be so ungallant 'as to remind the Baroness of the coronation, and ask her if the last sixty years have not passed like a dream to her.' [1]

All this was in the twilight; but to the politicians the twilight was comforting. Just why they felt the Roosevelt policies would pass with the Rough Rider is not yet clear. Taft had been a favorite — the court favorite — and had been literally lifted into the Presidency by Roosevelt, and in the campaign he had said nothing to justify the expectation of reaction. But the reactionary group were gathering about him with advice. When he was in Washington, the politicians were hailing him as the rising star, and it was all too evident that the long pent-up resentment against the retiring President was about to break out. To the sensitive Roosevelt this was pain.[2] It hurt, too, when gossips told him that Taft ascribed his nomination and election to his brother Charley. But worse than all was he hurt when he learned that his favorites in the Cabinet were not to be retained.[3] Henry Cabot Lodge, later to align himself with Taft against Roosevelt, was busy making mischief. He told Roosevelt he had heard that not one of the Cabinet would be retained, with the possible exception of Von Lengerke Meyer of the Navy, and that outside pressure alone would hold him in. This, Lodge understood, was in order to break all Taft's connections with the Roosevelt régime and influence. Butt, who had the story from a member of the President's family, was 'rather disgusted that Senator Lodge should come home and stir up discord between the two families.' [4]

At the moment, Lodge was still smarting under the indignity of being compelled to cool his heels two days at Augusta before seeing the incoming Executive. Others, besides Lodge, were busy on both sides. Neither man was well advised. There had long been much joking as to the 'incense-swingers' about Roosevelt — 'made up largely of the New England element, possibly more the Harvard type, who are supposed to stand around the President as acolytes do about a priest and swing incense at him and about him.' [5] And now Taft had his incense-swingers too. Unhappily, the incense-swingers knew how to swing clubs as well.

[1] *Letters of Archie Butt*, 211.
[2] H. H. Kohlsaat, *From McKinley to Harding*, 185.   [3] *Ibid.*
[4] *Letters of Archie Butt*, 271–72.   [5] *Ibid.*, 194.

II

Beveridge, listening to the gossip of the cloakrooms, saw what was going on, but still believed that Taft would continue the policies of his predecessor.

The statehood fight was still ahead of him, and to his chagrin he found Roosevelt no longer had the stomach to continue it. Before Congress met, he had written Beveridge that it were 'mere folly to kick longer against the pricks.' Roosevelt was evidently annoyed that he had been involved in the fight to refuse separate statehood to Arizona and New Mexico. Had he not said in the beginning that it would be much better to admit them? Of course he had acquiesced in the Beveridge plan, but the fight was lost. 'I do feel very strongly that no good whatever comes of any further delay,' he wrote. 'You will have to take them both in. You cannot take them both in together, and by keeping them out for a short time, which is all you can do, you merely irritate the people there against the Republican Party.' [1] Beveridge replied in a letter that a close friend of both parties in the correspondence thought 'sound and dignified and states-manlike'; but the mutual friend thought it best for Beveridge 'to go down with your colors flying.' Evidently Roosevelt had abandoned the fight. It was clear that Beveridge would not be justified 'in ever alluding to the question of him again, even in casual conversation.' [2]

But there was to be no time for action on the matter at that session. Rather worn by his phenomenal tour and ill, Beveridge was to be inactive on the floor. Vigorously he was to defend the Pinchot conservation policies in a running debate, for the re-actionaries were now confident of shunting them aside, and to propose a maximum and minimum tariff rate 'arranged accord-ing to the principle of protection,' with the minimum for coun-tries granting special commercial advantages to us in their markets, the maximum for those that would not.' [3]

But he was to have his worries over the situation in Indiana, where his enemies were casting covetous eyes upon his seat. The factions were showing their teeth; he saw the peril and sought to discourage the gossip about them. He would be up for reëlection in a year, and there were dangers ahead. Rothschild was report-ing some disaffection among the breweries and the liberals, be-cause of the feeling that Beveridge had aligned himself against them in the local option fight that year. It was a problem to know what to do. The Republicans had lost the State and

[1] Roosevelt to Beveridge, Nov. 19, 1908.   [2] Beveridge MSS.
[3] *Congressional Record*, Feb. 6, 1909.

Legislature on the local option issue. Would it come up in 1910? Rothschild had found an important party leader in a saloon in mellow mood, holding forth on what the liberals would do to Beveridge. 'The liberal element will take care of Beveridge,' he had said. 'He will go down like the rest of them did last fall.' And how would they get him? By doing nothing. That was what Rothschild feared. 'What I am fearfully afraid of,' he wrote, 'is that they will lie down and let the State go Democratic. Of course they can't throw it Democratic, but in a close fight, by inactivity on their part, they might give aid sufficient for it to go Democratic.'[1]

And the 'Baron' was uncannily wise in his generation.

There was injurious gossip about Beveridge, too, Rothschild reported: He did not stay in Indianapolis; in the last five years he had not averaged over six or eight weeks a year in Indiana. The 'Baron' had a number of agents, including one Democrat of some prominence, going over the State and listening. He was getting disturbing reports. The 'Louisville Courier-Journal' and the 'Louisville Times' were running stories calculated to hurt, and the 'Baron' thought them inspired. He had arranged with the Indiana editor of the 'Louisville Post' to counteract them. Everywhere he found evidence of 'a disposition to conduct a kind of guerrilla warfare in the hope of stirring up some semblance of an opposition.' Open opposition might then follow.[2]

Even the publication, in newspapers not unfriendly, of Beveridge's growing independence and opposition to the reactionaries was being used by his enemies to inflame the party spirit of the minor leaders against him.[3] He knew that he faced a fight for reëlection, but, despite his illness, he was in a fighting mood. When it was reported that warm friends and supporters of the University of Michigan were hoping he would succeed President Angell, he hastily disillusioned them with the announcement that he would remain in the Senate as long as the people of Indiana would permit.[4]

It was in the midst of these rumors of disaffection and conspiracy that the Indiana Republican Editorial Association was to hold its annual banquet, with Beveridge as the principal speaker. This would give him an opportunity to take a smash at factions. The State press was teeming with the gossip, and gossip is the food of faction. The speech was prepared with the utmost care, and submitted, through Rothschild, to three

[1] Rothschild to Beveridge, March 29, 1909.
[2] Rothschild to Beveridge, April 12, 14, 23, 1909.
[3] *Indianapolis Star*, Nov. 18, Dec. 6, 1908.
[4] *Ibid.*, Feb. 6, 1909.

trusted friends of ability and political acumen. But Beveridge had moved so far toward independence that he scarcely knew how to prepare a diplomatic address. All who read it [1] agreed that it was brilliant, but why drag in his views on the evils of injunction? they asked. The argument was able, but it went too far, thought a Federal judge. Why not silence? He was being thoroughly advertised as a leader of the progressives, so it was unnecessary to touch on the injunction and take 'extreme grounds.' He was admittedly 'strong with the workmen,' and it was unnecessary 'to stir up the employers.' All three took common ground, possibly after a conference, and the 'Baron' agreed with their conclusions.[2]

But when he came to speak, Beveridge took strong grounds in favor of the substitution of the primary for the convention, and thus accentuated the distrust of professional politicians. His appeal for the burial of the hatchet was accompanied by the unsheathing of a sword.[3]

Meanwhile, Fairbanks, Watson, and Hemenway were all going out of office together. These three astute politicians, and none friendly, would have abundant time to give attention to the creation of sentiment in Indiana in its relation to Beveridge. Never had he occupied a position so powerful and yet so perilous.

III

With an extra session summoned to revise the tariff and with Payne and the Ways and Means Committee busily framing the law after the old fashion of 'pick and take,' Beveridge was working desperately for a tariff commission. When, after the election, Payne invited James W. Van Cleave, president of the National Manufacturers' Association, to appear before the committee and furnish information, he declined. 'I very much regret to see the determination of our Republican statesmen to give us another tariff of the old kind. In politics, as in everything else, there is a hereafter. Much of the Republican success in the campaign of 1908 is due to the promise of an honest, equitable tariff revision contained in the party's platform.' [4] Payne replied coldly, regretting Van Cleave's declination, reminding him that a tariff commission was not before the committee, and saying that the leaders understood that the people would pass on their work.[5]

[1] Judge A. B. Anderson, of the Federal Court, Charles W. Miller, and Henry Bennett.

[2] Rothschild to Beveridge, Feb. 11, 1909.

[3] *Indianapolis Star*, Feb. 26, 1909.   [4] Beveridge MSS.

[5] Beveridge MSS.

About this time Alvin H. Sanders, chairman of the American Reciprocity Tariff League, was putting it up to Beveridge to watch the tariff moves in the Senate. 'We are depending upon you,' he wrote, 'to watch the tariff fight in the Senate. You will observe that the old crowd in the House have gone to work in the same old way.... I hope that La Follette and yourself and other friends, including our new Iowa Senator [Cummins], will roll up your sleeves and go out for the purpose of a good house-cleaning on this old question. The country will be with you upon it, and you should use every endeavor to induce the President-elect to enter aggressively into the fight for reform.'[1]

Meanwhile, a national convention of business men had been called to meet in Indianapolis to devise methods of persuading Congress to create a tariff commission, and Beveridge was in correspondence about it. He wrote Dr. Albert Shaw beseeching him to attend, and explaining that it was to represent 'a movement of business men and conducted exclusively by business men, together with great editors and students like yourself.' He was going himself, though he felt that 'no man in public affairs ought to attend.'[2]

Throwing himself with his tremendous energy into the movement and sponsoring the bill himself, he was not to escape treachery in the ranks of the National Manufacturers' Association. Some of the leaders of the organization were intimate political allies of some of Beveridge's most bitter foes, and soon it was evident that they would prefer failure to success if it contributed to the prestige of the senator they had asked to fight their battle. Was he not handing out invitations to the convention promiscuously? Might not some fall into the hands of Democrats?[3] James A. Emery, prominent in the leadership of the Association, was gravely concerned about Beveridge and the Democrats lest the convention 'degenerate' into a debate on schedules, and that 'free trade agitators' would air their views. 'Of course,' he wrote, 'the whole machinery of the convention must lie in committees, and I urge you to see that... any of the strong Beveridge men are kept off the chairmanships of committees like resolutions especially. I can see that Watson[4] is considerably worried on this point, and I can realize, quite apart from that, with the most apparent sympathy, the Committee on Resolutions could under suggestive leadership frame up resolu-

[1] Sanders to Beveridge, Nov. 13, 1908.
[2] Beveridge to Shaw, Jan. 26, 1909.
[3] Ferdinand C. Schwedtman from unknown, Jan. 20, 1909; hearings under Senate Resolution 92, 1913, III, 2551.
[4] James E. Watson.

tions which might be very pleasing to the Senator from Indiana and yet would be very offensive to our best friends there who believe that knowingly or unknowingly we had lent ourselves to propping him up, and I hope that you will not forget that while the Senator from Indiana is with you in this matter, he is opposed to you in principle on every other thing we stand for, and at the present moment is under pledge to use his influence to assist in the passage of a notice on hearing injunction bill. He is not and cannot be well disposed toward us in any real sense of the word, and I am sure you will agree with me that we cannot jeopardize the friendly influence of our real helpers to magnify a gentleman who has no real sympathy with us as a stepping stone to his own selfish ambitions.' [1]

All this was going on behind the back of the man who was leading the fight that the manufacturers at that time thought they wanted. It was not the first time in politics that an army, following a leader, has thought it would be an absurd thing to 'prop' him at the time of the battle. It is important, in view of the fight to come and of the result, to bear this letter in mind.

The convention was held and was successful on the surface; Beveridge spoke, but nothing special was done to 'prop' him.

Thus conditions shaped themselves as the extra session on the tariff approached.

IV

Meanwhile, despite the rumblings against the outgoing régime, it was going out with colors flying. If Roosevelt was saddened by the thought of laying the scepter down, he had no thought of putting it aside until he had to. Perhaps there was just a touch of bravado to the dynamic leader in his activities of the last weeks. Because he had been criticized for an order which was said to impose an impossible task upon army officers, he determined to prove that it was not beyond reason. He proposed, in mid-winter, to ride horseback to Warrenton, Virginia, and back, a distance of ninety miles. He invited Butt, Dr. Cary Grayson, and Admiral Rixey to accompany him on the jaunt. One day the party rose at two-thirty in the morning, and, after a beefsteak breakfast, the quartet, for all the world like characters from a Dumas novel, rode forth into the dawn. No one quailed at the ordeal. On the return trip they were pelted mercilessly by a sleet storm, and the danger was imminent. The slipping of the horses might prove fatal, but on they rode,

[1] Emery to Schwedtman, Jan. 20, 1908; Hearings under Senate Resolution 92, 1913, III, 2618–20.

almost boisterous in their mirth. When they approached the city, Butt ordered carriages to meet the party at the Aqueduct Bridge because of his fear of the slippery pavements, but Roosevelt would have none of it. The story of the ride attracted much attention.[1]

Never had the social affairs at the White House and in the homes of the social leaders been more lively. There was the December dance, with so many guests that it was a problem how to serve them supper until the resourceful Butt proposed that tables be laid in the basement. The usual receptions were gay and brilliant. But underneath it all was a suggestion of sadness. The King was dying. And Roosevelt was too sensitive and proud not to feel, in the atmosphere about him now, an undercurrent of hostility and jubilation. He was depressed when he learned that at the banquet of the Ohio Society in New York, which Taft attended, there had been no toast to the President.[2] Of mercurial temperament, his spirits soared when, on the journey to the birthplace of Lincoln in Kentucky, he heard the old familiar shouts of the crowds and saw the eager faces of his partisans at the stops. Perhaps, after all, the atmosphere of the capital city was not typical of that of the country.[3] It was not.

But he was none the less saddened by the all too evident decision of his successor to cut himself loose from the elements that had surrounded Roosevelt. He could not understand it. Taft had always seemed perfectly loyal, and now he was drifting away in the twilight. So sensitive had he become upon the subject that those of his immediate official household learned to be silent on what was taking place. Butt, the prophet among them, was quite sure that with the divorce from the Rooseveltian group there would follow a reversal of the Rooseveltian policies. He thought the new courtiers suggestive of 'the old weak days of McKinley,' and was sure he saw a drifting of government control into the hands of men whom Roosevelt would have considered the enemy. The old crowd, such as Aldrich and Wetmore, were literally licking their chops, and 'looking forward to seven fat years after seven lean ones.'

And Taft? He thought him well intentioned, but feared his amiability and his doctrine of expediency — and thus again he struck the note of prophecy.

As the hour drew near for the change of the régime, the reactionary forces in Congress, no longer fearful of the wrath of the strong man who had caused them so much anguish, broke forth in contemptuous phrases and open attacks upon the President and his administrations. Most of the Republican senators sat

---

[1] *Letters of Archie Butt*, 285–96.   [2] *Ibid.*, 313.   [3] *Ibid.*, 335.

mute. Most of Roosevelt's favored friends, like Henry Cabot Lodge, had no spirited reply to make. It was reserved for Beveridge to utter the final tribute. It was on March 3, the day before the change, that he was infuriated by the attacks of men who had not dared attack before. Getting the floor, he compared Roosevelt to Jackson and Washington. Both had been attacked, he said, but no one remembered the names of their detractors. Then he concluded:

Mr. President, I say, without fear of successful contradiction, more constructive laws have been passed, more great reforms have been advanced, than in any two administrations in our history, save only that which followed the adoption of the Constitution. Why is it that he has held the unparalleled affection of the American people for so many years? It is because he has gathered into his breast the wishes, the hopes, and the aspirations of the American people, just as the great Presidents I have named, before him....
Say what you will of the character of this man, of his conduct, no one can question the fact that he has achieved greatly; that he has wrought mightily; and that he has wrought for the permanent welfare of all the people, regardless of creed or color or party. At this time, when a few hours will see him stripped of power to punish or reward, I will no longer sit silent and suffer these accumulated assaults, and especially when I remember that many of them would not have been made even one short year ago.[1]

The spirited rebuke struck a responsive chord in the country and Beveridge was overwhelmed with letters and telegrams of appreciation. Roosevelt himself was touched, and when he learned of the popular response to the defense, he wrote Beveridge that he was 'very appreciative of your speech, my dear fellow, but... hadn't the slightest idea that your constituents would also appreciate it. I am greatly touched and pleased, both by what you said and by the response of your people.'[2] And two days later, writing of his concern over Beveridge's illness, he added: 'I wish to thank you again for your fine speech.'[3]

Soon after the delivery of the speech, and the same evening, the Tafts were to dine at the White House and remain throughout the night. It was an idea of Roosevelt's that the women scarcely would have approved had they been consulted. Because of the pressure upon him as the coming king, Taft was unable to reach the White House until eight o'clock. There were Senator and Mrs. Lodge, Senator and Mrs. Root, Mr. and Mrs. Longworth, Admiral and Mrs. Cowles, and Mabel Boardman. Of the politicians present, the first two were to align themselves

[1] *Congressional Record*, March 3, 1909.
[2] Roosevelt to Beveridge, March 10, 1909.   [3] March 12, 1909.

aggressively with Taft and against Roosevelt at a critical moment later on. It was not a lively dinner. The incoming and the outgoing Presidents sought, by jest and story, to cover the evident embarrassment, but Mrs. Roosevelt seemed depressed and Mrs. Taft ascribed it to uneasiness over her husband's hunting expedition in Africa.

That night a sleet storm beat upon the capital, encasing the trees on the White House grounds with ice, and Mrs. Taft was awakened by the raging of the storm, the cracking of twigs, the breaking of the overburdened tree limbs. Telegraphic communication all along the Atlantic Coast was paralyzed, and thousands, *en route* to the inauguration, were unable to reach the city. So impossible was the weather that it was necessary to hold the inaugural ceremonies in the Senate Chamber. Some eyewitnesses thought Roosevelt seemed unhappy, some even insisting that literally he 'ground his teeth.' But when Taft finished his inaugural address, the first to reach him with outstretched hands was the man whose favor had raised him to the Presidency.

But he did not, according to custom, ride back up the Avenue to the White House with his successor. Instead, he hurried from the Capitol to the station and was soon speeding to New York. Quite soon he would be on his way to the African hunting-grounds, and Taft would be alone, master of his destiny.

When the Roosevelt train pulled out of the Washington station, a new era dawned and an old one passed into history.

V

Meanwhile, Beveridge was paying the penalty of his super-exertions in the campaign for Taft. Years before, while in the Philippines, riding hours without end on horseback, he had incurred an injury that had not caused him much concern. The ordeal to which he had subjected himself in behalf of Taft had finished what the Philippines had begun. An operation for hernia was urged by his physicians as imperative, and early in March he went to Johns Hopkins Hospital, intending to conceal the fact. 'I am going away tomorrow for three or four weeks,' he wrote Rothschild — very confidentially — 'to have an operation performed. Nobody will know where I am, and it will be merely stated in the papers that I am off for a sadly needed rest.' [1] But hardly had he left Washington when the papers carried the news.[2] The operation disclosed a more serious condition than the physicians had suspected, and eleven days later

---

[1] Beveridge to Rothschild, March 8, 1909.
[2] *Indianapolis Star*, March 11, 1909.

he was still flat on his back, with a week more in bed before him.[1]
It was while he was in the hospital that he learned of the impending tariff struggle. He was told that President Taft wanted
the progressives to fight for reductions in the rates of the House
bill.

Soon he would be engaged in the most desperate and spectacular battle of his career, one of a band of Republican insurgents fighting the dictatorship of Senator Aldrich. Here we well
may pause for a more intimate view of the dictator and the men
who were to challenge his supremacy.

[1] Beveridge to Rothschild, March 23, 1909.

BOOK IV
INSURGENCY AND REVOLUTION

CHAPTER I

PORTRAITS OF THE DUELISTS

I

No one in the entire history of the Senate has ever dominated it more autocratically through sheer will power than Nelson W. Aldrich. A member of that body for many years, he had, from the beginning, made himself indispensable to the party organization there, rising step by step as the elders passed out, until in the end he made himself the dictator of a cabal which for a time was the master of the Government. In the years immediately preceding the insurgency, a little coterie of senators was in as complete control of the instrumentalities of government as the famous Council of Ten in another age and country. This coterie was composed of no ordinary men. Platt of Connecticut was a creator and builder, the constructive statesman of the group; Allison of Iowa was the diplomat who reconciled the dissatisfied to the situation; Spooner of Wisconsin was the spokesman who sallied forth in the shining armor of his genius when the occasion called for a defense of the machine; and Hale of Maine and Burrows of Michigan were lusty warriors when required. These men and their disciples ruled the Senate through the packing of the important committees with their creatures. And at the head of them all was Aldrich.

Anyone looking down from the gallery would have recognized him as a leader from his appearance and manner. Almost six feet in height, perfectly proportioned, neither heavy nor slim, he moved with a dignified assurance that seemed self-confidence to his friends and sheer arrogance to his foes. His hair, by now, was gray and a little thin, but there was nothing in his eye, the mirror of his soul, to denote any weakening of his power. His eye, in truth, was his finest and most remarkable feature. Dark brown in color, large and brilliant, it was so unusual that Zorn, the portrait painter, found it difficult to transmit to canvas,[1] and it had a penetrating quality that was disturbing.[2] It was a piercing, analytical eye and it did its work at a glance. In his powerful jaw, his projecting chin, and grimly firm mouth the student of mankind could not escape the conviction that his was a dominating personality.

There was little in his earlier career to associate with the

[1] N. W. Stephenson, *Nelson W. Aldrich*, 123.
[2] O. O. Stealey, *One Hundred Pen Pictures of Live Men*, 26.

making of a master of statecraft. Born in a drab mill town in Rhode Island, his common-school education was over by his seventeenth year. While fascinated by oratory, it was because of its advantage in the domination of men.[1] Though never to possess literary gifts, he appreciated them in others, and in early life he had a passion for books and pored eagerly over such authors as Emerson and Thackeray in bed by the light of a lamp until he fell to sleep from exhaustion.[2] He even entertained literary ambitions for a time. But his inherent qualities precluded success either in literature or in oratory, and marked him for the business life that was to follow. If he could not appreciate Browning, no one knew better how to value money, and he began its pursuit as a boy.

Aldrich entered upon his career as an employee of a wholesale grocery firm in Providence, and it is significant that he got his job without influence, and primarily because of a certain personal charm, an evident self-confidence, and a poise that carried the impression of inherent power. Then, too, he had had experience in clerking in a store in the drab mill town of his childhood. When the war of the States began, he enlisted; but sentry duty and indiscretion in drinking bad water sent him to the hospital. When he recovered, the war was mostly still to be fought, but he was mustered out after four months in uniform. The opportunities for profitable business beckoned through the battle smoke and he was soon back with the wholesale grocer. When the war ended, he was not oblivious of the fortunes being made by carpet-baggers in the South, and but for the offer of a partnership in the business, he would have hurried to New Orleans, where Warmouth was accumulating a fortune in politics. He had thought that the death or absence or the political opinions of the old business leaders of the Crescent City would leave openings for an alert young man of business acumen.[3] His biographer is quite willing to concede that in those sorry days he was not unimpressed with the 'thoroughness with which business men from the North were enriching themselves through the exploitation of war conditions,' resorting to profiteering and legislative privilege.[4]

In a debating society he was training himself in the management of men, and out of this came his election to the city council. Politically, we are told,[5] he 'held his ideas lightly.' His people were Democrats, but he instinctively affiliated with the dominant party. In 1872 he found nothing reprehensible in the first Grant Administration and was so enamoured of the

[1] Stephenson, *Nelson W. Aldrich*, 6.   [2] *Ibid.*, 24.   [3] *Ibid.*, 14.
[4] *Ibid.*   [5] *Ibid.*, 26.

President that he went to the convention that year to vote for his renomination.

Meanwhile, Aldrich was rising in the business world; and yet he was no ordinary business man. His letters from Europe about this time show him lamenting his inability to make a picture of words in writing of his emotions in the city of the Cæsars, though there is literary charm in his correspondence.[1] In the mean time he had been made president of a bank and of the Providence Board of Trade.

II

When, in 1878, he appeared in Congress there was nothing to foreshadow his future power. He was not conspicuous on the floor; he had no confidence in his ability to speak; and to the casual observer he seemed squandering time better spent in a grocery or a bank. But all the while, quite subtly, he was laying the foundations of his career and finding his forte. By attending meticulously to the individual claims of constituents, he was making himself invaluable in powerful quarters. Already he had developed an indifference to mass support in politics, and was carefully cultivating the influential and wealthy few. These, more and more, were to seem to him his real 'constituents.'[2] In three years he was elected to the Senate. That was the year a pale, shaggy boy from Illinois arrived at the seat of DePauw University and carried his trunk on his back to his humble quarters.

The seed Aldrich had been quietly sowing brought forth an early harvest. At once Allison and Platt of Connecticut took him into their inner circle. Capitalizing his very reticence, his clear scorn of the masses in addition made him real senatorial timber for those days. Thus he immediately found his place on the powerful Finance Committee, powerful as the distributor of privileges through the tariff. He had not lived in mill towns without profit. He had studied the tariff, mastered its intricacies, and acquainted himself with the wishes of the manufacturers of his State and New England. When in 1883 the great surplus in the Treasury impelled the Tariff Commission of that time, soon to be abandoned, to recommend many reductions in the schedules and the Senate acquiesced and the House did not, Aldrich, representing the Senate in the conference of the two houses, surrendered gracefully to the House. From that hour on he was a marked man, and the steel manufacturers of Pittsburgh claimed him as their own. No longer had he any doubt as to

[1] Stephenson, *Nelson W. Aldrich*, 29.　　　[2] *Ibid.*, 36, 38.

who were his 'constituents.' They were not the farmer and consumer, the masses of Rhode Island; they were the manufacturers of Pittsburgh and of Zanesville.

He was working now toward a definite end — to merge business and politics in the interest of business; to seize, through politics, the instrumentalities of government and use them for the profit of a favored few.[1]

And, meanwhile, he was spreading out. When in 1886 an attempt was made to pass an interstate commerce bill, he aligned himself aggressively against it, insisting that the railroads be left free in fixing rates as they saw fit. Under the Vanderbilt banner of 'The public be damned' he fought his earlier battles. He even insisted on the right of congressmen to vote on railroad legislation while riding on free passes and drawing a salary from the roads.[2]

Thus his constituents were not merely the manufacturers, but the railroads and the bankers — wherever they might live. When the Mills Bill, framed in harmony with Cleveland's plan, reached the Senate, it was Aldrich who prepared the report against it which was used as a campaign document in 1888. When, in the Republican National Convention of that year, Harrison's nomination was trembling in the balance, emissaries from Aldrich's camp made a hurried Sunday journey to Indianapolis to ascertain where the candidate stood on their program. Harrison was nominated. The McKinley Bill, passed on Aldrich's report, was the program.[3]

By this time the soft-spoken Aldrich was known as the real brains of the privileged and reactionary group and he began to pay the penalty in unpleasant publicity. The 'New York World' began to pry into the sources of his fortune, for now he was a very wealthy man, but he was encased in impenetrable armor as far as personal corruption was concerned. If he fought for higher tariff rates on articles in which personally he was interested, he was within the pale — nor was he alone. He had waxed wealthy in traction investments, and, later, in rubber, and he ignored the 'World's' attack. It only invited his superior scorn. Interpreting his reaction, his sympathetic biographer says that he continued to be 'himself, the man who refused to play to the crowd, the firm Hamiltonian, the rebuilder of the old social régime,' which temporarily had been overwhelmed by democracy.[4] And remaining 'himself,' he engineered the conspiracy of Democratic renegades which wrecked the Wilson Tariff Bill a little later.[5]

Thus he had continued in command, unmindful of gusts of

[1] Stephenson, *Nelson W. Aldrich*, 61.   [2] *Ibid.*, 68.   [3] *Ibid.*, 71, 78.
[4] *Ibid.*, 95.   [5] *Ibid.*, III.

popular disapproval, scornful of the rumblings against the tariff from the West, until Roosevelt succeeded to the Presidency. The impetuosity of the virile, dashing young Executive caused no end of consternation in the Aldrich group and there was much writing back and forth. Under the cover of a marriage of Aldrich's daughter and John D. Rockefeller's son, there was a gathering of the clans beneath the Aldrich roof; and in 1901, Aldrich went over the President's Message with him.[1] And later, when the business world was quivering under the lash of the muckrakers, with the Northern Securities Case and the anthracite strike exciting the people, Roosevelt cleverly was enticed to the summer place of Aldrich, where he found Hanna, Allison, Spooner, and Lodge in wait for him. But that was before Roosevelt got his overwhelming mandate from the people in 1904; and throughout the second Administration the two men had slept on their arms, smiling cordially when they met, while cautiously watching each other's hands.

Through it all, Aldrich had remained the master of the Senate.

III

A Washington correspondent, trained in the appraisal of public men, has given his interpretation of Aldrich's strength: 'He has a powerful and sometimes an imperious will. His cardinal principle is that mankind is composed of two parts — the rulers and the ruled.'[2] And there was another explanation of his strength — he stood for a theory of government which appealed to an embryo plutocracy and made him its spokesman and attorney. This theory has been defined by his biographer as 'the Hamiltonian gospel of a hundred years ago,'[3] as 'the conception of society as an economy hierarchy, which is the heart of Hamilton's vision.'[4] He had nothing but contempt for the notion that, in conflicts between the rights of man and the desires of property, the latter should give way. He believed that a divine right to rule had passed from kings to property, and the motivating ambition of his career was to make his party the party of property. His policy was to mobilize, regiment, drill, and direct the property interests, and while he hoped to bring even the corner grocer into the ranks of 'conservatism,' his eye was fixed rather upon the great property interests — bankers, manufacturers on a large scale, coal operators. These, in his dream, were to hand

[1] Stephenson, *Nelson W. Aldrich*, 182.
[2] Stealey, *One Hundred Pen Pictures of Live Men*, 26.
[3] Stephenson, *Nelson W. Aldrich*, 102. [4] *Ibid.*, 103.

down the law and the prophets to men of modest property-holdings.[1] For the farmers he had scant respect, again following the Hamiltonian lead. To him there was nothing of greater necessity than maintaining 'the balance in favor of manufacturers instead of agriculture' which came with the overthrow of Jeffersonian democracy,[2] and when the charge was made, in the debate on the McKinley Bill, that it discriminated in favor of the manufacturers against the farmers, he frankly admitted it.[3]

To the great body of the people he was utterly indifferent. He had a lofty contempt for the masses, upon whom he looked as inferior folk 'easily lead... easily deceived... easily betrayed.'[4] He was so completely scornful of these people that he found it repugnant to have any dealings with them, to notice their existence. So profound was his contempt for their weakness and vacillation that, when they misunderstood or misinterpreted his motives, he never took the trouble to disabuse them.[5] But when, later in his career, the worm turned and squirmed, and the spirit of insurrection arose, he was a little concerned. When the voice of these people was finally heard in the Senate Chamber through the progressive element, he thought it as degrading to the serene atmosphere of the Senate as the invasion of the Paris mobs was to the Convention of the Revolution. He considered it 'the voice of the street,' and to his concept of government the only voice worthy of that serene atmosphere of the Chamber was the voice of the counting-room. His sympathetic biographer and interpreter tells us that he 'could be indifferent to the fury of the proletariat while it raged beyond the Senate walls,' but that when it broke in upon the 'courtesy of that restrained body,' he felt that life in the Senate no longer was worth living.[6]

This ideal of government led him to revolutionary ideas as to what constituted the constituency of a Senator. It was not the whole people of the States, farmers, laborers, clerks, the middle classes, but powerful industries. 'The Senator from Sugar, the Senator from Steel, the Senator from Wool,' did not appeal to him as in the least grotesque. Firmly convinced — and honestly, we may assume — that industries, as such, and 'interests,' as such, had the right to open representation, he was frankly in favor of these forces, through their senatorial representatives or agents, using the agencies of the State for their selfish interest, with a cynical indifference to what his biographer describes as 'the delusions of the crowd.'[7]

As Aldrich grew in power, he concentrated more and more upon building up a clientèle of business interests that should be

[1] Stephenson, *Nelson W. Aldrich*, 218.   [2] *Ibid.*, 347.   [3] *Ibid.*, 80.
[4] *Ibid.*, 61.   [5] *Ibid.*   [6] *Ibid.*, 320.   [7] *Ibid.*, 100.

the firm foundation of his leadership.[1] Thus, long before the period on which we are now entering, he had become popularly known as the representative in public life of Big Business. He consulted with a small and select company of the financially powerful, not as a mere tool, but as one belonging to the group; and he dedicated his influence and genius to their service in legislation. He could see nothing reprehensible in senators speculating in products affected by tariff legislation, and when Senator Quay, accused of speculating in sugar, announced that he had, and asked defiantly what the Senate was going to do about it, Aldrich thought it heroic and splendid.[2]

Thus his idea of government was remote from the earlier American concept. It went back to feudalism, and he envisioned nothing less than a moneyed feudalism, with a few men at the top dictating the destiny of society and resting on the broad foundation of the masses confiding blindly in the superior wisdom of their masters.

IV

How did such a man attain such supreme power, dominating the course of legislation and dictating both to Big Business and Presidents?

Aldrich had a genius for leadership. His mind was clear and powerful, and always he knew precisely what he wanted. Seldom was he caught unprepared with a plan. While others knew they were opposed to something pending, he always knew what to propose as a substitute while the others drifted in confusion. He had superior facilities for familiarizing himself with all the intricacies of any question affecting the people he represented. A word from him — and the office force and the experts of the greatest industries would be set to work to furnish him with the data he desired. So seldom did he fail in his fund of information that he had the reputation of knowing what he was talking about, and lesser men were afraid to challenge his conclusions.

He understood, and made the most of his advantage. To senators who approached him in the spirit of disciples he was the pink of courtesy and helpfulness. All the charm of his personality was shed upon them, and usually he sent them away with a feeling of elation. Patiently he would listen to the most trivial suggestions or complaints. But all the while there was the iron hand within the velvet glove, and whenever he encountered too much independence, he did not hesitate to strike a resounding blow. His followers soon came to understand that he would not brook

[1] Stephenson, *Nelson W. Aldrich*, 60.   [2] *Ibid.*, 120.

opposition; when he met it, he put conciliation and argument aside and brought the full force of his tremendous will to bear. In the presence of stout opposition he assumed the arrogant manner of the autocrat and brushed it aside with a ruthlessness that was almost cruel.[1]

As a rule Aldrich met no opposition within his ranks, for he was a master in the judging of men. When those powerful, penetrating eyes had rested for a few moments on a new senator, he knew whether it would be worth while to attempt his cultivation. There were senators whom he almost scornfully ignored, though he had had no brush with them. Thus, Bristow of Kansas he instantly knew to be an incurable rebel with an offensively independent mind, and he passed him by as he would a servant in his house or an attaché of the Senate. More indicative of his rare penetration into character was his attitude toward Dolliver — a man with extraordinary gifts amounting to genius, a superb debater and therefore invaluable, a truly great orator, and seemingly a regular devoted to the fundamental policies of Aldrich himself. Yet from the beginning he did not like or trust him. The intensity of Dolliver's nature, his capacity for emotion shown in his orations, the floridity of his fine intellect meant to Aldrich a man given to impulses susceptible to the sentiment of the people. He was treated cordially, as one would treat a guest in one's house, but never was he to be invited into the inner circle. Time was to demonstrate the correctness of Aldrich's conception of his character.

Then, too, Aldrich was a genius in the organization of his forces and in the bargaining between interests involved in legislation. He was a clearing-house for the interests. When tariffs were on tap, he was magnificently effective in bringing all the importunate and selfish groups to a common understanding. He solidified the privileged as no one ever had. This was made the easier by the feeling that all depended upon him, that he was interested in each, and that he knew best just what could be accomplished.

Thus he ruled by faith and fear. The faith of his 'constituency' was unlimited, and there was reason for the fear of senators to cross him. A tradition of uncanny power for good or evil had grown up about him. He was thought to have the power to destroy. The timid studied his moods as carefully as a courtier studied the moods of Louis XIV. He could make a man of little courage unhappy and fearful by a glance or a cold salutation. This was enough for many senators. Why tempt fate? Why not take the easiest way, and that the way trod by the

[1] Beveridge on Aldrich, speech at Gary, Indiana.

dictator? Sometimes when without consultation a timid statesman would venture on the floor to make a proposition or modestly to suggest an amendment to an organization plan, he would
be all but terrorized by Aldrich's manner. He would find the
dictator sitting 'stiffly in his chair and leaning forward, his elbows on his desk, as if ready to spring into action.'[1] That would
be disconcerting enough. It suggested the tiger about to spring
upon its victim. But the expression on Aldrich's face was more
alarming still. Upon his lips a slight smile played, barely visible
through his white mustache, and his luminous eyes seemed
smiling too — but what a smile! There was something of cruelty
in it, a suggestion of mockery, an indication of a sneer. To proceed with confidence in the chill of that smile required greater
courage and strength of character than most men possessed.

And there was still another explanation of his power — the
common understanding that he was close to the source of campaign supplies. Everyone knew of his intimacy with campaign
managers throughout the country and that his will frequently
determined where campaign money should go. Thus, in 1904 he
was the contact man between the national organization and the
conservative forces numbered among his 'constituents.' It was
commonly understood that he was the spokesman of the great
corporations that supplied the sinews of battle in elections and
was in position to withhold or grant financial aid. This gave him
a powerful pull in putting legislation through. A despot? Yes,
but a benevolent despot he could be on important occasions.[2]

Thus, symbolizing material power, a genius in the art of legislative bargaining, a master of senatorial organization, the head
of the little clique that determined legislative programs and
organized committees, his position was commanding beyond
that of almost any other senator in generations.

V

And with it all Aldrich was a statesman, as reactionary as
Pobiedonostsev, but still a statesman with a constructive mind.
But his statesmanship did not concern itself with the social good
of the many; it was confined to the solution of business problems.
He was to assemble through his National Monetary Commission
a stupendous amount of information which others were to use in
the framing of the Federal Reserve Act after he had passed from
public life. He who in youth had so longed to be an orator and
thus sway multitudes never was to be one, but he had developed

[1] Beveridge on Aldrich, speech at Gary.
[2] Stephenson, *Nelson W. Aldrich*, 206, 246.

into a debater capable of taking care of himself in the give-and-take of senatorial controversy. When there was no escape, he spoke, and he seldom stumbled in his facts. A hard-headed business leader in politics, it was said of him that Burke's magnificent speech on the Nabob of Arcot's debts, with all its political and moral philosophy, would have bored him to tears, but that the illiterate employee of a Providence or Fall River mill who might accost him in a crowd with the announcement that he had a secret as to dyestuffs that would save five cents on the bolt of calico would be heard with rapt attention. But when he did speak, his language was chaste, his diction excellent, and he spoke with a fluency that sometimes almost amounted to eloquence.[1] Even so, his attitude toward orators of real eloquence was one of cynical amusement and disdain. Was it a touch of envy? More likely it was due to impatience with talkers who postponed the day of action. Usually his managerial genius had mobilized a majority, not always easily held in line, and when he had the votes, he wanted silent action. But when he had to descend to the arena, he made a good impression with his mastery of his subject, the clarity of his exposition, and the clear modulation of his voice.

There came a time when, as the head of the Senate machine dominating the course of legislation, he found his supremacy challenged by the rising power of Joseph G. Cannon at the other end of the Capitol — a man with a will power equal to his own. But Aldrich knew whom to crush and whom to placate. He took Cannon in; and thus assured himself that the plans of the Senate cabal would not be wrecked by the action of the House.

VI

Haughty, aristocratic, decidedly selective in his choice of intimates, at times arrogant toward those who did not bow to his yoke, no man could be more charming in social intercourse. Even toward his political opponents he found pleasure in a friendly gesture. Subtle as an Oriental, he managed by suggestion to direct the course of conversation, and thus, in charge of the agenda, he became the most flattering of listeners. He possessed the Jeffersonian secret of often holding the reins on others and directing their minds without their knowledge that something other than their whims had turned them this way or that.

Beveridge, on whom he was to turn in white rage, found him altogether charming in social intercourse. 'In social relations,' he said, 'it is impossible to imagine anybody more charming than

[1] O. O. Stealey, *One Hundred Pen Pictures of Live Men*, 25.

Senator Aldrich. He loved bright company, was fond of wit, jokes, repartee. He was one of the few leaders who had a bent for society; in this respect he resembled Alexander Hamilton, whom he admired more than any other character in history.' [1] While his social engagements were not permitted to interfere with his duties of leadership, he liked nothing better than the relaxation of the dinner-table. But here, too, he was as selective as an epicure, always making sure that the dinner would be very good and the company entertaining and worth while.[2] He was a thorough aristocrat, permeated with the idea of caste, contemptuous of the common lot, holding himself haughtily aloof from men of no particular importance, capable of cruelty toward his intellectual inferiors — a perfect replica of the Massachusetts Federalists of the days of George Cabot. It was his ambition to figure as a country gentleman.[3]

Moving about the Senate with physical grace, exuding a sense of power, complacently conscious of his strength, he wore his crown of kingship as one who did not feel its weight upon his head. Always self-possessed and self-contained, he seldom gave way to anger; but when he did, his fury flamed. His usual fighting mood was one of gayety, as one who likes a fight he feels confident of winning.

And yet, in his dictatorial rôle, Aldrich had his limitations, and all the triumphs that fell to him were not wholly of his contriving. We shall soon find him far from happy in fighting to maintain his supremacy; and men who noted the change were not in doubt as to the reason. He had outstayed the mighty group by whom he had been surrounded through almost all the period of his power. Allison was sleeping in the soil of Iowa; Platt of Connecticut had passed to his final rest; and Spooner, saddened by the progressive forces La Follette had let loose in Wisconsin, was in private life. The gentle persuasive power of Allison was gone. The resourceful diplomacy of Platt was missing. The parliamentary genius of Spooner no longer was available. Aldrich had been deprived of the genius of his lieutenants and the newer men of his school of thought were deficient in finesse. He was to do the best he could with the material left him, but it was none too good. The Aldrichian will of iron, audacity, directness remained, but the qualities that were lost in Allison, Platt, and Spooner were beyond replacement. The loss was to be fatal. Even as the last battle broke, the venerable dictator was growing weary of public life. The voice of the 'proletariat' was echoing more and more within the sacred

[1] Speech on Aldrich at Gary.   [2] *Ibid.*
[3] Stephenson, *Nelson W. Aldrich*, 39.

precincts of the Senate Chamber. The old gods had gone and Aldrich was growing lonesome. Soon even the people themselves would determine who would represent them in the Senate Chamber, and it was time to go. One last great battle that would wreck the party for a decade and leave scars that time could not easily efface, and he would follow Spooner into private life, to linger only a little while and die.

But he had written his name large in the history of two decades and made himself the greatest congressional dictator since Thad Stevens. 'One of the most extraordinary men in the public life of this or any other country' was the deliberate conclusion of Beveridge, who had no reason to pay him compliments.

VII

The senators who, with Beveridge, confronted Aldrich in the epochal struggle over the tariff of 1909 were all men of character and ability, and some among them had more than a spark of genius. They had arrived at insurgency by different routes and some by winding ways. The five who bore the brunt of the battle were more than merely emotional enemies of injustice. They were dominated by their intellectual processes, and they knew their facts because of herculean labors. Differing widely in personal traits, they fought as one man through that dreadful summer of 1909 for a principle.

The senior in insurgency was Robert M. La Follette, at this period a striking figure, short, stockily built, with a large head covered with a great mop of hair, brushed upward. His eyes were keen, penetrating, remarkably expressive; and anyone watching him in battle would note their capacity to express scorn, amazement, contempt, anger, and humor. His smoothly shaven face was strong in all its features, and in combat it was the face of a bulldog. He would walk into the Senate Chamber with a virile stride, and, seated at his desk listening to a debate, he was frequently found in the pose in which Joseph Davidson, the sculptor, has shown him in the vivid, animated statue now in the Capitol — his face alight with intense interest, his hands clasping the arms of his chair as in the act of springing to his feet. No one on the floor, noting that pose, was ever quite comfortable.

La Follette had entered public life years before as a regular, if not content with the *status quo*, not quite realizing what it was. Elected to Congress in his thirties, he had played his part usually after the fashion prescribed by political tradition. He had, in the course of time, learned of things and methods that shocked

ALBERT B. CUMMINS

ROBERT M. LA FOLLETTE

JOSEPH L. BRISTOW

JONATHAN P. DOLLIVER

MOSES E. CLAPP

and irritated him, but he had not crossed the Rubicon entirely.

It was in the gubernatorial office in Wisconsin, which he attained only after bitter contests with one of the most reactionary of machines that long had dominated the politics of the State, that he first attracted national notice. The reforms wrought in the regulation of the railroads in the days of the Granger Movement no longer protected the people against extortion; and the railroad interest completely controlled the State through its domination of the political machine. No longer were the roads subjected to a regulation that interfered in the slightest degree with their plans of greed; and they were immune from full taxation. They dictated to the machine; controlled the major portion of the press; influenced the banks; and through intimidation actually forced an acquiescent mood upon the shippers and merchants, who, no less than the consumers, were robbed in rates and methods. To challenge the power of this combination of political and financial interests, supported by the greater part of the press and superabundantly financed, called for a temerity almost beyond the human; and young La Follette challenged it.

Arousing the great unorganized mass of the people, he organized them, and plunged with his fiery zeal into a crusade for the democratization of the government — a crusade as fundamental as those led long before by Jefferson and Jackson. He took the enemy by storm.

Then had followed a series of reforms calculated to make democracy a reality in Wisconsin. He ended the literal stealing by the roads of millions in taxes belonging to society; and when he foresaw the inevitable purpose to transfer the taxes to the consumers through increased rates, he met them there with a scientific method of regulation.

These, however, were but symbolical of the things he did. He found children of tender age in factories and he made that unlawful and sent them back to the playgrounds and the schools. He found working-women laboring under intolerable conditions, and he stopped that too. The factories, without a sanitary code, operated to the serious detriment of the workers, and he forced sanitation into the shops. He learned that food adulterators were poisoning the people for profit, and he made that a crime.

No single man, perhaps, ever did more within the limitations of a State to reform abuses, political and social, or to make democracy something other than an academic dream. Thus did he incur the deadly enmity of the forces of privilege and pillage, and these were to hound him with unthinkable fury throughout his life. When the people transferred him to Washington, the embryo plutocracy, with knives in their hands, was waiting for him at the Senate door.

For more than a century, America had referred to her democracy, and yet La Follette was almost unique in his day in that he was a democrat. His political creed largely was that of Jefferson and Jackson — hostility to privilege. To him the only government fit to live was that which acted as an agency of the average man in working out his inalienable right to life, liberty, and the pursuit of happiness. He saw that privilege in government had made a mockery and a mess of democracy, and with a gay gallantry he fared forth to battle against privilege all along the line.

He differed from many others, sincerely devoted to democratic ideals, in that he was superbly equipped and munitioned for his crusade. His sympathies for the average man motivated his action, but there was more than emotion behind his blows. There was an intellect and a genius for research. There was industry of the most appalling sort behind the intellect. He never declared war on any evil until he had studied and mastered its meaning and methods in all their ramifications. This meant for him the most intensive labor with the aid of experts. Mobilizing all the facts, he studied them closely for their effects. Only when his preparation was complete did he declare war; and it was war to the death.

Where the average senator of commanding influence is satisfied to master some one subject — banking, railroads, the tariff, foreign relations, trusts — La Follette made a specialty of them all, because he sought the common thread of privilege running through them all. He spoke with equal thoroughness on each; and most of his major speeches literally were treatises. Each speech reflected enormous work and was so buttressed with authoritative facts that none were seriously challenged on the floor of the Senate. When his enemies were unable to meet the argument, they had recourse to the old device of sneaking out into the cloakrooms. 'I see a great many vacant seats in the Senate today,' he said one day with a smile to the crowded galleries. 'Many of the seats now temporarily vacant will be permanently so after a while.' He did not mind the absentee insult; he was using the Senate Chamber as a sounding-board to reach the millions in the corn rows and the shops.

To pursue this course required ineffable courage and a rare capacity to bear up under misunderstandings, misrepresentations, and loneliness. A woman who had never seen him before, but had admired his public conduct from afar, once met him in the Capitol grounds walking alone with his head bowed. As she greeted him she burst into tears. He stopped, startled. 'You seemed so lonely,' she explained. 'Yes,' he replied reassuringly, 'it is a little lonely sometimes, but we can stand it.' He always did.

Few men in American history have had greater moral courage. He could stand absolutely alone with an approving conscience. He never counted the cost. He was willing to save his life by losing it. He was never tempted to compromise with his convictions for the sake of a meaningless victory. Had he been of a more compromising nature, he might have won more battles, but the victories would have been dead-sea fruit. He sought the substance or nothing.

As an orator he was overwhelming before a popular audience. Summer after summer found him on the circuit speaking to great audiences for three hours in tents, under the boiling sun or the stars, and holding them spellbound, not with glittering rhetoric, but by a marvelous dramatic marshaling of facts. He had the art of an actor; and in his youth he hoped for a histrionic career. He had won the Interstate Oratorical Contest when in college with a brilliant analytic study of Iago. This instinct for the play stood him in good stead on the platform. He spoke with great vehemence — action, action, action. His modulation itself often was eloquence. In the Senate he did not vary his method greatly, and with the senators sourly seeking the cloakrooms as a storm cellar, the galleries hung upon his words. 'Fighting Bob,' his friends called him, and he never winced under a blow, and never failed to strike with all his might.

VIII

Quite different in temperament and training was Jonathan P. Dolliver of Iowa. Reared in the religious atmosphere of the home of his father, a Methodist circuit rider, he graduated at seventeen from the University of West Virginia with the highest scientific honors of his class, and found his way to Iowa where, at twenty, he began the practice of law. He became a protégé of Senator Allison, who was not the mentor for a progressive; and at twenty-six, he won renown by the majestic sweep of his eloquence as chairman of the Iowa State Convention. It was this speech that Beveridge, a college boy, heard in Des Moines, and that impelled Blaine, then the presidential nominee, to insist on the young man's presence on the stump in the East. Four years later, La Follette saw and heard Dolliver for the first time at the National Convention of 1888, where the young orator by his animation, eloquence, and flashing wit dominated and popularized the headquarters of Allison, candidate for the Presidency. That year he was elected to the House of Representatives, where the party leaders instantly recognized his value to the party organization. A natural orator of great power and charm, a veritable whirlwind in the wild charges of debate, it was soon found that whenever needed, on whatever notice, he could be relied upon to save the day for his party if it could be saved. During the greater part of this time, albeit never a superficial man, he was content to be the party managers' medium of expression. It was as an organization man and a 'regular' that he entered the Senate.

Physically he was fitted for the platform, for his was a commanding presence — a great body, a great head, a great personality. He had the artistic sense and temperament of a great orator. Perhaps out of his boyhood in the mountains he had brought something of the poetry and pathos which entered into the emotional appeal of his speeches. His intense humanity, his love and understanding of the mind and heart of ordinary folk, made him a perfect interpreter of the plain people. His musical voice could express the most delicate shades of feeling. His magnetism drew audiences, great or small, to him. His wit was brilliant, his humor mellow, his sarcasm devastating, his irony as fine as that of Junius. No one knew better where the line fell between pathos and bathos. Often there was a fine literary flavor to his speeches. The long evenings in his library with the masters of poetry and prose were reflected in his English, though he was not given to quotation. He assimilated what he read — it became a part of him. It was observed that he 'thought in pictures and epigrams.' He had the rare art of condensing an argument into a sentence of inspired illumination. His style was individual, patterned on that of no other orator, and yet possessing the best qualities of them all. Running through his arguments was a thread of homely philosophy often expressive of the most profound thought. Beveridge was to say, at the time of his friend's death, that Dolliver was 'beyond any possible doubt the greatest orator in the contemporaneous English-speaking world.'

He found his keenest joy in study, and there was no branch of literature he did not love. The Bible was a favorite because of the purity and strength of the English. The poets, from the masters to the minor figures, delighted him; the essayists, like Bacon, pleased him; and he was a careful student of history. It was not the events of the time alone that interested him — he saw their relations and applied their lessons to his own political thinking. Invariably in the latter part of his life, he got down to the fundamentals. He grew in poise.

But more than his genius entered into the deep affection he inspired. Dolliver was an incomparable companion. The lovable traits of boyhood never left him, and he was as full of fun as a child. His brilliant conversational gifts made any company in which he sat sparkle and flash. He liked nothing better than to gather a few congenial friends about him before a blazing hearth and then 'periodically he poured forth the riches of his mind.'[1] 'If I had been selecting a comrade for a journey,' said Senator Young,[2] 'either in a private schooner or a palace car, I would have selected Dolliver. Every day would have been a new one. When he looked out of a window, he saw more mountains and streams, he saw more prairies and crops. He photographed with a lens which poets and painters know. Nature delighted him. It is a surprise to know that he seldom attended a theater, though he loved music.... His charm of manner was in his simplicity, and he was willing to listen as well as to talk.' And he had no bitterness in his soul, no animosities, no hates.

As a public man Dolliver was not an organizer, for his mind was not for that kind of work. He was the thinker, the advocate, the expounder. He did not reach insurgency at a bound, for essentially he was conservative. But from 1901 to 1909 he had sought in coöperation with others to make government responsive to the needs of the average man. As time went on, gradually he became conscious of a cooling of the enthusiasm of not a few public men with whom he worked for these reforms. Finally, he was convinced that not only had these erstwhile reformers cooled, but that they had actually joined in the more powerful movement to commercialize government for a class. The discovery shocked him, and he was not happy in the thought that the hour was approaching when he would have to abandon his preference for popular government or face a fight.

That the inherent progressivism in the man was apparent to such as Aldrich is evident in the determination to exclude him from the Senate Finance Committee. This suspicion of his fidelity to reaction grew to conviction in the fight on the bill to regulate railroad freight rates; and he bitterly resented the action of Aldrich in bringing about the transfer of the floor leadership for the Roosevelt measure from himself to Tillman. A great light seemed to dawn upon him at that time. He saw the trend toward the consolidation of transportation companies and banks into a mighty system with the most sinister possibilities; and it was about this time that he began to call for 'the integrity, the freedom of the American market-place.'

When the extra session of 1909 was called, he was ripe for

[1] Hubbard, *Memorial Addresses.*   [2] *Ibid.*

revolt against that system. He was to play a memorable part in the fight; to labor day and night; to voice his protest in one of the greatest speeches ever heard at any time in the American Senate; and, broken by his labors, to go down to his grave. He was to be the actual martyr of the struggle — to leave behind the tender memory of a man who gave his very life to what he thought to be the service of his fellow men.

IX

Albert B. Cummins of Iowa, the oldest member of the group, had just entered the Senate when he took his stand with the insurgents in the tariff fight. It was the inevitable thing with him, for he had been fighting for tariff reforms for years. At the time he was of handsome presence, tall, slender, graceful in his bearing, with iron-gray mustache and hair, large, thoughtful blue eyes that, in repose, seemed a little sad, and with rosy cheeks. He conveyed the impression of one who looked seriously on life, for in public he seldom smiled. He lacked the vehemence of La Follette, the humor and wit of Dolliver, but there was a suggestion of solidity in his manner that was not belied when he spoke.

In the gubernatorial office Cummins had demonstrated to the Nation the qualities of courage and constructive statesmanship. He turned at once to the railroads, undertaxed, and with their hands at the throttle of the Commonwealth; he destroyed for a time their control of government and forced an equitable tax upon them. His railroad legislation deserves to stand alongside that of La Follette in Wisconsin. But this one victory did not suffice — he ended the domination of political conventions by the corporations in the making of nominations; he forced a primary system upon the politicians. But at the time of his entrance to the Senate, his national fame rested largely upon the association of his leadership with the tariff reform ideas, known as 'the Iowa plan.' He had not initiated it; but he agreed with it, accepted it, made it his own, and became its most powerful and convincing advocate.

Cummins was not a great orator, lacking the art, imagination, the fervor, but he was a persuasive speaker and an excellent debater, because of the clarity of his ideas and the simple force with which he set them forth. He never spoke without preparation; and when he spoke it was as one having authority. He had a penetrating mind that saw through the most complicated economic problems. He never sought to amuse or entertain, nor to stir emotions. He was a plain, blunt man who spoke right on.

Eloquence he did not have. Standing erect, he was a commanding figure; but his voice, though strong, was not musical, and he
had a precision of enunciation which gave one the impression of
a professor in the lecture-room of a university. But he had courage, energy, zeal, capacity, and was to associate his name with
some notable legislation before his death.

Altogether different from the others was Joseph L. Bristow of
Kansas, who, like Cummins, had just entered the Senate. The
aggressive editor of a small-town paper in Kansas, he had won
his way to the recognition of his party by the vigor of his editorial advocacy of its policies, and he had begun his official life
as Fourth Assistant Postmaster-General under McKinley. The
masterly and courageous manner in which he dealt with the
postal frauds in Cuba impelled Roosevelt to send him to Panama
as a special commissioner of the Panama Railroad. Thus he
had been something more than a Fourth Assistant Postmaster-
General — a valuable public servant in a field requiring independence, character, and courage — and his reputation was
national when he entered the Senate.

In personal appearance Bristow was not prepossessing. Very
tall, a little stooped and ungainly, he did not fit into the popular
picture of senatorial dignity. The rather heavy black mustache,
and the thick-lensed glasses, through which literally popped
dark, eager eyes, gave him a restive aspect. His voice was rasp-
ing and literally cut the air. Indeed, he had none of the graces
of the orator. Awkward in gesticulation, unmusical in tone, and
never given to the polishing of his English, which was, nevertheless, good and fluent, he commanded attention by his passionate
earnestness of manner, the forthrightness of his observations,
and the cutting sharpness of his tongue. He cared nothing for
'senatorial courtesy' or feelings. He was ruthless with his facts.
And he was a fighter — challenging, defiant, uncompromising.
He was soon to prove by his mastery of certain schedules that
his ability to delve for the truth was not confined to investigations of criminal proceedings. To Aldrich he was intolerable,
and consequently the dictator ostentatiously ignored him when
possible. But he was of the stuff of which insurgency is made.

If Bristow was a bit acidulous, the fifth leading member of the
progressive group had enough sweetness of disposition to serve
for all. Moses E. Clapp of Minnesota had entered the Senate
eight years before after a successful career at the bar. He had
held only such offices as were in the line of his profession. Tall,
heavily built, he was slow in his movements, but sure. Studious
and observant, he had long viewed, with grave mistrust and not a
little feeling, the economic trend toward the centralization of

financial and industrial power. He had no illusions, and yet he was of the breed that goes down fighting without complaint. No one could come into social contact with him without feeling the pull of his lovable personality. He had a contempt for hypocrisy and a hatred of dishonesty and trickery; and it was impossible to gild a wrong for him. He saw through the rotten fabric. And yet, withal, he was tolerant and just. No member of the group had a keener insight into character; and while he could deliver titanic blows, no woman could have been more considerate of the sensibilities of a friend. His political convictions were those of his section, which had suffered greatly from the impositions of the privileged. In sheer radicalism he resembled La Follette, to whom he was tenderly devoted. He had the courage of a great mastiff, and the supercilious condescension of the self-constituted leaders of the senatorial oligarchy merely amused him. He had a dangerous tongue when he wished to use it — one capable of the most annoying sarcasm and satire. Without vanity, he spoke only under the compulsion of a strong conviction, but when he did, it was with impressive power. During the strain and the multiplying irritations of the tariff fight, he was to be the peacemaker, the conciliator, the harmonizer.

x

These five, with Beveridge, were the outstanding leaders of the little group, but there was another, then new in the Senate and destined to great distinction, who met with them frequently, voted with them sometimes and sometimes against them, and in the end supported the bill. A little before, in the rôle of public prosecutor in Idaho, he had flashed upon the country by the brilliance and eloquence of his prosecution of some labor leaders accused of murder. He was typical of the robust Western country — powerfully built physically, with large generously carved features, a heavy shock of black hair, and a face of great mobility. He was an orator of a high order. His voice was strong and musical, his choice of words exceptional, and his reasoning robust. As a debater he has had few equals. But this new man, William E. Borah, was an individualist then, as always, and though he coöperated with the insurgents when he thought proper, he does not appear to have entered into the struggle with the abandon that characterized the rest. He preferred to plow his lonely furrow.

These were the men who had the temerity to challenge the authority of Aldrich and the courage to make history. With them were others less conspicuous, but of equal zeal.

CHAPTER II

THE EPOCHAL DRAMA OF INSURGENCY: I

I

Almost immediately after the inauguration of Taft, Congress was summoned in extraordinary session to revise the tariff. For six years or more the pressure of public sentiment had steadily been increasing upon the politicians for a saner adjustment of the schedules to new conditions and in favor of a revision downward. Beveridge had urged such action in the campaign of 1906, but Roosevelt, with whom economics was a mystery and whose political acumen warned him that a revision meant perils, had held off the inevitable until his retirement. In 1908, the Republican platform had pledged the party to a revision; and while it was not definitely said that the revision would be downward, this was generally assumed. There was no public clamor for a revision upward. But if the platform pledge was vague, its interpretation by Mr. Taft, the official spokesman of the party, was plain enough. In the course of the presidential canvass, he had repeatedly pledged himself and party to a revision downward. In his speech of acceptance,[1] he had said that he not only stood for a revision, but that he meant 'a revision which shall reduce excessive rates and at the same time preserve the industries of the country.' Two days later, speaking at Milwaukee,[2] he had declared that since the enactment of the Dingley Acts, the cost of production had been so reduced that 'the necessity for maintaining the tariff at the former rate has ceased.' He had gone so far in this speech as to suggest that the sole purpose of protection was to build up industries to the point where 'they can stand alone and fight their own battles in competition with the world.' Becoming more explicit, he had concluded that 'the tariff is greater than the differential between the cost of production at home and abroad, and that it therefore should be reduced.' Leaving no possible excuse for any misinterpretation of his meaning, he said: 'It is my judgment that a revision of the tariff in accordance with the pledge of the Republican platform will be on the whole a substantial revision downward.'

The next day, speaking at Des Moines, he reiterated his interpretation of his party's pledge in the identical terms used at Milwaukee.[3]

In his inaugural address, in the interpretation of the mandate

[1] At Cincinnati, Sept. 22, 1908.   [2] Sept. 24, 1908.
[3] *Des Moines Register and Leader*, Sept. 26, 1908.

given him and his party, he said that the change in conditions since the passage of the Dingley Act 'will permit the reduction of rates in certain schedules and will require the advancement of few, if any.'

Thus, when, in accordance with his promise, Taft summoned Congress in extraordinary session for the revision of the tariff, it was universally assumed that it was to be a revision downward. Certainly no one publicly gave expression to any other thought. Not one of the industries that were to secure increased rates during the saturnalia of logrolling and favor-seeking during the summer of 1909 uttered a word of complaint against the Taft interpretation of the platform pledge or of the mandate received from the people.

There was surprise, with some misgivings of the President's courage and intent, when, in his Message opening the extra session, there was no reference to a revision downward. The very brevity of the Message was a shock to those who had hoped for a militant call for the fulfillment of a campaign promise. In two minutes the clerk had finished. As he laid the paper down, the progressives exchanged startled glances. The document, which might have been historic, was nothing more than an announcement that tariff revision was to be that session's business and that no time should be lost in the process. Unwittingly, no doubt, the President had played into the hands of the enemies of a downward revision.[1]

With that, for the moment, the President seemed to wash his hands of all responsibility, and the Ways and Means Committee of the House immediately set to work. It had been holding meetings for many weeks, beginning in December, and its bill was practically completed when Congress met. It had been framed in the time-honored fashion. Lobbyists had appeared with their demands before the majority members of the committee, publicly and privately. Notoriously, as the press recorded, it had been a matter of vulgar barter and sale.

Without a single exception, the House leaders in charge were reactionaries on the tariff and on governmental problems generally. Cannon, in the chair, was a dominating factor. Sereno E. Payne was an honest devotee of privilege. John Dalzell, representing a Pennsylvania constituency, thought of himself as the attorney for the industrialists seeking favors and the public had long accepted his conception of his rôle. He had none other. Boutelle of Maine and Fordney of Michigan were as safe for sap-seekers as Blaine or Zack Chandler had been in the halcyon days of 'Pig Iron' Kelley.

[1] La Follette's *Autobiography*, 436.

Those apostles of the old system, laboring lovingly at their task under the approving eyes of industrial groups that had contributed always to the campaign funds, and not without the advice of Senator Aldrich, had their revision bill ready when the gavel fell. It was not to be materially changed when it reached the floor. Under the rules of the House reducing debate to a mockery, it was hastened to its passage. Champ Clark and Oscar W. Underwood, the Democratic leaders, made their protests, the roll was called, and the bill was passed.

It was a flagrant repudiation of the party's pledge — a revision upward.

Thus it went to the Senate, where Aldrich, the Senator of the industrialists, took it under his wing. From the moment it was reported to the House, the Republican members of the Finance Committee in the Senate began their work upon it. 'The Committee worked well,' Lodge was to write to Roosevelt in Africa. The 'scholar in politics' had never been so much impressed with Aldrich's ability and his unselfish devotion to the 'larger interests of the country.' Cullom of Illinois was old and did nothing, and Eugene Hale and Julius C. Burrows looked after 'one or two things in which they are interested.' Reed Smoot, a new man, was making an impression. Numerous changes in rates were made, and Lodge, with something less than frankness, assured Roosevelt, who was too remote to know what the press was saying, that there would be 'many reductions from the Dingley rates... but not of a character to come home to the mass of the people.' Nor did he intimate to his friend in the jungles that the Senate Finance Committee was increasing rates over both the House and Dingley bills that did affect the mass of the people.[1]

Thus did the Senate Finance Committee rewrite the House bill. No searching investigation was necessary. Aldrich knew precisely where he was going, and why. He knew precisely what was wanted, and who wanted it. He held the majority members of the committee in the hollow of his hand. A survey of the Senate had convinced him of his ability to get through any rates he wished, and the cotton, wool, and steel men thereupon demanded and secured rates in excess of those in the House bill and of those their own representatives had testified before the House committee were enough.[2] When at length the House bill reached the Senate, forty-eight hours were quite enough for a revision. But during those two days there was animated drama about the Aldrich committee rooms. The rooms and corridors

[1] Lodge to Roosevelt, April 29, 1908; *Roosevelt-Lodge Correspondence*, II, 333–34.
[2] Beveridge to Professor N. W. Stephenson, April 5, 1927.

were swarming with the representatives of the greater industries determined to make hay in the sunshine. It was a familiar scene — eager men in a hurry for honey. Now and then one was admitted to the sanctum of the Senator for a brief conference.

Thus, in two days Aldrich rose in the Senate to present the Senate bill carrying many and significant increases over the measure of the House, which had been a revision upward. The Senator, too, was in a hurry. There was no time for the preparation of the customary report. Not a word, written or oral, was offered in explanation of the reason for increasing the rates of the House bill on as many as six hundred items. These were to be accepted without question. Of course, the public would want to know the estimated revenue the measure would produce, but why should the public inquire how much money was to be extracted by due process of law from the pockets of the people? The important thing was haste. Business was waiting, nervous, anxious to 'get back to work.' Why waste precious time in talking, in asking questions, in investigating these mysterious proceedings? [1]

Senator Aldrich demanded immediate consideration.

II

Meanwhile, President Taft had been observing their weird maneuvers with increasing apprehension. He was an able and an honest man and wanted to keep faith with the people, but in the hands of cunning, designing politicians who knew precisely what they were seeking, he was as a child. Fate had taken a kindly man of judicial temperament and thrust him into a position of political leadership for which he was singularly unfit. He had not dealt with politicians and he knew little of popular psychology. From youth he had been the child of fortune; Fate had lifted him from one appointive office to another, and he had seldom faced the people at the polls. The action of the House, in increasing instead of reducing the tariff rates, had hurt as much as it had astonished him. When La Follette called upon him when the measure left the House, he had agreed that the bill submitted was 'not in compliance with the party platform.' He even said he would veto it unless changed. [2]

And it was changed by Aldrich — for the worse.

It was at this time that Taft sought to intimidate the reactionaries with a veto threat. The intimidative word was frequently on his lips. The moment the measure reached the Senate, he saw the drift. 'I fear Aldrich is ready to sacrifice the

[1] La Follette's *Autobiography*, 441.   [2] *Ibid.*, 439.

party, and I will not permit it,' he said to a member of his Cabinet when driving. 'I am not very anxious for a second term as it is, and I certainly will not make any compromise to secure one.'[1] Outraged and hurt, he was in the mood for battle. It was at this time that he said to La Follette: 'You and your associates in the Senate go ahead, criticize the bill, amend, cut down the duties — go after it hard. I will keep track of your amendments. I will read every word of the speeches you make, and when they lay the bill down before me, unless it complies with the platform, I will veto it.'[2]

It was at this juncture that Taft made a similar request of Beveridge and of Dolliver. The former, after his continental speaking tour for Taft, had, as we have seen, gone to the hospital for an operation. He had followed the tariff drama in the House through the newspapers, and, without an opportunity for a thorough investigation, was convinced that the tariff had been revised upward in defiance of the campaign pledge. He planned to return for the Senate fight and vote for reductions for the consumers, but to take no conspicuous part in the struggle. His surgeon had ordered him to do nothing more than sit and vote for four months.

Such was his intent, when, immediately after his return to his seat, he was approached by Senator Dolliver with the message that Taft wanted the progressives 'to fight for a downward revision of the tariff.' He had seen Dolliver personally and asked him to convey the request to Beveridge on his return.[3]

Beveridge and Dolliver had been the most conspicuous and brilliant advocates of Taft's election and had based their plea for him in part upon the promise of a revision of the tariff downward. Beveridge had traveled seventeen thousand miles on his campaign tour, and Dolliver twelve thousand. There was no other member of the Senate or of the party who had done so much. Taft's appeal to them was not unnatural. Beveridge had been an original advocate of a downward revision; and Dolliver had seen a light.

III

Both were ardent champions of the principle of a protective tariff; both had distinguished themselves in the support of all party principles; and both had been 'regular.' Beveridge had

[1] Butt, *Taft and Roosevelt*, I, 58.
[2] La Follette's *Autobiography*, 440.
[3] Beveridge to Ida M. Tarbell, Sept. 13, 1910. This letter was not sent and a shorter, less illuminating, one was sent instead.

broken away from the Aldrich domination on the battleship issue and Dolliver on railroad rate legislation. But neither was naturally insurgent; both were party and organization men. The pull of party more than once had held them to an organization policy they disapproved, and both had chafed under the yoke.

A little while before, Dolliver had surrendered his place on the Interstate Commerce Committee to make way for Cummins whose specialty had been railroads, and had applied to Aldrich for the vacancy on the Finance Committee created by the death of Allison. The request had been denied and the coveted place had been given to a new member with no experience or special qualification for the position. Dolliver had served for years on the Ways and Means Committee of the House and thus was thoroughly trained for the post he wanted. The explanation was not far to seek — Dolliver was a man with Western ideas and a spirit of independence. He pondered the meaning of the affront. He did not belong at heart with the Aldrich group — neither by temperament nor principle. He had thought so for a long time. Not long before he had told his mentor, the venerable Allison, that he could stand the bondage no longer, that he had to break away from the system. 'Don't do it, Jonathan,' Allison had pleaded, 'Don't do it now — wait till I am gone. I know it is wrong. It has grown up here gradually in the last quarter of a century. I have gone along with it. These men are my associates. I have only a little while left, and I haven't the strength to break away. It has got to come. It's a cancer; it's got to be cut out. But wait until I am gone, and then go into the new movement where you belong.'[1]

And Dolliver had waited; and Allison was gone.

It was at the beginning of the tariff session that La Follette made his appeal to Dolliver to take his stand with the progressives. For hours the two men sat in Dolliver's committee room and talked. And in the end the protégé of Allison took his stand. 'From this time on,' he said, 'I am going to be independent. I am going to judgment in the next twenty years, and I am going so that I can look my Maker in the face. I do not have to stay in public life. I can take my books, my wife and children, and if I am dismissed from the service for following my convictions, I will go out to my farm and stay there until the call comes.'[2]

Thus, in the spirit of a crusader, Dolliver crossed the Rubicon and took his stand for the people.

Taft had appealed to three men to make an insurgents' fight against the Aldrich tariff bill — La Follette, Beveridge, and

[1] La Follette's *Autobiography*.　　　[2] La Follette's *Autobiography*, 433–34.

Dolliver — and they were ready. It was not without advantage that these three men, with Borah, were the most effective orators on their side of the Senate Chamber.

IV

The tocsin was sounded, and quietly at first the progressives began to draw together. Cummins, Clapp, and Bristow were to share with Beveridge, Dolliver, and La Follette in the bearing of the burden. None of them had made an intensive study of the schedules. Not one of them but knew the task before them — the utter impossibility in the time they had for any one of them to master the intricacies of more than one of the schedules cunningly framed, with the aid of experts of the industries affected, to conceal their true significance.[1] It was arranged that Dolliver should master the cotton schedule, La Follette should help on cotton and master the wool schedule, Cummins should specialize on the metal and glass, Bristow on lead and sugar. At first, Beveridge, out of deference to his surgeon's orders, was to confine himself, as the oldest of the group in point of service and as a master parliamentarian, to the general leadership in the parliamentary battles on the floor. Some of them employed experts, paying for them out of their own pockets, to assist in the analysis of the schedules, in the gathering of the facts. All through the month of April, these men worked incessantly, literally day and night. At first even the correspondents of the press gallery found no indication of an organized resistance. More than ever before, senators prodded the members of the Finance Committee with embarrassing questions. It was suspicious, disturbing, but not conclusive of anything. As these questions multiplied, the annoyance of Aldrich grew, and he was prone to hasten from the Chamber when the barrage began. It was something new in his experience. He who had merely given orders through the years to be subjected to an inquisition? It was unthinkable; more, it was disrespectful! But it would pass.

Meanwhile, the reactionaries could insist that the tariff had been revised downward, citing an imposing number of decreases without going into their significance. Lodge had written Roosevelt that, while there were many reductions, these did not materially affect the masses. But among the six hundred increases, including cotton, wool, steel, zinc, linoleum, there were increases in cost to the people. When Aldrich and Cannon claimed reductions on articles entering into the consumption of the people to the value of five billion dollars, the insur-

[1] Beveridge to Miss Tarbell.

gents found that these were meaningless reductions so far as reducing prices was concerned. They included petroleum, agricultural implements, steel rails — in all of which we were the greatest exporting nation in the world. Much was made of the reduction of five cents on the hundred pounds of sugar, although this meant no reduction in the price of sugar at the store. 'Looking at the tariff bill as a whole,' Beveridge wrote, 'we see that increases were made upon many articles used by the people and which are their absolute daily necessities, while the decreases were upon articles most of which need no protection at all, and on the remainder of which even the reduced tariff is still prohibitive.' [1] In the case of cotton, Henry F. Lippitt [2] appeared before the House committee in behalf of the cotton interests of New England to ask for nothing better than the retention of the Dingley rates; but Aldrich and his associates insisted upon outrageous increases, particularly in the better grades of cotton.

No one was deceived as to what was being done, and all through April, Taft was threatening to use the veto. When, however, the press announced that he had served notice that he would veto an upward revision, the insurgents, while cheered, were not satisfied. Why did he not send a ringing Message to Congress to that effect and thus sound a clarion call to the people? [3] Instead, he was trying personal persuasion behind closed doors and converting the White House dining-room into a caucus room. But all was vanity. Aldrich knew he had the votes to put his measure through, and, as the faithful Archie Butt observed, of Taft, 'the feeling is pretty well abroad that he does not dare to veto any bill.' [4]

Throughout April there was more press publicity as to the controversy over an income tax than about the tariff schedules. The insurgents were probing, with the aid of experts, asking embarrassing questions in the Senate, and each night poring over statistics till long past midnight. It seemed a hopeless task. 'Now for the first time I am feeling discouraged and disgusted,' Beveridge wrote Shaffer. 'Perhaps this is due to my present physical condition, which is very, very bad because of my great loss of strength. I have come down from the Senate to write this letter and feel that I cannot remain in the Chamber very much longer, but will have to go home and go to bed.' [5] He had introduced his tariff commission bill and that was consuming much of his time. Only a few, like Aldrich, had seen anything

---

[1] Beveridge to A. L. Bodurtha, March 18, 1910.
[2] Later Aldrich's successor in the Senate.
[3] *New York World*, April 27, 28, 1909.   [4] Butt, *Taft and Roosevelt*, I, 58.
[5] Beveridge to Shaffer, April 22, 1909.

significant in the questions he was asking on the floor. As late as May 3, Beveridge was listed in the press as certain to support the bill, although the others of the insurgent group were put down as 'insurgents.'[1]

V

The struggle, with the two forces arrayed in open hostility, began in early May. It was only with the announcement of Beveridge's determination to fight for a reduction in lead ores that the metropolitan press discovered his position. 'Senator Aldrich,' said the 'New York World,' 'has taken notice of Mr. Beveridge's plunge from the fence and will punish him — sometime.'[2] Two days before, Beveridge had appeared in the rôle of floor leader of the insurgents, serving notice that senators would refuse to vote on the tariff act until they thoroughly understood its provisions and implications, and this was interpreted by the press as meaning that 'the tariff fight has just begun.'[3] Beveridge had burned his bridges now, and henceforth was to become increasingly obnoxious to the Senate dictators. He had no doubt as to the reaction of the people in Indiana to his insurgency. They had long favored a downward revision; and Rothschild, taking note of the gossip, was writing him that his opposition was 'causing a good deal of favorable comment' and was giving him 'a stronger hold upon the people';[4] and that a judge of the Supreme Court had expressed the hope that he would not only oppose the bill, but vote against it.[5] Beveridge was not oblivious of the dangers he was inviting or the herculean labor he was undertaking. 'I'm very tired and terribly confused on the tariff,' he wrote his wife two days before he appeared frankly in the rôle of insurgent leader. 'I'm sleepy, but I cannot sleep. But never mind — I'll come out all right. Don't worry about me.'[6] And the next day: 'Aldrich grows warmer and warmer.'[7] And the day after he had led the insurgents who 'paralyzed Aldrich' by presenting a solid front: 'It is better to be the leader of a growing band of men who now hold the balance of power than to be a cipher — a nought in a servile bunch of men.[8]

No longer was there any doubt as to the significance of the drama. The power of Aldrich, representing the power of privilege, was flaunted and challenged by an organized and militant

---

[1] *New York World*, May 3, 1909.   [2] May 8, 1909.
[3] *Indianapolis Star*, May 6, 7, 1909.
[4] Rothschild to Beveridge, May 7, 1909.   [5] May 12, 1909.
[6] Beveridge to Mrs. Beveridge, May 5, 1909.
[7] May 6, 1909.   [8] May 7, 1909.

minority composed of the most brilliant men on the Republican side of the Chamber. This was revolution. Henceforth these insurgents were to figure in the press, not as individuals, but as a group. 'These men,' said the 'New York World,' editorially, 'represent more than their region. They stand for the rank and file of their party throughout the country.... On the courage and constancy of such men is the best hope of improved conditions of living for the average American.' [1]

It was in the first days of May, when Beveridge took his stand, that Dolliver threw the fear of the Lord into the reactionary camp with the announcement that he would 'take his orders from his constituency' and not from Aldrich.[2] 'I want to see an end to the scandal that has accompanied the framing of every tariff bill,' he said. 'It has corrupted American industries and made great enterprises mere adjuncts to political agitation.' [3] It was the day after this declaration that Cummins, denouncing the party betrayal, when asked by Chauncey M. Depew what would be done when one concern, like the steel trust, controls the entire world, had answered that 'there will still remain the lamp-post and the common people.' [4] Here was a defiance to match La Follette's — and this was the spirit of the insurgents' battle.

Within a few days the insurgent group had met in conference and announced their program. They would continue the fight in the spirit in which it had been waged, and would continue to assail every item that impressed them as an attempt to legalize extortion from the consumer.[5] Thoroughly alarmed now, Aldrich and his group were eager for a speedy vote. Had not the 'New York World' said that 'in the course of the Senate discussions this week the country has learned more about the real methods of tariff-making than during the whole time the bill was in the House'? [6] Thus, on May 13, that very week, Senator Joseph W. Bailey, floor leader of the Democrats, and by many considered an ally of Aldrich, rose to move for a vote on June 1. There were instant objections; and thereafter Aldrich and his hard-pressed lieutenants were to whine insistently that politicians were 'talking business to death.' The illumination of debate was the last thing wanted. Rebuking insurgents for 'wasting time in talk' was to become the order of the day and to lead to a sharp exchange between Beveridge and Senator Eugene Hale, one of the Senate autocrats, in which the usually dignified New-Englander, losing his temper, lowered himself to personalities. 'I think he

[1] May 10, 1909. [2] *New York World*, May 5, 1909.
[3] *Ibid.*, May 6, 1909. [4] *Ibid.*, May 7, 1909.
[5] *Indianapolis Star*, May 16, 1909. [6] May 7, 1909.

was unusually sensitive,' said Beveridge with devastating serenity, 'because he realized that he had been responsible for this half-hour delay which, of course, he was very anxious to avoid.' [1]

As the insurgents emerged as a compact fighting body battling for downward revision and the sound of the clashing steel reached the White House, it appears, from the experiences of the insurgents, that Taft began to regret his request to them to fight. The Aldrich group were fighting back, and with increasing bitterness, and that made a difference. Apparently it had not occurred to the President that when men fight they do not fight with kisses and caresses.

One day in the latter part of May, Dolliver appeared at Beveridge's seat, 'his face as white as that of a dead man,' and with 'much emotion' asked the latter to accompany him to the terrace, as he had some 'terrible' news. Out on the terrace, walking back and forth, Dolliver explained that he had learned that Taft had turned against the insurgents and said he 'would not have anything to do with such an irresponsible set of fellows.' Dolliver was trembling with excitement and anger. Convinced that the story was without justification, Beveridge determined to put it to the test.

Retiring to his room, he assembled the various campaign speeches of the President interpreting the platform as a promise of a revision of the tariff downward, and the next day in the Senate called upon the party to keep the pledge. He quoted from Taft's interpretative speeches at Cincinnati, Milwaukee, Des Moines.

'It seems to me,' he said, 'that these are true interpretations of our party platform. They appear to me to be reasonable, carefully uttered, well balanced, and conservative. They defined, as far as my vote and my attitude was concerned, my position with precise exactitude as to what is protection. The President has perhaps expressed it with a nice precision it has not yet received from any other interpreter within twenty years.' [2]

This deadly appeal to the record naturally was not relished by the supporters of the bill; but the President had asked La Follette, Beveridge, and Dolliver to 'insurge.' And Beveridge merely was calling upon the party in the Senate to follow the party's leader and keep the faith. But when, the next day, Beveridge called on Taft at the White House, there was a perceptible chill in his reception. 'The coldest atmosphere I ever encountered in politics,' he wrote.[3] But very soon Taft would

[1] *Congressional Record*, May 21, 1909.   [2] *Congressional Record*, May 25, 1909.
[3] Beveridge to Professor N. W. Stephenson, April 5, 1927.

veer around again; and this was to continue until he was to become the object of contemptuous flings from both contending forces.

VI

All thoughts of conciliation were cast aside by June. Working like a galley slave day and night, with a reliable expert at his side, Dolliver was now prepared for a smashing attack upon the cotton schedule. When, worn by his labors, he faced the Senate in the most magnificent oration of his life, he had mastered every detail of his subject. He spoke with the easy familiarity of one whose life had been spent in the cotton industry. In a moment those long familiar with his eloquence realized that they were listening to a new Dolliver. The old felicity of phrase, the accustomed wit and humor, the familiar satire, the facility in exposition — these entered into the making of the masterpiece. But there was something better than all this which was new — a passionate earnestness, the zeal of a crusader, 'the fierce temper of the Scotch Covenanters, the militant revolt of Cromwell's Ironsides,'[1] and an undercurrent of righteous wrath. One who heard him that day was reminded of Webster's explanation of his famous speech — 'I only had to reach out my hand and grasp the thunderbolts as they went smoking by.'[2] Another competent critic was reminded of Junius in its irony, of Sidney Smith in its wit, of Mark Twain in its humor, of Lord Bacon in its philosophy.[3]

There he stood, in a chamber charged with electricity, now calm, now sweetly reasonable, now literally trembling with emotion, pouring forth a merciless fusillade of damning facts and figures, drawing an indictment of a whole system, while members of the Finance Committee fled in fear from the sound of his voice. Aldrich waited until the orator's back was turned and beat a hasty retreat. Beveridge observed aloud that not one member of the committee in charge of the bill was present. 'I do not care two and a half cents to the square yard,' Dolliver replied; and hurried on with his blighting analysis.[4]

When he had finished, there was not a senator or a correspondent in the gallery who did not know that he had heard one of the most memorable orations ever heard in the American Senate; and the cotton schedule was a stench in the nostrils of a nation.

Only a day or two before, La Follette had made a similar assault upon the sophisticated claims of Aldrich and Lodge that

[1] *Memorial Addresses*, Beveridge.   [2] *Ibid.*, Cummins.
[3] *Ibid.*, Champ Clark.   [4] *New York World*, June 6, 1909.

there had been reductions on three hundred and seventy-nine articles and increases on but thirty-three. He had spoken in the insufferable heat but a short time when he seemed on the verge of a collapse; a recess was moved by Senator Money on the Democratic side. Sending a reassuring word to his wife in the gallery, La Follette went to his room for thirty minutes and then returned to the floor. He had asked the Bureau of Statistics in the Department of Commerce and Labor to furnish him a report on the increases and decreases in rates as they affected importations. This showed that the increases affected ten million dollars in importations and the decreases but forty-five thousand dollars. These figures alone were enough to throw the friends of the measure into fever, but that was not what startled Aldrich and his friends most — the report had been made for La Follette on the request of the President! Aldrich hurried from the Chamber to evade an immediate reply. The next day he attempted an explanation laboriously, and Dolliver responded in a pulverizing speech.

Cummins on metals, Bristow on sugar — one after another the heavy artillery of the insurgents was put in action. 'Aldrich and the old crowd are gone,' wrote Beveridge jubilantly to his wife. 'He has lost his cunning. Thrice in two days has he gone all to pieces.' [1] And after La Follette's pitiless exposé of the cotton schedule: 'It was murder and sudden death today. La Follette tore the cotton schedule to pieces. I told Dillingham [2] that even if La Follette was the devil himself, his statements were unanswerable. Aldrich has utterly lost his composure.' [3]

This was the psychological background of the bitter two-hour altercation between Aldrich and Beveridge. The latter had ridiculed the idea that increased rates could have no effect upon consumers in increased prices, when Aldrich, his face flushed, rose to read him out of the party.

Mr. President, the influence and the dangers of association are well illustrated in the speech which has just been concluded. I have heard a few remarks of that kind before, rarely from Republicans, never from protectionists. The Senate has been voting in reference to these matters with men who believe that protective duties are added to the cost of all domestic articles.... The Senator's speech would have been made with great effect by any free trade or tariff reformer.

Beveridge faced his antagonist.

I thought it was utterly unworthy of the Senator to talk about asso-

---

[1] Beveridge to Mrs. Beveridge, June 1, 1909.
[2] William P. Dillingham, Senator from Vermont.
[3] Beveridge to Mrs. Beveridge, June 4, 1909.

ciations.... I could have retorted to the Senator, 'Did he account for his present state of mind by association — what association'?

Aldrich left the Chamber, but soon returned in more belligerent mood than before; and when Beveridge suggested that it might be possible to get an agreement on a vote, the dictator thought he had found his opportunity:

Aldrich — I am not sure that the Senator speaks for anybody else.
Beveridge — That is my opinion. I do not speak for anybody else.
Aldrich — I must confess that I am a little puzzled about the question of who is leading the opposition to the bill.
Beveridge — There again comes an attempt to becloud the issue by personal references.
Aldrich — I have been greatly puzzled for a number of days to know to whom to apply for an agreement to take a vote on the tariff.
Beveridge — Apply to the Senate.
Aldrich — I mean whose consent I would have to get.
Beveridge — You have to get the consent of the Senate.

When Aldrich referred contemptuously to the insurgent group as a 'heterogeneous mass,' Beveridge retorted with a reference to the 'combination,' and added:

I will ask the Senator if he thinks there is any one of the schedules over which we have fought hardest that had a chance of passing this body if it stood on its own feet and was not combined with the interest of other senators and other schedules? What does he think about it?

This open reference to Aldrich's genius in making trades and combinations was ignored; the debate continued with the dictator resorting to studied personal insults. He was in a rage; Beveridge was cool, and the triumph was his.[1]

But the whip applied to Beveridge was intended as a warning to the wavering ones in the 'combination.' More and more it was evident that the debate must be ended speedily. There was too much publicity. It was at this stage that Aldrich moved for night sessions. The Senate was meeting at ten in the morning. This would leave but little time for the insurgents to study the schedules still waiting for consideration.

VII

It did not lessen by an hour the time thereafter devoted to the study of the schedules; it merely put a superhuman burden on the insurgent leaders. They met this added burden grimly, good-naturedly. Night after night thereafter, Dolliver, Beveridge, La Follette, and the others returned to their homes at mid-

[1] *Congressional Record*, June 7, 1909.

night, retired to their studies and pored over their papers until two and three o'clock in the morning. The drain upon their vitality was deadly, and they knew it.[1] 'It is a fact little known,' Beveridge wrote Miss Ida M. Tarbell, 'that every so-called insurgent seriously impaired his eyesight during that session in the study of long intricate lines of figures.'[2] The letters of Beveridge to his wife, summering at Dublin, New Hampshire, are eloquent of his weariness. 'I'm tired of work — so tired — you can't imagine how tired.' 'I must work hard tonight,' he wrote, after Senator Crawford had dined with him and left late. 'I am lonely and weary and disgusted, and worn out.' 'Worked and worried all last night... I am very tired and almost at the limit of endurance.'[3]

And so it was with all the members of the insurgent group.

Throughout three months of intolerably deadly heat the little group met frequently in conferences to plan their strategy, to consider schedules, to compare notes. Often they met at Beveridge's apartment on Sixteenth Street; often at La Follette's; sometimes with one or another of the others. These were not social occasions — they meant concentrated work. Removing coats and collars, they fell to their task. Beveridge had insisted from the beginning that their effectiveness depended on their ability to compromise differences and present a solid front. Sometimes the search for the formula of compromise was prolonged, for all were individualists. Worn down by work and worry, irritable sometimes in the heat, the arguments were animated. It was when these men, agreed on principle, but nervously on edge, were verging toward serious dissensions that Senator Clapp was indispensable. He seemed to sense the coming of a storm and his was the rôle of the peacemaker. Big-minded, generous-hearted, he had a hold on the affections of them all and his intercession was enough to smooth the conferences over the rough places. There he sat in his shirt-sleeves, drinking his beer, for it was understood that whoever was host should 'have a case of beer for Mose.' Often Dolliver, with his never-failing sense of humor and pervasive kindliness, ended threatening disagreements with a witticism that brought laughter. Frequently he would visit Beveridge alone, and the two would sit and talk into the small hours of the morning. Usually they walked together to the Capitol. On one of these morning walks, Dolliver stopped for a moment to talk with an old white-haired negro. As they passed on, Beveridge said: 'You have

[1] La Follette's *Autobiography*, 442–43.
[2] Beveridge to Miss Tarbell.
[3] Beveridge to Mrs. Beveridge, June 1, June 28, July 8, 1909.

grown more in the people's trust and faith during the last twelve months than during your whole public life.' Stopping, he took off his hat, and, with a characteristic gesture, passed his hand over his brow: 'Yes,' he replied. 'I think that is so. It is because for the first time in my life I have determined to be intellectually free. That old gray-haired negro was not so much emancipated physically fifty years ago as I have been emancipated intellectually during the last year and a half.' [1]

Such was the spirit and such the methods of the insurgents. Not one but was a soldier, and all could have said what Beveridge wrote a friend:

You have no possible conception of what we are up against in getting a tariff bill that the people would endorse. My head is so jam full, and the situation from moment to moment changes with such dazzling rapidity, that I cannot very well get anything else into my head. By rights I ought to be sick, but still I never have felt so well — perhaps I am keeping up on my nerves. It is literally true that when I get up and begin work at six o'clock in the morning and do not cease my work until after midnight... I do not get time to see our baby to exceed five minutes a day at the outside, and this includes morning and evening also. As to Catherine, except as to breakfast and dinner, she is living almost in a state of widowhood.[2]

Thus, throughout the scorching months of June, July, and early August this little band was fighting, or planning to fight, on an average of eighteen hours a day. The sun poured down its frightful heat upon the pavements that even before sunrise were as hot as a stove, and the humidity was dreadful. La Follette had almost collapsed on the Senate floor on the second day of June. The atmosphere of the Chamber, without direct outside ventilation, was stifling and strength-sapping. The latter part of the month the press reported that 'even free lemonade furnished in large quantities from the storeroom did not help matters much'; that 'Senators sneaked out into the cloakrooms to sit under electric fans,' and that the few spectators in the galleries 'kept their hats busy.' [3] A week later, with the thermometer at 88 and the humidity at 85, Senator Tillman protested that the Senate was deliberating 'near the devil's kitchen,' and the body adjourned early in the afternoon.[4] And with the Aldrich forces with a safe majority constantly alert to push the schedules through, the whole of the insurgent group had to be at their posts in the Senate constantly.

The greater part of the Aldrich forces subjected themselves

[1] *Memorial Addresses*, Beveridge. [2] Beveridge to Shaffer, May 21, 1909.
[3] *New York World*, June 22, 1909. [4] *Ibid.*, June 29, 1909.

to no such torture. Few made any pretense at studying or understanding the schedules. They were under orders and had no special responsibility. During the long days of enervating heat, when the insurgents as a whole were gasping in the Chamber, these care-free privates in the Aldrich camp were enjoying the ball games in the park, watching the flights of the Wright brothers at Fort Myer, or sailing on the river by day and attending the theater at night.[1] Leaving enough senators on guard, Aldrich and his lieutenants would take turns in retiring to their cooler offices for naps.

VIII

Meanwhile, President Taft was puzzled and in distress. He had pledged the party to a downward revision; had asked three of the insurgent senators to fight the bill submitted and force reductions; and had, within a month, received Beveridge and Dolliver with marked coolness. To accentuate the inconsistency or vacillation of his conduct, he had persisted in demanding a downward revision and in threatening a veto otherwise. He was reported as holding the veto club over Aldrich two weeks after Beveridge had noted the coldness of his reception.[2] If, for a moment, he had resented the intensity of the insurgents' battle and had introduced Beveridge and Dolliver into a chilly atmosphere, he was soon receiving them again with great cordiality and expressing his sympathy with their fight. Two days after the 'World' reported him persisting in his determination to veto an upward revision, Beveridge had written his wife: 'One o'clock. Just home. Saw Taft — he is with us.'[3] Two weeks later he wrote again: 'I dined with Taft — Mr. and Mrs. Taft, and Mrs. Moore, Mrs. Taft's sister, at 7.30. Then we sat on the porch, then went automobile riding until 10.45.'[4] But within two days something had happened to destroy Beveridge's faith in him, for he wrote that Taft was impossible. 'When both Aldrich and I think so, it is so. The Administration is doomed.'[5] The very next day Taft was reported as saying at Yale University that 'unless the Republican Party lives up to its promises and the expectations of the people, there is no doubt that it will be relegated to the position of a minority opposition.'[6] When on returning to the White House the next morning, he found a group of senators and representatives waiting anxiously to inquire if he had said and meant it, he was reported to have

[1] Beveridge to Miss Tarbell.   [2] *New York World*, June 10, 1909.
[3] June 12, 1909.   [4] To Mrs. Beveridge, June 28, 1909.
[5] To Mrs. Beveridge, June 30, 1909.   [6] *New York World*, July 1, 1909.

smiled and asked them to use their own intelligence. The 'New York World' was sure this would mean a lowering of the rates.[1]

Meanwhile, he had caused no little consternation in the Aldrich camp by proposing a corporation tax and the submission of a constitutional amendment permitting the levying of an income tax; and this had speedily resulted in a compromise with Aldrich providing for a corporation tax on condition that the income tax be dropped. This had followed a dinner to the majority members of the Senate Finance Committee at the White House.[2]

It was an unhappy summer for the good-natured Taft with a genius for misunderstanding moves on the political chessboard. Mrs. Taft was ill, and he was greatly worried. He suffered from the heat. Honestly intent on keeping the party's pledge, he hoped through geniality, conciliation, and persuasion to induce the reactionary element to make concessions. Never had the White House dining-room known so many political breakfasts, luncheons, and dinners; never so many political automobile rides in the darkness. The housekeeper at the White House and Mrs. Taft never knew half an hour before how many guests the President would have for luncheon.[3] Archie Butt, the military aide, who had served in the same capacity under Roosevelt, observed that where the latter reserved dinner invitations as 'rewards of merit,' Taft was using them as 'a means to an end.'[4] The geniality and kindliness of the President pervaded the social scene, and in manner the guests took on the qualities of the host, persuading him that he was making progress. The adoring Butt was sure, after one of the dinners, that his chief had 'swallowed the entire Finance Committee,' and that, 'instead of being duped by Aldrich and the other senators, he has chloroformed them.'[5]

Throughout the summer Taft maintained close relations with Aldrich and Payne, entertaining them at dinners, with long talks afterward on the South Portico, and driving with them through the country in the night. But he did not confine these attentions to the upward-revisionists, for the insurgent leaders rode with him too, and dined with him, and chatted with him on the portico overlooking the park. Publicly he insisted on reductions in the House and Senate rates, and this was the position he assumed to the insurgents. It is incredible that he took any other position with Aldrich and Lodge. Throughout he kept his temper, perhaps too well, and found some enjoyment in the social activities of the town. Most of the non-official social leaders had

[1] *New York World*, July 2, 1909. [2] Butt, *Taft and Roosevelt*, I, 123, 124, 133.
[3] Mrs. William Howard Taft, *Recollections of a Full Life*, 352–53.
[4] Butt, *Taft and Roosevelt*, I, 61. [5] Butt, *Taft and Roosevelt*, I, 124.

fled from the heat, and the families of many of the senators had been sent to the mountains and the sea, but there were many dinners. Walter Johnson was pitching at the ball park; the Wright brothers were making exhibition flights at Fort Myer, and the capital scene was not without its gayety. The 'Night Riders,' under the leadership of Alice Roosevelt Longworth, were sallying forth at a late hour in the night to awaken friends with howls and cat-calls until their houses were opened and re-freshments served.[1] The summer was not without its gayety while an epochal battle was being fought in the Capitol.

It was toward the last of June that Lodge, continuing his highly colored reports to Roosevelt, complained of the necessity of meeting a body of insurgents, 'while Beveridge, who has not discussed a single tariff question, has been talking incessantly on every point of procedure that came up.'[2] It is true that Bever-idge's special function was that of floor leader of the insurgent group, but he had discussed schedules many times, and all too effectively for Lodge's peace of mind; had proved from the record the party's pledge to the enactment of a measure vastly different from that which Lodge was favoring. A sick man when the struggle began, Beveridge had determined to confine himself to the floor leadership; but he had abandoned his intention and plunged into a battle which was all his own.

Here we must turn, for a moment, to his personal fights.

[1] Butt, *Taft and Roosevelt*, I, 83.
[2] *Roosevelt-Lodge Correspondence*, II, 337.

CHAPTER III

THE EPOCHAL DRAMA OF INSURGENCY: II

I

FROM the introduction of his tariff commission bill in the previous session, public sentiment rapidly had been crystallizing in its favor. The National Manufacturers' Association, committed to the proposition and led in this direction by several men of tireless energy, had placed upon the measure the approval of the industrial forces. In January a notable convention had met in Indianapolis to demand its enactment. The press generally was sympathetic. The President was openly friendly. Such was the situation when Beveridge reintroduced his bill, which was referred to the Finance Committee, dominated by Aldrich. It was a sound, scientifically conceived measure providing for a permanent commission of seven members. These were to be representatives of the manufacturing interests, one a lawyer familiar with customs and tariff laws, one experienced in the administration of these laws, one familiar with commercial conditions in competing countries, and another was to be an economist and statistician. The members were to serve for seven years.

The commission was to investigate the comparative costs of production, including labor and raw material, in this and other countries covered by the tariff, and to assemble such other facts as would be useful in fixing tariff rates. The results of these investigations were to be tabulated and presented to Congress for use in tariff-making. In pursuing its investigations the commission was to have the power to take testimony under oath and to require the production of books and papers for examination.

This represented the best thought on the subject and was patterned after the German system. It had been approved by those in the National Manufacturers' Association who were in charge of the agitation for a commission. These, with men familiar with the personnel of Congress whom they had employed, immediately began a close canvass of the Senate. James E. Watson, who had just finished his last term in the House, was engaged by the Association to assist in its passage. He had opened an office for the purpose; thence he sent men from the different States to their senators, and there he received their reports.[1] The reports were favorable. Even Senator Aldrich gave the impression of heartily favoring a commission, though he had ideas of his own regarding its character. Mr. Watson himself, representing the Association, found the Beveridge bill to have broader powers than he thought feasible.[2] The sagacious Aldrich saw at a glance that most of the men representing the Association would be satisfied with something much less real; and when he was called upon by leading members of the Association [3] and Mr. Watson, he was in a complying mood. He outlined a measure that would suit and his visitors apparently were satisfied.[4]

After that meeting the president of the Association had daily conferences with Aldrich and with Beveridge. Finding the latter insistent on the kind of commission provided in the bill, the manufacturer could think of no other reason than the pride of authorship. When Beveridge, astonished to find him satisfied with the 'compromise' of Aldrich, said he would rather take six years to get a real commission than to accept a counterfeit on the spot, the president of the Association was dumbfounded. Had not Aldrich assured him that under the Aldrich plan the President would appoint big business men, and not mere government clerks, who would be 'the servants of the business men'? Thinking it over, he went to Beveridge's home one night and talked it over until after midnight. Reluctantly the latter agreed that if the recognition of the principle could be had, together with a commission, however crude, the fight could be renewed later.

Arrangements were made for a conference in Aldrich's office, with Beveridge, to agree upon the wording of the provision to be written into the tariff act. When the two senators and the representative of the Association gathered about the table, Beveridge presented a draft for consideration. Aldrich took it in his own hands and read:

To secure information to assist the President in the discharge of the duties imposed upon him by this section (maximum and minimum) and information which will be useful to Congress in tariff legislation and to the officers of the Government in the administration of the customs laws, the President is hereby authorized to employ such persons as may be required to make thorough investigations and examinations into the production, commerce, and trade of the United States and foreign countries, and all conditions affecting the same; and such persons shall have the power to examine witnesses under oath and to compel the production of books and papers.

[1] Hearings of House Committee, H.R. 198, IV, 2571.   [2] *Ibid.*
[3] James W. Van Cleave and Ferdinand Schwedtman.
[4] Hearings of House Committee, H.R. 198.

Beveridge was not unmindful of the significance of substituting the word 'employ' for 'appoint,' but this was Aldrich's idea and it had been accepted by the manufacturers. Aldrich summoned his legal adviser, and after a two hours' conference he announced that 'under no circumstances would he stand for the incorporation in the bill' of the provision for examining witnesses under oath or of compelling the production of books and papers. To Beveridge this was vital, but since the manufacturers had surrendered without the firing of a shot, he turned to their representative for his opinion. He was satisfied; and so, disgusted, but feeling that something had been achieved, Beveridge agreed, and that very day the Finance Committee adopted and reported the bill to the Senate.[1] It was to pass the Senate and strange things were to happen afterward, as we shall see.

II

But this was not to be the end of Beveridge's special work. One night he took up the report of Herbert Knox Smith, Commissioner of Corporations, on the tobacco industry, published a short time before. As he proceeded, he found it one of the most fascinating and incredible studies of the daring, ruthless, almost romantic methods of Big Business he had ever read. Even after all these years it is as exciting as a tale of piracy. It was, indeed, a tale of piracy, in which the pirates took their booty with the American flag floating from the masthead of their ship and under the benevolent protection and encouragement of the American Government. He found that the American Tobacco Company, dominating the tobacco business, had been built up to colossal proportions through a series of combinations forced by merciless might.[2] In 1898, ten men of vast prestige and power in the financial world, not previously associated with the tobacco business, literally broke in through the formation of the Union Tobacco Company. These were of the group popularly known as the 'Standard Oil Group,' and included such financiers as Ryan, Brady, Whitney, Payne, Elkins, and Widener. Thereafter, through manipulation and ruthless methods, they forced themselves into the control of the tobacco business and became the 'tobacco kings.' By imitating the methods of the American Tobacco Company they forced Duke, the head of the latter, to buy out the Union and let them in. Thus these financiers, with no practical knowledge of the tobacco business, took their places

[1] Van Cleave to H. E. Miles, May 3, 1909; Hearings on Maintenance of a Lobby under S.R. 92, 1913, III, 2846–49.

[2] Report of the Commissioner of Corporations on the Tobacco Industry, 1909.

on the board of directors. Finally the Consolidated Tobacco Company, really a holding company, was formed. This was in 1901. There was nothing apparent on the surface to justify financiers so cautious in taking the plunge they did. And yet Beveridge read, in the graphic language of the Commissioner of Corporations:

On the basis of the rate of earnings of the American and Continental, prior to the formation of the Consolidated, it would scarcely have been possible to pay dividends on their preferred stocks and interest on the consolidated bonds. During the three years and four months following the organization of the Consolidated, however, the earnings of the two companies were sufficient to pay those charges and also leave a profit of fully $30,000,000 to the Consolidated on its investment of $30,-000,000 (part of the time $40,000,000).

The reason for this financial wizardry was not far to seek. In 1898, as a war revenue measure the tax on all forms of tobacco had been raised. In increasing the tax, Congress permitted the manufacturers to reduce the size of the packages sold to the people. Thus the manufacturers, instead of paying the tax out of their profits, passed it on to the consumer. In 1902, one year after the organization of the Consolidated, Congress had removed the tax, but the manufacturers were permitted to continue the use of the short packages. Thus the consumers continued to pay the tax, which went into the coffers of the trust instead of into the Treasury of the Nation. Even more was done at this time: the anti-coupon provision of the Dingley Act, designed as a blow at the methods of the trust, was considerately repealed.

With much discussion of the amount of revenue the pending tariff act would produce, Beveridge determined to make a fight for the payment into the Treasury of the tax collected by the trust for its own profit; for the reënactment of the anti-coupon clause as a blow at the trust.

He observed that licorice and its extracts had been monopolized by the American Tobacco Company, forcing the independent companies to buy from it. He noticed that the House bill of 1909 had put licorice on the free list and that Aldrich's committee had taken it off. Beveridge proposed that it should go back.

Such was the background of his action in mid-May when he rose to offer his bill as an amendment to the tariff act. He was primed for his task. For the first time in his life he had momentarily impaired his sight by poring over the figures. He presented his amendment with a brief explanation. 'All told,' he said to a startled Senate, 'the Government has lost $184,090,-557.43 in the last eight years; most of this has come out of the pockets of the people and gone into the pockets of the manufacturers. Why should the trust be authorized still to sell the short-weight packages, and yet be relieved of the tax to collect which these short-weight packages were provided? Why should the trust be permitted still to collect the tax from the people and put it into the trust's treasury to swell the trust's profits, instead of putting it into the Government's Treasury to swell the Government's revenues?'[1]

There was something sinister in this story; something not easily explained on the ground of ignorance on the part of the lawmakers responsible for the action of 1902. It hinted at the working arrangements between the rulers of the Nation and the powers of pillage. There was a disposition at first to pooh-pooh as the tale unfolded, and Aldrich was furious. 'You are wrong about this and you will find it out,' he said angrily. 'I have two other parks of artillery to unlimber,' Beveridge replied, with equal heat. 'The first I will put in action in four weeks. If that is not sufficient for you, I will put the other in a little later.'[2] The tobacco trust and its tools were alarmed, but they hoped to smother the amendment in silence, and for some time nothing more was said.

Then, a month later, Beveridge went into action with his heavy artillery.

Despite the stifling heat in the Chamber, with the senators going and coming, he had a good attendance most of the time and made a profound impression. Even the conservative Root was to congratulate him on making an impression he had seldom seen.[3] He began with the promise that his amendment would add as much as $20,000,000 annually to the revenue without an unreasonable increase in the tobacco tax. Instantly he challenged attention with this statement: 'There are members of the Finance Committee at this hour who do not know that the House increase of the tax on cigarettes has been stricken out of the bill by their own committee.' He recalled what had been done in repealing the tax in 1902. Then, another startling statement on the tenderness of the revenue-seekers toward the tobacco trust:

If we taxed tobacco at the same rate that England taxes tobacco, instead of getting $84,000,000 all told from that source of revenue, we would get $380,000,000. If we taxed tobacco at the rate France taxes

[1] *Congressional Record*, May 14, 1909.
[2] Beveridge to Miss Tarbell.
[3] Beveridge to Mrs. Beveridge, June 25, 1909.

tobacco, instead of getting $84,000,000 as we do now, we would get $436,585,000 of revenue every year from that single source of taxation.

Showing from the record that we were taxing tobacco at a lower rate than ever before in history except from 1890 to the Spanish War, he hurried on to his attack:

Not only did we take the tax off [in 1902], but we specifically reënacted the war-time package, so far as smoking tobacco and snuff were concerned. I do not ask for an explanation as to why it was done. It was, of course, unwittingly done; but not only did we do that friendly act to the American Tobacco Company, but we were kind to it in another particular. When we took off the tax we permitted the manufacturer, which at that time had become chiefly the American Tobacco Company, to have drawbacks from the Government for all portions of its tobacco upon which it had then paid the tax and had not yet sold. There probably never was a more generous transaction.

But that was not all that was done at that time. The Dingley Act had in it an anti-coupon provision which prevented the giving away of coupons in packages of tobacco. The use of this coupon system had been one of the chief instruments with which the American Tobacco Company had been able to crush out independent competitors.

La Follette, who was smiling broadly at the gentle sarcasm, interrupted: 'Does the Senator think that remarkable legislation in 1902 was an oversight?'

'I question no motives,' Beveridge answered; 'I put the facts before the country; that is all.'

But why, asked Senator Crawford, has Congress, in decreasing the tax, authorized the short-weight package?

'That was undoubtedly done,' said Beveridge, 'for the purpose of enabling them to get the tax out of the people, and more; and they are still getting it.... When six cents was added to the tax in 1898, that tax was added by the Trust to the price of the article. When the tax was taken off, the price that had been increased by the amount of the tax was not reduced. In other words, the tax was added to the price when the tax was put on, and was retained in the price when the tax was taken off — the tax we took off was added to the trust's profits.'

Again La Follette interrupted, making the argument a veritable catechism so simple that he who ran could read:

'Was not attention directed in the Senate when the bill was pending to the results of the legislation?'

'Not that I can find.'

'It is very remarkable, then,' said La Follette, with delicious malice, 'and I agree with the Senator that it calls for some explanation from somebody.'

'It does indeed,' Beveridge agreed.

But Aldrich, a member of the Finance Committee in 1902 who angrily had told Beveridge he was wrong a month before, offered no explanation. No one offered an explanation. All sat mute.

Passing next to the background of the tobacco trust development against which the legislation of 1902 had come, the speaker told the bizarre piratical story of the trust and the sudden interest of the 'Standard Oil Group' in the tobacco business. Seer-like qualities, these financiering geniuses possessed, he observed in tones heavily laden with sarcasm:

The Trust managers thought the tax would be taken off, and the tax was taken off. They wanted to keep up the price notwithstanding the tax was taken off, and they did keep it up. They wanted again to use that weapon — the coupon — that they had formerly used with such terrible effect that Governor Dingley put the anti-coupon provision in the law of 1897. They thought it would be repealed, and it was repealed. And far more important than that — they thought the tax would be repealed, and it was repealed.

Passing now to a denunciation of the methods of the trust in crushing competition, he hurried on to the charge that it maintained a corps of corruption lobbyists, resorting to bribery to effect legislation. No method too wicked in the crushing of competition, and 'no method of the corruption of legislators that this company, which is the chief beneficiary of the reduction of this tax, has not practiced.'

And no one rose to protest. Aldrich, who had told him a month before that he was wrong, was silent. Had not Beveridge promised, if challenged, to open with more artillery?

Yet [he continued], though it has made scores of millions at the expense of the Government Treasury, though our laws have played into its hands, though its monopolistic control is admitted, though the Nation now know of its practices, yet this amendment to take from the trust its profits represented by the reduced tax which it still collects and give it to the Government again — this amendment is resisted. It is astounding, it is incredible, but it is true.

This speech on the tobacco trust, Dolliver's devastating exposé of the cotton steals, La Follette's on the wool graft, Bristow's on sugar, and Cummins's on steel, constitute in the *ensemble* one of the most damning indictments of a governmental system ever heard in the Senate.

The people were learning about their government from the inside.

III

But Beveridge was unable to get a vote on his amendment at the conclusion of his speech; for it was still pending before a sub-committee named by Aldrich and it was whispered about that the report would be adverse. Going forth to meet that danger, Beveridge publicly announced that in that event he would make another speech 'that will make his previous utterances on the tobacco trust and its domination of legislation seem tame in comparison.' The most suave and resourceful of the trust's big lobbyists were busily engaged, but the white light of publicity was beating upon them; and, worse still, the eyes of the public were upon the sub-committee. Soon it was to report in favor of a much smaller increase in the tobacco tax than that provided in the Beveridge amendment, but the lobbyists and their senatorial allies were reluctant to concede even that, and two days before the final vote on the tariff there had been no vote on the amendment. 'Worked and worried all last night on tobacco,' Beveridge wrote Mrs. Beveridge. 'Waited all day — no vote.' [1] But it went in. Two days before, the insurgents had met in conference at the Beveridge apartment on Sixteenth Street and agreed that nothing more could be accomplished by fighting against a vote on the bill. They had fought their battle. They would agree to vote; and then continue their struggle in the conference of the two houses.[2]

As the vote was about to be taken, Beveridge, speaking for the insurgents, took the floor. 'Any promise is a serious thing,' he said solemnly, 'and never should be made except to be kept; but a promise to a people is sacred. It has been the pride and glory of the Republican Party that it keeps its promises; and its promises have always been the people's matured demand.... Our votes shall be cast in harmony with our party's pledge as voiced by our party's leader — the Nation's President.'

The effect on Aldrich has been variously described. While Beveridge was speaking, he sat gazing at the ceiling, with no manifestation of feeling.[3] But the real effect was more accurately described by the 'New York World.' [4] 'When it became apparent that Mr. Beveridge would vote against the bill,' it said, 'Mr. Aldrich seemed to lose his accustomed self-control, and began reading the opponents of the bill out of the party.'

His eyes flashing, and speaking with evident emotion, he rose to reply:

The Senator from Indiana does not speak for the Republican Party.

[1] July 8, 1909.   [2] *Indianapolis Star*, July 5, 1909.
[3] *Indianapolis Star*, July 9, 1909.   [4] July 9, 1909.

... The Republican Party is a party of majorities and the views of the majority in matters of legislation control party policies and control governmental policies. The bill which will be voted upon in a few minutes is a revision which carries out every pledge of the Republican Party.[1]

He sat down, without a blush; without a smile. He was thinking of the majority in the Senate; Beveridge, of the majority in the country.

The next election would determine that majority.

IV

The day after the bill passed the Senate, Beveridge wrote Shaffer of his state of mind and body. 'It has been a fight for conscience,' he said, 'distinctly a fight for the people. But it has nearly worn me out... I am going to Indianapolis today... will meet Catherine there and look over the house,[2] and then immediately go to Dublin, New Hampshire, for a rest. I shall return when the bill comes out of conference, remain here until its final passage, and then go back to Dublin and do nothing but sleep for two months.'[3]

The next day, when he reached Indianapolis 'very tired,' the situation was tense in Washington. Taft, on the golf links with the faithful Butt, was frankly distressed. He was finding a veto difficult because the bill carried some reductions in the Philippine tariff on which his heart was set. But the conferees, appointed in House and Senate, promised little for reductions in the conference. Aldrich, Hale, Burrows, Penrose in the Senate; Payne, Dalzell, Boutelle, Fordney in the House — it looked 'as if the Aldrich school and the stand-patters in the House were in absolute control.' That day Taft was thinking of encouraging the insurgents 'to rally and defeat the conference report';[4] but he was weakening on a veto. When he asked La Follette what should be done, the latter had reminded him of his promise to veto the measure if it emerged from the Senate no better than when it left the House. 'Instead of being a better bill, it is much worse,' La Follette said. 'Well, suppose I find I can't do that. What changes ought I to insist upon in conference?' he asked. And La Follette had delayed his homeward journey for a day to write out a complete statement covering every point.[5] It was the gossip of the capital that Aldrich was planning to drop the

---

[1] *Congressional Record*, July 8, 1909.
[2] The new house on Washington Boulevard.
[3] Beveridge to Shaffer, July 9, 1909.   [4] Butt, *Taft and Roosevelt*, I, 140.
[5] La Follette's *Autobiography*, 439.

CARTOON IN THE NEW YORK WORLD, JULY 10, 1909

tobacco amendment as a punitive measure against Beveridge.
The dictator had been convinced to the last that the insurgent
would not go the length of voting against the bill he had denounced.[1] Every train entering Washington was bearing the
representatives of the interests to the capital and the conferees
literally were overrun. They were on hand to hold what they
had — to hold more than they had dared to ask originally —
and, if possible, to get more.[2] To most observers it seemed that
the insurgents were in a position of isolation, deserted by the
party leaders and the President. The 'New York World' editorially expressed the prevailing feeling:

The Progressive Republicans realize:
That they have nothing to expect hereafter from Aldrich and the
Republican leaders.
That they must make their own fights without any assistance from
them.
That they cannot rely upon the President for comfort and consola-
tion as he gave them never a whisper during their long struggle to se-
cure genuine downward revision.
The die seems to be cast with them, and they must depend upon
their own States for approval and continuance in public life.[3]

But depending on Indiana did not seem to Beveridge a forlorn
hope. The press of the State, as a whole, had supported him,
and he found on reaching Indianapolis that arrangements had
been made to give him a public reception in Tomlinson's Hall —
the first time anything of the sort had ever been done in the
history of the Commonwealth. On two days' notice, the Taft
Club had arranged the meeting, and the reception, in numbers
and enthusiasm, was memorable and significant. Beveridge's
reiteration of his stand was greeted with lusty shouts,[4] and John
Callan O'Laughlin, writing from Washington to the 'Chicago
Tribune,' found that the reception had been an 'eye-opener' to
the politicians in the capital.[5]
A brief sojourn in Dublin, New Hampshire, and Beveridge
was back in the steaming town on the Potomac. Most of the insurgents were on the ground. Taft now was exerting himself,
though his political ineptitude was painfully apparent, in trying
to persuade the reactionaries to disgorge a portion of the loot.
After a conference with members of the House, he authorized a
public statement that he 'was committed to the principle of a
downward revision.'[6] The insurgents thought the statement

---

[1] *Indianapolis Star*, July 10, 1909.   [2] *New York World*, July 12, 1909.
[3] July 10, 1909.   [4] *Indianapolis Star*, July 13, 1909.
[5] Quoted in *Indianapolis Star*, July 15, 1909.
[6] *New York World*, July 17, 1909.

had come too late. It should have come two weeks before. And it is not without significance that the reactionaries were not concerned. They continued to consult him regularly, evidently on the best of terms. No longer did they fear a veto, and a deferential attitude with a few minor reductions would be pleasant and do no harm. Taft was sweetly persuasive and not too exacting; and then he was so naïve about it all. Had he not summoned Warren of Wyoming to a luncheon at the White House and sought his agreement to a reduction on wool and hides? As Warren left that day, he met Aldrich and Cannon entering the White House; and it was men like these who literally lived with the President in those sweltering days of the conference.[1] But he was doing the best he could with his equipment for such a struggle. He did scotch the plan of Aldrich to drop Beveridge's tobacco amendment entirely, and he labored with the reactionaries for a congressional authorization of a tariff commission. When told that Cannon was opposed to a commission because there was no assurance that a protectionist would be put upon it and that Taft might appoint political economists from the colleges, he lost his temper. 'I am not a damn fool!' he exploded, 'and I am a protectionist, but I don't propose to say this much to the Speaker, and if the bill is passed, I will appoint the commission without his assistance.[2] Again he could not understand the men with whom he had to deal. Why mere protection under a commission when under the existing system extortion had been easy? Even so, while plodding a bit clumsily in the dark, he was honestly trying to force the party to keep the faith. But a veto — that he had now definitely put aside.

Anxiously, if cynically, Beveridge was awaiting the result on his two contributions — the tobacco amendment and the tariff commission. Taft, to whom he had explained the tobacco tax in detail while night-riding with him in the environs of the capital,[3] took his stand grimly against the elimination of that amendment and the conferees were forced to content themselves with a mere emasculation. They struck out the prohibition of the coupon system on which the trust set much store, and they cut the tax proposed in half.

But the weak tariff commission provision they fell upon with a murderous axe. At the last minute the conferees struck out the words, 'information useful to Congress in tariff legislation'; and not content with that, they struck out the authorization 'to make thorough investigations and examinations into the production, commerce, and trade of the United States and foreign

[1] Butt, *Taft and Roosevelt*, I, 145.   [2] *Ibid.*, 154.
[3] Beveridge to Mrs. Beveridge, June 28, 1909.

countries and all conditions affecting the same.' Thus they left but a ghastly shell — a body without dignity, authority, or power.

Aldrich had prevailed.

V

After ten days in conference the bill emerged, in isolated places worse or better, but still a revision upward. The insurgents met and put the finished product under the microscope. Nowhere did they find cause for jubilation. It was proposed by some of the more bitter that they issue a statement of their position, march to the White House in a body, and ask the President to join them in a battle for lower rates.[1] But they were not long left in doubt as to his position. Soon one after another of them was being invited to the White House to luncheons in an effort to reconcile them to the report. All who were invited went — Beveridge, Dolliver, and Cummins — but none were moved. 'Bob,' said Dolliver to La Follette, 'I was invited up to the White House to a tariff breakfast. The muskmelon he served was not very good.'[2] There was no hope for the redemption of La Follette, and Clapp and Bristow were ignored. It was the day Beveridge had a two hours' conference with Taft that the former wrote his wife: 'The tariff gets more and more disgusting. Taft seems to be "falling down" — weakening badly. I don't want to vote against the President, yet I don't want to vote for the report.... It's a hard situation.'[3] Others momentarily were in doubt, but that was before they had completed their study of the bill coming from the conference. On the last day of July the insurgents met in Beveridge's committee room and found the measure so honeycombed with trickery and 'jokers' that ten of the number, then and there, determined to vote against the report. The night before, and on the morning of that day, Taft had been laboring with some of them. That was the day that Beveridge positively determined on his final stand and wrote his decision to his wife. 'I've made up my mind to do the right thing and leave the results to the people. If they don't see it, they are not worth my slaving my life out for them in politics, but then, we'll see.'[4]

The next afternoon, with the House considering the report, Beveridge, Dolliver, Cummins, Clapp, Knute Nelson, and Bristow created consternation in the reactionary ranks of that body by appearing on the floor to point out to individual members

[1] *New York World*, July 21, 1909. [2] La Follette's *Autobiography*, 451.
[3] July 25, 1909. [4] July 30, 1909.

the most notorious 'jokers' in the bill and to announce their caucus decision to vote against the report. This stiffened the opposition there, and the party whip [1] was busy scurrying over the floor to 'watch over his doubtful voters like a motherly hen.' [2]

And so, the lines drawn and held, the last scene of the drama opened in the Senate in the discussion of the report. The utter mockery of the tariff board provision was disclosed by Hale, who said explicitly that 'the attitude adopted by the conference absolutely excludes not only the idea of a tariff commission, but of any authority to be given to the President in any way to open the subject of investigation himself.... When this subject came up, I went over the whole situation with the President as to his scope of duties. I showed him that it was not intended to keep the subject open, but to confine him to the question of discrimination, discriminating duties and discriminating processes of other powers.... I have no fear the President will undertake to exceed that.'

Thus was Beveridge relieved of the necessity of showing that the idea of a tariff commission had been rejected. But it fell to him to point out what had been done to the tobacco tax and for the tobacco trust. Right mercilessly he did it. Only a few days before, the trust had made public its report for the year. It had paid interest on more than $105,000,000 of bonds, and dividends on more than $78,500,000 of preferred stock, and made a net profit of nearly $20,300,000, or more than fifty per cent profit on its $40,000,000 of common stock. Quoting the figures, Beveridge asked an explanation for the reduction of the tax he had proposed.

'Not only did the conference committee decrease the amount of taxes that I proposed,' he said, 'but, in addition, actually reduced once more the weight of the package.... In plain words, it took every dollar of this new tax off the shoulders of the trust, where I had placed it, and put it on the shoulders of the people.'

And then, concluding: 'I demand that these outrages be remedied and remedied speedily. I demand that the new short-weight packages which the conference committee provided shall be abolished.... I demand that the anti-coupon provision of the Dingley law, which Congress without debate repealed in 1902, which the Senate passed again at its last session, but which the conference committee struck out, shall again be enacted.'

Thus did the insurgents go down fighting — with undiminished vigor to the last. The prolonged battle in the hot and humid atmosphere, with little rest or sleep and no relaxation,

[1] John Wilbur Dwight, Representative from New York.
[2] *New York World*, Aug. 1, 1909.

had left its imprint on them all. Some were much thinner, and haggard; some were sick; and one had written his own death warrant. From the orators of the group, Beveridge, Dolliver, and La Follette, had come speeches challenging comparison with the most powerful ever heard in the Chamber: they had done something to lift the standard of public service and to revive faith in the sincerity and courage of public men. Not one who did not know that he had taken his political life into his hands, and not one cared. If ever men fought in an exaltation of spirit, this gallant, brilliant group fought thus, and worn, weary, but happy, they hurried from the blistering pavements of the capital to their homes in the proud consciousness of duty nobly and bravely done.

VI

But the President was happy too. He had forced a few concessions and these relieved him of the necessity of carrying out his veto threat. Although the major portion of the press denounced the measure as iniquitous, he somehow had persuaded himself that the people would be content. His cup of happiness ran over on the night he learned he had prevailed in his plea for a reduction of the proposed tax on gloves. He received the news at the home of friends, and seemed for a moment unbelieving. 'He sat perfectly silent, staring incredulously at the paper before him.' Then the attractive smile the country knew spread over his face, and he said, 'Well, good friends, this makes me very happy.' His host took him by the hand in congratulations, and his hostess went over and kissed him.[1]

It was his moment of triumph — his last during the remainder of his term. Convinced of a triumph, and happy in what he thought a victory, he gave the last of the famous political dinners of that memorable session. About the board were the real victors who had made him a victim, unknown to himself. There was Aldrich, never more the head of the table; and there was Cannon, with Hale, Lodge, Penrose, Burrows, McCumber, Crane, Root, Wickersham, and Knox. Conspicuously absent were those whose names were then on the tongues of the people — Dolliver, Beveridge, La Follette, Clapp, Bristow, Cummins, and the rest of the little band of rebels. It was a merry dinner, with its sherry, hock and water and champagne. Butt had been asked by the President to get some 'extra fine wine,' and when an effort was made to confine the most exquisite to Root, Hale, Cannon, and Wickersham with exacting tastes, Nick Longworth

[1] Butt, *Taft and Roosevelt*, I, 162.

saw the trick and added to the merriment by protesting that two kinds were being served and inferior brands were being palmed off on the unsuspecting.[1] Strangely enough, Taft, smiling and happy, called it a 'harmony dinner'; and while the witticisms passed and the glasses clicked, the best orators of the party were speeding westward to arouse the people, already in revolt.

[1] Butt, *Taft and Roosevelt*, I, 169.

CHAPTER IV

AFTER THE BATTLE

I

WITH the adjournment, Beveridge joined Mrs. Beveridge at a summer home in Dublin, New Hampshire, and there he lingered until in late September resting and trying to forget politics. Sleeping, reading, and walking consumed his time. Many hours he spent wandering with Mrs. Beveridge through the woods, or rowing — his favorite exercise. This open-air existence soon restored his depleted strength, and it was a happy vacation, free from worry; for he was convinced from all he heard and observed that the sentiment of the country, and the greater portion of the party, would justify the action of himself and his little group. Contrary to his custom, he devoted but little time to literary work, but he accepted the invitation of the 'Saturday Evening Post' to prepare an article setting forth the progressive point of view on the tariff fight:

The insurgents sought to keep faith with the people. 'They felt that the promissory note of their party should be redeemed at a hundred cents on the dollar. They felt, too, that these promises were based on justice. So that, from the very beginning, the revision of the tariff presented itself to them as a moral question. And the deeper they went into it, the plainer it became.... They considered the business side of it as well — the common sense and practicability of it. And so the insurgents fought for moderation.... All of them feel that protection has become the settled policy of the Nation. But because they wanted protection beyond attack, the insurgents did fight for many reductions and against any such increases as seemed to them unnecessary and wrongful.[1]

This article met with the hearty approval of the insurgent group, and Senator Cummins wrote from Iowa:

I have read your article in the last 'Saturday Evening Post' and I say sincerely that while you have done many good things you have done nothing better than this article. You are a born writer, and I am coming gradually to believe that as strong as you are in the work of the Senate, you are stronger as an author, and I am gradually also becoming reconciled to your foolish resolution to give up public life at the end of your next term and spend the remainder of your days covering good white paper with sound and instructive thought.

The very day I read the article I was playing golf with the Attorney-

[1] *Saturday Evening Post*, Oct. 16, 1909.

General of Iowa, who is a good deal of a man and close enough to take the same liberties with me that you do, and he said: 'Have you read Beveridge's article in the "Saturday Evening Post"?' I answered, 'Yes, what do you think of it?' He replied, 'I hope it won't pain you too much when I say that it is altogether the best thing that has appeared on the subject. It puts the case so plainly and simply that those of us who know nothing of the subject can understand it.' I think it will strike everyone in about the same way, so I congratulate you heartily upon a successful and effective blow planted squarely on the Aldrich jaw.[1]

Meanwhile, President Taft at his summer home at Beverly was constantly growing more belligerently hostile to the progressives and making no effort to conceal his feelings. Scarcely had he reached his summer place when he dined at the home of Henry C. Frick, the steel magnate, whose industry had been so handsomely treated in the tariff act. Even so faithful a friend as Archie Butt, his military aide, thought the time not politically auspicious for such social intimacy. And Taft was becoming a militant supporter of Ballinger, his Secretary of the Interior, in the bitter feud with Gifford Pinchot growing out of the manifest purpose of the Cabinet member to wreck the conservation policy of Pinchot and Roosevelt. When Walter Fisher, of Chicago, called to remonstrate with him for supporting Ballinger against Pinchot, the President flew into a rage and raised his voice in anger.[2] When, a few days later, Ballinger reached Beverly 'laden with portfolios' bearing on the Pinchot controversy, Butt became uneasy. He thought 'it would be a pity to cut off Pinchot in the work he is doing,' but found Taft 'not overindulgent toward reformers.' That which alarmed Butt most in the prospect of the dismissal of Pinchot was the certainty of the resentment of Roosevelt.[3]

Then, emerging into the open, Taft began the fatal journey to Winona. He commenced his blundering in Boston, where he lavished praise on Aldrich. Later he found occasion to give the presidential blessing to the notoriously reactionary Senator Tom Carter. Meeting Cannon on the way, he posed with him for photographs, and whenever the two spoke together, conveyed the impression that he admired the Speaker greatly; though privately he always spoke of him with contempt. Endorsing the Roosevelt policies in words, in every State he entered he allowed himself to be monopolized by the reactionary element. In the case of Cannon he was permitting his geniality to betray him; but his belief in Aldrich was sincere. When a storm of protest

[1] Cummins to Beveridge, Oct. 19, 1909.
[2] *Letters of Archie Butt*, I, 189.   [3] *Ibid.*, I, 193.

from progressive sections greeted his praise of the dictator of the Senate, he admitted privately that he had made a 'political mistake,' but added that he 'had the satisfaction of knowing that I said what I believed.' [1] The distressed Butt, struggling between his devotion to both Taft and Roosevelt, concluded that the President had 'been largely won over by Aldrich.' [2]

But the supreme blunder was reserved for the speech at Winona, Minnesota, where Taft had planned to help Representative Tawney, whose support of the tariff had met with the vociferous disapproval of his constituency. It was here that he deliberately cut himself off from the insurgents, and, in so far as his speech could effect it, practically stamped them as poor party men. After a labored defense and explanation of the tariff act, he concluded:

> When I would say without hesitation that this is the best tariff bill that the Republican Party has ever passed, and therefore the best tariff bill that has been passed at all, I do not feel that I could have reconciled any other course to my conscience than that of signing the bill.[3]

Out over the country in their various homes the insurgent senators, some of whom had entered the fight against the bill on the solicitation of Mr. Taft, read this speech with utter amazement, and even, in the case of Beveridge, with incredulity. This is clear in their correspondence, for they were in communication with one another throughout the summer and autumn. Their reactions to the speech and to the attitude of the people is best shown in these letters. Bristow had vigorously challenged Taft's Winona speech in an interview given the 'Kansas City Star.'

Clapp to Beveridge, Aug. 17, 1909
Matters seem to be in fine shape in Minnesota. Am out at my camp near Pine City. They wanted to get up a demonstration at St. Paul and may yet, although I feel that it would not be the best thing to do, as it would sort of accentuate the position taken by Mr. ——. From all I can hear, the general sentiment is with us. Am glad to learn that matters look well in Indiana.

Cummins to Beveridge, Aug. 24, 1909
Everything is going quietly here, and I find that the great majority of the people are in harmony with what I did in respect to the tariff bill.

Beveridge to Bristow, Sept. 5, 1909
I am getting the same kind of reports [good ones] from some of the

[1] *Letters of Archie Butt*, I, 220.   [2] *Ibid.*, I, 198.
[3] Winona speech, Sept. 17, 1909; Senate Doc. 164, 61st Cong., 2d Ses.

most substantial people of the country who spend their summers in this place [Dublin]. I am astonished, and a good deal puzzled at the strength and persistence of popular opinion, and especially at the individual opinion of strong men whom I might reasonably expect to be the other way.

Cummins to Beveridge, Sept. 13, 1909

It is very plain that the air of New Hampshire is lifting up your spirits to the point, which every man must reach before he fights well. ... I have not had a moment's vacation in the ordinary sense of the word, and when I wrote you it seemed to me that three or four days of loafing on a steamboat would be a good preparation for the work of the fall and winter. I have done nothing as yet except to talk with the people who wanted to see me, try to keep up with my correspondence (which is voluminous as it is gratifying), and play golf. I omit from this recital some very painful hours with the dentist.

I began a series of speeches on Wednesday and I suppose for three weeks I will be in the old harness. Bristow is whacking away at the tariff in Kansas.... Clapp is as cocky as ever in the serene knowledge that nine out of ten of his constituents are with him. La Follette is reading his roll calls. Borah is stripping himself for a real progressive fight. Dolliver is nursing his wrath; and the rest, the Lord knows what they are doing or thinking.

I intend to be in Washington about November 10th with a corporation regulation program; but I feel in my bones that I will be turned down by the closest friends and advisers of the President, who are just now consulting upon how not to do it in all the dialects of equivocation and uncertainty.

From the brilliant Dolliver came a characteristic letter referring to his physical collapse, due to the superhuman labors of the session:

Dolliver to Beveridge, Sept. 14, 1909

Fact is that I was about played out when I first came home, and have been for a month trying to get even with the doctors by getting well.... I can't tell you how much I enjoyed your letter. Should like a good long talk in our shirt-sleeves at Meade's hotel. But you are wrong about what is going on in the country. If we had had a direct line from the skies we could not have done a better job for ourselves than we did when we stood on our convictions against all comers, including the Big Chief. The penalty of doing right exists only in the imaginations of grafters and time-servers. If you never see the inside of the Senate Chamber again, the last three months of your labors will make your life notable and famous when biographies are written....

It is an incredible thing that as sensible a man as Taft should start out by tying the Aldrich millstone about his neck and traveling like a pedlar of damaged goods. 'Leader of the Senate' — we will jar that myth in the next three years. Wait for results, my boy. We will see how the public will take to a tariff revision made by its intimate friends and certified up by a total stranger.

Everything is O.K. out here. No voices heard against our position except a few old-timers whose intellectual advancement is that of twenty years ago. I want you to go into the bank question. Master it as you did the tobacco question, and we will see a pretty spectacle in the Senate. We have got to fight. They can't hurt you in Indiana without hurting the party. We don't need money to fight them. We will go in with the common weapons of justice and common sense and make a new era in national life. With Pinchot knocked out and Aldrich put in command, I think you can hear a lion roar in East Africa.

I have not been much in evidence since I came home... but I never saw so clearly my duty and yours, and our opportunity. I am in a happy frame of mind. I would give more for one more session in the old Senate with the right to think for myself, speak my own thoughts, and hit the big heads than to have a guaranteed term of twenty years more as the servant of a syndicate of played-out New England politicians. Mrs. Dolliver and the children are all well. All join in love to you and Mrs. Beveridge and the baby. With a thousand cheerful and blessed memories of our three beautiful months, I am, sincerely...

Bristow to Beveridge, Sept. 20, 1909

I enclose you a clipping from the 'Kansas City Star' which was published by Kansas City papers Sunday morning.[1] I am free to say that I am very much surprised at Taft's attitude. He seems to have surrendered absolutely to Aldrich. There is but one course for me to take, and that is to fight it out along the lines outlined; first, because I know it is right; and second, because it is representing accurately the sentiments of the majority of the people who elected me to the Senate.

Beveridge to Bristow, Sept. 25, 1909

Just got your letter and your interview. You strike straight from the shoulder. I can't believe that our friend, the President, ever said what he is reported to have said in Winona. I was in the East at the time his speech was printed. It raised an awful howl in New York and Philadelphia, and little else was talked about on the trains. I am just as sorry as I can be, sorry not for us, but for the general effect.

Let me know your observations since the speech was made — the exact facts, whatever they are, good or bad. After all, nothing but facts — the truth — cuts any ice; and you are a perfect Vidocq when it comes to the facts.

Bristow to Beveridge, Sept. 27, 1909

I have yours of the 25th and will write you frankly my views. The situation, however, must rest more on judgment than facts. Last week I made four speeches in four different counties in Kansas, to audiences

[1] This clipping was a vigorous attack on Taft and Aldrich, apropos of the rubber schedule.

varying from six hundred to thirty-five hundred. Previous to the Taft Winona speech I had probably made twenty or twenty-five speeches in different parts of our State. Now I am writing you confidentially and frankly. Before the Taft speech there was marked enthusiasm and an overwhelming sentiment. Since the Taft speech I have not noticed any change in the sentiment, but there is not the enthusiasm there was before — that is, it is not so general. In the audiences there will be a number who will vigorously applaud, and who are more intense in their earnestness, but the rank and file, while sympathetic and earnestly attentive, seem to have a rather depressed expression.

I have inquired of the best informed men in each community where I go as to the effect of Taft's speech on the insurgent sentiment, and the universal reply is that it will not change a vote or in any way affect the various communities. Yet I have noticed two marked results following the speech: the old Machine crowd in this State, the corporation gang have taken courage.... That is one result. The second is that there is developing a most bitter and relentless hostility to Taft himself. This has been developing ever since Taft signed the tariff bill. Half the congratulations I have received have been coupled with regret as to Taft's course, or a pronounced criticism. Since his speech, the letters I receive — and I receive a good many — are intolerant in their criticisms of Taft.... If the election of President were to be held again this year, Bryan would carry Kansas by 60,000 over Taft. There is no doubt of that. Taft's majority last year was 36,000....

Now I have given you the facts, as nearly as I have been able to secure them. My judgment is that Aldrich has completely captured Taft. Aldrich is determined to crush and destroy the insurgent senators. It is the program he has outlined and he will use the Taft Administration at his will until after the next congressional election when there will be an overwhelming Democratic victory unless Taft changes his course. Then the President may be forcibly impressed by the fact that he has wrecked his Administration, or is wrecking it.

As I wrote you before, there is just one thing for us to do and that is to fight. Taft makes our fight a great deal harder. Everything was our way until he took the Aldrich side with such force, and my opinion is that in Indiana you will find him strengthening and encouraging the old gang that the people so completely put out of business last year. The President's attitude may make it hard for you because it will be hard on the party; but I trust that you will be able to win in spite of that fact. If you should lose, remember that you are still young, and you had better lose fighting valiantly for what the party ought to stand for than to lose going along and being one of the betrayers of the party and the faith of the people.

Cummins to Beveridge, Oct. 1, 1909

The situation in Iowa is just as I would have it. Our crowd is always in danger when things are quiet, and when they are stirred up they can win hands down. Taft's speech at Winona (and especially his break in Boston) has made an issue in this State which we could not ignore if we wanted to, and we don't want to. We shall find out in the next State Convention whether the Republicans of Iowa support Dolliver and myself or Aldrich and his crowd. I am as serene as a May morning in regard to the outcome.

I am speaking every day or two, and the way the people receive me is so gratifying that I cannot describe it, lest I be accused of overweening vanity. As yet I am skirting around the edges of the vital public problems, for I am talking to Old Settlers' meetings and the like. I am to follow Cannon next week at one of these, and if I know the man as well as I think I do, he will give me an opportunity to kick up a row, which I will do as promptly and effectively as possible.

... Bristow has suggested, and I am in hearty concurrence with him, that a few of us ought to get together about the 20th of October in Chicago, to look over the ground and see where we are. Can you make your arrangements to be there about that time?

Beveridge to Cummins, Oct. 7, 1909
Answering your bully letter of Oct. 1st: it delights me because it shows you to be in splendid fighting fettle, and that means in superb health. I find things in surprising good shape here. The wider and more complete the reports I get, the better the situation appears.

Your interview is a trumpet blast. Truth about it is this whole thing is a part of a movement to get American business, and indeed, American life, down to a plain simple honest basis.

There isn't any possible question that the important point on which we want to concentrate is the tariff commission. We have the country back of us on that particular question.

About the meeting in Chicago, I doubt the strategic wisdom. As a matter of fact what could the meeting be for? As I look at it, it would only attract attention, get a lot of sensational stuff printed about us, and come to nothing. It would be all right if it did come to something — in that event the more publicity the better; but if it can come to nothing at all, every syllable of publicity would hurt.

Thus through the summer and autumn the insurgents maintained their contacts. The country seethed with insurgency, but even these men were sometimes doubtful, as the letters show; and the reactionaries were so blind to the realities that they were jubilant. Such was the situation when Congress met in December.

II

'Saw Taft yesterday — looked tired and puzzled. Very nice to me. Think all will be well in that quarter — but you never can tell.' Thus Beveridge wrote his wife after his arrival in Washington for the session.[1]

Not only was Taft puzzled; he must have felt harassed and deeply distressed by the accumulating frictions within the party.

[1] Dec. 13, 1909.

The stubborn refusal of Pinchot to acquiesce in the wrecking of the Rooseveltian policy of conservation was annoying, and Roosevelt would soon be home again. And the big men of the business world who knew just what they wanted were not letting him forget their wishes. Already they were assuming a sort of domination over him that ruffled his dignity and disturbed his sense of proportion. Aldrich, more than ever contemptuous of the 'mob,' was riding rather hard. Thus, in December, when at his brother's in New York City, the President was informed that Aldrich was in the city and anxious to see him. 'Tell him to come here,' said Taft. 'That is not what he wants,' replied his brother. 'He is at the home of J. Pierpont Morgan and they are having a conference there and they want you to come to it if possible.' It was an astounding piece of impertinence. The President of the United States summoned like an underling to wait upon Mr. Morgan at the beck of Mr. Aldrich! Taft rebelled. 'Telephone Aldrich that if Morgan wants to see me he can come to Washington. Aldrich ought to know that what he suggests is impossible. There is just one place where men like Morgan can see me, and that is in Washington.' And it was in Washington that Morgan saw him — immediately.

When Taft returned to the capital at eight o'clock the next morning, he found Morgan waiting patiently in the Red Room of the White House. He had reached the White House at seven, long before Washington makes its bow to the sun. Thus the newspapers missed an interesting story.[1]

There was to be some railroad legislation that session and hell was popping. The insurgents would be 'unreasonable' to the railroads too, and the reactionaries were lining up their forces. The 'Leader of the Senate' and Mr. Morgan had consulted and agreed, but the President could not be entirely ignored. The faithful Butt, noting the twists and turns of intrigue, was worried. 'The fact that strikes me as inauspicious is that Senator Aldrich was back of the interview. I feel that the Rhode Islander is the most sinister influence around the President. The President thinks he has captured Aldrich and can make him do anything he wants, but I fear it is the case of the wolf in sheep's clothing.'[2]

As the irrepressible issue of the Pinchot-Ballinger controversy deepened, Taft became more despondent; and finally determined to act and take the consequences. Pinchot had written a letter to Dolliver which amounted to an attack on the Administration. Early in January, Taft announced that he would not exercise that day, but would 'wrestle with Pinchot.' He was haggard,

[1] *Letters of Archie Butt*, I, 244.   [2] *Ibid.*

and during that day of wrestling he seemed ill to Butt, who observed him closely. That afternoon he dismissed the Chief Forester — the bosom friend of Roosevelt — and gave his enemies more ammunition.[1] He had been advised by Root, who at first opposed a dismissal, that the letter to Dolliver made it necessary for the President to act. He hoped that when Roosevelt saw all the correspondence he would be satisfied.[2]

Meanwhile, Henry Cabot Lodge was working on the big hunter, bombarding him with letters. The day of the dismissal of Pinchot, Lodge wrote Roosevelt, ascribing it to the Dolliver letter, and, with a fine Machiavellian touch, regretting that Pinchot had not realized that his 'first duty was to the great service he had built up,' and had permitted the 'muckraking magazines' to involve him in an assault on Ballinger.[3] A week later, Lodge was warning Roosevelt that newspaper men would meet him at Khartoum and try to arouse his indignation against Taft. Of course Roosevelt should say nothing about American politics until he reached home.[4] Pinchot, he wrote, was reported to be planning to meet Roosevelt in Europe, which would be most unfortunate, and certainly would cause 'misapprehension.'[5] When, about that time, Lodge heard from the man in Africa that a news agency had sent a runner to his camp with a cable on the dismissal, the former President had written that he 'sincerely hoped it was not true.'[6] That was disquieting enough; but the statement in a later letter, that 'if Gifford Pinchot comes abroad I shall certainly see him as intimately as though nothing has happened,' was positively alarming. But it was still another letter, from Rome, that put the fear of the Lord into the reactionaries. Of course, Roosevelt wrote, he would not make a general appeal in the congressional campaign. Clearly 'the tariff issue was not met as it was necessary to meet it,' and it seemed probable that it never could be met properly through the methods of the Cannons, Paynes, Dalzells, and Aldriches. Was Roosevelt going into the Beveridge camp on the tariff commission?[7]

This was bad; but there was worse: 'I don't agree with you about not seeing Pinchot. I am delighted to see him. The only man I invited to see me was Root, and Root said he could not come; but when Pinchot said he wanted to see me, I said I would be more than delighted.'[8] The closer he was getting to the situation, the more threatening Roosevelt's shadow became.

Then, from Porto Maurizio, came another letter that gave a critical aspect to the prospects. 'You do not need to be told that

[1] *Letters of Archie Butt*, I, 253.   [2] *Ibid.*, I, 258.
[3] *Roosevelt-Lodge Correspondence*, II, 356.   [4] *Ibid.*, II, 357.   [5] *Ibid.*
[6] *Ibid.*, II, 360.   [7] *Ibid.*, II, 365–66.   [8] *Ibid.*

Taft was nominated solely on my assurance to the Western people especially, but almost as much to the people of the East, that
he would carry out my work unbroken; not (as he has done)
merely working for somewhat the same objects in a totally different spirit, and with totally different results, but exactly along
my lines with all his heart and strength.' How, then, could he
go into a 'wholesale campaign for the Administration'? Had
not the party leaders 'shown with the utmost possible distinct-
ness that, while they welcome my help in carrying an election,
they are cynically indifferent and contemptuously hostile to
doing themselves anything after the election which would show
the slightest regard to what I have promised'? [1] The trouble was
with the leadership, he continued. Aldrich had 'no real following
whatever among the people at large, not even in his own State.'
The fact was, he thought that the Aldrich-Cannon type of leadership did not represent 'ten per cent of the rank and file of the
party's voting strength.'

By this time, Lodge, finding that he had been found out, fell
back on pleading. Of course the party would be defeated. But
Roosevelt, surely, would say a word for it — tell the people that
'it is the best instrument for carrying out the policies you have
at heart.' [2] And, harping on the same note later: 'All I want you
to say, all I think it would be wise for you to say, is that you
want the Republican Party to win.' [3]

But he got no promise — and Roosevelt would soon be home.

III

Meanwhile, Taft, utterly under the spell of Aldrich, was constantly making matters worse. His Attorney-General, George
W. Wickersham, made a speech in Chicago belaboring the insurgents, and Dolliver and La Follette had replied in the Senate,
and with deadly effect. The Wickersham speech had been gone
over with the President and it was accepted as his expression.
Beveridge thought the La Follette reply 'the ablest thing he has
ever done.' [4] The reason for the fierceness of the attacks by the
two insurgents appears in Beveridge's letter to Shaw:

Wickersham's speech, which voices the real sentiments of the Administration, has made things much worse than ever, and I haven't
the slightest doubt Dolliver is going after him horse, foot, dragoons,
mounted batteries, and heavy artillery. The unfortunate thing about
it is that Wickersham's speech was carefully prepared, read over and
O.K.'d by the President, and yet on the very night of its delivery, the

---

[1] *Roosevelt-Lodge Correspondence*, II, 367–72.   [2] *Ibid.*, II, 374–75.
[3] *Ibid.*, II, 377.   [4] Beveridge to Shaw, April 14, 1910.

President pats us on the head at the same time Wickersham, for the President, is knocking our heads off.[1]

All the while, though only a part of it was known at the time, Taft was consorting with the most deadly enemies of the insurgents. Beveridge knew that the President had two of his most powerful enemies in Indiana for lunch and conferred with them for hours. 'It was all about my candidacy,' he wrote Mrs. Beveridge.[2] Months before, while walking with Butt and Frank B. Kellogg, the latter had urged Taft to use the patronage of both House and Senate to force his renomination, and patronage was being withheld from the insurgents with a few exceptions.[3]

IV

Thus, thanks to the presence of Archie Butt, who recorded the incident the day it occurred, we have a strange side-light on presidential politics. It was in March — a raw windy month in Washington. Taft, on entering his car, had directed that it be driven to the home of Senator Aldrich. Knowing that something interesting was 'on the tapis,' Butt, instead of having the car driven by the usual route, 'directed the chauffeur in a low voice to go out the unfrequented thoroughfare of Nineteenth Street,' and as they reached 'byways and side streets' he gave directions until they finally reached Fourteenth Street. It had turned cold and the wind was blowing a gale. Aldrich, who joined the party at his home, complained of the cold and proposed that the top of the open car be put up. Instead, one of the President's sweaters was fished out for him, and Butt observed, with mirth, that 'it would encircle his body twice.'

Butt found that Taft had many 'important things to say to Aldrich.' He admitted that in Aldrich's absence everything had gone wrong, and 'begged him to remain in Washington as much as possible until his bills had passed.' But the special subject he wished to discuss was his plan 'to defeat the Cummins and Dolliver faction in the next election in Iowa.' He had had Hepburn and 'some of the other stalwarts, as he called the old Allison Republicans, to dinner.' These had concluded that with some outside financial aid they could cause the insurgent senators serious trouble. Taft had not favored the participation of National Chairman Hitchcock in the fight, since he felt the work should be done within the State. Aldrich agreed he was right, and promised he 'would see what money could be raised

[1] Beveridge to Shaw, April 11, 1910.   [2] June 29, 1910.
[3] *Letters of Archie Butt*, I, 260.

among certain friends of his to help Hepburn on the ground that it would be a campaign of education.' Money, he was sure, could be raised by private subscription. He would contribute himself; and Taft added that he also would contribute his share.

The idea appealed strongly to Aldrich, who insisted that Dolliver, Cummins, and Beveridge should not go unscathed for their independence. 'Senator Aldrich agreed with the President that Senator Beveridge, while apparently acting with the Administration, was organizing the insurgent element for its most effective operations,' and Aldrich urged Taft to withhold as much patronage as possible from these three, 'for the sooner they are made to quit the party counsels, the better it would be for the party.' [1]

Two days later, the President took another ride, this time with Cannon as his guest, wrapped up, as Aldrich had been, in the President's enormous sweater. The discussion was on the postal savings bank bill which important banking interests were attempting to influence, with the insurgents seeking to eliminate the 'jokers.' Cannon was 'damned tired of this everlasting yielding to the popular outcry against wealth,' and had so much contempt for Taft's enemies that he would give him his support. [2]

Thus, throughout the winter, spring, and early summer, Taft, while hoping for the approval of Roosevelt on his return, was going over bag and baggage to the reactionary elements in the party. His resentment of the insurgents who had begun their fight at his request was becoming more and more bitter. When Franklin MacVeagh, his Secretary of the Treasury, had the temerity to speak to him in the interest of Beveridge's forthcoming candidacy for reëlection, he was outraged. He began to feel that MacVeagh himself was 'tinged with the insurgent doctrines.' When MacVeagh told of his desire to assist as much as possible in Indiana, Taft replied that he 'would do anything to aid the Republicans in Indiana but... do nothing for Beveridge.' Besides, if he did anything for Beveridge, 'Watson, Cannon, and their friends will do nothing to aid me.' [3]

Thus, so far as Beveridge was concerned, he was outside the Administration breastworks; and the President had staked his political future on the support of the Aldrich group.

V

This session was to witness the last act of the long-drawn-out drama of statehood for Arizona and New Mexico. Beveridge had

[1] *Letters of Archie Butt*, I, 299-301. [2] *Ibid.*, I, 301-03.
[3] *Ibid.*, I, 355-56.

fought separate statehood for years, but the Republicans had pledged themselves to it in their platform of 1908; the people of the Territories had voted against joint statehood; and accepting the inevitable, Beveridge determined to push through a statehood bill free from 'jokers' against public interest. The House bill he found 'unspeakably bad' in some respects. On the land features of his own bill he put to work four experts, detailed from the Reclamation Service, the Department of the Interior, and the Department of Justice.[1] In this he worked in complete accord with the Administration. Frequently he saw Taft, and the semblance of good relations was preserved, but it was Frank Hitchcock who gave him the most powerful support in Administration circles.[2] He drew the bill in its final form embodying the agreement between the President and the committee. But because of its protective features the bill encountered the opposition of some leaders and he was forced to fight for its passage, just as he previously had fought for joint statehood. Thus in the end his was the triumph, after all, and he was invited to Arizona to receive the applause of the people. Taft made a ceremony of the signing of the bill, and his first act on affixing his signature was to turn to Beveridge with congratulations.[3]

But that was to be his last friendly gesture for a while. In the statehood matter he had needed the Indianian; thereafter he felt he would need him no more. Beveridge was content with the approbation of the people, expressed in a formal statement by Delegate Cameron of Arizona: 'Beveridge has treated us white in this matter and the people of Arizona owe him a debt of gratitude.'[4]

The session also brought in the Child Labor Report of a thousand pages with exhibits that Beveridge thought 'simply awful,' but he had to indulge Senator Smoot with a row over its printing for distribution.[5]

But his most important work, as chairman of the Committee on Territories, was in framing a bill for a more adequate civil government in Alaska. In this, too, his views coincided with those of the President. He wrote his civil government bill in Indianapolis during the Christmas holidays.[6] It was to be stoutly opposed because it provided for the appointment instead of the election of the legislative council. The scheme provided

[1] Beveridge to Shaffer, Jan. 25, 1910.
[2] Beveridge to Sims Ely, June 20, 1910.
[3] *Indianapolis Star*, June 21, 1910.
[4] *Ibid.*, June 20, 1910.
[5] Beveridge to Mrs. Beveridge, June 1, 1910.
[6] *Indianapolis Star*, Dec. 12, 1909.

for the appointment by the President, with the consent of the Senate, of a Governor to serve four years, an Attorney-General, and a Commissioner of the Interior and of Mines. All of these were to reside in Alaska; and these, with eight others to be similarly named, were to serve as a legislative council. The eight were to be *bona-fide* residents of the Territory.

Instantly Senator Borah opposed the bill as not being an American scheme in its denial of the right of the people to elect their legislative council. Objecting to the treatment of the people of Alaska as 'aliens,' he declared that ninety per cent of the people were against it. Beveridge met this issue frankly: 'It was clear to a majority of the committee that on account of the sparse population, the enormous extent of the territory in which they are located... the difficulty of communication in physical hardship and in time and expense, the question of an elective legislature is impracticable.' [1] But the opposition, together with the concentration of the session on railroad legislation, prevented a vote, and nothing was done until after Beveridge had left the Senate.

Toward the close of the session he presented a plan for the establishment of a national coal reserve in Alaska. Four years before, Roosevelt, by executive order, had withdrawn these lands, and the purpose of Beveridge was to leave no doubt as to the legality of the withdrawal and to safeguard the Roosevelt conservation principles.

These principles [he said] are that where there are deposits of coal... the surface above shall be separated from the deposits below — the surface to be open to entry by homesteaders or others like any other public lands, but the deposits to be retained forever as the property of the Nation.

The second principle is that these fuel or mineral deposits shall then be developed under the leasing system; that any person who wants to develop the coal or other deposits may do so by paying the Nation, for every ton of coal taken, a royalty which shall be agreed upon between the Nation, which owns the coal, and the person who is developing it. This principle is that the title to these deposits shall remain forever in the people. [2]

This plan precipitated a discussion with some Westerners objecting to the leasing system and insisting that the scheme was a discrimination against Western in favor of Eastern mines. The measure was lost, and even a roll-call was refused.

Thus the session gave Beveridge one personal triumph on the statehood bill, and two rebuffs on Alaska.

[1] *Congressional Record*, Feb. 14, 1910.
[2] *Congressional Record*, June 15, 1910.

VI

To the country generally the one exciting topic of the session was the railroad rates bill which again arrayed the insurgent group against the Administration. During the preceding fall, Cummins, a specialist on railroad legislation, had been invited by Taft to consider with him the measure written by the Attorney-General, George W. Wickersham. As we have seen, he loathed the idea, knowing the impossibility of an agreement. To the insurgents the Administration measure was vicious in some particulars, and not framed in the public interest. Two of their number, La Follette and Cummins, were better equipped by experience for the discussion than any senators on the other side. Dolliver and Beveridge moved to their side, and while the group occasionally divided on some sections, they were a unit in their determination to destroy the Wickersham measure and to write a new one on the floor. So effective and devastating were their arguments and exposés, that the Administration forces were sometimes forced to the open abandonment of whole sections and a humiliating retreat from the light of the exposure.

The Administration measure clearly was railroad-made. It created a new Court of Commerce in which the roads might enjoin the Interstate Commerce Commission, but the public was denied a similar privilege. It even gave the Court the right to set aside the findings of the Commission on grounds other than those of jurisdiction or of a constitutional nature. A judge of the Court, without notification to the Commission and upon an *ex parte* showing, temporarily could enjoin the enforcement of the Commission's orders reducing rates. The communities, corporations, or individuals or shippers were refused admission to the Court to assist in sustaining the Commission's orders. Quite as remarkable as anything else, it legalized agreements as to rates and classifications and denied the Commission any rights in the matter. This was equivalent to repealing the anti-trust laws in so far as they applied to the railroads. It denied the Commission the existing right to appear in appeal cases, and left its representation entirely to the Attorney-General with the power to abandon them if he saw fit. And under the guise of controlling the capitalization of the roads, it actually gave the sanction of the Congress to the existing capitalization, no matter how notoriously fictional and fraudulent.

The insurgents fell upon this measure with zest, riddled, and rewrote it. Before they were through, it had been amended to permit the Commission to engage counsel and appear in court to defend its orders; to make it impossible for an Attorney-General to discontinue one of its cases or otherwise dispose of it; to compel the proposed Court of Commerce to give five days' notice to the Commission and an opportunity to be heard before the issuance of a temporary restraining order. It forced the abandonment of the Administration's attempt to legalize the capitalization claimed by the roads, and permitted such interested parties as the shippers to appear in court to defend the action of the Commission undertaken in their behalf. And it denied the right of the Court to set aside the Commission's orders.

Thus the battle was a slaughter, and one of the utmost humiliation to the Administration whose spokesman at Chicago had written the measure. La Follette and Cummins led naturally in the onslaught, and Beveridge made no extended set speech. But most of the time he voted with his two associates and made himself still more obnoxious to Aldrich by entering the debate aggressively against the bill on the long and short haul. He did not support La Follette on his amendment for the physical valuation of the roads, but neither did Cummins; though neither voted against it. He supported La Follette's amendment, which amazingly enough was defeated, making it unlawful for any judge of the Court of Commerce to have official relations with the roads, to own their stock and bonds, or in any other way to be pecuniarily interested. He went down with La Follette, too, on the latter's amendment against working men in the railway service more than fourteen hours a day. And he offered an amendment of his own forbidding members of Congress, or members of their official household, or judges or employees of the Court of Commerce, or any employee of the Government to accept a fee, or gift, or anything of value from any person or corporation engaged in interstate commerce. Not only was this defeated, but a roll-call was refused.

Even so, the victory was with the insurgents, and Aldrich realized more than ever that his domination was being challenged. Bitterly resentful of Beveridge, who once had been considered one of his 'regulars,' his resentment flamed into something very like hate.

The flare-up came during the consideration of the Sundry Civil Appropriation Bill when an attempt was made to strike out the appropriation for the tariff board. Beveridge, in his speech, disclaiming any thought of considering the board a real commission, sustained it as the recognition of a principle for which he had fought. In the reiteration of his commission arguments, and in reviewing the fight of the previous session, he made it a matter of record that Aldrich had been responsible for striking out the provision permitting the board to take evidence under oath and to summon persons and papers.

The next day found Aldrich in a fury, and he was weakest thus. He entered upon a personal attack — an astonishing speech. He was the father of the board, he said. Beveridge had done nothing at all. Beveridge replied with a smashing detailed story of the conferences and conversations — none of which Aldrich could remember. When Clapp interposed to remind Aldrich of his own personal conversation with the tottering dictator, the latter's memory was equally at fault. When Aldrich sneered at the idea that popular agitation had influenced him one whit in agreeing to a tariff board, Beveridge retorted that but for the agitation 'not one line or syllable or punctuation mark of this legislation would have been written.'

'I am wondering,' said Aldrich, 'if the Senator thought that agitation had something to do with my action, or whether the Senator thought it was his persuasive eloquence that influenced it.'

'Not at all,' Beveridge answered. 'I do not imagine that anything of that sort would influence the Senator, and I acquit the Senator of being influenced by the popular demand of millions of people continued for years.'[1]

Quite definite by now was the break with the President. Toward the close of the session, when Beveridge called upon him in regard to an Indiana appointment, Taft flew into a rage and announced he would not appoint the Senator's candidate because he was an insurgent and had tried to defeat the Administration's measures.[2]

However, Beveridge was not flying recklessly and ignorantly against Fate. For months he had known of the sharpening of knives for him back in Indiana; of the intimacy of his enemies at the White House. But he was losing no friends; and one was hurrying back from Africa. Taft now was deeply concerned as to Roosevelt's position, and soon Beveridge would see him at Oyster Bay.

The party schism was hurrying on. It was to be a death struggle. When on the last day of the session Taft went to the Capitol as usual to sign belated bills, not one of the insurgents called to bid him good-bye; and strangely enough, the President felt hurt.[3]

[1] *Congressional Record*, June 11, 1910.
[2] Beveridge to Mrs. Beveridge, June 29, 1910.
[3] *Letters of Archie Butt*, I, 413–14.

CHAPTER V

'BLOODY BUT UNBOWED'

I

WITH the adjournment, Beveridge was forced to concentrate on his battle that year for reëlection. He was not oblivious to the bitter hostility to his fortunes from powerful party figures in Indiana, but more than ever was he convinced that among the people there was a strong undercurrent of resentment against the dominant element of the national party and its policies. In a letter to Gifford Pinchot he had analyzed the cause of the restlessness and resentment of the average man. He found it in Taft's complete accord with the Aldrich element, the tariff, the wrecking of the Pinchot program, the Administration's railroad rates bill, the 'joker' introduced into the postal savings bank bill, designed to draw the money away from the communities where deposited. Because of this record of complacency or subserviency to privilege, he had concluded that the Republicans would fight a losing battle in the autumn.[1] He knew he would have a hard battle even with the sincere support of all the party leaders. But he had dedicated himself to the fight. The spirit that possessed him at the time is shown in a letter to a favorite cousin: 'Generally speaking, we have got to straighten things out in this country; for not only business, but the whole structure of our national society is going to be imperiled before many years to come. The people won't stand injustice — they simply will not.'[2]

He had abundant evidence that his independent course on the tariff had alienated some of his earlier supporters. One of the most valued friends of his earlier years had warned him not to urge his tariff views upon the State Convention. 'It is rumored,' he wrote, 'that you will make the convention speech along the lines of your letter to me. That would carry condemnation of a party act and of the President.'[3]

And yet he had no thought of turning back. When Samuel Blythe wrote a militant article, favorable to Beveridge's position, for the 'Saturday Evening Post,' on the division on policy in Indiana, one of his early friends, who had been a power in his first election, wrote him that the article had given 'no relief,'

[1] Beveridge to Pinchot, March 23, 1910.
[2] Beveridge to E. L. McClain, March 18, 1910.
[3] Robert A. Brown to Beveridge, March 29, 1910.

and urged the wisdom of not vigorously attacking the Aldrich-Payne crowd in the convention speech.[1]

But it was not public sentiment so much as manipulation by the politicians that he feared; and throughout the spring he was in constant communication with his followers urging the utmost vigilance in preventing the reactionaries from capturing the convention in the election of delegates. He was sure they would 'use money or any other kind of influence' to control the convention and pack the committee on resolutions. 'It is absolutely necessary,' he wrote, 'that men who have the people's welfare at heart should be chosen on the resolutions committee from every single district. Not only that, but they should be strong, determined men.'[2] He knew that the Administration leaders in the State were moving mysteriously about organizing for the defense of the Payne-Aldrich Act; that former Governor Winfield Durbin was trying to organize a public meeting of business men to demand an endorsement of the measure. 'This will not succeed,' he wrote Shaffer. 'Should such a thing be done it would be perfectly useless for me to make a campaign. I most emphatically would refuse to stand on any such platform or to enter the campaign myself.' He looked forward with dread to the strenuous campaigning before him. 'I am not going to wear my life out in such a way any more. Whether we win or lose, and we will win, I am going to cut out campaigning after that.'[3]

Thus thoroughly confident and not unmindful of his handicaps, he put aside the counsels of the timid, and prepared his convention speech, determined to make it ring true to progressive principles.

II

For three days before the convention, he shut himself up in his quarters in the University Club in conferences with his advisers. With trusted friends he went over the speech, holding out firmly against the importunities of some to modify or moderate some expressions. A number begged him to change the first sentence: 'The coming battle is not so much between political parties as between the rights of the people and the powers of pillage.' This, he was told, was 'too strong for a party convention'; but he retained it despite his expectation that it would be heard in frigid silence.[4]

The atmosphere was charged with electricity. His enemies

[1] C. E. Coffin to Beveridge, March 31, 1910.
[2] Beveridge to C. W. Miller, March 6, 1910.   [3] March 10, 1910.
[4] Beveridge to Phillips, April 12, 1910.

were on the ground. James E. Watson, representing the Administration forces, maintained headquarters at a hotel, and everything possible was done to secure an approval of the tariff act. The bitterness of the struggle heightened the drama. The friends of Beveridge were in fighting mood, and when he appeared upon the platform he was given an ovation. His first sentence, 'The coming battle is not so much between political parties, as such, as between the rights of the people and the powers of pillage,' came with the force of a discharge of artillery. A tremendous burst of applause rewarded his audacity. It foreshadowed a fighting speech, and the delegates were on the edge of their chairs in expectancy.

A moment later:

A political party is not a group of politicians, each with his following, combining to win the spoils of place and power. Such an organization is not a party — it is a band of brigands; and its appeals in the name of the party are mere attempts to beguile and defraud the voter for its selfish purposes. Such organizations and men are the tools and agents of lawless interests which know no party, attempt to use all parties, and practice only the politics of profit.

Foreshadowing, thus, his forthcoming attack upon the tariff, he anticipated the inevitable challenge to his Republicanism with a vigorous partisan assault upon the Democrats in Congress. Pledged to put all trust-made articles upon the free list, they had voted for the highest duty on iron ore proposed. They had voted for excessive schedules, and, for the most part, sat mute while the progressive Republicans waged the fight against the tariff bill. These members of Congress, constituting the Democratic organization, had wantonly betrayed the rank and file. Had not Bryan — then an idol of the Indiana Democracy — said as much? The great party of Jefferson and Jackson had fallen under the domination of local machines interested solely in the spoils of office, allies of the powers of pillage.

Having thus fired the partisan heart, he turned abruptly to the tariff:

The Republicans of Indiana are for a protective tariff which covers the difference between the cost of production here and abroad. Less than that is unjust to American laborers; more than that is unjust to American consumers. And injustice is the only foe that protection need fear.

And then, the challenge:

The great masses of American voters — protectionists nearly all of them — refuse to permit the great doctrine of protection to be used to excuse and cloak tariff excess. Perpetrate injustice in the name of a principle, and the friend of that misused principle will fight to save it.

A moment later he had reached the crest of his defiance. Calling the roll of the more outrageous schedules — iron ore, raw material, wool, lumber, cotton cloth, structural steel, sugar — he closed each attack with an effective reiteration:

I could not stand for the duty that was proposed and passed, and I cannot stand for it now.

Time and again the delegates broke in on his fiery sentences with fierce cheers. More than once the convention was on its feet.

Passing rapidly to generalities, he threw a bombshell into the reactionary camp:

Certain men believe that the reasonable prosperity of all American citizens depends upon the gigantic prosperity of a few dozen American citizens. I believe that the reasonable prosperity of a few dozen American citizens should depend upon the common prosperity of all American citizens.

And then, more:

The Nation would be healthier and the moral tone of the people better if these great masses of individual wealth which are now being dispersed as gifts had been distributed through the long years in better wages and salaries to their owners' employees and smaller largess to their owners' lobbyists.

Turning to the tariff commission, he boldly attacked Republican Senate leaders by name — the acts of Aldrich, the remarks of Hale. And did the friends of the tariff act tell the people that the purpose of a tariff commission had been met? It was false. 'We asked for reality; they gave us a mockery. We asked for power; they gave us palsy. We asked for bread; they gave us a stone.'

Thus, contemptuously ignoring party strategy, he ruthlessly bore down with the truth with defiant courage. With equal courage he turned upon the greed and arrogance of the trusts he had been the first to defend years before, with a demand for their governmental control:

Uncontrolled, they will grow stronger than the Nation itself. They must be brought under the guns of national authority, stripped of their unrighteous power, and made to serve the people by honest methods and for fair profit, instead of being permitted to rob the people by dishonest methods and for outrageous profits.

A denunciation of child labor, a demand that in injunction cases labor should have its day in court, a defiance of the 'powers of pillage' and their campaign funds, concluded the most militantly progressive speech ever heard in a Republican convention. And as he closed with the words, 'Up, then, with the holy

flag of justice and human rights, for "by this sign we conquer,"'
the orator sat down as the Convention rose *en masse* and cheered
wildly.

For the moment he seemed triumphant. The righteousness of
his position, the fine audacity with which he had burned his
bridges and thrown himself upon the people, was thrilling. His
friends were jubilant, none more so than the ever-faithful David
Graham Phillips.

The speech was magnificent [he wrote] you at your best; you yourself, God bless you... I see the *motif* of your campaign. I hope that
the other crowd will pour the money in and order Taft and the rest
of them to speak against you... I hope and pray they will make it
obvious to even the muttonheads just what they are up to. Then there
is sure to be a tremendous reaction in your favor... You may have
your left wing repulsed, or your right wing checked, or your center
possibly routed, but the army will win the battle. Oh, you Jeremiah![1]

Even the Democrats, a little concerned over the stealing of
their thunder, could not deny their admiration. But the gage
had been thrown down to the reactionary element, and it was
taken up.

To these, the performance was a mortal offense. Slyly they
began their subterranean operations against him. It was clear
to the experienced politicians that there would be treachery behind him, and that only strong Democratic support could save
him. On that hope Beveridge relied.

III

The action of the Democratic Convention dealt him a deadly
blow. The strategy of the campaign he had planned contemplated an appeal to the progressive Democrats from whom he
hoped to recoup in strength all he expected to lose among the
reactionaries of his own party. He was to pitch his campaign
above partisanship, to strike no partisan note, to lead the people,
irrespective of party, against the powers of pillage. He had won
the admiration of the Democrats by his daring in the tariff fight.
He had earned the respect of the independent Democrats by in-
curring the enmity of the machine politicians of his own party.
He would enter the campaign the one known quantity — his
record plain. And no one would know, in the event of a Democratic Legislature, whom the Democrats would choose. It
would be an easy matter to convey the impression that a Democratic victory would mean the election of a reactionary to the
Senate, or of one totally unfit for the position.

[1] Phillips to Beveridge, undated.

But all this was ruined, when under the aggressive leadership of John E. Lamb, with the countenance of Governor Thomas R. Marshall, the Democrats in convention nominated as its senatorial candidate the popular John Worth Kern.

No one could doubt the progressivism of Kern; he had been preaching it for forty years. And he was beloved by the rank and file. Thus Beveridge's proposed appeal for progressivism against reaction became absurd. He could scarcely put forth a reason why any progressive Democrat should reject his party's nominee and vote for him.

Thus the nomination of Kern accentuated the seriousness of the dissensions in the Republican Party — and the State Convention did not put an end to these. Watson and Hemenway were now turning their attention to the district conventions, determined wherever possible to get endorsements of the tariff act. Soon Beveridge was hearing from Will Hays, chairman in the Second District, which had acted favorably to Beveridge, that there had 'been a great change since the district convention'; that the workers are not taking off their coats; that Watson and Hemenway have so many friends over the State who have got to be placated.[1] Then the Sixth and Eleventh district conventions met and approved the Payne-Aldrich Act. 'This thing must not continue in the other districts,' Beveridge wrote. 'The other districts must follow the State platform.'[2]

Meanwhile, Hemenway and Watson were on their travels, and when, in July, they succeeded in getting an endorsement for the tariff act in the First District, Beveridge lost all patience, even with his friends. 'Where were all our men?' he wrote in angry mood to a lieutenant. 'This will be a bad blow to us. Under no circumstances must it occur again. Of course they will get the news of this to Roosevelt by telegraph, letter, by visitor, and in every other way.... I cannot comprehend how it came about.'[3]

And yet it was easy to comprehend. It was Hemenway's own district, the convention was held in his own town, and he and his followers were completely in control. The faithful Rothschild sent the explanation. 'Hemenway absolutely had the convention. In fact, many of the fellows who were claiming that Hemenway was down and out a year ago were red-hot with him and howling for the stand-pat resolution. He has been all over every corner of every county and knows every in and out.'[4]

---

[1] Beveridge to C. W. Miller, March 17, 1910.
[2] Beveridge to Miller, April 23, 1910.
[3] Beveridge to Miller, July 15, 1910.
[4] Rothschild to Beveridge, July 16, 1910.

Thus, quite early, it was apparent that the Aldrich group were gunning for Beveridge, even though the nominee of his party. With district after district repudiating the action of the State Convention, his position became well-nigh untenable. An issue had been made among his own people in Indiana between him and the Administration, and there was nothing to do but to burn the bridges and fight. With Taft clearly hostile, his one hope was in bringing the more popular Roosevelt to his support, and even Roosevelt, at this stage, seemed to be hedging. His repeated statements that his was a neutral attitude in the tariff controversy was damaging, and in letter after letter to their mutual friends, Beveridge was remonstrating. 'Our great friend is making a mistake in a statement appearing in the morning papers that he wants to occupy a neutral position,' he wrote Albert Shaw. 'It will not have a good effect upon the public. It looks too much like playing politics, and it is just what he cannot afford to do.' [1] And to James R. Garfield he wrote: 'I think there is no doubt that the reactionaries will use every effort... to confuse... the public mind. They will try to make it appear that he is holding the scales evenly between the two factions — just as though this progressive movement and the reactionary forces are factions. Absurd! Their chief effort will be to get him to commit himself in some fashion to the Payne-Aldrich tariff law — this I know to be a fact. Of course if they could accomplish that, they feel, and feel rightly, that they have shorn our Samson of his lock.' [2]

All the while politicians of all varieties were going in a stream to Oyster Bay, and Roosevelt was under pressure from both sides. It was on his way to his vacation in July that Beveridge was a guest and carried away the pledge of the 'man of the hour' to make a personal appeal for him in Indiana. A similar promise was given William Dudley Foulke, Lucius Swift, and Shaffer. Even so, Roosevelt felt it necessary to explain away the promise in a letter to Lodge. 'My aim is to support Beveridge in such a way as will soothe the feelings of the sensible men who can be gotten to support you, although on account of their general sympathy with the Insurgents a little unwisdom on our part would drive them into violent opposition,' he wrote. [3] Strangely enough, he thought a political speech of Lodge's 'the keynote on the tariff'!

But on one thing he was determined — there should be from him no flaming general endorsement of Taft, whom he had seen at the time of Beveridge's visit to Oyster Bay. Soon Beveridge

[1] July 16, 1910.   [2] July 13, 1910.
[3] *Roosevelt-Lodge Correspondence*, II, 385.

would be sending him Dolliver's speech and a 'Scribner' article on the cotton schedule, and pressing the importance of his tariff utterances 'because they would be universally quoted.' [1]

On his arrival in New York, Roosevelt had received an invitation from the White House which had been declined, and this was worrying the President, who told his friends there would be no second invitation. The last of June a machine bearing Roosevelt and Lodge had driven up to the summer house at Beverly, but the meeting was more disconcerting than encouraging to Taft. He had hurried to the porch as the machine drew up, with both hands outstretched and the exclamation: 'Ah, Theodore, it is good to see you!' But the mighty hunter had addressed him as 'Mr. President.' Slapping his visitor on the shoulder, Taft protested against the formality. 'See here, now, drop the Mr. President,' he said, laughing. 'Not at all,' was the reply. 'You must be Mr. President, and I am Theodore. It must be that way.' There was a barely perceptible chill in the atmosphere, evidence of strain and embarrassment. Butt, wondering if the two men should be left alone, consulted Lodge, who replied that Roosevelt on the way there had expressed the wish to the contrary; and so the two men chatted gayly enough after a while in the presence of witnesses, and politics did not enter into the conversation.[2] No misunderstandings had been cleared up, but Butt thought the visit would be interpreted by the public as proof that the two leaders were in accord. 'I know this man better than you do,' said Jimmy Sloan, the secret service man. 'He will come to see the President today and bite his leg off tomorrow.'

Meanwhile, Taft was regularly playing golf with Henry Frick, the steel man, and receiving a secret visit from J. Pierpont Morgan, who, dressed in yachting clothes, appeared mysteriously in a motor boat, slipped into the house, and after an hour's conversation slipped out again without betraying his presence to the press correspondents.[3] More and more Taft was aligning himself with the elements against which the sentiment of the country was rising. Aldrich appeared in his yacht in August in response to a demand from Taft that he publicly deny the charge of Senator Bristow that the dictator had manipulated the rubber schedule to his personal financial profit. Profoundly contemptuous of public opinion, Aldrich had no taste for denials, but Taft had insisted that the Administration was involved; whereupon the dictator had proposed a visit to Beverly with John D. Rockefeller. To this plan Taft had dissented, and Aldrich had

[1] Beveridge to Roosevelt, July 25, Aug. 1, 1910.
[2] *Letters of Archie Butt*, I, 427.   [3] *Ibid.*, II, 443.

gone alone.[1] But even this visit was to have annoying repercussions because of the impression given the press by the President's secretary that Aldrich had appeared without an invitation.[2] The Senate leader resented this as an insult, but this wrinkle in the relations of the two men was ironed out; and soon Aldrich and Senator Murray Crane, notoriously ultra-conservative, 'slipped into Beverly... and slipped out again as if bent on some criminal errand.' Even the secret service men on guard had been instructed not to look into the machine, as the two men were bent on the concealment of their presence. The purpose of the visit was to restore the old relations between Taft and Aldrich, but members of the presidential household were afraid the insurgents would learn of the conference.[3]

Then came Roosevelt's Western journey, without a word of commendation for the Administration, and to his household Taft made no secret of his bitterness. The two men were rapidly becoming the centers of two hostile groups. Taft had declined to go to Indiana; Roosevelt had agreed to go, and thus Beveridge entered to some extent into the long-distance quarrel.

IV

All the while Beveridge was preparing for his campaign, physically and oratorically, at Dublin, spending his time outdoors in the sunshine, hatless and coatless, roaming the mountains and chopping for exercise. Day after day found him in mountain shoes, old khaki trousers, and a workingman's shirt, meandering through the woods with an axe, prepared to chop if the impulse came. He had a house three miles from the village on the side of Monadnock, pretty and solitary. But absolute rest was impossible with him at any time, and he, better than most, knew that there was work to do that summer. There were campaign speeches to prepare, articles to write, and heavy political correspondence to demand attention; and, as he went out into the mountains with his secretary and stenographer along, he would stop every half-hour, sit down under the trees, and dictate. He had interesting home diversions, too, for a daughter, Abby, was born in the spring. He wrote Phillips that his enemies were 'unparking, unlimbering, and otherwise bringing into action all their artillery, little and big, financial and oratorical, and everything else'; and that 'Indiana is certain to be the bloody angle of this great national Shiloh.'[4] His lieutenants in Indiana were scouting about listening and reporting on his enemies, and some

---

[1] *Letters of Archie Butt,* II, 474.   [2] *Ibid.,* II, 477.   [3] *Ibid.,* II, 501.
[4] Beveridge to Phillips, July 30, 1910.

of these were powerful. But there was no mistaking the insurgency of the country, and this was his hope. Bristow had swept Kansas easily, and Cummins, in control of the State Convention in Iowa, had made a notable speech along progressive lines that had attracted favorable national attention. The man in the mountains was in frequent communication with the insurgent senators through the summer, and all of them were planning to take the stump for him in Indiana.

But the terrible strain of the tariff fight was taking its toll among them. Cummins was in the hands of a physician, Dolliver was now desperately ill, and La Follette sorely stricken. It was in correspondence with Cummins that Beveridge outlined the tone and temper of the campaign he had in mind. The Iowa statesman had written for suggestions: 'I would like you to tell me frankly just what you intend to say and do,' he wrote. 'It would be a fatal error for any of us to go into Indiana and rip up the work of the Administration unless you intend to pursue that course.'[1]

Beveridge replied:

I am going right down the line for progressive principles in Indiana. ... Of course I shall lay a great deal of stress on a genuine non-partisan tariff commission; I shall speak for the national control of railway and trust capitalization, for physical valuation of railroads, for eight hours a day labor, for the abolition of child labor, Canadian reciprocity, etc.

I shall not attack the Administration. I see no call for that, notwithstanding the way we have been treated. I do not think this either good politics or indeed just the right thing to jump onto the President of the United States. The people will do their own thinking on that subject. It has been my policy all through my life not to attack any man personally and by name. Even when Bryan was a candidate for the Presidency the first time and feeling was running bitter and high and our fellows were denouncing Bryan bitterly, in all my speeches I took exactly the opposite course — said I thought he was sincere, honorable, but a mistaken man. So personally I shall not attack any of the reactionary leaders by name. I certainly shall attack reactionary principles, if there are such things.[2]

Thus passed the summer; and in September he returned to Indiana, his principal speeches prepared, and physically hard as nails, browned, in perfect condition, and outwardly radiating confidence. The attention of the Nation was centered on the Indiana contest. Many magazines were publishing commendatory articles on his career, and his literary friends, Phillips, William Allen White, Arthur W. Little, and Sam Blythe, had taken up their pens. He was sure of his personal organization,

[1] Cummins to Beveridge, Sept. 6, 1910.
[2] Beveridge to Cummins, Sept. 9, 1910.

but was fearful of the fidelity of local county organizations, and soon he was to observe much to disturb him. Before opening the campaign he had accentuated his differences with the Administration by addressing a conservation convention in St. Paul, where his tribute to Pinchot brought the cheering audience to its feet and moved the great conservationist to tears.[1] La Follette wrote him gratefully from Wisconsin, promising, if his health permitted, to enter the fight in Indiana — but this was not to be.

V

With the delivery of the opening speeches of Beveridge and Kern, it was evident that the campaign was to be pitched upon a higher plane than usual, for both passed buncombe by to get down to cases. But just in the beginning Beveridge was embarrassed by the action of Roosevelt, on whom he was depending, at the Republican State Convention at Saratoga, New York. Just before, Roosevelt had delivered a ringing progressive speech at Osawatomie, Kansas, and the somersault at Saratoga, accepting the high tariff platform there, was a blow certain to weaken the effect of Roosevelt's speeches for Beveridge. It was sure to make confusing a speech in behalf of an insurgent against the tariff act by the chairman of a convention that had adopted the position of Taft at Winona.[2]

Thus Beveridge opened his campaign in Indianapolis before an audience vociferously sympathetic. He spoke with great deliberation and emphasis, and his mien was serious. Gone now the superficial sparkle of his old efforts. He was fighting for his political life, and it depended upon his capacity to reach the conscience of the people, and scarcely less upon his ability to pitch his plea above partisan politics.

I appeal to the people [he began]. This is the war of the citizen against giant interests that wrong him. Many politicians of both parties would have this campaign a mere partisan struggle for office. It shall not be. 'The old order changeth, giving place to that which is new.' This is the day of such a change.

And then, charging at those who questioned his right as a Republican to break with tradition:

Hospitality to righteous ideas is the life of political parties; intolerance of ideas their death. A party can live only by growing, and it can grow only by deserving the approval of men to whom citizenship is stronger than partisanship.... An organization that depends upon reproduction only for its votes, son taking the place of the father, is not a political party, but a Chinese tong; not citizens brought together

[1] *Indianapolis Star*, Sept. 8, 1910.   [2] *Indianapolis News*, Sept. 30, 1910.

by thought and conscience, but an Indian tribe held together by blood and prejudice. The Republican Party is no such tong or tribe.

Were the people thinking of the cost of living? Railroad rates and trust prices based on overcapitalization was one cause; 'the century-old policy of giving away to private interests the people's natural resources, thus increasing our taxes by destroying this source of income, is another; extortionate tariff rates, so far beyond the limits of protection that they insult and betray protection, is still another.'

Thence on to meet the charge of his enemies within the party that he was disloyal to its policies, with a sweeping condemnation of Democrats who had helped to enact the existing tariff act. Logrolling legislation — it must stop. Lobby legislation — it must end. And a tariff commission for scientific revisions must come. What would that mean? 'For example, you would have had the wool schedule changed and lowered. It is more than forty years old. Such changes as have been made by both parties during the last forty years have been for the special benefit of those men who have now grown into the wool trust.' A tariff commission would mean legislation in the public interest. And the cotton schedule — why should it have been increased? Were the Republicans who opposed the increase disloyal to protection?

What did we Republican Senators who fought this increase contend for? For the Dingley tariff on cotton. Was not the Dingley cotton tariff a protective tariff? The cotton manufacturers themselves said so. And if the Dingley cotton tariff was high enough, what was this increase? If the Dingley rates were protective, were not these increases extortion?

Thence on to a plea for the conservation policy of the Roosevelt régime; for child labor legislation; for the eight-hour day for all working indirectly for the government.

It is wrong that Mr. Schwab should pile up scores of millions of dollars while his workingmen are sent to the human scrap-heap at fifty years of age by the murderous process of seventy hours a week of desperate toil — ten hours a day for every day in the week including Sunday.

Then, turning to a defiance of his foes:

It is said that great sums of money are coming into Indiana to defeat me. I advise the sources of this corruption fund to save their cash. Indiana voters cannot be bought before an election, and Indiana legislators cannot be bought either before or after election. Let the interests that are parting with their currency, including the tobacco trust, put that in their pipe and smoke it.

It was a militantly progressive keynote, strong in its application to Beveridge personally, weak in an appeal for his party. The 'Indianapolis News,' none too friendly, thought it 'radicalism, but mainly on safe and proper lines... an honest speech, as different as possible from the old political buncombe of which we believe the country is heartily sick.' But it thought he had underestimated the progressivism of the Democratic Party under the leadership of Woodrow Wilson and Thomas R. Marshall.

Five days later, Kern opened his campaign at Evansville, free from the party embarrassments of his opponent. The Republican Party had in the tariff betrayed the interests of the people, he said — violated its solemn pledge of a revision downward; and with four fifths of its members of Congress supporting the treachery, its President not only signed the bill, but praised it.

All this Beveridge himself had denounced, arraigning his party for high treason and ending with an appeal for its continuance in power. 'The impudence of such an appeal reaches a degree of sublimity never before approached in the history of American politics.'

And did not Beveridge favor the taxing of the people for the private profit of private industries? — the very essence of protection. A keen and clever strategist, Kern made the most of Roosevelt's connection with the New York Convention and its laudation of the tariff that Beveridge damned.

Having attained this eminence, Roosevelt's strength departed, his valor oozed away, and the war-cry which struck terror to the hearts of the Standpatters at Osawatomie died upon his lips and could no more be repeated. That temporary chairmanship apparently did for the mighty Roosevelt what the silly and seductive Delilah did for his valorous predecessor, the mighty Samson. While Samson slept, he lost his hair and his strength; while Roosevelt, intoxicated over his victory over the Old Guard, his power to serve the people departed. The powers of pillage took advantage of his misfortune and through their accredited representatives wrote and caused to be adopted a platform which led those luminaries of protection, Aldrich and Cannon and Payne, to sing together with even greater joy than the morning stars manifested in the days long gone by.

And Beveridge's arraignment of the Democrats in the tariff fight? Why, only one had failed to vote against it! Was the principle of pillage involved only in the Payne-Aldrich Bill? Why had Beveridge voted for the 'outrageous rates' of the Dingley law?

Senator Beveridge stands committed to the principle that in the exercise of its power of taxation it is the duty of the Government to so frame its tax laws as to create a class of beneficiaries and confer upon that class the right to levy tribute upon the earnings of the great mass of the American people. He only balks on a schedule, here and there. With him the act of larceny is justifiable. He would only regulate the amount of plunder to be taken in certain particular and isolated cases.

It was a speech perfectly framed to hold the Democrats within their party fold; and further to drive a wedge between the two elements of the party of Beveridge. It was a strong speech in answer to one of strength, and the 'Indianapolis News' thought that 'the speakers on both sides are going to deal with real things and the real issues.' They were both off to a good start.

Strategically the advantage was all with Kern. He voiced the sentiments of a united party and its traditions. And the effect of Roosevelt's forthcoming speech for Beveridge had been neutralized by his acquiescence in New York's laudation of the tariff act. His enemies were not to permit the people to forget it. The 'Indianapolis News' editorially was making the most of it:

Mr. Beveridge is making his campaign on his record in opposing the Payne-Aldrich enormity. He has pointed out that measure's defects and shortcomings and treasons to the party promise with incisive vigor. But Mr. Roosevelt's whipped and subservient convention at Saratoga — 'beaten to a frazzle' as he declared — lauded the Payne-Aldrich performance in terms more sweeping than Mr. Taft used in his unfortunate Winona speech; in phrases as enthusiastic as Cannon or Watson or the Vice-President could frame. Standing on that platform, how can even the greatest man in history consistently support our insurgent senior senator? It looks as though it were a dilemma that could not be ignored by silence.[1]

This only accentuated the embarrassment when men like Charles B. Landis were pleading for Beveridge's election in the same speech in which they were denying all the charges against the Payne-Aldrich Act.[2] And Kern was asking every day how Mr. Roosevelt on entering the State could ask for the reëlection of Beveridge who voted against the tariff bill and also the Republican congressmen who voted for it. Meanwhile, Kern was making the most of all the vulnerable points in his opponent's record before the days of his insurgency. Why had he voted for the ship subsidy? Why against the income tax? Why for ten years had he defended the Dingley tariff and the trusts? Why had he voted for the $40,000,000 appropriation for battleships? Day after day he was hammering away upon these questions. No one ever pitched a campaign upon a higher plane than Beveridge; no one had ever been more powerful in attack than Kern. The entire country was deeply interested.

It was not until toward the close of the contest that Beveridge took cognizance of the bombardment of questions.

[1] Oct. 10, 1910. [2] *Indianapolis Star*, Oct. 27, 1910.

The ship subsidy? He would have preferred a lower tariff on imports carried in American ships, but treaties with other countries made it impossible.

So, when the question came up, I voted for the bill, doubtful as it was. But the ship subsidy plan is dead, and I am glad of it. Its absolute and final collapse is due chiefly to the weakness and wrong of the plan itself as revealed by study, and also by the settled opinion of the people.

And the income tax?

Years ago, I declared that an income tax, increasing as incomes increase, was a rational and just method.... But the Supreme Court has said that the Constitution forbids Congress from laying an income tax.... The question was, should Congress again pass practically the exact law which the Supreme Court declared the Constitution forbids; or should we take the necessary steps to amend the Constitution so as to give Congress this power.... To have done the former would have been to have struck a serious blow at popular respect for the courts, at present none too strong at best. To do the latter was to respect the decision of the Supreme Court and to follow the course prescribed by the Constitution itself for just such an emergency — its amendment. And this is what we did. We followed the method of orderly liberty.[1]

Then, demanded Kern in reply,[2] if Beveridge preferred another subsidy method, why had he not proposed it? And if he was against the subsidy, why, in all the years it had been pending, had he not made his position plain on the Senate floor instead of waiting until ten days before the election 'to have it corkscrewed out of him by the herculean methods of a political opponent'? And was the subsidy dead? Had it not been recommended by Roosevelt; and supported by the leaders of the Republican Party; and had it not been pushed more vigorously the last year than ever before?

And the income tax for which Cummins, La Follette, Clapp, Bristow, and Borah had voted when Beveridge was voting 'with Aldrich' — had these men no respect for the Supreme Court or the processes of orderly liberty?

Thus throughout the campaign Kern was seeking to isolate Beveridge wherever he could from the other insurgent Republicans, in order to hold the Democratic progressives in line.

VI

Meanwhile, the most notable political figures of America were speaking in Indiana: Cummins, Clapp, Bristow, Pinchot, Garfield, and Winston Churchill, the novelist, were forcibly urging

[1] At Rockville, Oct. 27, 1910.   [2] At Huntingburg, Oct. 28, 1910.

the reëlection of Beveridge; but two of the group — and these the most powerful with the people — were absent. La Follette, with tears of chagrin coursing down his cheeks, was tied to his home by illness. And Dolliver was hopelessly stricken now. Early in October he had written Beveridge a pathetic explanation:

It is with deep regret that I dictate this to you. I find it impossible to tell what I can do in the way of campaign work, as, for the first time in my life, I am entirely disabled and unable to do anything. For three weeks I have been confined to my house, unable to eat my meals, and just barely able to get my breath. Under these circumstances I have been compelled to give my entire attention to getting on my feet again. I think I am better, although I have not yet recovered strength enough either to travel or speak. The probability is that it will be a long time before I am able to make a speech of any sort. I regret the situation, but I am up against the real thing. I have got to have absolute rest and quiet.[1]

Eight days later, the great orator was dead, and Beveridge, sorely stricken, was saying that 'Senator Dolliver died for his country as literally as any soldier who ever expired on a battle-field.' A real affection had developed between the two men. Momentarily tempted to abandon his campaign to attend the funeral, he was dissuaded by Cummins. 'Your first duty,' he telegraphed, 'is at home. It would be an irretrievable disaster if, after losing Dolliver by death, we should lose you by defeat. I will explain everything here.' [2]

In the mean time Roosevelt had come and gone, giving momentum to the campaign. Speaking to thirty thousand people in Monument Place he had paid tribute to Beveridge's public services on meat inspection, overcapitalization, the tariff commission, child labor; but unhappily he dared not broach the tariff bill which was of paramount interest to the people. The opposition press made the most of this omission, the outstanding feature of the speech; and Kern took full advantage of all the holes in the armor, not overlooking that at Saratoga. Roosevelt left in his wake much ugly gossip concerning his failure to speak with Beveridge at Richmond as announced. The gossips among the latter's enemies in his own party gave currency to the story that Roosevelt had refused to leave the train at Richmond because Beveridge was 'drunk'; and others, to make the story better, had it that both were drunk. The truth was that the special train, scheduled to reach Richmond from Indianapolis within three hours, lost an hour and a half by being shunted on sidings, was stopped at water-tanks, held up in transfers, and slowed down in speed, and this made it impossible for Roosevelt to speak without missing his connection for New York. The

[1] Dolliver to Beveridge, Oct. 7, 1910.   [2] Oct. 18, 1910.

representative of the Pennsylvania Railroad on the train was offered five hundred dollars to run a special from Richmond to Columbus, Ohio, but refused. Roosevelt was informed that the road was holding its regular train for him, but that it could not be responsible for getting him to New York on time for an engagement if he left the special at Richmond to go uptown. It developed that he was to be held up in the railroad yards at Richmond for half an hour and could have made the speech. Thus the Roosevelt visit ended in a fiasco.

To offset the effect of his plea, Bryan was traversing the State on a special, addressing record-making crowds in behalf of Kern. The one offset the other; if, indeed, Bryan, reaching more people, and remaining longer, did not have the advantage.

VII

Toward the close of the fight both candidates were verging on exhaustion. Kern spoke the last week literally holding onto a table, his legs trembling with weakness. Beveridge, mentally harassed by multiplying evidence of treachery in his own party in addition to his physical exhaustion, was irritable and occasionally offended his friends. For he had gone into the fight at top speed and had never slackened. As the end approached, he gave his fight more and more the character of a moral crusade. At a Corn Show at La Grange, he literally preached a nonpartisan sermon from a Bible on the table before him, on the theme that righteousness exalteth a nation.[1] Sundays not infrequently found him speaking in churches on 'The Bible as Literature.' The fervor of his denunciation of 'invisible government'[2] and 'the powers of pillage' increased. He gave no peace offering to privilege. He accepted the enmity of the reactionary politicians in his own party and dragged it into the open. In Terre Haute he made a sensational attack upon the organization leaders there. 'For years,' he said, 'various petty chieftains with a band of followers which Bulwer tells us of in his great novel, "Rienzi," have flourished here, waging their little factional wars. They are like the *condottieri* in Italy in mediæval times except in this particular — that whereas the Italian *condottieri* were led by men of great ability with noble blood in their veins, the little groups here are led by men who have no claim to any sort of leadership.' It had become futile to ignore the movements of his enemies in his own party. They were

[1] *Indianapolis Star*, Oct. 7, 1910.

[2] It was at Jeffersonville, Oct. 10, 1910, that Beveridge coined the phrase 'invisible government.'

bending every effort to accomplish his defeat, and more than one Democratic speaker was secretly entertained after the meeting at a Dutch lunch of Republican politicians.[1]

Thus neither giving nor asking quarter, Beveridge swept over the State, accompanied by Frederick Landis, an attractive orator, by a secretary, and correspondents, traveling mostly in automobiles, and stopping for brief talks at crossroads and country towns. To keep himself in condition he took advantage of every opportunity for a brisk walk, and the correspondents found it difficult to maintain his pace. Enthusiastic crowds greeted him everywhere. Not once did he mention Kern's name, and, seeking independent and progressive Democratic votes, he discussed governmental questions without reference to parties. When, in the last days of the campaign, he was presented with a basket of flowers at South Bend, he asked permission to send them to his Democratic colleague, Senator Shiveley, then in a hospital there. He closed his campaign at a great meeting in Indianapolis, realizing that the result was uncertain, but satisfied with the fight he had made. Just as he was uttering his last word in the canvass he was handed a telegram:

We know you are going to win. We are sure of it. We send you our best wishes for success. Neither we nor the American people can get on without you in the Senate. Go in and win.

It was signed by David Graham Phillips and Robert W. Chambers, the novelists, and Joseph H. Sears, the publisher.

But it was not to be. The Democrats, for the most part, were satisfied with the progressivism of Kern; too many Republicans, encouraged by their leaders, voted against Beveridge. In his office, surrounded by friends, the most cheerful and the least downcast of all, he received the returns. At ten o'clock the indications were bad and he went home and went to bed. The next morning his one comment was:

Fortunes of war. It is all right; twelve years of hard work, clean record; I am content.[2]

From the faithful Phillips came a touching letter:

Well, Jeremiah, now you've got a very valuable measure of just how your campaign of education is progressing; for an election is of no importance except as a measure. The people have to go where you are leading and they have to have you at the head of the procession. But it takes a long time to rouse them to a sense of their own interest. You've done wonders in educating them, but nothing compared with what you are going to do. I don't feel sorry for you, for you've got plenty of time.... I do feel sorry for the people. Poor devils, they

[1] The author had two such experiences.　　[2] *Indianapolis Star*, Nov. 10, 1910.

haven't got any time to spare, and they are anything but comfortable while they wait to get sense enough to look after their own interests.

So get busy, Jeremiah, and become a bigger and saner and stronger radical than ever. You didn't begin soon enough. You must make up for lost time — and you will.... As I always say about you, you never have been and never will be beaten except by death. All you've got to do is to take care of your health and march on. Office is an incident. If you are in office you can use the office to help your plans. Office is like epaulettes on a uniform. The general in his shirt-sleeves is still the general.[1]

From the Administration one sincere note of regret — from Franklin MacVeagh, Secretary of the Treasury:

I am awfully sorry that the tidal wave has engulfed you. You held the majority down extraordinarily well, however. I know that you and Catherine did not set any great store on a continuance in the Senate, and I know, therefore, that the general result of the election will bring as little regret to you and her as it will to any family that is involved. You are a young man and the way is long before you, and there is nothing to prevent your being one of the national forces, in or out of office. There are so many things involved in this great party over-turning that it will take time to make anything like an adequate study of it. But I suppose that in due course we may be able to understand it.[2]

And, from the insurgents, an editorial by La Follette in his magazine:

The loss of Senator Beveridge is very hard to bear. A brilliant and able debater, a trained parliamentarian, alert, aggressive, persistent, undaunted, he is one of the best all-around fighters in the progressive group.... Fighting against big odds, Beveridge fought out the entire campaign on progressive issues, without compromise. Though de-feated temporarily, he comes out of the campaign true to his faith, with unsullied record, and practically victorious. Beveridge is an athlete, with thirty years of game fight in him. He never quits. He is sure to come back.[3]

He had fought hard to save his party from the *débâcle* that overcame it; and his personal defeat was meager compared with the enormous Democratic majorities in President Taft's and other States. Replying to an encouraging letter from Roosevelt, he said that he was 'not in the least cast down,' and that 'the propositions for sound economic reforms laid before the people are virile needs which will yield their sure and abundant har-vest.'[4]

And so, impenitent for his insurgency, he turned his thoughts to his last short session of Congress with undiminished zest.

[1] Phillips to Beveridge.   [2] MacVeagh to Beveridge, Nov. 10, 1910.
[3] *La Follette's Magazine*, Nov. 19, 1910.
[4] Beveridge to Roosevelt, Nov. 17, 1910.

CHAPTER VI

FIGHTING TO THE LAST

I

BEVERIDGE returned to Washington chipper and in fine fettle, bearing no grudge. Within a few days he had inquired of Senator Smoot of the Finance Committee when it would be ready to report on the anti-coupon tobacco legislation and had received a hedging answer. The committee, said Smoot, had met but once thus far, but would soon meet again, when he hoped for a speedy report. But, asked Beveridge, had not the committee held meetings once upon the bill, and reported favorably? Smoot was forced to agree.[1] A month was to elapse before Beveridge made further inquiry of the committee's progress, and then received the reply that Smoot had discussed the matter with Aldrich and that an agreement had been reached to refer the coupon legislation to a sub-committee. But why, persisted Beveridge, when the full committee had acted upon it once before? This time Smoot had an answer: some manufacturers had requested further hearings — some 'independent manufacturers' who had expressed themselves absolutely against it.

'How many of them are independent?' asked Beveridge. 'Is there more than one?'

'Yes, there are three,' said Smoot.

'How many independent manufacturers that are undoubtedly independent demand the passage of this bill?'

'Oh, a great many of them.'

'Practically all — is that not true?' Beveridge pressed.

'No, I do not think so.'

'All but two or three?'

'All but three appeared at the last meeting,' Smoot admitted.

'Then, as a matter of fact,' said Beveridge, 'it appears that this is opposed most powerfully by the tobacco trust, and one or two, possibly three, so-called independent concerns, and is earnestly demanded and prayed for by the great bulk of the independent manufacturers of the country. That is the situation, is it not?'

But Smoot backed off from a direct answer, and could 'only say' that 'just as soon as the matter could be reached, it will receive attention.'[2] But no attention was to be given; the

[1] *Congressional Record*, Dec. 19, 1910.　　[2] *Ibid.*, Jan. 17, 1911.

tobacco trust had scored on the coupons, just as the meat-packers had scored on labels on the can.

Beveridge was to find it equally impossible to persuade Aldrich's committee to report on his tariff commission measure. Within a few days after Congress met, he had referred to the long pendency of the bill and the crystallization of sentiment in its favor, and had asked Aldrich when his committee would report. The reply was, the committee would consider it.

'The Senator does not object to the designation of this crystallization of sentiment, does he?' asked Beveridge.

'No,' said Aldrich, 'though there may be a difference of opinion as to the interpretation to be placed upon it.' [1]

But Aldrich had no intention of advancing the Beveridge bill toward its passage; and as Beveridge's term was nearing its close, he knew that his fight for a tariff commission, for child labor legislation, and against the use of the coupon by the tobacco trust would have to wait on other times.

Other and new matters were pressing and he turned his attention to these. Taft had set his heart on a tariff reciprocity treaty with Canada and was urging its speedy ratification by the Senate. Not a few of the high protection reactionary wing of the party, sympathizing with the predicament of the President, supported it reluctantly, but the greater part of the insurgents continued to 'insurge.' To Beveridge the idea of reciprocity was in harmony with the principles for which he had fought in the tariff session; in accord with ideas he had advanced for years. He owed nothing to Taft, whose influence had not been thrown in his favor in the election; whose personal hostility he felt. But putting personal considerations aside, he aligned himself with the President for the treaty. Among the insurgents he stood alone. In this connection he had amicable conferences with Taft, and early in February he entered the debate with a carefully prepared speech, which, contrary to custom, he read. From no one in the reactionary group did Taft's policy receive a more brilliant and intelligent support, and the bigness of Beveridge in rising above personal resentment attracted national attention. The 'New York World' thought it an act of statesmanship, and from Andrew Carnegie, the day following, came a note of appreciation:

I wish to congratulate you on your stand in regard to reciprocity. You made the speech of a statesman. There is no possibility of injury to our own people from free-trade Canada.... The economic question can safely be discarded, but the moral and friendly results to flow

[1] *Congressional Record*, Dec. 12, 1910.

from this opening of the doors are incalculable. I talked with President McKinley on his way to make the great speech at Buffalo, which the President has quoted, and rejoiced that he recognized that conditions have changed; that we have no more infant industries needing protection.[1]

Not content with this one effort, Beveridge wrote a strong article for the 'Saturday Evening Post' along the lines of the speech.[2] But the treaty was doomed by the President's own party, and he would soon be calling an extra session, with numerous Democratic accessions, to get it through the Senate.

II

Meanwhile, not long before the delivery of the reciprocity speech, Beveridge had suffered an irreparable loss. On the afternoon of January 23, as he was entering the Princeton Club in New York City, David Graham Phillips was shot five times by a demented violinist with a persecution complex. Phillips had been receiving threatening letters for days, and just as he was leaving the National Arts Club, where he lived, he was handed a telegram bearing his own signature telling him to 'look out for yourself.' He was carried into the Princeton Club, and after emergency treatment, hurried to Bellevue Hospital. Beveridge took the first train to New York, reaching the hospital at four o'clock in the morning, and was one of the few admitted to the sufferer's room. Because of the novelist's robust health and strength, it seemed for a while that he might recover; and happy in that assurance, Beveridge returned to Washington. Scarcely had he turned away when Phillips began to sink. 'I could fight two wounds, but not six,' he murmured. Then came the collapse.

Beveridge had just reached Washington when he learned that the most loved and loyal companion of his DePauw days had succumbed. Taking the next train back, he reached New York at three o'clock in the morning, went to the hospital, and took charge of the funeral arrangements. The pallbearers were all friends — Sears the publisher, Lorimer of the 'Saturday Evening Post,' John O'Hara Cosgrove, Sam Blythe, and himself.

'Of course no one will ever know how hard hit I am by the death of Graham,' he wrote.[3] Their relations had been those of intimacy and militant loyalty, from the far-off days at DePauw. The novelist had rejoiced in the triumphs of the orator and statesman, and he in the literary successes of Phillips. The mu-

[1] Carnegie to Beveridge, Feb. 10, 1911.
[2] March 25, 1911
[3] Beveridge to C. E. Coffin, Feb. 6, 1911.

tual affection was deep and tender; and to the day of his death, Beveridge never visited New York without calling on Phillips's sister, with whom the novelist had lived. Before me lies a batch of letters between the sister and her brother's closest friend, in which he tenderly sought to soothe her sorrow, and lift her from her gloom — letters too sacred to quote.

Thus Phillips's end came almost at the moment Beveridge was passing to private life. The writer had cheered him on, with a college friend's enthusiasm, and had shared in the joys of his triumphs, and in the hour of defeat had sought to cheer him still, as we have seen.

The world was changing for Beveridge now.

III

But there was work to do — work Phillips would have had him do. That last session witnessed the initial battle over the seating of Senator Lorimer of Illinois. Charges had been brought that he had been elected to the Senate through the bribery of members of the Legislature; and the case was referred to the Committee on Privileges and Elections of which Beveridge was a member. The reactionary element in the Senate for the most part sympathized with the 'blond boss,' as he was called. There was, in truth, much that was appealing in his personality. He had risen from extreme poverty, and his personal habits were good. He had a family. And, after all, said some, he was not the only man who had entered the Senate through bribery. Then, too, the 'Chicago Tribune,' a powerful paper, politically hostile to him, was attacking him and his right to a Senate seat with a vigor that some resented. But the issue never had been more clearly put to the American people — Can Senate seats be bought and sold with impunity? It was an issue on which the Senate had to pass. The interest of the Nation had been aroused — the issue transcended the boundaries of Illinois, and, in the minds of many, came to be a test of the integrity of the Republic. The action of Roosevelt in Chicago in refusing to sit down at a banquet with Lorimer present had added fuel to the flame; some, and notably Mr. Taft, criticized his action as an unfair prejudging of the case.

When, after the evidence was in and published throughout the country, it was learned that the majority of the committee would report in Lorimer's favor, there was a general cry of protest. And when it was found that Beveridge had refused to sign, and was considering the submission of a minority report, the entire country pinned its hopes on him. The 'New York World' editorially said that 'Mr. Beveridge cannot close his senatorial career more honorably or more usefully than by leading the fight against Lorimer's tainted title to his seat.' The argument made, that since without the purchased votes Lorimer had enough for his election his seat was safe, outraged Beveridge's sense of ordinary decency.

While working on his report, he was overwhelmed with letters of commendation or abuse. The abusive letters were for the most part anonymous, demanding to know how much the 'Chicago Tribune' had paid him. Others were denunciatory of Roosevelt, and expressed the hope that Beveridge would 'keep aloof from any contaminating influences' that might interfere with his 'occupying the chair of Washington, Lincoln, Garfield, and McKinley.' To these he paid no attention. From Professor A. C. McLaughlin, the historian, head of the Department of History at the University of Chicago, he found that sentiment there was not at all with Lorimer. Ridiculing the findings of the majority of the committee, he wrote 'only because I do not think that senators should be left to suppose that intelligent people are going to accept this finding and its whole tone and temper without a grimace.' [1]

To such letters he made the same reply:

Of course I cannot discuss the matter privately. I have always held the position so clearly stated by Senator Hoar — that members of the committee considering such a case sit in the nature of a court, and that they are bound to refrain from outside discussion the same as a judge in the hearing of a case. Whatever action I may take will be dictated solely by conclusions formed after a careful and thorough study of the testimony. [2]

But there could be no doubt of his intentions. He had refused to sign the majority report and was at work on his own. It was a devastating analysis of evidence unmistakably denoting bribery. When Roosevelt congratulated him upon the document, Beveridge replied that 'it is intolerable that if a successful candidate for the Senate has bribed fifteen or twenty votes, yet if without these bribed votes he had a majority of other votes not proved to be bribed, his election is valid'; and 'even more intolerable that, though it be proved that a sitting senator has himself bribed one or more members of the Legislature that elected him, this fact does not vitiate the election so as to require a majority vote in the Senate to declare his seat vacant, but only

[1] McLaughlin to Beveridge, Dec. 22, 1910.
[2] Beveridge to McLaughlin, Dec. 24, 1910.

taints the sitting member so that he can be expelled only by a two-thirds vote.'[1]

The congressional session was nearing its close, and the excitement in the Senate was reflected throughout the country. Senator Elihu Root shocked the reactionaries by speaking powerfully against Lorimerism, but the most overwhelming philippic of the two was that of Beveridge. After making a study of the evidence, he had looked for some law on the subject, but he could find nothing in the prior debates to aid him, beyond the meager references of Conkling and Caldwell on opposing sides in the Caldwell case of years before. He therefore searched the records of all countries, ancient and modern, and everything he could find upon the subject he incorporated in his speech. 'I did this,' he wrote Roosevelt, 'so that hereafter, when any senator finds himself in a like plight, he will not have to go through the work I went through, but can find in this speech all existing authorities.'[2]

Expectant throngs of men and women packed the galleries to hear him. Every Senate seat was occupied, and around the walls and peering in from the cloakrooms were members of the House. The atmosphere was electric. The scene suggested a drama — all the more so because, pale and calm, and looking the part of a Christian martyr under the torture of men who knew not what they did, sat Lorimer.

And never had Beveridge been in better oratorical form. Dividing the speech into two parts — the Issue and the Evidence — he proceeded with remorseless logic, at times with inspiring eloquence, occasionally with wit and irony, utterly to demolish the majority report and to establish the guilt of the accused. An exhaustive speech, it required forty pages in the printing, and when he had finished, there could have been no exoneration consistent with logic or official honor. Impressively he closed, bringing the issue back to the fore:

Mr. President, the deepest students and the most sympathetic with our institutions more and more are asking the question. What is going to become of the American experiment of liberty? Is it to succeed or is it to fail? And there have not been wanted the ablest minds that doubted its success, because they have thought that the love of money and the love of office and finally the vice of bribery might undermine us.

I confess that to me it has been for years a serious matter what our future holds for us. Let us safeguard it, Senators, by our votes. And when in that future, American institutions ask of the sentinel upon

[1] Beveridge to Roosevelt, Jan. 19, 1911.
[2] Beveridge to Roosevelt, March 3, 1911.

their walls, 'Watchman, what of the night?' let us pray that the watchman shall not answer in the words of the Hebrew prophet of old, 'The congregation of hypocrites is desolate and fire has consumed the tabernacle of liberty.' No, Mr. President, let us hope and pray and vote that when the question is asked, 'Watchman, what of the night?' the answer shall be, 'Lo, the morn appeareth.' [1]

Beveridge had closed his last great speech in the Senate, and the galleries enthusiastically applauded. The applause was echoed by the press of the country, and Roosevelt wrote, 'Good for you! That was an admirable speech about Lorimer. I must heartily congratulate you.' [2]

But that session was not to see the expulsion of the 'blond boss'; the fight would be renewed in the next, and under the leadership of Kern.

And so the brilliant senatorial career of Beveridge came to its close, his last words a warning against corruption in public life.

IV

But retirement meant no rusting.

Almost immediately he was off to Canada, which had deeply interested him, to make a study of its methods in dealing with its problems. In accordance with his custom, he went loaded down with letters to statesmen, business men, bankers, railroad men, labor leaders, and writers. From James Bryce, the British Ambassador, he carried letters to the Governor-General, Premier Laurier, and the presidents of the Universities of McGill, Toronto, and Manitoba. 'I am sure you will enjoy your visit to Canada,' Bryce wrote, 'for there is much there to hear. You will, I am told, find opinion much divided and rather hot on the reciprocity question, so that in mixed company it is a subject to avoid rather than to raise.' [3] With Mrs. Beveridge, he dined with the brilliant Laurier; and at Senator W. P. Caspain's, with the Premier, the President of the Senate, Mackenzie King, and Sir Frederick Borden. Soon the American Consul-General [4] was strenuously engaged in collecting facts for him.

He meant to prepare six articles dealing with the Canadian management of currency problems, the trusts, the railroads, immigration, and industrial wars. Leading Canadian statesmen, like Mackenzie King, responded generously; and Beveridge sat with the Board of Railroad Commissioners when in session, and had long conversations with Sidney Fisher, the labor leader, to

---

[1] *Congressional Record*, Feb. 24, 1911. [2] Feb. 24, 1911.
[3] Bryce to Beveridge, March 27, 1911. [4] John G. Foster.

whom he had a letter from Samuel Gompers. Preparing these articles with the utmost care, he submitted them to competent Canadian authorities before publishing. Soon they were running in the 'Saturday Evening Post,' keeping him in the public eye during the months he was sojourning in Switzerland.[1] So accurate, fair, and entirely sympathetic and appreciative were these articles that the Canadians were pleased, and Mackenzie King wrote him, apropos of his article on the trusts, that it was 'comprehensive, clear, and accurate, forming in fact one of the best compendiums regarding the Act which I have yet seen.'[2]

But even in the whirl of the work of gathering material, he was not too busy to remember his friends; and when in the home of Earl Grey, the Governor-General, the latter produced 'with gusto' a copy of 'La Follette's Magazine,' which he 'read regularly,' Beveridge wrote of the incident to La Follette, and of Grey's comment: 'I get it regularly. But I roared with laughter and turned over on the floor when I read Senator La Follette's article on "The Progressive Republican League," of which I see you are a member. Good God! man, has it taken you people a hundred years to find out that you have not got popular government? It rejoices me because I am a Liberal and I am for popular government to the very limit.'
'And what do you think of that, Bob?' Beveridge added. 'Isn't it a dandy?'[3]

Nor was the reciprocity fight overlooked, for Taft, with a new Senate and Democratic support, was getting his treaty through. As Bryce had warned, Beveridge found that the sentiment in Canada was as badly divided as in the United States, if not more so. He had more than one talk with Laurier on the subject, and was entrusted by the Premier with an important message to Taft — under no circumstances in any public speech even to mention the word 'annexation.' Returning to Washington, Beveridge spent an hour with the President on the Canadian outlook and delivered the Laurier warning.[4] Instead of observing the admonition, Taft, within two weeks, was mentioning the forbidden subject, and although pronouncing it 'bosh,' creating a very live issue in Canada. Laurier had to go to the country battling against the fear and prejudice thus created. The Con-

[1] 'Our Cousins: How They Handle Their Currency Problems,' June 17, 1911; 'How They Break Their Trusts to Harness,' July 1, 1911; 'A History of a Railroad Triumvirate,' July 22, 1911; 'How They Handle the Immigration Problem,' Aug. 26, 1911; 'Profiting by Our Mistakes,' Sept. 9, 1911; and 'How They Solve the Problem of Industrial Wars,' Sept. 25, 1911.

[2] Mackenzie King to Beveridge, July 20, 1911.

[3] Beveridge to La Follette, April 1, 1911.

[4] *Indianapolis Star*, April 14, 1911.

servative press was making the most of the President's reference
to Canada at 'the parting of the ways,' and his amazing statement that the 'tie that binds Canada to the mother country is
light and almost imperceptible.' The Liberals were swept from
office on the issue, accentuated by Taft's strange disregard of
Laurier's warning conveyed personally by Beveridge.

But at that time Beveridge was enjoying the pure air of
Switzerland.

V

It was to be his first real vacation in years, free from the cares
of official life, but Mrs. Beveridge was ill, and he could not wholly
relax. Nor could he otherwise — for investigation beckoned
him. The Swiss form of government, and particularly its initiative and referendum, interested him, and he made it the subject of an intensive study. The fruit of his observations was to
appear later in an article on 'The People Who Govern Themselves.'[1] But even in his remote retreat in the Villa Griswolden,
Lucerne, he heard, through many correspondents, the reverbera-
tions of the controversy among the Republicans at home. Nothing that he heard indicated any healing of the wounds of the
old quarrel. The insurgents were even more incensed with Taft
for summoning an extra session on the Canadian pact. Scarcely
had he reached Switzerland when he heard from Bristow:

Taft is making a desperate fight for reciprocity, and of course has almost the united support of the Democratic Party, and a minority
of the Republican Party. There has been no material change in the
political situation since you left. But Lucerne, Switzerland, is a more
agreeable place, in my opinion, to spend the summer than in the Senate
Chamber discussing reciprocity and the tariff.[2]

From Senator Norris Brown, another of the insurgents, he
got news of a different tenor:

I would not for the world disturb your peace of mind, but... I
wish with all my heart that you were here to give us the benefit and
the inspiration of your example.... From my viewpoint the situation
is critical. There seems to be a shortage of wisdom and an oversupply
of animosity on the part of some who would be likely to listen to you,
but who are indifferent to advice from other quarters.[3]

More interesting was the letter from Cummins, foreshadowing
the presidential contest of the next year and criticizing the

[1] *The World Today*, December, 1911.
[2] Bristow to Beveridge, June 10, 1911.
[3] Brown to Beveridge, June 29, 1911.

'blunder' of the President in forcing the reciprocity issue upon a party sadly divided.

The newspapers, of course, are boosting Taft in every issue, and everywhere, and undoubtedly they are helping him, but the help is of a sort that will not be effectual when it comes to votes. La Follette is gradually organizing his candidacy for the nomination, and while he will have a good deal of strength, it is not possible for him to get more than two hundred votes in the convention.... Every member of the Senate, no matter how he feels about reciprocity, is dispirited and somewhat sullen. We are in no temper to legislate properly, and yet we must crawl through the hot days of July and probably August in order to reach an end that will satisfy nobody. I congratulate you on being out of it all.[1]

By contrast with these dour reports, one was received from Loeb, Collector of the Port of New York, to the effect that Taft was 'growing in popularity,' and the insurgents slipping because of 'their inconsistency on the tariff in the case of the Canadian pact.' [2]

But within a few days, to emphasize the continuing division, a contradictory note from Clapp:

As was inevitable, Senator La Follette is being pressed to stand as a candidate for the Republican nomination, and I do not see how he is going to be able to resist. From all over the country there is a demand that there shall be a candidate who stands for old-time Republican policies as exemplified in men like Lincoln... and Roosevelt.... I believe that Mr. Taft has weakened himself terribly throughout the country with the Canadian bill.[3]

Two days after Clapp wrote, three other friends were signing their names to reports on conditions. From Frank Munsey the man in Lucerne learned that 'the political situation is still badly mixed, but Taft has his renomination well in hand'; [4] from George Perkins, that while the Democrats had not made much headway, 'it does seem to me as though the Republican Party were still moving down the toboggan slide'; [5] and from Ira E. Bennett, of the 'Washington Post,' that 'Taft is steadily growing in strength,' and that 'his renomination seems to be a certainty,' since La Follette was handicapped 'by the failure or refusal of other insurgent leaders to fall in behind him.' [6]

To Beveridge all this was far from illuminative of conditions. And when a few days later, he heard from Gifford Pinchot that men were after Taft's scalp and might get it in the convention,

[1] Cummins to Beveridge, July 13, 1911. [2] Loeb to Beveridge, July 5, 1911.
[3] Clapp to Beveridge, July 11, 1911. [4] Munsey to Beveridge, July 13, 1911.
[5] Perkins to Beveridge, July 13, 1911. [6] Bennett to Beveridge, July 13, 1911.

and that 'the insurgents are picking up again,' it was confusion worse confounded.[1]

In August, Beveridge began to receive letters dolefully describing conditions and urging him to keep out of the controversy. Senator William Alden Smith wrote that the Senate had been 'in the trough of the sea during the session,' and paying tribute to the spirit and energy of La Follette. But, he added, 'in some respects it is fortunate that you are far away, as I am afraid that you would have been involved in controversial politics much to your disadvantage. As I said to you one night while walking in the Mall, the thing for you to do is to try to bring the reactionaries up to the color line and the progressives back to the column.'[2]

Almost two months later, Senator Smith in a more general discussion wrote, in evident fear that his friend of years might be considering some rash political alignment, and indirectly held forth an olive branch from the reactionaries.

Taft's visit to Michigan was very successful from every point of view — the people liked him, and turned out well. His speeches were intelligent, manly, and frank, although he has no political sagacity at all.... He got a terrible blow when reciprocity was defeated by the Canadian electorate. He was disappointed. It did not disappoint me, however....

Everything is going well with us here, and I am taking things pretty easy. I am not worrying at all over the political situation, even though a rump ticket were to be nominated by disaffected Republicans. You will remember that Grant went through that when Sumner, Schurz, and Horace Greeley nominated a separate ticket, though they did not succeed in winning anything.

I am glad you are out of the country, because there is only one thing possible for you to do, Albert, and that is to be loyal and regular — you have been rebellious enough to give you a good standing with the belligerent *vox populi*, and if you sustain the party organization you are bound to be the most available man in the party after Taft is through. Now I feel certain of this, as do other good friends; even Taft admitted this the other day. I talked to him about you considerably. In my opinion you are the biggest asset we have in the Middle West, and all you have to do is to be true to your party, reasonably conservative in your views, and with the aggressiveness and progressiveness, which you have heretofore shown, you will come back with a whirl after the present difficulties are closed.[3]

There was no mistaking the meaning of this letter. There was, it seemed, the possibility of a 'rump convention,' of a third

[1] Pinchot to Beveridge, July 18, 1911.
[2] Smith to Beveridge, Aug. 6, 1911.
[3] Senator Smith to Beveridge, Sept. 28, 1911.

party, and in some quarters there was a fear that Beveridge, driven by his militant insurgency, might align himself with the movement. At the moment there was not the most remote possibility of such a thing. In none of the letters received in Switzerland was there any reference to a possible Roosevelt candidacy. Balancing the letters of both groups against each other, it was possible to conclude that the situation had not greatly changed since Beveridge left America; and, though interested, he was not in the least excited. He was finding the scenery of Switzerland inspiring and charming, the air invigorating, his associations delightful, and the initiative and referendum more interesting at the moment than American politics.

His old friends in Indiana had not been lax in keeping him advised on the Indiana angle, which concerned him more. Taft had been to Indianapolis and had been lionized by Beveridge's enemies, but the crowd had been disappointing. The throngs expected from outside the city did not appear. But there had been a banquet at the Marion Club, and it seemed that 'Taft's visit will undoubtedly strengthen him.' The efforts of 'the old crowd to gobble up the situation,' had done more harm than good with the people. And then, the old note, so familiar in the Swiss letters:

I think it is the best time in the world for you to be out of Indiana and doing just what you are doing during the period things are taking shape.... The movement against Taft is making little or no headway. In my belief he is growing stronger and will certainly be renominated unless factors not now in the situation appear.... The greatest weakness is the lack of spirit among Republicans everywhere — a sort of resigned determination to be defeated. If they could only be inoculated with a little enthusiasm, I would be far from predicting Republican defeat in the next election.[1]

But again, in the Indiana letters, contradictions. The State Chairman wrote that 'conditions in Indiana are not satisfactory,' and that 'if the National Convention and election were to be held this month, Mr. Taft would be renominated and defeated.'[2] From the watchful Rothschild came the opinion that Taft's visit to Indianapolis had 'undoubtedly strengthened him,' since 'his mannerisms and style set those old hard-headed business men wild.'[3] It was only from Lucius B. Swift, the venerable reformer among the Hoosiers, that Beveridge caught the tone of militant insurgency, in a letter introducing with enthusiasm the name of

[1] Beveridge MSS.
[2] E. M. Lee to Beveridge, Aug. 1, 1911.
[3] Beveridge MSS.

Woodrow Wilson. 'As to Taft, I may vote for him and I may not. As it is now, Woodrow Wilson would bury him out of sight.' [1]

Evidently returning to Indiana then would mean venturing into the arena of controversy and inviting the intrigues of his foes. Early in September, his friends in consultation had agreed that he 'should not return before the middle of October.' They wrote him that it was becoming clearer every day that Taft would be renominated and defeated, and that Beveridge's enemies planned to simulate devotion to Taft to get the organization.[2]

On October 18, he reached New York on the Kaiser Wilhelm II, and, refusing to discuss politics, he took the first train for Indianapolis. He found many requests for speeches, which he declined, and, shutting himself up in his library, turned to literary pursuits. He had his article on 'The People Who Govern Themselves' to write; and it was at this time that, responding to the urging of Lorimer, he began the writing of an autobiography, soon to be abandoned. La Follette was in the field as a candidate, and there was nothing as yet to indicate that Roosevelt would enter the lists. When La Follette was about to enter the State for two speeches, his supporters asked Beveridge to be one of a committee to meet him at the State line; and there was much scurrying around among his friends to dissuade him. There was not any possibility of his acceptance; he liked and admired La Follette, but he was not ready for such a definite commitment to any candidacy.

Thus the year 1911 dropped from the calendar; and soon, with Roosevelt in the field, Beveridge would have enough to do.

[1] July 25, 1911.   [2] Beveridge MSS.

CHAPTER VII

'NO, SIRE, THIS IS REVOLUTION'

I

LONG before Roosevelt determined to contest with Taft for the nomination, Senator La Follette, not without definite encouragement from the former President, had entered the race. Almost from the beginning his candidacy had been sapped and mined by counterfeit supporters seeking to persuade the Rough Rider to mount again. Previous to Roosevelt's announcement, Beveridge had refused to commit himself in any way, but he had scant patience with those pretending to be progressive who were constantly criticizing his friend from Wisconsin. While far from being in complete accord with all the latter's views, he had a profound admiration, amounting to affection, for the audacious courage, ability, and brilliancy of La Follette; and on most matters he thought him fundamentally right, though too much in a hurry. Thus, when Governor Chase S. Osborn, a warm personal friend, made a savage attack upon the Wisconsan, Beveridge took exceptions.

Frankly, old man, I am sorry you felt it your public duty to criticize Senator La Follette so severely, or, indeed, to criticize him at all. Personally, I am exceedingly fond of him. During our six years of mutual service in the Senate, I found him always standing fearlessly for what he sincerely believed to be right. Usually I found that he was right. I must say that during the hard fights we made together in the Senate, I came to believe in him and in what he stands for generally; though not in all he says. Neither are his methods mine. Yet the general tendency of the man is toward righteousness.[1]

Two weeks later, when the press was vague regarding La Follette's plan to speak in Indianapolis, Beveridge wrote for definite information, 'so that if you do contemplate coming... Mrs. Beveridge and myself can have you at our house and take care of you while you are here.[2]

In the bitter controversy to follow between the supporters of the two candidates, never at any time was Beveridge to give utterance to a disrespectful word about the Little Giant.

In time Roosevelt launched his campaign for the nomination in his startling Columbus speech, demanding, among other new departures, the recall of judicial decisions, and Shaffer, thoroughly

[1] Beveridge to Osborn, Jan. 6, 1912.
[2] Beveridge to La Follette, Jan. 22, 1912.

THE HOUSE IN INDIANAPOLIS

alarmed at the revolutionary tone, wrote Beveridge of his inability to agree to changing the Constitution with such levity. 'I think you attach too much importance to Constitution changes,' Beveridge replied. 'Don't forget your years of enthusiastic approval of my speech on "The Vitality of the Constitution." Today's document [1] must be taken as a whole, and as such is an able and comprehensive expression of the advance movement in American life. Constitution parts reflect the latest and wisest conclusions of ripest scholars on this subject.' [2]

The moment Roosevelt tossed his 'hat into the ring,' Beveridge hurried to his corner. Thenceforth, until the party was disrupted in the Chicago Convention, he exerted himself to the utmost for his nomination. From the moment he announced his stout adherence to the Colonel's cause,[3] appeals to take the stump flowed in upon him from the States in which primary elections were held to choose delegates to the National Convention. The opening of his campaign in Indianapolis at Tomlinson's Hall was one of the notable oratorical triumphs of his career. So intense the enthusiasm, so tumultuous the throng, that an hour's speech required an hour and forty-five minutes in the delivery, because of the interruptions. He himself compared it to his Chicago speech in 1896.[4] Refraining from the lurid personalities that marred most of the pre-Convention speeches, from Roosevelt's down, Beveridge urged the necessity of nominating a winner, and thus eliminated Taft; declared the necessity of an Executive capable of coping with existing evils, and pronounced Roosevelt the man. Thence he launched into a brilliant, stirring review of the achievements of the Roosevelt régime.[5]

A few days more, and he was opening Roosevelt's campaign in the Auditorium in Chicago to an equally tumultuous meeting. When Shaffer, who preferred Taft, wrote that the great outpouring and the acclaim were tributes to the orator and the people's faith in him, he took exception. 'That Auditorium audience did not go there merely to hear me or because of their faith in me,' he wrote. 'It was a tribute to the man and cause for whom I spoke.' [6] From Roosevelt himself came a grateful note: 'What a fine speech you made at the Auditorium,' he telegraphed.[7]

A few days more, and he was at Bay City, Michigan, to address the State Convention, but the rioting that was to run its course through the National Convention had begun. The fac-

[1] Roosevelt's Columbus speech.   [2] Beveridge to Shaffer, Feb. 20, 1912.
[3] *Indianapolis Star*, March 1, 1912.   [4] Beveridge to Shaffer, March 13, 1912.
[5] *Indianapolis Star*, March 13, 1912.   [6] Beveridge to Shaffer, March 22, 1912.
[7] Roosevelt to Beveridge, March 21, 1912.

tions split, named contesting delegations, and in the violent tumult, Beveridge, in disgust, refused to speak, and left the hall.[1]

April found him battling in Massachusetts, presumably the hotbed of the enemy, speaking at Lynn, to the textile workers at Fall River, at an imposing meeting in Tremont Temple, Boston. 'Your Tremont Temple rally turned the tide for us in Boston and was a very great help throughout the State,' wrote Matthew Hale, the Roosevelt manager.[2] Thence through other portions of New England, where Taft had the advantage in the leadership of his forces.

When Beveridge, anxious at the time about his children's health,[3] sought release from further engagements, he was refused. The campaigning was tiresome, he was worried, and the traveling was expensive; but when the committee sent him a check to cover the expenses, he returned it promptly. 'When it came to cashing it, I simply could not do it,' he wrote Dixon. 'Somehow it goes against the grain. As you know, I have made it a rule not to accept even my traveling expenses on such matters as this.'[4] And he was distressed because Roosevelt had said it might be necessary for him to go to California. Another continental tour! It was too much. He begged Dixon to spare him if he could. 'Honestly, Joe, I don't want to go.'

But soon he was speeding westward with an itinerary that was reminiscent of the mad crusade of 1908. 'I've done many foolish things in my life,' he wrote his wife from Montana, 'but none so foolish as this absurd trip. It takes me from midnight tonight until 1 P.M. Monday to get to San Francisco. Then a week of desperate campaigning.... The Amalgamated [5] literally owns this State.... It was really funny last night to see the politicians on the stage shiver and shake when I defied the Amalgamated — and the crowd went wild.'[6]

Always popular in California, his meetings in San Francisco, Los Angeles, and in smaller cities were personal triumphs and contributed materially to the triumph of his cause.

But scarcely had he returned to Indianapolis when Roosevelt personally urged him to go to South Dakota; and he was on his way. A whirlwind campaign there, and he was through.

The pre-convention campaign had established beyond all

---

[1] The speech, printed for the press, is in the Beveridge MSS.
[2] May 13, 1912.
[3] Beveridge to Senator Dixon, Roosevelt manager, April 18, 1912.
[4] Beveridge to Dixon, April 28, 1912.
[5] The Amalgamated Copper Company.
[6] Beveridge to Mrs. Beveridge, May 4, 1912.

doubt the overwhelming popular demand for Roosevelt's nomination, but the reactionary element, bent on rule or ruin, had no thought of permitting it. Wherever possible it arranged for contesting delegations, since the convention machinery would be in their control. The certainty of a desperate struggle persuaded the followers of Roosevelt that he should crash through precedent and personally assume command of his forces in Chicago. That Beveridge had something to do with Roosevelt's decision to hurry to the convention city, the records show. 'Conforming with your request in reference to the attendance of Mr. Roosevelt here in Chicago during the Convention,' wrote a Roosevelt supporter, 'I have consulted with a number of the leaders, and, considering the closeness of the vote provided the Taft delegates contested are seated, I believe that the Colonel's presence would add material strength and enthusiasm to his followers. We have broken all precedents in our campaign to nominate Mr. Roosevelt and we might as well go even further and have him personally at the head of his forces.... I firmly believe that you are the one to put this up to Colonel Roosevelt and convince him that the best interest of the cause demands his presence.' [1] 'Just have your letter and have already communicated as you suggested,' Beveridge replied.[2]

And Roosevelt electrified the country by appearing personally on the battle-field.

II

But the reactionaries held their lines and grimly set about their task of seating the Taft contestants; and, in the chair, Elihu Root ruled with a hand of iron. With the drama of that convention we are not concerned save with the closing scenes. The ghastly cynicism with which the men in charge of the machinery drove over the protesting followers of Roosevelt was maddening, and Roosevelt was beside himself with rage. When the inevitable result was all too clear, there was a dramatic meeting in Roosevelt's room. He himself was utterly worn out with impotent rage and outward striving against Fate. Back and forth in silence he paced the room. In the northeast corner, Perkins and Munsey stood apart, talking in rapid whispers; the others in the room — and there were but few — were merely spectators. Somehow they knew that great events hung on the whispered conference, and all eyes were turned on the two participants. Munsey was the more agitated of the two. Sud-

[1] Charles H. Campbell to Beveridge, June 6, 1912.
[2] Beveridge to Campbell, June 8, 1912.

denly the whispering ceased when he made a decisive gesture. The two men straightened up, and moved together toward Roosevelt, meeting him in the middle of the room. Each placed a hand on one of Roosevelt's shoulders, and one said:

'Colonel, we will see you through.'

That, in later years, was to impress Amos Pinchot, one of the spectators, as marking the birth of the Progressive Party.[1]

As the audience drifted out, the real conference began, lasting from midnight until dawn. There was Roosevelt, fagged and haggard, with flushed face, sitting on the bed; and, grouped about him, Munsey, Perkins, and Henry L. Stoddard. The first two were urging the defeated leader to launch a third party fight, pledging him their fortunes. 'My fortune, my magazine, and my newspapers are with you,' said Munsey in tense tones.[2]

The first step was to be a bolt, the holding of a rump convention, the nomination of Roosevelt, and an appeal to the people.

In none of this did Beveridge have part. Only twice during the convention did he have a personal talk with Roosevelt, and in the last of these he refused to have any part in the Orchestra Hall mass meeting to put Roosevelt in the field as a third candidate. He himself has left a record of these talks:

I had only two private talks with T. R. The first was late in the afternoon of the first day of the convention. We sat together alone in his room for, I suppose, upward of an hour. I recall nothing more curious than that conference. Here we were with his fate, the fate of the party, almost the fate of the country at stake; yet both of us felt it so keenly that our talk was about almost everything else. It was casual, even trivial. T. R. was in one of his sweetest and most human moods, and I felt pretty human myself. I was interested in his health, how he was standing the strain, etc.; and he wanted to know all about the campaign I had made for him, how much it had cost me, whether my voice stood up well, how Mrs. Beveridge was, and what she thought about it. And I on my part wanted to know how Mrs. Roosevelt took it and what her judgment was, etc. In this talk T. R. grieved about Taft; what a disappointment he had been, how shamefully he had betrayed T. R., and the trust all of us had in him. Strangely enough, T. R.'s talk was not bitter — its tone was that of a deep regret....

The second talk was brief. On the afternoon that Taft was nominated and that Orchestra Hall 'convention' was held to nominate T. R., he sent a message to me in the convention to come to his room. When I got there, he asked me to be chairman of the committee to notify him of his nomination by the Orchestra Hall 'convention.' I refused to do so and said something like this: 'No, no, Colonel, that will be just as bad a mistake in tactics as the series of mistakes we have made through-

[1] Pinchot's 'The Progressive Party,' MS.
[2] H. L. Stoddard, *As I Knew Them*, 305.

out this convention.... To hold a rump convention is not the way to act if we are going to stay in the party, and it certainly is not the way to act if you intend to start a new party.'

He did not complain nor appear resentful, but said, 'You may be right; but it is too late to change things now. The matter has been determined.' [1]

It was to be determined later that a real convention would be necessary, with a platform of principles; but Beveridge left Chicago with no definite idea as to his course in the campaign.

III

He was ardently attached to the party of his youth and manhood; and while he differed in principle on vital things and on policy on many things for which the party organization stood, he could not have been a Democrat. His deep prejudice against Jefferson and his utter devotion to Hamiltonian principles were of the very texture of his being. But against this was his intense fidelity to Roosevelt and the alignment under his banner of three of the closest friends he ever had. Perkins, Munsey, and, above all, Shaffer — how could he part company with them? He saw the possibilities and felt the need of a new party, based elementally upon the principles of the old, but more progressive, more national, more scientific in its governmental methods, more sympathetic toward human needs. For the moment he had utterly lost faith in the Republican Party. But he knew that any party, to live, had to be built on something more substantial and permanent than the personal grievances of an individual. Was this new party to come into existence merely to advance the personal ambitions of Roosevelt? Then it was doomed to a short life and he wanted nothing to do with it, however ardent his devotion to the Colonel.

During his brief sojourn with his family at Seal Harbor, Maine, his mind was in turmoil. Back at home, the faithful Rothschild was reporting on sentiment with meticulous honesty and sending his usual wise advice. 'My judgment is,' he wrote, 'that you want to absolutely lay low for a considerable time, whatever you do. You have so much to take into consideration. If the Democrats succeed in launching a progressive candidate and a progressive platform at Baltimore, I don't believe that Roosevelt and his new party would have a look-in, or would live more than one campaign. The conditions will not exist sufficiently strong to make it permanent.' [2]

[1] Beveridge to William Allen White, Dec. 8, 1919.
[2] Rothschild to Beveridge, June 28, 1912.

But the same mail that brought this letter carried another from Lee, the State Chairman, reporting a rising sentiment for the new party. 'Many of your friends do not agree with Rothschild or Miller,[1] but are of the opinion that if a third party is started, you will almost of necessity have to cast your lot with it in order to be consistent, taking the position that you cannot align yourself with the old machine.[2] With the nomination of Woodrow Wilson by the Democrats, however, Rothschild was more than ever sure that Beveridge should stay out. He should 'give no interviews, get busy at something, and drop out for four or five months.' Had not the Democrats nominated a militant progressive? Would not progressives, bent on defeating Taft, vote for Wilson to make sure? Would not the overwhelming defeat of Taft call for a new leadership in the Republican Party? And 'the men who go with the third party will never get control of the Republican Party.' More:

I get information from some friends who have been playing with the other people [3] to the effect that... they are in hopes that you will join in the Roosevelt movement. They figure that... it will place you in such a position that they will not have to contend with you in the future. Of course Roosevelt has practically bolted; is up against THE proposition now... and has nothing else to do but go on with it. This is no reason why you, who always prided yourself on standing on your own feet, should give him the asset of your wonderful record to help him in his predicament.[4]

Meanwhile, Senator Dixon had informed him his name would be signed to the call for the Progressive National Convention unless he telegraphed his disapproval. Harassed by the pressure, he telegraphed Shaffer, who replied that his decision 'should be controlled entirely by your own views and those of Mrs. Beveridge.' That was enough. He refused to sign.

A little relieved now, he wrote frankly to Lee, in Indiana, of his refusal:

There are too many reasons to go into in a letter, but what do you think of this one item as an example: While T. R.'s immense popularity may give the third party greater strength in the present campaign than it might otherwise have, yet, being purely personal, it cannot be expected to last over other campaigns.

In case the third party has not enough vitality in fundamental principles to endure more than one campaign, only the Republican Party remains. The Republican Party could go on with its great pro-

---

[1] Charles W. Miller.   [2] Lee to Beveridge, June 28, 1912.
[3] The Anti-Beveridge crowd in Indiana.
[4] Rothschild to Beveridge, July 3, 1912.

gressive work if only it were rid of the evil men and the evil influences back of them, who have brought disgrace and humiliation to our party.

Mr. Taft, of course, will be defeated in any event — he would have been defeated overwhelmingly even if Colonel R. had not been a candidate and if Mr. Taft had been the unanimous choice of the Chicago Convention. The failure of his Administration would have assured that. What occurred at Chicago only adds to the defeat.

Will not this defeat rid the party of the men whom Mr. Taft has gathered about him and who constitute the party's weakness? What do you think of that? [1]

It was immediately after this that conferences momentous in Beveridge's career were held both in Chicago and New York, where he was urged to cast his lot with the new party, accept the chairmanship of the convention, deliver the keynote speech setting forth its principles and purpose. In these conferences sat three intimate and trusted friends — Shaffer, Perkins, and Munsey. He conditioned his acceptance on one positive assurance: that the new party would adopt a vital program of political and social reforms, and, if defeated that year, as he thought it might be, would continue aggressively into future campaigns as a permanent party. The assurance was given, the duty assigned him was accepted, and in a letter to the 'Indianapolis Star' [2] he announced his adherence to the Progressive Party. The next day his selection as the keynote speaker of the convention was given to the press.

Meanwhile, Beveridge was wrestling with another personal problem. As early as the first of July, Rothschild had warned him that he would receive many letters, inspired by an active canvass, urging his acceptance of the Progressive gubernatorial nomination. [3] The letters came, and again he appealed to Shaffer for advice. At first he refused, and then under increasing pressure he relented, and just before the National Convention he was nominated in a wildly demonstrative State Convention. 'I made a short fighting speech,' he wrote Shaffer, 'sending delegates home full of battle, murder, and sudden death for the enemy.' [4]

He left at once for Chicago and the Progressive National Convention.

IV

Immediately after agreeing to make the keynote speech, Beveridge turned to its preparation. He wanted to make it

[1] Beveridge to E. M. Lee, July 12, 1912.   [2] To W. H. Dye, July 25, 1912.
[3] Rothschild to Beveridge, July 3, 1912.   [4] Beveridge to Shaffer, Aug. 1, 1912.

fundamental, concise, stirring in the simplicity of the expression of striking truths, and within the comprehension of men in the factories and the corn rows. Hiding away from interruptions in Chicago, beyond the reach of anyone but Shaffer, Dixon, and Perkins, he sat down to the happy task of writing precisely what he thought. Having taken his stand, he was content, whatever might befall. 'What I have done and what I stand for has forced me into this,' he wrote his wife. 'But win or lose, it is the very last. My friends can think that I have lost my energy and initiative if they like; the people can think what they please, but this sacrifice is the final one.... The old party is gone.... We really are founding a new and great party. Albert and Abby can be proud of that — and that's something.'

The night before the convention met, a few men gathered in his room to hear him read his keynote speech, which Perkins thought the best he ever made. There were Roosevelt, Perkins, a few of the leaders. He read on in tense silence. This was the first official interpretation of the principles and purposes of a new party. It was a definite breaking with the past. One who was present noted that Beveridge, as he read, was 'laboring under emotion,' and that Roosevelt was 'visibly affected.' But for some reason his old friend Perkins was most deeply moved. The tears were coursing down his cheeks; and when Beveridge reached the part dealing with a course of justice for the men who make the Nation, an audible sob from Perkins startled everyone. He rose abruptly and left the room, pacing the corridors until he recovered his composure.[1]

V

It was a remarkable assembly of men and women that Beveridge faced in the National Progressive Convention, one of the most emotional in the story of American politics. One of the more enthusiastic and intelligent of the delegates, looking down from the gallery of the Coliseum upon the upturned faces, had a moment of misgiving. All bore the imprint of grim determination, and great numbers were lighted with a kind of exaltation. These were the men and women who thought they were forming a new party that would persist and purge the public service of corruption, and, through a program of social justice, contribute to the happiness and well-being of the whole people. Women like Jane Addams were conspicuous — women of high ideals of service to humanity. Here and there were men of character who, in their various communities, had fought for a generation

[1] Amos Pinchot to Joseph M. Dixon, *New York Times*, June 10, 1914.

against local grafting politicians, now happy in the thought that they were to have a real instrument for their purpose. College professors, social workers, business men of vision and independence, farmers tired of seeing Agriculture on the cross — these were enlisting in a cause they loved for unselfish service. But the delegate, looking down from the gallery, saw others who disturbed him — Socialists, in a hurry and impatient of the tactics of their party; sentimentalists, more moved by their emotions than by any processes of their mind, to whom Roosevelt later was to refer as the 'lunatic fringe'; but most disturbing of all were the cynical, hard-faced professional politicians with no ideals and no purpose beyond the possible collection of the loaves and fishes that Roosevelt's popularity might put within their reach. There were too many of these, perhaps; but to the casual observer they, too, were in a state of righteous exaltation. The man in the gallery was skeptical.[1]

The scene was one of drama. The delegations entered the hall cheering, and those already there cheered back and waved banners. A distinguished-looking man with a masterful manner, whom few recognized as Hiram Johnson, marched at the head of the California delegation bearing a banner that was greeted with cheers and laughter:

> 'I want to be a Bull Moose,
> And with the Bull Moose stand,
> With Antlers on my forehead,
> And a Big Stick in my hand.'

Soon the entire convention, under the incitation of the Michigan delegation, was parading the hall to the tune of their song:

> 'Follow! Follow!
> We will follow Roosevelt
> Anywhere! Everywhere
> We will follow on!'

But it was the New York delegation that gave the touch of religious fervor, as it marched down the aisle, led by Oscar S. Straus, noted Jewish philanthropist, singing:

> 'Onward, Christian soldiers!
> Marching as to war.'

This was more in accord with the spirit of the sincere souls, men and women, who really were moved to the depths of their being by lofty ideals of social and civic service, old Scotch Covenanters, Cromwell's Roundheads. Time and again during the demonstrations the martial air of the religious song was

[1] Amos Pinchot's observations, in 'The Progressive Party,' MS.

heard above the turmoil, and later, in a thousand meetings from coast to coast.

Thus the stage-setting and the mood of the convention was perfect for the kind of speech Beveridge had prepared. When, sober-visaged and immaculately attired, he appeared upon the platform, he was given an ovation; and instantly, without the customary preliminaries of such an address, he plunged to the heart of his theme. The convention, seeing in the first paragraph that it was to be a fighting speech, prepared to respond in fighting mood.

VI

We stand for a nobler America. We stand for an undivided Nation. We stand for a broader liberty, a fuller justice. We stand for social brotherhood as against savage individualism. We stand for an intelligent coöperation instead of a reckless competition. We stand for mutual helpfulness instead of mutual hatred. We stand for equal rights as a fact of life instead of a catchword of politics. We stand for the rule of the people as a practical truth instead of a meaningless pretense. We stand for a representative government that represents the people. We battle for the actual rights of man.

Thus he began; and the convention cheered.

A moment later, he had brushed aside the charge of its enemies that the convention met on a mission of revenge in protest against the grievance of an individual:

We found a party through which all who believe with us can work with us; or rather, we declare our allegiance to a party which the people themselves have founded.

For this party comes from the grass roots. It has grown from the soil of the people's hard necessities. It has the vitality of the people's strong convictions. The people have work to be done, and our party is here to do that work.

Lifting his theme above the level of mere partisanship as it appealed to many, he continued:

The people vote for one party and find their hopes turned to ashes on their lips; and then, to punish that party, they vote for the other party. So it is that partisan victories have come to be merely the people's vengeance; and always the secret powers have played the game.

Developing the idea that party warfare no longer meant a conflict between principles, but merely a struggle for patronage and power, he went on:

So there is no national unity in either party, no stability of purpose, no clear-cut and sincere program of one party at frank and open war with an equally clear-cut and sincere program of an opposing party.

Pointing out the incongruity in both old parties at war with each other on fundamental principles, he proceeded:

The condition makes it impossible most of the time, and hard at any time, for the people's legislators who believe in the same broad policies to enact them into logical comprehensive laws. It confuses the public mind. It breeds suspicion and distrust. It enables such special interests as seek unjust gain at the public expense to get what they want. It creates and fosters the degrading boss system in American politics through which these special interests work.

Turning now to the bosses, who were to be the special targets of the Progressives throughout the campaign, and appealing to all but the politicians in the audience, grown cynical with experience, he hurried on:

Under this boss system, no matter which party wins, the people seldom win; but the bosses almost always win. And they never work for the people. They do not even work for the party to which they belong. They work only for those anti-public interests whose political employees they are. It is these interests that are the real victors in the end.

This led on to a denunciation of the 'invisible government':

These special interests which suck the people's substance are bipartisan. They are the invisible government behind our visible government. Democratic and Republican bosses alike are brother officers of this hidden power.... The root of the wrongs which hurt the people is the fact that the people's government has been taken away from them — the invisible government has usurped the people's government. Their government must be given back to the people. And so the first purpose of the Progressive Party is to make sure the rule of the people.

And then he who had been infatuated in Switzerland with the initiative and referendum pledged the new party:

The rule of the people means that when the people's legislators make a law which hurts the people, the people themselves may reject it. The rule of the people means that when the people's legislators refuse to pass a law which the people need, the people themselves may pass it. The rule of the people means that when the people's employees do not do the people's work well and honestly, the people may discharge them, exactly as a business man discharges employees who do not do their work well and honestly. The people's employees are the people's servants, not the people's masters.

Asking what the absence of a real rule of the people has meant to the people, he answered:

We have more than enough to supply every human being beneath the flag. There ought not to be in this Republic a single day of bad business, a single unemployed workingman, a single unfed child. American business men should never know an hour of uncertainty, discouragement, or fear; American workingmen never a day of low wages, idleness, or want. Hunger should never walk in these thinly peopled gardens of plenty.

And yet, in spite of all these favors which Providence has showered upon us, the living of the people is the problem of the hour. Hundreds of thousands of hard-working Americans find it difficult to get enough to live on. The average income of an American laborer is less than five hundred dollars a year. With this he must furnish food, shelter, and clothing for a family.

Women whose nourishing and protection should be the first care of the State not only are driven into the mighty army of wage-earners, but are forced to work under unfair and degrading conditions. The right of a child to grow into a normal human being is sacred; and yet, while small and poor countries, packed with people, have abolished child labor, American mills, mines, factories, and sweatshops are destroying hundreds of thousands of American children in body, mind, and soul.

At the same time men have grasped fortunes in this country so great that the human mind cannot comprehend their magnitude. These mountains of wealth are far larger than even that lavish reward which no one would deny to business risk or genius.

And what would the Progressives do?

We mean to remedy these conditions. We mean not only to make prosperity steady, but to give to the many who earn it a just share of that prosperity instead of helping the few who do not earn it to take an unjust share. The Progressive motto is, 'Pass Prosperity around.' To make human living easier, to free the hands of honest business, to make trade and commerce sound and steady, to protect womanhood, save childhood, and restore the dignity of manhood — these are the tasks we must do.

Then he passed rapidly to the means to bring all this about and to a definition of the new party's attitude toward business. It was not to destroy Big Business, since this is necessary now, but —

We mean to try to make little business big, and all business honest, instead of striving to make Big Business little, and yet letting it remain dishonest.

And this meant the elimination of business evils: 'overcapitalization which taxes the people's very living,' 'the manipulation of prices to the people's damage,' and the 'running of the people's government in the unjust interest of evil business.' And how was the Government thus run? Hastily he sketched the story of the tobacco tax, and of the beef trust, by way of illustration:

Behind rotten laws and preventing sound laws stands the corrupt boss; behind the corrupt boss stands the robber interest; and commanding these powers of pillage stands bloated human greed. It is this invisible government we must destroy if we would save American institutions.

And how destroy it? Not through the Sherman anti-trust law, through which we 'have struck at Big Business itself and have not even aimed to strike at the evils of Big Business.' Instead of that, a national supervision of Big Business, to wipe out its evils and direct its power to the service of the people; to end the uncertainty of business men as to their rights and duties.

And the tariff? The new party would stand for a protective tariff, framed through scientific methods and the creation of a genuine tariff commission. The measure of 'protection'?

A tariff high enough to give American producers the American market when they make honest goods and sell them at honest prices, but low enough that when they sell dishonest goods at dishonest prices, foreign competition can correct both evils.

These, he continued, are 'samples of the reforms in the laws of business that we intend to put on the Nation's statute books.' But there were others that were pressing too. 'Child labor in factories, mills, mines, and sweatshops must be ended throughout the Republic'; women must be given the ballot; and there was something more:

The care of the aged is one of the most perplexing problems of modern life. How is the workingman with less than five hundred dollars a year, and with earning power waning as his own years advance, to provide for aged parents or other relatives, in addition to furnishing food, shelter, and clothing for his wife and children? What is to become of the family of the laboring man whose strength has been sapped by excessive toil and who has been thrown upon the industrial scrap-heap? It is questions like these we must answer if we are to justify free institutions. They are questions to which the masses of the people are chained as to a body of death.

Did the opposition challenge their right to make such reforms by citing the Constitution?

The Progressive Party believes that the Constitution is a living thing, growing with the people's growth, strengthening with the people's strength, aiding the people in their struggles for life, liberty, and the pursuit of happiness, permitting the people to meet all their needs as conditions change.

As he approached the close, his manner increased in fervor, his voice rang like a clarion. He ended with a note of defiance and a battle-cry. He was addressing many who had broken with the political associations of a lifetime, and at them his last words were aimed:

Knowing the price we must pay, the sacrifice we must make, the burdens we must carry, the assaults we must endure — knowing full well the cost — yet we enlist and we enlist for the war. For we know the justice of our cause, and we know, too, its certain triumph.

Not reluctantly, then, but eagerly, not with faint hearts, but strong, do we now advance upon the enemies of the people. For the call that comes to us is the call that came to our fathers. As they responded, so shall we.

> 'He has sounded forth a trumpet that shall never call retreat,
> He is sifting out the hearts of men before His judgment seat,
> Oh, be swift our souls to answer Him, be jubilant our feet,
> Our God is marching on.'

As he concluded, the convention burst into rapturous applause. The band blared forth with 'The Battle Hymn of the Republic,' but it could not be heard above the frenzied cheering of the standing crowd. Richard Harding Davis, reporting the convention for 'Collier's Weekly,' concluded that 'until Beveridge spoke, the delegates lacked cohesion; they wanted for something to weld them into a unit. With his speech, Beveridge did that. It was a really big speech, delivered earnestly, with no theatricalism, with no consciousness of self. It was full of food for thought, full of good lines, full of swift home-thrusts that brought the delegates cheering to their feet. It pulled them together, sent them out into the night with something to bite on, and, incidentally, through that speech the man who delivered it "came back."' [1]

Not one who heard but knew that he or she was listening to one of the most remarkable speeches ever addressed to a party convention. At first some, and especially the politicians seeking loaves and fishes, were stunned at the audacity of the performance. These things were said about the dinner-table, and these things were thought by average men and women, but when before had a public man proclaimed them from a platform with such clarity and power? No elaborate rhetoric had obscured the meaning of the short, crisp sentences, and each had come like the cracking of a whip. Its art was in its simplicity; its power was in its truth; its novelty was in its honesty. That day was Beveridge day at the convention. Roosevelt was delighted; the downright frankness had pleased the press correspondents surfeited with speeches written with the Talleyrand concept of the purpose of language; and even from stand-patters came

[1] *Collier's Weekly*, Aug. 24, 1912.

praise. Soon the orator would be reading a letter from Chauncey M. Depew from Aix-les-Bains:

I have read your speech at the Roosevelt Convention as published entire in the 'Chicago Tribune.' You and I are as far apart as the poles in the present campaign, but I admire a good speech, and love to tell a friend so when he has made a brilliant effort. As a speech, and for the purpose for which it was delivered, it is the best of your life. It is a masterpiece, and your statements are put with singular epigrammatic force, and antithesis was never more attractively utilized.[1]

VII

That night the platform committee labored over the resolutions while Roosevelt, Perkins, Munsey, and others sat in rooms upstairs, pencils in hand, going over each plank as it was sent up. The incidents of the evening were to disclose a lack of unity on economic questions. It was almost dawn, the members fagged and nervous, when Professor Charles McCarthy, Legislative Librarian of Wisconsin, phrased the committee's thought on the Sherman anti-trust law in these words:

We favor strengthening the Sherman law by prohibiting agreements to divide territory or limit output; refusing to sell to customers who buy from business rivals; to sell below cost in certain areas while maintaining high prices in other places; using the power of transportation to aid or injure special business concerns; and other unfair trade practices.

Beveridge, in truth had long publicly urged the repeal of the Sherman anti-trust law, but Roosevelt had agreed to some such plank as McCarthy had written. It was sent upstairs. When the industrial planks came down again, the committee was stunned to find the trust plank stricken out. They knew it was a direct challenge to the Morgan interests with which Perkins had been connected; and indirectly struck at the International Harvester Company, then under fire for such practices as were specifically condemned, and with which Perkins was associated. It was concluded that the blue-penciling was the work of Perkins, and the committee incorporated the plank.

The next day Dean Lewis, chairman of the committee, was reading the platform to the convention. He reached the plank on the Sherman Act. Perkins, seated beside Amos Pinchot, turned excitedly to him: 'Lewis has made a mistake. That does not belong in the platform. We cut it out last night,' he whispered. Springing to his feet he left the hall. A conference was called. Oscar King Davis, secretary of the Progressive National

[1] Depew to Beveridge, Aug. 21, 1912.

Committee, was sent hurrying to the press associations and newspaper offices with instructions to prevent the printing of the offending declaration. This was done; the press did not carry it; and the platform printed for distribution in the campaign also omitted it. No one noticed. Everyone was thinking of Roosevelt and too few of economic issues; but there was to be an explosion later.[1] In the wild tumult which followed the nomination of Roosevelt, no one cared. With the nomination of Hiram Johnson for the second place on the ticket, the delegates surged into the streets shouting, singing:

> 'Onward, Christian soldiers!
> Marching as to war.'

VIII

There was only one possible result — the election of Wilson. The country was convinced of the genuineness of his progressivism. Unembarrassed by the vituperations of his two opponents, he was free to confine himself exclusively to the discussion of principles and policies. Soon, in the turmoil, his seemed the one serene voice. Roosevelt successfully was dramatizing himself as a crusader of civic righteousness opposed by unscrupulous bosses; and, sweeping across the country, was receiving hysterical ovations. The Republicans took alarm. There was a notable lack of fervor in their meetings and experienced politicians were soon convinced that Roosevelt would poll more votes than Taft. The contest speedily resolved itself into a contest between Wilson and Roosevelt.

The conditions were similar in the gubernatorial contest in Indiana, where it was early seen that either Beveridge or Samuel M. Ralston, the Democrat, would win. The intense bitterness among the Republicans pointed from the beginning to a large and secret support of Wilson and Ralston to beat Roosevelt and Beveridge.

A vacationless summer it was for Beveridge. A few days with his family at Seal Harbor, and he was off to the war. Opening the Progressive fight in Vermont,[2] he tried to convince the public that Wilson would be a tool of the bosses because the New Jersey bosses had nominated him for Governor. 'Do you imagine those bosses would do it without first making their deal?' he asked. It was a blunder. Wilson's defiance of the bosses was table-talk across the continent.

Keenly conscious of the difficulties of his task, Beveridge, who seldom opened his campaigns before the last of September,

[1] Amos Pinchot, 'The Progressive Party,' MS.   [2] Aug. 21, 1912.

formally opened on September 7 at Indianapolis. On national issues he reiterated and reënforced the views he had set forth in his keynote speech; he localized the 'boss' issue by attacking the two 'machines' in Indiana. He then set forth his program for Indiana — an eight-hour day, workingmen's compensation, a minimum wage for women, an adequate public utilities commission, free text books for children in the public schools. He would fight for tax reforms, road improvements under a State highway commission, and for the initiative, referendum, and recall.

Closing with an appeal to the progressives of both old parties, he paid eloquent tribute to Jefferson and Lincoln. Never before this campaign had Jefferson elicited his admiration; never was he to give expression to it again. The frequent approving references to Jefferson this year were made as a gesture to the Democrats.

IX

Immediately he was in the full tide of his campaign, speaking daily, sometimes five times a day, to large audiences that responded fervently. In his fierce denunciation of the 'bosses,' he continued to treat Woodrow Wilson as their tool until the Democratic nominee took notice and dismissed it as a rare bit of humor.[1] The two opponents in the gubernatorial race were attacked as boss-owned and corporation-controlled; and Ralston responded with a denunciation of Beveridge's defense of trusts.[2] Soon Bryan, never more than at this period the idol of the Indiana Democrats, was making another of his triumphant tours through the State, speaking from nine in the morning until midnight, and treating the 'tardy reformation' of Roosevelt and Beveridge ironically.[3]

And Beveridge was striking back lustily, though handicapped by the knowledge that progressive Democrats, whose votes he sought, believed in Bryan. All the while, as the Progressives were defending trusts as inevitable and promising regulation, Woodrow Wilson was satirizing their position. 'Have we come to the time,' he asked, 'when the President of the United States who wishes to be President must doff his cap in the presence of this high finance and say, "You are our inevitable master, but we will see how we can make the best of it"?' Thus, as the campaign progressed, the strategy of the Democrats was to belittle the sincerity of the pretensions of the new party; and the at-

[1] *Indianapolis Star*, Sept. 17, 1912.
[2] *Ibid.*, Sept. 20, 1912. [3] *Ibid.*, Oct. 18, 1912.

tempt to align Wilson with the bosses had unhappy repercussions.

But Roosevelt and Beveridge were making enormous inroads on the Republicans, and soon these, abandoning all hope of victory, were directing their efforts solely against the new party's nominees. The word was going down the line to vote for Wilson and Ralston to make certain the defeat of the Progressives. It was the Republicans, more than the Democrats, who raised the hue and cry that millionaires and trust magnates were flooding the State with slush funds in the interest of Beveridge. Was he not the friend of Perkins, of the Morgan interests, and the harvester trust? There was no twilight zone in that campaign between moderation and bitter personalities — no gradual approach to fury. The bloodhounds of hate were unleashed early in September and they were howling at Beveridge's heels until the end.

X

And then, at Milwaukee, a maniac's bullet wounded Roosevelt, and the wounded man, hurrying to his meeting, pulled back his vest, revealed the bloodstain, and proceeded with his speech. There was a moment of awesome silence. No one knew how serious the wound. Woodrow Wilson canceled his speaking engagements for the moment. And Beveridge hurried to Chicago to the bedside of his chief.

The purpose of the summons was to ask Beveridge to act as the ambassador and spokesman of the stricken leader in Louisville, and for more than an hour in the sick-room the two men conferred on the message to be delivered. The chief had fallen and had passed the banner on to Beveridge.

Not a man, but a cause [Beveridge began at Louisville]; not even a personality, but a principle. This is the word the shot at Milwaukee speaks to the American people. For had that shot done the work that it was meant to do, yet it would not have stayed the cause. Had it laid the great leader low, still the principle would have marched onward. But our great leader is spared to lead that forward movement in American life, which God meant him to lead to final victory. Over slander and abuse; over falsehood and libel, over craft and cunning, over plot for his ruin by criminal wealth and the crazed mind which was the shot's sure fruit — over all the forces of evil and their workmen the great American prevails.

And then he read Roosevelt's message:

It matters little about me, but it matters all about the cause we fight for. If one soldier who happens to carry the flag is stricken, another will take it from his hands and carry on. One after another the standard-bearers may be laid low, but the standard itself will never fall. You know that personally I did not want ever to be a candidate for office again. And you know that only the call that came to the men of the sixties made me answer it in our day, as they did more nobly in their day. And now, as then, it is not important whether one leader lives or dies; it is important only that the cause shall live and win. Tell the people not to worry about me; for if I go down, another will take my place. For always the army is there, and it is the cause for which the people should care, for it is the people's cause.

Meanwhile, again the guns were roaring along the whole line, unsilenced by the Milwaukee shot, and Beveridge hurried back to the battle-front in Indiana.

XI

It was toward the close of the fight that his enemies aimed their poisoned arrow at him. A senatorial committee, under the chairmanship of Clapp, was inquiring into the scandal of campaign funds, and suddenly the press announced that the fund of Beveridge was under scrutiny, and more was heard about his close relations with Perkins.

Nationally the rumor was afloat that millionaires like Perkins and Munsey were pouring untold sums into the coffers of the new party — offerings of the great corporations with which they were connected. Beveridge long had been mindful of the danger. Long before, despite his affectionate friendship for Perkins and Munsey, he had said to Amos Pinchot: 'Perkins, Munsey, and Littauer are too much in evidence. If we're not careful we'll be labeled as a Wall Street promotion.' [1] And now the attempt was being made to paste the label on his back, and the enemy press was making the most of it!

The reaction of Beveridge and his friends was that of indignation. Scrupulously throughout his career he had refused large contributions to his campaign funds from Perkins, and others like him; meticulously he had turned their checks over to Charles E. Coffin for safe-keeping; and invariably they had been sent back after the election. In the winter of that very year, when he was momentarily embarrassed, and Perkins had offered to relieve him, he had refused: 'I simply cannot bring myself to accept your generosity,' he had written. 'My debts are my own, and I should, and must, take care of them myself. I can do this readily, but even if it involved sacrifice, that would be no reason or excuse for permitting even a lifelong friend to

[1] Pinchot, 'The Progressive Party,' MS.

help me out. The fact that I am not in public life does not change this.'[1]

And now he stood accused!

His friends, infuriated, ascribed the move to 'political assassins,' and it was denounced as 'dirty and dishonest business.'[2] Soon the Senate Committee learned that in 1904, the campaign concerning which the charge was made, Beveridge had returned many thousands of dollars in uncashed checks; and Clapp, who knew him, knew this to be true. The summons to appear before the committee therefore was withdrawn.

But that did not satisfy Beveridge.

Dramatically, he appeared in Washington demanding a hearing. Conscious of his rectitude, he was easily the master of the situation, and he opened his testimony with a rebuke to the committee in the comment that in 1904 twenty-nine senators had been elected, and of this number he alone was the subject of a senatorial investigation.

'I have been wondering,' he continued, with sarcasm, 'whether the committee has been entirely fair in neglecting the other twenty-eight gentlemen and favoring me.'

Profuse apologies instantly were offered by individual members. Ignoring these Beveridge hurried on with his statement. In 1904 he had received checks for substantial amounts from George W. Perkins and Edward L. McClain. The latter was his cousin, to whom he had been close as a brother since boyhood; the former had been his intimate friend from early manhood. Both checks had been inspired by friendship and that alone.

On receiving the checks, his first thought had been, 'I can't use this money; I'll return it at once.' Thomas R. Shipp, his secretary, and John Hayes, assistant, suggested the wisdom of taking the opinion of Rothschild first on the wisdom of an immediate return. He was summoned. Commenting that the contributions had been offered in a spirit of disinterested friendship, he advised against the immediate return of the checks lest such precipitate action offend the contributors. Shipp agreed — and Hayes.

'If you fellows think it is best to hold them for a while, then I guess it is best,' Beveridge had said. Then, in the presence of these men, he placed the checks in an envelope, instructed Shipp to seal it, wrote his name upon it with the date, and had each of his 'kitchen cabinet' write theirs. 'Now, Tom, take it to the bank and put it in a safety deposit box.' This had been done.

The day after the election he had called Rothschild, Shipp, Hayes, and his friend Larz Whitcomb into his room to witness

[1] Beveridge to Perkins, Jan. 20, 1912.   [2] *Indianapolis Star*, Oct. 23, 1912.

the return of the checks and drafts. To a duplicate copy of the letter to Perkins the four men appended a certification:

We hereby certify that we have compared the enclosed with the original; have seen two certificates of deposit, No. 19415 and No. 19437 of the First National Bank, New York, each for $10,000, and one draft payable to the order of the Central Trust Company for $10,-000, or $30,000 in all, endorsed to George W. Perkins by Albert J. Beveridge, enclosed in said letter, and we have seen same sealed and mailed.

A similar certification was made in the case of the other contribution.

'And here,' said Beveridge, 'are the certifications' — as he passed them to the committee, with the request that they be returned to him. 'I want to keep them for my children.'

It was all sheer drama — the very simplicity of the recital. The members of the committee sat in silence. Then one of them asked what reply Perkins had sent to the letter returning the checks and drafts.

'I would rather not answer,' he replied.

The committee insisted.

'It was in the form of a telegram reading, "An honest man is the noblest work of God."'

Thus did his enemies play into his hands and dramatize his honesty in the permanent records of the Nation.[1]

But the incident, so base in its inception, intensified the bitterness of the personalities, and the campaign closed in a sort of rage. Intensive as was his campaign in Indiana, Beveridge had found time to assist the national cause with speeches in Madison, Wisconsin, in Philadelphia, and in Columbus, Ohio. Only the appeal of Perkins and Pinchot for speeches in New York to counteract the ultra-conservatism of the campaign there, was denied because of the demands at home.

The contest closed with victory for Wilson and Ralston; but Roosevelt and Beveridge polled more votes than their Republican opponents, and but two States gave their electoral votes to Taft. In one campaign the Progressives had become 'the party of the Opposition.'

And after the election, the Marion and Columbia Clubs in Indianapolis removed Beveridge's picture from their walls.

[1] 'Campaign Contributions,' Testimony, II, 1235–50, 62d Cong., 3d session, U.S. Senate.

CHAPTER VIII

CRUMBLING FOUNDATIONS

I

IN VIEW of the astonishing vote polled by the new party, most of its leaders and the rank and file assumed immediately after the election that it had come to stay. There was no reason why Roosevelt should not lead it in the next campaign, but, should he prefer to lay aside the scepter, there were brilliant men to take it up. Insistently it had been dinned into the public consciousness that the new party was more than a mere instrument for the advancement of the personal ambitions of a single man. But it was soon evident to a few that Roosevelt was not entirely happy in his new alignment. Aside from a group of brilliant and able orators, statesmen, journalists, and social workers, he found little in his new associations to appeal to him.

This state of mind was not at first apparent to the leaders, who eagerly prepared to press forward in the reorganization of the Progressive forces for the next election. To this end a conference of the leaders with Roosevelt was called at Chicago for mid-December, but opinion was not harmonious as to the character of the meeting; Medill McCormick wished to take advantage of Roosevelt's presence to hold a great town meeting, while others questioned the wisdom of an open meeting or of exploiting an individual. For a time McCormick prevailed, and it was arranged to hold the meeting in Orchestra Hall, with Roosevelt presiding and Beveridge making the principal speech.[1] The latter questioned both the open meeting and the propriety of his making the principal speech.[2] In the end a dinner was substituted, with everyone, including Roosevelt, Beveridge, and Perkins, paying for his own ticket. These three would be called upon to speak.[3] But the conference was to accentuate dissensions and narrowly escape ending in an open rupture.

A strong sentiment had been developing against the continuance of Perkins in the chairmanship of the executive committee. His corporation affiliations were thought disadvantageous in appealing to the masses. He was suspected of responsibility for the mysterious suppression of the anti-monopoly plank. Thus, with the calling of the conference, some, under

[1] Shaffer to Beveridge, Dec. 2, 1912.
[2] Beveridge to Shaffer, Dec. 4, 1912.
[3] Shaffer to Beveridge, Dec. 5, 1912.

the leadership of Amos Pinchot, proposed to make it the occasion for the dropping of Perkins. The first gun in the skirmish was fired by Pinchot in a letter to Roosevelt. 'Unless we keep the great issue clear,' he wrote, 'unless we make plain beyond a suspicion our stand on the great economic question whether the trust shall or shall not be allowed to exploit the people by dictating the terms upon which the people shall obtain food, fuel, and clothing, we will lack a cause and our party will be a flash in the pan. I believe that under the circumstances the selection of a trust magnate as a leader of our party would be bad politics and bad ethics.' He concluded with the direct charge that Perkins had been responsible for the emasculation of the platform.[1]

So incensed was Roosevelt and the first draft of his reply was so intolerant in tone that he was persuaded to moderate it on the train *en route* to Chicago. The answer finally sent did not reach Pinchot until after the conference. It was a denial of the sole responsibility of Perkins for the dropping of the trust plank, which the Colonel thought 'utterly unimportant'; a challenge to the charge that trusts increase prices; and a protest against a program calculated to make the property interests apprehensive.

I believe that our vote would have been cut in half at once if we had not been able to persuade two or three millions of good men and women that we were not engaged in an assault on property, or in wild and foolish radicalism. I believe that the suspicion that we were over-radical, were jeopardizing property and business, cost us a million or two votes. I further believe that if we put out Perkins, and then did the only logical thing by putting out all men like him, we should gain one or two hundred thousand votes and lose two or three millions.[2]

In the absence of an answer from Roosevelt, Pinchot determined to launch his fight with a demand on Senator Dixon, who would preside, for the immediate restoration of the trust plank. Scarcely had he reached the La Salle Hotel when an irate delegation, including Oscar Straus and Dixon, warned him that an attack on Perkins would instantly disrupt the party. He disclaimed any intention of attacking Perkins, explained that he would confine his fight to the restoration of the suppressed plank, and proposed that they all go to Roosevelt's room to discuss the situation. But Roosevelt refused to receive them. When the conference convened, a fight was averted when, after a conference with Roosevelt, Dixon announced that the plank had been inadvertently dropped, read it in a monotone, and said

[1] Pinchot to Roosevelt, Dec. 3, 1912.
[2] Roosevelt to Pinchot, Dec. 5, 1912.

that, in the absence of an objection, it would be taken as the will of the conference that it should be included in future printings.[1]

But a struggle involving Perkins's status in the party had begun which was to be distressing to Beveridge and dangerous to party solidarity. It was to gain in momentum for more than a year and end in an open rupture. Within six months, in the midst of the Wilson Administration's suit against the International Harvester Company, Perkins added oil to the flames in an interview declaring that in Canada they knighted men for doing what the creators of the Harvester Company had done. Another six months, and he was engaged in an acrimonious debate with Senator Borah on monopoly, insisting that a successful attack upon the steel trust would be a national calamity.

It was after this that Amos Pinchot brought the fight into the open in a letter to Senator Dixon demanding the retirement of Perkins, and with its publication there was a general drawing of swords. Beveridge aligned himself aggressively with Perkins, and wrote Gifford Pinchot inquiring if he had known of his brother's intended attack. The reply was far from comforting. The great forester thought it unfortunate that it had been necessary to publish the letter, but agreed heartily with its sentiments. 'It is, of course, utterly out of the question,' he wrote, 'that our party should gain or hold the confidence of the working people of this country with Perkins at the head of the organization.'[2] In the mean time, others high in the party counsels had joined in the demand for Perkins's dismissal or resignation. Medill McCormick had written him that he should resign from the chairmanship of the party or retire from the steel and harvester trusts. It was not his opinion alone, he wrote — it was shared by Dixon, Hiram Johnson, William Allen White, and Raymond Robins. The latter was strong in the conviction that a million workingmen never would join a party 'whose executive head is also the head of two corporations, of which the labor policy is anti-union.'[3]

But Roosevelt was adamant and Beveridge loyal to his friend. When William Allen White wrote him that 'no man should long continue as the real active managerial head of the party who combines all the points of attack that Perkins combines,' Beveridge wrote a spirited defense:

I have known George Perkins intimately for more than a quarter of a century. He was a progressive before any of us. Years before I went

[1] Pinchot, 'The Progressive Party.' MS.
[2] Gifford Pinchot to Beveridge, June 24, 1914.
[3] McCormick to Perkins, July 14, 1914.

to the Senate, George Perkins was talking about the very things for which we are standing now. And look at George Perkins's personal work. Let me give you a few instances: It was George Perkins, who, when the Steel Corporation was formed, after a long and arduous struggle succeeded in getting that great corporation to adopt publicly as its policy and publish in the newspapers its assets and liabilities every year, and this, too, before there was a law in the country requiring such publicity and before the agitation for it had started. It was George Perkins who finally got that corporation, and others with which he was connected, to adopt the minimum-wage scale, the old-age pension, the profit-sharing system, and other similar things for the men who work for those corporations.[1]

Thus the contest over Perkins, beginning within a month of the election and continuing with increasing feeling to within three months of the congressional elections, was doing desperate damage to the party solidarity. It was doing something more — it was demonstrating the inability of even the leaders to agree upon a definition of progressivism.

II

But even more destructive was the constant undertone of conversation on the possible amalgamation of the Progressives with the Republicans. It suggested a party eager for its shroud. This was certain to hasten the return of the timid and the time-servers among the local politicians to the party they had left. Within three months of the election of 1912, Beveridge was engaged in a correspondence with his friend Frank Munsey which perilously approached the acrimonious. The latter had broached the subject to Beveridge in conversation, and there had been an explosive remonstrance. Munsey left no doubt of his position, and little as to the real feeling of Roosevelt, in a letter to Beveridge later:

Dear Albert: For the most part you and I have seen things much the same way in national affairs, but this is one of the times that we are occupying divergent paths, and must continue to occupy them unless you get a new view of my attitude.

This is one of the times, Albert, that I know I am right all the way through. There is no guessing about it, no fine balancing of one idea against another — it is positive certainty.

I have gone into this matter a good deal further since seeing you, analyzing it more deeply, and have talked with a good many men of both parties, little men and big men, including the Grand Chief himself, Mr. R. And he is a grand chief, a very big broad man whose eyes sweep over the whole political field and sees things. Not much escapes him.

[1] Beveridge to White, July 6, 1914.

If you stand stiff-backed where you did the other day when I first flung out the idea of amalgamation, a conference would not help matters. On the other hand, if you begin to see some wisdom and hard-headed business sense in my proposal, I am sure it would be very much worth while to both of us if we could talk the problem over. Of course, I am always glad to see you, whether we agree or not.

I am especially anxious, however, that you should open up to a receptive view of this scheme and get busy with me in helping bring it about. It has survived the stage of satire and ridicule, and it is now occupying the serious thoughts of the people. Believe me, Albert, it is sinking into productive soil. We have got to get together the people who think alike, have got to get them together as a fighting force to go into the field against our common enemy, the Democratic Party.

You have had years of experience in statesmanship and I have had years of experience in business. The business side of politics is a very important one. It takes money to organize and maintain a political organization and to maintain a fighting force in the field.

There is no considerable money in the Progressive Party, save in the pockets of a very few, and the very few will not feel called upon to fight another campaign alone. We need the Republican voters and they need us. We need their money and they need our idealism.[1]

Thoroughly alarmed by this insidious undermining of the party that had polled more votes than the Republicans, Beveridge took up his pen to combat it in the 'Saturday Evening Post.' How, he asked, are you going to merge with the Republicans when millions of Democrats voted with the Progressives? How merge Cannon and La Follette; Penrose and Cummins? And what terms did these Progressives, hoping for amalgamation, expect to get? Had not Senators Smoot and Gallinger served notice that they must return as penitents, in sackcloth and ashes? And why the defeatist attitude when more organization work was being done by the Progressives than by both the old parties combined? And Republicans and Progressives stand for the same thing? Absurd! They differ on trust regulation, on the initiative, referendum, and recall, on the idea that labor was a commodity. And child labor, too. 'How can the Progressive Party, which has this concept of nationalism as one of its basic principles, be merged with another party that denies that principle? Will the Republican Party put a child-labor plank in its platform? Let the merger promoters try it.'[2]

Then, in the late summer, returning from Arizona, Roosevelt gave an interview which, not without reason, the Republican press interpreted as showing a disposition to bargain with the Republicans for a return. Beveridge felt that Roosevelt should

[1] Frank Munsey to Beveridge, Feb. 3, 1913.
[2] Saturday Evening Post, June 28, 1913.

have met the charge with an instant challenge. The Colonel, stressing the importance to the Progressive cause of making a good showing in the Maine elections that September, had written him in June that he had a 'very earnest hope' that Beveridge would speak there because of the 'real importance' to the 'future of the Progressive Party in New England.' Wishing publicly to denounce the interpretation of the Roosevelt interview with his sanction, Beveridge had written for authority; and receiving no reply, telegraphed just as he was starting for Boston:

Just starting for Maine. Have received no answer to my letter of last Thursday.... Have I your authority...? Please wire me care Touraine hotel. I shall be there until nine o'clock tonight.

A letter awaited him at the Touraine:

I am awfully glad that you are going to Maine. By all means treat that preposterous story just as you suggest (but don't speak of dishonor ever in a hypothetical case about me). As you know, I have for a year and a half been explaining to the Republicans just how they can get together with us — that is, by adopting our platform in its entirety, by retiring their own leaders of the Root, Penrose, Barnes, Smoot variety — and then I am afraid we should have to insist upon their changing their name, not that to me personally names mean anything, but because they do mean so much to many people. This month I have an article in the 'Century Magazine'... which I think you will approve. But I speak sincerely when I say that it does not approach your really great article in the 'Saturday Evening Post,' which was the finest justification of our position which I have as yet come across.[1]

But Beveridge still felt that Roosevelt himself should scotch or crush the story, and so wrote him; and Roosevelt replied with some impatience:

Now, you say 'the lie must be handled without gloves.' The trouble is, where am I to stop when I begin to handle lies without gloves? The Republican 'Standard Union' of Brooklyn, the big Republican paper there, has just come out with a detailed lie, far more detailed than the one you quote, and far more openly stated, saying that my purpose is to secure the election of the Democracy; that my whole purpose is to help Tammany. Now, it is a mere question with me just when it becomes necessary to deny these lies. If I deny too many of them, I weaken my own position, and really the statement which you wished me to deny is such a rank absurdity that it is hard for me to make up my mind to deny it at all.[2]

Beveridge could not see the comparison and was disheartened at Roosevelt's reluctance to make a personal denial. He turned

---

[1] Roosevelt to Beveridge, Sept. 2, 1913.
[2] Roosevelt to Beveridge, Sept. 9, 1913.

on the National Committee with a hot remonstrance against
the failure to denounce the common gossip that Roosevelt 'wants
to go back to the Republican Party and is planning to get the
Republican nomination in 1916.' This, he wrote, 'has hurt.'
'Our people hardly know what to think. The one thing we cannot and must not permit is any suspicion of our political and
moral integrity, or that of our great leader.' What did Ormsby
McHarg mean by his Detroit statement that Roosevelt was
really conservative at heart and would be the Republican
nominee in 1916? Such comments from one associated with the
Roosevelt fight in 1912 was destructive.[1]

Two months later, at a Progressive conference in Indianapolis,
addressed by national leaders, Beveridge, who was not on the
program, asked the audience if they wished to amalgamate.
There was a thunderous 'No.'

But the rumors poisoned the air, and too few of the leaders
seemed to care. Beveridge began to bombard Perkins with
protests and warnings. Walter Brown of Ohio was said to have
talked pessimistically of the prospects. 'It would break my
heart if it turned out that Walter is fooling us. I simply cannot
believe it,' he wrote Perkins. And what of the organizer in the
pay of the committee who was telling the Progressives in South
Dakota that a merger with the Republicans would be all right?[2]

But even Perkins was not disturbed, and replied in jesting
mood. 'Like wildfire the rumor is spreading that you have left
the Progressive Party,' he wrote. 'You have been so prominent
in the Progressive cause that these persistent rumors of the
last three or four days are doing a great deal of harm.' Perkins
would not credit these rumors but for the proof in his possession.
'The proof comes in the shape of unmistakable evidence, viz.,
a photograph taken in Indianapolis of the members of the Progressive Club at the formal opening on November 25, 1913.
It is pointed out that you are absolutely the only Progressive
in the State who is not in the photograph.'[3] And, pleased with
the joke, Perkins wrote again the next day. 'I was so disturbed
about not finding you in the photograph that I had it X-rayed
and hasten to let you know that you were found hiding behind
the chimney toward the left hand of the picture. So that everything is once more serene, and our minds are relieved of a great
load.'[4]

So, with Munsey aggressively demanding amalgamation,
Perkins was treating the matter lightly! Not in the least reas-

[1] Beveridge to O. K. Davis, Sept. 10, 1913.
[2] Beveridge to Perkins, Nov. 29, 1913.
[3] Perkins to Beveridge, Dec. 11, 1913.   [4] Dec. 12, 1913.

sured by the levity of Perkins, Beveridge put aside his letter to
write Medill McCormick urging that the 'Chicago Tribune'
sound a battle-cry and make it clear that 'under no circumstances or conditions shall there be any merger, amalgamation,
or connection of any kind with any other party whatever.' [1]
The 'sincerity and integrity of the Progressive Party' was 'at
stake.'

III

Not content with merely combating amalgamation propaganda, Beveridge was exerting himself to strengthen the new
party. In heavy demand for speeches all over the country, he
responded to all he could. He was passionately in earnest about
creating a great party, liberal according to his lights, and he
saw no hope in the party he had left.[2] This was to be his theme
at a Northwestern Progressive conference in St. Paul in January.
'I am going to try to make this speech a really big one,' he
wrote Shaffer, 'and shall try to show the Republicans that that
party has finished its mission just as the Whig Party had finished
its mission when the Republican Party was formed.' [3] The next
day he was speaking to the Progressives in Iowa. The next
month found him talking with Roosevelt at a New York banquet,[4]
and thence he went to Burlington, Vermont, where he addressed
the Progressives in a speech described as 'one of the greatest
ever given on economics and the industrial situation in New
England.' [5] When Governor Hadley of Missouri recanted Progressivism, it was Beveridge who replied in an address at
Detroit.[6] At Springfield, Illinois, he explained the Progressive
concept of the tariff.[7]

But of all the non-campaign speeches of the year, that at
New Orleans was the most important and significant, prepared
with the greatest care, in the hope of strengthening the party
in the South. Speaking at the Athenæum to a responsive audience, Beveridge did not question the abiding hostility to the Republican Party in the South; he knew its history when in power
there. He aimed to show it a political advantage to the section
in a divided allegiance; glowingly expanded on its industrial and
commercial possibilities; took it to the mountain-top and showed
it all the kingdoms of the earth. Thence he passed to a powerful

[1] Beveridge to McCormick, Dec. 15, 1913.
[2] Beveridge to Rothschild, Aug. 24, 1913.
[3] Beveridge to Shaffer, Jan. 24, 1913.
[4] *Indianapolis Star*, Feb. 13, 1913.   [5] *Ibid.*, Feb. 15, 1913.
[6] *Ibid.*, April 6, 1913.   [7] *Ibid.*, April 30, 1913.

exposition of the program of the Progressives on the tariff, the trusts, the initiative and referendum.

Meanwhile, as he hurried from conference to conference, from one speaking engagement to another, he did not lose sight of the individual. Well — too well — he knew that the professional politician who had joined the party in the hope of reaching the heaven of patronage on the tail of the Roosevelt kite was returning to his old love. If other and bigger leaders could be brought in, there would be no loss. And so he pondered the problem of Cummins. He had announced in 1912 that he would not join the Progressives, but would vote for Roosevelt. That, however, was not enough. 'Dear me, I do wish Cummins would come over to us,' Beveridge had written Clapp. 'He belongs to us; and I am very fond of him. Why will he persist in fiddling along trying to patch up the unpatchable?'[1] Clapp agreed that Cummins should be with the new party because 'one of the most intellectually honest men I ever knew.' He could only account for Cummins's hesitation by his 'devotion to the Republican Party for what it has stood for in days gone by.'[2] But it was not until December that Beveridge personally appealed to his comrade from Iowa in the insurgent fight:

I cannot help writing you, even if it makes you impatient for me to do so. It is so powerfully borne in upon me that now is your time to do what you told me in New York that you intended to do in case your convention plan failed.[3] You then said you would openly leave the Republican Party, or at least I so understood you. Of course, dear friend, you know how I have felt and how I feel more strongly every day. From every possible point of view, logically, morally, politically, you ought to be with us. Surely the conduct of the Republican National Committee[4] cannot leave you any further hope.[5]

But Cummins was immovable. He was not annoyed, for his reply was affectionate. But it was decisive:

I am profoundly convinced that it is easier to substitute a new leadership in the Republican Party, so that not only will the rank and file of our party be progressive, than to build up a new organization to such power as to enable it to influence legislation. You think otherwise, and I know you are absolutely honest about it, and we must await the lapse of time to see who is right.[6]

[1] Beveridge to Clapp, June 27, 1913.
[2] Clapp to Beveridge, July 1, 1913.
[3] An attempt to secure reforms in the rules of National Conventions.
[4] In rejecting the Convention reforms.
[5] Beveridge to Cummins, Dec. 19, 1913.
[6] Cummins to Beveridge, Jan. 14, 1914.

IV

Two years of confusion and readjustment — and nothing definite. Where was the trumpet of Roosevelt? All but silent. Where was the militant challenge to the propaganda for amalgamation? Even Perkins was merely amused. And there was something more that caused the Progressives no little concern — the Wilson Administration was moving smoothly, speedily, onward along progressive lines. The tariff bill enacted had been such an improvement on the old ones that La Follette had voted for it. And all the reports that reached Beveridge indicated the growing popularity of Wilson. Even a month before his inauguration, Rothschild, whose perspicacity surpassed that of more eminent leaders, was writing Beveridge that public interest was concentrated upon Wilson; that Progressive meetings would be useless at the moment. Almost a note of prophecy, the conclusion of the 'Baron':

I believe that Mr. Wilson is going to develop into a very clever man. He undoubtedly has the good will of the masses, and it appears as if he is trying to get entrenched in this strength in order to make the party follow him. If it does not follow him, he can go to the masses and become stronger, in a sense, than his party. If they make a halfway creditable Administration I cannot see how they can be overthrown for some years.[1]

When, following the enactment of the tariff act without a scandal, Wilson pressed on with the Federal Reserve Act, the Progressive leaders were all the more embarrassed in their strategy. Toward the close of August, Beveridge received a pessimistic note from the secretary of the Progressive National Committee. There was no line of attack yet open, he wrote. Wilson's handling of the tariff had been 'adroit.' When the stand-patters sought to create a scare and induce a panic, he had diverted attention by his warning to the lobby and sent it scurrying. By bringing in the currency bill immediately, he had forestalled 'the possibility of panic and commercial disaster.' Crops were short and prices were going up. Wilson would probably be as successful with his currency bill as with the tariff, and 'his handling of the Mexican situation has been fortunate up to this date. In brief, I believe he is now strong enough in the country that if he finally decided to intervene, it would not react against him severely.'[2]

A year later, no good opportunity for an attack on the Administration had appeared. The tariff and currency measures,

[1] Rothschild to Beveridge, Feb. 18, 1913.
[2] O. K. Davis to Beveridge, Aug. 27, 1913.

both handled adroitly, and pressed with the persistency of a courageous leadership knowing its destination, had made a favorable impression upon the country. Thus, when Roosevelt launched his bitter attacks on the President, Beveridge heard from Ernest Bross, editor of the 'Indianapolis Star,' that these assaults would 'not get him anything because people seem inclined to feel that [Wilson] is doing the best he can, and so long as he keeps us out of trouble it is profitless and pointless to say that he should have done this or that instead.' [1] Even Shaffer had written that he was in 'hearty accord with the President for removing Ambassador Wilson' because 'he talked too much and did not show the right spirit toward his superior,' and was 'also in hearty accord with him [Wilson] in not recognizing Huerta.' [2]

Thus it went — amalgamation, dissensions among the Progressives over Perkins, and from every quarter commendation from Progressives for Wilson. The loss of the militant spirit would be fatal, and Beveridge took sharp issue with his correspondent on Mexico. It was a mistake, he wrote, not to recognize Huerta. 'All agree that strong methods are necessary to stable government there' — a reversion to the Beveridge of the earlier days. Indeed, should it develop that Mexico is unable to establish a stable government, 'we ourselves must go there and administer her affairs for the next two or three generations.' [3]

By the spring of 1914, Beveridge felt he had found a legitimate issue against the President in his demand for the repeal of the Panama Canal tolls; for Wilson had been hotly challenged and the debate was bitter. 'There is one issue of tremendous importance,' he wrote — 'the Administration's fatal blunder on the Canal tolls question.... The Progressive Party in Congress will be solid against the repeal.' [4]

Meanwhile, the campaigns of 1913 had found him energetically engaged, but in the Maine campaign he was convinced that Roosevelt's failure to sound a clarion call, following the interpretation put upon his interview, was playing havoc with the party. The divergence of the old insurgent group widened when Cummins went to Maine for the Republican candidate, described by Beveridge as 'owned by the old stand-pat Hale machine.' [5] But Beveridge went wherever the fight was hottest — in New Jersey, Maine, and Massachusetts. Engaged at the time in literary work, he finally rebelled when Perkins sought to send him to West Virginia. Why shouldn't Roosevelt go?

[1] Bross to Beveridge, Aug. 25, 1914. [2] Shaffer to Beveridge, Aug. 7, 1913.
[3] Beveridge to Shaffer. [4] Beveridge to W. C. Bobbs, March 22, 1914.
[5] Beveridge to Clapp, Aug. 27, 1913.

he asked. It would be his last opportunity for a bugle blast before leaving for South America.[1]

But it was not only Roosevelt's aloofness from the campaign that troubled Beveridge. He had assumed that the farewell dinner to the Rough Rider as he set forth for South America would be utilized for the sounding of a militant battle-cry to rally the wavering columns of the Progressives, but Perkins had written him that 'the Colonel is going to speak in a very broad way at the dinner, and I am heartily in favor of it.'[2] 'I do not agree with you about the theme of the Colonel's speech,' Beveridge replied instantly. 'If ever there was a time when the whole situation demands from him a battle-cry that will sound from ocean to ocean and which will reassure those who have rallied to his colors, that time is the present.'[3]

But there was no 'battle-cry,' and so the Colonel sailed, and the winter passed, and the second national congressional election came with 1914.

V

It was to mark the last stand of the new party, and in several States its leaders of national repute were candidates. In Pennsylvania, Gifford Pinchot was making a brilliant fight for the Senate against Penrose. In Illinois, Raymond Robins was in the field; in Ohio, James R. Garfield; in California, Hiram Johnson. In Kansas, where Bristow was running for reëlection as a Republican, the Progressives put up Victor Murdock against him, with Henry Allen running for Governor. In New York, strenuous efforts were made to persuade Roosevelt to bear the banner in the gubernatorial race, but he had other plans.

Beveridge, busy with his literary work, was eager to plunge into the speaking campaign from coast to coast, but was determined to accept no nomination for himself. But the Indiana Progressives, literally on their toes, were pressing onward with their organization with no other thought than of making him their senatorial nominee. 'Confidentially,' he wrote Shaffer, 'I am in terror that our party will nominate me for Senator at the State Convention. It must not be done. It would mean the absolute and final end of my book — two years of desperately hard work thrown away; and the one real ambition of my life — the writing of a Life of Chief Justice Marshall — completely defeated.'[4]

[1] Beveridge to O. K. Davis, Sept. 10, 1913.
[2] Perkins to Beveridge, Sept. 22, 1913.
[3] Beveridge to Perkins, Sept. 23, 1913.   [4] March 28, 1914.

But there was unanimity among the Progressives that he bear the burden of the battle. From every nook and corner the demand rolled in. He had agreed to preside, but had determined to limit his address to no more than fifteen minutes. But there was no mistaking the will of the convention. All too clearly he was the dominating mind and the man to bear the banner. Time and again demonstrations had followed the mention of his name; and when, in a fiery and brilliant speech, Frederick Landis placed him in nomination and the delegates rose with an ovation seldom equaled in the history of the State, there was no escaping the summons to battle. 'I did not mean to, but I will,' he said, 'and I cannot answer your devotion except with a full heart.' The delegates were on their feet shouting and waving flags. Above the din the band marching down the aisle could scarcely be heard. The cheering partisans paraded before the platform where Beveridge sat. For fifteen minutes the turmoil continued, and was terminated only when the band played 'Onward, Christian Soldiers,' and the convention joined in the singing of the hymn.

And so Beveridge left Tomlinson's Hall with the banner in his hand again. The literary work was laid aside; the desperately needed rest was curtailed; and through the summer, until mid-August, he was traversing the State assisting in the organization of his forces. The Democrats renominated Senator Benjamin F. Shively, a strong campaigner with the Wilson sentiment behind him; the Republicans, Hugh Miller, a clean and cultured gentleman without magnetism or eloquence. Long before the campaign opened in September, Beveridge had written to each of the thirty-two hundred precinct committeemen, to the fifteen hundred county and township candidates, to every county chairman; and, with the State Chairman, had personally participated in many organization conferences. July found him sweeping across Illinois on a speaking tour for Robins — and on the trip receiving the deadliest blow that either he or his party nationally was to feel.

VI

This was the 'Hinman incident' in New York.

In midsummer, Roosevelt, evidently in pursuance of the amalgamation plan, proposed that the Republicans and Progressives unite in the gubernatorial nomination of Hinman, a Republican. There was no doubt of his Republicanism, since he had frankly announced his candidacy for the Republican nomination and his fidelity to the Republican Party, whether nominated or not. It was sensed by the rank and file everywhere that the 'Hinman deal' was to be the bridge over which Roosevelt would leave his followers and return to the Republican camp. The reason given for the strange proposal was that there should be a unification of reform forces against the political machines of the two parties, but unhappily, for appearances, the Democrats did not enter into the calculation of the amalgamationists at all. Thus, the common interpretation that Roosevelt was seeking an avenue of escape from the party he had founded to that which he had left with resounding denunciations.

The effect was as a clap of thunder from a cloudless sky. And so it was true? — Roosevelt was going back? Those among the Progressives who were in the party for the loaves and fishes began preparations for a hasty flight back to the old homestead. The fact that the New York Republicans, in haughty mood, promptly vetoed the Roosevelt plan, and as a result that Roosevelt announced that 'of course' he would 'support the Progressive ticket,' did not remove the apprehension. The New York Progressives entered the campaign discredited, and, after a pitiful fight, suffered a humiliating rebuke at the polls.

The startling story of the 'Hinman deal' reached Beveridge in the midst of his tour of Illinois for Robins. With Medill McCormick and other Illinois leaders he had opened at Danville, and had been receiving ovations in enthusiastic meetings everywhere — and then came the report of the 'Hinman deal.' The effect was deadening. 'From that hour on,' he wrote later, 'the local committees on the Illinois tour who met the train looked like men who had been stricken with illness.' [1]

Beveridge was furious and made no secret of his indignation. He wrote Perkins:

I am very, very sorry that the Colonel's statement about Hinman and the New York situation made an exceedingly unfavorable impression on our workers in Illinois, and, I fear, on the general public. There is some danger that it may stop scores and hundreds of thousands of Republicans from coming over to us, who are ready to come and anxious to come, provided they think that the Progressive Party is here to stay.... The Colonel's statement may give this important class an unfavorable opinion on this subject.... So it is not very nice, is it, after all the work we have done out here in Indiana — yes, Illinois and Ohio too — and the sacrifices we have made, to have this bombshell thrown into us? The Republican papers and politicians, and the 'Indianapolis News' are making the most of it. They are printing columns about T. R.'s abandonment of the Progressive Party. [2]

[1] From an article on the 'Launching and Wrecking of the Progressive Party,' sent Lorimer of the *Saturday Evening Post*, but not for publication. Beveridge MSS.

[2] Beveridge to Perkins, July 25, 1914.

Everywhere he turned thereafter, as he rode on his campaign through Indiana, he was confronted by flaming billboard advertisements of the Republicans — 'Eventually, why not now?'

But the damage was done, and there was no turning back for him. The banner was in his hands and his very indignation increased the intensity of his fighting. Feeling he must fight his own battle, after being betrayed in the house of his friends, his correspondence with Perkins became more acrid. When the latter asked him to make speeches in Maine, he refused. 'We have got to win the Indiana fight and are going to win it,' he wrote. 'The New York performance has made our work harder, but not impossible.... There are two definite, tangible things I shall expect Colonel Roosevelt to do for me in Indiana in order to make up in a very small way for the large handicap his action has placed upon me out here.' [1] This was nothing more than the delivery of a few speeches in his behalf, and for a time a favorable response seemed probable. In New York, Roosevelt had told Shaffer that if 'we can elect Beveridge in Indiana, we can nominate him for the Presidency in 1916.' [2] And he had written Beveridge for a complete record of his public work to be used in the speeches planned. But all this was to dwindle to one half-day in Indiana, while two days were given to Ohio, three to Illinois, and a week to Pennsylvania! It was incredible.

Beveridge grimly set himself to the task of plowing his lonely furrow.

VII

He formally opened his campaign in Terre Haute, only incidentally touching on the Wilson Administration. It proposed a shipping bill, with Government ownership and operation, and he described it as no better than a subsidy, and warned that in days of war it might embroil us in the struggle. His most vitriolic denunciations were of the reactionaries in both parties; his strategy to convince the people of a bi-partisan combination of the bosses against him; his necessity, somehow, to combat the effect of the 'Hinman deal.' Mentioning names in his excoriation of the reactionaries in the beginning, he soon passed to a more sober exposition of Progressive principles — the tariff commission, trust regulation instead of trust destruction, child slavery, the initiative, referendum, and recall. The speech, in striking contrast to his earlier orations, was singularly calm in tone and unrhetorical in phrasing.

[1] Beveridge to Perkins, Aug. 10, 1914.
[2] Shaffer to Beveridge, Sept. 14, 1914.

Thenceforth he engaged in one of the most intensive campaigns in the history of the Commonwealth, going into almost every town and city, to hamlets and crossroads, speaking under every imaginable condition, in theaters, halls, and from the automobile in which he traveled accompanied by his secretary and press correspondents. The first week of the tour called for twenty-two speeches — he made more. Time and again he was interrupted by hecklers set upon him by the Republicans, but here his felicity in rough-and-tumble debate stood him in good stead.[1] Riding through the countryside from town to town, crowds gathered at the hamlets and he paused for unscheduled speeches — brief but telling.[2] More than one day, speaking many times and in inclement weather, he did not take time to eat. One day he made twelve speeches. Once, when the machine was stalled in a narrow mud road, he walked with a companion nine miles through the slush and rain and kept his engagement. Everywhere big crowds, unrestrained enthusiasm, and yet he was not unmindful of his handicaps. When Borah entered the State to speak against him, his momentary impulse was to strike back personally, but Clapp, the kindly, tolerant, even-tempered friend, strongly advised against it.[3] 'Many thanks for your wise counsel,' Beveridge wrote; and he promised to act accordingly. But, with Borah attacking him vigorously, he was unable to remain silent, and in his final speech in Indianapolis he made a vigorous reply and counter-attack. The two men had strangely jarred on each other from their first meeting, and it was not until some years later that they were to establish friendly relations on the basis of their mutual admiration and common views on international affairs.

And so, fighting to the last, the campaign closed, and the Progressives found themselves third in the poll. The Democrats, delighted with the Wilson Administration, stayed with their party, and not a few Progressives of 1912 joined them. Others, convinced that there was no possibility of permanence in the third party, had gone back to the Republicans.

To Beveridge the result was not a shock, for he had measured in his mind the psychological effect of the propaganda for amalgamation. When, immediately after the election, Perkins called a conference at Chicago and wrote Beveridge it had not been thought wise to have Roosevelt present, he received a blunt reply:

I have not thought that our people in New York, even T. R. himself,

[1] *Indianapolis Star*, Sept. 25, 28, 1914.   [2] *Ibid.*, Oct. 24, 1914.
[3] Clapp to Beveridge, Oct. 21, 1914.

had a clear understanding of the feelings of our rank and file, and of our local county and district leaders.

They expect and depend upon a sturdy, aggressive leadership at all times; but especially in an hour of disaster.

It is not hard to lead troops who are flushed with victory; the time when leadership really is needed and indispensable is in the hour of defeat.

Believe me, George, and do give heed when I say that if ever there was a time for T. R. to rise above any height to which he has hitherto risen, this is the hour.

I am very emphatically of the opinion that the Colonel should attend the Chicago conference. I know you will scoff at this, but I wish to set it in black and white as my opinion.

Aside from the positive necessity, more, the imperative duty, for him to speak out clearly and bravely, it is the fact that it seems absurd for him to refuse to attend a conference of a party he founded, especially when that conference is held at an hour when the very life of his party is at stake.

I see no reason why he should not attend, and every reason why he should; and I would not be surprised if this will prove to be the feeling of the rank and file.

Can anything be more absurd than the counsel given him about running for Governor of New York — that he ought not to do so because he ought to save himself; and the counsel now being given him that he must not commit himself by going to this conference?...

He wrote me a letter of which I enclose a copy. How does it happen that he writes me such a stirring trumpet blast, and then says to us that he will not say anything at all? [1]

Beveridge himself did not attend the conference. An Archduke of the House of Austria had fallen victim to a Serbian assassin in a Balkan town three months before; and the war lords of Europe were strutting gayly at the head of marching columns; and in America the press was reeking with propaganda to involve the United States, at least in sympathy. Intensely moved, interested, curious as to the real meaning of the most desperate struggle in world history, Beveridge had agreed to visit the warring nations, interview their statesmen and other leaders, and write a series of articles for 'Collier's Weekly.' If not a rest, it would mean a change, and a welcome release from the increasing confusion of American politics.

With Paxton Hibben, a linguist with ten years' experience in the diplomatic service, as secretary and interpreter, he sailed from New York on December 12, 1914.

[1] Beveridge to Perkins, undated.

BOOK V
WAR AND POLITICS

CHAPTER I

AT ARMAGEDDON

I

THE close of the campaign of 1914 had left Beveridge physically exhausted, his nerves on edge, and depressed, because of his enervation, with forebodings of the future. The tragic struggle across the sea had been in progress for three months, and in America the people still were groping in the dark in search of the real cause and motives of the participants. President Wilson's proclamation of neutrality was being bitterly challenged by the partisans of the opposing forces, and the machinery of the most shameless and unscrupulous propaganda had been put in motion. No American yet had undertaken an interpretation of the war, based on personal investigation. The temptation to Beveridge to accept the mission was all the stronger because his enthusiasm for the military life had persisted from boyhood; and the opportunity offered a diversion for his thoughts from the gloomy political prospects at home. But he had his misgivings too. The hue and cry against the Germans had been raised and the poisoned American imagination was picturing them as wanton assassins of women and children, given to deeds of cruelty, torture, and mutilation. Would the American public tolerate a record of impressions not in harmony with the hideous picture painted? Beveridge doubted it. Three times he sought release from his engagement on the ground that the minds of the people had been closed to mere facts that did not fit in with their prejudices. But Mark Sullivan, editor of 'Collier's,' was insistent. 'The best advice I can give,' he wrote, 'is to look upon everything with the eyes of a child and to write whatever you see and hear.'

With this intention Beveridge pushed his preparations for the journey. His first disappointment came in the general advice against taking Mrs. Beveridge with him. The State Department warned of dangers. Jules Jusserand, the French Ambassador, wrote of an uncomfortable voyage, of the demoralized railroad service in France, and of Paris 'very gloomy, or if not gloomy, at least very serious.' [1] Again he was disposed to abandon the journey, but Mrs. Beveridge urged him to go alone.

Thus he boarded the New Amsterdam, physically exhausted and depressed. The journey was to be brightened by the presence on board of Henry van Dyke, the American Minister to

[1] Jusserand to Beveridge.

Holland. His personal log of his war-time adventure on the sea may be read in daily letters to his wife:

Sunday.

Van Dyke asked me to sit at his table.... I like him immensely, and I think he likes me.... Walked until 11 o'clock and went to bed and slept until 3.30 today — had breakfast and luncheon in bed. I feel much rested and a great deal quieter. The stateroom is ideal. You and I would have had a sure-enough honeymoon.... I can feel the inflamed nerves cooling and relaxing. If you were with me I would like the voyage to last for a month.

Monday.

Slept from ten P.M. to one P.M. today. Breakfast in bed. It's so comfortable there that I have had a reading-light rigged up, for it is very cloudy and the deck is dark. Also my room gets more air than the stuffy deck.

Began Von Bülow's book — very good. It is getting quite rough and will be worse. Most people are down. I hope I won't succumb. Thank Heaven Hibben is immune. He is very attentive and helpful. ... Van Dyke said I couldn't have found a better man for my purpose....

Met the German woman — she knits all the time, very sad, and in terror that the British may take her off the boat when they search the ship in the Channel. Van Dyke reassured her.

Tuesday.

Slept until 11 this A.M. Roughness vanished during the night; went on deck to a glorious sunny day.

Am reading Von Bülow's 'Imperial Germany' — diffuse, but enough good points here and there to make the reading necessary.

Van Dyke and I get on well. Am so glad he is on board — I really like him immensely. It is going to be a great help and a base to retire upon....

Am looking eagerly to the Channel and the boarding by the British warship.

Wednesday.

So I've got through Von Bülow's discursive 'Imperial Germany'; Martin's (of 'Life') little volume of essays on the war; and now on Treitschke's lectures. Van Dyke attended Treitschke's lectures and tells me all about him.

Saturday.

The ocean has been deserted — only two ships sighted, small tramps. ... I loathe the thought of going to Berlin and having to see all those people. I want to get out among the country folk. I fear my articles will be dreary stuff — the whole trip is on the knees of the gods.... We got German news today — picked it out of the air. The Captain let me and Van Dyke see it — no one else. In the German bombardment of the English coast a day or two ago a German submarine sank a British light cruiser.... This German news is very different from the English and French versions. I fear the American people know very little of what is going on.

From the moment he came within sight of the English coast until the vessel entered the Maas leading to Rotterdam, the war became a stark reality. The searchlights from the Lizard glowed in the distance, flashed and circled over the water near Dover. The ship was halted by a British war-vessel and investigated as to cargo and passengers. The last night was one of peril as the ship cautiously nosed its way through a narrow channel lined with mines. The passengers were assigned their life-belts. The sunrise revealed, floating on the water face downward, a victim of the war — one of the British or German sailors who had fought in the North Sea battle a few weeks before. Such was Beveridge's introduction to the tragedies of the war.

II

At The Hague he learned from O'Loughlin, newspaper correspondent, of Hindenburg's victory and the capture of three hundred thousand prisoners, and of Italy's entering with the Allies in a few days. That first morning Van Dyke took him to call on Loudon, the Foreign Minister, whom he had known in Washington, and later to the German Minister. He had a long talk with the former, and the latter arranged about his passports for Germany. That night he dined with Van Dyke, finding him 'nicer and nicer' and 'very valuable,' and the next morning found him at the camp of the interned Belgian soldiers. His observations on the scenes here were not to contribute to his popularity among the partisans of the Allies at home, where all the Belgians were being pictured as fighting heroically for their country with their backs against the wall. The thirty thousand who had wandered across the Dutch border and into an internment camp remote from danger were as the lost tribe. In conversations at The Hague Beveridge found a note of distinct hostility to them, and in the cafés he overheard the natives describing them as 'dirty,' 'shiftless,' 'idle,' 'ungrateful.' A little while before there had been rioting among them against what they thought exorbitant prices at the canteen. Determined to fathom the secret of the resentment among the Dutch, Beveridge went to the camp at Zeist, where he found the interned living in roughly built barracks, the ground surrounded by barbed-wire fence. Warmly clad, apparently well fed, rosy-cheeked, and care-free, he found them clumping about in their wooden shoes.

In the canteen he found no evidence of a melancholy brooding over the fate of their country. As he entered, he got the impression of a huge social hall or rathskeller, with hundreds of soldiers sitting about tables drinking beer, munching chocolate, talking, playing cards.[1] In conversation with them, he heard that they were underfed and poorly rationed, but an inspection of the dining-room convinced him that the food, though simple, was nutritious. In the city he had heard complaints that the prisoners refused to work, and he got their explanation — that for them to work would deprive the Dutch workingmen of employment.[2] Altogether he found them uninspiring, unheroic, none too eager to escape to resume their places on the firing line. 'They look well fed,' he wrote Mrs. Beveridge, 'and as content as men with nothing to do but tramp around in the mud can be.'

Returning to The Hague, he continued his investigations among the natives, and found them equally resentful of the rich Belgians living luxuriously in the best hotels and contributing nothing to the care of their interned soldiers.[3] As an honest recorder of realities, there was nothing to do but to set down what he saw and heard; but he did suggest that the anti-Belgian feeling he found so prevalent had 'its roots deep down in the soil of history.'[4]

A bit dubiously, he wrote his first article at The Hague and sent a copy to his wife. 'Don't know whether Sullivan will use it,' he wrote. 'It is accurate. And I did work so hard to get the material.... Don't scold if you think the article poor.'[5]

Amusingly enough, the real source of his worries as he prepared to enter Germany was in regard to his wardrobe. He wrote his wife:

Hear from every source must have a frock coat and a silk hat in Germany, Austria, and elsewhere. If so, must get a suit from Berlin tailor.... But don't worry, for I won't have my time wasted by worthless social functions. It is busy men I want to see, and they, I always have found, respect, listen to, and grant the wishes of another busy man. Also I hear nothing is to be heard at these luncheons, teas, and dinners but second-hand reports, mostly wrong, and worthless small talk — one could use up a year in that way and know no more for certain at the end than at the beginning. When I was in Berlin and St. Petersburg on my Manchurian journey, I found everything without red tape, frock coat or silk hat. Von Bülow, Witte... were quite simple and more plainly dressed than I, and seemed to like my directness — it saved their time. And this in a time of peace. So I'm praying that now in time of war they will not insist on a Prince Albert coat and a tall hat. Maybe they may even relish the change of an American without

[1] *What is Behind the War*, 2.   [2] *Ibid.*, 10.   [3] *Ibid.*, 11.
[4] *Ibid.*, 13.   [5] Beveridge to Mrs. Beveridge, Dec. 27, 1914.

these adornments, who goes directly and quickly to the point and saves their time and his own.[1]

The next day he was in Berlin, established at the Hotel Adlon, on the Unter den Linden, and henceforth we hear no more of his sartorial complications.

III

Beveridge had no trouble at the frontier. Traffic was heavy, and the train to Berlin was crowded, mostly with business men. In the capital he found nothing remotely suggestive of war. Everything seemed normal — the Berlin he had seen before. He thought it 'delightful in its living conditions.' That first night he got his first impression of the popular reaction to the war when he went with James Gerard, the American Ambassador, to the Winter Garden, a music-hall where the best number was a recitation on the conflict. He observed that it was directed, not against France or Russia, but England. His plan of action was thoroughly mapped. He proposed to talk with rulers, statesmen, military and naval leaders, manufacturers, bankers, publicists; and, in addition, to converse with the common people, the laborers, cab-drivers, farmers. Thus did he hope to form a fairly accurate opinion of each nation's concept of the war — the reason for it. His impression of his function was carefully thought out and written down:

The writer acts merely as a reporter — a medium through which the ideas prevailing and the facts existing, as they really are, in three countries at war, are conveyed to the American public. While the student of people at war must maintain sympathetic seriousness in order to get the real spirit of the belligerent countries visited, yet he must at the same time have ever in his heart the getting and the stating of the facts regardless of whether they fit anybody's preconceived ideas.[2]

Thus it was not only opinions, but facts that he sought — facts as to food supplies, cost of living, the state of the armies, the extent of their resources. And he soon found facts that did not harmonize with 'news' he was reading in American newspapers. He had understood that Germany was feeling the pinch of food scarcity. But on the train from Berlin to Posen he had large veal cutlets, with rice, asparagus, and beans, for fifty cents. In Berlin restaurants he had a very large pork steak, sauerkraut, and lentils for twenty-two cents, and could have had three shirred eggs for fifteen cents and half a young pheasant for thirty-seven cents. The bread, it is true, he found 'noticeably

[1] To Mrs. Beveridge, Dec. 27, 1914.   [2] *What is Behind the War*, 165.

darker, from five to ten per cent of potato flour being used.' [1]
Dining with Albert Südekum, leader of the Social Democratic
Party, at the Gewerkschaftshaus — the workingmen's house
and the labor center of Berlin — the meal for three was but $1.10,
though one man had rabbit pot-pie, and the other two large
thick pork steaks, and all three potatoes, beans, peas, cheese.[2]
Thus, all surface indications belied the stories he had heard in
America. Food was abundant and cheap, the Berlin stores and
shops were open and normal, even to the usual January sales;
the cafés, amusement halls, moving-picture houses, theaters,
were crowded. Within a few days he was writing his wife that
'from what I have picked up already, the Germans have been
frightfully lied about.' [3]

Impatient to get to his interviews, Beveridge presented his
letter of introduction to Baron von Munn, in charge of such
matters, and was asked to dine; but when a courteously worded
note postponed the dinner, he resented the delay. Were they
suspicious or was it merely red tape? But almost immediately
the barriers were down, if they ever had been up, and he was
moving at a dizzy pace from one of the German leaders to another. Within three days he had lunched with Prince and
Princess Hatzfeldt, who had been gracious to him eighteen years
before, finding them, in old age, more charming than ever; and
dined with Professor von Harnack and his daughter in his simple
home, and as we have seen, with Südekum, leader of the Social
Democrats, at the labor center in Berlin. In Germany it was his
invariable rule to state the case against the Germans as it had
been presented in America, and to get the answer.

The interview with Von Harnack, 'the unchallenged leader of
German theological thought' and an intimate friend of the
Kaiser, was granted at the scholar's suburban home in Grüne-
wald, his daughter acting as translator. No one was to delight
Beveridge more. 'Professor Harnack,' he wrote Mrs. Beveridge,
'is the dearest old man — one's ideal of a German man of learning, so gentle and childlike.' [4] It was in the days when Americans
were being convinced that Treitschke, the historian, had influenced German thought with the philosophy that might makes
right, and that General Bernhardi's book, represented as enormously popular in Germany, was representative of German
ruthlessness. 'Incorrect both,' said the old savant. 'Treitschke
merely interpreted history as it actually was, not as it ought to
be.' And Bernhardi's book? 'I never read it,' said this leader of
German thought. 'I do not know anyone who has read it. I

[1] *What is Behind the War*, 150.   [2] *Ibid.*, 193.
[3] To Mrs. Beveridge, Dec. 28, 1914.   [4] To Mrs. Beveridge, Jan. 1, 1915.

never heard of it until long after the war began. It could not have had much of a sale.'[1] This, to an American at that time, seemed incredible, and Beveridge, making his own investigation, found that only six thousand copies of Bernhardi's book had been printed, and not all were sold.[2]

From Südekum, the orator representing Nürnberg in the Reichstag, who spoke English fluently, Beveridge sought the workingmen's interpretation, both of Germany and the war. He was told that the workingmen were fighting for the preservation of the industrial life on which they depended. The Germany of Goethe and Schiller? 'It could not have fed nearly seventy million of people; it did not even feed the people it had in those days.'[3] The military system? 'Modern militarism was not made in Germany. Napoleon III was its father and it was made in France.'[4] Bernhardi's book? 'I doubt if many of the German people know that Bernhardi ever wrote a book.'[5] The invasion of Belgium? 'It was a question of life or death with us. If we had not marched through Belgium, England and France would have done so. That is proved now.'[6] Warring on humanity and civilization? 'Is our care for the aged through old-age pensions, our industrial insurance, our provisions against sickness and accidents, our system of labor exchanges to bring the employers and laborers together — are these examples of barbarism?'[7]

For a business man's interpretation, Beveridge selected Albert Ballin, of the Hamburg-American Line, and Walter Rathenau, president of the General Electric Company of Germany, and both ascribed the war to the commercial rivalry between Germany and England.

In every interview with responsible leaders in Germany, England, and France, Beveridge never deviated from a system to assure absolute accuracy. Having reduced the interview to writing, he sent it to the leader concerned for his corrections; and when corrections were made, he rewrote it and submitted it again. In not one instance was an interview published until it had received the absolute approval of the person interviewed. 'I thank you so much for sending me the manuscript,' wrote Ballin. 'It is absolutely correct and I have no alterations to suggest.'[8]

In the case of responsible military leaders, he was to take even greater precautions.

[1] *What is Behind the War*, 169.   [2] *Ibid.*   [3] *Ibid.*, 195.
[4] *Ibid.*, 198.   [5] *Ibid.*, 199.   [6] *Ibid.*, 205.   [7] *Ibid.*, 206.
[8] Ballin to Beveridge.

IV

In the home of a rich Frenchman in the town where the Grand Headquarters were located, he found Admiral von Tirpitz, in a blue uniform, with the regulation gold lace at the wrists, but without decorations. The interview was in English, and the Admiral's conversation was 'clear, simple, sometimes eloquent, and all the time forcible.' Expressing his amazement at the American attitude, he was told that Americans believed Germany had forced the struggle.

'Our ships were abroad,' was the reply. 'Many of our warships were in foreign ports; much of our vast merchant marine was far away in the harbors of every country — do you think that if we had planned war, or even foreseen it, we should not have got all our ships home before war was declared?'[1] But what of the German naval toast, 'To the Day?' asked Beveridge.

'A lie,' was the quick response. 'I say on my honor as a man and an officer that I never heard such a toast proposed, never drank such a toast, never heard of such being proposed or drunk. ... I am sure no honorable English officer will say otherwise.'[2]

'But why the building of a Navy?' Beveridge asked.

'And why not?' was the retort. 'Why should England build a navy? Had not Germany colonies and trade to protect as well?'

'But submarine warfare — what about that?' asked the interviewer. 'Well, why not?' was the answer. 'England is trying to starve us. Are we not to retaliate?'

But a submarine blockade gives the blockade-runner no chance, persisted Beveridge.

'What chance does a mine give the merchant ship?' asked Von Tirpitz. 'It gives less chance than a submarine.'

This interview was typed, submitted, accepted, but Beveridge asked that on each page should be placed the official stamp of the Navy Department as evidence of approval, and the manuscript with the stamp is before me as I write.

V

This interview was given the day after Beveridge's first experience at the front in Northern France. He reached the captured city of Lille on January 6, in the rain. There was little to suggest the tragic operations not far away. The sidewalks were filled with men, women, and children, the stores were open, shoppers were making purchases. But at the station two hospital trains with the wounded filed by; soldiers swarmed everywhere;

[1] *What is Behind the War*, 61.   [2] *Ibid.*, 63.

from afar off came the booming of cannon; and at the leading café the German officers had monopolized the tables. The next day he wrote his experiences and impressions to Mrs. Beveridge:

You never would think this is a captured city with fighting going on only ten miles away, except for the crowds of soldiers and the roaring of the heavy artillery which I can hear quite plainly — shops are open and doing a brisk business. Big crowds on the streets.

Dined with the Crown Prince Rupert of Bavaria — speaks English, very simple, informed, and even sweet. I really like him very much. Parade of the Bavarian troops in Public Square this morning in honor of the birthday of the old King of Bavaria, reviewed by the Crown Prince.... Very impressive with their deep-throated 'Ra's.'

Lunched with the General Staff — pleasant gentlemen. Major Xylander, who won the iron cross for taking Lille, my especial entertainer; about forty-five years old, speaks English, mother English — and quite nice. Also Prince Loewenstein, greatest Bavarian Catholic noble leader of the Center in the Reichstag — very handsome, perfect English, most attractive.

Dined with officers of the staff in honor of the King's birthday — pleasant, quite informal. Very little drinking — made a good impression on me. I go Sunday to the Grand Headquarters to see the Chancellor. Then to Berlin.[1]

The next day, with officers, he was whirled away to the firing-line. Gaunt walls of shelled buildings flashed by... wagons with provisions driven by soldiers... a train loaded with munitions covered with canvas... coffins on a station platform... the central street of a town smashed and crumpled. And, in contrast, a flock of sheep grazing... a peasant plowing peaceably in a field... the houses of Dinant, shell-riddled... and then 'the pale green of winter wheat already faintly coloring the fields...'

Then to the trenches in the night, through villages without a light, the cocks heralding the coming dawn. And then into a hamlet at the break of day as the cannons began to roar; and into a riddled church where Beveridge rescued a prayer-book from the litter; and into the church-tower, soldiers holding the ladder. Through the great slats he looked down upon the French and German trenches, startlingly close. 'Be careful,' he is warned. 'Don't show yourself or we may get a shot.'[2] And then into the trenches, through mud and water.

VI

It was while at Grand Headquarters in conversation with Chancellor von Bethmann-Hollweg that Beveridge expressed a wish to meet the Emperor, though with faint expectations.

[1] To Mrs. Beveridge, Jan. 7, 1915. [2] *What is Behind the War*, 24–25.

Abandoning hope, he was in a restaurant at the station waiting for the train for Berlin when a young officer attached to the Foreign Office rushed in to inform him that Wilhelm would see him that afternoon. The appointed time found him at the temporary quarters of the Chancellor in conversation with Von Jagow, Minister of Foreign Affairs, when the Emperor's aide appeared to escort him to the walled-in garden, where he found Wilhelm walking with Von Bethmann-Hollweg. The Emperor wore a simple uniform of the field, with the familiar gray fur-lined cloak about his shoulders, and the cap of a German officer. The Chancellor was in khaki-colored uniform with boots and cap. Beveridge was dressed as he had come from the trenches.

The two men walked for two hours along an oval gravelled path under the leaden skies, and we find in a letter to Mrs. Beveridge a more intimate impression of the supreme war lord than is given in the published article.

Most interesting and important of all, I was presented to the Emperor and had a long conversation with him at Grand Headquarters located at a place I do not think it right to name.... I went to the Chancellor's at 2.10 and was taken to the garden, where the Emperor was walking at 2.45, and we walked and talked until exactly 4.45.

Judging from appearances, he is in fine form physically. Although we walked and talked for two hours, he was as fresh or fresher at the end than at the beginning. His voice was vibrant and full of force, and his stride, attitude, and gestures strong and even powerful, his eyes blazing with vitality. His talk was snappy, full of color, teeming with ideas. And what charm!... It is a loss to history that I am in honor bound not to repeat verbally or in writing this brilliant and impressive conversation. I cannot tell even you of it when I get home, for, alas, Von Jagow, Secretary of State, asked me not to do so, and of course I gave him my word that I would not. And yet that talk, if given to the world in the right way and with proper setting, would do Germany more good than an army corps. Perhaps the Emperor may come to see this himself.... So all that I can say to you now is that it was as two gentlemen talking together. He is the kind of man you would like regardless of what station he filled.[1]

But Beveridge did not easily abandon the hope of securing an interview for publication, and after reaching Berlin he approached the Chancellor again, in a letter. Preparing a long list of questions, he asked that these be submitted to the Emperor in advance that he might choose the topics on which he would talk.

Excellency: Herewith I enclose you points on which the American public would be glad of enlightenment.

It is suggested that comment be prepared on the points which the

[1] To Mrs. Beveridge, Jan. 16, 1915.

Emperor chooses to discuss, and on others which may occur to him, or you.

Then, when this material is ready, I shall go to Grand Headquarters when notified, and while there prepare the interview from this material, making the interview in the form of questions and answers, just as the conversation developed last Monday and just as weighty conversations always do naturally develop.

When this is prepared, it should be gone over by His Majesty in its completed form, and corrected and changed so as to state His Majesty's meaning exactly. This form of an interview is attractive, easy to read, and makes a stronger impression on an ordinary person than a more formal expression. For that reason, and that it may be read as widely as possible, it is preferable.

Finally, the Emperor should sign a statement at the end of the completed interview that he had read the manuscript and that it is an accurate statement of what he said...

May I suggest that the Emperor's comment be allowed to have the color and life which was his conversation of last Monday? The less detailed and involved the interview is, the better. It should be as simple as possible so that the average man can understand it. It should have none of the formality and tediousness of a State paper. It should deal with the big aspects of this historic controversy...

May I again thank His Majesty for the honor of receiving me, and Your Excellency for your kindness in arranging it.[1]

But Von Jagow's prohibition stood, and the Beveridge article could be no more than an impressionistic portrait of the Emperor. So finicky were the Secretary of State and the men surrounding Wilhelm that for a moment Beveridge even hesitated about entering upon the monarch's personality in his article. He took the precaution to inquire of Baron von Munn whether it would be permissible. Even this request was clearly made the subject of a solemn conclave, as shown in the letter from the Baron's office:

You asked Baron von Munn the other day whether there was any objection to your describing your impressions of His Majesty's personality in your publication in America. I am requested to inform you that Baron von Munn would not like to take the responsibility of a decision in this matter upon himself. But he would request you to submit it to the Foreign Office — that part of your publication dealing with His Majesty's personality. Baron von Munn will then put it before the Acting Secretary of State and will let you know that gentleman's decision in the matter.

I trust that this arrangement will meet with your approval.

I am, sir, your obedient servant,

D. G. ROEDIGER [2]

[1] Beveridge to Von Bethmann-Hollweg.
[2] To Beveridge, Jan. 23, 1915.

The article accordingly was submitted and approved.

To the day of his death, Beveridge kept his word, never divulging even to his wife the nature of the interview in the two hours' conversation in the walled-in garden within hearing of the thunder of the guns.

VII

Soon after returning to Berlin, he was on his way to the Russian front to see Von Hindenburg. On Sunday, in Berlin, he had gone to the great Lutheran Church service, and later to the Catholic Cathedral, to note the effect of the war, and heard 'an amazing sermon supporting the war like the evangel of the sword.' Both churches were crowded, with officers and soldiers, some recovering from wounds, sprinkling the congregations.[1] A few days before, he had attended the wedding of Cecelia May, whom he had known in Washington, at the American Embassy, and had met the Baroness von Sternburg, widow of the former Ambassador who had been a favorite of Roosevelt's. After the church services he had gone for tea to the home of the Countess Oppersdorff, one of the most brilliant women in Berlin and a friend of Henry White; and meeting Baroness von Sternburg there, had accompanied her home for a long talk. 'I can't help remembering that she was a good friend in Washington,' he wrote Mrs. Beveridge.

Almost persuaded that his hope to see Von Hindenburg was futile, he was making preparations to leave, when a message from Colonel Hoffmann inviting him to Posen reached him, and immediately, he was on his way. It was a hard journey. Going to Posen by train, he there transferred to an automobile for a nine-hour drive at top speed in the face of a bitter wind 'which stung your face like wasps.' To bed by midnight, he was up again by four-thirty and away in the speeding machine. 'The bellowing wind' he wrote — 'you had no idea it could howl with such a penetrating voice.[2] Happily, he was to see the battle of Bolimoff. In preparation for the drive to the field of action, he dressed warmly, wearing three suits of woolen underwear, riding-breeches, shirt and coat, thick long woolen hand-knitted socks; riding-boots with thick woolen socks over these. To protect the head, he wore a thick wool knit headpiece covering his forehead, ears, and chin, and warmly circling about the neck.[3]

His guide was a 'gentle-spoken Jewish youth,' a trusted messenger of the military headquarters, who had won the iron cross

[1] To Mrs. Beveridge, Jan. 17, 1915.
[2] *What is Behind the War*, 81.　　　[3] *Ibid.*, 82.

and knew every road and by-path. The sky was dark, gloomy. The landscape, as it flew by, was 'a study in black and white,' and 'patches of pine forests' stood out 'like sections of midnight on the snowy plain.' On the right and left were deserted Russian battery pits and rifle trenches... towns and hamlets... and at crossroads 'a tall cross of rough-hewn timber bearing the Holy Image.'... Another town — people walking indifferently in the streets, an old woman on a stool at a doorway selling bread.... Women peasants, in bizarre costumes, trudging through the snow to church, for this battle day was Sunday.... And then the road was more congested — wagons, field kitchens, field guns, mounted officers... a side-road packed with infantry, awaiting orders... a regiment of Uhlans riding in an open field... horses slipping and falling on the ice.

And then, in an open field by the roadside, General von Mackensen and his staff — a tall slender man with gray hair and mustache, walking to and fro with an officer. Again that day Beveridge was to see Von Mackensen, sitting alone in his machine; and again, alone, pacing back and forth, 'his head bent forward in thought, his long gray military overcoat, with cape about the shoulders, reaching almost to his heels.' And then — the German artillery in action with twenty-centimeter guns, seeking to silence the Russian batteries four miles distant, and the Russians answering, 'not plentifully nor with good aim.' Near by a Russian shell explodes, throwing 'geysers of earth in the air.'

Noon — and he eats with the common soldiers, a thick soup of navy beans with slices and chunks of pork, and plenty of brown bread.

He learns that, despite the seeming placidity of the scene, a furious artillery duel is in progress preparatory to a dash upon the Russian trenches. Would he go to the church-tower where he could see the fighting? He ascends winding black stairs, and with powerful field-glasses looks upon the most dramatic picture he has ever seen... a long line of men march by — Russian prisoners. Another line — the wounded, temporarily bandaged, pale, smoking cigarettes, awaiting their turn in the field hospital.

And then, his greatest thrill, when his automobile is caught between the German and Russian fire. An alarmed sentry orders him back. Twice that day the officers' machines had drawn the enemy fire. The machine quivers as the driver throws on every ounce of power, but 'the shells sing an intimate song as they fly above us.' Thus for twelve hours he made dangerous contacts with a battle he was to learn, after all, was but a strategic move.

'Now I can tell you,' he wrote his wife, 'that I saw a real

battle yesterday — shells tearing up the earth, men killed, the wounded, the prisoners, the earthquake of artillery, etc. It was splendid! I was surprised to find I was not afraid, and shocked to find I was not shocked. The German troops were splendid.'

But he did not mention the perilous moments between fires.

VIII

It was after this that he saw Von Hindenburg, finding him in a newly built castle called Posen Schloss, whence he was directing the successful movements of a mighty army from the Baltic Sea to Cracow. Before leaving Berlin, Beveridge had written out in lead pencil on the stationery of the Hotel Adlon the questions he would ask, and each was numbered. On the same stationery the answers were written in pencil. No military figure impressed him quite so much as this massive man whose mingled dignity and simplicity suggested the ideal soldier. Military matters he could not discuss, and Von Hindenburg's impressions on the causes of the war were those of the political leaders. Was there a military party in Germany? he was asked. 'Nonsense!' he exploded. 'The German army is the German people.' Who made the war? 'The English merchants.' The violation of the treaty of Belgium? France had violated it first. Almost as much as in the case of the Kaiser, Beveridge was forced to rely on the vividness of the portrait to give value to the article.

But scrupulously the typed interview was submitted, and the original is before me, the stamp of the General Staff on each page in proof of its authenticity and accuracy. In his interview with Von Tirpitz, he had foreshadowed the ruthless submarine war that was to follow; in his article on Von Ludendorff, then scarcely known in America, he had predicted he would be a field marshal within a year — and he was. Never had a correspondent or publicist within six weeks made a more exhaustive and intelligent survey. Soon he was to hear from Mark Sullivan: 'I have never in my life seen so much journalistic work of extraordinary thoroughness and importance as you did in six weeks.' Before leaving Germany he made a journey to Bayreuth for a memorable visit to Houston Stewart Chamberlain. He was now prepared to write the story, to set down the truth, and the very veracity of his account later was to be turned against him in a dastardly manner by a New York paper.

Wishing to write his German articles in a neutral atmosphere and beyond the reach of censorship, he moved on to Switzerland and established himself at Berne.[1]

[1] Beveridge to Mark Sullivan, Feb. 9, 1915.

IX

As soon as he reached Berne, Pleasant A. Stovall, the American Minister, gave a tea for him to meet the French, British, and Italian Ministers and their wives. The editor of the 'Revue des Deux Mondes,' was there — 'a brilliant, funny little man and a great friend of Shaw's,' Beveridge wrote. But the company lingered until seven, and, eager to get to his articles, Beveridge seethed inwardly. 'I talked about the Lincoln Highway, books, climate, odd places and people in the Orient, but NOTHING about the war,' he wrote Mrs. Beveridge.[1] But the French Minister was gracious and helpful, and Beveridge's fears that he would have difficulty in France began to subside.[2]

Soon, his German articles written and on the way, he proceeded to Paris, where he stayed at the Hôtel Vouillemont on the rue Boisy-d'Anglas. It was not the Paris he had known, but a Paris 'of sadness and mourning... of heroism and resolve.' There, as in the French villages and in the vineyards, he was impressed by the absence of young men — all at the front. Depressing, too, the darkened streets at night, for, aside from subdued lights in the most frequented thoroughfares, the city was 'somber after sunset,' and he was to lose his way in returning from the residential section to his hotel. The spirit of the city, too, had changed. The gayety was all gone. The 'intellectual pessimist' was nowhere in evidence. The people were thoughtful, serious, industrious. Everyone was attending to a task, and the work being done was 'noble, pure, unspotted of gain.' Thus he found the atmosphere thrilling. 'Not in the most glorious days of the great Napoleon,' he wrote, 'did the sons of France pour out their blood with greater prodigality than their descendants have done up to the present hour of this mighty conflict.' His enthusiasm for the French literally flamed.[3]

Just as in Germany he had submitted the claims of the Allies and recorded the answers, he stated and wrote down the answers to the German charges; and just as frequently found these answers convincing. But he had just reached Paris when he had warning that a mere record of actualities would be intolerable to the pro-Ally circles in America. Meeting his friend Gifford Pinchot, he found him 'so violent as to be incoherent mentally about Belgium and German outrages.'[4] Just as in Berlin he had sought the responsible leaders of the Government for opinions, he interviewed President Poincaré and Foreign Minister Delcassé. Both received him with cordiality, and

[1] Feb. 14, 1915.   [2] Feb. 15, 1915.
[3] *What is Behind the War*, 246–50.   [4] To Mrs. Beveridge, Feb. 21, 1915.

talked freely, but neither would permit him to ascribe the interview to them by name. This deprived their interviews of the weight that went with the statements of the German leaders, and laid him open to the charge of his political enemies of making a one-sided investigation.

Within two days of his arrival in Paris, he spent an hour and a half with Delcassé, whom he found 'very nice and very able.' But that same day he wrote Mrs. Beveridge: 'It is too bad that he has a rule never to be quoted by name, for his talk, if given out under his name, would make a great presentation of the French case.' Delcassé told him the 'real reason of the conflict is to maintain the equilibrium of Europe'; that if Germany came to be the first power in Europe, France would cease to be a first-class power.[1] The interview submitted to the Foreign Minister is before me, with Delcassé's corrections, mostly of a minor nature. There is one elimination:

'Is there any commercial rivalry?'
'No, substantially none. Some, of course, but not important.'
This is stricken out in the manuscript.

That day he lunched with Paul Bourget and Henri Bergson, the philosopher. Everyone he found helpful and 'open-hearted.'[2] It was at luncheon at the home of the clever Countess Greffuhle, a leader of Parisian society, that he met Léon Bourgeois, the militant peace advocate. He thought the war a struggle between peoples, an attempt by Germany to impose her ideals upon France and the world, and to acquire French territory to increase her man-power for military purposes. France had entered the war only because she was invaded; the Russian alliance was not decisive. The defeat of Germany would mean the recovery of Alsace and Lorraine and the destruction of the German military system. But Bourgeois refused the use of his name, and his interview, ascribed to 'an eminent French advocate of peace,' was weakened in its effect. Beveridge had found 'the great peace advocate at his best, and the society leader very brilliant.'[3] The typed interview submitted to Bourgeois was returned with numerous changes, mostly as to phrasing. But it was at the luncheon that arrangements were made for the Countess's brother, Prince d'Ahrenberg, to accompany him to the fighting. Working day and night under high pressure, Beveridge needed a change. He was 'almost dead for want of sleep and from overwork' and 'in a daze sometimes,' almost persuaded he should 'not have undertaken the trip.'

[1] *What is Behind the War*, 276.
[2] To Mrs. Beveridge, Feb. 21, 1915.
[3] To Mrs. Beveridge, Feb. 23, 1915.

X

This journey to the battle-fields of Flanders was to be one of Beveridge's most memorable experiences. The democracy of the French army impressed him, the quick accuracy of the men firing the famous '75' guns and the easy action of the cannon delighted him, the sense of danger thrilled him. And he was charmed and impressed by General Franchet d'Esperey, who had played his part in the battle of the Marne, and who took him under his wing on tours of inspection. 'His table-talk makes you forget your appetite,' he wrote.

So away toward Rheims, still under fire, he rode with d'Esperey. He learned that the town was shelled the day before and bombarded that morning, though there were no French troops there; that movements there were under the field-glasses of the enemy; that more than one automobile would attract attention. 'That is the reason I sent back the other automobiles,' the soldier explained. They flashed into the town and Beveridge viewed the 'ruins' of the Cathedral, astonished that so little damage had been done. 'The irreparable loss,' he found, 'is the shattering of the priceless thirteenth-century stained glass which made the glorious windows of the Cathedral of Rheims artistic monuments of the craftsmanship of the Middle Ages, now lost to the world.'

But the lure of the trenches drew him, and they turned away. Disappointed at the absence of a thrill in Rheims, he entered the military automobile when — 'Boom!' — and a shell exploded but a short distance away. A great column of earth and smoke — and he knew the machine had been marked by the Germans.

Out through the open country flashed the motor car, and soon he entered the 'approach' — a long, deep trench leading to the village where the local trench headquarters were located. The commanding officer — 'attractive and gentle-mannered, delicate of face and figure,' accompanied him to the village which appeared deserted despite the feeling that it teemed with life. A moment he lingered in a partly demolished church, once picturesque, where Mass was being said in a corner still intact; and thence into the trenches. The living-quarters of the officers, with soap and bottles of eau de Cologne, amused him. He saw no signs of danger. 'I must ask you to remain here a moment,' said the officer. He was in a bomb-proof retreat. 'We might as well sit down,' added his companion. Candles were lighted. 'We shan't have to wait long,' the officer continued. 'They are shelling us.' 'I hear no explosions' — from Beveridge. 'There have been twenty of them, and there will be more.' In truth there were twenty-nine. The automobile had been seen from an enemy plane and reported. The shelling was inspired by the suspicion that the machine contained a French General or a French civilian of importance.

'Especially shelled,' Beveridge chortled, happy in the thought.[1]

XI

Back to Paris, refreshed by the experience. 'The French are very nice to me,' he wrote his wife. 'Just back from the front batteries in Flanders. Heavy cannonade — my party were shelled especially. Now I am back at the grind of seeing people. Feel like a new man from my outing at the front, but by tomorrow I'll be rags again.'[2]

With a letter from an intimate mutual friend he found easy access to Gabriel Hanotaux, former Minister of Foreign Affairs, and father of the Franco-Russian alliance. He was willing to be quoted by name, and Beveridge found him 'direct, simple, outspoken,' stating his points 'clearly and with great emphasis.' The reason for the war? The taking of Alsace and Lorraine against the will of the people, was the reply. But how about Morocco and Algiers? Beveridge asked. A people, not civilized, and in a state of anarchy, Hanotaux replied — just like your Philippines. Beveridge was pinked, and passed to other topics. It was from Hanotaux that the interviewer received the most direct answer to the question whether there was a secret understanding with Belgium that in the event of war France could move her troops through Belgian territory.

'Just a conversation between a British military attaché and somebody in the Belgian Government,' Hanotaux replied.

The first draft of the interview was returned to Beveridge with many changes, but merely in the phrasing.

Having seen the military and political leaders, Beveridge now turned, as in Germany, to the scholars, and, substituting Henri Bergson, the philosopher, for Von Harnack, he lunched with him and his wife at the Villa Montmorency, Auteuil, Paris. It was a bright moment in a gloomy journey, for no one pleased him more than this man, with the 'long, thin, intellectual face; the expansive brow, the large blue eyes whose lights reflect keenness, mysticism, and kindness.' His was a tolerant view — a plea for the retention within themselves of the different cultures of the nations. But he found the war a German plot against the liberties of the world, and he painted a drab picture of the fate of

[1] *What is Behind the War*, 216–43.
[2] To Mrs. Beveridge, Feb. 28, 1915.

BEVERIDGE AND A 'SEVENTY-FIVE'
On the French front, February 27, 1915

France in the event of defeat.[1] His corrections of the first draft were submitted in the form of a letter:

I am sending back to you the account of our conversation, so vividly written down by you. I felt whilst reading it as if I was seeing my own image in a magic looking-glass, where I was transfigured and yet most resembling. You have made me speak much better than I ever spoke, but you have stated my meaning exactly. On two or three points only have I made additions and corrections.

Page 1: When I said that between Germany and England there was a commercial rivalry, I did not mean that England would ever have transformed that rivalry into actual war. On the contrary, if England had wished to get rid of German competition by force, she would have done so before the German navy became so strong. I believe that the real cause of the present war was Germany's intention to crush France and Russia first, so that England would have to stand alone when Germany chose to attack her. I know England well, and I am perfectly convinced that up to the beginning of August no English Government would have been able to persuade the nation to go to war against Germany; it was the violation of the neutrality of Belgium that set the English people against Germany. So I have added one or two sentences in order to explain that it was Germany, not England, that intended to transfer the commercial rivalry into actual war. Only Germany hoped that England would stand still while France and Russia were being crushed; her turn would have come later on.

Page 3: I have struck out the words, 'by equally important and valuable,'[2] because I believe that the various ideals developed by evolution have a right to exist on account of the greater richness that they give to the world, although no one can say whether they are equal....

Page 4: I see that what I said about the two souls of Germany is not at all clear. I have added one or two sentences to explain my meaning. That is what I mean by speaking with two minds and souls. To which I have added: 'One of the two souls may be concerned, as you say, with philosophy, poetry, music, art'; but the other is below the ordinary level of humanity. We have seen that other soul at work since the beginning of the war and we know what it is worth.

We shall all keep vivid remembrance of the time, much too short, which you spent with us, and we hope that you will soon come back again.[3]

The French search for opinion ended with conversations with Eugène Schneider, owner and manager of the famous Le Creusot Works, producing the noted artillery, representing the industrialists, and with Monsieur Hervé, editor of the 'Social War,'

---

[1] *What is Behind the War*, 289–90.

[2] This had been: 'Let Germany keep her *Kultur* and develop it; but also let France keep her culture and develop it; and England keep her culture and develop it. It is a manifestation of human evolution at different but equally important and valuable angles.'

[3] Bergson to Beveridge, March 4, 1915.

representing the Socialists. With the former he lunched at his home, and the latter he met at a luncheon in the home of one of the richest of the French bourgeoisie. From the industrialist he heard that the war was a German plot to acquire the rich iron and coal fields of northern and eastern France, along with the iron, steel, and textile works, and to take the ports of Havre, Dunkirk, and Cherbourg, with the view to Germanizing the country.[1] From Hervé he heard a defense of the French Socialists fighting with reactionary Russia against Germany with her social reforms — a defense that approached prophecy. 'Russia is far better prepared for socialism than Germany,' said the agitator. 'There is more liberal spirit in Russia than in Germany. Wait until her mujiks are educated and you will see. And the end of this war will be a warning to any military party that does exist in Russia. The end of this war will open the Russian eyes, I assure you.'[2]

Thus Beveridge left France with a profound admiration for the fighting spirit of her people, convinced of their unity of purpose, their confidence and determination. He found but one thing to resent — the pictures and cartoons showing women being raped and tortured by the Germans. But he had been warmly received, graciously served, and he carried away the impression of something 'noble, inspiring, beautiful, and even touching in the spirit of self-sacrifice and high purpose.'[3]

XII

Early March found him in London at Brown's Hotel in Albemarle Street, with every expectation of having his work facilitated. He had known Lord Bryce in Washington, and he carried a letter from Roosevelt to Lloyd George. He found London literally swarming with soldiers, with traffic constantly halted to permit marching companies to pass. In the streets and parks, khaki-clad privates with natty caps were promenading; and they thickly sprinkled the music-halls and restaurants.[4] Almost immediately he sensed that unity — and the grim determination of the masses which had impressed him in Germany and France — was lacking.[5] He was to verify this impression in conversations with all classes later. The unrest in labor circles was something new in his experience. But he thought that the aristocracy or hereditary class had never shown such courage and patriotism.[6]

[1] *What is Behind the War*, 296–305.   [2] *Ibid.*, 319.
[3] *Ibid.*, 255.   [4] *Ibid.*, 323.
[5] *Ibid.*, 324.   [6] *Ibid.*, 326.

He was particularly anxious to have satisfactory conversations with Asquith, Lloyd George, and Sir Edward Grey, and on reaching London he solicited the good offices of Walter Hines Page, the American Ambassador, in making the connections.[1] Sir Gilbert Parker cordially welcomed him to England and invited him to lunch. But with the personal recommendation of Bryce and the letter from Roosevelt, he found it impossible to see Lloyd George. On the receipt of the Roosevelt letter, the latter's secretary had responded with frigid formality to Hibben: 'Mr. Lloyd George would be glad if you would inform him how long Mr. Beveridge intends to stay in town.'[2] No engagement ever was made, although America at the time was more interested in the picturesque Welshman than in any other British statesman. Sir Edward Grey saw him at the Foreign Office one afternoon, but after the discouraging warning: 'Sir Edward Grey feels sure that Mr. Beveridge will understand that the visit must be considered as of a private nature.' This meant another interview anonymously ascribed. Even so, Grey was to be the only one of the outstanding members of the Ministry to set forth the English point of view in an interview. The purport of it was that the invasion of Belgium was the immediate reason for England's entering the war; that, this aside, she could not afford to acquiesce in the crushing of France; that Britain's situation imposed upon her the maintenance of the equilibrium of Europe; and that the existence of a predominant power would mean the imposition of that nation's will upon the other countries.[3] The interview, ascribed to 'one of Great Britain's foremost statesmen,' was sent to Grey for his corrections. But one, of any significance, was made. In the conversation he had said: 'If Germany had not made that mistake [the invasion of Belgium] Great Britain would not have taken the hostile action she did take.' To this, Grey, in his correction, added the words, 'so promptly and unanimously.'

With Asquith, Beveridge was to have a more annoying experience. The Premier perfectly understood the nature of the interview desired when Beveridge was invited to luncheon at 10 Downing Street on March 12. But when the latter arrived, he found Paderewski at the table, and the conversation was most casual. This meeting with Asquith was precious time wasted and no interview was written. This attitude of English leaders in power was in painful contrast with that of those in Germany and France. The Duke of Devonshire courteously received him

---

[1] Beveridge to Page, March 4, 1915.
[2] Lloyd George to Beveridge, March 9, 1915.
[3] *What is Behind the War*, 364–68.

at Devonshire House, but afterward wrote his own interview which was bromidic in its studied conservatism of expression. [1]

But Bryce was frank and helpful. He had opposed the war, disapproved of the Government's policy, but was positive that the violation of the neutrality of Belgium was responsible for Britain's participation. He took issue with Grey's idea that the creation of a predominant power in Europe necessitated the challenge of England; and denied that economic or commercial considerations determined England's course. When the first draft of the interview was returned to Beveridge, it bore many corrections. Where Bryce had said that he had not approved of the Government's policy, he added, 'and I think the same still.' Where he had said he did not think it had the aggressive moral support of the English people, he preceded the word 'moral' with 'general.' To the statement that England had not been moved by economic motives he added: 'She is losing economically far more by it than any man would have fancied she would gain.'

In submitting the manuscript for correction, Beveridge had asked if there had been any agreement between England and France to attack Germany through Belgium. In returning the paper, Bryce wrote:

You will not, I trust, suppose that British Liberals accept either the 'balance of power' doctrine or the notion of undoing German unity. Certainly I don't. Our people have not, I hope, any hatred of Germany, heartily as they condemn Prussian militarism.

P.S. As to the other question in your letter, there was never any arrangement between Britain and France to attack Germany through Belgium. Any statement to that effect is a malicious fiction. What Britain did discuss with Belgium was the contingency of a violation by Germany of Belgian neutrality. In that case, and in that case only, would Britain have entered Belgium, and she would have entered it in fulfillment of her own guarantee of Belgian neutrality.

My impression is that our views here are just those of your and my friends in the United States, who, as lovers of free democratic government, of peace and humanity, desire the fall of a baleful system of militarism which denies the fundamental principles of international morality and of Christianity. We wish to see the German people deliver themselves of that system. [2]

XIII

Unhappily for the general effect of the English articles, where the supporters of the Ministry and of Grey's policy were reticent,

[1] Devonshire to Beveridge, March 12, 1915.
[2] Bryce to Beveridge, March 15, 1915.

their opponents were eager to set forth their views; and these were men of too much consequence to ignore in determining the nation's thought. William Archer urged Beveridge to see H. W. Massingham, of the 'Nation,' who not only represented 'advanced Liberal thought,' but would be able to help him in estimating 'the personal equation of other people whom you have been seeing.'[1] L. Buckler, of the American Embassy, had brought him in contact with Charles Trevelyan, who was at the head of the New Union of Democratic Control, seeking to curb the power of Sir Edward Grey. Trevelyan, in turn, had taken it upon himself to arrange a meeting with Ramsay Mac-Donald. And Archer and Gilbert Murray had arranged a meeting with George Bernard Shaw.

Trevelyan had resigned from the Ministry on account of the war, and impressed Beveridge as a 'young man of fine ability.' Bitterly opposed to secret diplomacy, he thought it outrageous that Grey should have given his opinion to France ten years before that, in case of war, England would support her; and even more outrageous that no one should have known of the assurance.[2] He was not interested in the 'balance of power,'[3] and was sure the war would lead to a spread of democracy.

Even more damaging to the official version of events was the interview with Shaw — which was written wholly by himself. Before me lies the manuscript of the interview as it was returned to Beveridge by the brilliant dramatist and socialist. With a fine-pointed pen he had completely obliterated every line of typewriting with a circular movement, and in between the lines, in astonishingly tiny but perfectly legible writing, Shaw had interviewed himself. Cleverly, and bitingly, too, he arraigned Grey for the secret 'opinion,' which he declared the sole reason for England's participation, and scoffed at the idea that England was pained or surprised at the violation of the neutrality of Belgium. 'Why, everyone knew for years,' he wrote, 'that Germany would march through Belgium in case of war with France. There were Germany's strategic railroads built right up to the Belgian frontier — what other object could they have had? There was no secret about it at all.'[4] No, he concluded, it was the balance of power and England's dominion of the seas that drew her into the conflict.

Thus there was ample justification for Beveridge's conclusion that England lacked the unity of the other nations. While he was in England, workers were striking on the Clyde and dock laborers in Liverpool; the Commandeering Bill had been passed

[1] Archer to Beveridge, March 11, 1915.
[2] *What is Behind the War*, 378.   [3] *Ibid.*, 380.   [4] *Ibid.*, 387.

to meet the situation, and, at a labor mass meeting he attended, he had listened to bitter denunciations of the Government, and heard it charged that business profiteers were squeezing the poor. He had read a pamphlet, 'Why Starve?' protesting against the rise in the cost of bread. And all he heard from public men he recorded with meticulous care, and all he saw he wrote down. His mission was that of a recorder, not a propagandist, and writing for a publication of a neutral country he was not concerned with the prejudices and prepossessions of those who scouted the President's call for neutrality. If the partisan views of the governmental leaders of Germany and France were recorded, and not those of England, it was their fault, not his. He had not been responsible for Lloyd George's refusal to talk; for Paderewski's presence at the Asquith luncheon; for Grey's prohibition of the use of his name.

His general conclusions have now taken on the color of prophecy. He saw 'an immeasurable advance in democracy, expressed in terms of collectivism.'[1] 'It is not extravagant to say,' he concluded, 'that time may show that the war marked the passage of an old economic dispensation and the coming of a new social and industrial period.'[2] But most striking of all was his foreshadowing of unemployment and the dole:

I was willing to fight for my country and the Government cared for me while I was doing it; now I am willing to work for my country... I am not willing to starve; I am not willing to see my wife and children perish from hunger and cold. If the nation could feed, clothe, and pay me for the destructive work I did for it in time of war, why cannot it now pay, feed, and clothe me for the constructive work I am anxious to do for it in time of peace?

Thus, in the first year of the war Beveridge anticipated the demands that were to come. Satisfied with his investigations, he sailed from Liverpool for home.

[1] *What is Behind the War*, 408.   [2] *Ibid.*, 410.

CHAPTER II
WAR AND POLITICS, 1915–17

I

THE first reaction Beveridge got to his attempt impartially to
describe what he had seen, and to record what he had heard,
came immediately after his return, on the occasion of his address before the Sphinx Club, New York, in which he said the
press here gave no proper idea of the war, which was a war of
peoples. This idea, held by leaders in all the warring nations,
generally was ridiculed. He found that even his first article on
the interned Belgian soldiers in Holland was bitterly resented,
though Mark Sullivan, in London, had written him that 'the
people who have read it describe it as a very obvious effort to
write the most fair and unpartisan kind of article.' [1] But the
war party in America, howling like hyenas at the heels of Wilson
because of his neutrality position, appreciated no such 'obvious
effort.' Dr. Albert Shaw had written him that his articles were
'a great success,' in 'marked contrast with the writings of mere
newspaper correspondents'; and that they would add greatly to
his reputation 'as a writer and as a publicist.' [2] Perkins had
written before that the current article 'is by long odds the best
thing you have ever done written in the most convincing style,
simple, direct,' and was making 'a very favorable impression.' [3]
And Sinclair Lewis, whose triumphs were still in the future, wrote
from his desk at Doran's publishing house 'to express my extreme interest in your series of impressions of Europe.' Lewis
was moved to write after reading the article on 'A Visit to the
Kaiser and his War Lords,' which gave 'a very vivid picture of
these men.' [4] From Elmer Roberts, a classmate at DePauw, and
then representing the Associated Press in Paris, he heard that
the French articles were 'admirably written and sympathetic
toward France.' [5]

But the article Lewis had liked had caused Beveridge no end
of embarrassment. He had scarcely reached Paris when he received a cable from one of the editors of 'Collier's' asking
'whether the interview with William will ever be released.' It

[1] Sullivan to Beveridge, Feb. 11, 1915.   [2] Shaw to Beveridge, May 11, 1915.
[3] Perkins to Beveridge, April 3, 1915.
[4] Sinclair Lewis to Beveridge, April 2, 1915.
[5] Roberts to Beveridge, July 14, 1915.

reached him, bearing the stamp of the French War Office. He cabled 'Collier's' a sharp rebuke:

You apparently forgot that you were cabling me at the capital of a country at war, with the enemy not an hour and a half automobile ride away, and... about a supposed interview with the ruler of the invading country. Your cablegram went to the War Department and was delivered to me with the stamp of the Minister of War upon it. It might have caused serious complications.[1]

But that was not to be the end of the embarrassment. He had given the article the title, 'The German Emperor and Two of the Fighting Chiefs,' and 'Collier's' had changed it to 'A Visit to the Kaiser,' implying an interview. The 'New Republic' seized upon the misleading title as a deliberate misrepresentation. The 'North American Review' jocularly explained the absence of an interview in a two hours' talk on the theory that Beveridge got started talking first. 'But even so,' it added, 'it would seem as if one of them might have squeezed in a Wie gehts or two.'[2]

Then, too, 'Collier's' did not want to publish a number of the articles Beveridge thought the best. To Albert Shaw he offered the interviews with Von Harnack, Rathenau, Ballin, Südekum, Bergson, and Hanotaux that 'Collier's' did not take, and a number of articles dealing with France and England were run in the 'Review of Reviews.'

Meanwhile, the press ran copious extracts from the articles and many editorials upon them, some bitter and offensive. The 'Springfield Republican' was outraged that a 'cub reporter' should presume to enlighten America by writing of what he had seen and heard. Much of the editorializing was in denunciation of the prediction that the war would lead to the socialization of industry in Europe; some, of the suggestion that democracy would win.

Soon Beveridge was being pronounced 'pro-German'; and finally, in August, both the 'New York Telegram' and the 'New York Herald,' under flashing headlines, announced 'Scores of Prominent Persons Now Involved in German Conspiracy,' naming, among the 'leading conspirators,' Beveridge, William Travers Jerome, the famous District Attorney of New York, and S. S. McClure, editor of the 'Evening Mail.'[3] The Beveridge articles in the mean time had been published in book form, and the 'Herald,' one of the American war-hawks, said in double-column headlines that the 'Revelations throw a new light on

[1] March 31, 1915.   [2] May, 1915.
[3] *New York Telegram*, Aug. 16; *New York Herald*, Aug. 17, 1915.

Mr. Beveridge's pro-German book on the war,' and that he would lecture in the Kaiser's cause giving a one-sided view of the conflict.

Thoroughly aroused, Beveridge's first impulse was to sue the two papers, and he advised with New York friends on the choice of a lawyer familiar with the law of libel. 'This is the first time in my life,' he wrote Shaw, 'that anyone ever so much as faintly insinuated that anything I did or said was corruptly and improperly influenced. Such an insinuation I will not submit to.' [1]

But no one was impressed with the story, and the absurdity of a suit was soon manifest. The press reception of the book had been almost wholly favorable. Sir Gilbert Parker wrote that it was 'most valuable, absorbingly interesting,' showing 'great skill at analysis, prodigious memory, and a fine political instinct.' [2] Buckler, of the American Embassy in London, thought it 'the most illuminating book that I have seen upon the war.' [3] And Senator Cummins wrote: 'It stands alone in all the writing about the war, its causes and its consequences. No one else has approached it, either in thought or in style.' [4]

II

As the darkness deepened for the Allies, there was an intensification of the war propaganda in America. 'You would see a great change here from the careless London you saw six months ago,' wrote Buckler in October. 'The Allies' prospects have never seemed darker, and London streets are so dark as to be dangerous. Trevelyan, with whom I was lunching last week, derives consolation from the fact that we have kept out of the fight, and sees in that the one hope for sanity and civilization.' [5] Beveridge heartily concurred in Trevelyan's idea. Having seen and talked with the leaders of the warring nations and viewed the fighting in the field, he was astounded at the audacity and absurdity of much of the propaganda; more amazed at its acceptance at face value by friends of keen intelligence and customary mental poise. A famous novelist, and a close friend, wrote, 'I begin to shake, shriek, and dribble at the mouth whenever there is a pro-German whisper.' It was a common malady, but not all realized, as did Tarkington, that it had become a disease. Quite as incomprehensible to Beveridge as the ready acceptance of the most patent propaganda was the seeming inability of the Nation to grasp the stupendous significance of the world struggle.

[1] Beveridge to Shaw, Aug. 20, 1915.
[2] Parker to Beveridge, Oct. 13, 1915.
[3] Buckler to Beveridge, Oct. 2, 1915.
[4] Cummins to Beveridge, Oct. 13, 1915.
[5] Buckler to Beveridge, Oct. 2, 1915.

'It has been a great shock to me,' he wrote Shaffer, 'to find that when the foundations of the world are quaking, when a whole dispensation is passing away in blood and fire, America, apparently, does not know what is going on.'[1] And a week later: 'Do not forget that this hour, this very hour, is the greatest in all the history of all the ages. Vast issues will arise beside which the small playing of politics will be so trivial that our children will wonder how we ever could have endured it.'[2]

Then, in May, came the sinking of the Lusitania by a German submarine and the loss of American lives; the clamor of the war-hawks for a declaration of war; the resignation of Bryan from the Cabinet, because unable to agree with Wilson on the tenor of the note of protest. Beveridge sympathized with Bryan's view that Americans had no moral right to endanger the peace of their country by taking passage on the ships of the belligerents — ships carrying ammunition. He had foreseen the vigorous use of the submarine by Germany ever since his interview with Von Tirpitz. Warning had been given. Neutral ships could have been taken. But those who had criticized Wilson for not pushing us into war over the invasion of Belgium, naturally made the most of the shocking tragedy of the sea.

'I am gravely concerned over the development of our national policy,' Beveridge wrote Shaffer. 'When we say that the United States insures a belligerent ship carrying ammunition and war material in case it has one American citizen on board, we take a position which is absolutely indefensible.'[3] Shaffer answered hotly, and Beveridge replied at length, defending his position. 'You cannot state a hard-and-fast rule of international law, and ... disregard all history and also the actual existing conditions. This country is a neutral country; that means that it must act like a neutral.'[4]

But the Lusitania crisis passed when Germany yielded to Wilson's demand that she sink no liners without warning and without providing for the safety of the non-combatants, unless the liner resisted or sought to escape. Beveridge was pleased with Wilson's triumph, and thought it might increase his strength greatly. 'Conversely,' he wrote Shaffer, 'our friend's [Roosevelt's] bitter utterances... I fear weakened him, especially in view of Wilson's success.... A few weeks ago Mr. Wilson's strength was very doubtful; today it apparently is supreme. But tomorrow? Who can tell?'[5]

But he was not blind to the increasing difficulty of maintain-

[1] Beveridge to Shaffer, April 1, 1915. [2] April 8, 1915.
[3] Beveridge to Shaffer, July 10, 1915. [4] Beveridge to Shaffer, July 21, 1915.
[5] Beveridge to Shaffer, Sept. 3, 1915.

ing a position of neutrality. When, in the spring of 1916, Shaffer wrote that Chicago business men were a unit in thinking it would be a disaster for the Germans to win, Beveridge replied: 'Yes. Unless the Allies win these bonds become very poor securities; and... the enormous bills for the munitions which have been and are being furnished... cannot be paid speedily, if at all.'[1]

In the earlier stages he was passionately opposed to America's participation in the war.

III

Through 1915 and the early part of 1916, Beveridge was critically observing the maneuvering within the camp of the Progressives, and with no little cynicism. After the 'Hinman incident,' he was convinced that Roosevelt was seeking a realignment with the Republican Party on his own terms and in his own interest. Perkins, in charge of the organization, was busily exchanging views with Progressive leaders throughout the country regarding the attitude of independent voters, and calling attention to the reactionary tendency in the Republican legislatures closing in the spring.[2] But Beveridge was waiting impatiently for a militant note from Roosevelt.

'My judgment is,' he wrote Perkins, 'that the party is disintegrating. This is largely due to the feeling... that T. R. is flirting with the Republicans. Unless he comes out mighty soon with a tremendous bugle blast calling our people to arms, my judgment is he won't have anybody to call to arms — or, to put it in terms of politics, he won't have anybody to deliver.'[3]

In July he attended a conference of leaders in New York and was disgusted by the domination of the meeting by the New York contingent and the adoption of a resolution authorizing the party in each State to take its own course locally. He wrote Perkins:

This is the same thing as dissolving the party; the same thing as going over, body, boots, and breeches, without terms either as to platform or candidates. With some little experience in politics, and an intimate acquaintance with the ability and character of the stand-pat leaders... it makes me laugh to hear men, like our Illinois friend, talk about making terms with Deneen; and one faints with mingled mirth and disgust at Flynn's [of Pennsylvania] scheme of 'following Brumbaugh.' In New York, Barnes won't pay as much attention to Davenport... as the buttons on his coat; in Illinois, the Lorimer-Cannon-

[1] March 6, 1916.
[2] Perkins to Progressive State Chairmen, May 4, 1915.
[3] Beveridge to Perkins, May 6, 1915.

McKinley machine will play marbles with our friends who talk of going back there; in Pennsylvania, what Penrose and Brumbaugh will do to Flynn and our fellows will be too pathetic to describe.... So that 'releasing' each State to do as it likes is not only to dissolve the party, to throw away all our assets, but it hasn't the dignity of self-respect.[1]

Unimpressed, but still anxious apparently to preserve the new party's entity, Perkins was soon writing Beveridge of a Progressive conference and the attempt of Davenport and Robinson [2] to have the party organization advise its members in New York to enroll as Republicans in the fall. 'We had a regular knock-down, drag-out fight of it, but they were overwhelmingly defeated in the meeting,' he wrote Beveridge. But in New Jersey the progress of disintegration had gone so far that George L. Record had openly returned to the Republican Party. 'What do you think of that?' wrote Perkins. 'The worst, most extreme Progressive joining the rankest and most reactionary political organization.' [3] And on top of it all, Roosevelt issued a statement on the return of Progressives to the Republican Party in New York expressing his appreciation of their previous support, sending them back with a blessing, but saying that if his advice were asked he would advise Progressives to stay with the party.

But Beveridge expected little of it. 'As I have told you several times,' he wrote Perkins, 'what our people have needed, waited for, prayed for, is a tremendous call to arms by Colonel Roosevelt himself. For since the Hinman affair there has been a wide-spread and growing feeling among our rank and file, as well as among our party workers, that the design of Colonel Roosevelt and the New York leaders was to abandon the party.' [4]

Tramping through the woods at Beverly Farms, Beveridge had ample opportunity for clear thinking, and he could not share Perkins's confidence that the Republicans would turn their party over to Mr. Roosevelt and his supporters. As autumn came, his skepticism increased. He declined Perkins's invitations to conferences, refused to advise his friends in Indiana, and was not surprised when Perkins found it necessary to repudiate the erstwhile Progressive, who proposed, at Washington, a merger through a Republican pledge to nominate a Progressive candidate. When Beveridge was asked to sign a statement by Progressives, he refused because Roosevelt's name was not to be on it. 'If the signature of a number of gentlemen appear and that of Colonel Roosevelt is absent, it would confirm the suspicion that our great leader is no longer active for the

[1] Beveridge to Perkins, July 21, 1915.   [2] New York Progressives.
[3] Perkins to Beveridge, Aug. 2, 1915.   [4] Beveridge to Perkins, Aug. 18, 1915.

party,' he wrote Perkins. 'It would be an admission in writing of what Republican workers, from the highest to the lowest, have been charging for more than a year. The Republican organization all over the country would cite that call... as documentary proof of their wretched assertions that Colonel Roosevelt has deserted us.'[1] To letters from Indiana inquiring if Roosevelt was seeking the Republican nomination, Beveridge now replied that he did not know.[2] But when the New York wing of the new party proposed that the Progressive Convention should be held at the same time and in the same city as the Republican, he thoroughly understood the strategy. To Shaffer, who favored such a course, he wrote that it would 'put us in a ridiculous light and make a bad impression throughout the country, and that the Progressives, if in earnest, should meet before the Republicans.'[3]

Six days before the writing of this letter there had been a mysterious gathering at the home of Judge Gary, of the Steel Corporation, at 856 Fifth Avenue, New York. A smoke screen was thrown about the meeting to escape publicity. There, in the Gary house, were August Belmont, Jacob H. Schiff, George F. Baker, A. Barton Hepburn, Frank A. Vanderlip, Cornelius Vanderbilt, Daniel Guggenheim, Clarence Mackay, and George Cortelyou — and the central figure was Colonel Roosevelt. And Perkins was there, too. When the press discovered the dinner, Judge Gary explained that it was given to discuss preparedness.[4] But practical men like Beveridge drew their own conclusion. After that, he knew that Roosevelt would seek the Republican nomination, but he had no faith in the success of the plan. It was at this time that he summed up the situation in a letter to Shaffer:

... Then along came the T. R. campaign in 1912 which I thought was a mistake as a matter of political tactics, but a noble thing if the real purpose was to establish a great national liberal party. Finally persuaded that it was the latter, I went with the Colonel, with misgivings. But, as it turned out, the movement was not a genuine one to the great end of founding a new party, as Lincoln, Jefferson, and Jackson had founded new parties, but a mere political maneuver....

Since it is now plain that the Progressive Movement was never intended to be a sincere effort to found a great new liberal party, the situation is this:

The Republican Party has both its legs broken — badly broken, a compound fracture. You cannot jam the sundered parts of the broken bones together and make the leg so that it can run or even walk. The

[1] Beveridge to Perkins, Nov. 27, 1915. [2] To H. L. Kitselman, Dec. 1, 1915.
[3] Beveridge to Shaffer, Dec. 23, 1915. [4] *New York Times*, Dec. 19, 1915.

splints must first be put on, the leg put in a plaster cast, and then time given for the broken parts to knit. The Chicago Convention may succeed in putting on the splints and applying the plaster cast; but it will take from two to four years more for the broken bones to grow together.[1]

And so it was to be.

IV

The two conventions met at Chicago at the same time, as planned; and the Progressives were made as ridiculous as Beveridge had foreseen. Not tempted to inject himself into such a comedy, he stayed away. Perkins was in charge of the Progressive Convention, even to the steam roller. Raymond Robins, the chairman, would not tolerate any opposition to the Perkins program. The first move to force the nomination of Roosevelt by the Republicans appeared in the appointment of a joint committee of the two conventions to seek a common ground on which both could stand. Not long were the Progressives to cherish their illusions. Senator Reed Smoot, representing the Republican Convention, began proceedings with the blunt announcement that his party would accept 'anyone but Roosevelt.' And so the fair expectations tumbled like a house of cards.

The leaders rushed to the telephone to consult their chieftain; and the outcome was a letter from him to the convention urging that they unite on Henry Cabot Lodge. The Progressives listened to the letter in a daze. Why Lodge — in Heaven's name, why Lodge? He had been a consistent reactionary all his life; had hated the Bull Moose Movement with all the venom that went with his hostility; had made speeches furiously assailing the Progressive program and had them published as Senate Documents and distributed at the public cost. There was scarcely a line in the Progressive platform that was not, to him, as the red banner of the picador to the bull. It was incredible — and yet there it was — the letter!

A wave of resentment, bitter and deep, swept over the convention. Perkins lost control. Bainbridge Colby, who was to have placed Roosevelt in nomination and had been held back, literally was pushed to the platform. Deliberately, not without a touch of irony, he put Roosevelt in nomination. Hiram Johnson, in ringing tones, seconded the nomination, and called upon the Colonel to meet his responsibilities. The nomination was made; and instantly a declination came by wire. Roosevelt had washed his hands of the Progressive Party.

[1] Beveridge to Shaffer, June 3, 1915.

That day, too stricken to leave town, Bainbridge Colby shut himself up in his room at the hotel. At his feet lay a crumpled telegram from the 'New York World' asking for an expression on the future. Finally he recovered it and sent a reply. The purport was that the army had been deserted by the General, and that real Progressives would have to determine their course. Many were to go over to Wilson, Colby among them. Many, a bit bedraggled, dragged themselves like poor relations back to the party they had left four years before. The great adventure was over.

With the nomination of Charles Evans Hughes, the old day returned. The silence of Beveridge concerned his friends, and Shaffer wrote him that six months before, Roosevelt had said he could support Hughes, that the new party was organized only as a protest against the methods used to nominate Taft, that there had been no thought of promoting a new party.[1] But Beveridge could not gracefully accept such an interpretation of the revolt of 1912. He replied:

It is rather melancholy, however, that the most inspiring movement, with only two exceptions in American history, to organize American liberalism into a great national party should be looked upon as nothing but a protest against the work of the bosses four years ago.... What has become of the wonderful platform, especially the economic features? Has it all been abandoned for what you say is now 'Americanism, preparedness, and a protective tariff'? I feared that was the case [merely a protest], which was why I went into the Progressive Party very reluctantly and with grave misgivings. My memory must be seriously at fault as to the conversations in Chicago and New York that preceded my final consent to be chairman of the National Convention; and of many conversations at Oyster Bay since 1912.

Beveridge liked Hughes, personally, and thought him a strong man, but had Shaffer forgotten the conversation on the grave issue of dragging the Supreme Court into politics? 'Marshall considered it about the most hurtful thing that could happen to our institutions. I must think the matter over very carefully.... Look out for Brandeis four years hence.'[2]

Meanwhile, Beveridge was by no means overlooked in the calculations of Mr. Hughes and the party managers. Soon after the convention, Perkins wrote him of a dinner with the nominee, his complimentary references to Beveridge, and a desire that he should participate in the campaign. The reply was that if Hughes wished to see him, he could write him and make arrangements.[3] In less than two weeks he was dining alone with Hughes in his

[1] Shaffer to Beveridge, June 13, 1915.   [2] Beveridge to Shaffer, June 19, 1916.
[3] Beveridge to Perkins, July 7, 1916.

New York apartment, whither Roosevelt had found his way before him. After a four-hour conference, Beveridge retired to another room and prepared the statement announcing his return to the Republican Party and gave it to the press, after submitting it for the approval of the new leader. The meeting had been altogether pleasant. 'Although I have known Mr. Hughes for many years,' he wrote Shaffer the next day, 'and always have liked him, I have never been so favorably impressed with him, and very seldom by any other man, as I was last night. Indeed, it is this impression which he made upon me of his trustworthiness and straightforwardness that finally determined me, and I told him so.' [1]

The announcement of his return to the fold was received with delight by most of his former associates who had not strayed. The Columbia and Marion Clubs in Indianapolis, that had removed his portrait from their walls four years before, quite as ostentatiously restored it. Charles G. Dawes, friend of his early days, wrote him cordially: 'Time has wrought no special changes except to make me more tolerant with those who disagree with me. It is many years now since you and I used to face each other like two rhetorician bantams, wasting nervous energy, perhaps, but enjoying to the full the mental exercise of vigorous discussion. It did us both good.' [2]

Beveridge enjoyed the resumption of his old relationships, but even so, something had been taken out of him by his excursion into new fields. He returned a bit disillusioned, with the realization that even the greatest of heroes have feet of clay. It was at this time that he sat down and wrote the article, 'The Rise and Wrecking of the Progressive Party,' which he sent to Lorimer with the admonition that it was not for publication. He ascribed the wrecking to treachery and stupidity, tracing the beginning back to the 'Hinman incident.' 'I think,' he wrote Lorimer, 'that history has not one single example of a party or a movement which was used so coldbloodedly and wrecked so cynically and selfishly as the Progressive Party has been used and wrecked.' [3] Having thus worked off his wrath, he put behind him the four preceding years and turned to the preparation of his speeches for the campaign.

V

This was not to be an easy task, especially for him. He had long urged currency reform upon his party without effect, and

[1] Beveridge to Shaffer, July 20, 1916. [2] Dawes to Beveridge, July 22, 1916.
[3] Beveridge to Lorimer, June 24, 1916.

Wilson had created the Federal Reserve System over Republican opposition. He had vainly sought to interest his party and Mr. Roosevelt in child-labor legislation — and Wilson had forced its enactment. When this bill was on its passage, Senator Kenyon reminded the Senate that, almost ten years before, Beveridge 'fought alone for something that has come to be a bill in principle at least,' and now was 'entitled to the utmost credit.' He had been the first in years to fight for a tariff commission, and Wilson had created one. He had proposed the establishment of a clearing-house where business men might learn their rights and find protection against unscrupulous competitors, and Wilson had given them the Federal Trade Commission. He had bitterly denounced the tariff lobby in 1909, and in 1913 Wilson literally had scourged it from the Capitol. And if the Underwood Bill did not meet his approval, it more nearly accorded with his views than the last Republican tariff act which he had fought heroically. Clearly, it was not to be a simple matter to frame a militant campaign address against an Administration with such a record.

Nor could he see the slightest possibility of a Republican victory. 'The whole situation is a cave of the winds for the Republicans and Progressives,' he wrote Lorimer. 'Together, they may defeat Wilson, but I'll be hanged if I can see how they are going to do it — corn at seventy-five cents a bushel, wheat out of sight, farmers prosperous, workingmen all employed at high wages and striking for higher, currency law passed, and perhaps my tariff commission bill will be passed before Congress adjourns' — and it was.[1]

In August he was studying Wilson's Message on the Panama Canal tolls, his speech in favor of 'disentangling alliances,' the congressional debate on the Japanese exclusion part of the immigration bill, and on Philippine independence.[2]

Finally he finished the speech, devoted largely to other matters; and one night he sat down in his home at Beverly Farms, with Professor Archibald C. Coolidge of Harvard, an authority on foreign relations, James R. Williams, editor of the 'Boston Transcript,' and one or two business men, to the reading of the manuscript for criticism. They pronounced it excellent. Beveridge himself, strangely enough, thought it superior to his keynote speech in the Progressive Convention.[3] He was content.

He spoke first before the Middlesex Club, Boston, savagely assailing Wilson on his prevention of a threatened railroad strike

[1] Beveridge to Lorimer, June 3, 1916.
[2] Beveridge to J. K. Julian, Aug. 16, 1916.
[3] Beveridge to Shaffer, Sept. 30, 1916.

by forcing an eight-hour day act into the statutes, and the prosperous business men who heard him applauded warmly. But the treatment of the speech by the National Committee aroused his suspicion. The publicity bureau had not given it to the Associated Press and the 'dumbfounded' National Chairman was told by the bureau that the press association did not send such matter out. This was unconvincing to a veteran campaigner.

But the Chicago speech was a triumph of astuteness. Beveridge began with a demand for the nationalization of industry — a gesture to the old Progressives. He passed to the tariff, demanding higher rates to meet the 'revolutionized economic conditions of Europe.' He criticized the Wilson Administration's failure to take steps to increase our foreign trade in South America, the Orient, and Africa to offset the loss of European trade. He denounced Wilson's refusal to sustain with arms the railroad investments of Americans in China. He assailed the Administration's Mexican policy at length, denounced it for its threatened abandonment of the Philippines, attacked it for forcing an eight-hour law upon the railroads, and ridiculed the claim that Wilson had 'kept us out of war' — when no one wanted to go in. Unhappily, at the moment Roosevelt was sweeping over the country denouncing Germany and demanding that we go in. Beveridge literally had raked the record of the Administration and made the most of every possible opportunity. The audience was enthusiastic; the press carried the speech; praise flowed in from every partisan quarter. Frank Hitchcock, who heard it, telegraphed Mrs. Beveridge: 'Albert made a wonderful speech last night. Everybody most enthusiastic about it.' A. T. Hert, in charge of the Western Republican Headquarters, wrote her that it was 'the greatest of his career,' and Dawes wrote that he was 'very much pleased,' though he did not agree with the first part on the nationalization of industry.

As in other years, Beveridge swept westward from Chicago, speaking to responsive audiences in Minneapolis, Sioux Falls, Billings, Portland, San Francisco, Los Angeles, Tucson, Albuquerque, Denver, Omaha, Kansas City, Louisville, and Indianapolis. Always a prime favorite, he extended himself in the West, and the strain on his vocal cords was such that, on orders of physicians, he rested for three days at the Grand Canyon, not using his voice even in conversation.

But, despite the enthusiasm, he sensed an undercurrent running against Hughes. He found it first in Minnesota, where the Republicans were dangerously apathetic and the farmers contented and not prone to get into the fight.[1] The Republican

[1] Beveridge to Shaffer, Oct. 8, 1916.

chairman thought Wilson might carry the State.[1] Prosperity, high wages, and high prices were not easy to combat, and the Republicans were blundering. Through the Western country they were speeding the 'ladies' special,' carrying women of great wealth, none too prone to conceal the evidence, and this was doing no good. 'The special is hurting Hughes terribly,' he wrote Mrs. Beveridge. 'Handbills scattered everywhere about the "Billionaire Special," giving names of heavy guarantors like Mrs. Guggenheim, Mrs. Vanderbilt, Mrs. Whitney, etc.' [2]

Thus the reëlection of Wilson did not surprise him. He was right — the bones of the broken legs had not yet knit. Pleased that the ordeal was over, he turned instantly to his literary work and closed the door on politics.

VI

But with the exit of politics, war entered. The genius of the German leaders for blundering reached full flower in the repudiation of the pledge to abstain from unrestricted submarine warfare. It was a defiant challenge and was instantly accepted. Von Bernstorff was handed his passports, and Congress was summoned to hear Wilson's demand for a declaration of war and to make response. To Beveridge, this was tragedy. He always was to feel that our participation in a war he considered primarily a European quarrel could have been prevented; and he was unable to sympathize with the unmeasured abuse of the German people or even of their rulers. He had hoped that the United States would stand aloof, and nothing would have pleased him more than the realization of Wilson's ambition to be the medium of peace.

For some months he had been appalled by the tendency of perfervid patriots to see in their neighbors of German blood potential enemies of the country. He had written Shaw of his apprehensions. 'I think it is the duty of every citizen,' he wrote, 'to take for granted the equal loyalty of his fellow citizens. It must be intolerable to loyal citizens of German blood to have their fidelity to this Government questioned. We have all got to live together after the war is over; and any and every thing said and done at this time is wicked which will leave dissensions among ourselves when peace is restored.' [3]

Throughout the greater part of the struggle, Beveridge was to be engrossed in important literary labors, declining the greater part of the invitations that poured in upon him for speeches and

[1] Beveridge to Mrs. Beveridge, Oct. 8, 1916.   [2] Oct. 14, 1916.
[3] Beveridge to Shaw, Feb. 13, 1917.

emerging occasionally only in response to some patriotic summons. As early as February, at a dinner in Indianapolis in his honor, he had set forth his concept of the duty of an American should war come. 'When in a foreign controversy our Government takes its stand,' he said, 'the result of which may be the gravest that can befall a country, all citizens, of course, support it. There is among them at such a time only one competition — the competition of patriotism.'[1]

On the night of Decoration Day, in a powerful oration at Tomlinson Hall, he took the position from which he did not deviate throughout America's participation in the war. Enumerating the acts of war against the United States, he said it had been forced to draw the sword:

So it was, that the German Government made the greatest and most fateful blunder in German history; for when it compelled the American people to enter the conflict, the German Government then and there lost the war. Then and there it wrote the sentence of Germany's inevitable defeat. So insane was the German decision that forced the United States into the war that it almost seems the decree of Fate that Germany, through sheer madness, shall work her own undoing.

For, he continued, by Germany's action she had imposed upon all Americans the necessity of a united front:

Before the direct assault and open insult to the American Nation that forced Congress to declare war on Germany, the people were divided in their foreign sympathies and opinions, as always has been and always will be the case.... But when the American Nation was attacked, and the American Congress passed the great and fateful resolution, the effect was universal and instantaneous. It was no longer Great Britain, France, Russia, Italy, and other nations against Germany — it was Germany against the United States. On that plain issue there is but one side for American citizens, and they take that side with every means at their command.

Soon after the Nation entered the war, Beveridge formally offered his services to President Wilson and the Governor of Indiana for any task assigned him. He had no doubt that the added impetus of the American arms would speedily terminate the conflict. That which concerned him most was the aftermath. Time and again, in letters to his friends he protested against the increasing trend to look upon Americans of German blood or birth as legitimate targets for vilification or suspicion; and the proposal of a League to Enforce Peace after the war aroused his wrath.

But he was remote from the centers of war activities and the

[1] *Indianapolis Star*, Feb. 5, 1917.

controversial discussions. For the most part his knowledge of what was going on was gleaned from the newspapers at which he glanced hastily at the breakfast-table before hurrying to his study to work upon his book. Buried in the house at Beverly Farms, he found even the social activities of the North Shore suspended — everything 'extremely quiet — almost oppressively so.' [1]

Even so, the knowledge that great and heroic actions were impending sometimes irked him, as he pored over his manuscript. From boyhood, he had found a glamour in the moving of armies and the shouting of the captains. Only an unfortunate giggle had kept him out of West Point; and in the Spanish War he had tried to find an opening in the army. The old yearning returned, and soon he was writing Shaffer that should the war last much longer he was 'mightily tempted to go into the service,' though he then was in his fiftieth year. [2] In Indiana, he put himself at the disposal of the Council of Defense, and his eloquence was utilized at great mass meetings in support of war activities. But in none of his speeches did he attune his voice to the Hymn of Hate, nor indulge in the usual references to the 'inhuman Huns,' nor the customary sentimental banalities about 'our Allies.' Instead, he described the war as one waged in vindication of American rights, and called upon Americans to support it to the utmost.

The Armistice found him deeply engaged in Boston with his 'Life of Marshall,' from which the war had not diverted him.

[1] Beveridge to W. C. Bobbs, July 16, 1917.
[2] Beveridge to Shaffer, July 17, 1917.

CHAPTER III

THE LEAGUE OF NATIONS, 1917–20

I

BUT the study at Beverly Farms was not sound-proof against the rumblings of the impending struggle over the League of Nations. The public in general knew nothing of the importance of his participation in the organization and conduct of the fight against America's adherence. The position he assumed was not motivated by party considerations. Long before the League had become intimately associated with Woodrow Wilson, and at a time when Henry Cabot Lodge's advocacy of something of the sort was fresh in the public mind, and William Howard Taft was urging it, Beveridge took his stand. The former President for some time had been urging the creation of a League to Enforce Peace. Republicans like Senator Burton of Ohio were supporting it, and Elihu Root was understood to be in sympathy with it. There had been no alignment of political parties, nor was there anything to indicate that there would be. It was at this time that the literary labors of Beveridge were disturbed with increasing frequency by the crystallizing sentiment that, following the war, some international agency should be created to protect the peace of the world. As early as February, 1917, before his country entered the war, Beveridge was writing Dr. Albert Shaw in denunciation of the proposed League to Enforce Peace:

By the way, I do hope you have not committed yourself to the program of the League to Enforce Peace. They nearly got me into that thing; but luckily I read the literature of the propaganda, and this aroused such misgivings that I have studied it as thoroughly as I am capable of studying anything. The result is that I am against it with all my might. I do not think that it has a redeeming feature. Some of the articles and speeches made by these propagandists, although they are supposed to be scholars, would disgrace boys at school, to quote one of Edmund Burke's speeches.' [1]

As the horrors of the war increased and the popular mind began to set in favor of something of the sort, he sought, through correspondence and conversations, to arouse his friends against it.

At first blush, his position seemed incongruous to those familiar with his career. In the advocacy of the Philippines

[1] Beveridge to Shaw, Feb. 13, 1917.

policy, he had declared that destiny had imposed upon America the position of a world power. He had scoffed at the idea that we could longer remain aloof. He had shamed as cowardly souls those who were afraid to venture forth to meet the obligations and the dangers of world leadership. The supporters of the League had now grasped his banner and were echoing his very phrases. But there was this difference — the Beveridge of 1899 was the chauvinistic imperialist with the Napoleonic concept. America, powerful and omnipotent, would pursue her independent course and dictate in the field of international politics. She would act when she saw fit and remain aloof when she wished. But here was a new proposition — to limit the Nation's independent action by international agreements. The very intensity of his nationalism, which made the swashbuckling imperialist of twenty years before, made the isolationalist of 1918. Instantly he found the catch-phrase suited to his end — 'Nationalism versus Internationalism.' It was to become the shibboleth of his party.

And yet his hostility to the League was not born of partisan thought, as we have seen. He was quite willing to point out the party advantage of opposition, in dealing with politically minded men, but it was his intense nationalism that dominated him. In one of the most notable of his speeches on a non-partisan occasion he concentrated in three paragraphs the motivating thought and feeling behind his action:

Consider our position and advantages — a position and advantages which all the money that ever was issued could not purchase, all the labor that ever toiled could not create. Nature has placed this Republic on the throne of the world — midway between Europe and Asia, from which we are separated by thousands of miles of ocean. We are perfectly situated for defence; and perfectly situated, too, for world trade, world friendship, and world helpfulness. Our forefathers cut with the sword all political relations with the Old World, so that, under our institutions of orderly freedom, we could work out American ideals.

Shall we abandon these advantages? Shall we sacrifice our heritage? Shall we enter into a government which places us in the same position as if we were a physical, integral part of Europe and Asia? Shall we poison American idealism and American aspirations with the age-old racial hatreds, ambitions, and intrigues of alien races and distant lands? Can anyone doubt what the answer of the American people will be?

Were any one of the nations that are now so anxious to have us carry their loads of historic woe, pay their debts and do their work — were any one of them in our place, would that nation surrender what we are ordered to yield? Were England or France or Italy situated as we are situated, having the resources that we possess, blessed with the history and traditions that make America peculiar and glorious among the nations of the world, would France, would England, would Italy do what is now demanded of us? Every sane man knows that nothing on earth or in heaven would induce them to do so.[1]

Thus, from the beginning he threw himself heart and soul into the fight, never doubting that he was playing the patriot's part.

In July, 1918, he had dinner with Roosevelt at Oyster Bay and the battle-scarred veterans talked over the trend of the times; and Beveridge left with the impression that their minds ran in the same groove. As though to verify his interpretation of the talk, he wrote immediately afterward:[2]

Thank you and Mrs. Roosevelt for a delightful evening. I think I enjoyed the conversation more than any we ever had. The whole evening was altogether charming to me, and I shall never forget it.

After leaving, I thought of so many things suggested by your talk that I more and more regretted the engagement that took me away.

As soon as I returned to this place, I got the June and July numbers of the 'Metropolitan' and read your articles. By this sign we conquer. You are doing the best and biggest work of your life thus far.

Wilson has hoisted the motley flag of internationalism. Thank God that he has. That makes the issue, does it not? Straight Americanism for us. There is both sense and sentiment in that....

You have become the voice of America. Wilson knows that, so he is trying to become the voice of the world. But he can't. His tones are too thin. No man can, for that matter. Good thing, too. One does not care to have brothers wished on him. What rot it all is! Old men who are through and don't know it, and young men who have not started, think they can fix up a scheme — an old maids' pacifist club.

If Roosevelt only would denounce the League to Enforce Peace — by name!

A little later, Beveridge wrote again with this in view, and the Colonel replied reassuringly. 'You understand exactly how we feel,' he wrote. 'In my speech at Springfield, the end of the month, I give expression to your and my views on nationalism and internationalism.'[3] This opened the way for a reiteration. 'So glad you are going to make the Springfield speech,' Beveridge replied. 'Now we shall have an issue. I hope you will specifically name the League to Enforce Peace and state those big and simple reasons why it will be ruinous to this country. It will stir up amiable old male grannies who, over their afternoon tea, are planning to denationalize America and denationalize the Nation's manhood. May your speech be a call to arms for the defense of American nationalism!'[4]

[1] Pennsylvania State Bar Association speech, June 24, 1919.
[2] Beveridge to Roosevelt, July 14, 1918.
[3] Roosevelt to Beveridge, Aug. 14, 1918.
[4] Beveridge to Roosevelt, Aug. 19, 1918.

Meanwhile, Will Hays, Republican National Chairman, starting on a tour, offered an opportunity. Of course he would talk with the party leaders, and perhaps a hint as to conditions would be helpful. 'In informing me of the subjects most acceptable,' Beveridge wrote, 'Wood [1] writes that the attack upon Wilson's League will be extremely well received.' [2]

He was not at all sure of Hays upon the issue, and just at this juncture he had a disconcerting letter from Roosevelt:

My own judgment is that in dealing with the League of Nations we should not say that we totally reject the idea, but that it is probably chimerical, and while we are willing to experiment with it, it must be merely in addition to, and never as a substitute for our own real purpose to prepare for our defense. [3]

Alarmed that any concession should be made, Beveridge pointed out the perils of the course suggested:

All right. But if we acquiesce in Wilson's scheme, will he not try to put us at a logical disadvantage in our advocacy of universal military training?... At the very least, ought we not to insist on a thorough, nation-wide debate of the whole question before it is adopted, since, once adopted, there will be an infinite difficulty and complication in extricating ourselves, no matter how much we may find ourselves injured? This would not seem to be unreasonable in view of the fact that it is one of the gravest questions the Nation ever has been called upon to decide.... As the matter stands, the people have heard only one side, and that side has been presented dogmatically and superficially. Also, as a matter of practical party politics, if we are to abandon the issue of Nationalism versus Internationalism, as exemplified in Mr. Wilson's League of Nations scheme, what issue have we? [4]

Yes, Roosevelt answered, but

I feel that we have more than one issue; but I agree with you as to Nationalism vs. Internationalism. You may see I have taken it up strongly in my speeches and articles. My advice, however, is to say that we will accept internationalism in the sense of just treatment of all other nations, and as an addition but not as a substitute for our own military preparedness, and cultivate a spirit of intense American Nationalism. [5]

This was not at all what Beveridge had in mind for Roosevelt to do, and he wrote him to that effect.

Roosevelt answered:

I think your suggestions are probably right. But don't make any mistake about me. I am insisting upon Nationalism as against Inter-

[1] General Leonard Wood.   [2] Beveridge to Hays, Oct. 10, 1918.
[3] Roosevelt to Beveridge, Oct. 16, 1918.
[4] Beveridge to Roosevelt, Oct. 19, 1918.
[5] Roosevelt to Beveridge, Oct. 21, 1918.

nationalism. I am saying with a bland smile whatever Nationalism demands. I will then adopt with that extra consideration any wise and feasible plan for limiting the possible area and likelihood of future wars. Mine is merely a platonic expression, designed to let Taft and his followers to get over without too much trouble, and also to prevent any accusation that we are ourselves merely Prussian militarists.[1]

This was not so encouraging — especially when there were no doubts on the other side. Some of Beveridge's most cherished friends were taking issue with him too. Worthington Ford had just written that the Republicans were 'playing a losing game,' since 'the criticisms of the management of the war have not yet developed anything so startling as to warrant a change in leadership.' Had not even Europe admitted that 'what has been done by the United States has bordered upon the miraculous?' And the League — was there not an analogy between the Union of the States and the League?[2]

At this juncture, Beveridge seemed lonely in his view that his party should declare bluntly, unequivocally, against the very principle of a league. Even Henry Cabot Lodge, from whom he heard, was inclined to a policy of dissimulation.

I think it would be a mistake to admit that the League is a good thing, but I think we should make a mistake if we met the proposition with a flat denial. The purpose of the League — that is, the preservation of the world peace — we are all anxious to see, but what we oppose is the method. Now the strength of our position is to show up the impossibility of any of the methods proposed and invite them, when they desire our support, to produce their terms. They cannot do it. My own judgment is that the whole thing will break up in conference. There may be some vague declarations of the beauties of peace, but any practical League that involves control of our legislation, of our armies and navies, or the Monroe Doctrine, or an international police, and that sort of thing, then our issue is made up, and we shall win. We can begin by pointing out these dangers, and that I am sure will be done.[3]

'Soundest statesmanship and wise politics,' Beveridge replied. 'I endorse every word of it,'[4] — but he didn't.

Lodge had written before of his plans and strategy and difficulties. When Congress met, he certainly would attack the League. Reed of Missouri had already made a strong assault, and it was well, since he was a Democrat. His own speech in 1917 in favor of a League — well, 'it was not a question that was up then.' Nothing could come out of the attempt to create a

[1] Roosevelt to Beveridge, Oct. 31, 1918.
[2] Ford to Beveridge, Oct. 23, 1918.
[3] Senator Lodge to Beveridge, Dec. 3, 1918.
[4] Beveridge to Lodge, Dec. 9, 1918.

League in Paris, nothing but 'empty words.' But that was no reason why the warfare should not be kept up.[1]

II

With the idea of persistent warfare, Beveridge was in complete accord. About this time he made the first of numerous attacks he was to make on similar occasions against the principle of a League before the Massachusetts Bar Association. The tendency toward a timid dissimulation among most Republican leaders distressed and dismayed him. Then, in March, he heard from Lodge, a frank exposition of his plans. He proposed to demand in the Senate that the advocates of a League to Enforce Peace explain precisely what they meant. But he was going to take a different tack from that of others:

The point is this. We are all agreed that we want peace and that we are against war. Now, the first step toward a world peace is to make peace with Germany, then carry out that peace effectively and settle the questions growing out of it. That is, in reality, the work of a generation, and is beset with great difficulties. If we can do that, we shall have done more to promote the world's peace than will ever be done by any League constituted as some people seem to think they want it constituted. Now, why embarrass these great questions with which we must deal at this moment by bringing in a question of a league to take care of an unknown future?[2]

That, at least, was not half bad. Put the League idea to sleep with the opiate of faint praise for a generation and there would be no awakening.

After all, the Republican leaders were clearly bent on making opposition to ratification the party policy, some way or another. When both Lodge and Knox opened with their heavy artillery in December, Beveridge was delighted and sent his congratulations. He had never had any reason to be partial to Lodge, but now he wrote Knox that the Massachusetts Senator was 'a tremendously big man, and kind and gentle as courageous' — a characterization that would have made Woodrow Wilson smile.[3] When George Harvey denounced the League in New York, he, too, was warmly congratulated. 'We ought to thank Wilson for having given us this issue,' wrote Beveridge, 'for it is an issue and a winning issue — the greatest issue the American people have ever been called upon to decide.'[4]

[1] Lodge to Beveridge, Nov. 23, 1918.
[2] Lodge to Beveridge, Dec. 14, 1918.
[3] Beveridge to Knox, Dec. 28, 1918.
[4] Beveridge to Harvey, Dec. 26, 1918.

But there was still one fly in the ointment, for his dear friend and ardent supporter, Shaffer, still was pleading with him for the League and throwing the weight of the 'Indianapolis Star' in its favor. In a letter with the salutation, 'Best Beloved,' Beveridge sought to coax him into line with the party bait. Had he not read the speeches of Borah, Poindexter, Knox, and Lodge? 'So you see the party is lining up solidly and in disciplined ranks in support of the American traditional policy and against those who would surrender the American position in the world,' he wrote.[1]

But Shaffer was not convinced.

More disturbing, however, was the seeming uncertainty of Hays, the National Chairman, and Beveridge urged George Harvey to get in touch with him.[2] And Lodge again — he seemed afraid to attack the principle of a league — a league of any kind. When Beveridge wrote in January urging a more aggressive fight, Lodge replied that he was doing the best he could, and that caution had to be exercised until after the organization of the Senate to get control of the Foreign Relations Committee. 'If we seem to you... to be not as effective as you desire, I am sure you will make allowances for the difficulties which confront us.'[3]

But this failed to curb Beveridge's impatience. 'What is the matter with our men in Washington?' he wrote George Harvey. 'Have they neither courage nor sagacity?'[4] And to Lodge he wrote at the same time that the future of the party was in his hands 'more than in those of any other man' and that its prospects would be 'seriously, perhaps fatally, injured by the acceptance of Mr. Wilson's international plan, or any variation of it.'[5] When George Harvey was planning a speaking trip to Indianapolis, Beveridge urged him to talk exclusively on the League, to 'hit the whole scheme directly between the eyes,' and 'not give the Leaguers the least opportunity to say that you agree with the scheme in principle.'[6]

III

A few days later, Beveridge had the opportunity to act on his own advice. This was at a mass meeting in Tremont Temple,

[1] Beveridge to Shaffer, Dec. 21, 1918.
[2] Beveridge to Harvey, Feb. 25, 1919.
[3] Lodge to Beveridge, Jan. 30, 1919.
[4] Beveridge to Harvey, Jan. 26, 1919.
[5] Beveridge to Lodge, Jan. 28, 1919.
[6] Beveridge to Harvey, March 3, 1919.

Boston, where he presided and Borah and Senator Charles S. Thomas spoke. Said Beveridge:

It has now been four months since the cannon ceased to thunder — and yet we are still at war. By now, peace could have been established and the peoples of the world could have begun the resumption of normal life. But the nations are kept waiting while the additional billions of expenses mount, misery increases, and anarchy spreads.

Peace knocks at barred doors and is not admitted. Why? Because behind these doors sit men weaving a net that would entangle the American Nation in a European-Asiatic balance of power. Let the so-called 'Peace Conference' take notice that when it puts off peace to contrive permanent political alliances with America, it is engaged in useless labor.

Open the doors, gentlemen, and bid Peace enter without further delay; for we Americans refuse to be inveigled into a partnership where Europe furnishes the liabilities and the United States supplies the assets. That is just what the League of Nations amounts to.

No longer isolated, say the proponents of the League?

How have we ever been isolated? Not financially, not commercially, not socially. We have been isolated only in a political sense — only in the sense that we have not bound ourselves to take part in alien quarrels.

And then, the point he pressed persistently on all occasions:

God forbid that the American people shall ever allow themselves to be chained to that body of death, a permanent foreign political alliance, involving them forever in historic and alien animosities, in racial and alien hatreds.

Try the experiment? But we cannot try it and drop it if we do not like it — unless we break a treaty.

The duty of the hour? To make peace, to call our soldiers home, and then in leisurely fashion make the decision on a League. We ought to take plenty of time to decide whether we want to make the United States an insurance company which, itself, pays the premiums for the insured as well as the benefits to the insured.

And why the objection to a popular vote upon the League? It will not take a hundredth part of the time, nor a thousandth part of the difficulty, nor a millionth part of the expense, to vote upon it, that it will take to carry out the scheme if we get into it.

And why the hurry — the determination to jam the project through in a single session of Congress, without a popular mandate? According to their way of procedure, secret diplomacy is the true method, after all, for the settlement of the destinies of nations — frame up a scheme in secret, and then rush it through in haste.

But on the very day Beveridge was speaking, Lodge was writing him he 'could not agree that we are against any League

at all,' and that such a position 'would drive away support.'
However, they would talk that over when they met.[1] It was a
clash of temperaments — of methods. Beveridge put his faith
in open fighting, Lodge in the finesse of the diplomacy of dissimulation. It was that month that Lodge, meeting President
Lowell of Harvard in debate on the League, and manifestly
embarrassed, made a rather sorry presentation of the opposition
cause. He explained to Beveridge that his embarrassment grew
out of the fact that under his leadership thirty-nine senators had
signed the round robin proclaiming their sympathy with a
union of the nations to promote peace, while refusing to accept
the Wilson scheme. He was unable to go beyond the limits
therein set, and Beveridge would therefore 'understand with
what reserve it was necessary for me to speak.'[2]

But Beveridge had not signed and was unbound, his opposition
going, not only to the method, but to the principle. Others
among Republican senators shared his view — Borah, McCormick, Hiram Johnson; and outside the senatorial group, George
Harvey, brilliant, caustic, tireless, a bit unscrupulous, whose pen
flashed over reams of paper in bitter denunciation of the covenant and ridicule of Wilson. 'Before long,' Beveridge wrote
him early in April, 'within the next five or six weeks, we must
sound the battle-cry, "Get out of Europe and stay out." Unless
human nature has been repealed, nothing is more certain than
that this is what the people want.'[3]

But at this time he was not a little alarmed. The amendments
had been offered instead of a straight-out opposition to the principle, and he was in deadly fear that Wilson would turn a trick.
His intellectual poise made it impossible for him to share in the
real or simulated contempt of Roosevelt and Lodge for Wilson's
capacity. 'I consider Wilson a master politician — have so considered him from the very beginning,' he wrote William Edward
Dodd, the historian.[4] When Borah wrote him of the apparent
weakening of some of the opposition senators, he was not surprised. 'I cannot get rid of the idea,' he answered, 'that they
will come around all right and fight a good deal harder than ever
when they realize the trick played upon us in the so-called
"amendments" and played for the purpose of ensnaring the votes
of some of our men.'[5] But three days later, Lodge informed him
that he and Borah had agreed 'as to the amendment line,' and

[1] Lodge to Beveridge, March 8, 1919.
[2] Lodge to Beveridge, March 21, 1919.
[3] Beveridge to Harvey, April 3, 1919.
[4] Beveridge to Dodd, April 14, 1919.
[5] Beveridge to Borah, April 27, 1919.

that the important thing was to assure Republican control of the Senate.[1]

Meanwhile, the enemies of the League were by no means sure of the popular reaction to their fight, and Medill McCormick proposed a continental speaking tour for Beveridge 'from Boston to Seattle.' But Beveridge's literary labors interfered, and he proposed instead that James M. Beck be sent. 'Let him start a week or two after Taft begins his tour for the League,' he wrote. 'He is one of the very best speakers in the country; he has a wide reputation, and a pretty big following.'[2] A few days later, Harvey discussed the plan for trailing Taft with the opposition leaders in Washington, but found them all intent on having Beveridge make the tour. 'I made the best reply possible,' he wrote, 'but did not impress Borah and Lodge.' However, ten senators had agreed to follow Taft, 'with the understanding, of course, that their expenses would be paid.' Harvey had thought it over in the mean time and concluded it inadvisable to adopt the trailing plan lest it serve to 'advertise Taft.' 'Mr. Root agreed with me on this,' he added, 'so there is where the matter stands.'[3]

Meanwhile, Taft was on his tour, clearly causing Hays, the National Chairman, some concern. When the former President in his Kansas City speech scored Beveridge, Hays wrote him about it and sent an excerpt of the attack. 'Do you not think it very wrong and most impolitic for him to go into States where our party leaders have taken their stand... and attempt to start back-fires on them?' Beveridge replied. 'The party has lined up on this question and it is inevitable that it will be a party issue. No power can prevent that.'[4]

But had Hays 'lined up' yet? Beveridge was not at all positive. In less than three weeks the press carried the report that Hays had lined-up with the League and favored a reservation plan. Utterly dumbfounded, Beveridge took up his pen. He wrote the party chairman:

This morning's paper distresses me. You will recall the letter which I wrote to Borah at your request, and which I read to you over the 'phone; yet the paper this morning says that you have announced yourself for the League and appear to favor the reservation plan. I greatly fear that, after my letter, Borah will not place the confidence in my judgment which he heretofore has exhibited. Furthermore, dear Will, I tell you, in strictest confidence, and for your own information,

[1] Lodge to Beveridge, April 30, 1919.
[2] Beveridge to Harvey, May 13, 1919.
[3] Harvey to Beveridge, May 24, 1919.
[4] Beveridge to Hays, July 7, 1919.

that what appears to our people up here [Beverly Farms] to be the higgling, piddling side-stepping and shifting of some of our men down at Washington in the face of a practically united Democratic support of this scheme is producing a pretty ugly feeling on the part of our strongest men.[1]

Hays sent an immediate denial, and Beveridge replied, urging him to stay close to Harvey. When it was reported that senators resented the appearance of Hays in Washington about this time, Harvey wrote Beveridge it was not true, and that Hays had gone to Washington 'in response to a formal request from Lodge, reënforced by Borah,' and had gone reluctantly. 'He returned before I did and I expect to meet him and Root in New York on Monday or Tuesday,' he added.[2] About the same time, Beveridge heard from Senator Knox that he had 'spent six or seven hours with Root yesterday,' and that the man at Beverly Farms would be pleased with what he would see in the paper the next day. He had also had a talk with Hays over the telephone, and he had promised to 'make a helpful statement.'[3]

But Beveridge could not rid himself of the feeling that Hays was not unequivocably committed to whole-hearted, downright opposition, and kept hammering away at him in correspondence. 'If Wilson gets this thing through,' he wrote him, 'especially if he gets it through with Republican support, I think that our prospects of winning, which three months ago seemed a certainty, will be very gravely diminished.'[4] This called forth a frank avowal of the embarrassments that beset the National Chairman. He agreed that the party was 'split this way and that way,' and that was 'just the trouble.' It had been impossible to persuade forty-nine senators to take a united position; and if they did not represent forty-nine different positions, it was almost that bad. 'I know of no way,' wrote Hays, 'to commit the party, as such, and to get the party position taken, when the party is divided as it is.' But he hoped that a plan could soon be worked out 'which we can assume as the party's position and go to the bat on it.'[5]

Overcoming his reluctance to lay aside his literary work, the latter part of July found Beveridge entering upon a brief speaking tour which was abandoned before it had really begun. He was to address a mass meeting in Chicago and thence go on westward, but when he reached Chicago, he 'ran into hell.'

[1] Beveridge to Hays, June 27, 1919.
[2] Harvey to Beveridge, June 28, 1919.
[3] Knox to Beveridge, June 21, 1919.
[4] Beveridge to Hays, July 7, 1919.
[5] Hays to Beveridge, July 8, 1919.

The race riots were at their most dangerous stage, and it would have been perilous, if not impossible, to hold a meeting. Then, too, he learned that the proposed meeting at St. Paul was 'in very bad hands,' and, in conference with Hays and McCormick, the entire tour was abandoned.[1] This was all the more provoking because Beveridge was increasingly alarmed over Wilson's strategy in trying to pin the Republicans down to how few reservations they would take. If they fell into the trap, would not Wilson pronounce these reservations 'harmless' and accept them? 'Thus,' thought Beveridge, 'we shall be euchred out of a perfect political situation, and, what is far worse, the country will be buncoed, since reservations won't get us anywhere.' In Heaven's name, would not Harvey hurry to Washington and stiffen up the opposition? 'This fight is won if we only have the guts to stand firm and only have common sense enough to see the trap Wilson is laying for us.'

It was at this juncture that Lodge tried to reassure him on the reservations. He wrote:

You must remember, in judging this situation, that the votes are all here in the Senate and nowhere else. To those votes and voters I have been devoting all my strength ever since April. It would take me too long to tell you how much advance has been made. But the votes to defeat the treaty squarely are not there, for the simple reason that the League is tied on to the treaty of peace, and we cannot get votes to separate them. I am not arguing the right or wrong of it, but telling you what the situation is. My business was to unite the Republicans so far as I could, and they are united now on strong and effective reservations. Any that go on will be effective, and Mr. Wilson's maneuver will be without result. The situation is one of extreme difficulty. I cannot go into all the details, but in addition to having all the Republicans practically united on strong reservations along the lines indicated by Mr. Root, we have a good deal more than a third who will vote down the treaty if the reservations are not adopted.... I tell you this in confidence, for I wanted you to know the situation.[2]

But Beveridge's mind ran with Borah's rather than with Lodge's. The latter had written Beveridge that, while opposed to Article X, 'to respect and preserve as against external aggression the territorial integrity and existing political independence of all members of the League,' he would support a simple proposition that, in the event of an attack by Germany, we should go to the rescue of France.[3] This was a recognition of the very international policy to which Beveridge was fun-

---

[1] Beveridge to Harvey, July 31, 1919.
[2] Lodge to Beveridge, Aug. 4, 1919.
[3] Lodge to Beveridge, Aug. 11, 1919.

damentally opposed on principle. But Lodge, not Beveridge, was in command of the forces in the Senate.

IV

On the platform, however, Beveridge was his own master, and in June, in an address before the Pennsylvania Bar Association at Bedford Springs, he had confined himself to an attack upon the very principle of a league. It was a smashing assault all along the line, based on the assumption that the League meant a super-state with power to dictate American policies in their relation to the world.

Then, in September, Woodrow Wilson, on the verge of a physical collapse, disregarded the orders of his physicians and set forth on an arduous speaking crusade in favor of the League which was born of his strivings. On September 19, he was stricken. For a moment the Nation was appalled and a wave of sympathy and admiration for a man willing to die for a cause swept over the land. To Beveridge, Wilson's act in setting forth to do or die was one of heroism. His speeches against the League and even his private letters had been singularly free from the personal vilification of Wilson which had characterized the utterances of many others. He had admired the intellectual qualities, the brilliancy, and the fighting strength of the man. Later he was to say that if, instead of becoming merely incapacitated, Wilson had fallen dead upon the platform, his martyrdom to a cause would have lifted him overnight to a position higher than Lincoln's.[1] But with the stricken leader silenced and confined to his room, the fight went on. The Senate was yet to act.

In October, Beveridge was preparing a new speech against the League, 'with reservations or without reservations, with amendments or without amendments';[2] and trying to explain to Hays why Lodge was defeated in the Massachusetts Convention by the supporters of the covenant. 'He made a brave and noble speech,' he wrote, 'but made it at the wrong time.' He could have prevented the endorsement of the League had he spoken before the adoption of the platform, and easily have kept out the words 'without amendments,' but for the fear of disturbing harmony. 'It was a policy of weakness,' he thought.[3]

In November, the test vote was taken in the Senate and the treaty with the covenant was defeated by a vote of fifty-five for,

[1] This statement was made to the author.
[2] Beveridge to Hays, Oct. 4, 1919.
[3] Beveridge to Hays, Oct. 5, 1919.

and thirty-nine against — the proponents of the treaty lacking eight votes of the two thirds necessary. But the struggle was not yet over and would be resumed after a short recess.

To Beveridge this was the critical period. The Senate vote had a sobering effect upon the people, and the demand for a compromise arose in the land. He wrote Senator Brandegee expressing the hope that 'our men are strong enough not to be stampeded or seduced,' since 'it would be tragic, after the victory is won, to throw it away.'[1]

Nor was it without reason that Beveridge was uneasy, for powerful forces were at work to effect a compromise, and the press teemed with the gossip. Lodge again wrote to reassure him. 'Don't be disturbed about the talk of compromises in the newspapers,' he said. 'The situation is a very simple one. I stated on the floor of the Senate that if they had any modifications to propose they had only to formulate them and present them and we would consider them. It would have been a great mistake for me to have taken the attitude that we would not even consider modifications.'[2]

Unfortunately for the cause of the League, Woodrow Wilson was a very sick man and in no temper for a compromise. Thus nothing was done, and the fate of the League passed to the arbitrament of the people in the fall election.

V

It was during the interval between the Senate fight and the opening of the presidential campaign that Beveridge delivered three of the most important speeches of his career. On December 22, 1919, he was the orator at the celebration of the two hundred and ninety-ninth anniversary of the landing of the Pilgrims at Plymouth. In this oration he returned to his earlier concept of the relations of the state to the citizen — an uncompromisingly Hamiltonian position. Although the occasion was not partisan, and he mentioned no party names, it was aggressively political in that it was a bitter denunciation of one important act of President Wilson. In 1916 the Nation had been threatened with a railroad strike involving practically every branch of the service. The railroad employees were both united and determined. A nation-wide strike had been planned and the day set. Congress was then in session, and Wilson personally intervened in an effort to prevent what threatened to be a catastrophe. On his insistence, Congress speedily passed the Adam-

[1] Beveridge to Brandegee, Nov. 24, 1919.
[2] Lodge to Beveridge, Jan. 3, 1920.

son law fixing a legal eight-hour day for railroad labor, with *pro rata* for overtime. Thus was the strike prevented; but instantly business men denounced the settlement as a surrender on the part of Government. The answer that the settlement made was in accord with Wilson's sense of social justice did not satisfy the critics. To Beveridge, it was an abject surrender of Government to the organized force of a group, and to the development of this thought he addressed himself:

The method of forcing that law upon the statute books brought into conflict fundamental principles — principles which are utterly antagonistic, absolutely irreconcilable. Of such a conflict there can be no compromise. One principle must yield to the other. And that is just what happened. The threat of force by a special interest prevailed. The Government yielded.

And the issue raised was this — 'Whether the American Nation is to be governed by the constitutional representatives of all the people or by the non-constitutional representatives of predatory groups. The real issue is whether we are to have constitutional government at all.'

That issue must be met, he said, if we shall not witness 'the disintegration of American institutions.' The right to strike? Yes, but 'if, as organizations, they refuse to do their social duty, then they must not prevent others from performing that function, and doing that duty.' Permit labor organizations to dictate terms to Government? 'Every human being who does not belong to the organization, which exacts from the Nation as a whole compliance with the demands of that organization, pays tribute to it, toils for it, is driven under its lash.' And if real grievances exist, what can labor organizations do? 'They must invoke the law, rather than strike at society.' And if no law? 'They must appeal to all the people until public opinion, expressed at elections, demands and compels the enactment of such a law.'

The speech instantly attracted wide attention; favorable in business circles and unfavorable in trade-union quarters. It was direct enough as a challenge to labor-unionism in itself; but unfortunately, it was printed and circulated by enemies of union labor with comments of their own. It was a daring challenge, and labor bided its time to strike back.[1]

In the further development of his thought on current problems, Beveridge made the occasion of his oration at the tomb of

[1] The Adamson Law was held constitutional by the Supreme Court. The speech was printed by the *Shield Press*, with the statement that 'a most hopeful omen of the present day is the turn of public sentiment against labor unions.'

Washington [1] the opportunity for an attack upon the League of
Nations, based on the warning of Washington's Farewell Address.

In his address in January at the McKinley Club celebration
in Detroit there was no need to dissimulate the political purpose.
Many times he had spoken in that city, and he was among
friends and admirers who were delighted to find him back
in the party fold. It was the launching of the Republican campaign in Michigan, and one of the largest and most demonstrative audiences that ever crowded Arcadia Hall heard him.
To Beveridge, it offered an opportunity for plain speaking, and
the sheer audacity with which he touched on topics on which
everyone was thinking, but few had the temerity to talk, electrified the crowd. Hysteria had seized on many because of
subversive doctrines from abroad, and there was a loud clamoring for the suppression of free speech and the denial of constitutional rights. The orator began with a denunciation of this
spirit. Unpopular doctrines? 'It is a man's constitutional right
to try to make them popular.' More: 'The right of every citizen,
by the lawful exercise of free speech to try to change our institutions themselves by peaceable methods, is the very heart
and soul of those institutions.' The Legislature of New York had
just unseated Socialists duly elected, and he denounced the
expulsion. 'Attempts to smother thought by force only make
converts to the very doctrines thus sought to be destroyed,' he
said. 'Denial of lawful free speech is the noxious culture in
which crazy radicalism is propagated most rapidly.'

Yes, the right of free speech was an American fundamental,
and there was another — the right to work; and that had been
denied of late by labor unions; and he struck out at the Adamson
Law. 'Organized labor's assault on American institutions!' he
thundered.

Thence to the League of Nations, with a reiteration, in stinging phrases, of his previous arguments. 'We take up the gage of
battle and will fight to the end for the interests, the security, and
the independence of the American Nation.'

And then came a note of prophecy, in the warning that
'criminal wealth' should not be permitted to resume its hidden
sway. 'Such a reaction will inevitably cause counter-reaction
that will throw the country into the extremes of the wildest
radicalism,' he warned. 'The man is blind who does not see in
operation every day influences that are making for these two
developments.'

But the high cost of living — was that due to the conspiracies

[1] April 20, 1920.

of predatory wealth? Could legislation cure that evil? Demagogues would say so, but was it true? Can politicians affect the
laws of economic change? Not all the increases in the cost of
living could be traced to human greed. Thus:

In my boyhood everybody pastured milch cows on village commons
without expense; today pasturage must be paid for. In former times
immense herds of cattle and sheep were fed on vast free ranges belonging to the Nation, without any cost but the wages of herders; today
these free ranges have disappeared, and every blade of grass nipped by
an animal raises the cost of beef and mutton, of leather and of wool.
The average citizen today actually lives in greater comfort than kings
and nobles of bygone ages.

No abnormal causes for the increase, then? Yes, there was
one — inflation — 'which has raised to the dangerous height of
over fifty per cent.' Deflation, then, was imperatively required.
'Economy must take the place of extravagance.... All of us must
work harder, and save more.... Whatever the inconvenience,
whatever the deprivation of indulgences, we must get back to
normal.'

And there was another abnormal reason — 'the levering up
of wages, which instantly, permanently, added to prices.' And
if members of labor unions are already getting reasonable wages,
and in addition force still higher pay and shorter hours by
attacking or threatening to attack the very existence of economic
society, they merely 'lay all the other citizens under tribute for
the special benefit of labor unions.'

Did demagogues complain of profiteering in business? 'The
average American business man does less profiteering today than
ever was practiced by any business men in this or any other
country.' Robbers there were, but these could be jailed without
persecuting all business men — and that was the practice of the
Wilson Administration. It had set spies on business, and made
business a crime.[1]

And there was still another abnormal reason — the constant
draining of American money to Europe through 'foreign propaganda.' 'This has spread until even among ourselves a frenzy
has grown up for collecting funds for every imaginable purpose
— a frenzy which is a clear and distinct form of insanity.'

And the Republican program? The ending of the League; the
revision of the tax laws; the abolishment of the excess profits
tax; the repeal of the Sherman anti-trust law; the repeal of the
shipping law; and a ship subsidy, if necessary.

When, in a moving peroration, reminiscent of his earlier

[1] This was a reference to the income tax and the Federal Trade Commission.

oratory, he closed, the audience rose, and, standing, cheered lustily for minutes. Seldom outside a national convention had such an enthusiastic demonstration been seen.[1] Business, and especially Big Business, had been waiting for just such a defiance, and it had come. It was the Beveridge of pre-Rooseveltian days, in substance and in manner — the youthful Hamiltonian had emerged again, a little older, but with undiminished fire and brilliance. It was the political Beveridge that remained until the end.

Thousands of copies of the speech were circulated from Seattle to Boston, and overnight, as never before since he fought the Payne-Aldrich Bill, he resumed his place among the foremost leaders of his party and expounders of its faith.

Again he had reached the high tide of popularity among his fellow partisans — and the campaign of 1920 was beginning. He moved to the front in the calculations of his party.

[1] *Indianapolis Star*, Jan. 20, 1920.

CHAPTER IV

THE DRAMA OF 1920

I

THIS new popularity mounted, when, voluntarily and decisively, Beveridge took himself out of consideration for the senatorial nomination, and the friends of Watson fairly surfeited him with praise.[1] When, at a party conference, National Chairman Hays paid him tribute for his self-abnegation in the interest of party solidarity, the party workers rose and cheered for more than a minute.[2]

Almost at the turning of the year, aspirants for the presidential nomination made their appearance, and the certainty that General Leonard Wood would be a candidate instantly determined Beveridge's allegiance. As one of the inner circle of the Rooseveltians, he belonged naturally under the banner of the intimate friend of the Colonel. Roosevelt had passed in his sleep to the ultimate verdict of history, at Oyster Bay in the preceding September, and Beveridge had been a mourner at his grave and had paid tribute at a memorial meeting in the Academy of Music in Brooklyn. Had the former President lived, his nomination would have been all but inevitable, and his death was a blow to his followers. Most of these rallied around the banner of Wood. The decision to enter him in the Indiana preferential presidential primary was momentarily held in abeyance when the rumor spread that Beveridge himself might be a candidate; and Senator George Moses, in charge of the Wood campaign, wrote the Indianian that Wood would go in if Beveridge stayed out. And then, cannily, he added: 'I am looking to see you the Prime Minister of the next Administration.'[3] The bait was unnecessary, and from the first Beveridge gave his allegiance to the intimate friend of Roosevelt.

In due time, Wood, Senator Hiram Johnson, Governor Frank Lowden, and Senator Warren G. Harding were entered in Indiana, and a spirited battle began. There was no doubt regarding the real preference of the two Indiana senators, Watson and New; they were for Harding, favorite of the senatorial cabal. However, it was evident that Harding's supporters were confined almost exclusively to the professional politicians. He entered the State and made a number of perfunctory speeches to

[1] *Indianapolis Star*, Feb. 15, 1920.   [2] *Ibid.*, March 5, 1920.
[3] Moses to Beveridge, Feb. 2, 1920.

undemonstrative audiences. The real enthusiasm was for Wood and Hiram Johnson, and the latter's bitter attacks upon the League made him a formidable contender. Racial groups, antagonistic to the Versailles treaty, flocked to his support. 'Johnson is gaining fast,' Beveridge wrote from Atlantic City, 'and that shows what courage can do.' [1]

But it was Wood who won, and won without victory, for he got a plurality of the vote, without carrying the majority of the districts. Nor was the clear mandate of the State to be respected by the State Convention in the selection of the four delegates-at-large. Beveridge, who had been placed at the head of the Wood slate, was compelled to fight for his place; and it was soon the gossip that Shaffer had been forced to serve an ultimatum on the bosses that the support of the 'Indianapolis Star' in the election would depend on the selection of Beveridge as one of the 'Big Four.' This malicious story continued in circulation for two years and was finally denounced by Shaffer in a telegram to the 'Indianapolis News,' which gave it renewed currency in 1922. There had been a conference, lasting thirty minutes, at the Claypool Hotel, between the organization leaders and Shaffer, regarding Beveridge's recognition. Senator Watson previously had agreed to yield to Beveridge; but having been chosen by the senatorial cabal for the chairmanship of the resolutions committee, making necessary his presence in the convention, the State Chairman withdrew from the slate to make way for Beveridge.[2] Even so, the primary vote was disregarded, and Beveridge aside, the delegates-at-large were supporters of Harding, who had polled an insignificant vote in the primaries, running fourth and last. The convention instructed the four men [3] to vote for Wood, but the politicians accepted the instructions in the Pickwickian sense.

II

Meanwhile, the indications pointed to a place of prominence for Beveridge in the convention. No one, in the expression of the party's principles, policies, and purposes, had approached Beveridge in the months preceding the convention. He had been made chairman of a sub-committee on 'Law and Order and the Administration of Justice' to prepare a memorandum for the platform committee and had submitted a report prepared with the thoroughness and meticulous care of a lawyer's brief, which

[1] Beveridge to Mrs. Beveridge, April 22, 1920.
[2] *Indianapolis Star*, May 24, 1922.
[3] Senators Watson and New, Governor Goodrich, and Beveridge.

the 'New Republic' thought the best thing that had come out of the convention.[1] In the early spring the discussion of the temporary chairmanship had centered on either Lodge or Borah, but the latter favored Beveridge for the position. That, however, had been preëmpted by Lodge, and the current gossip was that the permanent chairmanship would go to Beveridge. Harvey was interested in seeing that it did, and early in May, Borah publicly proposed him for the place. So nearly settled did it seem that Beveridge wrote the speech he would have delivered. It was a condensation of the Detroit speech, brief, but packed with political dynamite, brilliantly phrased, and calculated to lift the delegates from their seats. But it contained one sentence intended to pledge the party against the League, even with the reservations the party had proposed:

Do the reservations safeguard our country? If so, we can abandon our one traditional policy, and become a part of the alliance establishing a new European balance of power which the covenant creates; because, although we have nothing to gain by entering that alliance, we have little to lose, provided the reservations make us secure.
But is this the case? We dare not be in error on this point because the fate of America is at stake. We must be certain and without doubt, since our understanding of the reservations is denied, both here and abroad.

But the senatorial cabal had other plans. It was not the intent that anyone so conspicuously identified with the Progressive Movement should be featured in the convention. There was uneasiness among the organization leaders in Indiana lest the increasing popularity of Beveridge sweep him into the senatorial race against New two years later.

Thus a way was found to put Beveridge aside for the permanent chairmanship. Hays, of Indiana, was National Chairman. Watson, of Indiana, was selected by the senatorial cabal for the chairmanship of the platform committee. And an Indianian for permanent chairman, too? That would be too much. The plan had been perfected long before the convention met, and the proceedings in Chicago were mere mummery. An hour before the time set for the choice of a permanent chairman, the resolutions committee met, and, according to plans and specifications, elected Watson as its chairman, and the word was hurried to the Committee on Permanent Organization, with the suggestion that, since another Indianian could hardly be honored with the permanent chairmanship, it would be just as well to continue Lodge in that position. And so it was.

[1] *New Republic*, June 16, 1920.

Old and weary, Lodge's keynote speech, as temporary chairman, had been a keen disappointment, the bromidic, uninspired utterance of a cynic. But the practical men in the convention could dispense with another speech, and all the easier since the selection of a second man for permanent chairman would let down the bars to Beveridge. And so the word went down the line that Lodge was to be the sole chairman; and when the friends of Beveridge insisted on a vote in the committee, the better trained, hearkening to their master's voice, voted for Lodge. Eleven members, including the representative of Borah's State, went to Beveridge. Thus, with Lodge's disappointing speech as the sole message, the convention proceeded to its work, and Beveridge filed his unspoken speech among his papers. He presided over the convention on the day of the nominating speeches, but he did not speak at all.

Throughout the convention, Beveridge was living comfortably in a private house, and watching the maneuvering with some amusement and more astonishment. 'The things that went on on the inside were perfectly amazing,' he wrote Albert Shaw.[1] And two days later he wrote Mrs. Beveridge: 'The Presidential muddle grows worse and worse. The delegates are desperate — literally so. No candidate will do, and they don't know where to turn.'[2]

But the senatorial cabal in charge were muddling toward their appointed end, and in due time, with the telegraphed blessing of Penrose, Harding was nominated. The news was passed to the convention, which, with its characteristic docility, acquiesced.

Beveridge had voted for Wood to the finish.

III

A few days later, Harding invited him to a conference in Washington. He had not been wholly easy concerning the nominee's attitude toward the League, since he had seemed sincere in his advocacy of ratification with reservations. The two men discussed the issues, with Beveridge bearing down hard on the League and urging the nominee to confine his speaking to the front porch. A little later, he wrote at length on the advantages of such a course. He was motivated by the feeling that, unless Harding were constantly surrounded by the enemies of the League, he might backslide from the position of the irreconcilables. These gravely concerned themselves through-

[1] Beveridge to Shaw, July 6, 1920.
[2] Beveridge to Mrs. Beveridge, June 8, 1920.

out the campaign, and especially during the weeks preceding the delivery of the acceptance speech.

Early in July, Beveridge sent Harding some suggestions on the preparation of this speech. He urged that, to prevent pressure being brought upon him by organized labor on the Adamson law, he should clearly state that 'any attempt of any organization, group, or combination to coerce the Government, by force or threat of force, to do its bidding, will be fought to a finish and without compromise.' And the nominee should make it positive that 'the League Covenant, with or without reservations, will not again be submitted to the Senate.' Otherwise, he was warned, 'you will be expected to submit it, and will be viciously attacked if you refuse to do so.'[1] And with special emphasis he added another warning: 'Opposition to the League affords the strongest vote-getting issue we have; if our differences with the Democrats is merely that of the nature and wording of the reservations, that issue is lost.'

Ten days later, Harding sent a copy of the speech, expressing the hope that 'it will meet with some degree of your approval,' and complaining of the difficulties of his task: 'It has been a difficult task to proceed along the lines which are calculated to bring the party together, and I have done my best in that direction and shall hope to have your friendly consideration.'[2]

The tentative draft fell short of Beveridge's hopes, but, diplomatically he replied that the speech 'is admirable'; that no one could have done better, and that he was 'delighted.'[3]

Throughout the summer and fall, the enemies of the League were to be in close communication on Harding's tactics. Within a few weeks he was to be suggesting some new form of international coöperation for peace, to the deep distress of those who opposed anything of the sort. It was at this time that Beveridge heard from Hiram Johnson:

Of course you were absolutely right in your suggestions to Harding. Within a short period, Harding will have to tell (that is, if the Democratic side of this fight has any sense and energy) whether he is going to ratify the League with reservations, whether he is going to return it to the Senate, and what he is going to do with the treaty. He cannot get by, if our opponents are sufficiently insistent, with generalities and platitudes. He ought to anticipate the attack, as you suggest, and tell the country that he does not ever intend to send the League of Nations back to the Senate....

This morning's newspapers contain press dispatches from Marion

[1] Beveridge to Harding, July 10, 1920.
[2] Harding to Beveridge, July 20, 1920.
[3] Beveridge to Harding, July 26, 1920.

that Harding is soon going to elaborate upon his plan of international coöperation, and tell in detail just what he proposes the nations of the earth will do. The instant he attempts this, he gets into difficulties.... And just the moment he undertakes it, he transmutes the issue from Wilson's League to Harding's proposed international convenant.[1]

Even the acceptance speech failed to relieve the apprehensions of the League's foes. Its hints at some new league were disconcerting to those who had taken their stand, four-square, against any such thing at all. 'Harding's speech was not satisfactory to me,' Beveridge wrote a personal friend. 'Part of it was extremely satisfactory; but that part in which he in substance advocates a new League of Nations (for that is what it amounts to) does not strike me as either statesmanship or good policy.' [2]

Nevertheless it was necessary to appear pleased, and gently to push a puzzled candidate into a more positive, unmistakable position. With this in view, Beveridge wrote to encourage a more uncompromising position on Harding in the speech on the League alone, which he was planning to deliver.

I am delighted that in your forthcoming speech you will further emphasize our position on the League — and our foreign policy in general. Clear and forthright as was your superb speech of acceptance, certain well-meaning, but not politically wise, friends have so confused the public mind upon these matters that the Democrats are quietly trying to convince those of their people who are with us on this supreme issue that there is really very little practical difference between the parties on the League — and I fear that they are making some impression.[3]

To help keep the candidate in the straight and narrow path in the League speech, George Harvey was hurried to Marion and all but slept with Harding for nine days. He had written Beveridge that his 'stock is high in this vicinity,' and that 'Harding certainly admires you hugely'; and Beveridge had replied that he was 'overjoyed' that Harvey had gone to Marion, since he had 'been very anxious about Harding's forthcoming speech.' [4] But, alas, even this speech was not without alloy, and Beveridge, in congratulating the candidate upon the general tone, expressed regret that he had felt it necessary to commit himself to any particular course of action after becoming President. 'The whole situation is changing so constantly,' he wrote, 'that it appears to me desirable not to lay down any specific program so far in advance.' [5]

[1] Johnson to Beveridge, July 27, 1920.
[2] Beveridge to W. C. Bobbs, Aug. 30, 1920.
[3] Beveridge to Harding, Aug. 21, 1920.
[4] Beveridge to Harvey, Aug. 23, 1920.   [5] Beveridge to Harding, Aug. 31, 1920.

The reply of Harding was almost alarming:

I think we are in entire accord in believing that there should be no delay as to our foreign affairs which would prevent our working out with the people of other countries some plan to promote peace and amity, and to make war the last resort in matters of international difference.

The League of Nations, as it appeals to many of our people, is purely an ideal and they have no conception of its profits, effects, or ramifications. Certainly I realize that any understanding which may be worked out in the future is not a thing which can be formulated by any man, or even by any one country, but this is something I can talk with you about at greater length, and especially if any power in connection with it is lodged in my hands.[1]

Thus, with no little nervous twitching, the campaign dragged through August; and September brought a real fright.

IV

One morning at the breakfast-table, Beveridge was startled to find that Elihu Root had proposed and outlined a plan for the organization of a World Court connected with the League. Instantly he telegraphed Harding:

Am much concerned over the Root Court League proposition. If accepted, will it not lose all you and other senators have won? Trust you will not commit yourself to it.[2]

And the same day he wrote at greater length:

Might it not be well for you to cut the Gordian knot — to cut loose from the whole miserable business, and say simply, plainly, and positively, that we will have nothing whatever to do with the League in any shape or form?

Instantly, the enemies of the League brought all their heavy artillery into action. The very day he wrote Harding, Beveridge wrote Frank Munsey, the publisher, indicating what he had set in motion:

After talking with you, I talked with Senator Knox. He was savagely aroused; told me he had already sent a smashing telegram to Harding, and asked me to do the same. I did so, and also wrote a letter, as requested to do by Frank Brandegee,[3] who wrote Harding at the same time.... Unless the Root superstition is smashed, we shall certainly have trouble with the Taft-Wickersham-Root crowd. I was so much impressed with what you said to me over the 'phone from Lewiston,

[1] Harding to Beveridge, Sept. 10, 1920.
[2] Beveridge to Harding, Sept. 16, 1920.
[3] Senator from Connecticut.

that I wired you that your idea of having a great editorial, entitled 'The Passing of Root,' is nothing short of genius.[1]

Two days later, he wrote Harvey urging that pressure be brought to bear to force the cutting of the 'Gordian knot,' apropos of Root's Court:

We have fiddled and fuddled with reservations and all that sort of thing long enough. The country's mind is made up; they are against the League or anything like the League.[2]

And to Borah:

I am deeply troubled by the publication of Root's World Court League plan. It seems to me that if that is endorsed, we shall lose practically all that you and the rest of our men have won by such historic and fearless fighting.[3]

In a telephone conversation, Beveridge and Brandegee had agreed that the leaders in the fight against the League should pound Harding with 'smashing' telegrams and letters, protesting against a favorable consideration of the Court.

Two days later, Beveridge had a reassuring letter from Brandegee:

I have just been talking with Lodge over the telephone about his coming here to speak, and incidentally he told me that he had written Harding, and that Harvey had also. Lodge says that Harvey is going to meet Root as soon as he gets off the steamer. I hope he will get at him first.[4]

There was a rallying of the anti-League clan and a descent in force on Harding, and, for the moment, the crisis seemed to pass.

V

In the mean time, with Republican leaders like Charles Evans Hughes and George W. Wickersham preparing to appeal to the Nation in full-page advertisements to support Harding as the surest way to get into the League, pressure was being brought on Beveridge, whose views were well known, to take the stump on another continental tour. The positions of Root and Taft definitely took them out of the campaign; Knox physically was incapable of making a speaking tour; and Lodge would make but few speeches, and none west of New York and New

[1] Beveridge to Munsey, Sept. 16, 1920.
[2] Beveridge to Harvey, Sept. 18, 1920.
[3] Beveridge to Borah, Sept. 21, 1920.
[4] Brandegee to Beveridge, Sept. 20, 1920.

Jersey. Much as he was interested in the issue of the campaign, it was with some reluctance that Beveridge consented to assume the burden. No longer did the old war-horse snort impatiently at the sound of the bugle. The serenity of the scholar's closet had cooled the ardor of the orator, but he consented.

Starting out in early October, he spoke to great audiences, largely in denunciation of the League, in Chicago, Lincoln, Denver, Madison, Salt Lake City, San Francisco, Los Angeles, San Diego, Kansas City, St. Louis, and Louisville. At times the vacillation and vagueness of Harding appalled or disgusted him, and once he was tempted to cancel his engagements and return home. 'Am much disturbed by Harding's whirling dervish performance,' he wrote his wife. 'It's all I can do to keep myself from writing the committee to cancel dates. He is surely leaving Johnson in for a sorry predicament if they fight for their convictions.'[1]

It was a sad campaign for Beveridge's friend Shaffer, whose faith in the League remained unshaken. An editorial in the 'Star' expressing dissent, but complete faith in Beveridge's sincerity and Americanism, is not without its pathos.

VI

When the polls closed with victory for the Republicans, Beveridge entered upon a long series of non-partisan speeches, and it was not until the latter part of December that he was invited to Marion by the President-elect. Wishing no appointment that he could get, he was more embarrassed than gratified by the invitation. In a letter to Harvey, he set forth the reasons:

The papers say that I am to be called to Marion. I sincerely hope this is not the case. I am, as you know, opposed to any league or political association whatever with foreign nations; and I don't want to be put in the position of opposing such plans as Senator Harding may be developing. The rumor is also flitting around that I am to be offered a place in the Cabinet. I depend upon you to prevent that catastrophe. There is only one place I would have that I can afford to take, and that will not be offered me — I mean the position of Secretary of State. Unless you are to be appointed to that important post, I hope and pray it will be given Knox and that he will take it.[2]

But the invitation came, and Beveridge spent some time with Harding agreeably, but the very next day he was annoyed by a press report that he had opposed the appointment of Will Hays

[1] Beveridge to Mrs. Beveridge, Oct. 18, 1920.
[2] Beveridge to Harvey, Dec. 22, 1920.

to a Cabinet position. It was the very opposite to the truth, for he had urged the selection of Hays for the portfolio of Commerce. Realizing that the story had been inspired by political enemies to embarrass him in Indiana, he sent the clipping to Harding with comments:

The enclosed astounds and irritates me. As far as opposing Will, I am for him most heartily for a Cabinet appointment. As I said to you yesterday, it has seemed to me that his powers of coördination should be of peculiar value at the head of the Department of Commerce.

Not by word or look did I indicate to anybody anything upon which the enclosed could possibly be justified. I did not even see the 'Times' or 'Ledger' men....

I am sorry to trouble you with this insect incident, but feel that I cannot let such an untruth pass without comment.

Let me say how much I enjoyed our talk and how highly I value your confidence.[1]

Asking and expecting nothing for himself, Beveridge did earnestly urge upon Harding the appointment of Senator Moses E. Clapp as a member of the Interstate Commerce Commission, but later he was to understand the absurdity of proposing the selection of such a Progressive to such a strategical position in the Administration. A non-committal acknowledgment of the recommendation closed the Clapp incident.[2]

In the Marion conference, Harding had approached his visitor on a Cabinet appointment, without indicating the portfolio he had in mind. It was evidently not that of State, and Beveridge dismissed from his mind all thought of an official association with the Administration. But, a little later, he was offered the ambassadorship to Japan, and promptly declined it. Later still, but yet in January, Harding was intent on placing him in the diplomatic service. Medill McCormick was sent, as the President's emissary, to New York to see Frank Munsey and beg him to use his influence in persuading Beveridge to accept the ambassadorship to Germany. It was admitted by McCormick that the Administration was 'terribly worried about Indiana,' and convinced that three congressmen might be lost in the next election. A contest between Beveridge and New for the senatorial nomination would be a dreadful calamity and might lose the State. If Beveridge could be eliminated through an appointment to Berlin, it would be good, but Harding could not renew the offer previously rejected without the assurance that it would be accepted.

Munsey summoned Beveridge to New York to submit what

[1] Beveridge to Harding, Jan. 7, 1921.   [2] Harding to Beveridge, Jan. 11, 1921.

he called 'an order from the President.' Beveridge listened to the story and instantly rejected the new offer. The two friends then reviewed carefully what Munsey should say to McCormick, and afterward to Harding. Then, dismissing the subject, they sat down to the enjoyment of their visit.

Even then pressure was being brought to bear on Beveridge to contest for New's seat in the Senate, and while not enthusiastic over the idea, he was toying with it. 'You and I, and we alone, will decide whether I go to the Senate or write Lincoln,' he wrote Mrs. Beveridge. Throughout the whole of 1921 he was responding generously to requests for speeches on John Marshall from bar associations from Denver to Boston; and while he spoke mostly upon Marshall and the Constitution, he found ample opportunity for the discussion of political and economic questions. For a time the old eagerness for the platform, which had diminished during his cloistered days with the 'Marshall,' returned, and throughout the entire year it was as though he were in the midst of a political campaign. Everywhere he was enthusiastically received, and never had he spoken with greater effectiveness or art. The profundity and scholarship of his 'Life of John Marshall' had dissipated wholly the impression, long encouraged by his enemies, that the very brilliancy of his platform performances was proof of the superficiality of his thinking. To the moron and the ignorant, the stammering expression and the solemn silence are apt to be confused with depth and wisdom. No one noting the fluency of Beveridge's oratory and its graces realized that the speech had been prepared after intensive research and submitted to the criticism of competent authorities on the subject treated. Thus, for many years the orator had been forced to fight against the impression given by his enemies that he was merely a 'glib young man,' not to be taken seriously.

With the appearance of the 'Life of Marshall' this was no longer possible. He reached new heights of popularity. With his seeming withdrawal from the political arena, the old jealousies died down, and men of all factions and parties united in praise. As he went about Indiana that year, the constant importunities of his admirers to return to public life almost persuaded him. But he would have to think about that. He would have to be convinced of a real demand.

His observations and conversations throughout the country left him more than dubious about the prospects of his party. He found much to distress him in the business situation. During the campaign of 1920 he had the feeling that the Republicans would win easily, and four years later 'go out with a bang,' because of the inability of any man or party to effect the economic readjustments necessary to prosperity.[1] This feeling had been accentuated since. Nine months after the election of Harding, he was writing pessimistically to a personal friend of a report on business conditions he had received from business men and politicians:

> It is really terrible. It put the melancholy capstone of a gloomy and even sinister account of conditions given me by various business men.... I came back feeling very blue.... It seems reasonably certain that the Administration is due to pass through a series of storms, each more tempestuous than the one before; and I am poignantly fearful that their estimate is not wholly inaccurate of the wretched state of the equipment of the Government to meet these storms, not only in the House and Senate, but elsewhere also.[2]

A month later he wrote Rothschild that the political drift was against the Republicans.

Throughout the summer, after he had gone to Beverly Farms, his friends had been active in directing the movement for his nomination for the Senate. He listened to all he heard, but made no promise. In the serenity of the late summer and early autumn, out under the trees and along the walks of the North Shore, and camping in the pine woods of Maine about Churchill Lake, he refused to be stampeded. While his friends in Indiana were busily creating sentiment summoning him again into the political arena, he was writing home from his camp in the woods that he and his young son were going to bed at eight or nine o'clock, and sleeping 'like iron.' 'And, Heavens! how we eat — corn bread, butter, marmalade, eggs, bacon, flapjacks.'

On his return to Indiana, he would have to make a decision. but 'sufficient unto the day is the evil thereof.'

[1] Beveridge to E. L. McClain.
[2] Beveridge to W. C. Bobbs, Oct. 17, 1921.

I

IF, ON returning home, Beveridge intended a return to public life, his manner and public expressions were not those of one cultivating popular acclaim. If there was to be no positive popular recall from official exile, he could return to the ivory tower, and, in the writing of another book, make an even surer bid for lasting fame. At any rate, he would be free — free and frank, whatever the result. With the appointment to the State Department of Charles Evans Hughes, who had promised that the election of Harding would assure America's entrance to the League, Beveridge was prepared for anything in Washington. And when the Washington Disarmament Conference was called, he looked upon it with misgivings. Was this to be the blazing of a path to the organization at Geneva through the back door? Such rumors were afloat. Lodge, indeed, was to be one of the American delegation, but Lodge had favored some kind of league before Wilson had proposed one. At any rate, Beveridge would make his protest against any form of surrender to the 'internationalists.' Thus, early in October, Lodge was reading a letter from him:

But for the fact that you are a member of our delegation at the approaching Peace Conference, I should feel more apprehensive than I do as to the outcome of that parley. The increasing talk about that gathering somewhat disturbs the complacency with which, at first, I accepted it. The 'Weekly Review' now advocates an Anglo-American entente; Lloyd George suggests a British-Japanese-American 'understanding'; London dispatches inform us that France and England have decided to insist that we shall enter the League, of course with 'reservations'; and those who are so ardently championing the international arrangement are now asserting, seemingly with confidence, that, after all, the Conference will produce something very much like the League.

Of course I do not really know what the situation is, but the growing rumors are a little bit disquieting to me, and I imagine that a feeling of uneasiness is spreading among the public. If attempts should be made at the Conference to denature our victory of last year, you may be certain that, in repelling these attempts, you will be supported by the vast majority of those who voted our way in the Presidential election.[1]

Lodge replied reassuringly. There was no cause for anxiety, he thought. In the treaty with Germany, about to be ratified, it

[1] Beveridge to Lodge, Oct. 3, 1921.

was specifically stated that no obligations under the League had been assumed. 'This is the first time,' wrote Lodge, 'that in a great diplomatic transaction and in a diplomatic instrument, this has been stated, and I think it very important on that account.' Of course Harding, in his Message, had 'taken the best possible ground' upon the League, 'but to have put it in an international instrument is very valuable.' Lodge had no apprehension of the dangers feared by Beveridge, but if they developed he thought they were 'pretty well prepared to meet them.'[1]

Even so, Beveridge was by no means satisfied, and a little later, in an Armistice Day address to the American Legion at Warsaw, Indiana, he demanded absolute publicity of the proceedings of the Conference as essential to its success.[2] Thereafter he followed the course of the negotiations with interest and hailed the result without enthusiasm. Later he was to write Mark Sullivan that in traveling about the country he had convinced himself of several things: 'For instance, I will tell you, very confidentially, that the average citizen, man and woman, is not in the least worked up about the Four Power Treaty. He and she do not care a whoop about it; but if they do, they are suspicious and mildly hostile — even a little sullen about it.'[3]

In all this he was not endangering his political prospects. But after his return home and before the announcement of his senatorial candidacy, he threw discretion to the winds in two speeches that inevitably would be used against him. In November, 1921, he addressed the Chamber of Commerce of the State of New York on 'The Plight of Business.' 'It is a time for plain speaking for men who have graduated from ambition,' he began; and hurried on to the expression of views utterly incompatible with the cultivation of popular favor. These were a hot denunciation of the Adamson law, and 'the methods by which the Adamson law was forced upon the statutes'; of the increase in the wages of the railway workers by McAdoo under Government operation; and a demand for the repeal of the Adamson law, and for the consolidation of the roads. Attacking income and corporation taxes as destructive of business enterprise, he proposed a sales tax on the consumption of the people. He called for the repeal of the Sherman anti-trust law, and the substitution of a national incorporation act 'to prevent the wrongs and frauds of dishonest business.'

The speech offered his enemies every opportunity to charge

[1] Lodge to Beveridge, Oct. 6, 1921.
[2] *Indianapolis Star*, Nov. 12, 1921.
[3] Beveridge to Sullivan, May 27, 1922.

him with enmity to organized labor and high wages; and with seeking to benefit the rich at the expense of the poor by shifting the burdens of taxation. Soon it was to be used against him. Undaunted by the criticism of laboring men and merchants, he soon reiterated his plea for a sales tax to check the mounting income taxes in the higher brackets and for the abandonment of the excess profits tax.[1]

Meanwhile, despite the grumbling, he was adding to his prestige in notable addresses outside the State, expounding his views on the treaty powers of the Senate to the Iowa State Bar Association one day,[2] and the next paying tribute to Senator Knox at a memorial meeting in Philadelphia. It was at this time, too, that the council of the Historical Society of Pennsylvania notified him of his unanimous election to an honorary membership. 'It may interest you to know,' said the notification letter, 'that you are the first American ever so chosen, and that in ninety-eight years of existence the honorary membership has been conferred only upon the late Lord Bryce and Mr. George Otto Trevelyan.'[3] Day by day the 'Indianapolis Star' was reporting a lengthening procession of 'Beveridge-for-Senator' clubs throughout the State; Washington correspondents were writing of popular interest in his candidacy,[4] and metropolitan papers were discussing it encouragingly in editorials.

Just at this juncture, his enemies, in control of the Indiana Republican State Editorial Association, made the stupid blunder of excluding him from the list of speakers, and the public gasped in astonishment at the flagrancy of the affront. Resenting the discourtesy, Beveridge was not displeased. 'Did you ever hear of anything so stupid?' he wrote a friend.[5] The reaction was wholly in his favor, and the 'Indianapolis Star' made the most of it. 'We are left to infer,' it said, 'that they see no danger or impropriety in holding out the idea that the nomination of Beveridge would be a rebuke to the Harding Administration.'[6]

II

November came, and passed, before Beveridge could satisfy himself that there was a real demand. That month a number of his most faithful friends in the office of William C. Bobbs,

[1] At Anderson, *Indianapolis Star*, Jan. 17, 1922.
[2] *Indianapolis Star*, Dec. 31, 1921.
[3] Hampton L. Carson to Beveridge, Feb. 1, 1922.
[4] Notably Mark Sullivan and Samuel G. Blythe.
[5] To the author.
[6] Jan. 30, 1922.

the publisher, conferred on whether or not he should enter the contest. Almost a quarter of a century before there had been a similar conference to advance his first candidacy for the Senate, and all participants, still living in 1921, were in the publisher's office — as zealous as in youth. Bobbs had not been a member of the group of 1899; his affectionate friendship, which had developed later, came to be one of Beveridge's most cherished associations in later life. In the publisher's personal charm, his responsiveness, and appreciation he found the qualities that appealed strongly to his needs. But at the time of this meeting, Beveridge was still unconvinced. 'I told the boys last night,' he wrote his wife, 'that I will not run unless public sentiment powerfully demands it. They said my nomination is absolutely certain — but I won't make a fight.'[1]

More than two weeks later he was still in doubt. 'The pressure very heavy,' he telegraphed Mrs. Beveridge. 'Friends absolutely confident of victory. Not satisfied myself, but if showing continues may change my mind.'[2] On the night of December 1, in the Beveridge home, the decision was definitely made, but the announcement was postponed while organization work was pressed; and it was not until the middle of February that he was ready formally to enter the contest. Then one noon, men and women from every quarter of the State crowded into the living-rooms and halls of the Beveridge home to inform him that 'at first it was a sort of universal desire; it became a request; and then a demand; and now it is a movement.'[3] Speaking conversationally, as to friends, Beveridge touched upon the gravity of the national problems for a decade to come; said they were too vital for any man to aspire to a Senate seat without a 'genuine and voluntary movement of widespread and unmistakable character'; confessed himself convinced of the reality of such a movement, and announced his candidacy. Here he was interrupted with lusty cheers — 'three cheers.' 'Issues of the utmost gravity have already been raised,' he continued. 'At an appropriate time... I shall publicly discuss those issues, as well as public questions which affect the prosperity and happiness of all the people.' And then, with a smile: 'The flag is unfurled. Go to it. Keep sweet. God bless you, every one.'[4]

Thus again Beveridge appeared before his party as a candidate, supported by a militant organization loyally directed by Clarence Martin.[5]

[1] Nov. 1, 1921.   [2] Nov. 26, 1921.
[3] Judge James B. Wilson, Bloomington.
[4] *Indianapolis Star*, Feb. 17, 1922.
[5] Later Judge of the Supreme Court of Indiana.

III

He formally launched his campaign with a speech at Fort Wayne. It was inevitable that the contest would be hardly fought. The traditional enemies were in the saddle, booted and spurred, and he whose seat was now endangered was a prime favorite of the group in power. Senator Harry New owed his political career to ingratiating personal qualities and rare powers of organization. Temperamentally, and in their concept of politics, Beveridge and New were antipathetic. It was the 'machine' against the rank and file. Soon the supporters of New were spreading the propaganda that President Harding was actually behind him, and the friends of Beveridge forced the President to announce through the Associated Press that he was not interesting himself in the Indiana contest.[1] But, even so, it was generally assumed that the party organization was using its influence against Beveridge, and that large sums of money would be used against him. Attempts were made to alienate the regulars because of Beveridge's support of Roosevelt, but more than half the Republicans of Indiana had followed Roosevelt against Taft.

Carrying the fight to the people, as Beveridge had to do, he determined to make his initial speech a sounding-board for the whispering campaign against him. He was to find it no easy task to frame the Fort Wayne speech, and before the campaign started he was wishing he were out of it. 'Am writing the Fort Wayne speech,' he wrote his wife. 'Goes slowly — can't say much about the real issues. What a campaign! — Harding losing ground fast. Sometimes I wonder if he has lost his mind.... Am well but tired. This kind of work is too much even for a man of twenty-five. I was a fool to go into it.'[2]

In his Fort Wayne speech he touched but lightly on the issues, reserving these for the real campaign. His record? He reviewed it. 'So let specifications be provided,' he said. 'Let the voters be informed of laws written, policies formulated, debates made, as well as votes given, that makes the record of both candidates. That is only fair, is it not?' He would 'stand by Harding' — but he added quickly: 'On matters of fundamental principle I will never yield my convictions to any man or set of men. On such sacred things I hold and shall hold myself answerable only to God and my conscience.' Was it charged that he was incapable of 'team work'? 'If by doing team work is meant the refusal of a Senator to investigate for himself grave public matters, and, at the very least, constructively help to devise

[1] *Indianapolis Star*, March 2, 1922.   [2] March 1, 1922.

appropriate laws, but instead, to vote as leaders dictate, such "team work" does not appeal to me.' And the party organization's attitude? 'If, as reported, the organization anywhere is taking sides in this contest, which I refuse to believe, then the issue is forced and is unavoidable: Does the party belong to the organization or does the organization belong to the party?' Was the point raised against him that he had 'stood by that glorious American, that matchless soldier of the common good, that unrivaled captain of righteousness, Theodore Roosevelt? Is that wise party counsel? Is that sound party policy? Is that even good party common sense?' In other States the party had reunited — was the fight still on in Indiana?

And closing with a reference to the rumors of unlimited expenditures by the candidates, he met it with a challenge:

Cannot my opponent and myself, with our respective committees, at once get together and agree to the limitation of the amount to be spent, which amount will appeal to the common sense and common honesty of all the people as a proper sum? I am willing, and even eager, to have just such a conference in the friendliest spirit, and as soon as possible; make such a compact; reduce it to writing; both of us sign it; and then publish it in every newspaper of the State.[1]

The idea, warmly endorsed by many leaders, was rejected by the followers of New. But Beveridge kept the issue alive by announcing at frequent intervals his expenditures up to the time of publication.

Thereafter, for a month, he spoke almost exclusively on governmental problems, setting forth the views we already know.[2] But, making progress as he was, his foes grew desperate and launched a whispering campaign against him which he speedily dragged into the open. An attempt was made to evoke against him the passions of the war. Had he not been friendly to the Germans? Had he not 'slacked' in the war? Had he not written 'What is Behind the War' — in 1915, two years before America entered? Had it not been banned in public libraries when we entered?[3] Had not Will Hays just spoken, in an interview, disparagingly of the book?

The bitter stage had now been reached, and Beveridge's friends responded with denunciations of the slanders; with an enumeration of his war activities; and with a letter from Hays in lavish praise of 'What is Behind the War,' written at the time of its publication.[4] Meanwhile, Beveridge made triumphant

[1] *Indianapolis Star*, March 10, 1922.
[2] Lafayette speech, *Indianapolis Star*, April 9, 1922.
[3] During the hysterical period.   [4] *Indianapolis Star*, April 13, 14, 1922.

progress, with enthusiastic receptions everywhere, and New, wholly incapable of coping with him on the stump, was at a disadvantage. The latter was depending on organization, Beveridge on the people, and they responded. He carried the State by more than twenty thousand, and fifty-seven of the ninety-two counties marched under his banner.

IV

Again Beveridge was unfortunate in the nomination made against him by the Democrats. Samuel M. Ralston, an able campaigner, with an enviable record in the gubernatorial office, was a man of irreproachable personal integrity. 'Ralston is to be the Democratic candidate,' Beveridge had written Mrs. Beveridge before the primary. 'He is my friend.' Not only was he his friend, he was an admirer, who had a keen appreciation of Beveridge's oratory and a profound admiration for his 'Marshall.' There could be no personal issue between two such men; the fight would have to be on issues.

Though worn by the primary campaign, Beveridge was to wait almost two months longer for his vacation. Through May and June he was constantly occupied with conferences and organization meetings, and it was not until July that he was able to take the rest he needed. Going to the Rocky Mountains where he could rough it and sleep in the open, he spent a few weeks tramping the trails, cutting down trees, splitting wood, eating the plain wholesome food of the camp. But his mind was occupied, too, with campaign plans and speeches. He had always found that the silence and solitude of the woods and hills not only rejuvenated and invigorated his body, but put his thoughts in order. He returned to the battle-field in August.

Meanwhile, he was busy with a voluminous correspondence with friends throughout the country, some of whom sought to coax him away from his position on international affairs. All these he answered with ill-concealed impatience. When Irving Fisher, the Yale economist, wrote the expression of his hope that Beveridge would not commit himself against the League of Nations, he replied: 'But, my dear Fisher, on this question we are in an elemental disagreement, and, as I have said, on principle. I supposed that you knew that.' [1] And when Mark Sullivan wrote to warn him that no American statesman in the future could ignore world problems, he replied that 'the mass mind — the public — do not take your view of foreign affairs, or of the attitude and design of the United States.' [2]

[1] Fisher to Beveridge, June 5, 1922; Beveridge to Fisher, June 8, 1922.
[2] Sullivan to Beveridge, May 16, 1922; Beveridge to Sullivan, May 27, 1922.

However, his position on the League was to be the least of his worries, for Senator Joseph T. Robinson of Arkansas, opening the campaign for Ralston, had thrown the covenant to the wolves in that campaign.

But, as he faced the cheering crowd at Evansville, there were embarrassing hurdles to take. There was the Republican tariff act of 1922, strongly reminiscent of the method of the making of the act of 1909 that he had opposed. He had to endorse it, and he did; differentiating this one from the other on the ground that it had been more deliberately framed and carried the flexibility clause making possible a presidential shifting of the rates up or down. There was a defensive note, too, in this portion of his keynote speech: 'Every Progressive who followed Theodore Roosevelt, and who since has been sent to the Senate or the House as a Republican, worked and voted for the present tariff.' Ralston and the Democrats were smiting it hip and thigh, and Beveridge's defense was evidently reluctant, and without his customary strength.

It was on the new issues that he struck his boldest blows, and some of these were fatal to his cause. Again he lunged at 'banded labor' on the Adamson law; again attacked the wage scales of the employees of the railroads and demanded that they be changed; again assailed the income taxes in the higher brackets and the corporation tax, and called for the substitution of a sales tax that would fall equally on all.

Labor was almost a unit against him on the wage question and the housewife on the sales tax, but he persevered along this line until the campaign closed. It was 'magnificent, but it was not war.'

Then, toward the close, fell another deadly blow. It was at the time that the Ku-Klux Klan fairly swarmed in Indiana from the river to the lake, and Governor Henry Allen of Kansas made it the object of a bitter attack at Richmond, where it was strong.[1] The news of the attack flashed instantly to every quarter of the State — and Allen was speaking for Beveridge! The latter unconsciously had been 'Burchardized,' for Allen was his devoted friend. The forces of the Klan moved silently and speedily to secret hostility, and prepared to vote, not for Ralston, but against Beveridge, in retaliation.

The hostility of the Klan and labor was serious enough, but there was another danger beneath the surface. Many of the supporters of New were out for their revenge; and the old 'stand-patters' in rubber heels were on the march with tomahawks. The organization was in the hands of his enemies, and though

[1] *Indianapolis Star*, Oct. 25, 1922.

his friend, Charles W. Miller, was chairman of the executive committee, he was, throughout the fight, unknown to Beveridge, a desperately worried and harassed man, and was soon to die at his own hands. Everywhere, while the people cheered him in his brilliant and spectacular campaign, the cards were stacked against him. Even the Harding Administration and its appointees in Indiana were unfriendly, as was generally suspected. And this was strange. Had not Harding personally begged him to open the campaign for the party in Ohio, and had he not held the great crowd spellbound at Columbus?[1] Had he not taken time from his own campaign in response to importunities to speak in Chicago under the auspices of the Union League?[2]

Meanwhile, the 'Indianapolis Star' was waging a notable campaign in his behalf, and day by day was printing conspicuously in a front-page frame, tributes to his statesmanship and worth from notable men throughout the country.[3] But these were doing more harm than good. Who were these men that they should presume to instruct the people of Indiana on their duty?

And so the campaign, fated from the start, came to a close in a memorable meeting in Cadle Tabernacle, packed to capacity long before the hour, with automobiles parked for four blocks in every direction. This final speech was a masterpiece of eloquence, with a peroration suggestive of his younger days.

A few days before the meeting a close friend had said: 'Albert, this is the last speech of the campaign. You will have a tremendous audience. I want you to give them a peroration such as you can give and send them home on their tiptoes.'

'No,' Beveridge replied, 'you know I can't do that. I quit that years ago. I haven't given that kind of peroration for many years, and I don't intend to now.'

'Well, do it this time. You can do it in such a way as to inspire your friends, reaching their ideals and touching their hearts as well, and send them out to work Tuesday with a lot of enthusiasm.'

Beveridge had made no reply; but his peroration in that closing speech brought thousands to their feet with frenzied cheers, and sent them forth to battle in fine fettle.[4]

But his enemies within his party were impervious to perorations, and the resentments he had aroused by some of the policies he had proposed were beyond the softening influence of words.

---

[1] *Indianapolis Star*, Oct. 4, 1922. [2] *Ibid.*, Oct. 20, 1922.

[3] Senators Lodge and Moses, Nicholas Murray Butler, William Roscoe Thayer, Albert Shaw, Irving Bacheller, Raymond Robins, Lawrence F. Abbott, Henry L. Stoddard, Dean Bates of the University of Michigan, and many others.

[4] Told the author by James W. Noel, who made the request.

He went down to defeat. Instantly he telegraphed his congratulations to Ralston, and, in no sense dispirited, turned to other things.

V

Henceforth until the end he was to be engrossed with his biography of Lincoln — a drama within itself. But he remained keenly alert to public affairs and by voice and pen continued to play his part. All through the spring, however, he was poring over the papers he had assembled for his Lincoln biography and turning over in his mind a series of articles he had agreed to write for Lorimer. In June he spoke at the annual Bunker Hill dinner of the Sons of the Revolution at Boston, striking at the World Court, reiterating his views on international relations. Politically, he found things gloomy. He was convinced, just before sailing for Europe in July, 1923, that the Democrats would sweep the country the next year. 'The cause,' he wrote Shaffer, 'is the public indifference to and disapproval of Harding. The estimate is that he amounts to nothing — is weak and procrastinating. Anyhow, the people simply are not for him and their minds are made up.' And apropos of the President's Western tour, which was to end in his death, and in the course of which he spoke earnestly for the World Court, Beveridge wrote: 'His trip has not changed this in the smallest degree. It is very much like the swing of Taft and Harrison and Hughes — big crowds cheering, etc., and then defeat.' [1]

That summer of 1923 he was to have his first real rest in a quarter of a century. After a few days in London and Paris, he went with his family directly to Schinznach-les-Bains, Switzerland, and took up his quarters in an old hotel built in 1704, standing alone in a valley almost on the banks of the river Arre. Years before, it had been famous for its waters. He found here precisely what he wanted — simple living, excellent food, and serenity. Because of the absence of English-speaking guests, he was not called upon to talk, and for three weeks he 'slept most of the time, literally.' [2]

Returning in the autumn to Beverly Farms, he plunged into hard and intensive work in the preparation of his articles for the 'Saturday Evening Post.' He proposed to discuss our foreign policy, the five-to-four decisions of the Supreme Court on constitutional questions, railroads, taxation, and bureaucracy. He planned to phrase the articles so simply that 'the chauffeur,

[1] Beveridge to Shaffer, July 9, 1923.
[2] Beveridge to Shaffer, Nov. 17, 1923.

workingman, the farmer, and the housewife can understand them.' But there was to be nothing of simplicity in their preparation. On taxation he had talked, on the return trip from Europe, with Professor E. R. A. Seligman of Columbia University, and he was to consult with Professor C. J. Bullock of Harvard on the same subject, and to discuss the railroads with Professor W. Z. Ripley of Harvard and with railroad presidents. 'I hope to shape the Republican platform by these articles,' he wrote. He was in the mood for concentration, for he found that the clouds on the political horizon had not lifted in his absence. 'The average voter is still in a state of great dissatisfaction, or rather of great mystification,' he wrote — 'the sentiment is to be against everything and everybody that can be hit.'

The 'Post' articles began to appear in the fall and extended into the spring. That setting forth the danger to public confidence in the Supreme Court in five-to-four decisions on constitutional questions added heavily to the burdens of correspondence. He had proposed that no act of Congress be declared unconstitutional without a vote of as much as six to three. Admitting that this could not be achieved by legislative enactment, he suggested that the Court itself establish a rule to that effect, and cited the action of John Marshall in fixing a rule against decisions on constitutional questions without a majority of the whole Court. To one of his hostile critics he wrote of his fear 'that rigid adherence to the so-called majority decisions of grave constitutional questions will so augment the steadily growing antagonism to the principle of judicial review itself that the end will be an abolition of that principle by constitutional amendment.'[1] And to a friend he wrote frankly of his fears: 'I do not care a whoop what policy the Court adopts with reference to the two-to-four decisions, but I do care profoundly... about the preservation of the principle of judicial review. And that principle will be in grave peril if another epidemic of five-to-four decisions occurs. Don't make any mistake about it.... Most of us haven't the remotest idea of how deep, widespread, and increasing the general sentiment is against these five-to-four annulments of a national law which involves a settled and definitive national policy.'[2]

But his correspondents were not all hostile. President Coolidge wrote him that he kept the article on the Supreme Court on his light-stand at the head of his bed for a month, intending to write him of his admiration of it. 'It is so plain, so simple and

[1] Beveridge to Frederick R. Kellogg, New York, Jan. 9, 1924.
[2] Beveridge to Louis A. Coolidge, Jan. 25, 1924.

strong, that I am sure it will do a vast amount of good,' the President concluded.[1]

It was at about this time that the pleasant relations of President Coolidge and Beveridge began. Bascom Slemp, the President's secretary, had written that the President 'would appreciate an opportunity of talking over matters with you if your plans are bringing you this way.'[2] A little later the President himself wrote, apropos of an intended visit of Beveridge to Washington, that he was expected to stay at the White House. 'We can promise not to make you a guest, but just one of the family, privileged to go and come as you wish,' he wrote. 'If you will telegraph, the car will meet you at the station.'[3]

It was at this time, too, that Beveridge and Borah, originally antipathetic, drew close together. The Western orator and statesman had won Beveridge's warm regard because of the stout position he had assumed on international affairs.

From the quiet watch-towers at Beverly Farms and Indianapolis, Beveridge was looking over the political scene with misgivings and disgust. Senator Thomas J. Walsh of Montana, Democrat, had launched his great fight on the oil conspiracy and was pressing hard upon his prey. It appalled Beveridge that Republicans, with ample warning, had done nothing, and had surrendered the task of purging the public service to the opposition. It was at this time that he wrote his friend, Worthington C. Ford, of his feelings and observations:

I am gravely concerned about the state of the public mind. Out in this neck of the woods, ordinary citizens are coming to the conclusion that nobody is straight about anything.... I am alarmed at the course our men have taken in Washington — I mean men of our party, Republicans. If they thought these [oil] leases and the policy right and wise, they ought to have stood up and fought to the uttermost all attacks upon them; but if, on the contrary, the whole thing is rotten, then our men should have led the attack — beat the Democrats to it. But they have shilly-shallied, side-stepped, dilly-dallied, etc., until members of our own party out here think that we are all in the wrong.[4]

Just before this, Borah had sent him his speech calling for the impeachment of Secretary of the Navy Denby as the only

---

[1] President Coolidge to Beveridge. These articles were later published in book form, *The State of the Nation*.
[2] Slemp to Beveridge, Jan. 23, 1924.
[3] Coolidge to Beveridge, May 1, 1924.
[4] Beveridge to Ford, Feb. 25, 1924.

constitutional method of removing him. At the moment the President was standing by him. 'You are right at every point,' Beveridge replied.[1]

As the investigation into different departments proceeded under Democratic leadership, Beveridge was soon to put politics aside and favor the pushing of the inquiries to the utmost. 'The nasty mess in Washington must be cleaned up, and the whole place fumigated and sterilized,' he wrote Gifford Pinchot. 'These investigations positively must not be allowed to peter out, as I hear others have in the past. They must go on until every last person — and I don't care who he is — who has been faithless to the public interest is at least exposed, and, if possible, punished.'[2]

It was, therefore, with mixed feelings that he contemplated the approach of the campaign of 1924. He was in the midst of the most gruelling literary work, but habit turned his thoughts to the coming battle, and for a time it seemed he might be called upon to play a conspicuous part. His availability for the Vice-Presidency and as temporary chairman of the National Convention had been canvassed at a conference at the White House. He would have been pleased to serve as chairman. He had no desire for the Vice-Presidency. 'If elected, what would a man do, either in politics or literature,' he wrote.[3]

But there was little probability of his nomination if his enemies in Indiana could prevent it; and, later, when sentiment turned in his direction, two other Indianians appeared in the field as aspirants. Even so, just before he left for the convention at Cleveland, photographers descended upon the house on Washington Boulevard, in anticipation of a possible nomination. 'It will be Hoover, thank God,' he wrote Mrs. Beveridge. 'We're in for an awful licking.'[4]

He went to Cleveland and in sheer disgust went through the motions of participating. The letters written during the convention to Mrs. Beveridge scarcely mentioned politics, but touched mostly on the book he was writing. But he had been entrusted with a mission by Senator Borah. Great pressure was being brought to bear to effect Borah's nomination for the Vice-Presidency. The reactionaries were in the saddle, and it was planned to strengthen the ticket with a progressive; the farmers were discontented, and it was thought that a Western man would help; the party had been sadly smeared by the various

[1] Beveridge to Borah, March 28, 1924.
[2] Beveridge to Pinchot, March 7, 1924.
[3] Beveridge to Stanley Washburn.
[4] June 6, 1924.

scandals in Washington, and it was hoped that Borah, whose integrity was beyond question, and who had not joined with other Republican senators in attempts to obstruct the investigations, would do good. But Borah had no intention of being drafted, and he had asked Beveridge to make his decision known in the event his name was presented. When Secretary of War Weeks was saying he had Borah's assurance he would accept and Beveridge telegraphed as much to Washington, Borah replied that 'Secretary Weeks has no such assurance and you may rely on what I have telegraphed.' When in the midst of the convention, Borah was summoned to the White House and urged by the President to accept, he telegraphed Beveridge:

Have just conferred with the President and there is absolutely no change in my position. Do not accept any statement to the contrary.

And, then, having talked with Beveridge on the telephone, he sent him a positive refusal, to be read in the event his wishes were disregarded:

I 'phoned you last night to withdraw my name in case it is presented. Please be sure to do so, but if they should nominate me, anyway, then I authorize you to read the following telegram to the convention:
'Mr. Chairman and Gentlemen of the Convention: I greatly appreciate your manifestation of confidence, but I must be permitted to serve in the way in which I can serve best. Therefore, most respectfully, but positively, I decline the nomination for the Vice-Presidency. This is final. I thank you all.' [1]

Beveridge was not called upon to read the declination.

After the convention he remained of the opinion the Republicans would lose until the successful two-weeks effort of the Democrats to commit suicide in the New York Convention. He attended with Mrs. Beveridge to hear the Klan debate, with Bryan in the stellar rôle, and left with the conviction that the Democrats had squandered their opportunity.

Soon after the nominations, he heard from President Coolidge:

As this campaign is about to start, and I am preparing my address of acceptance, I think it will be a great help to me if you would send me a very short statement indicating what you think may be the principal issue or issues, and on what you think I should put special emphasis as the policy of our party. [2]

After complying, Beveridge again sought to put politics out of his mind, but he was importuned to take a prominent part

[1] This telegram is in the Beveridge MSS.
[2] Coolidge to Beveridge, July 16, 1924.

in the speaking campaign. At length he agreed to spend two weeks in Indiana, but not in other States. Again he heard from the President:

The National Committee people have seemingly been a little divided between their sentiments of satisfaction that you are going to make a number of speeches in Indiana and their disappointment that you do not make more than a couple of addresses outside the State. I wish you would make it possible to give them a little more time for strategically important places outside your own State. I shall not suggest where, because my suggestions might conflict with the plans of the management. But if I were the management and had your consent, as I hope you may be able to give it, I should have some highly important things for you to do. Isn't it possible for you to give the Committee at least a half-dozen addresses outside Indiana? [1]

Beveridge thereupon agreed to speak in Louisville and Chicago, but he would go no farther away; and so it was. It was not a happy experience, that campaign. 'The campaign sickens me,' he wrote Mrs. Beveridge in the midst of it. 'It will be hard for me to keep going even for this short time — such buncombe, falsehoods, and mush. It really is not worth the effort and time.' [2] His audiences were large and enthusiastic as usual, but he was much perplexed by things he heard. 'What our men and women told me in private conferences,' he wrote Borah, 'showed a swirl of cross-currents beneath the surface which I could not and cannot make heads or tails of. So I am not altogether at ease about the future.' [3]

VII

With the President committed to the World Court, Beveridge was much concerned over the attitude of Republican senators and was in correspondence with Borah. 'To my mind,' he wrote, 'it all comes to this: If I were for the League, I would be for the League Court. It is merely a method for getting us into the League — by far the cleverest method that has yet been devised.' [4] Borah consoled him with the assurance that he would oppose any court connected with the League, and 'not completely and absolutely a judicial tribunal, wholly divorced from international politics.' [5] Less than a week after he received this letter, Beveridge, a guest at the White House, spent four hours

[1] Coolidge to Beveridge, Sept. 25, 1924.
[2] Oct. 21, 1924.
[3] Beveridge to Borah, Nov. 13, 1924.
[4] Beveridge to Borah, Nov. 25, 1924.
[5] Borah to Beveridge, Nov. 28, 1924.

alone with Coolidge in his study, discussing 'many things.' But just what these were was never divulged by him.[1]

Thereafter, with a few speaking excursions and one temptation to reënter politics as a candidate, the remainder of his life was to be one of concentration on his literary work. For ten years he had been engaged in research and writing on biographical works of the highest importance, and after each diversion, he had returned to his closet determined to remain. Now, at length, he took leave of the arena, and henceforth we shall find him in the ivory tower. The old enthusiasms on politics had been cooling gradually and now there was little more than ashes.

[1] Beveridge to Shaffer, Dec. 5, 1924; *Indianapolis Star*, Dec. 2, 1924.

BOOK VI
THE IVORY TOWER

CHAPTER I

THE 'LIFE OF JOHN MARSHALL'

I

'As I feel now,' Beveridge wrote three years after he had begun work on his 'Life of John Marshall,' 'I consider it a Godsend that I am out of politics. It has furnished me an opportunity for quiet, for study, and for thought which political activity utterly forbids. I would not exchange the life of delicious liberty which I now enjoy; the opportunity of conversation and close intercourse with friends, among them the first scholars in America; the chance for investigation and undisturbed thinking; the normal living, the walks through the forests, the regular hours of refreshing slumber, the new birth of mental and physical vigor which I feel every morning when I awake — in short, all that makes life worth while — I would not exchange all this for the hectic, hurried, shallow, insincere life of politics, if, in addition to high office, were added great pecuniary reward.' [1]

The genesis of the monumental biographical history on which he was to be engaged intensively for six years goes back to the early days in the law office of Senator McDonald. It was there that, taking down the noted decisions of the Chief Justice, Beveridge, the youth, came under the fascination of his style and thought. We have observed the impression made in his enthusiastic comments to the amused and yet sympathetic old statesman. This discovery of a man who so vividly gave expression to his own instincts, as yet stumbling in articulation, set him on a hurried journey to the library for a biography of Marshall. He found none that was more than fragmentary; and then he determined, if the want were not supplied otherwise, sooner or later to undertake the task himself. But as he matured, the diversions and duties of a political career postponed the undertaking, though it never was abandoned. The desire grew with the years, and in 1908, with three years before him in the Senate, he began to perfect his plans. At the moment he had no conception of the magnitude of his task. His first thought was to write a biography in one volume that might be published serially at first in a magazine. It was with this in mind that he turned to Robert Underwood Johnson, editor of the 'Century Magazine,' and an old friend, with whom he had had some literary correspondence. In a letter, which is historically interesting as the first approach

[1] Beveridge to Edwin M. Lee, April 17, 1916.

to a publisher for a work destined to rank with the classic biographies of the English language, he set forth his purpose and plan:

As I said to you... it has been in my mind for a long time to write a life of John Marshall — one that would be not only an accurate statement of the facts of his career and the philosophy of his opinions, but also one which would be readable, attractive, and popular. When Mr. Oliver's notable book on Alexander Hamilton appeared, I found that he had done the work with reference to Hamilton in the manner that I had hoped to do with reference to Marshall.

I am sure that the most readable book can be written upon the life, work, and times of the greatest of jurists. I am sure that it can be made a work that will appeal, not only to lawyers and those particularly interested in public affairs, as such, but also be made attractive indeed to the general reader.

During the last decade the powers of the Nation have been in the public mind much more than they have ever been in our history, excepting only during the Civil War.

It is the talk of lawyers and business men in their offices; it is the subject of discussion upon the stump and lecture platform; and even where men and women get together socially, it is seldom that this subject is not discussed. There is hardly an issue of a newspaper that has not either an editorial or an article or a news item bearing directly upon it. For this reason, Marshall's work is coming more and more under public consideration and the reading public is more and more interested in him every day.

Upon examination, I find that only two or three lives of Marshall have been written, and only one of these — the Life of Marshall in the American Statesmen Series — is at all known or read. Even this excellent little volume does not pretend to be comprehensive. It contains too little of the color of Marshall's very picturesque life — hardly any of the human interest features of his career....

My thought, therefore, is this: that the time is ripe for an entertaining work upon this subject. It seems to me that it should appear first in a serial form in the very greatest and most dignified of American periodicals. While there are other magazines that might dispute with the 'Century' this title, I suppose, that, generally speaking, the consensus of competent opinion would be that the 'Century' more nearly answers this description than any other periodical in this country.

So would it not be a good thing?

If you and Mr. Gilder [1] think that this would prove an attractive feature to 'Century' readers, I would be extremely glad to do the work. After a little rest, I intend to begin it, in any event; but if the chapters are to appear in serial form in the 'Century,' of course I should like to know it beforehand, as it would, to a certain extent, influence the style of the writing. [2]

Apparently the idea made no impression on the editors of the

[1] Richard Watson Gilder. [2] Beveridge to Johnson, July 10, 1908.

ALBERT J. BEVERIDGE
A late portrait

'Century,' for within a week Richard Watson Gilder replied with almost curt brevity: 'Your letter about a work on John Marshall is very interesting, but on consultation here, we feel unable to go into the scheme. It unfortunately does not seem to fit into our plans.' [1]

Rebuffed on the first advance, Beveridge appears to have done nothing more until in the autumn, when he wrote the 'Century' proposing a conference with Johnson and Gilder the following week, but the reply was in his hands by the return mail from Johnson: 'We have been discussing with Mr. Scott the question of the project you propose. Alas, he sees no chance of being able to make any money out of it for you.' [2]

Thus, not for the first time nor the last, did a publisher's lack of perspicacity or imagination rob his house of a golden opportunity.

By the time the definitive refusal reached Beveridge, he was ready to start on his seventeen-thousand-mile continental tour for Taft; and then came the bitter enervating battle of the extra session on the tariff; then the election and defeat of 1910, followed by the epochal struggle of 1912. During these four years nothing more was done, but the idea was not abandoned. However, with his release from pressing public and political obligations, his thoughts turned again to the 'Marshall,' and in the summer of 1913 he actually began the writing. He had written Shaffer of his intention in the winter.[3] That summer he had taken another cottage at Dublin, New Hampshire, and there he entered with zest upon his labors. Early in the spring he had spent some time in Virginia in search of material on Marshall's early life.[4] Through the summer he was literally groping his way. He had no more idea of the methods and obligations of historical scholarship than the average casual reader. In the preparation of lawyers' briefs and speeches he had learned something of the importance of citations in an authoritative work. But he was an amateur — stumbling through. He still believed he could write an interpretative biography of his subject in one volume. After all, it would not be different from the preparation of a speech or the writing of a magazine article on a current topic. We find him appealing to Albert Shaw to assist him in making contacts with some Marshall letters,[5] and complaining of the political diversions in the woods.

[1] Gilder to Beveridge, July 17, 1908.
[2] Johnson to Beveridge, Sept. 25, 1908.
[3] Beveridge to Shaffer, Feb. 26, 1913.
[4] Beveridge to Caroline Frevert, April 26, 1913.
[5] Letter in possession of Professor Charles W. Dabney, of the University of Cincinnati.

'It seems to me,' he wrote Shaw, 'that no sooner do I get started on my book — well into the spirit of it — than something... happens and throws me out of tune; but, by the everlasting jumping Jehoshaphat, when I get back here Thursday morning of next week, the world, the flesh, and the devil will not be allowed to draw me away from my real work again.' [1]

He had misgivings, however, as to his concept and method and was anxious to talk with Shaw. Would he not spend the week-end at Dublin? 'We could just talk and talk and talk, with nobody to interrupt us except the trees, and to them we could say, "Hah, hah," and also, "Ho, ho, you inanimate flora — you have just got to listen — and you can't talk back."'

That summer he wrote four chapters, and in the easiest way. Retiring to the woods with his stenographer, he would sit under the trees and dictate from his notes. It was a method soon to be abandoned for the pencil, but the first page of the completed biography is precisely as it was dictated in the Dublin woods. But when he had finished four or five chapters, he found himself less pleased with the product and began rewriting. Even the encouraging note from Shaw, who had read the manuscript, failed to satisfy him that what he had written could stand. 'I am glad you take this work so seriously,' wrote Shaw, 'and intend to give to every chapter ample and unsparing criticism and rewriting.' And Shaw put in a word of warning, lest the author, seeking dignity and solidity, become heavy. 'You need not be at any effort to make the book sprightly by any tricks of style or manner,' he wrote. 'The book has got movement in it, and since it is going to be largely the presentation of constitutional doctrine before you get through, it is not best that the early part should, in point of style, strive for what is supposed by some magazine editors to be popular and taking diction.... This does not mean that you are to try to put a heavy and dull style in the early chapters, but only that you are to carry your natural vivid but dignified style through every page of the book.' [2]

Such was the work of the first summer, to be interrupted again by the senatorial campaign of 1914, and then by the trip to the battle-fields of Europe. That European diversion was to be the salvation of the book. Something clicked in his mind. It was on the sea going and coming that the magnitude of his enterprise came to him in a flash. Everything would have to be done over; this subject justified and demanded something more than a pebble among others; it had to be a monument.

[1] Beveridge to Shaw, June 27, 1913.
[2] Shaw to Beveridge, Sept. 29, 1913.

II

By this time Beveridge had worked out a definite idea of the art and science of writing a biography. The stenographer was put aside; he took up the pencil. He had found, too, that the work of collecting material could not be delegated, but that even that drudgery must fall upon the author. His experiences with the early dictated chapters had convinced him that any such writing, to have permanence, must be gone over and over again. He had found that 'nothing is harder than to write a plain sentence; nothing so easy as easy rhetoric.' Had not Gibbon rewritten one chapter of the 'Decline and Fall of the Roman Empire' fifteen times? But this prospect did not appall him. 'If the product is clear and simple — a work of art — it is worth all the trouble,' he concluded.

And facts about the subject of the biography were not enough — 'indeed they are only the beginning.' Personal incidents, disassociated from the setting of the times and their relations with others, might mean literally nothing and could be misleading. He concluded that the biographer should 'take into equal consideration what others said and did, and everything that happened which influenced the hero or heroine.' Thus he reached the very foundation of his theory: 'That in reality the story of a public man, to mean anything, to be truthful, or even to be entertaining, is part of the epic of the nation into which that man's deeds and words were woven during the period in which he wrought.'

Here, then, was the task he had undertaken — to write the epic of the Nation in the period of Marshall's life. And this meant endless labor, the ascertainment of all the facts, little and big, concerning every character, great or small; and more than that — these facts must include the manner of living of the masses of the people. These facts, too, had to be susceptible to proof. He recognized that 'official records' have a basic value, but his personal experience in public life had taught him the necessity of going behind the 'records' for the whole truth. He knew the importance of private letters that so often throw a new and different light on official actions.[1] To create color and atmosphere, he sought all possible information about the houses and places associated with his subject. His correspondence of the first two years of his actual writing of the 'Marshall' teems with letters of this sort. Where did Marshall, Pinckney, and Gerry stop in Paris on the X.Y.Z. mission? Was the hotel still standing? What was its appearance? Did the Paris press discuss their mission?[2]

[1] On 'The Making of a Book,' *Saturday Evening Post*, Oct. 23, 1926.
[2] Letter to Vicomte Benoist d'Azy.

As he proceeded, the one-volume project was found impossible; and then, within a year, two volumes seemed scarcely adequate. Worthington Ford, whose advice to Beveridge was precious, wrote to warn him on the length. 'The subject is a great one and deserves full treatment,' he wrote. 'But the public no longer reads, and the libraries complain that fiction holds the center of the stage. So it may be judicious to limit it to two volumes if possible.'[1] But even this seemed hopeless now. It was clear that two volumes would be necessary to take Marshall to the Supreme Court; and then was to follow the history and dramatization of the important decisions. He would do the best he could.

III

Within a year nothing seemed so worth while to Beveridge as the 'Marshall.' The work absorbed him. More and more he became impatient with diversions. Politics had become ephemeral and unsatisfying. During his absence in Europe, Mrs. Beveridge, with his consent, had purchased the house at Beverly Farms on the North Shore of Massachusetts, which they together had admired some time before. At first he feared it would become 'a white elephant'; he soon came to love it because of its association with his literary work. Set back from the road, concealed by trees and shrubbery, it offered beauty and a kind of solitude. Back of the grounds stretched the primeval woods of Pride's Hill, and there was a walk to the beach in front. The builder of the house had included in his plans a small stone house, one room, one story, separated from the main house by a porte-cochère. With windows on two sides, and a fireplace for winter and autumn, it might have been designed as the study of a scholar or statesman. Instantly Beveridge pounced upon this as his own. It was to be his work den, nothing else. The table he had used while in the Senate, bearing the burnt marks of his cigarettes, occupied the center of the room; shelves for the books he would require were built along the walls, and there, through the remainder of his life, with intervals, he was to bend to literary tasks, while Wally, a collie devoted to him, lay curled contentedly at his feet. When the hot days came, he worked out in the open, under the trees, on an uncovered platform built at the beginning of the woods. While engaged on his two biographies, he followed a routine which fitted in with his work and gave him the exercise he needed.

Rising early, he had his breakfast on the terrace overlooking

[1] Ford to Beveridge, April 2, 1914.

the little lake on the grounds, and immediately afterward he set forth, with the collie at his heels, on a vigorous hour's walk into the woods. Returning, he shut himself off from interruptions in his study, and worked steadily until four o'clock, when invariably he had tea. Then again he went out for a walk. If he took the forest walk in the morning, he went to the sea in the afternoon, or the reverse. The end of the afternoon walk found him again in his study, where he worked until the dinner hour. After dinner it was his custom to spend an hour or more in the drawing-room with Mrs. Beveridge, but even then it was not an hour of utter relaxation. It was then that Mrs. Beveridge would read aloud to him the chapter he had written, and in this way he caught the rough passages not so easily detected by the eye alone. By nine-thirty or ten o'clock he would again seek his study, and there he wrote steadily until midnight; and sometimes, when in the fever of composition, he would continue until two o'clock in the morning. These were the precious hours — at night.

In the writing of his biographies he seldom was much more than one chapter ahead with his notes. These notes, literally thousands of them, were written with a pencil on small sheets of paper and fastened together with clips or rubber bands. When satisfied that he had exhausted all possible sources, he reëxamined the notes with the utmost care; and then he was ready for composition.

After that first summer at Dublin, he wrote with a pencil on rough paper and then turned the composition over to a stenographer, who sometimes, in his loyalty and zeal, worked on into the small hours of the morning. With the typed manuscript before him, Beveridge entered upon the rewriting and revision. Usually the chapters were much too long; sometimes the problem was to condense a manuscript long enough for three chapters into one, without slighting a single essential feature. That done, the revised work went to the stenographer again; and then, more revisions for proportion, or further condensation, or the amplification of some point.

While he worked, it was almost impossible, physically, to enter the study, for he had books, pamphlets, Government documents he was using spread all about him on the floor, apparently in chaos, but he knew precisely where to put his hand for anything he wished. The table was kept clear.

Finally, the chapter on which he had been working would be completed, and he was ready for criticism from someone presumably a specialist on the subject treated. During 1914 alone, some of the chapters written were read critically by Worthington

C. Ford, Lindsay Swift of the Boston Public Library, Edward Channing, J. Franklin Jameson, William E. Dodd, Albert Shaw, Charles A. Beard, H. J. Eckenrode of Richmond, and Archibald C. Coolidge of Harvard. His first experience with the historians was painful. Manuscript on which he had worked with meticulous care was returned with many marginal notes of corrections. It seemed incredible, absurd, and yet, on checking up, he found the critics were right. This had a pronounced effect upon his work thereafter, and upon his character. The old cock-sure days were gone forever. Never again was he to be intolerant of disagreement. And much as he had respected the quiet scholars of the colleges before, his respect expanded into profound admiration.[1]

IV

Later, he was to feel that the purchase of the place at Beverly Farms was providential. It made possible an easy contact with three scholars for whom he soon was to feel a deep affection. At the Boston Library, he found Lindsay Swift the best of friends, because the most ruthless of critics. Some of the scholars were tender of his sensibilities; Swift was not. Whenever he found flaws, he pointed them out without apology, and almost invariably he was right. But his was the ruthlessness of a scholar's friendship, and Beveridge came to love him for his uncompromising fidelity to facts. Through him, in large measure, he was to be indebted for the extraordinary privileges accorded him of taking some of the most precious documents and books to Beverly Farms.

Then there was Edward Channing, whose interpretation of American history was in such close harmony with Beveridge's own. Even their mutual dislike of Jefferson drew him to the historian he was frequently to describe as the ideal. A quiet, dignified gentleman of the New England school, the effervescent Mid-Westerner, bubbling with enthusiasm and high spirits, and bursting at times with boisterous merriment into the orderly serenity of Channing's office, must have been alarming at first. But the very intensity, sincerity, and tireless energy of the disciple came to appeal to Channing, who continued, through the life of Beveridge, to be one of his most trusted councillors. The Harvard Library, like that of Boston, was thrown wide open to the man from Beverly Farms, and everything there was done to facilitate his researches.

In Boston, too, he found Worthington C. Ford, to whom he

[1] Told the author by Beveridge in 1919.

became warmly attached. Through his connection with the Massachusetts Historical Society, Ford was able to place the treasures of that great library at his disposal. Believing him to be one of the soundest historical scholars in America, Beveridge came to lean more and more upon his judgment. To him he went frequently with his tangles, and seldom without relief. To him went the major part of the manuscript as it was completed, for his criticism; and while he was more tender with the sensibilities of the author than Swift, he was invaluable in advice. The charm of his personality, the soundness of his judgment, his quiet humor, soon converted a professional relationship into one of intimate personal friendship, and Beveridge never was happier than when he could relax for an evening in his company. 'What a perfectly charming time you afforded me last night,' he wrote Ford after such an evening. 'Not for many moons have I had such adequate hours. They furnish me with another golden memory. Also your companionship and that admirable dinner have restored my strength and given me a new grip on my work.' [1]

To make Beverly Farms all the more ideal for his work, it was not long until he had found a publisher in Houghton Mifflin Company, and in Ferris Greenslet and Roger Scaife he was so fortunate as to find congenial spirits and friends, as well as publishers. In and out of Boston, as he was, in his visits to the Library and Harvard, he frequently was dashing into Greenslet's office looking out on the Common, in high boyish spirits, demanding and receiving applause when he had unraveled a mystery, or encouragement when he found himself, as he frequently did, in a blind alley.

Thus Beverly Farms was providential, and once or twice he remained there throughout the winter; but usually, the early winter found him in the house on Washington Boulevard in Indianapolis, where he worked in the library looking out upon the trees. When Wally, the faithful collie, was not there to accompany him on his walks, which he never neglected even in inclement weather, the numerous dogs of the neighborhood soon learned of his habits, and when he appeared a numerous company had assembled to take the collie's place at his heels.

V

The correspondence, which was voluminous, throws a vivid light upon the meticulous care he took with all his facts. Many copies of the mimeographed chapters were made and sent to

[1] Beveridge to Ford, Jan. 22, 1916.

historians and scholars, and they returned with minor corrections as to facts; more frequently with questionings of interpretations; occasionally with suggestions regarding style. At one time he was appalled at the cumulative nature of his difficulties. 'The task is so great,' he wrote Shaffer after the first two volumes, 'that I do not dare think of what is before me or behind me; for if I do, I become so depressed that I feel like abandoning the remaining two volumes altogether, and, of course, I shall not do that.'[1] Four months later, he wrote that it would be good if he could 'slow down,' but doubted if he could. 'The subject is so big and perplexing, and the research is so extremely intensive and involved, that if it were possible for me to get discouraged, I sometimes feel that I would be.'[2]

This was written at the time he was planning the interpretative chapters on the great decisions and finding that the dramatization of them or the painting in of the background called for deep delving into the social, business, and political history of the times. But he was exaggerating when he wrote of 'discouragement' or 'abandonment.' Temperamentally he was incapable of turning back, and, though tired and sometimes harassed by problems, his enthusiasm did not wane. He had a genius for turning labor into a lark. 'You have no idea what this kind of work means, and you will not until you see the work itself,' he wrote Rothschild, as he was making the final revision of the first two chapters. 'But all the work you ever saw me do in the law or in getting up a speech— the long, hard, toilsome hours of investigation so as to get the facts correct — all that was nothing at all compared to this painstaking and brain-racking scholarly labor.'[3] In the anxiety to omit no essential detail in the story he was telling, and in the frequency of his revision, Ford thought there was a danger, and warned him. 'Being conscientious as you are,' he wrote, 'the danger lies in the direction of too much detail, and in giving detail one loses a swing which is apt to go with the first composition. As an old hand, I merely mention the caution not to polish too much — much energy is lost.'[4] He was referring particularly to the French Revolution chapter — on which Beveridge set much store.

Beveridge essentially was a Federalist, a Hamiltonian, and he shared the feeling of that school against the French Revolution. He was using Jefferson as a foil for Marshall throughout the biography, and the former was convinced that, with all its excesses, the upheaval which was leveling the walls of feudalism

[1] Beveridge to Shaffer, March 29, 1917.   [2] July 17, 1917.
[3] Beveridge to Rothschild, Dec. 9, 1915.
[4] Ford to Beveridge, March 22, 1916.

would work for the betterment of mankind. Marshall was to figure in the X.Y.Z. episode. Thus Beveridge had elaborated upon the Revolution to such an extent that Ford had urged him to prune and cut. 'Eliminate one third,' he wrote.[1] The author promised; but when the chapter came back from Channing with enthusiastic praise, Beveridge hastened the news to Ford, probably in the hope he would recant. 'I am puzzled, but I will stick to your suggestion,' he wrote. But Ford was not compliant in the real sense. 'Channing speaks with authority,' he wrote, 'and he always praises what gives him material for his college lectures. I should like to see Channing's face when you tell him this; but he is a competent critic, and you would be safer in following his view than mine, for he is more in touch with teachers of history and knows better what they want.'[2] Beveridge turned at once to the condensation.

But he was not receptive to suggestions concerning the condensation of the trial of Burr, which was to require four chapters. Albert Shaw had hailed it with enthusiasm as a 'marvelous narrative' and had begged him not 'to chop it down on any theory you may have as to the size of volumes.'[3] The trial fairly reeked with politics, with Jefferson in the background as the villain in the piece, and with Luther Martin, 'the Federalist bull dog,' in the center of the stage. At the time all the Federalists had rallied to the zealous defense of the man who had shot Hamilton one quiet summer morning, and proclaimed his innocence. Beveridge shared this view, and he fell with enthusiasm to the task of dramatizing the trial.

VI

Accepting suggestions freely as to method and facts, he was immovable in regard to his theories or interpretations; and this brought him into numerous conflicts with his friends among the historians in his treatment of Jefferson. Fundamentally a Hamiltonian, temperamentally a champion of a strongly centralized government, and a bit skeptical of democracy, he had not been unaffected by the days of his youth when the passions of the Civil War were flaming still. As a boy in the partisan household of a veteran of the war, he had heard that States' rights was a theory of secession; that the Virginia and Kentucky Resolutions were the inspiration of disunion; that Jefferson was the author of it all. In addition, was not Jefferson sympathetic toward the

[1] Ford to Beveridge, Jan. 10, 1916.
[2] Ford to Beveridge, Feb. 1, 1916.
[3] Shaw to Beveridge, April 30, 1918.

French Revolution, and was he not the champion and philosopher of democracy in America? And an enemy of Hamilton — the centralizationist? And of the Federal judiciary? Even the historians of the school of his youth had treated the author of the Declaration of Independence with scant respect, and none yet had gone into the record of the early Federal courts when partisan judges delivered bitter political harangues as charges to grand juries, to be published with much *éclat* in Federalist newspapers, and when the Chief Justices of the Supreme Court sat in Federalist Party caucuses.[1] Jefferson was an enemy of these courts, and Beveridge would not have tolerated them in his time. But these conditions, determining Jefferson's attitude, had been hidden by the historians for generations.

Thus Beveridge had a pronounced dislike of Jefferson. Five years before he began his 'Marshall,' in one of his debates with Bryan he had referred to Jefferson in France 'as wild with the doctrines of Rousseau as any Jacobin,'[2] though there was nothing of record to show that the Frenchman had exerted the least influence upon his thinking, and the recent publication of Jefferson's 'Commonplace Book' shows that Rousseau did not enter into Jefferson's reading. But it was the popular conception, carefully nourished by a school of historians, that Jefferson was a disciple of Rousseau. In beginning his work on Marshall, Beveridge had written his brother-in-law in Paris that he understood that while in France Jefferson was a member of 'the Jacobins.' This he was to find untrue and to discard. Even so, while he was scrupulously fair toward most of the Jeffersonians, his feeling against Jefferson was to creep into his narrative and to meet the challenge and remonstrance of some of the critics of his manuscript.

Soon after he began the work upon the biography, Senator Clapp had written to ask how he was going to satisfy his devotion to popular government with the anti-democratic views of Marshall and a disapproval of the philosophy of Jefferson. Beveridge replied gently, for he was fond of Clapp, that Jefferson had been too radical or advanced for his day; that the restraining hand of Marshall was necessary then; that with the progress of the years the philosophies of the two men had merged into that of America. But with the critics of his manuscript he sometimes went to battle. The correspondence indicates that Channing was in hearty accord with the treatment of Jefferson, and that was enough.

The first adverse criticism reached Beveridge from Professor William E. Dodd of the University of Chicago, a profound

[1] Jay and Ellsworth. [2] *Reader's Magazine*, April, 1907.

specialist on Jefferson, and Beveridge replied that 'the careful reading of his letters and study of his career has disillusioned me,' and that he was 'sometimes almost sorry' he had made the investigation which the biography of Marshall had made imperative.[1] A few months later, Gaillard Hunt, who had read the manuscript, wrote to remind him that 'Jefferson disliked Marshall as much as Marshall disliked Jefferson,' and that he 'would as soon expect them in political and mental friendship as to find Mr. Justice Brewer and Mr. Roosevelt agreeing with each other.'[2]

But it was Professor Dodd who persisted in his protest. 'My reading of history, especially the sources of history, compels me to believe and say that we are getting away from democracy every day, and you and your friends are pushing us a little faster than the conditions of American life might carry us; you do not seem to realize it.'[3] He thought that Beveridge hated Jefferson as had the Hamiltonians. 'Oh, yes, about Jefferson,' Beveridge replied, 'I don't hate Jefferson. But I am perfectly disgusted to find the sort of man he was personally' — referring to Jefferson's one notable misrepresentation on the assumption of the State debts.[4] 'Your ideal,' Dodd replied, 'is found in the past in men like Marshall; mine, unlike yours, is in the "lying" Jefferson. But when it comes to the matter of truth-telling, you will not find one of them who does not sin in the same sort of way. Marshall, Hamilton, and the rest prevaricated about innumerable things.'[5] But Beveridge was unmoved; and when Dr. J. Franklin Jameson warned him against the use of the word 'populace' he replied with a slashing attack on Jefferson as a 'reckless demagogue.'[6]

The next year gentle remonstrances continued to roll in from the scholars over the Jeffersonian phase. It was not so remarkable that Dr. Eckenrode of Virginia, who had been helpful on the chapters dealing with Marshall's Virginia life, should write that 'you are perhaps a little hard on Jefferson. Machine politician that he was, his point of view was, nevertheless, a thousand times loftier and juster than that of the narrow-minded Federalist leaders, and it was for the benefit of the world that he prevailed.'[7] But it was a bit disturbing to hear from Professor Max Farrand of Yale that 'I have a feeling that you inherit a Republican prejudice against Jefferson.'[8]

[1] Beveridge to Dodd, Feb. 4, 1915.　　[2] Hunt to Beveridge, Aug. 24, 1915.
[3] Dodd to Beveridge, Feb. 22, 1916.　　[4] Beveridge to Dodd, Feb. 28, 1916.
[5] Dodd to Beveridge, March 6, 1916.　　[6] Beveridge to Jameson, Feb. 12, 1916.
[7] Eckenrode to Beveridge, Aug. 27, 1918.　　[8] Farrand to Beveridge, Sept. 13, 1918.

Annoying though these criticisms were, they did not influence Beveridge in the slightest degree. His anti-Jeffersonian feeling was of the very fiber of his nature. It was not until long after the publication of the biography that he was to conclude he had been too severe in his strictures on the democratic philosopher. Only a short time before his death, in an after-dinner chat with Lawrence F. Abbott, editor of 'The Outlook,' the latter observed that later reading and a visit to the University of Virginia had modified his own opinion of Jefferson. 'I, too, have modified my views,' said Beveridge. 'If I were rewriting the "Life of Marshall" today, I should not be quite so positive in my criticisms of Jefferson.' [1]

This was the sole controversial point in the writing, though he had innumerable worries and perplexities. For a long while he was unable to justify to himself Marshall's action in the Fairfax land case, and he was greatly relieved when further investigations exonerated the Chief Justice to his satisfaction.

VII

It was generally known that he was working on a biography of Marshall, but few, beyond the small circles of historians and scholars who had read the manuscript, had any conception of the scope of the work. Something thoroughly readable was expected, something interesting, but would it be scholarly and throw a new or vivid light on history? Few of his warmest friends expected this. When, therefore, the first two volumes appeared in the early spring of 1917 and were found not only fascinating but profound, the general reaction astonished Beveridge himself. The reviewers uniformly were enthusiastic. Roosevelt reviewed it for 'The Outlook' with unstinted praise and wrote the author: 'I could not forbear pointing out that the biographer of Marshall had himself for twelve years been one of the great champions of Marshall's principles — with Lincoln's democracy.' [2] Men never before numbered among his friends joined in the general acclaim, and these included Lodge, from whom nothing had been expected. 'He has been big and generous enough to write me this letter,' Beveridge wrote Shaw. 'Lodge's letter, in addition to being one of praise, also makes some suggestions about Hamilton, Jefferson, and Burr.' [3] Statesmen, historians, lawyers, and laymen were equally delighted, and, as with Macaulay's History, fashion gave it a place on the library table and it entered the list of 'best-sellers.'

[1] *The Outlook*, May 11, 1927. He said as much to others.
[2] Roosevelt to Beveridge, July 31, 1917.   [3] Beveridge to Shaw, Feb. 8, 1917.

But after the exaltation of the triumph came the reaction of depression and fear lest the last two volumes should fail to realize the expectations awakened by the first. These presented a greater problem than the others, for these were to deal with judicial decisions and constitutional interpretation. Could he make these reasonably readable to the layman? And how? He buckled down to the problem with grim determination and found a way. Behind every court decision was a controversy; in every controversy there was a human drama. He would dramatize the story of the issue. Before the decisions of the court was the argument, and he would humanize the court proceedings with portraits of the great lawyers who appeared. Behind some of the Marshall decisions, such as in the trial of Burr, there was no dearth of action, picturesque and dramatic; he would make the most of these. But this was a challenge, not alone to the historian but to the artist. It would be no easy task. The next two years were to find him chained more than ever to his desk, working longer into the night. Toward the close he felt the strain of the confinement. The dispatch of the last of the corrected proof-sheets to the publisher left him in a state of nervous exhaustion and depression.

But a veritable inundation of praise poured in upon him and revived him. Everywhere the biography was proclaimed one of the classics of the language, one of the four or five greatest biographies in the English language. He had written something that would live — and that was enough.

Nothing delighted him more than the commendation of two men — Justice Oliver Wendell Holmes and Lord Haldane of England. Many times during the tortuous days of the writing, he had strolled over to the near-by home of the venerable American jurist at Beverly Farms and discussed his problems with Holmes, and the latter had seen portions of the manuscript. From Washington, Holmes wrote:

Supreme Court of the United States
Washington, D.C., Feb. 14, 1920

Dear Beveridge:

This moment sees the conclusion of reading your four volumes, which once begun in the leisure of recess, I have devoured. They seem to me to deserve every praise, even more than I foresaw from the fragments that I had read. I admire the work for the most opposite virtues — for the strenuous labor of pursuing every fact to the sources — for the capacity to tell a never flagging tale in such a way that one's interest is always on the alert — for the judgment that comes from your knowledge of, and participation in politics, and from the impartiality hardly to be expected from a man of strong beliefs upon political subjects. I feel as if I had gained an understanding of the... antecedents of Marshall's opinions, of the whole history of the times, such as I had never had before, and that it would have been my duty to read the book as a judge of the court, even if it had not been my delight as a student and a friend. Also you have kept it mighty human.

Sincerely yours

O. W. HOLMES

All the more gratifying because unexpected was the letter from Viscount Haldane, the English statesman and philosopher, to whom he was not known personally, expressive of the 'pleasure and profit' he had derived from reading the 'Marshall':

It is not only the light you have thrown for me on the legal aspects of the Constitution of your country that has appealed to me. It is the picture which is embodied in your narrative of a great statesman, a man, who, as a judge, did a piece of work unexampled in the history of the world in putting flesh onto the bones of a written Constitution. How he developed that Constitution into what was essential for the growth of a very great nation, you have made appear before us. In your hands, the task of Marshall, as well as his solution, grows as a living growth. The book is one which should instruct the civilized world about a problem which raises its head everywhere, and which, in the case of the United States, required for its solution a new and great combination of qualities in Marshall. His was a genius of a type as extraordinary as it was fresh.[1]

Acclaimed by statesmen, historians, and critics, the book made an unequaled appeal to lawyers, and invitations poured in on the author from their organizations, local, State, and national, and for the rest of his life he was to make many speeches on Marshall and the Constitution; to be welcomed whole-heartedly into the fraternity of historians; to receive the Pulitzer Prize for the best biography of the year, and that of the Roosevelt Foundation for the book best interpreting the American spirit; and to be invited into the Academy of Arts and Sciences.

He had literally lost himself in the herculean labor of his task; and losing himself thus, he had found himself.

VIII

After the success of the 'Marshall,' Beveridge had no thought of laying down his pen. He had found a work he loved that brought rewards without bitterness or regrets. The moment he completed his task, he was deluged with suggestions for another biography, and some of his friends sought to interest him in a particular subject. For a long time he had wanted to write a definitive biography of the younger Pitt, whom he resembled in so many ways, and he had numerous talks with Ford about it, but he finally felt that his inability to go into the French sources

[1] Haldane to Beveridge, July 18, 1920.

in the original would be a serious handicap and it meant living in England for some years. The abandonment of this project disappointed Ford, who wrote: 'You say you are growing cold on the Pitt proposition. I am sorry for that.... The enormous power of Pitt and his failure to accomplish his ends would make a story dramatic in the extreme, but you could not tell it on the scale of Marshall because that would require more than a dozen volumes, and life grows shorter every year.' [1] He then sought to interest Beveridge in a life of Roger B. Taney, the successor of Marshall, and in this there were co-conspirators. Eight months after Ford urged it, Beveridge had a note from Felix Frankfurter:

Mr. Justice Brandeis and I talked about you and your 'Marshall' the other day, and he made a suggestion that I think you'll like to hear. He said your next piece of work seemed clearly cut out for you — Taney. There is the chance to continue the great contribution to the history of the country and Constitution, and the more so because Taney's régime, almost as long as Marshall's, is practically a dark chapter of American history. [2]

This interested Beveridge, who replied:

I am much impressed by the suggestion of Justice Brandeis. I should like to talk with you and with him about it.... It occurs to me that Taney wouldn't do as a companion piece of the 'Marshall.' While the period was of critical importance, and while the story of each opinion rendered by Taney and of the decisions of the Supreme Court during those years is vivid and entertaining, still the treatment of the subject, as a whole, does not admit of what some call 'movement and color' and 'human interest' stuff, you know. All the time I was writing 'Marshall' there was in the back of my head the idea that the work ought to be continued, but built up around a character which, in itself, is attractive. Up to this time it seems to me that there was only one such personage — Abraham Lincoln, of course. [3]

There was another reason, however — Beveridge did not belong to the political school of Taney, and it was not until he entered upon his studies for the biography of Lincoln that he was to rid himself of the prejudices against the former Chief Justice. His mind was fixed on Lincoln — the Lincoln of his youthful conception, and he had so notified Greenslet some months before. 'I do find an amazing interest in Lincoln,' he wrote. 'So I have made up my mind to do the Lincoln, and on exactly the same scale, on the same plan, and by the same method that I did the "Marshall."' [4]

[1] Ford to Beveridge, Nov. 19, 1920.
[2] Frankfurter to Beveridge, July 1, 1921.
[3] Beveridge to Frankfurter, July 11, 1921.
[4] Beveridge to Greenslet, Nov. 30, 1920.

CHAPTER II

'LINCOLN': A VOYAGE OF DISCOVERY

I

As soon as the polls closed on his defeat in 1922, Beveridge turned with zest to the biography of Lincoln. He had served his apprenticeship in historical scholarship in the writing of the 'Marshall,' and had passed through the experimental stage in method. This he had worked out to his definite satisfaction — delving, writing, rewriting, verifying, and submitting the rough draft to the most competent scholarship he could find.

The new task he had assigned himself seemed simple. He proposed to continue, in the biography of Lincoln, the interpretation of the development of American nationalism, begun in the 'Marshall.' Speedily, he had no doubt, he would dispose of the earlier life of his subject and plunge into the major political controversies that were to culminate in the War of the States. For generations historians, apparently, had exhausted all possible sources in the study of Lincoln's early life. Their findings had entered into the folklore of the people. No one doubted the truth of any of them. Thus, in a general way, when Beveridge sat down in his house in Indianapolis to the new biography, he knew what he would find in the studies he would make.

Of course, he would find that as a child Lincoln had a burning hatred of slavery, and a determination, if the opportunity should come, to 'hit it and hit it hard.' He had no thought of lingering long on the career in the Illinois Legislature, since none of the biographers or historians had found it worth more than a few inconsequential lines or paragraphs. The congressional career would require but little research, for nothing distinguished it aside from Lincoln's opposition to the Mexican War, which had been arranged by the slave power to extend its domain. The fighting in Kansas interpreted itself — the ruffians of slavery had pushed in with guns and liquor to overcome the champions of freedom, backed by the Abolitionists, to control the State for slavery. The Missouri Compromise and Douglas — he had always known about these; and about how Douglas, an unscrupulous politician, had sold himself to slavery for the Presidency. And the Dred Scott decision and the infamy of Taney and the 'wicked conspiracy' were all part of his boyhood knowledge. He had known all these things through all his life; had heard about them from his father and from the schools, and when men like John A. Logan spoke; read about them in the histories and biographies; and talked about them sometimes on the platform and in the Senate.

But he would take nothing for granted, would depend on no secondary sources, would go back to the originals, and uncover new information if possible. It would be an onerous but a pleasing task, for, as in the writing of the 'Marshall,' he would be following the direction of his inclination and his preconception.

But at the very beginning he was to encounter obstacles in his search for the whole truth. Eager to examine the Lincoln manuscript in possession of Robert T. Lincoln, the emancipator's son, he sent his request to the latter, then old, feeble, and suffering with a nervous disorder. There was no reply. Assuming the letter had miscarried, he wrote again and sent it by special delivery, and this brought a petulant refusal. This distressed him, while arousing his curiosity. He wrote Ford that he was 'willing to use dynamite, or chloroform, soothing syrup, or quinine, cocaine, or T.N.T. to get hold of that manuscript.' [1]

It was while he was annoyed by this first rebuff that he was shocked by another. He had counted heavily on the manuscript diary of Senator Orville H. Browning for intimate details and the atmosphere of the times, and, while it was placed at his disposal, it was 'under certain restrictions' as to the references to Mrs. Lincoln. 'Now doesn't that beat the devil!' he wrote Ford. 'I am wondering if something like that is not in the back of Robert Lincoln's head. Sometimes I feel like dropping the whole business.' [2]

Meanwhile the Lincoln papers had been sent to the Congressional Library with the stipulation that they were not to be accessible to historians for twenty years. Robert Lincoln had justified his act to Beveridge on the ground that his father might have reflected on the fathers of some of the son's friends. Beveridge appealed to Nicholas Murray Butler,[3] who, in turn, appealed to Lincoln, but without success. The latter was 'obdurate.' [4] Undiscouraged still, the biographer now sought the aid of Henry White, the diplomat, and an intimate friend of the Lincolns, but White found, on calling, that Lincoln was in such a nervous condition that he did not mention the papers; and when he called a little later, Lincoln had gone to his summer home at Manchester, Vermont.[5] The pursuit of these papers had continued for more than a year when Beveridge gave up the chase.

---

[1] Beveridge to Ford, Jan. 30, 1923.   [2] Feb. 14, 1923.
[3] Beveridge to Nicholas Murray Butler, April 19, 1924.
[4] Butler to Beveridge, April 25, 1924.
[5] Henry White to Beveridge, May 15, 18, 1924.

In the mean time he had been poring with increasing amazement over the Herndon-Weik Lincoln manuscripts, the most valuable in existence, and until then inaccessible to students of Lincoln's life. He had it at his home, along with important newspaper data sent him by the University of Illinois, and was 'constantly alarmed lest something should happen to it.' [1]

II

For years Beveridge had accepted the popular theory that William H. Herndon, partner, political adviser, and Lincoln's most intimate friend and associate, was an unreliable biographer, because of the storm of abuse that descended upon him after the publication of his famous biography. It had broken in upon the process of canonization and deification and aroused the wrath of the myth-makers and the politicians. But Beveridge had talked with his friend Jesse Weik, who had collaborated with Herndon on the biography, had lived with him and known him intimately for years, and had made an exhaustive study of his character and credibility. He knew the Herndon biography had been the basis of most of the Lincoln studies that had followed, with the biographers accepting his credibility where the facts fitted in with their purpose and rejecting it otherwise. In the end, Beveridge was to conclude him the most dependable of sources as to facts. 'About Herndon,' he wrote, 'do not get wrong about that old man. I have gone into his credibility as if I were a lawyer trying a murder case. There is absolutely no doubt whatever about his entire truthfulness and trustworthiness generally. When Herndon states a fact as a fact, you can depend upon it. It is only when he gets to analyzing the souls of others... that he is not to be relied upon.' [2]

But the Herndon manuscripts disturbed him, and some of the newspaper data astonished and distressed him; he was facing facts that did not fit in with the preconceived theories of a lifetime.

That spring he went to Springfield and wrote Ford that he had made a hasty journey through the 'Lincoln and Douglas country in a sort of preliminary survey,' while suffering tortures from an ulcerated tooth.[3] The tooth sent him to the hospital and interrupted his summer's work.

But six months of research had convinced him there was a mythical and a real Lincoln. 'I become more and more puzzled

[1] Beveridge to Ford, May 23, 1923.
[2] Beveridge to Professor Frank H. Hodder, Dec. 15, 1925.
[3] Beveridge to Ford, May 21, 1923.

about Lincoln,' he wrote Ford. 'Sometimes I feel like throwing it up altogether. I am doubtful whether the Mid-Victorians will permit any truthful and scholarly life of Lincoln to be written.'[1]

With the summer he moved to Beverly Farms, where he continued his work until in August when he went to Switzerland for a rest, taking his family with him. He had not written a line. He had read the biographies, including that of Nicolay and Hay, which did not impress him; the Herndon manuscripts, the newspaper data from the University of Illinois; and he wrote Channing that he was ashamed of the slight progress made, since he had taken no more than 'five thousand notes, all put together.' He had made contacts with 'a lot of manuscripts, which nobody seems to have gone over' — such as the David Davis papers and the Browning diary. But he had gone far enough to reach the definite conclusion he wrote Channing: 'You are dead right when you say that the Lincoln of that time could not by any possibility have been the father of the Lincoln of 1862. I have not yet gone over the data sufficiently to form a sound judgment, or any judgment at all; but it is already fairly clear that the Lincoln of youth, early and middle manhood showed few signs of the Lincoln of the second inaugural.'[2] It was at this time he wrote Greenslet he would not accept any of numerous invitations to speak on Lincoln, since he did not positively know what he thought.

III

Meanwhile, from the ivory tower he was watching political developments with curiosity and some misgivings. In the summer Frank Munsey, of the 'New York Sun,' had sent him an article, as yet unpublished, reflecting gravely upon a member of the Harding Cabinet who later was to involve the Administration in scandal. 'From the political point of view,' he wrote Munsey, 'I am frankly sorry that such a state of things exists; and strictly from the political point of view would rather not see the article published. But here again, you as a journalist and a Republican, and I as a citizen and a Republican, are up against the condition that constantly recurs. If those in our party who are in authority so act shall journals to which the public looks for information and guidance suppress the facts... or shall the facts be told?'[3]

Along with the premonitory rumblings of approaching scandal,

[1] Beveridge to Ford, May 23, 1923.
[2] Beveridge to Channing, Dec. 19, 1923.
[3] Beveridge to Munsey, June 27, 1923.

he was distressed by Harding's St. Louis speech, made on his Western journey, on the World Court, which he thought 'a fatal blunder.' 'If still in favor of the Court, he should have stood by his guns; if convinced of his mistake, he should have dropped it; instead, he concedes the validity of the objections and proposes as a substitute the incredible proposition of a self-perpetuating tribunal.'

Even in the ivory tower, remote from the hurly-burly of politics, Beveridge could not get beyond the voice of the siren. 'Peering into the deep mists and mysteries of politics,' wrote Munsey from Paris, 'I see a figure looming large. The features and figure are not quite clear, but I ask myself, are they not like my friend Beveridge? It may be all fancy. It may be something else.' [1]

But he had no illusions, and he turned grimly and with zest to the 'Lincoln' in 1924.

IV

Throughout that year, in the midst of the drudgery of reading old manuscripts, poring over the yellow pages of old newspapers and legislative records, and writing, he was engaged in a correspondence of appalling magnitude on every phase of Lincoln's life. Temperamentally incapable of ignoring any clue, he frequently found at the end of a voluminous correspondence that the hint was worthless. At the same time he was in constant communication with numerous historical specialists on all the major matters of Lincoln's day. Interest in the public in his work burdened him with innumerable Lincoln stories that turned out to be pure fabrications, but he investigated everything regardless of its source.

In February he was more than ever puzzled by his discoveries about the early Lincoln. 'The cold fact is,' he wrote Greenslet, 'that not one faint glimmer appears in his whole life, at least before his Cooper Union speech, which so much as suggests the radiance of the last two years.' [2] All this discouraged and distressed him and he took his troubles to Ford. 'How in the world am I going to be able to tell the truth without raising a storm from the Mid-Victorians, I do not yet know. But of course scholarship cannot compromise with falsehood; and although I am not a scholar, I have got from you and from others, but especially from you, what I hope and believe is the spirit of scholarship. My soul revolts against the practice of

[1] Munsey to Beveridge, Aug. 21, 1923.
[2] Beveridge to Greenslet, Feb. 2, 1924.

suppressing vital facts or distorting them in order to placate unfounded sentiment or to advance some political cause.'[1]

When, in April, he was studying his notes preliminary to a visit to Kentucky, southern Indiana, and Illinois, he had concluded that a scientific biography of Lincoln had not been written at all, and the obstacles before him seemed to brush the sky. 'I am blue about it,' he wrote Mrs. Beveridge ' — and the whole job. It's a bad mess. I feel like chucking it sometimes.'[2] And again: 'It's a big job — infinitely harder than the "Marshall." I must step lively if I do it before I bump off.'[3] Two months before, he had retraced his steps over the same ground because, in Kentucky, 'one or two matters turned up which interest and puzzle me.' He wrote Ford that 'the farther I go into this morass, the deeper and more confused it appears to me. I sometimes almost get blue, and if it were in me to get discouraged I am afraid that I should have fits of melancholia nearly as bad as those which Lincoln enjoyed — for he did seem to enjoy his sadness.'[4] He needed some one to 'buck him up.' Dr. Jameson had done it for him in Washington the week before — but couldn't Ford help?

But just as he was about to begin the trip, the grippe 'struck him like a load of brick,' and his physician held him to his bed. But not for long would he be held a prisoner, he wrote Ford. 'I am going, anyway, even if it causes my early demise.'[5]

Thus the original plan to hurry through the pre-political phase of Lincoln's life went glimmering with the discovery that fancy had so frequently taken the place of fact, and Channing began to warn him about going too minutely into the earlier years. 'Lincoln needs someone schooled in affairs and the wiles of politicians to penetrate under his mask and under their masks and tell the truth,' he wrote. 'You are the man to do it, and if I can hang on to your starboard or larboard coat-tail and steer you away from doing some awful thing, you will produce a book that will be the "Life" of Abraham Lincoln for half a century.'[6] When Beveridge insisted on the necessity of going into Lincoln's earlier career, Channing suggested that he write the last part first, and then go back. 'I simply cannot do the end of my task before I do the beginning,' Beveridge replied. 'The neglected part which I know I shall have to do later would be on my mind all the time, nagging and worrying me.'[7]

He had become obsessed with the work, and his letters to Mrs.

[1] Beveridge to Ford, Feb. 25, 1924.   [2] April 19, 1924.
[3] April 18, 1924.   [4] Beveridge to Ford, Feb. 14, 1924.
[5] May 25, 1924.   [6] Channing to Beveridge, June 9, 1924.
[7] Beveridge to Channing, July 26, 1924.

Beveridge from the Cleveland Convention touched more on the book than on the convention. With the certainty of another interruption in the autumn for campaign speeches, he turned grimly to the writing in the open-air study under the trees at Beverly Farms. But in August he needed a change, and with Mrs. Beveridge and two guides he made the Allagash trip from Moosehead Lake to Fort Kent on the St. John's River. Just before he entered the woods he received a telegram announcing the death of Rothschild in Indianapolis. The trip was hard, with some excitement, as when they were overtaken by a great windstorm, and he overtaxed himself. Returning to Beverly Farms, he worked day and night until forced to take the platform for the party. But by early October he had finished the first three chapters in the rough.

Sending the manuscript to Ford, he hoped he would 'be able to find the development of personal character and the appearance of the *motif* of the book in the third chapter,' which introduced the Webster-Hayne Debate and the Nullification Movement.[1] To Professor Theodore Pease, of the University of Illinois, he explained that he purposely had 'overannotated' these three chapters because 'this is the controverted period,' and he wished 'at the very beginning to inspire the reader with confidence in the more important chapters to follow.' [2]

With these chapters making the rounds of the 'historical sharks' for criticism, Beveridge plunged grimly into the research for the succeeding chapters, for he wrote as he completed his study for each part. December found him in Springfield, going over the Springfield papers 'with a fine-tooth comb,' and concluding that biographers had spared themselves this task. 'I had not been at work a single day,' he wrote Ford, 'until it was plain to me that nobody else had made a careful and scientific search through the dim columns of those thousands of musty old pages. What a task it is! What drudgery! Still it has to be done, of course. I am finding out things all the time.' [3]

V

He was finding out many things by subjecting himself to an onerous duty that every other historian and biographer had ignored, by reading through the eight huge volumes of the Journal of the Illinois Legislature covering the period of Lincoln's membership. It seemed incredible that the long legislative

[1] Beveridge to Ford, Oct. 21, 1924.
[2] Beveridge to Pease, Oct. 16, 1924.
[3] Beveridge to Ford, Dec. 24, 1924.

record of Lincoln had been passed by without a glance. And yet, finding the Journal printed in small type, with dim ink, on rough paper, and with an index to but two of the eight volumes, Beveridge thought he understood. With the aid of a magnifying-glass, he turned thousands of pages, 'finding out things' that were a complete refutation of things he had always heard and believed. Before the unimpeachable testimony of the record the accepted theory that Lincoln always had been a foe of slavery was definitively discredited. In these neglected yellow pages it appeared that he had voted against the abolitionists and at no time disclosed a marked antipathy to slavery. The Lincoln of prohibition suffered a similar fate. 'The facts are,' Beveridge wrote Channing, 'that in the Legislature he several times voted against prohibition amendments in the liquor law, and every time against putting more teeth in liquor legislation.'[1] Astonished as he was by these discoveries, he was even distressed by his inability to find in the member of the Legislature the most remote resemblance to the Lincoln he had imagined all his life. The Lincoln of these years seemed shifty, with no other definite purpose than to pursue a safe and comfortable course. 'I wish to the Lord he could have gone straight-forward about something or other,' he wrote despairingly to Ford. 'Of all uncertain, halting and hesitating conduct, his takes the prize.'[2] Being honest, Beveridge could do no other than set down what he found, but more and more he wished he had not undertaken the work, and now and then he was tempted to abandon it. 'I am blue as blue about my Lincoln,' he wrote his wife. 'Work so huge and complicated! It really never has been done.... So I'm disgusted and tired and blue and I'd seize any excuse to drop Lincoln — politics or anything. I am pouring out my life and more than my money in it.'[3] The gloom persisted, and a few days later he wrote at greater length: 'It may be because of my intensive ten months' toil, but I am so discouraged and blue that I feel that I cannot go on with the Lincoln. At each step through the jungle I have expected that the next step would bring me into the open, but instead the thicket only becomes more dense. Also I am convinced that the public, and scholarship also, does not want minutiæ — only the high spots; and to me the high spots are not intelligible without the facts that lead up to them. The task is prodigious and utterly confusing, and I am very tired. So why keep on?'[4]

[1] Beveridge to Channing, May 19, 1926.
[2] Beveridge to Ford, Jan. 28, 1925.
[3] April 3, 1925.
[4] Beveridge to Mrs. Beveridge, April 15, 1925.

But just then a letter from Professor Charles A. Beard, who had read the manuscript on Lincoln in the Legislature, buoyed him up. Beard had thought there was too much detail at first, but he had taken a walk in Central Park to think it over and it came to him 'in a flash' that Beveridge had 'done a revolutionary piece of historical writing, the kind of masterly analysis by detail of fact which the great novelist attempts.' Indeed, Beveridge had 'revealed the early Lincoln in a blinding light.' [1]

He had not discontinued work in the meantime, but now he pressed forward with renewed zest and confidence. But he had scarcely entered upon the congressional career of Lincoln and the Mexican War when he found more of the cherished illusions of his youth going. It was at this stage that he began to resent the methods of the abolitionists. 'I am now in the Mexican War and the confusion of it makes me a little crazier if possible,' he wrote Channing. 'I was amazed at the clearness, simplicity, and courage of your treatment of the ancient Whig-Abolitionist bunc about the powerful and superhumanly foresighted slave power compelling us to go to war against a poor little weak country in order to extend the domain of human bondage. Wow! What stuff! And to think that I and most other people have believed it!' [2] Again he wrote the truth as a meticulous investigation revealed it; and when one of the historians suggested he had made too strong a defense of the war, Beveridge replied, stoutly defending his position: 'So just tell me, old man, wherein our diplomacy in Mexico was so confoundedly thievish. I have not been able to find it myself, notwithstanding the fact... that I had that general notion at first. On the contrary, it seems to me that we were incredibly slow in asserting our rights.' [3] Again he had been puzzled by Lincoln's conduct — his war speech at the beginning in Springfield; his failure to utter a word against it in his congressional campaign, leaving the people to believe he approved it; and then, in Washington, his attack upon it, and on Polk. In submitting the congressional chapter to Channing, Beveridge set forth his own explanation of the mystery:

It is as plain as plain to me that nine tenths of the Whig assault on Polk's Administration was party politics. I have seen the same thing myself, and possibly I have taken part in such performances. The fact that Lincoln's paper, the Sangamon Journal, attacked Polk for his leniency in Mexico; that Lincoln said nothing upon the subject; that he did not even open his mouth about Texas except to write that amazing letter to the two 'liberty men' in Illinois; that not until he

[1] Beard to Beveridge, April 23, 1925.
[2] Beveridge to Channing, May 19, 1925.
[3] Beveridge to Beard, Aug. 19, 1925.

met the big National Whig leaders in Washington did he show any opposition whatever to the Mexican War, and that he then fell in line with the Whig program — all these facts fit in perfectly with what has happened hundreds of times. I have seen it myself many times.

Neither is it a mystery to me that Lincoln fell in with Stephens, Toombs, Preston, and other Southern Whigs who were as much against the Mexican War as John Quincy Adams himself. Also the scheme to beat the Democrats by nominating Taylor, and Lincoln's ardent support of that scheme, is exactly what one might expect from such a politician as he was.... I know men today who do exactly the same thing.[1]

All this was contrary to everything he had been taught, at home, in the schools, in the histories, and he found no real pleasure in the recording of the truth as he found it.

VI

As he proceeded into the political phase, he found Stephen A. Douglas, the horned devil of his youth, looming larger and larger in intellectual and moral stature, and he was horrified and disgusted with the flagrant misrepresentations of the politicians and partisan historians. Aside from the resentment of the injustice, there were reasons for his sympathy in the similarity of Douglas's career to his own. Both were orators; both fighters; both chairman of the Senate Committee on Territories and, as such, engaged in the making of States; both had fought bitter senatorial contests without the sympathy of a President of their own party; and both had suffered defeat through the treachery of their own people.

The correspondence of the 'Lincoln' years is thickly sprinkled with enthusiastic praise of the Little Giant. When Channing suggested that Douglas was a great man,[2] Beveridge replied: 'Douglas! You bet Douglas was a great man, and he grows bigger all the time.... It becomes clearer and clearer to me... that the literary Lincolnites had almost a hijacker conspiracy against Douglas — and against any other man of power who for any cause happened to run counter to their hero; and especially is this true of Douglas.'[3]

It was later, after reading Douglas's famous and misrepresented Chicago speech of November 9, 1854, that he again wrote Channing: 'What an incredible quantity of "bunc" has been written about Douglas! How shamefully he has been

[1] Beveridge to Channing, Sept. 16, 1925.
[2] Channing to Beveridge, May 19, 1925.
[3] Beveridge to Channing, May 21, 1925.

written down — and written down in order to write Lincoln up. That is neither history nor art. Against all the teachings of my boyhood and young manhood, and in opposition to every prejudice, my admiration for Douglas grows all the time — and it grows solely from what he said and did.[1]

As he penetrated deeper and deeper through the thickets of propaganda in the search for truth, he returned time and again to the topic in his correspondence with the scholars. 'How Douglas does loom up!' he wrote Channing. 'And what rotten treatment he has had at the hands of so-called "historians"! I am beginning to think that, after all, writers of history in former, and even in recent years are not above being propagandists.'[2]

VII

All through the summer of 1925, without a rest, he was bending over his desk at Beverly Farms, writing, rewriting, day and night, to finish the first volume. Occasionally the replenishment of his notes called him away, but only to work. In the spring he spent some time in Chicago going over 'a large collection of letters written from the South during the four or five years preceding the outbreak of the Civil War,'[3] and at Springfield giving wearisome but fruitful hours to the newspaper files from 1848. All the while the earlier chapters were returning with comments from the scholars, and some were amazed to find Herndon's story of Lincoln's fits of melancholia and his strange action on the day first set for his wedding substantiated by the facts. 'I do not know,' wrote one, 'whether it has occurred to you to call the psychologists and psychiatrists into consultation, but it seems to me they would be more useful advisers than historians.'[4] Within two weeks another made the same suggestion,[5] and Beveridge sent the manuscript to his friend Dr. Morton Prince for an opinion.[6]

In the early autumn he was working on the last two chapters of the first volume with all the more zest because Channing had been clamoring for more about Lincoln the man. With boyish satisfaction, Beveridge sent these chapters to Channing at Cotuit, Massachusetts — 'since you are down there looking at the deep blue sea, the monarch of all you survey, and a pirate captain at heart, and with nothing at all to do.' More about

---

[1] Beveridge to Channing, Feb. 9, 1925.   [2] April 18, 1925.
[3] Beveridge to Channing, March 30, 1925.   [4] S. E. Morison, June 15, 1925.
[5] Ellery Sedgwick, *Atlantic Monthly*, July 8, 1925.
[6] See Beveridge's *Abraham Lincoln*, I, 315, footnote.

Lincoln, did he want? 'Huh! If you glance through these pages, I think you will get your belly full of him.' [1]

And so the first volume was finished in the early winter and he turned to the next encouraged by the generous praise of Ford, who pronounced the first 'a real achievement,' with Lincoln 'pictured as never before.' 'It is a wonderful story,' wrote Ford — 'drab, disgusting at times, hopeless of any real good, and convincing; but so given as to picture the growth of character and to leave us eager to see how this man will deal with the responsibilities laid upon him.' [2]

Soon he was deep in the first chapter of the second volume and 'learning things' all the while.

VIII

In this first chapter, 'Seeds of War,' he planned to review the controversy on slavery, putting all prejudices aside and setting forth the case of both sides impartially. He had scarcely skimmed the surface before he found that, historically, the period had been treated with exaggerations and significant suppressions. He wanted to know what sort of abolition pamphlets had been sent into the South; and, if the South had resorted to pamphleteering, he wanted to know what it had said. Historians generally had ignored the Southern answers, and soon Beveridge was to find that they had considerately censored a goodly portion of the abolitionist attacks. Scouring the libraries of the country, he soon was in possession of this literature on both sides. He read the abolitionist pamphlets first, and was unutterably shocked at the nature of some of it, especially with the foulness of the attacks, not only on the morals of Southern men, but of Southern women. It was while he was in the midst of the reading of this 'literature' that he said to me, with intense feeling: 'If I had lived in the South and had a wife, a mother, sister, or sweetheart, and anyone had sent such an infamous thing to me, I would have felt like taking the first train North, shooting the wretch, and taking the consequences.'

As he studied these abolitionist expressions and found them interspersed with contemptuous flings at the Constitution and the Union, his amazement grew. He had heard nothing of this before; it had not been told him in his boyhood or taught him in the schools; and he had not read it in the histories. And there it was — in black and white — accessible to anyone in search of truth.

[1] Beveridge to Channing, June 29, 1926.
[2] Ford to Beveridge, Dec. 6, 1925.

He turned to the Southern pamphlets, which had been generally ignored, and found them pitched upon a more argumentative and higher plane, and less abusive. He noted that almost all of them concentrated their fire upon the abolitionists; and he concluded that the South, interpreting the bitter abolitionist attacks as expressive of the opinion of the North, began to think of separation in self-defense and self-respect. Why had the historians given but one side? He wondered.

In doubt whether he should even refer to some of the foulest reflections on Southern people, because so loathsome, he wrote Jacob M. Dickinson, Secretary of War under Taft, and a Southern man, for advice. He replied that a 'solemn duty' had thus been 'imposed' upon him, but that his 'deliberate opinion' was they 'should not be omitted.'[1] Beveridge thereupon included them, but later struck them out.

It was while writing the 'Seeds of War' that he wrote Ford of his utter impatience with the abolitionist propaganda. 'Those furious maniacs who did not hesitate to lie if they could make their point, and whose stock in trade was personal abuse... carried the red flag; and as they made progress, the South began to associate their doctrines with the Northern people.'[2] Just before, he had written Channing that he was in the midst of this chapter and that it was 'the worst yet.' Promising to tell him of his troubles when he saw him, he continued: 'I warn you that you will be in the presence of a desperate, dangerous, and not altogether sane person. So watch your step.'[3]

The wealth of untouched or rejected material and its significance led him to write on and on, and the work of revision and condensation became a problem.

'I have condensed and condensed, and cut and cut until I can do no more,' he wrote Ford.[4] But, putting into it the hardest work of his life, he was almost disheartened when Ford returned the manuscript with the comment that there was too much detail. Beveridge replied with an explanation of his motive:

I attempted to show what was in the back of the heads of the Southern men and women that made them take the desperate and well-nigh hopeless hazard of leaving the Union and going to war to maintain an independent government of their own. What slavery actually was — the essence or even the externals of it — has nothing whatever to do with my plan.

As I have told you many times, it has been very hard for me to

[1] Dickinson to Beveridge, Jan. 19, 1926.
[2] Beveridge to Ford, Dec. 19, 1925.
[3] Beveridge to Channing, Oct. 15, 1925.
[4] Beveridge to Ford, Jan. 14, 1926.

write this chapter, because of the circumstances of my birth and up-bringing. I was born when the Civil War was reaching its red climax; and my father and brothers were all officers in the Union Army. From earliest infancy I was taught that 'Uncle Tom's Cabin' and the speeches of Wendell Phillips, Sumner, and others like them, were the real truth.

As a result, I have somewhat to this day the notion, which I find on examination to have been absurd and wickedly false, that Mrs. Stowe drew a faithful picture of Southern society and conditions. I looked at Charleston, for instance, as a mosquito-bitten, filthy spot inhabited by low-browed, lustful, brutal, and cruel men, and cringing women whose chief outdoor sport was to flail saintly negroes to death.[1]

He was to feel that this chapter, with the one that followed on the Compromise of 1850 would be the 'heart of the whole biography,' since 'without them everything that happens is meaningless, just a series of unexplained albeit dramatic events.' And he wrote Channing, 'I am going to keep them in the book if I hang for it.'[2]

IX

But it was when he turned to the treatment of the Missouri Compromise that his amazement grew into disgust. He had determined to treat it fully, since 'an extensive, detailed, and even minute account of the repeal is indispensable to any intelligent narrative of Lincoln's political career.'[3] Again he found all the teachings of his youth, all the impressions of his manhood fading out before the light of the torch. In March he was 'plodding through' the evidence, 'running up against the most amazing negligence or worse,' and wondering why 'the other fellows or felleresses didn't condescend to look at the sources... big and outstanding as precipitous mountains rising from a plain.' And he was writing Channing: 'Instead of Douglas being a sneaking villain, the record shows him to have been one of the greatest intellects this or any other country ever produced. I hate like the devil to say this, because in doing so I have to eat crow, for like everybody else who did not know what they are talking about, I have repeated the usual war-time propaganda about him.'[4] He had been taught that the repeal of the Missouri Compromise was a deep-laid plot of the 'Slave Power,' and had believed it up to the hour he began his research. He was to find nothing but the afterthought of partisan politics to

[1] Beveridge to Ford, March 2, 1926.
[2] Beveridge to Channing, Jan. 15, 1926.
[3] Beveridge to Channing, June 29, 1926.
[4] Beveridge to Channing, March 9, 1926.

justify the conclusion. Writing Professor Arthur C. Cole, he said:

Lincoln never studied harder in his life than he did during the first nine months of 1854. He read everything he could get hold of — studied the census, etc.; and as a result he did not think that the repeal of the Missouri Compromise was the outcome of a plot of the 'Slave Power.' At least he did not say so.

On the contrary, in his Peoria speech, he declared that the Southern people had not asked for the repeal... did not expect it, and were surprised by it. It is as certain as certain that if Lincoln had believed that the South planned and secured that repeal, he would have said so; for it was a legitimate as well as a powerful argument, and he was too good a politician to overlook so strong and so obvious a point on his side.

I have dug and dug around this hole until there is no hole left, and I can't find a particle of evidence — lots of argument, but no evidence — of the Slave Power plot theory.[1]

He wrote honestly what he found, believing that to be the function of an historian, and was encouraged by the letter of a specialist on the period that the chapter had stirred him 'as no other production ever has.' The correspondent was able to see Douglas 'in his true magnificence for the first time.' 'I had taken the abolition view of Douglas and had always believed that he had sold himself for the Presidency, but now I see that he was a true patriot and that the Presidency would not have purchased him.'[2]

But the moment he felt himself to be in the clearing, and turned to the next chapter on the warfare in Kansas, Beveridge found himself in the underbrush of myth and propaganda again. He was not wholly unprepared, for Channing had written him that in his own researches he was 'never so appalled at the amount of lying.'[3] And Beveridge, already entangled in the underbrush, replied that he had found the same thing. 'Such a number of lies have been woven, and cunningly woven, with a modicum of facts, that to pull out the threads of falsehood destroys the whole fabric.[4] He found it 'devilishly hard work,' with 'the twists and tangles sometimes well-nigh maddening.'[5] And while writing the Kansas chapter he had confessed to Channing that he was 'flabbergasted, hornswoggled, and in other abnormal states,' because the facts revealed had given him 'a smash on the head which makes me see stars, to find that most

[1] Beveridge to Cole, June 29, 1926.
[2] W. E. Connelley, Kansas Historical Society, June 9, 1926.
[3] Channing to Beveridge, July 30, 1926.
[4] Beveridge to Channing, Aug. 3, 1926.
[5] Beveridge to Connelley, Oct. 13, 1926.

of the teachings of my youth were sheer bunc, and the result of political propaganda.'[1] In August his head was whirling from numerous rewritings and attempts to reconcile the irreconcilable among the 'facts.' 'I have literally sat with Lane, Robinson, and Conway in their caucuses,' he wrote, 'have met with Atkinson and Stringfellow in the Blue Lodges, have watched both sides plot and drink whiskey, and have snooped around generally.'[2]

More and more life grew less glamorous, for the moment he extricated himself from one wilderness he found himself in another. Thus still another illusion of his life went glimmering when he came to write of the founding of the Republican Party. 'Isn't it amazing,' he wrote Channing, 'that I have always supposed that Lincoln founded the Republican Party, whereas he steadfastly refused to join it for more than a year and a half after the historical assemblage under the oaks at Jackson, Michigan?'[3] Channing wished it were possible to 'hitch him onto the Republican Party in some more graphic way,' but supposed it could not be done.[4]

But it was when he began his researches for the Dred Scott decision and its consequences that Beveridge found the undergrowth both rank and nauseous. Since this was to carry him into the next year, we may pause here to note the effect generally upon the biographer.

The myths and fabrications had been as sacred to him as religion from his boyhood, and he now was sixty-four. It was like parting with his faith. At times the deception of his youth by parents, teachers, histories, enraged him. 'Such was the kind of trash that was fed to Northern children for more than two generations,' he wrote Professor S. E. Morison. 'Politicians, who were out for office, contracts, and cash, had a good deal to do with these hideous legends. They used the Grand Army and all similar patriotic organizations for political ends.'[5] Only his firm fidelity to the truth held him to his task, but he sometimes suffered. Writing Channing of a 'sudden cold with pneumonia in the offing,' he confessed that he had troubles not physical. 'These troubles relate to the question which is constantly before you: Shall the facts be told, or shall we continue to write as "history" statements made long ago which were sheer political propaganda without anything of truth in them?'[6]

[1] Beveridge to Channing, May 26, 1926.
[2] Beveridge to Professor Theodore C. Pease, University of Illinois, Aug. 12, 1926.
[3] Beveridge to Channing, Sept. 28, 1926.
[4] Channing to Beveridge, Sept. 28, 1926.
[5] Sept. 25, 1926.   [6] Nov. 12, 1926.

Some of the older historians, reading his manuscript and finding it bomb-proof as to facts, wrote frankly of their own distress. One wrote that at eighteen he had read the whole of Henry Wilson's 'Rise and Fall of the Slave Power,' and that much earlier his mother had read him 'Uncle Tom's Cabin.' 'So you see how I came to be.' 'Your account of the origin of your political feeling is almost identical with mine,' Beveridge replied. 'As I look back on it now, it is almost incredible that intelligent persons could, for any cause, get into such a state of mind as that of my parents and family for nearly a generation after the war was over. The atmosphere in which I was brought up was well-nigh lurid; and the things that all of us were told by the politicians, and which all of us took for granted, formed a very tissue of hatred. So you see... it is very hard for me to write this book at all.' ¹

The work and worry took its toll, though, but for a moment of ineffable weariness, he did not notice. In midsummer his physician warned him that he was 'traveling on his nerves' and ordered him to take a month's rest and a sea voyage, and he thought something of taking 'one of the Scandinavian liners, creeping to Norway and Sweden, and then turning around and coming back.' ² But at the last minute this plan was abandoned because Mrs. Beveridge was loath to leave the children. A little later he was as buoyant as ever. 'I am in fine shape,' he wrote. 'While I work continuously from ten to twelve hours each day, I nevertheless have my two walks, one in the early morning and one in the afternoon, two miles and a half; sleep like a log; and so the machine seems to keep running splendidly.' ³

In May, however, he had a warning. He had agreed to deliver an address before the Historical Society of Pennsylvania at the Academy of Music in Philadelphia on the 'Sources of the Declaration of Independence,' and he prepared it with his usual care. Not since he began on his 'Marshall' had he dictated speeches. He now wrote them with a pencil, subjecting himself to the drudgery. Always he had delivered his speeches without notes, and his really marvelous memory made this easy. But this time overwork or absorption in the book made it difficult. From Washington, where he was working on the Trumbull Manuscript, he wrote his wife: 'Have to commit speech.... Very hard. Really I must not drive my engine at such speed.' ⁴ And two days later: 'Don't let me try to do so much at the same time again. Can't get speech into my head. It is now midnight

---

¹ Beveridge to Professor James A. Woodburn, Feb. 5, 1927.
² Beveridge to Channing, July 13, 1926.
³ Beveridge to W. E. Connelley, Oct. 13, 1926.   ⁴ May 29, 1926.

and I'm really desperate. If I succeed it's by God's grace. Coolidge 'phoned me and we talked for an hour and a half.' [1]

But he passed the ordeal satisfactorily and showed in his treatment of Jefferson that other of the myths of his youth had passed. Even when he wrote his 'Marshall,' he was accepting the propaganda that Jefferson got his ideas from Rousseau, but in Philadelphia he no longer was deceived. 'Some have insisted that the theory of human equality was derived from Rousseau,' he said, 'but every word of the Declaration on that subject, and also on the purpose of government and the consent of the governed, is in the Second Treatise on Government written by the English philosopher, John Locke, almost a generation before the eccentric French adventurer was born. And Locke was more widely read in America than in England — Jefferson especially was a disciple of the great English philosopher.'

Beveridge no longer found pleasure, however, in making speeches, and politics now seemed drab. Writing from Washington in the spring, he said: 'It makes politics seem trivial. Politics has again lost its hold on me. Just now it is child's play and women's needlework.' [2]

But even in these last months of his life, he could not remain entirely aloof nor isolate himself from the tempter even in the ivory tower. Here we must pass for a moment, from the biography to politics again.

[1] June 1, 1926.
[2] Beveridge to Mrs. Beveridge, May 30, 1926.

CHAPTER III

THE ADVENTURE'S END

I

IN 1926, Senator Watson was up for renomination and reëlection, and the Progressives determined, if possible, to persuade Beveridge to enter the contest for the nomination. Such a fight would have been a joust of principles, for the two men were fundamentally opposed in their philosophies of government. The issue had been similar in the contest with New four years before when the result proved the predominance of Progressive over reactionary Republicans in the State in a clear-cut fight. Early in the year, Frederick Joss, one of the little coterie of young men who had managed Beveridge's first race for the Senate when he, too, was young, went to Beverly Farms, but found Mrs. Beveridge and the former Senator's friends in Massachusetts hostile to the plan. This did not deter the friendly conspirators from conferring and concluding that the best interests of the party demanded Beveridge's nomination; and two days later, they met again, agreed upon a list of party workers in each district to be invited to a State conference in January, and adjourned for lunch to the Columbia Club, where they were informed that the 'Indianapolis Times' would support their favorite if he were 'the same old Beveridge' and, had not gone over to 'the reactionaries, as the last campaign indicated.' Meanwhile, the conclusion of the State conference was that he could be nominated and elected and a formal organization was perfected to push his candidacy. A telegram was sent to Beverly Farms asking Beveridge's consent at once; but one of the group, sleeping upon the plan, and wondering if the conspirators had been too optimistic, telegraphed the next day to disregard the first telegram until further notice. Great numbers of letters had been sent over the State and ninety per cent of the responses had been favorable. Petitions were in circulation and were being signed rapidly. Soon these petitions, signed by an enormous number, were before Beveridge, as they are before me as I write. The signers were strong men in their communities.

But Beveridge had lost zest for internecine battles and was by no means sure he wished to return to the Senate. He announced that he would take no part in a primary contest, thinking thereby to put the whole thing behind him, but it had scarcely any effect. The demand continued and grew. 'I am

going to stand pat,' he wrote Shaffer. 'If they want to nominate
me without my opening my mouth or lifting my finger, all right;
but I absolutely will not, because I cannot, go out and make a
hammer and tongs campaign for votes.' [1] The temptation was
strong, however much he sought to dissemble with himself. He
admitted finally [2] that he would like to be in the Senate during
the next three years because of the vitally important problems
of reconstruction that would be pending. 'But the trouble is
that the campaign has to be made right now, and I cannot drop
my work to make the campaign.' It was at this time that I
had tea with him at the Plaza in New York. He was tempted,
but he had no stomach for a contest for the nomination, and he
knew his nomination and election would mean the abandonment
of his 'Lincoln.' 'And,' he said, 'that means throwing away four
or five years of the hardest kind of work.' When a delegation
called upon him in Indianapolis urging that since he had grown
enormously in public esteem, regardless of political affiliations,
the party had a right to use him as an asset, he asked, with a
smile: 'How does it come about? Because of politics or my
books?'

His decision really was made subconsciously even as he
thought he pondered, and finally he took his stand decisively.
'I must choose either between the Senate or the "Lincoln,"' he
wrote, 'and of course I cannot drop the book.' [3]

In truth, he found little in the general political situation to
draw him to the political arena. The conditions were drab
enough. The nauseating corruption of three years before was
history, and there was nothing inspirational nor exciting on the
agenda of the statesmen. Government was drifting, doing as
little as possible and making a virtue of it. Its face was grimly
set against crusading or reforming of any sort. The public
conscience had given way to individual appetite for gain. The
talk of the counting-room and the club, as of the breakfast-
table of the average family, was that the country wanted no
governmental interference with business, big or little, and Beveridge measurably shared this opinion and expressed it in private
conversation. It was the twilight of the gods; and some thought
it the millennium of the minnows.

What he did see of politics did not please him. He was shocked
by the vast sums spent in the senatorial primaries in Pennsylvania; even more by the amount spent on Prohibition.
'The expenditures of the Anti-Saloon League,' he wrote, 'from

[1] Beveridge to Shaffer, Jan. 26, 1926.
[2] Beveridge to Asa J. Smith, Jan. 15, 1926.
[3] Beveridge to Judge Ulric Z. Wiley, Feb. 2, 1926.

the viewpoint of the good of the country is much worse, because everyone had been led to believe that the concern was battling for righteousness and could do no wrong. I have been shocked beyond measure to learn that they have spent scores of millions of dollars "putting over Prohibition," and six millions in the last four or five years.... In short, we seem to be indulging in even worse practices than are resorted to in war. I sometimes wonder if these dear people realize that they are undermining the very foundations of republican government.' [1]

When the campaign opened in the autumn, he found nothing that was not petty and insincere — with nothing worth talking about. From the window of his ivory tower everything political seemed sadly scrambled. He saw the Republicans divided on the tariff, or farm relief, and 'the wet and dry fight as confusing as it is senseless.' [2] He had about determined to make no speeches — certainly not a continental tour. 'There is nothing big,' he wrote, 'hardly anything worth while, in the political mix-up just now. From this detached position, where I cannot do forced thinking on such matters, there seems to be nothing at present but retail politics. In any case, the party is split on every question which, if the party united, might give high ground for a great fight.' [3]

As the campaign in Indiana waxed warm, and Beveridge lingered in his cozy study at Beverly Farms, some of his friends urged him to take the stump in Indiana at least, but he was unresponsive. And when one wrote that his failure to campaign there might affect his future in politics, he replied impatiently: 'If my political fortunes depend upon my taking part in this particular campaign, they are frail, indeed, and not worth consideration.'

But the State organization was in the hands of his enemies, and in the twenty campaigns of forty years since his first while at DePauw, this was the first year he had received no invitation from the State Committee. For the first time since he had entered the Senate, twenty-seven years before, the organization had not asked him to attend the State Convention.

And so he lingered on at Beverly Farms late into the winter, busy with his manuscript, and giving no heed to a political contest that to him seemed meaningless.

He had been serving as national chairman of a committee that was trying to raise a million-dollar fund for the American Historical Association, and he was urged to attend the annual meet-

[1] Beveridge to Shaffer, July 4, 1926.
[2] Beveridge to Shaffer, Sept. 20, 1926.
[3] Beveridge to Shaffer, Sept. 30, 1926.

ing of the organization in December, but the month found him with conflicting engagements, and worried. As honorary chairman of the D.K.E. fraternity, he was expected to attend its national convention and make the presidential speech. A week before he was hurrying to finish Chapter VII of the second volume of the 'Lincoln,' and to pack up his material and household effects to get to Chicago by January 15 to do the final work on the last three chapters.

The D.K.E. speech was utilized to make a smashing attack on the nation-wide movement to end the primary system and go back to conventions. He was thinking of the fight threatened that winter to repeal the primary law in Indiana. He had been among the first to demand the primary, and had been a beneficiary of the system, and never had he believed so firmly that a return to the old-fashioned convention would be a step backward and toward the domination of government by the bosses. More than once before he had rushed into the breach when a fight to retain the primary seemed lost.

Almost immediately after the enactment of the law, the old-line politicians began to plan for its repeal, and periodically, as legislatures met, the agitation was set on foot anew. Invariably Beveridge had been summoned to the firing-line, and the moment he assumed the leadership of the fight to preserve the primary, and began making his appeals above the heads of the politicians to the people, the repealers had postponed their plan. Now again the agitation was renewed, and Beveridge had written two powerful arguments for the primary, published originally in the 'Saturday Evening Post.' In the last days of his life nothing engrossed him more in public affairs. He saw in the primary system the one and only hope for popular government, and he had called his articles, 'Of, By, and For the People' and 'Yes or No.' Thus, with a cause that enlisted his deepest feeling, he spoke that night at the dinner of the D.K.E.[1] with his accustomed vigor and with even more than his usual earnestness.

It was to be his last speech. 'You cannot take from the people rights they have won and enjoyed.... Why try to turn back the hands on the clock of progress.' With these words his long and brilliant career as a speaker came to a close. That night the curtain fell finally on the orator.

II

He was to be delayed in reaching Chicago, however. On arriving in Indianapolis, an irritation of the throat drove him to a

[1] In New York City, Dec. 29, 1926.

physician, and he was found to have an infected antrum, and for three weeks his work was stopped. Then, with Mrs. Beveridge, he hurried on to Chicago, where he took up his residence at the old home of Mrs. Beveridge's aunt, on Prairie Avenue and worked feverishly on the book. By this time the scholars, historians, and jurists were returning his manuscript chapter on the Dred Scott decision and its political significance.

Nowhere had he found more of the tangled underbrush of legend and falsehood, and again the understandings and beliefs of a lifetime were swept away. He began his research for the chapter still saturated with the poisonous propaganda of generations; here surely, he thought, he would find corroboration of the things taught him in childhood and in school. Of course the Dred Scott decision involved a wicked conspiracy between President-elect Buchanan, President Pierce, and Chief Justice Taney to serve the 'Slave Power'; of course the Justices were large slave-owners; of course the opinion of Taney was utterly indefensible — and he knew it; and of course the Republican leaders and the country instantly met the opinion with vehement denunciation. Naturally, wherever men met together, this 'monstrous act' of Taney was the subject of indignant conversation.

Under the compulsion of the facts, Beveridge was to change his mind.

Very quickly under his investigation the charge of 'conspiracy,' born of the delay of the Court, was relegated to the junk heap of political canards. 'The delay in the decision,' he wrote Channing, who was entirely sympathetic, 'was caused exclusively, solely, by the request of Justice Nelson for reargument. The statement of Republican senators in their combined assault in 1858 that this delay was part of a conspiracy was mere and sheer campaign stuff.'[1] Quite as astonishing was the discovery that among the great mass of the people, and even among the politicians, there had been no excitement. Poring over hundreds of the letters exchanged during 1857, he failed to find more than an occasional mild mention of the decision. A careful combing of the letters of John P. Hale, in possession of the New Hampshire Historical Society, failed to disclose any popular interest at all. 'I have gone through them,' he wrote, 'and as you said would be the case, no mention is made of the Dred Scott decision during the whole of 1857, except one request immediately after the decision was handed down, from a Republican club for Hale... to make them a speech about it. This is precisely what the letters of Trumbull[2] show; from the time the decision was given down

[1] Beveridge to Channing, April 4, 1927.　　[2] Lyman Trumbull, of Illinois.

to the end of 1857 only one person that wrote to Trumbull made mention of the decision; and that was done casually and incidentally in the course of a long letter on political subjects.' [1]

And the Justices? He went into their lives and records as meticulously as though he were examining them for jury service in a murder trial — and the slave-owning fabrication went glimmering. Taney had freed his slaves long before, and while two or three of the Justices owned house servants, none were the great slave-owners they had been pictured by the abolitionists. Beveridge found them men of high-minded patriotism and great legal erudition. But he did find one among them who shocked his sense of judicial propriety, and this was Justice John McLean, one of the dissenters, who had been hiding presidential aspirations beneath his judicial robes from the hour of his appointment by Andrew Jackson. Never had he abandoned hope for the Presidency; and Beveridge was to hear from the very highest sources that 'McLean stirred up the whole mess, and that Curtis [2] probably would not have peeped if McLean had not ripped and torn around so much.' [3] This Taney, the infamous slave-driver of his lifelong imaginings, emerged from Beveridge's researches in a vastly different light. 'The more I study the matter, the more I think that you are right in your praise of Taney; he seems to me to have been an able, upright, patriotic old man,' he wrote to Professor Hodder.

Sternly he set down what he found, however much it went against the grain; but when the manuscript copies of the chapter returned from the foremost scholars and historians with their approval, he was content. Some thought he treated the incident at too great length. To Ford he sent an explanation:

I have given a great deal of attention to it because, as you know, it still is a landmark in American history, for it has been represented as having precipitated the Civil War, and because Lincoln jumped on it so hard — but he did not jump on it for more than a year after the decision was made, nor for three or four months after the Republican senators had made it the principal object of Republican attack.[4]

To Ferris Greenslet, he wrote a similar explanation:

Up to this very day we have been taught that the Dred Scott decision aroused the North to the fighting point. The Republican press and the anti-slavery pulpit show this to be true; but the letters from

[1] Beveridge to Otis G. Hammond, New Hampshire Historical Society, Dec. 1, 1926.
[2] The other dissenter.
[3] Beveridge to Professor F. H. Hodder, University of Kansas, Feb. 22, 1927.
[4] Beveridge to Ford, Feb. 11, 1927.

the people themselves to the men named and to the others show exactly the reverse to be the case.[1]

Beveridge was to believe that 'the biggest historical discovery' he had made was that there had been no popular excitement over the decision for almost a year, and until it was made the object of a campaign attack.

But it was to Professor Charles A. Beard, who doubted if the decision was so important in the 'Life' of Lincoln, that he set down his full reactions on the chapter:

Perhaps I was influenced by my own reactions. Up to last year when I began my researches on this decision I believed so firmly, that it never occurred to me that there could be any doubt about it, every bit of the 'bunc' which I had been taught from my childhood. So when I came up against the court records themselves... and the shocking changes in the attitude of Republican newspapers, and old McLean's political sculduggery, I was astounded.... Moreover, I never had the least doubt that the charge of Greeley... that the Court itself was a lot of slave-holders and under the influence of the 'Slave Power' was true; and when I found that Taney had no slaves, Campbell had no slaves, and that only Daniel, Wayne, and Catron may have had a house servant or two, I was interested beyond measure.... These are some of the reasons for my paying so much attention to the Dred Scott decision. Just how the 'Life' of Lincoln or the story of the Civil War can be written with less attention to that decision and the partisan use of it, I cannot see.[2]

No one's criticism meant more to Beveridge than that of Justice Oliver Wendell Holmes. Many times during the writing of the 'Marshall' and the 'Lincoln,' in the summer and during the recess of the Supreme Court, he would fare forth with his dog at his heels for a little visit with the venerable jurist in the rambling frame house at Beverly Farms, and discuss his problems. In his criticism of the Dred Scott chapter, Holmes thought he had used some over-strong words in his characterizations and quoted too copiously from the newspapers. Beveridge thought the first criticism possibly just. He had felt a fierce resentment time and again during these five years of research because of the misrepresentations on which he, in common with all, had been fed and poisoned. He promised to go over the manuscript and strike out all such evidence of feeling. But he refused to budge on the press quotations. 'That decision brought out more editorials than any other in our judicial history,' he wrote, 'and the Republican press made it its own great point of attack, although the conservative press stopped talking about it very soon. On

[1] Beveridge to Greenslet, Feb. 7, 1927.
[2] Beveridge to Beard, April 7, 1927.

the other hand, the correspondence from the people themselves to men in public life shows that the people had well-nigh no interest at all in the decision.'[1]

Satisfied, at length, with the Dred Scott chapter, he was working feverishly on the last three chapters he was to write — on the senatorial contest of Lincoln and Douglas in 1858.

III

It was a winter of incessant labor, with the Barrett collection of Lincolniana and the material of the Chicago Historical Society, and with one or two excursions to Springfield to verify his notes from the newspapers in the State House basement. For a year he had been troubled with arthritis, and he was worried over Mrs. Beveridge's health, but there was nothing in his appearance to indicate illness, and with undiminished enthusiasm and persistency he pushed on with his work by night and day. Early in March he spent two days with the newspapers in the basement at the State House, going directly to his drudgery from the train. That month he was satisfied he could finish the second volume by the first of June, and he planned then to devote eleven months to a final revision.[2]

It was at this time that Frederick Joss, who had been one of his young champions in the Senate fight of 1899, spent a day with him. Many years with their manifold changes had come and gone since youth was served; and while there had been times when the two friends had not been able to see alike in politics, the old friendship had survived. Beveridge laid his work aside, and talked. Joss was to remember afterward that he seemed rugged and rich in vitality. The years had dealt with him kindly, despite his burning of the candle at both ends. His face was stronger and ruddier, but he had retained the slenderness of his youth; and his spirit was unquenched. The affectionate manner, the enthusiasm, the bubbling good nature of his brilliant dawn beautifully linked the man of thirty-six with the man of sixty-four. And throughout the day the old friends relived the intervening years and celebrated anew the victory of 1899; discussed old friends, the old ambitions, and what had become of them; and Beveridge went over the work he was doing and talked entertainingly of his voyage of discovery in American history. That evening the friends parted with nothing to suggest that they might not meet again.

At length the work in Chicago was finished. There were some

[1] Beveridge to Oliver Wendell Holmes, April 8, 1927.
[2] Beveridge to Albert Shaw, March 21, 1927.

odds and ends to attend to in the basement at Springfield, but that could be done on the way to Indianapolis. The last of March, the Beveridges, with their daughter Abby, went by train to Springfield, where their car was waiting for them; and after two more days of labor they started home. It was on the motor trip to Indianapolis that they passed the old tool shed at Illiopolis, associated with the bitter logging days of boyhood, where, in a momentary fit of despair, Beveridge had thrown himself face downward on the floor and sobbed. Now the bitterness was all gone — it had vanished long before; they paused at the shed, and, as they rode on, he talked of his laborious boyhood and boyish struggles.

It was the first day of April when they reached the Indianapolis home on Washington Boulevard, built immediately after their marriage. There still was work to do, but soon the great trees on the grounds would be in leaf and the odorous Hoosier spring would come.

Instantly Beveridge returned to his task, working day and far into the night; but almost every morning he and Mrs. Beveridge would walk along the tow-path from the present site of Butler University to the Michigan Road, where the car would meet them and take them home. He loved this walk more than any other, for in the spring it was indescribably beautiful. He had always loved the tow-path — from the days when, as a young lawyer, he followed the fashion and pedaled his bicycle under the trees.

With only a chapter and a half to write of the second volume, taking Lincoln into the period of his glory, and with every expectation of finishing by the first of June, he was jubilant. He had passed through the disillusioning part of his task — he was sure of that. He had written Channing he would finish by the first of June 'in spite of hell and high water,' and would soon be in Boston, where 'the first darn thing I do will be to come around and get the inspiration of your presence, as well as your blessing.'[1]

Ten days later he was stricken with a heart attack. Dr. Emerson, his physician, was at first hopeful of his recovery, but after a day or two, he asked permission to summon Dr. Thayer, of Johns Hopkins. No longer was there any doubt of the seriousness of his illness.

Thus Beveridge was forced to put his work aside; but for almost two weeks longer, Mrs. Beveridge read to him by the hour from the manuscript chapters of the book, the last on the Dred Scott decision.

It was just dawn on the morning of April 27 that he had an attack more severe than any before. Physicians were hastily

[1] Beveridge to Channing, April 4, 1927.

CARTOON BY McCUTCHEON IN THE CHICAGO TRIBUNE, APRIL,
1927

summoned. That morning the news flashed over the country that Beveridge would write no more. He, too, had passed into history.

The country was shocked, for his had seemed, to those who knew him, a perennial youth. Telegrams poured in from the White House and from the lowly for whom frequently he had fought gallantly against overwhelming odds. Newspapers everywhere paid editorial tribute to the statesman, orator, and biographer. Learned societies spread resolutions on their records.

But in Indiana it seemed incredible — he had not grown old with the years and had not greatly changed. Always he had seemed as he was when first he went to the Senate — youthful, brilliant, and colorful. For he had not rusted in inactivity, and to the end he had continued a marvel of industry, eager for the adventure of high achievement.

THE END

BIBLIOGRAPHY

MANUSCRIPTS

BEVERIDGE MSS. These papers comprise many thousands of letters to and from Senator Beveridge from 1898, when he was elected to the Senate, until his death in 1927. The greater part of this correspondence is with the political leaders of his time on party policy, principles, and strategy. A great number are of a social and personal character, but all these teem with side-lights on the political drama. The more than two thousand letters to and from historians and scholars, written during the preparation of the biographies of John Marshall and Abraham Lincoln, throw a vivid light upon the problems of the meticulous biographer.

Among these private papers is the manuscript of an autobiography begun during Beveridge's senatorial career, on the suggestion of a leading editor. After writing the chapters covering boyhood, youth, college days, and early days at the bar, the project was abandoned. This fragmentary autobiography throws a vivid light on the training of an orator.

Another unpublished manuscript of value is an article written after the final passing of the Progressive Party, on its rise, and the reason for its passing. It was sent to George H. Lorimer, of the 'Saturday Evening Post,' with the admonition that it was not to be published.

Among the manuscript speeches, not published, the most interesting is that prepared as the Keynote Speech for the Republican National Convention of 1920 when Beveridge had every reason to believe he had been selected for the chairmanship. Through political manipulation a shift was made and the undelivered speech was filed away with his papers.

More interesting and revealing is the Philippine Notebook, in which, during Beveridge's searching survey of the islands before the American governmental policy there had been determined, he wrote each day the interviews he had with all sorts and conditions of men. These interviews were read, without the names, into his famous Philippine speech. The one with Ito, the great Japanese statesman, is of the greatest interest and importance.

I found among these papers, too, the paper written for the Indianapolis Literary Club, before Beveridge entered the Senate, to prove, through the lawyer's method, that the Shakespearean plays were written by Sir Walter Raleigh.

The Beveridge MSS. are in possession of Mrs. Beveridge at Beverly Farms.

PINCHOT MS. Through the courtesy of Mr. Amos Pinchot I was permitted to read his manuscript history of the Progressive Party. It is in possession of Mr. Pinchot.

DOCUMENTARY MATERIAL

The *Congressional Record*, 1899–1911, and numerous Senate and House Documents and Hearings have been used, and cited, whenever used, in the footnotes.

MAGAZINES AND NEWSPAPERS

Saturday Evening Post, 1900–1927.
The Review of Reviews, 1900–1915.
The Reader's Magazine, 1907–1908.
Indiana Magazine of History, September and December, 1928. ('The Senatorial Career of Senator Beveridge,' by John A. Coffin.)
The Quarterly Journal of Speech, February, 1932. ('The Education of an Orator,' by Herold Truslow Rose.)
Indianapolis Journal.
Indianapolis Sentinel.
Indianapolis News.
Indianapolis Star.
Indianapolis Sun.
New York World.
New York Times.
New York Herald.
New York Tribune.
New York Sun.
  Where other magazines and newspapers are quoted, they are credited in the footnotes.

BOOKS

BEVERIDGE, ALBERT J. *The Russian Advance.* New York, 1903.
  The Young Man and the World. New York, 1905.
  The Meaning of the Times. Indianapolis, 1907.
  Life of John Marshall. 4 volumes, Boston, 1916–19.
  The State of the Nation. Indianapolis, 1924.
  What is Behind the War. Indianapolis, 1915.
  Abraham Lincoln, 1808–1858. 2 volumes, Boston, 1928.
BOWERS, CLAUDE G. *Life of John Worth Kern.* Indianapolis, 1918.
BISHOP, JOSEPH BUCKLIN. *Theodore Roosevelt and His Times.* New York, 1920.
BROWNE, WALDO R. *Altgeld of Illinois.* New York, 1924.
BUSBEY, L. WHITE. *Uncle Joe Cannon.* New York, 1927.
BUTT, ARCHIE. *The Letters of Archie Butt.* Edited by Lawrence F. Abbott, New York, 1924.
  Taft and Roosevelt: The Intimate Letters of Archie Butt. 2 volumes, New York, 1930.
CLARK, CHAMP. *My Quarter Century of American Politics.* 2 volumes, New York, 1920.

COOLIDGE, LOUIS A. *An Old-Fashioned Senator: Orville H. Platt.* New York, 1910.

CORTISSOZ, ROYAL. *Life of Whitelaw Reid.* New York, 1912.

CROLY, HERBERT. *Marcus Alonzo Hanna: His Life and Work.* New York, 1912.

CULLOM, SHELBY M. *Fifty Years of Public Service.* Chicago, 1911.

FORAKER, JOSEPH BENSON. *Notes of a Busy Life.* 2 volumes, Cincinnati, 1916.

HOAR, GEORGE FRISBIE. *Autobiography of Seventy Years.* 2 volumes, New York, 1903.

KOHLSAAT, H. H. *From McKinley to Harding: Personal Recollections of the Presidents.* New York, 1923.

LA FOLLETTE, ROBERT M. *La Follette's Autobiography.* New York, 1913.

LODGE, HENRY CABOT. *Selections from the Correspondence of Theodore Roosevelt.* New York, 1925.

LEWIS, W. D. *Life of Theodore Roosevelt.* Philadelphia, 1919.

MITCHELL, EDWARD P. *Memoirs of an Editor.* New York, 1924.

NEVINS, ALLAN. *Henry White: Thirty Years of American Diplomacy.* New York, 1930.

OLCOTT, CHARLES S. *Life of William McKinley.* 2 volumes, Boston, 1916.

PRINGLE, HENRY F. *Theodore Roosevelt.* New York, 1931.

ROOSEVELT, THEODORE. *Autobiography.* New York, 1913.

RHODES, JAMES FORD. *The Roosevelt and McKinley Administrations.* New York, 1922.

STEALEY, O. O. *One Hundred Pen Pictures of Live Men.* Washington, 1910.

STEPHENSON, N. W. *Nelson W. Aldrich.* New York, 1930.

STODDARD, HENRY L. *As I Knew Them.* New York, 1927.

SULLIVAN, MARK. *Our Times.* New York, 1926.
Pre-War America. New York, 1930.

THAYER, W. R. *Life and Letters of John Hay.* 2 volumes, Boston, 1915.

THOMPSON, C. W. *Presidents I've Known.* New York, 1929.

TAFT, MRS. WILLIAM HOWARD. *Recollections of a Full Life.* New York, 1914.

WISTER, OWEN. *Roosevelt: The Story of a Friendship.* New York, 1930.

INDEX

INDEX

J1.